D0912332

Latino Pentecostals in America

Latino Pentecostals in America

FAITH AND POLITICS IN ACTION

Gastón Espinosa

Harvard University Press

Cambridge, Massachusetts

London, England

2014

Copyright © 2014 by Gastón Espinosa
All rights reserved
Printed in the United States of America

First printing

Library of Congress Cataloging-in-Publication Data

Espinosa, Gastón.
Latino Pentecostals in America : faith and politics in action / Gastón Espinosa.
pages   cm
Includes bibliographical references and index.
ISBN 978-0-674-72887-5 (alk. paper)
1. Hispanic American Pentecostals.   I. Title.
BR1644.5.U6E87   2014
277.3'08208968—dc23   2013037062

*This book is dedicated to my father, Rafael Jimenez Espinosa (1929–1978),
who taught me to stand up for what is right no matter what the cost,
and to Jesse Miranda (1937–), without whose support this story would have
never broken the silence.*

Contents

Acknowledgments   ix

Introduction   1

1. Holy Ghost and Fire: Azusa Street and Mexican
   Pentecostal Origins   22

2. Victory Is Coming Now: Mexican Pentecostals in Texas   60

3. Their Salvation May Depend on Us: Missionary
   Origins in Texas   83

4. The Gringos Have Control: Francisco Olazábal's
   Reformation in the Borderlands   109

5. Pentecostal Origins in the Southwest and the Struggle
   for Self-Determination   134

6. The Challenges of Freedom: Mexican American
   Leadership in the Southwest   164

7. We Preach the Truth: Azusa Street and Puerto Rican
   Pentecostal Origins and Expansion   192

8. The "Puerto Rico Problem": The Struggle for Integration,
   Independence, and Rebirth   233

9. Spirit and Power: Puerto Rican Pentecostalism in
   New York City   255

10. Your Daughters Shall Prophesy: The Uphill Struggle of
    Women in Ministry   282

11. Righteousness and Justice: Faith-Based Action
    for Social Change   322

12. Balancing the Horizontal with the Vertical: Latino
    Growth, Social Views, and Influence in National Politics   361

    Conclusion   406

    Notes   421
    Index   491

Acknowledgments

This book would not have been possible without the vision and support of Jesse Miranda. I first met him in Harvey Cox and Eldin Villafañe's course on Pentecostalism and Liberation Theology at Harvard University Divinity School in 1992–1993. That proved a critical encounter, as he noted that little had been published on the origins of Latino Pentecostalism in the United States and Puerto Rico. In the fall of 1994, I entered the Ph.D. program at the University of California at Santa Barbara to work with Mario T. García and Catherine Albanese in American history and religion. Although I had initially planned to write on religion and the Mexican American civil rights movement, on the advice of García and Albanese I explored the origins of the Latino Pentecostal movement in the United States, Mexico, and Puerto Rico. I focused particularly on the Latino Assemblies of God (hereafter Latino AG) because it was and remains the largest Latino Pentecostal tradition in the United States. After painstakingly amassing a mountain of material over the past two decades, I decided to write a history of the Latino AG, for which Miranda has offered his steadfast and strategic support. I have original, photographic, or duplicate copies of all written, transcribed, and oral history sources and national data sets or results cited in every chapter of this book. These materials and others are contained in my Latino Pentecostal History Collection.

This project would not have been possible without the generous support of the National Endowment for the Humanities (NEH) and the National Humanities Center Institute for Advanced Studies, which helped provide funding, release time, and office space to complete this book. AG General Superintendents Thomas Trask and Dr. George O. Wood and the following ten Latino Superintendents of the then eight Latin District Councils offered their support and provided invaluable sources and photos for this book: Sergio Navarrete (SPD), Lee Baca (NPLAD), Dennis J. Rivera (CD), Edward Martínez and Saturnino González (SESD), Clemente Maldonado (MLAD), Rafael Reyes and Manuel A. Álvarez (SED), Juan H. Suárez (PRD), and Gary Jones (GLAD).

Finally, I thank the following individuals (some of whom are now deceased) and their families for their interviews, keen insights, and/or primary source letters, reports, artifacts, diaries, photos, and periodicals: Rev. Ricardo Tañon, Rev. José Girón, Rev. Josue Sánchez, Frank Olazábal Jr., Florence Olazábal, Rev. Jesse Miranda, Rev. Daniel De León, Rev. Adolfo Carrión, Rev. Rafael Reyes, Rev. Manuel A. Álvarez, Rev. Sergio Martínez, Rev. Felix Posos, Dr. Eldin Villafañe, Rev. Sergio Navarrete, Rev. Saturnino González, Rev. Samuel Rodríguez, Dr. Shaun Casey, Rev. Joshua DuBois, Rev. Wilfredo de Jesús, Dr. Juan Hernández, Rev. Alex and Anita Bazan, Rev. Gloria Garza, Rev. Aimee García Cortese, Rev. Leoncia Rosado Rosseau (a.k.a. "Mama Leo"), Rev. Eva Rodríguez, Rev. Maria Camarillo, Rev. Anita Soto, Rev. Abigail Alicea, Jessica Estrada, Yanina Espinoza, Sophia Garcia, Rev. Fidel Martínez, Rev. E. F. Martínez, Rev. Arturo Santana, Rev. José Leyva, Rev. Tomás V. Sanabria, Rev. Alejandro Vargas, Dr. Efrain Agosto, Dr. Tommy Casarez, Rev. Eleazar Rodríguez Jr., Rev. Tony Martínez, Rev. Joe A. Leyva, Rev. Efraim Espinoza, Sherri Doty, Todd Johnson, Peter Crossing, and many others. Most important, I want to thank the Latino AG community for allowing me into their world and for giving me access to their untold stories and struggles for voice and agency in the church and society.

Tracking down these sources would have been even more difficult without the assistance of Glenn Gohr and Wayne Warner of the Assemblies of God Flower Pentecostal Heritage Center. Over the past twenty years, they provided key documents that have enabled me to piece together this Latino AG mosaic. On more than one occasion, Glenn went the extra mile to secure sources, and for this I am most grateful.

I also want to thank a number of archives and other centers for their assistance: the International Church of the Foursquare Gospel; the Church of God (Cleveland, Tennessee); the Church of God of Prophecy; the Apostolic Faith (Portland, Oregon); the Latin American Council of Christian Churches; the Methodist Archives at the Claremont School of Theology; the Evangelical Seminary of Puerto Rico; and the University of Puerto Rico. Appreciation is also due to my research assistants Ian Fowls, Brian Cottle, and Joshua Newton. I would also like to thank Presidents Pamela Gann and Hiram Chodosh and Deans Gregory Hess and Nick Warner at Claremont McKenna College for their support, and Ulrike Guthrie and Melody Negron and the Harvard University Press team for their editorial assistance. Finally, special thanks are due to Kathleen McDermott and Andrew Kinney. They have been wonderful to work with in the negotiations and production of this book.

Finally, and most important of all, I thank my family for their support and for accompanying me on this journey.

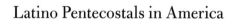

Latino Pentecostals in America

Introduction

In 1979 VICTOR DE LEON published *The Silent Pentecostals: A Biographical History of the Pentecostal Movement among Hispanics in the Twentieth Century.* This was the first book-length history of the Latino Assemblies of God (AG) in the United States. It spanned the period from 1915 to 1979 and focused primarily on the Southwest. He titled it *The Silent Pentecostals* not because Pentecostals are quiet, but because their story had never been told before outside of the Latino AG community and because they had not "receive[d] the recognition they deserved," De Leon said.[1] The fact that he had to self-publish the book only seemed to underscore the movement's marginality. Hidden from society by their working-class social status and location in barrios and migrant labor camps just beyond the railroad tracks of suburban America, their story has long been overshadowed by the larger narrative on black-white race relations and Pentecostal origins. Over thirty years after the publication of his book, Latino Pentecostals still languish in the shadows of American, Latino, and Pentecostal history, politics, and society, though this is beginning to change.

The lack of literature on the Latino AG is not due to a paucity of histories of the General Council of the Assemblies of God. Indeed, the AG has commissioned, supported, and/or published eight histories stretching back more than a century.[2] Unfortunately, Latinos do not figure very prominently in most, and in some cases are not discussed at all in them.[3] Furthermore, despite De Leon's work, there is not a single book in English or Spanish that critically traces the history of the Latino AG across the United States and Puerto Rico from 1914 to 2014.[4] Although there are publications about other Latino Pentecostal denominations and some of the fourteen Latino AG districts, most were written in Spanish or occasionally English by denominational writers and leaders.[5] While there are publications that touch on the Latino AG in English, most of them are either book chapters, sections of chapters, articles, or books that focus on a specific leader, district, period, city, region, church, school, doctrine, or topic.[6]

However, there is a need to understand the Latino AG movement because of its size and the growing influence of its leaders in American public life. In April 2013, *Time* magazine ran a front-page cover story titled "The Latino Reformation," which spotlighted the work and activism of Latino AG leaders Rev. Samuel Rodríguez and Rev. Wilfredo de Jesús. They serve as president and vice president of the National Hispanic Christian Leadership Conference (NHCLC), which is the largest interdenominational Latino Protestant Evangelical organization in the United States. Despite the Latino AG's growing influence, most know surprisingly little about the movement that shaped them and the various ways they have exercised influence in American religion, politics, and society.[7]

This book seeks to help fill this gap in the literature by providing a history of the Latino AG that can also serve as a case study and window into the larger Latino Pentecostal, Evangelical, and Protestant movements along with the changing flow of North American religious history. Indeed, Latino actors invite scholars to reimagine and recast the narrative and flow of it as a multidirectional story that moves south to north, not just east to west.

This book's title, *Latino Pentecostals in America: Faith and Politics in Action,* was selected by the publisher and is much broader than the originally proposed title. Despite this fact, the book focuses almost exclusively on the Latino AG, and for this reason it does not tell the story of all Latino Pentecostals. Indeed, there are at least 225 Latino Pentecostal/

Charismatic denominations and Spanish-language branches in the United States that invite further research and study.[8] It should be stated at the outset that all of them have made their own unique contributions to Pentecostalism and North American religions.

Demographic Shifts in U.S. Latino Religions

Despite the book's disclaimer about the Latino AG being one of many Pentecostal traditions in North America today, there are important reasons for studying it. It is the largest Latino Protestant, Evangelical, and Pentecostal denomination in the United States and the second largest in Puerto Rico.[9] The largest denomination in Puerto Rico was also affiliated with the Assemblies of God until it severed its loose ties in the 1950s to become a separate independent denomination for reasons discussed in Chapter 8. National surveys report that more than one million Latinos self-identify with the AG across the United States and Puerto Rico, 700,000-plus of whom are noted in AG statistical analyses. The rest are Latinos who do not regularly attend church for various reasons, but who still self-identify with the AG. They attend approximately 2,665 Latino-serving AG congregations and are led by more than 3,900 Latino ministers, 1,100 of whom are women.[10] To put the above figures in national comparative perspective, there are more Latina clergywomen in the AG than in all other Latino-serving mainline Protestant denominations in the United States. There are also almost as many Latino AG churches as all other Latino mainline Protestant churches combined (2,863) and more Latino Protestants than Jews or Muslims in America.[11] The 2012 Latino Religions and Politics (LRAP) survey found that Latino AG members make up almost 25 percent of all Latino Pentecostal Christian voters in the United States and 22 percent of all Latino Protestant Christian voters, which underscores their political importance in national politics. The Latino Protestant electorate (3 percent out of 10 percent) is about the same size as the national Asian American electorate (3 percent) and is now slightly larger than the Jewish (2 percent) and the Muslim electorates (less than 1 percent).[12]

The Latino AG is important because it is also contributing to the growth of Latino Protestantism and Evangelicalism in America. There are 53 million Latinos across the United States today, and they are the largest racial-ethnic minority group in twenty-three states. The number of Latinos is expected to climb to 128 million people, or 29 percent of the American population, by 2050.[13]

Approximately 93 percent of Latinos self-identify as Christian and/or with a Christian tradition, movement, or experience such as being born-again, Pentecostal/Charismatic, and/or independent/nondenominational Christian. Of the 53 million Latinos, approximately 66 percent are Catholic and 27 percent are Protestant and non-Catholic Christian, though some put the figures at 62 percent Catholic and 33 percent Protestant and unaffiliated. Over 80 percent of all Latino Protestants self-identify as born again, or Evangelical, and/or attend an Evangelical, Pentecostal, or Charismatic denominational or nondenominational/independent church.[14] There are 23,189 Latino Protestant churches across the United States, 12 percent of which are mainline Protestant (2,863), 41 percent Pentecostal/ Charismatic (9,420), and 88 percent Evangelical/Pentecostal/Charismatic (20,326). In total, 37 percent of Latinos across all denominations (Protestant, Catholic, independent, and so on) report being born again and 28 percent report being both born again and Pentecostal/Charismatic.[15] Pentecostals make up approximately 64 percent of all U.S. Latino Protestants and 65 percent of the U.S. Latino Protestant electorate.[16] The Latino Evangelical and Pentecostal movements have also influenced Latino mainline Protestants, 43 percent of whom report being born again and 22 percent of whom report being Charismatic. They have similarly influenced Latino Catholics, 26 percent of whom report being born again and 22 percent of whom report being Charismatic.[17]

The growth of the Latino AG and the larger Protestant Evangelical movement is not likely to taper off any time soon. Catholic sociologist Andrew Greeley estimates that up to 600,000 Latinos may be "defecting" annually from Catholicism to Protestantism, largely Evangelicalism and Pentecostalism.[18] Recent national surveys seem to confirm this when they found that for every one Latino who "recently converted" or returned to Catholicism, four (more than 3 million) left it and "recently converted" to Protestantism.[19]

The Latino AG is contributing to this seismic shift from Catholicism to Protestantism. The 2012 LRAP survey of likely Latino Christian voters found that the Latino AG was the destination of almost one out of four (23 percent) Catholic converts to Protestantism. This, along with the growth of other Evangelical and Pentecostal/Charismatic churches, may also help explain why 71 percent of all Latino Protestant converts also self-identify as born-again Christians.[20]

In light of these developments, it should not be surprising that Latinos make up an increasing share of Protestantism in general and the AG in particular. This trend reflects a growing racialization of Protestantism and Evangelicalism and what R. Stephen Warner calls the de-Europeanization of American Christianity.[21] The Assemblies of God National Leadership and Resource Center confirmed this when it noted that in 2012 Latinos made up 20 percent of all churches, 22 percent of all AG adherents across the United States, and 55 percent of all national AG growth from 2002 to 2012. Over the past two decades, the AG has witnessed an increase of 837,871 adherents, 414,031 of whom were Latino. Since 1992, the number of Latino churches has grown by 30 percent and Latino adherents by more than 150 percent. This growth has taken place at precisely the same time that the number of those classified as "white" AG parishioners has decreased by about 0.3 percent.[22] For these reasons, Latinos remain vital to the future growth, health, and vitality of the AG. This trend reflects a similar development in many other ostensibly "Euro-American" denominations. We are entering what Davíd Carrasco calls "the Brown Millennium," wherein the Latino experience will profoundly shape the spirit, ethos, and cultural complexion of American religion, politics, and society. Indeed, the Latino AG may be one of the movements in the vanguard of the browning of American Evangelicalism and Christianity.[23]

The Latino AG story is important, finally, because it also sheds light on the religious, class, gender, and racial dynamics in North American religious history. The story provides a window into Latino, Mexican American/Chicano, Puerto Rican, and Latin American religions; Pentecostalism; women's history; immigration studies; working-class religions; and religion, politics, and activism. Indeed, there is every reason to believe that, given the browning of America, the Latino AG will continue to play an ever-increasing role in the story of American history, religion, and politics in the twenty-first century, all of which makes telling this story timely.

History and Definitions of Protestants, Evangelicals, Pentecostals, and Charismatics

A problem one immediately encounters in any discussion of Latino Pentecostalism is defining "Pentecostal," "Latino," and related terms. What and who exactly do we mean by these terms, and what are their historical origins? Pentecostals are a subset of Evangelicals, and Evangelicals are a subset of Protestants. All Pentecostals and Evangelicals are Protestant in their core doctrinal beliefs. Protestants trace their roots back to Martin Luther (d. 1546) and John Calvin's (d. 1564) Protestant Reformation (1517–1648) in Europe. These reformers taught a number of core Protestant beliefs such as that people are saved by the grace of God alone; the saving grace of God comes only through Jesus Christ and not through the Catholic Church; salvation is by faith alone (versus faith plus good works); there are two sacraments (baptism and communion) rather than seven; the Bible alone teaches all that is necessary for salvation and ethics (versus the Bible plus Catholic tradition); the church is an association of believers and not an intermediary between God and man; good works and virtue are a natural by-product of genuine faith and do not contribute to one's salvation; and there is no longer any need for praying to the saints or the Virgin Mary, indulgences, penance, or purgatory, or to follow one supreme religious leader like the pope. Protestant reformers promoted the priesthood of all believers and translating the Bible into the vernacular so that everyone could read and study it in private devotions and in church. Their beliefs can be summarized in the five solae: *sola scriptura* (divine revelation by Scripture alone), *sola fides* (salvation by faith alone), *sola gratia* (salvation by grace alone), *sola Christo* (salvation through Christ alone), and *soli deo Gloria* (glory to God alone).[24]

Calvin's teachings gave birth to the Protestant Reformed and Evangelical traditions in western Europe, which in turn influenced the rise of the Calvinist-oriented English Puritans, Congregationalists, Anglicans, and Baptists, the Dutch Reform Church, and the Scottish Presbyterians, all of whom settled colonial America. Calvinist ideas were spread throughout the colonies during the First Great Awakening (ca. 1731–1755) led by Congregationalist, Anglican, and Presbyterian evangelists like Jonathan Edwards, George Whitefield, and Gilbert Tennent. John Wesley left Calvinism to spread the Methodist movement from England to the American colonies during the 1730s to the 1780s. They promoted many Arminian teachings, which were popularized during the Second Great Awakening (ca. 1790–1840) through Presbyterian, Methodist, and Baptist revivalists like Charles Finney, Francis Asbury, Peter Cartwright, and in the late nineteenth and twentieth century by Dwight L. Moody, Billy Sunday, and Billy Graham. The Methodist movement in turn helped give birth to the Holiness movement from the 1850s to the 1890s led by Dr. Walter and Phoebe Palmer, Thomas Upham, William and Catherine Booth, Robert Pearsall and Hannah Whitall Smith, Alma White, Charles Price Jones, Frank Sandford, and Daniel S. Warner. Their writings and ministries in turn influenced Charles Fox Parham, William J. Seymour, and the rise of Pentecostalism after 1900.[25]

The Methodists, Holiness, and Pentecostals tend to promote some of the theological ideas of Dutch theologian Jacob Arminius (d. 1609). His views were summarized in *The Remonstrance* (1610), and were drawn up by his followers: (1) although due to the fall, people are totally depraved in their mind, will, and affections, the Holy Spirit provides all people with the prevenient (enabling) grace necessary to freely chose and exercise faith in God, thus counteracting the effects of the fall and giving man a "free will"; (2) God elected people because He foresaw via foreknowledge that they would have faith in Jesus; (3) Jesus died to save all men, but only in a *potential* fashion and only on the condition that they first believe in Him; (4) humans can resist and thwart the grace of God and the work of the Holy Spirit; and (5) people who are genuinely saved can lose their salvation.[26]

In response to *The Remonstrance,* John Calvin's followers drew up the five points of Calvinism at the Synod of Dort (1619), which they later summarized by the acrostic TULIP: (1) Total depravity—people are totally depraved in their mind, will, and affections and thus need the Holy Spirit to elect, regenerate, and save them; (2) Unconditional election—God elected people as an act of divine grace and mercy, not due to their good works or on the condition and foreknowledge that they would choose Him; (3) Limited atonement—Jesus's sacrificial death is limited and applied only to the elect; (4) Irresistible grace—God's grace and love via the Holy Spirit are irresistible and results in people wanting to be saved; and (5) Perseverance of the saints—God will enable those whom He saves to persevere in their faith until the end of their lives, even though they may go through struggles and backslidden periods in their life. While some Evangelicals draw the theological lines firmly in the sand, others adapt what can be described as a "Calminian" perspective, whereby they blend these doctrines.[27]

What Protestant Evangelicals and Pentecostals generally share in common across denominational and theological lines is their conviction that a person must have a personal, born-again conversion experience with Jesus Christ to go to heaven. They base this belief on New Testament passages like John 3:3, John 14:6, and Acts 4:12. The word *evangelical* traces its roots to the Greek *evangelion,* which means "good news." An Evangelical is therefore someone who preaches the good news about Jesus's life, death, and resurrection from the dead, his sacrificial love for humanity, and the need for people to repent of (or turn from) their sins and have a personal born-again conversion experience with Jesus Christ. While the vast majority of Pentecostals are "born again" and thus "evangelical," not all evangelicals are Pentecostal/Charismatic because they do not believe that all of the spiritual sign gifts in I Corinthians 12 and 14 should be practiced in the church today.[28]

While born-again Christians can be found in almost every Christian denomination, the term *evangelical* is largely applied to politically, theologically, and morally conservative Protestants. In the U.S. Latino community and in Latin America, the term *evangélico* (Evangelical) normally refers to all Protestants, not just Evangelicals and Pentecostals. Latino Evangelicals point out that although they are theologically and morally conservative, like their African American counterparts, they tend to vote Democratic; though a large share of them swung over and voted for George W. Bush in the 2000 and 2004 presidential elections, for reasons discussed in Chapter 12.

Throughout this book, "evangelical" will normally refer to socially progressive but theologically and morally (but not necessarily politically) conservative Protestants who promote the fundamentals of the faith, but who are not Pentecostal, Charismatic, Neo-Charismatic, or fundamentalist. "Fundamentalist" refers to theologically and socially conservative antimodernist Protestants who struggle to preserve the fundamentals of the Protestant faith from skeptics and liberal Protestants. They often hold to a premillennial dispensationalist and cessationist position on the gifts of the Holy Spirit. Fundamentalists have historically rejected Pentecostals as a "fanatical menace" to Christianity for promoting speaking in unknown tongues, divine healing, the ordination of women, and the spiritual sign gifts listed in I Corinthians 12 and 14.[29] Like Evangelicals, Pentecostals, and fundamentalists, "historic" or "mainline" Protestants also trace their roots back to the Protestant Reformation in Europe. Although originally evangelical in theology and ethics, many mainline Protestants today are moderate-liberal in theology, social ethics, and politics, though there are conservative elements throughout almost all mainline denominations, especially among racial-ethnic minorities because they were largely converted by evangelically oriented pastors and laity.

Pentecostals differ from most traditional Evangelicals (for example, Southern Baptists, Free Methodists, Church of Christ) and mainline Protestants (for example, Episcopalians, United Methodists, Presbyterians [PCUSA]) in their belief that speaking in tongues and the spiritual gifts listed in I Corinthians 12 and 14 are available to all born-again Christians today and that speaking in tongues did not cease with the death of the Apostles, which is called the cessationist view. The Assemblies of God and some other Pentecostal denominations also affirm the distinctive "initial evidence" theory, that speaking in unknown tongues (glossolalia) is the initial, physical evidence of the baptism with the Holy Spirit.[30]

While Evangelicals, mainline Protestants, Catholics, and Orthodox Christians have not historically affirmed or practiced the spiritual gifts and speaking in tongues, during the 1960s the Pentecostal movement entered into their churches and helped birth the Charismatic movement (for example, Charismatic Episcopalians, Charismatic Presbyterians, Charismatic Catholics).[31] A number of independent Charismatic movements also emerged out of the classical Pentecostal movement during this period, such as Calvary Chapel (Costa Mesa), Vineyard Christian Fellowship, and Victory Outreach International, along with a growing number of independent and nondenominational churches. Charismatics normally believe that the spiritual gifts are available for all born-again Christians today, but either choose to remain in their mainline Protestant, Evangelical, or Catholic denominations or attend independent or nondenominational charismatic churches. They also normally do not affirm the initial evidence theory. The Charismatic movement entered into Latino Spanish-language districts in Evangelical, mainline, and Catholic traditions. This is why (as noted above) such a high percentage of Latino mainline Protestants and Catholics reported being born again and/or Pentecostal/Charismatic Christians.[32]

Latino Diversity

The Latino community in the United States is diverse and includes more than twenty-two nationalities, though in many locales it can and does take on particular national and/or regional identities. This rich diversity has made it difficult to find a suitable umbrella term to describe it. In general, Latinos born in the United States refer to themselves as "Americans" or by their country of origin (for example, "Mexican American"). Similarly, Latino immigrants refer to themselves almost exclusively by their country of origin or by the umbrella term given to them by the larger Euro-American society—Hispanic or Latino. Unless otherwise noted, all Mexican Americans and Mexican immigrants will be referred to as "Mexicans" because Euro-Americans and Latinos themselves tend to lump both groups together as "Mexican." While some college-educated people of Mexican descent refer to themselves as "Mexican Americans" or "Chicanos," most noncollege-educated people and immigrants still prefer to be called by their country of origin or "Hispanic" because this is the term used by Euro-American society and the United States government on many documents and applications. The word *Hispanic* was created and used by the government as an umbrella term to include people from twenty-two Latin American countries and Spain. Hispanic also tends to point to the community's roots in Spain (ancient Hispania) rather than its immediate roots in Latin America (Latino), which includes Spanish, indigenous Indians, blacks, and other multi-ethnic people. For this reason, many college-educated Latinos in the

Southwest reject the term *Hispanic* along with its implied homogeniza-
tion of the community's rich diversity and instead use "Latino" because
it has also been the most commonly used term in Spanish literature in
the United States and Latin America throughout the twentieth century.
However, working-class Latinos on the East Coast, along with many
Puerto Ricans, Cubans, Latin Americans, and Mexicans, still prefer
"Hispanic" instead of "Latino," though most are fine with either desig-
nation. In the Latino AG and Latino Evangelical and Pentecostal communities, they normally prefer to be called by the country of origin, Hispanic, or Latino.

With respect to the spelling of Spanish names, diacritical marks have
been applied to all relevant first and last names, except in instances
where the subject never used them. This will explain any inconsistency
in usage. This respects the social and cultural identity, location, and
preferences of the subjects. Although the names of the Spanish-language
districts have changed over the years (for example, conference, convention, district), to be consistent throughout the book, all of the Spanish-
language Latino conferences, conventions, and districts will simply be
referred to as districts (which is what they are called today), and all fourteen current Latino AG districts will collectively be referred to as the
Latino Assemblies of God or Latino AG.

Method, Sources, and Perspectives

This social-cultural history of the Latino AG takes an ethno-
phenomenological approach to the study of North American religious
history. It seeks to examine and understand religious actors and movements, in the words of Mircea Eliade, on their own plane of reference
from a critical scholarly perspective in order to see how they contribute
to the larger culture.[33] It draws on archival, qualitative (oral histories,
solo and focus group interviews), and quantitative research, including
eight national surveys. Since 1993, I have visited over a dozen archives
and private collections in the United States, Mexico, Puerto Rico, and
Europe and have secured thousands of pages of primary and secondary
sources and loose-leaf materials on Latino Protestantism, Evangelicalism, and Pentecostalism. These sources include denominational annual

reports, private letters, periodicals from 1900 to the 1980s, tracts, hand-bills, self-published autobiographies, biographies, poems, hymnals, no-tarized statements, telephone and electronic interviews, 150 photo-graphs, audio recordings, cassette and videotaped interviews, services, and revivals, silent and modern film footage, and denominational and national survey data. This book also draws on qualitative findings from approximately forty interviews with thirty-two people and the quantita-tive findings from eight national surveys, six of which I managed or di-rected in 1998, 2000, 2008, and 2012. All combined, these sources pro-vide rich insight into Latino AG beliefs, moral and social views, and political attitudes and voting patterns from 1914 to 2014.[34]

I have attempted to examine these sources as judiciously as possible. When dealing with sensitive matters, I have also sought to find corrobo-rating evidence to confirm the veracity of the original report. Although the historian Peter Novick reminds us that complete objectivity is im-possible this side of heaven, I have endeavored to write a history that is critical and fair-minded and that reflects a close reading of the archival sources, interviews, and survey data. Since it is impossible to cover ev-ery facet of any movement in one volume, I hope that others will build on, refine, and, where the evidence permits, expand, revise, and correct the history that follows.[35]

This history differs from traditional church histories in several ways. Although it covers the origins and development of the Latino AG and some of their most important leaders, since they are almost completely unknown to the outside world, it also includes the stories, comments, and views of ordinary pastors and lay leaders not mentioned in previous histories. Also woven into this archival and qualitative work are the ag-gregate quantitative views of rank-and-file Latino AG parishioners via the national surveys. This study also focuses on topics normally left out of traditional church histories, such as sociological and political science research on women in ministry; race relations; civil rights and social jus-tice struggles; political, civic, and social action; religious and moral be-liefs; and political identity, attitudes, and voting behavior. It also ex-pands the geographical boundaries of traditional American church histories by including Puerto Rico.

It discusses not only the perspectives of insiders and those who have always remained loyal to the movement, but also in relevant cases those who left the AG and went on to organize their own denominations and churches. A movement's history is best told not only from the sources of those who won the battle for control of their organization, but also by considering those who lost. This approach is important because it also reveals the larger influence of the Latino AG's beliefs, practices, and social views on new denominations and movements that emerged out of these conflicts and schisms. As this history will reveal, very few schisms were driven by doctrinal differences; more commonly they were the result of personal conflicts and power struggles, so for this reason the Latino AG's doctrinal and social influences remain influential even in some non-AG denominations.

Thesis, Argument, and Contributions

Contrary to the image of the compliant and silent Euro-American-led Latino AG, this book argues that Latino Pentecostals have struggled over the past 100 years to exercise voice, agency, and leadership in the Assemblies of God, in Latino Protestantism, and in American public life. It contends that the Latino AG has been one of the most important catalysts in the growth of denominational and religious pluralism in the North American Latino community and has exercised a modest but significant influence in American public life relative to other Latino Pentecostal and Evangelical traditions and leaders.[36] Although some scholars argue that this shift toward Latino Protestantism and Pentecostalism is a phenomenon that made "few inroads among Mexican Americans" until relatively recently,[37] I argue that the movement's origins trace their roots back more than 100 years among Mexican Americans and other Latinos and that it has witnessed significant growth throughout the twentieth century. This book also challenges the claim that Pentecostals make up only 2 percent of the Latino community nationwide by noting that recent surveys found that 64 percent of all Latino Protestants reported being Pentecostal or Charismatic and that 28 percent of Latinos nationwide reported being the same.[38] This growth is due to a number of overlapping factors: a strong and stable indigenous Latino leadership; organizational independence and autonomy; fostering transformational rather than transactional leaders; emphases on youth evangelism, women in ministry, and planting indigenous Latino-led churches; decentralization from one Latino AG district in 1939 to fourteen today; cultural hybridity; a focus on personal conversion, healing, and community-based spiritual empowerment; and a constant desire to exercise voice, agency, and self-determination in the church and in society. Perhaps the most important factors are its strong and stable transformationally oriented indigenous leadership and focus on theological education, evangelism, and church planting and women in ministry. The Latino AG and its leaders seek to transform and empower their followers to identify and unleash their unique spiritual gifts in order to bring about Christian renewal and social change in the Latino community and American society.[39]

Despite its historically marginal status and a lack of scholarly attention, the Latino AG and its leaders have emerged out of the shadows of American history, politics, and society. Today Latino AG leaders are among the nation's most influential Latino Christian voices in American public life. This leadership and influence have been garnered through Jesse Miranda and the Alianza de Ministerios Evangélicos Nacionales (AMEN), Samuel Rodríguez and the NHCLC, and a number of other leaders, churches, and faith-based organizations. Similarly, they are also increasingly exercising leadership and influence in the academy. For example, Latino AG minister Dr. Eldin Villafañe was a founder and the first president of La Comunidad of Hispanic Scholars of Religion at the American Academy of Religion and the Society of Biblical Literature, a founder and the first president of the Center for Urban Ministerial Education in Boston, a founder and president of the Association of Hispanic Theological Education, and the first Latino scholar of religion to be a visiting professor at Harvard Divinity School, where he and Harvey Cox team-taught the first course on Pentecostalism at an Ivy League university. He is not alone. The Latino AG has also influenced other scholars, among them Dr. Efrain Agosto, Dr. Samuel Solivan, Dr. Tommy Casarez, and others who have served in national leadership roles over the past thirty years.[40]

This book challenges De Leon and almost 100 years of Pentecostal historiography by revising the claim that Euro-American missionaries Henry C. Ball and Alice E. Luce alone founded the Latino AG in 1915, one year after the larger AG movement was founded in Hot Springs, Arkansas, in April 1914. Instead, it posits that the Latino AG traces its origins back to Latinos and Euro-Americans at William J. Seymour's Azusa Street Revival in Los Angeles in 1906 and to followers of Charles Fox Parham's Apostolic Faith ministry in Houston around 1909. They in turn influenced several key Latino and Euro-American pioneers like Juan Lugo, Francisco Olazábal, and many others who in turn helped spread the work throughout the United States, Puerto Rico, and Mexico. Parham's Euro-American followers converted Enemecio Alaniz in Deepwater, Texas, in 1909. He and others organized a number of independent Latino Pentecostal missions in Texas from 1909 to 1915, which after 1914 became affiliated with the AG. These Latino AG pastors and evangelists began preaching throughout Texas before Ball first began preaching Pentecostalism to Mexicans in Texas in July 1915. Moreover, Ball's initial work tends to be overstated in the Latino AG literature because he did not exercise any major influence over all of the independent Latino AG churches and missions in Texas until after the first convention that he and Isabel Flores organized in 1918. Prior to that time, he pastored a very small and struggling mission and worked sporadically with other missions. The future of his Latino AG mission and work in Texas was in doubt. Ball secured his future after he and Flores persuaded most of the independent Pentecostal missions to attend their convention in 1918, during which Ball assumed and secured the leadership of the newly formed convention. Ball then used his administrative skills to develop and provide stable leadership for it throughout the early twentieth century. The single district that Ball helped organize has now developed into fourteen independent and autonomous geographical districts, each with its own superintendent, constitution, bylaws, and Bible schools. The contributions of Isabel Flores and other Latinos have until now been left out of the history of the Latino AG.

In addition to challenging a number of myths and stereotypes about the origins of the Latino AG, this book also explores the Latino Pentecostal contributions to Latino history, politics, and civil rights struggles. It shows how Latino AG and other Pentecostal leaders and laity indirectly and sometimes directly influenced and/or contributed to Latino, Mexican American/Chicano, Cuban, and Puerto Rican struggles, such as Reies López Tijerina and the Hispano Land Grant struggle in New Mexico; César Chávez's United Farm Workers' struggle in California; Operation Pedro Pan and the Mariel Boat Lift in Florida; and the NHCLC's push for comprehensive immigration reform on Capitol Hill from 2006–2014. Latino AG leaders led criticisms against Arizona governor Jan Brewer's SB 1070, which authorized law enforcement to identify (profile), prosecute, and deport undocumented immigrants. They also wrote open letters to President George W. Bush, the Republican Party, and *Christianity Today* criticizing Republican and Euro-American Evangelical leaders for allowing nativist and racialized sentiments to emerge within their ranks and they likewise criticized President Barack Obama for not following through on his 2008 campaign promises to pass comprehensive immigration reform in his first year in office and to support traditional marriage. In short, they have exercised a small but growing voice in some of the most important struggles in contemporary U.S. Latino history and American public life. Latino AG leaders like Miranda and Rodríguez have also placed a growing emphasis on righteousness and justice, by which they mean the reconciling (vertically oriented) message of Billy Graham and the (horizontally oriented) faith-based civil rights and social justice activism of Martin Luther King Jr.

As a result, U.S. presidents from Ronald Reagan to Barack Obama have invited Latino Assemblies of God leaders to the White House. Miranda has been invited to the White House to meet every American president from Reagan to Obama. George W. Bush reached out to Miranda and his Alianza in 2000 and especially in 2004 to win over the Latino Evangelical community. The strategy worked because despite voting for Clinton in 1996 and Gore in 2000, Latino Evangelicals switched over and voted for Bush in 2004, which helped him win 40–44 percent of the Latino vote.[41]

In 2008, Barack Obama worked hard to reclaim lost ground among the Latino Evangelical electorate by appointing a Latino AG minister, Wilfredo de Jesús, senior pastor of the 4,000-member New Life Covenant Church in South Chicago, to serve as his campaign adviser and surrogate in the Latino Protestant community. Obama also invited Samuel Rodríguez to participate in campaign forums on faith and social justice. As a result of these efforts and many others, Obama reversed the trend in Latino Evangelicals voting Republican by winning their vote by a margin of 58 to 40 percent. To underscore his commitment, Obama invited Rodríguez to pray at his 2009 presidential inauguration prayer service and appointed him to White House task forces on fatherhood and abortion reduction. From 2009 to 2014, Rodríguez has also provided regular advice to President Obama on immigration, health care, and job creation. Despite these developments, almost nothing has been written about the important contributions of Latino AG leaders in American public life. This book will discuss the origins and development of these leaders, organizations, and movements.[42]

The Burden of Racial-Ethnic Minority History

Tracking down the sources, interviews, and national survey data for this history has not been easy. Scholars trying to piece together racial-ethnic minority history face a number of obstacles—what I call the burden of racial-ethnic minority history. The biggest is the paucity of sources. Simply put, racial-ethnic minorities left relatively few sources behind when compared to some of their Euro-American counterparts. This is due to low levels of literacy as a result of dropping out of school to help support their families and to a lack of the financial resources needed to write and create these histories. Those sources that are available are not generally housed in a single major archive or location and are scattered across North America largely in private collections or at district offices, some of which lack the staff to maintain accurate records. Furthermore, many denominations were simply unwilling to invest time, personnel, and scarce resources in preserving the past because most were struggling to survive. This dearth of sources forces scholars to carry out time-consuming and complicated qualitative research with eyewitnesses. This is made even more difficult because minorities are cautious about sharing their stories with outsiders. There are also linguistic barriers in the study of racial-ethnic minority history that require language training for nonnative speakers, since much of the literature remains buried in foreign-language periodicals, letters, and documents and in-person interviews.

All of the above results in racial-ethnic minorities being left out of many histories or included in only a truncated or incomplete form, which invariably gives disproportionate weight and voice to Euro-Americans who left behind accounts of their own contributions and accomplishments. When racial-ethnic minorities are mentioned, it is generally in passing, along with a few brief statistics. Securing these documents is also remarkably time-consuming and expensive because it involves building relationships to gain the trust of one's subjects and extensive travel to far-flung locations often not in major metropolitan areas. Some racial-ethnic minorities are reluctant to tell their stories because they are often checkered with struggle, conflict, pain, and despair, something few are eager to report, let alone write about and read. Finally, sometimes their theological outlook, eschatology, and worldview undermine any incentive to write down their own stories for posterity. All of the above burdens, in addition to publication costs, resulted in racial-ethnic minorities producing relatively few full-length histories of their own.

While almost all historians in American religion, history, and politics face some of the above restrictions to one degree or another, their number is compounded and multiplied—in some cases exponentially—for those working in racial-ethnic minority communities, where archives and historical preservation are almost unheard of. Many racial-ethnic minorities have also been very reticent to share their stories for fear that they would be scorned, mocked, exoticized, and misunderstood. They worry that their stories will be used against them to reinscribe their own marginality.

This concern is not without basis. The ease with which minority faiths such as Latino Pentecostalism are misunderstood and exoticized by the mainstream media was evident in the above-cited *Time* magazine article. Although the author offers a largely fair-minded treatment of Latino Pentecostals throughout parts of the essay, she also reinscribes their exoticism and otherness when she describes a woman at a Spanish-speaking Latino Pentecostal church who was so "extreme" and "praying so hard that she vomited" or "exorcised a demon" and later "fell to the ground in convulsions," which—the author noted—"was not uncommon."[43] This approach simultaneously enhances the exotic nature and novelty of the story and reinscribes the subjects' marginality and otherness. For without the extreme prayer, vomiting, and demon-possessed woman falling to the ground in convulsions, one is left only with the story of the unvarnished and desperate faith of a Latin American immigrant woman trying to find hope, voice, and agency in her struggles—something not particularly attractive to some hard-nosed editors driven by an "if it bleeds, it leads" mentality.

All of the preceding was not unlike a similar story told more than 100 years ago by the *Los Angeles Daily Times* in April 1906, which described William J. Seymour's Azusa Street Revival as a place where an "old colored exhorter" (Seymour was thirty-five years old) with a "stony optic" and "big fist" (he was five feet nine inches) preached the "wildest theories" and "mad excitement" to his "howling . . . worshippers who spent hours swaying back and forth in a nerve-racking attitude of prayer and supplication."[44] The vortex of race and religious otherness—even by people occasionally sympathetic or even associated with the community—has remained remarkably powerful and constant over the past 100 years despite the progress that has been made in post–civil rights movement America. Perhaps this progress may have been more favorable to African Americans than to Latinos, whose new day has yet to dawn.

The two larger professional and academic burdens that scholars face when studying racial-ethnic minorities are the assumptions that these topics are not mainstream enough for job openings in American religions and that people writing on them are invariably less objective and rigorous than historians writing on Euro-American topics. The problem is exacerbated if the scholar is from the same racial-ethnic community and/or religious tradition, no matter how broadly defined or loosely affiliated.

This suspicion has led some Euro-American scholars to call such scholarship "racial-ethnic" and "multicultural" history,[45] often with the implicit assumption that this work is somehow less rigorous and objective and more partisan and politically committed than their own. However, few of these same historians define or label their own work on

Euro-American subjects "white" or "Euro-American" history. Nor do they assume that they are any less rigorous or objective than any other historian. This double standard and burden has prompted a number of minority scholars to refrain from writing about their own community or to write about the traditions in a mocking and condescending tone to demonstrate their objectivity and impartiality, but at the price of reinforcing and reinscribing their community's social, intellectual, and historical isolation and marginalization within the academy. A more tempered approach might seek to understand their subjects on their own plane of reference from a critical scholarly perspective based on their archival, qualitative, and/or quantitative research.[46]

This above view and implied historical normativity in the mainstream academy tends to privilege an East Coast intellectual history paradigm and the rationally oriented religious traditions that have dominated American history, politics, and society for more than two centuries. An alternative historical remapping and renarrating might revise and redirect the flow of U.S. history, politics, and society from multiple directions, but especially from south to north. They would follow the movement of Spanish, Mexican, black, mestizo, Indian, and mulatto conquistadores, missionaries, settlers, and laborers from Mexico City (al norte) to the Southwest and from Puerto Rico and the Caribbean to Florida, New York, and up the East Coast and across the country. They could also add another flow of African Americans from the Deep South to the North and West in the wake of a failed Reconstruction, and still more streams from Africa and Asia via the Chinese, Japanese, Filipinos, Vietnamese, Indians, and other racial-ethnic minorities. The present East Coast, east-to-west paradigm clearly represents a political rather than a historical defining of the field. Although these views are slowly beginning to change in the academy and society, they still contribute to the burden of writing racial-ethnic minority history because they marginalize these subjects and their stories, religious experiences, and political outlooks to the periphery, by implicitly implying they are not part of the mainstream core "American" experience—by which they mean (however well intended) their own projected normative patterns, experiences, and beliefs of good Americans.

These kinds of selectively applied distinctions between marginal and mainstream, center and periphery, and normative and extreme, invariably contribute to the racialization, marginalization, and politicization of history and religion and stunt their academic growth and potentially expansive contributions to the larger field. Perhaps it is time to bring them out of the shadows not as parallel, tangential, or exoticized histories, but rather as an integral and often central dimension that provides scholars and readers with a richer and more complete—if at times painful—understanding of American history, religion, and society. This recalibration, renaming, and shift in focus from marginal to mainstream may also help scholars, the media, and the general public better understand the seismic demographic shifts currently taking place across the nation and help them to realize that they are not new phenomena, but rather an ongoing part of a regular dynamic and flow in the North American experience.

In short, this book seeks to weave into the American tapestry one admittedly small but important chapter, and by so doing help readers understand Latino Pentecostals and their contributions to North American history, religion, and society. Perhaps by so doing, it may also have the unintended consequence of giving voice to a hitherto silenced community that is struggling to be silent no more.

CHAPTER 1

Holy Ghost and Fire

Azusa Street and Mexican Pentecostal Origins

T HE BIRTH of the Latino Pentecostal movement in the United States
and Puerto Rico traces its origins to William J. Seymour's Azusa
Street Revival in Los Angeles in 1906. Latinos participated in the revival
the first week it opened and in the first manifestation of the Holy Spirit.
In October of that year, Abundio and Rosa López testified about the
impact of Seymour's revival and the baptism with the Holy Ghost on
their lives:

> We testify to the power of the Holy Spirit in forgiveness, sanctifica-
> tion, and the baptism with the Holy Ghost and fire. We give thanks
> to God for this wonderful gift which we have received from Him,
> according to the promise . . . [at] the Azusa Street Mission . . . on
> the 5th of June, 190[6]. . . . We cannot express the gratitude . . . we
> feel moment by moment for what He has done for us . . . we want to
> be used for the salvation and healing of both soul and body. I am a
> witness of His wonderful promise and marvelous miracles by the
> Holy Ghost.[1]

The Lópezes' burning testimony captures the heart and passion of the
Latino Pentecostal movement throughout the Americas. Despite their

Figure 1.1. Abundio L. López, Los Angeles, California, date unknown.
(Gastón Espinosa Latino Pentecostal History Collection)

powerful descriptions of Azusa, little has been written about the involvement of Latinos.[2] Their participation has long been overshadowed by an emphasis on the black and white origins of Pentecostalism. This is ironic because they were actively involved in the revival for three years, participated in key turning points, and helped spread Seymour's message throughout the Latino community in the Southwest and around the world through the ministry of Mexican American evangelists like Adolfo C. Valdez, who spread his message throughout the United States, Latin America, Asia, and Australia and New Zealand. The image of Abundio López (Figure 1.1) was taken at the end of his forty plus year Pentecostal ministry.[3]

This chapter, along with those that follow, argues that the Latino AG movement in the United States, Mexico, and Puerto Rico traces its genealogy directly back to William J. Seymour and the Azusa Street Revival in Los Angeles and to followers of Charles Fox Parham's Apostolic Faith Movement in Houston. Although followers of both converted Latinos, primacy of origin and importance goes to Seymour and the Azusa Revival because the evidence indicates he personally interacted with, converted, and ordained the first Euro-Americans and Latinos to Pentecostalism, some of whom in turn influenced the future Latino Assemblies of God work in the United States. In Texas, on the other hand, it was primarily Parham's converts rather than Parham himself who converted and ordained Latinos to Pentecostalism in Texas.[4]

In order to understand the origins of the Latino AG, it is important to examine the origins of Pentecostalism through the life and ministries of Parham, Seymour, and the Azusa Street Revival. Approaching the story from this perspective challenges a number of misperceptions. Seymour did not simply popularize Parham's message. In fact, he crafted his own message. He taught that the outpouring of the Holy Spirit was ushering in a new age that made everyone level at the foot of the cross, regardless of race, class, and education. The Spirit reportedly poured out spiritual gifts so that people could cross race, class, and nationality lines, spread the love of Christ to all nations, and usher in the Second Coming. This story challenges the largely biracial black-white narrative of the Azusa Revival in view of the role that Latinos and other ethnic minorities played. Finally, the popular perception that conversion to Latino Protestantism and Pentecostalism is of recent, post-1960 origins is challenged by a genealogy that stretches back more than 100 years in California and Texas.[5]

Outpouring of the Holy Spirit on Azusa Street

"Weird Babel of Tongues" read the headlines of the *Los Angeles Times* on April 18, 1906. The "night is made hideous . . . by the howlings of the worshipers, who spend hours swaying back and forth in a nerve-racking attitude of prayer and supplication," the reporter recounted. An "old colored exhorter" with a "stony optic" and "big fist" preached the "wildest theories" and "'mad excitement'" to his large multiracial crowd for almost an hour. The reporter's contempt for Azusa was evident when he stated that although Los Angeles was home to almost numberless creeds, this "new sect of fanatics" surpassed them all.[6]

The reporter's racialized reaction to Seymour's "weird babel of tongues" reflected the sentiment of the Progressive Era (1870–1920), a period of tremendous social change. The rise of a new middle class and the decline of rural island communities created an impersonal society. Society was increasingly driven by industrialization, mechanization, and the clock. This, along with the migration of countless blacks to the north and the influx of millions of southern European, Asian, and Latin American immigrants, created a period of tremendous social upheaval. The landed Euro-American middle-class response was a search for order that stressed continuity and regularity, administration and management, functionality and rationality, and the centralization of authority. Suppression and social control were key ingredients in the psychosocial make-up of the Progressive Era.[7] Seymour's multiethnic revival seemed to challenge these ingredients.

Most Protestant denominations embraced the new middle-class ethos and search for order. With its emphasis on Scottish commonsense realism, the new scientific interpretation of Christianity and the Bible was gaining ground not only in Christian Liberalism but also in Evangelical/Fundamentalist circles.[8] While Christian Liberalism was outright skeptical of most supernatural truth claims, conservative Protestants and Presbyterians like B. B. Warfield of Princeton Seminary criticized selected supernatural ecstatic manifestations in *Counterfeit Miracles*.[9] He denigrated what he considered primitive religious practices, especially those associated with supernatural, miraculous, and ecstatic experiences.[10]

Those unready or unwilling to embrace this new ethos found solace and meaning in metaphysical, occult, and new religious movements advertising their wares in the religious marketplace.[11] In short, people had choices. However, they generally had to choose between a more orderly and rationalistic approach to religion and an intensely personal and supernatural one represented by metaphysical and occult traditions such as Spiritualism, Spiritism, and Theosophy.[12] Pentecostalism provided a third alternative that seemed to combine trappings of historic Christianity and experiential religion. Seymour's vision of Pentecost also wove in one more very important stand, and that was a blending of a prophetic social consciousness on the one hand and a theology of racial reconciliation and multicultural, transformative, egalitarian Christianity on the other. He challenged the American church and society to live up to its professed ideals of unity in Christ and liberty and justice for all regardless of race, color, or nationality.

Charles Fox Parham

The exact theological roots of Pentecostalism are hotly debated.[13] Although shaped by nineteenth-century black slave religion and black and white Holiness, Keswick, Dispensational, Premillennial, divine healing, and other social and religious movements, it is generally believed that modern Pentecostalism began in the United States in the early twentieth century. Today the worldwide movement numbers over 630 million people on six continents and 135 million people throughout the Americas.[14] Many credit the slightly built, eccentric evangelist Charles F. Parham (1873–1929) and the sturdy black Holiness minister William J. Seymour (1870–1922) as two of its key U.S. founders.[15] Still others see them as two of a number of pneumatically inspired leaders around the world simultaneously promoting the outpouring of the Holy Spirit.[16]

Parham was one of the first to systematically preach the distinctive Pentecostal doctrine that speaking in unknown tongues is the physical evidence of the baptism with the Holy Spirit. His pre-Pentecostal religious experiences directly influenced his theology. Born in Muscatine, Iowa, on June 4, 1873, as a child he suffered from a virus that stunted his growth and left him looking handsome but physically impaired. Plagued by rheumatic fever, Parham and his mother moved to the wheat fields of Kansas in 1878. Upon his mother's death in 1885, Parham vowed to see her in heaven and gave his life to Jesus Christ in a Congregational Church near Cheney.[17]

As his newfound faith took root, he became an earnest and spiritually minded youth who stressed holy living and personal purity. He began wrestling with the idea of becoming a minister. Pushing the idea aside in favor of medical school, the fragile youth entered the Methodist-affiliated Southwest Kansas College around 1890. This took tremendous heart, given his physical handicap. Walking was difficult because he suffered from clubfoot. Despite long stares from his peers, he hobbled to classes on the sides of his feet.[18]

A critical turning point came after another severe bout of rheumatic fever left him at death's door. He interpreted the illness as divine punishment for refusing God's calling to the ministry and now promised to give himself 100 percent to spreading the Christian message. At that moment, he reported, his ankles were "instantly healed." He stood up and walked away from a medical career, dropping out of college in 1893 and joining the Methodist Episcopal Church, North. In March, he was licensed as a "local preacher" and later pastored two small Methodist churches in Eudora and Linwood, Kansas, despite not then being formally ordained.[19]

He soon became "enamored" with the Holiness movement and its belief in divine healing—the latter of which seemed to elude him until later in life. The Holiness movement grew as a renewal movement primarily in the Methodist church in the 1860s and 1870s. It emphasized complete sanctification and moral perfection in this life and was popularized through the writings of Phoebe Palmer, Charles Finney, and Hannah Whitall Smith. After the Methodist church expelled the Holiness movement from its ranks in 1895, Parham, along with 100,000 other Holiness-Methodists left and began their own independent ministries.[20]

In 1896, Parham married Sarah Thistlethwaite, a Quaker. Her grandfather, David, had a profound influence on the twenty-three-year-old Kansan. He persuaded the impressionable Parham to reject the traditional beliefs in water baptism, hell as a place of eternal torment, and mandatory church membership. Parham later wrote that the doctrine of hell as a place of eternal punishment was a "Pagan-Catholic doctrine" "concocted by Augustine and adopted by Protestants" for anyone who would not join their churches.[21]

Indeed, during this time Parham also formulated his controversial views on white supremacy and other theologically heterodox positions that differentiated him from traditional Protestants. He embraced the British Israelism theory, which claimed that those of the Anglo-Saxon race were the lineal descendants of the ten lost tribes of Israel and therefore God's chosen race. He adopted a sacred genealogy that traced Queen Victoria's ancestral pedigree all the way back to the ten lost tribes of Israel and Adam and Eve. In his 1902 theological treatise, *Kol Kare Bomidbar: A Voice Crying Out in the Wilderness,* he argued that Adam and Eve were the founders of a white race of people created by God on the eighth day of creation. They were morally and spiritually superior to blacks, Latinos, Native Americans, and Asians, who were created on the sixth day and were "nearly all heathen still." He argued that it was important to segregate the races and avoid interracial marriage because miscegenation between the races had caused God's wrath to be poured out through Noah's flood. He warned that if the present intermarriage between the races did not stop it would lead to the further dilution of the Anglo-Saxon race and to the eventual demise of America. His British Israelism theory gave him a sacred genealogy by which to support Manifest Destiny, Jim Crow segregation, the Ku Klux Klan, and white supremacy. Parham, like many people in his day, saw no contradiction in mixing his Christian faith and white supremacy.[22]

The year 1897 changed Parham's life for two reasons: his first child was born and Parham claims he was "miraculously" healed of heart disease. From this time on, he became a faith healer and preached that medicine was not necessary. Not wanting to waste any time before Christ's imminent return to Earth, the restless Parham in 1898 opened up Beth-el Healing Home in Topeka, Kansas, and started a Holiness periodical called the *Apostolic Faith.* In the summer of 1900, Parham and eight of his students traveled across the country, visiting prominent Holiness centers like Alexander Dowie's Zion City, Illinois; A. B. Simpson's Nyack College in New York; and Fred Sandford's Shiloh commune in Maine. Parham stayed at Sandford's commune for six weeks, listening intently to Sandford's Holiness teaching and stories about foreign missionaries speaking in tongues (xenolalia, the ability to speak in a human language one has never studied). He became convinced that Christ's Second Coming would not take place until after a worldwide religious revival. Tongues, Parham believed, were the key to world evangelization because they enabled people to preach to non-Christians around the world in their own language without having to waste valuable time studying a foreign language. Energized by his newfound theology, Parham returned to Kansas, where he started Topeka Bible School on October 16, 1900. He opened the school to prepare his followers for the imminent outpouring of the Holy Spirit and Christian missions. He rented Stone Mansion from the American Bible Society for $16 per month. The school was free of charge and eventually forty students enrolled.[23] Little did they know they were about to make history.

The Pentecostal movement in the United States began after Parham challenged his students to search the Bible for evidence of the baptism with the Holy Spirit. According to Pentecostal tradition, on New Year's Day 1901, Miss Agnes Ozman (1870–1937), a student of Parham's, received the "gift of tongues" (ecstatic utterances) after he prayed that she might receive the baptism with the Holy Spirit.[24] Ozman claimed that the Holy Spirit gave her the ability to speak Chinese. Three days later, twelve more students were reportedly baptized with the Holy Spirit and allegedly spoke in different languages.[25] From that time on, Parham became convinced that speaking in tongues was the physical evidence of the baptism with the Holy Spirit. Parham also taught that in the New Testament book of Acts, speaking in tongues accompanied all known instances of the baptism with the Spirit and should thus be a normative experience for all true Christians. Figure 1.2 captures the spirit and energy of Parham's Apostolic Faith ministry team at Bryan Hall in Houston, Texas, in 1905.[26]

Parham's controversial beliefs and aggressive proselytism attracted sharp criticism from the otherwise mild-mannered Kansans and prompted him to flee Topeka in April 1901. With his Bible school disintegrating and his foes criticizing him on all sides, Parham retreated from the world he sought to convert—at least for a short while. His powerful revival meetings two years later in Galena, Kansas, reignited his ministry. The rough-and-tumble mining region of Galena was ripe for Parham's message of divine healing and spiritual empowerment. Thousands converted to his fledgling Apostolic Faith movement. Emboldened by his recent campaigns in Kansas, Parham and his roving bands of tongues speakers "invaded" Houston, Texas, in 1905. In October he opened the Houston Bible School, his base of operations and the training ground for his Pentecostal "shock troops."[27]

Figure 1.2. Charles Fox Parham and Apostolic Faith workers, Bryan Hall, Houston, July/August, 1905. (Flower Pentecostal Heritage Center)

William J. Seymour

In December 1905, the fledgling Pentecostal movement took a decisive turn when a thirty-five-year-old, unschooled, black Holiness preacher named William J. Seymour asked Parham if he could attend Houston Bible School. Seymour was an unlikely prophet and even more unlikely founder of a global religious movement. The son of slaves, the five-foot nine-inch tall Seymour was born to Simon and Phyllis Salabar Seymour in Centerville, Louisiana, on May 2, 1870. Brought up in the Deep South during Reconstruction, Seymour was keenly aware of both his theoretical Fourteenth Amendment "freedom" and the ugly reality of Southern racism. The lynch man's rope and the Ku Klux Klan cast a long shadow over Reconstruction and black civil rights as over 2,500 blacks were lynched between 1880–1920. In the early 1890s, Seymour left his family in the South and journeyed north to Memphis, Tennessee, and to St. Louis, Missouri. He then traveled to Indianapolis, Indiana, around 1900, where he attended the all-black Simpson Chapel Methodist Episcopal Church. Over the next couple of years he moved to Chicago and then to Cincinnati, Ohio in search of a color-blind society. In Cincinnati, he joined Daniel S. Warner's Evening Light Saints. This socially progressive, radical Holiness group preached racial equality at the height of Jim Crow segregation and aggressively reached out to blacks. While with the Saints, Seymour rededicated his life to Jesus Christ. He also had one of his first visions of a racially egalitarian church—something he was true to for the rest of his life.[28]

After resisting his divine calling to ministry, Seymour gave in to what he interpreted as God's will when smallpox nearly cost him his life. He was ordained an evangelist. A few years later, Seymour traveled to Jackson, Mississippi to attend a conference led by Charles Price Jones and possibly Charles H. Mason. He left in search of his relatives in Texas with an even deeper commitment to premillennial theology, prophecy, and divine revelation and found not only his family but also Pentecostalism. He joined a Holiness church pastored by a former slave, Lucy Farrow, niece of Frederick Douglass, the great African American civil rights leader and statesman. After becoming governess of Parham's growing family, Farrow asked Seymour to take over her church until she returned. It was while pastoring Farrow's church that Seymour met Parham and was later invited to Los Angeles.[29] In January 1906, Seymour asked Parham if he could attend his Bible School. Because of his support of Jim Crow segregation laws in Texas and racial views, Parham agreed—but only if Seymour took notes outside the classroom in the hallway.[30]

Seymour agreed and spent the next two to eight weeks listening carefully to Parham's teachings. Although he embraced Parham's view that baptism with the Holy Spirit was evidenced by speaking in tongues, he disagreed with his writings on white supremacy, Jim Crow segregation, annihilationism, that miscegenation caused Noah's flood, and that the Anglo-Saxon race were the lineal descendants of the ten lost tribes of Israel and therefore God's chosen race. Despite their growing differences, Seymour and Parham conducted joint evangelistic and revival services in the black community, taking turns preaching and ministering

to blacks. Parham's followers and perhaps Parham himself reached out
to Latinos. Although it is unclear if Parham himself converted any Latinos to Pentecostalism (we know that at least one attended his services),
we know that Parham's followers converted a number of Mexican American and Mexican immigrants to Pentecostalism in the Houston area
in April 1909. These converts developed small independent Mexican
Pentecostal missions in the farm communities near Houston and San
Antonio.[31]

A classic opportunist and careful propagandist, Parham saw the hard-
working and mild-mannered Seymour as a way to reach the large number of blacks in Houston and the Deep South. Yet after listening to Parham's lectures, reading his books, and conducting services with him,
Seymour began to realize that Parham's understanding of the Pentecost
described in Acts 1–2 differed from his own. Parham segregated his revival services along racial lines and did not allow Seymour to "tarry" at
the front altar with whites. In fact, this is why Seymour did not receive
the baptism with the Holy Spirit under Parham's ministry. While Parham affirmed white supremacy, Seymour believed that the outpouring
and baptism of the Holy Spirit broke down all unbiblical racial, class,
educational, social, denominational, and gender barriers. Seymour's
central message was not tongues or eschatology, but rather that a person
must be born again to enter the kingdom of heaven and that a regener-
ated person had to demonstrate their faith through brotherly love and
the fruit of the Spirit manifest in how they treated their fellow man, ir-
respective of race or class. Seymour's desire to convert a dying and lost
world to faith in Jesus Christ was the engine that drove his ministry and
Pentecostal vision.[32]

Seymour's opportunity to break free of Parham's control came in late
January or early February 1906 when a visitor to Farrow's mission named
Mrs. Neely Terry asked Seymour to be a candidate for the pastorate of
her Holiness church back home in Los Angeles. Seymour jumped at the
opportunity, even though Parham strongly admonished him to remain
in Texas and preach among his "own color." Seymour gently insisted
that he had to follow God's calling and go to California. By invoking
God, he pulled rank on Parham, which was the only way he could alter
the unequal power relationship. Although not entirely happy about Sey-

mour's "calling" to a Holiness church outside of his own Apostolic Faith movement and control, there was little Parham could do. He relented and even financed part of Seymour's trip, but only after he heard that he would be preaching to blacks. Parham's patronage left Seymour in his debt—one that he would call in soon enough.[33] Had Parham known the future, he would have done all he could to stop Seymour from going west.

Traveling in a segregated railroad car to California, Seymour dreamed of a new life and ministry in California. Soon after his arrival at the Holiness mission on Santa Fe Street in Los Angeles, he began preaching Parham's doctrine that baptism with the Holy Spirit must be accompanied by speaking in unknown tongues. Conflict erupted several days after he began preaching that although he had never personally spoken in tongues, such speaking should be practiced by all true Christians of his day. Julia Hutchins was shocked by his outlandish claims, she said. Acting as the new interim leader of the mission, she sought to silence Seymour. On the fifth night of Seymour's candidacy, she padlocked the door and forced Seymour to leave the mission. Penniless and without a place to stay, Seymour turned hat in hand to Ed Lee, a black member of Hutchins's congregation. Not having the heart to turn a black man out onto the streets of white Los Angeles, Lee agreed to let Seymour stay at his home until he could raise the train fare back to Texas. He did so despite his skepticism about Seymour's claims. Over the next few months, the Lees were struck by Seymour's spirituality, grasp of theology, humility, and persuasive abilities. Shortly after the conflict, two mission leaders, Richard and Ruth Asberry, asked Seymour to conduct a prayer meeting for revival at their home on 214 North Bonnie Brae Street, in the black Temple district of Los Angeles.[34]

Winds of Revival on Azusa Street

On April 6, 1906, Seymour led the small interracial prayer group on a ten-day fast for revival. Four days into the fast, on April 9, Pentecostal tradition has it that "the fire came down," meaning that God poured out the Holy Spirit on the Bonnie Brae participants as on the Day of

Figure 1.3. Seymour and Azusa Street leadership team. First row (left to right): May Evans, Hiram Smith, Mildred Crawford (young girl), William Seymour, Clara Lum. Second row (left to right): G. W. Evans, Jennie Evans Moore (later Mrs. William Seymour), Glenn Cook, Florence Crawford, Thomas Junk. (Flower Pentecostal Heritage Center)

Pentecost account in Acts 2. Eyewitnesses claimed tongues of fire swirled around the room and above the heads of the band of "prayer warriors." Ed Lee spoke in tongues. Later that evening Jennie Evans Moore (Seymour's future wife) was also baptized with the Holy Spirit and reportedly spoke in six languages—Spanish, French, Latin, Greek, Hebrew, and Hindustani—none of which she knew prior to that night.[35] News of this supernatural event attracted a growing host of curious and spiritually "hungry" washerwomen, cooks, laborers, janitors, ministers, and housewives.[36] A spiritual fire had been ignited that would spread around the world. To guide and nurture this Pentecostal fire, he and his leadership team, depicted in Figure 1.3, mentored, trained, and commissioned the next generation of leaders to fulfill their divine callings.

The Bonnie Brae Street prayer meetings began on Monday, April 9, 1906. The growing throngs of parched souls and curious onlookers forced Seymour to move his small interracial flock to the former Stevens African Methodist Episcopal Church at 312 Azusa Street. The first meeting at Azusa Mission was slated for Saturday, April 14.

Biddy Mason initiated the congregation in the 1870s long before the Stevens African Methodist Episcopal Church was built in 1888. It was abandoned not long after a fire in 1903. Seriously damaged, the dilapidated 40- by 60-foot, two-story whitewashed building had been converted into a horse stable on the first floor and apartments on the second. The low ceilings, sawdust-covered dirt floor, and redwood plank pews gave the services a rustic flavor reminiscent of old Methodist and Holiness campgrounds. Located on a short dead-end street half a block long, not far from the Los Angeles railroad terminal, the Azusa Mission was surrounded by a lumberyard, a tombstone shop, stockyards, wholesale houses, and "less saintly businesses" in black Los Angeles. The "barn-like" atmosphere of the mission was not lost on the participants, who compared it to the manger in Bethlehem where Christ was born 1,900 years earlier.[37] Despite its location and dilapidated state, scores of curious spectators and spiritual searchers from all over the city and every walk of life descended on the old church.

Mexicans and the First Supernatural Events on Azusa Street

Eyewitnesses claim that the Spirit fell the night before the Azusa Mission formally opened its doors. Although often overlooked in most histories, the first supernatural manifestation of the Spirit took place one day before the first revival on Friday, April 13. Arthur G. Osterberg reported that a Mexican American day worker was the first person touched by the power of the Holy Spirit at the Azusa Mission after three black women from the Bonnie Brae prayer group went over to the mission to clean it. After a spirited conversation about holy living with one of the black women, the Latino youth fell to his knees and burst into tears. He was the first of many Latinos at Azusa touched by the power of the Holy Spirit. In fact, Osterberg stated that "hundreds" of Catholics attended, "many" of which were "Spanish" or "Mexicans."[38] He noted that this event was the first manifestation of the Holy Spirit at the Azusa Mission and was a premonition that something historic was about to happen.[39]

Despite the powerful descriptions of Latinos at Azusa by Abundio and Rosa López and Adolfo C. Valdez, little else has been written about the Latino participation and their contributions.[40] However, we know that Latinos participated at Azusa from 1906 to 1909. Their involvement has long been overshadowed by an important if uneven emphasis on the black and white Pentecostal origins.[41] However, Latinos were important because they took part in the first supernatural manifestation of the Holy Spirit, the first instance of divine healing, prayed for people at the altars to receive Christ, served as both lay and ordained leaders, carried out Azusa evangelistic work throughout southern California, and helped contribute to its international and multilingual flavor. They also participated in a conflict that according to Frank Bartleman foreshadowed the Azusa Mission's decline. Latinos helped transform what was a largely biracial, American, and English-language prayer meeting on 212 Bonnie Brae Street into a multiethnic, multilingual, and international revival at 312 Azusa Street.[42] Although most of the Latinos who participated have long since been lost to the pages of history, we do know the names of ten: Abundio and Rosa López, José, A. C., and Susie Villa Valdez, Brigido Pérez, Juan Navarro Martínez, Luís López, and possibly Genaro and Romanita Carbajal de Valenzuela.[43]

Cadence and Spirituality of the Revival

Latinos and other participants believed that miraculous healing was evidence of the long-awaited outpouring of the Holy Spirit prophesied to take place "in the last days" of the world. The first issue of Seymour's the *Apostolic Faith* newspaper read, "Pentecost Has Come: Los Angeles Being Visited by a Revival of Bible Salvation and Pentecost as Recorded in the Book of Acts."[44]

The article claimed, "The power of God now has this city agitated as never before. Pentecost has surely come and with it the Bible evidences are following, many being converted and sanctified and filled with the Holy Ghost, speaking in tongues as they did on the day of Pentecost . . . some are on their way to the foreign fields, with the gift of the language."[45]

This supernatural outpouring of the Spirit led many at the mission to believe that God was unleashing a citywide revival that would spread around the world and could help usher in the Second Coming of Jesus.

The daily schedule at Azusa was mind-boggling by today's standards. Services took place seven days a week, often three times a day (morning, noon, evening) for three years straight from 1906 to 1909, and off and on from 1909 to 1912. In contrast to more traditional mainline and Evangelical Protestant services—which tended to be highly liturgical, orderly, time-sensitive, and structured—Azusa reportedly had no set format. However, one could expect to regularly see enthusiastic prayer, song, testimony, and preaching at almost every service, along with "singing in the Spirit," speaking in tongues, and prayer for divine healing. Services went on for hours and sometimes with only a slight intermission between them. After the services, A. C. Valdez wrote that about one hundred "black, brown, and white people" would ascend to the "Upper Room" (so named after the room where Jesus's disciples were baptized with the Holy Spirit on the Day of Pentecost), where they sought the baptism with the Holy Spirit and spent time in prayer and quiet meditation. It was here that the races would intermingle and lie prostrate across the floor or kneel in prayer and supplication. Seymour, Abundio López, Hiram Smith, and other mission leaders would cross the racial lines of the day by laying their hands on people of any race, gender, or economic background and praying for those wishing to receive the Spirit's baptism or for healing, although men generally prayed for men, and women for women.[46]

Other Protestants sharply criticized Parham's insistence that speaking in unknown tongues was the physical evidence of the baptism with the Holy Spirit. Although not emphasized in contemporary Pentecostalism, most people at Azusa equated tongues with the God-given ability to speak a real human language they had never studied.[47] Seymour adopted this position for several years, but then later taught that tongues was simply one of several evidences of the baptism with the Holy Spirit, which included divine love and the fruit of the Spirit. A good number of missionaries left the mission believing that God had given them the ability to speak one or more human languages previously unknown to them.[48]

However, more than one—like Alfred and Lillian Garr—returned from the foreign mission field after realizing that he or she did not in fact speak the language they thought God had given them. As a result, later leaders taught that the initial evidence of the baptism of the Holy Spirit could be a real human language (xenolalia), an unknown human language known only to God (glossolalia), or any gifts of the Holy Spirit. While today the AG teaches that tongues can be expressed as xenolalia (a public human language one has hitherto never studied) or, primarily, glossolalia (a personal language known only to God), the AG also affirms the initial evidence theory, which holds that speaking in unknown tongues is the initial, physical evidence of the baptism with the Holy Spirit. Some Pentecostal bodies like the Church of God in Christ (COGIC) do not affirm this initial evidence view.[49]

Yet it was not tongues speaking but the heartfelt spirituality and powerful singing that stood out most to seekers and spectators. Singing was done at first *a cappella* and from memory. Black spirituals and Holiness and Methodist camp songs were crowd favorites. Glenn Cook described how the singing created a "holy awe" and "indescribable wonder" and a place where "evil speaking and evil thinking was all departed."[50]

Indeed, contrary to the stereotype of the revival as a wild service of hand-waving fanatics grasping after experiences with the Holy Spirit, there was a quieter side. Early eyewitnesses tell of long periods of soft singing, hushed prayers, and gentle quietness in the "Upper Room." Bartleman wrote the "Upper Room" was "sacred, a kind of 'holy ground.' "[51] It was here that "men sought to become quiet from the activities of their own too active mind and spirit, to escape from the world for the time, and get alone with God. There was no noisy, wild, exciting spirit there." For Bartleman, Latinos, and others, it was a sort of " 'city of refuge' . . . a 'haven of rest,' where God could be heard, and talk to their souls."[52]

Message and Theology of the Azusa Street Revival

Contrary to popular perception, some early Pentecostals were knowledgeable students of doctrine, church history, and larger social and religious trends.[53] Seymour believed that theological education was important to deepen one's faith and understanding of the gospel, and he ran a lay Bible school on the second floor of the Azusa Mission, encouraging people to attend it in preparation for life and ministry.[54]

Seymour saw Pentecostals (a term he popularized) in spiritual and theological continuity with great Protestant leaders and teachings like Martin Luther's doctrine of justification, John Wesley's teaching on sanctification, and the more recent revivals in Europe among the Quakers, Irvingites, Swedes, Irish, and Welsh.[55] In fact, many people like Frank Bartleman, Joseph Smale, and others at Azusa had been following the revival directed by Evan Roberts in Wales in 1904 and praying for a similar outpouring in Los Angeles.[56] Frequent references to theologians, Bible scholars, figures in church history, and other theological terms and distinctions also indicate a level of theological knowledge not often ascribed to early Pentecostals.[57]

Despite Seymour's theological literacy, his main message was focused on spiritual transformation, the kind that affected one's body, mind, spirit, and society. He taught that a person must be "born again" to enter the kingdom of heaven. "Now don't go from this meeting and talk about tongues, but try to get people saved," Seymour often stated.[58]

Seymour's theology represents the coming together of five major theological streams in late-nineteenth-century Christianity: (1) African American spirituality, (2) the Holiness and Wesleyan idea of entire sanctification, (3) the Reformed idea of power for Christian service, (4) Dispensational premillennialism, and (5) a robust belief in faith healing.[59] The Azusa participants did not originally see themselves as ushering in a new movement, but as reformers seeking to restore existing denominational churches back to their New Testament roots. Seymour and his colleagues wrote in the *Apostolic Faith,* "We are not fighting men or churches, but seeking to displace dead forms and creeds and wild fanaticism's [*sic*] with living, practical Christianity."[60]

Indeed, Seymour and his followers believed that the spiritual gifts gave them the ability to restore the New Testament church to its original purity, something often emphasized by focusing on sanctification and holy living. Far from ceasing with the death of the Apostles as some taught, they believed that the spiritual gifts were still available to all Christians. They emphasized the spiritual gifts (charismata) listed in 1 Corinthians

12 and 14: wisdom, knowledge, faith, healing, miraculous powers, discernment of spirits, tongues, interpretation of tongues, and prophecy. It was precisely the belief in tongues as the physical evidence of Holy Spirit baptism that separated Pentecostals from other Evangelical Christians. The purpose of tongues was not self-gratification or ecstasy, but being endowed with power to build up other Christians in their faith and to preach a transformative message of faith, repentance, and conversion to Jesus Christ both at home and on the mission field.

Yet Seymour and his colleagues also recognized the social conditions that left many of their converts in poverty. This is why he and Latino leaders like Abundio López and A. C. Valdez stressed the salvation and healing of the body, mind, and spirit. It is also why he encouraged Susie Villa Valdez, a Mexican, and Emma Osterberg, a Swedish immigrant, to preach Pentecost in the migrant farm labor camps in Riverside and San Bernardino and why Susie reached out to the prostitutes and others living on skid row in Los Angeles. Memorializing his mother's evangelistic-social work, Valdez wrote:

> As if it were yesterday, I remember her [Susie Valdez's] hard but rewarding spiritual-social work with prostitutes and skid-row alcoholics done in the Lord's name. . . . At midnight police picked up drunks and unloaded them at Pisgah Home [a Pentecostal social service mission], instead of jail. . . . On nights when Dr. Yoakum didn't need her, my mother visited the slums, playing her guitar and singing sacred songs in the poorly lighted streets for anyone whom would listen. Without fear—she was armed with the Lord—she heard the troubles of many lonely and depressed people and usually introduced them to Christ. Around midnight she would walk the long way home, often arriving as late as two a.m.[61]

Seymour and his colleagues held that the outpouring of the Holy Spirit was also evidenced by "signs and wonders" and divine healing. Healing testimonies are found on virtually every page of the *Apostolic Faith* newspaper. If love, transformation, and speaking in tongues were the central attractions at Azusa, healing was not far behind.[62]

In fact, the first major healing at the Azusa Revival involved a Mexican with a clubfoot, which made him limp. Swedish immigrant and future

California AG Superintendent Arthur G. Osterberg stated that this healing was the first great miracle of the revival:

> All at once a man who had come in walking haltingly with a club-foot, got up and went out into the aisle and he was clapping his hands and his face was uplifted. His wife looked at him and pretty soon she followed him. They walked toward the back and then toward the front [of the Mission], and by this time they were walking arm in arm and he [was] clapping his hands and his face [was] uplifted. That must have taken place for four or five minutes, then it quieted down, then he came down with his wife. I noticed when he came up the aisle . . . he wasn't stumbling like he was when he walked into the meeting. I knew something had happened to his foot. . . . For the first time he noticed—he stood there [in the Mission] moving it and then started to walk—then he started to shout "Hallelujah."[63]

The healing left an indelible impression on Osterberg. He was so moved that he merged his own mission with the Azusa Mission.[64]

Latinos also participated in a number of other healing episodes at the revival. In the very first edition of the *Apostolic Faith,* it describes a rough "poor Mexican Indian" from central Mexico laying his hands on a young white woman named Ms. Knapp and praying for her healing, after which she was reportedly healed. Mexican American A. C. Valdez claimed to have witnessed many healings at the mission, including the healing of his father. Mexican immigrants Abundio and Rosa López wrote that divine healing was part of their ministry. They wanted "to be used for the salvation and healing of both soul and body" and as "a witness of His . . . marvelous miracles by the Holy Ghost."[65]

The Pentecostal focus on divine healing, the supernatural, and miracles tapped into similar preexisting beliefs in the Latino community. One writer attributed Latino receptivity and conversion to Pentecostalism to their "immemorial traditions and belief in divine healing." Pisgah Home Mission reported that one-fourth of their southern California missions were made up of "Spaniards and Mexicans, among whom are many cripples and deformed."[66] In a day and age where white doctors were expensive and medical insurance unheard of, many Latinos preferred a more holistic approach to health and wellness by visiting curandera/o folk healers and, after 1906, Pentecostal missions and ministries that prayed for the sick. This focus on divine healing, perhaps more than any other factor, explains the attraction, power, and influence of Pentecostalism in the Latino community.

Latinos were not alone in their healing testimonies. The *Apostolic Faith* newspaper is chock-full of reports by people claiming to be healed of cancer, epilepsy, tuberculosis, asthma, blindness, fever, deafness, head injuries, hemorrhages, hernias, lung infections, mental illnesses, paralysis, pneumonia, rheumatism, tuberculosis, smoking addiction, alcoholism, drug addiction, and other ailments. Reportedly invoking the saving and healing power of Jesus Christ, Azusa leaders stated, "canes, crutches, medicine bottles, and glasses are being thrown aside as God heals."[67] Seymour and his colleagues prayed and wept with tears of joy and compassion over these letters and testimonies.[68] A. C. Valdez wrote how Seymour hung objects (e.g., crutches) from the mission walls as public evidence of the miraculous healings at Azusa.[69] Focus on divine healing was shaped by the conviction that Christians should not rely only on medicine since some of the causes of the ailments were spiritual, not just physical.[70] Seymour claimed that some sicknesses were from the devil and that the body itself could be sanctified in healing. Today most Pentecostal leaders believe that God heals through *both* prayers of faith and medicine, since they believe the latter is God-given.[71] Latinos adopted Seymour's view and continue to regularly pray for the sick during and/or right after their Sunday and often mid-week services.

Seymour's Leadership and Ministry Standards

Although Seymour was a very soft-spoken, compassionate, and forgiving man, he had high standards for the ministry. He believed God could only speak and work through a holy and deeply spiritual man or woman. As a result, he wrote that a minister of the Gospel should be diligent, serious, converse sparingly, believe evil of no one without good evidence, speak evil of no one, praise his congregation and encourage believers, and, if necessary, tell people under his care what he considered wrong in their conduct and temperament in a very loving and simple manner so it does not fester in their hearts. He also admonished ministers to pay close attention to their actions since other believers and an unbelieving world were watching.[72]

Seymour encouraged ministers to avoid talking too much, especially about themselves. One hour should be the maximum limit for a home or hospital visit, he advised. A minister should be punctual, ashamed of nothing but sin, and should always pray when they begin and end a meeting. Above all else, a minister was an evangelist. Their primary goal should be to "save souls." He reminded ministers that it is "not your business to preach so many times and to take care of this or that Mission, but to save as many as you can; to bring as many sinners as you can to repentance."[73]

At every church, a minister should convince people of their need for Christ, give an altar call at the end of most services, and then encourage and disciple them in the faith. When preaching, a minister's whole persona should be joyful, weighty, and solemn. He wrote that the duty of a minister is to preach, regularly meet and minister to each congregation member, visit the sick, and make disciples—especially of leaders. A minister should frequently ask his members: "Do you walk closely with God? Do you spend the day in the manner with which the Lord would be pleased? Do you converse seriously, usefully and closely?" All ministers should read and meditate daily on the Bible and should always take a Bible with them wherever they go.[74]

One of a pastor's primary goals should be to plant new churches for his new converts in areas without a good church; otherwise many will fall away from the faith. For this reason, Seymour said it is critical to disciple converts and "build them up in that holiness." This should be done through Sunday school classes, discipleship classes, church-sponsored Bible schools, and Christian conferences. All of this should be bathed in prayer and fasting. Seymour was open to different styles of ministry. However, he said that a minister should never disappoint a congregation and that he should begin and end at the appointed time, and not go overtime.

Finally and most importantly for Seymour, he said that a successful minister must not disappoint his family. He must lead a Godly home. He warned that Christians needed to be more careful in how they raise their children. Family prayer and devotion should be joyous, loving, and well planned out. Fathers needed to be patient with their wives and children. Seymour taught that a Christian home should be one of the "sweetest places" on God's green earth for the parents and children. It should never be harsh, but rather a place full of God's love. In a two-parent home, the father should take the lead in devotions as the spiritual head of the home and where a father was not present, the mother should fulfill this role. Seymour lived what he preached by leading devotions in his own home with Jennie and his adopted daughter, about the latter of whom we know nothing.[75]

The Pentecostal emphasis on the spiritual gifts, speaking in tongues, enthusiastic worship, and divine healing went beyond the pale of orthodoxy for many traditional Protestants. The result was ridicule and expulsion. With no place to go, the homeless Pentecostals began to form their own missions and movements. Despite his openness to people of diverse races, classes, and walks of life, Seymour's commitment to biblical doctrine and historic Protestant Christianity prompted him and his followers to criticize Spiritualism, Theosophy, Seventh-Day Adventism, Christian Science, Mormonism, and the Jehovah's Witnesses as unbiblical non-Evangelical Christian traditions.[76]

Conflict with the Religious Establishment and a Global Revival

While the Azusa Revival converted many "non-Christians," most of those who joined the mission came from Protestant churches in Los Angeles. As pastors saw their church attendance dwindle and the Azusa Mission grow, many became agitated. This decline in church attendance and Seymour's radically egalitarian message threatened some in the religious establishment. In June 1906, the Los Angeles Ministerial Association filed a formal complaint with the city against the mission on the grounds that it was disturbing the peace and should thus be closed. The police investigated but found no grounds to close the mission, in large part because it was located in an industrial, not residential, section of the city. The Azusa Mission, depicted in Figure 1.4, provided a large open space for the revival on the first floor and living accommodations for

Figure 1.4.   Azusa Street Mission, Los Angeles, 1920s.   (Used by permission of the Apostolic Faith, Portland, Oregon)

Seymour and guests on the second floor, as well as a room (which they called the "Upper Room" after Acts 1:13) for those tarrying for the baptism with the Holy Spirit.[77]

Criticism of Azusa did not end with the Ministerial Association. Other critics called it foolish and fanatical. The free press, although negative, attracted people seeking a deeper Christian faith or the latest religious fad. Azusa participants spread like a flash flood across a sunscorched Los Angeles preaching "waves of power."[78]

The revival also attracted future leaders in the Assemblies of God like Ernest S. William (AG General Superintendent, 1929–1949), A. G. Osterberg, John G. Lake, Fred Greisinger, Rachel Sizelove, G. N. Eldridge, F. F. Bosworth, and George and Carrie Judd Montgomery.[79] The free press, reports of miraculous healings, and scores of street-corner preachers attracted crowds of 800 to 1,500 people. Eyewitnesses reported that twenty nationalities attended the revival.[80]

The hordes of people who descended upon the revival in Los Angeles came from across the country. William H. Durham, Charles H. Mason, Ophelia Wiley, Lucy Farrow, F. W. Williams, J. A. Jeter, D. J. Young,

Garfield T. Haywood, Gaston Barnabus Cashwell, Ernest S. Williams, and many others traveled from the Midwest, East Coast, and South to attend the Revival. Durham, who came from Chicago, described Seymour as "the meekest man I ever met. He walks and talks with God. His power is in his weakness. He seems to maintain a helpless dependence on God and is as simple-hearted as a little child, and at the same time is so filled with God that you feel the love and power every time you get near him." Durham's opinion would later change. For the time being, Azusa became a sacred center from which Pentecostalism spread across the United States. By 1914, Pentecostals could be found in almost every U.S. city with a population over 3,000.[81]

The sensational newspaper coverage, traveling evangelists, foreign missionaries, attacks by denominational leaders, and the over 405,000 copies of Seymour's *Apostolic Faith* newspaper (1906 to 1908) quickly spread the Pentecostal message around the world. Andrew Johnson was one of the first foreign missionaries sent overseas by the mission. He left to pioneer the work in his native Sweden in April 1906.[82] A. G. Garr and four others left in July to carry the revival to India and later China and elsewhere. The missionary impulse was so strong that it took Seymour just fifteen minutes to raise the $1,200 Garr and his associates needed to travel overseas. A few months later, Lucy Farrow, Julia Hutchins, J. S. Mead, and G. W. Batman and family spread Seymour's message to Liberia, while Tom Hezmalhalch carried it to South Africa. A. S. Copley took the message to Toronto, Canada, A. H. Post took the message to Egypt, South Africa, England, India, and Sri Lanka, and Lucy Leatherman carried the message to Jerusalem and the Middle East. George and Carry Montgomery carried it to Mexico, and A. C. Valdez spread it throughout California and in the mid-1920s led evangelistic crusades in Australia and New Zealand.[83] Azusa Street participants converted Thomas Ball Barratt during their stopover in New York City. He left the Methodist ministry in his adopted Norway to pioneer the Pentecostal message through his Filadelfia Church in Oslo. During his stopover in England, Barratt persuaded his friend and ministerial colleague Anglican Vicar Alexander A. Boddy to embrace the Pentecostal message, something he did with great fervency and, as a result, he visited the Azusa Mission in 1911. By 1908, Azusa and other Pentecostals claimed missionaries in over fifty nations around the world.[84] All of this missionary work led Alexander Boddy to write in 1912 that Azusa had become a sacred center for the global Pentecostal movement and was "a sort of 'Mecca' to Pentecostal travelers . . . [who] like to kneel where the fire fell."[85]

Seymour's Transformational and Egalitarian Social Vision

In a period dominated by Jim Crow segregation, the Ku Klux Klan, Nativism, Social Darwinism, and racial purity, Seymour's message of racial equality, integration, and multicultural Christianity ran against the grain of U.S. society. The first edition of the *Apostolic Faith* newspaper declared, "God makes no difference in nationality. Ethiopians [blacks], Chinese, Indians, Mexicans, and other nationalities worship together."[86] The Azusa leaders claimed, "It is noticeable how free all nationalities feel. If a Mexican or German cannot speak English, he gets up and speaks in his own tongue and feels quite at home for the Spirit interprets through the face and people say 'amen.' No instrument that God can use is rejected on account of color or dress or lack of education. That is why God has so built up the work."[87]

Blacks at the Azusa Revival shared this sentiment. Mattie Cummings stated, "everybody was just the same. It didn't matter if you were black, white, green, or grizzly . . . Germans and Jews, blacks and whites, ate together in the little cottage at the rear. Nobody ever thought of race."[88] Bartleman summed up the attitude of many Azusa participants when he declared, "The color line was washed away in the blood." It was precisely this kind of message of racial reconciliation that caused a number of former white supremacists such as Cashwell to "crucify" their racist beliefs at the Azusa Street mission, where he asked blacks to pray for him.[89] Boddy remarked after his visit in 1912 that the interracial activities at Azusa Street were "extraordinary." He was particularly struck by how Southern whites like Cashwell would come to the revival, lay aside their white supremacist attitudes, and then take their racially reconciliatory message back to the South, and even lead integrated revival services despite warnings to keep them segregated.[90]

The Azusa Revival was also a transformative and egalitarian social space for women. Seymour claimed that on the Day of Pentecost God "called them all into the upper room, both men and women, and anointed them with the oil of the Holy Ghost, thus qualifying them all to minister in this Gospel. . . . In Christ Jesus there is neither male nor female, all are one."[91] He supported women in the ministry and they served as evangelists, missionaries, and church planters, and coedited the *Apostolic Faith* newspaper. Susie Villa Valdez and Emma Osterberg teamed up to minister to prostitutes, alcoholics, and single mothers in Los Angeles and Mexican labor camps in Riverside and San Bernardino, California.[92]

Seymour attempted to erase the deeply embedded class and educational distinctions. He and his followers declared that God "recognizes no man-made . . . classes of people, but 'he be willing and obedient.'"[93] Azusa Revival eyewitness Frank Bartleman echoed this: "We had no 'respect for persons.' The rich and educated were the same as the poor and ignorant, and found a much harder death to die. We only recognized God. All were equal."[94]

Parham's Confrontation with Seymour

Physical contact driven by fears of miscegenation between the races led some to condemn the revival. Seymour said the revival had been a "melting time" where "God is melting all races and nations together."[95] Stories of men and women kneeling together, falling across one another, greeting one another with a "holy kiss" as noted in the Bible, and laying hands on one another to pray for healing or to receive the Spirit served for many as proof positive in the minds of some that Seymour's revival crossed the boundary of appropriate interaction.[96] Alma White, who clearly disliked Seymour's interracial services, claimed he was a "devil-possessed" "religious fakir" whose revival in the "worst slums" of Los Angeles was the scene of kissing and shocking familiarity between the sexes.[97]

The most painful accusations of all came from his former teacher, Charles Fox Parham. The revival had been running about six months when Parham finally arrived at Azusa in October after numerous delays. Rather than praise Seymour, after several visits he walked to the pulpit uninvited and stated to his stunned onlookers: "God is sick at his stomach!" Parham later explained: "To my utter surprise and astonishment I found conditions [at the Azusa Mission] even worse than I had antici-pated."[98] Disappointed but not entirely surprised by Parham's reaction given his racial views, Seymour tried to be positive. Seymour hoped to receive his blessing. Threatened by Seymour's growing success and emerging leadership, Parham later condemned the meetings in the sharpest terms possible.[99] This was nothing more than a "hotbed of wildfire," he claimed.[100]

Although Seymour said little in his own defense, his white elders led by Glenn Cook asked Parham to leave the mission. Seymour and his leadership team flatly denied all of these charges as patently false. Angry and disgraced that a black man and his white coworkers thwarted his attempt to take over the mission, Parham set up a rival mission in Los Angeles. Siphoning off 200 to 300 white followers from Azusa at first, Parham split the fledgling Pentecostal movement in Los Angeles. Like the ocean tide, however, Parham's followers quietly receded until he was left with just a handful. The frustrated Parham went back to Illinois and then Texas, where he later faced an accusation about moral misconduct.[101]

Parham had gone to Azusa at the height of his popularity, claiming 13,000 followers throughout the United States. His insensitive actions cost him hundreds of followers in California and the country. He could no longer count on their support for his evangelistic services. This fact, along with his failed attempt to take over Alexander Dowie's Zion City in Illinois after Dowie's death, left Parham's public image seriously tar-nished. The most devastating blow was yet to come. In December news broke that Parham had been accused of moral misconduct in San Anto-nio, Texas.[102] In the morally strict world in which he lived, that accusa-tion alone was the kiss of death to his ministry. Parham insisted that his enemies like Wilbur Viola of Zion City had framed him and the charges were dropped. As Parham's star dimmed, Seymour's was rising. Parham spent the rest of his life living in the shadow of Seymour's Azusa Street Revival.[103] Parham's criticisms of Pentecostal leaders and other concerns led future AG leader E. N. Bell to publicly repudiate Parham's leadership over the Apostolic Faith Movement in 1912.[104] By the time Parham died in 1929, some claim he was largely unknown among second-generation Pentecostals outside of the Midwest.

Seymour's transformative message of equality had its own limits, however. While Seymour taught that women could exercise a prophetic voice in the ordained ministry, he also stated that they should submit to their husbands at home.[105] He also increasingly recognized the value and necessity of order during the worship and revival services. As a result of these concerns and Parham's criticisms, in January 1907 he noted that he would run his services "decently and in order."[106]

Love Triangle and Broken Friendships

By May 1908, Seymour was printing 50,000 copies per month of the *Apostolic Faith* and distributing it around the world. Seymour joyfully stated, "We are on the verge of the greatest miracle the world has ever seen." Seymour spoke too soon.[107]

Conflict erupted immediately after Seymour unexpectedly announced that he and Jennie Evans Moore had married on May 13, 1908. Jennie was an African-American woman, revival pianist and worship leader, and a leader at Azusa. Their marriage, which took place in an unannounced and private ceremony conducted by Reverend Ed Lee and witnessed by just a handful of people, surprised many in the mission. Stunned by the decision, Clara Lum (a key leader of the mission and editor of the newspaper) and other Azusa participants interpreted the marriage as a betrayal of their "end-times" message of self-sacrifice.[108] Lum questioned Seymour's virtue, wisdom, and spirituality. Like a jilted lover, Lum, who reportedly had fallen in love with and wanted to marry Seymour, raised a hornet's nest of opposition.[109] She accused Seymour of having compromised on "sanctification," a serious accusation among the holiness-minded Pentecostals. Lum left the mission in protest to join Florence Crawford's now-independent work in Portland, Oregon, but not before she grabbed the only copies of the national and international mailing lists. Crawford had broken earlier with Seymour because she disagreed with his views on sanctification and because Seymour changed his views on divorce and remarriage. He stated that a person who divorced without biblical grounds could not stay in the ministry or remarry another person if his or her first spouse was stilling living, because of the scandal it might bring upon the ministry. Crawford was recently divorced.[110]

Lum's public protest shook the mission to its very core. Without the newspaper to spread his message, Seymour was voiceless and invisible across the nation and around the world. Not willing to give up so easily on their dream, the newlyweds traveled north to Portland in hot pursuit of Lum and the mailing lists. After rejecting Seymour's overtures for reconciliation, Lum refused to see the couple or give them the mailing lists. They returned to Los Angeles disappointed, but not without hope. Still, Seymour's moral and pastoral authority had taken a serious hit from which he would never recover fully.[111]

Birth of Latino Pentecostalism

Mexicans had faithfully attended the Azusa Street Revival for three years. Seymour's confidence in their growing leadership abilities led him to ordain Abundio L. López and Juan Navarro Martínez in 1909 (Figure 1.5). They were the first Latinos ordained to Pentecostalism in the United States.

Frank Bartleman reported that around 1909 the leader of the Azusa Mission at that time had a conflict with a group of "poor" and "illiterate" Mexicans. For Bartleman, this conflict signaled the beginning of the revival's end and the loss of its spiritual and transformative social power. He wrote:

> The Spirit tried to work through some poor, illiterate Mexicans, who had been saved and *baptized* in the Spirit. But the leader deliberately refused to let them testify, and crushed them ruthlessly. It was like murdering the Spirit of God. Only God knows what this meant to those poor Mexicans. Personally I would rather die than to have assumed such a spirit of dictatorship. Every meeting was now programmed from start to finish. Disaster was bound to follow, and it did so.[112]

It is unclear whether Bartleman is referring to Seymour or more than likely someone else like African American associate pastor J. A. Warren.

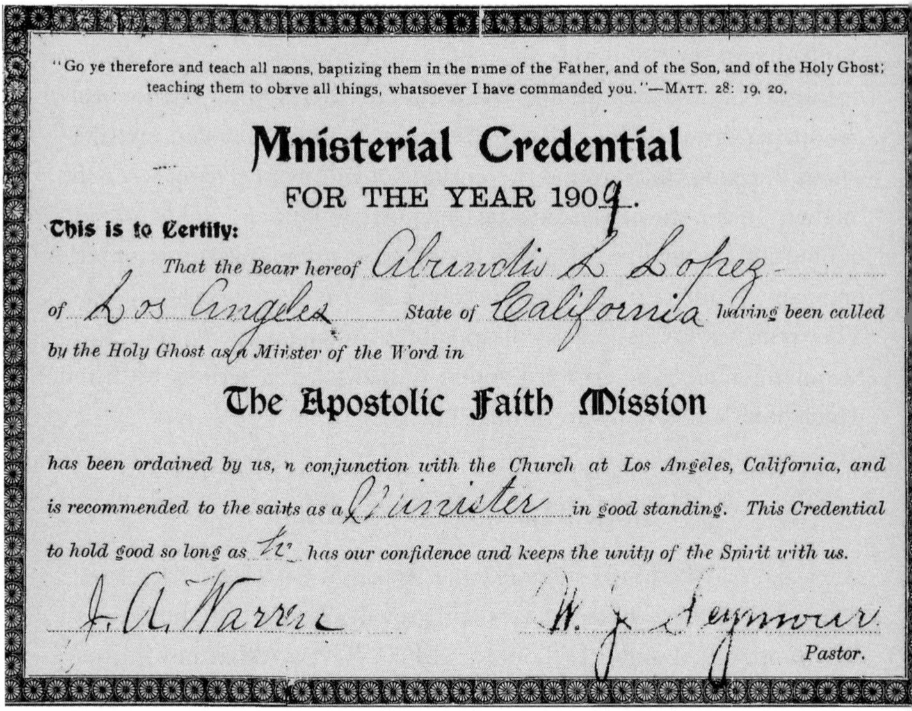

"Go ye therefore and teach all naons, baptizing them in the nime of the Father, and of the Son, and of the Holy Ghost; teaching them to obrve all things, whatsoever I have commanded you."—MATT. 28: 19, 20,

Mnisterial Credential

FOR THE YEAR 190*9*.

This is to Certify:

That the Bearr hereof *Abundio L. López*

of *Los Angeles* State of *California* having been called

by the Holy Ghost as a Minister of the Word in

The Apostolic Faith Mission

has been ordained by us, n conjunction with the Church at Los Angeles, California, and is recommended to the saints as a *Minister* in good standing. This Credential to hold good so long as *he* has our confidence and keeps the unity of the Spirit with us.

J. A. Warren   *W. J. Seymour*

Pastor.

Figure 1.5.   Abundio L. López ordination certificate signed by William J. Seymour and Joseph A. Warren, 1909.   (Gastón Espinosa Latino Pentecostal History Collection)

Regardless, we do know there are no confirmed reports of Latinos regularly attending Azusa after 1909. Furthermore, A. C. Valdez said the revival ended (for him and his family) in 1909, even though Seymour continued to hold services until 1922. There was also a large influx of already Spirit-baptized Mexicans at Elmer Fisher's Upper Room Mission in Los Angeles in 1910. Finally, not one person ever came forward to deny the widely publicized charges. Even if it was Seymour, it appears that he and his Latino followers patched up any differences since Abundio López and Genero Valenzuela pastored a "Spanish Apostolic Faith Mission" in Los Angeles, thus borrowing the name of Seymour's mission, and there are unconfirmed reports that the Valenzuelas visited the Azusa Mission around 1911.[113] Regardless of the conflict, Seymour appears to have had a warm and friendly relationship with Latinos, and his Azusa Street Revival directly gave birth to the Latino Pentecostal movement.[114] There is also absolutely no evidence that the conflict with the Mexican contingent was motivated by any racial animosity by Seymour or anyone else against Mexicans. Whether the conflict was before or after the ordination of López and Navarro Martínez is unclear, though perhaps it was before and the ordination was a way of later healing the conflict and reaffirming Latino leadership and ministry at Azusa and beyond.

Durham's Betrayal and Seymour's Decline

Despite these conflicts (which were often limited to factions within the mission), the Azusa Revival continued to run peacefully, although meetings were considerably smaller than in its glory days. In 1909, the Reverend W. B. Godbey, an influential Bible scholar and Holiness leader, attended the mission and claimed that Los Angeles was "electrified with the movement."[115] Things changed in February 1911 after William Durham returned to Los Angeles to serve as Seymour's interim pastor for ten weeks while Seymour was on a speaking tour across the country. Durham's dynamic preaching abilities and unbounded conviction attracted hundreds of people, including many who had left the mission years earlier. The mission was packed again like in the old Azusa days. Durham wrote Seymour that a second Azusa Revival had erupted. Unbeknown to Seymour, however, Durham was preaching the "Finished Work of Calvary," which denied the Wesleyan view of sanctification held by Seymour and most other Pentecostals. He argued that the believer received complete sanctification at conversion, not as a second unique experience. Durham used Seymour's pulpit to propagate his own unique views and criticize others who disagreed with him. The Pentecostal community was now divided. Unable to bite their tongues any longer, Seymour's elders wired him and requested that he return home immediately. In an ironic twist of events, Seymour's elders locked Durham out of the Azusa Mission. Seymour tried hard to find common ground and persuade Durham to reject the "Finished Work" theology, but Durham would not budge. Like Parham, Durham immediately set up a rival mission in Los Angeles. It was May 1911.[116]

As a result of Durham's powerful preaching, his congregation swelled to over 600 people within days, with 1,000 people attending on Sundays.[117]

Durham's zeal, strong personality, "firm determination to rule or ruin," and nonstop campaigning for the "Finished Work" doctrine all seemed unstoppable. For this reason people were shocked to hear of Durham's sudden death on July 7, 1912. Only thirty-nine years old, Durham lost his battle with tuberculosis.[118] His meteoric success, however, had come at a devastating price. The schism decimated Seymour's revival. Rather than return to Seymour's mission after Durham's death, most joined existing white missions or formed their own independent churches. By 1912, there were at least twelve Pentecostal missions in Los Angeles, many of which ministered to particular immigrant groups.[119]

The Oneness Division and Azusa's Declining Influence

The final blow to Seymour's vision of a united Pentecostal community was the Oneness controversy. Pentecostalism was divided at the Worldwide Pentecostal Camp Meeting held in the Arroyo Seco campground just outside of Los Angeles, which took place April 15 to June 1, 1913. In sharp contrast to the first camp meeting six years earlier, Seymour was not invited to speak or even sit on the stage with the rest of the ministers. Seymour nonetheless attended. Just as the 1,000 white, black, Mexican, and other participants were about to proclaim Maria B. Woodworth-Etter's healing services a great success, controversy erupted over doctrine. A number of Durham's followers, led by the Canadian evangelists Robert A. McAllister and John G. Scheppe, began preaching throughout the camp that the Apostles baptized only in the name of Jesus Christ (Acts 2:38), not in the triune formula found in Matthew 28:19. They rejected as unbiblical the Council of Nicea's Trinitarian teaching that God is one essence in three distinct persons. They instead argued that the Trinity is the same one person (Jesus) in three modes. Oneness leaders taught that Matthew 28:19–20 calls on people to baptize in the "name" of the Father, the Son, and the Holy Spirit. The "name," they claim from the context, is Jesus. The "Oneness" or "Jesus Only" Pentecostals required Trinitarians to be rebaptized in Jesus's name only. The new controversy split Pentecostalism into two theological camps. Seymour was powerless to stop it. Most of Durham's followers embraced the "Jesus Only" position, including a number of blacks and Mexicans. Today the most popular Oneness traditions in the Latino community are the Apostolic Assembly of the Faith in Christ Jesus based in Rancho Cucamonga, California, the United Pentecostal Church based in Hazelwood, Missouri, and the Apostolic Church of the Faith in Jesus Christ based in Mexico.[120]

Many of Durham's followers accepted the "Jesus Only" position because they thought it was a more literal reading of the Bible. The Oneness movement also attracted some of Seymour's strongest white and black followers such as Glenn Cook and G. T. Haywood—which only further isolated William Seymour in the growing movement. The Oneness movement spread like wildfire throughout emerging Pentecostal denominations such as the Assemblies of God, which almost destroyed it since one-third of its ministers defected to the Oneness movement, including E. N. Bell and Howard Goss, though the former returned to the AG.[121]

The Oneness controversy in 1913 marked a major turning point in the history of the Pentecostal movement. The movement, which had spent so much time preaching unity, was now divided due to a small group of people claiming a more literal reading of the Bible. The conflicts with Parham, Lum, and Durham prompted Seymour to make a historic decision. In 1915 he published his revised Articles of Incorporation and Constitution in his Apostolic Faith minister's manual to state that only "people of color" could serve on the board of trustees and as bishops, although exceptions were made. He stated, "Now [that] we don't take [whites] for directors . . . is not for discrimination, but for peace. . . . We are sorry for this, but it is best [for] now." He also made it clear that he would not tolerate racial discrimination among blacks: "If some of our white brethren have prejudices and discrimination . . . we can't do it." In fact, he commanded them to "love our white brethrens and sisters and welcome them . . . so that the Holy Spirit won't be greaved [*sic*]." He also called on whites to love their black brothers and sisters.[122]

Seymour wrote that some whites not only divided the Azusa Mission, but also brought in a divisive and fanatical spirit by being too dogmatic in their insistence that speaking in tongues was the only physical evidence of the Holy Spirit baptism. This led him to make the historic decision to reject Parham's theory that speaking in unknown tongues was the only evidence of the baptism with the Holy Spirit.

Seymour wrote, "Wherever the doctrine of the Baptism with the Holy Spirit will only be known as the evidence of speaking in tongues, that will be an open door for witches and spiritualists, and free lovism . . . because all kinds of spirits can come in" by counterfeiting the outward manifestations and practices. However, Seymour still strongly believed in the baptism with the Holy Spirit. He wrote, "It is all right to have the signs following, but not to pin our faith to outward manifestations. We are to go by the word of God." Tongues should simply not be the only defining mark of Holy Spirit baptism, but rather it should be accompanied by brotherly love and the fruit of the Spirit.[123]

Seymour's once powerful revival had receded like the waves of a storm. By 1914 the mission was reduced to about twenty to forty black and white participants, many of whom had been part of the original prayer group at Bonnie Brae Street eight years earlier.[124] Latinos like Abundio and Rosa López and Genaro and Romanita Valenzuela led Spanish Pentecostal missions in Los Angeles. Nightly meetings at Azusa had been reduced to just one meeting all day Sunday. Seymour continued to pastor his small flock for almost another decade and to push for Christian unity, love, and cooperation in Los Angeles. The Roaring Twenties brought great prosperity to millions of Americans and growth among the scores of emerging Pentecostal denominations like the Assemblies of God, but the Azusa Mission struggled to survive. In contrast to its glory days, when Seymour could raise $1,200 in fifteen minutes, now the Sunday offering amounted to barely seventy-five cents. This regression prompted Seymour to ask his congregation to at least cover his expenses.[125]

Despite this struggle, Seymour was still a highly sought-after speaker across the country. William and Jennie went on lengthy speaking engagements across the country, preaching his prophetic egalitarian vision of Pentecostalism. He regularly visited churches in Indianapolis, Chicago, Cincinnati, New York, Washington, Baltimore, Houston, and other places. Between 1916 and 1917, Seymour made one last attempt to bring the various Pentecostal missions together in unity. Only two pastors attended.[126]

In 1918, Seymour attended Aimee Semple McPherson's first Los Angeles campaign, not as a speaker but as a silent spectator. A new star was rising. Not ready to give up, the creative Seymour organized an Azusa Street anniversary celebration in 1920, although with little fanfare. A year later he went on another preaching tour across the country. On September 28, 1922, the fifty-two-year-old Seymour had a small heart attack in the morning and then died of a massive heart attack later that same day at 5 p.m. while dictating a letter. Despite the fact that the revival touched thousands around the world, only two hundred people showed up to pay their last respects. People testified at the funeral of the impact he had had on their lives. His body was laid to rest in Evergreen Cemetery, East Los Angeles, in a plot not far from where another Pentecostal leader would rest—the Mexican American evangelist Francisco Olazábal.[127]

After her husband's death, Jennie Seymour took over the Azusa Mission, but refused to accept the title of bishop because of the bylaws William had put in place. Despite one last attempt by a white man named R. C. Griffith, who claimed to be a Coptic priest, to take over the mission from Jennie, it remained firmly in her control until it was torn down in 1931 on the pretext of it being a fire hazard. In her hour of need, she turned to the Assemblies of God to save the Azusa Mission from imminent destruction. It chose not to do so, saying they did not believe in collecting "relics." The Azusa Mission was torn down. Jennie took her flock back to the old Bonnie Brae Street house, where she continued to hold meetings until 1936. On July 10, 1938, Jennie Seymour died at the age of sixty-two.[128]

Despite the decline of the revival, by 1914 there were an estimated 70,000 Pentecostals throughout the United States, missionaries in at least fifty countries, and literature published in at least thirty languages. Seymour's Azusa Revival along with other leaders and centers helped give birth to many other denominations, periodicals, and independent churches and ministries across the United States and around the world. Latinos also contributed to the revival in various ways. Today there are 23,000 Pentecostal and Charismatic denominations, many of which in one way or another trace their spiritual genealogy back to Parham and especially William J. Seymour and the Azusa Street Revival.[129]

Seymour's Azusa Revival is important to Latino Trinitarian Pentecostalism in general and the Latino AG in particular because it attracted a number of people like George and Carrie Judd Montgomery and other Azusa missionaries, who were directly responsible for persuading Latinos to embrace Pentecostalism like future Assemblies of God leaders Francisco Olazábal and Juan Lugo. They and many others went on to pioneer the work in the Southwest, New York, and Puerto Rico.

The Latino Pentecostal movement in the United States traces its roots back to William J. Seymour's Azusa Street Revival in Los Angeles in 1906. Seymour was a quiet but powerful leader whose prophetic social consciousness and theology of racial-ethnic reconciliation and multicultural Christianity challenged the church and society to live up to its professed ideals of unity in Christ and liberty and justice for everyone regardless of color or nationality. Because he preached and practiced a message of racial reconciliation, Latinos were attracted to Pentecostalism. No longer could a pious Christian make blacks, Mexicans, and others sit in the last pews in the back of the church. No longer could truly spiritual Christians keep the pulpit from bright but uneducated men and women. No longer could devout Christian men require women with a passion to preach to sit silently in their churches. The fact that Seymour was an economically poor, unschooled, and marginalized black man has everything to do with his racially egalitarian message and church that he felt led by the Holy Spirit to lead and guide.[130]

While Seymour's Azusa Street Revival was not a blatant protest against the social order of the sort we are used to seeing in the post–Civil Rights Era, it was nonetheless a profound populist critique of the religious and social order. In an era that did little to stop the lynching of over 3,400 blacks and Mexicans across the United States between the 1880s and 1920s, it is not surprising that people who were not part of W. E. B. DuBois's "Talented Tenth" of black college-educated elites found other creative ways to use their beliefs to transform society.

Despite Seymour's efforts at racial integration, by the 1930s Parham's vision had largely won the day as denominations began to split along racial lines. However, there have always been preachers and churches that have preached his message of integration. Latino churches in particular have kept alive Seymour's message and spirit.[131]

Latinos played a small but still-important role in the Azusa Street Revival. They were the first people reportedly touched by the power of the Holy Spirit and healed. They also contributed to its international and multilingual flavor. They ministered to participants across racial lines during worship, prayer, and altar call services and publicly testified to the supernatural, transformative, and healing power of the Holy Spirit. Latinos conducted evangelistic work for Seymour's Azusa Mission, carried out social work, wrote testimonials for the Azusa Mission newspaper, helped introduce the spiritual gifts and Pentecostal experience to Catholics,[132] participated in large numbers, were ordained by Seymour, and participated in a conflict with an unnamed mission leader that signaled the routinization of the revival and according to Frank Bartleman a lack of freedom in the Spirit that ultimately signaled the revival's decline. Indeed, Latinos helped transform what was an essentially biracial, American, and English-language prayer meeting on 212 Bonnie Brae Street into a multiethnic, multilingual, and international revival at 312 Azusa Street.[133] Seymour's Pentecostal DNA was passed on by Mexican and Euro-American evangelists who in turn spread it to other Mexicans, Puerto Ricans, and Latin Americans.

CHAPTER 2

Victory Is Coming Now

Mexican Pentecostals in Texas

W ILLIAM J. SEYMOUR'S AZUSA STREET REVIVAL and Charles
Parham's Apostolic Faith Movement were the two primary catalysts in the birth of the Latino Pentecostal movement in Texas. Their
followers converted a number of Mexicans to Pentecostalism who in
turn founded their own independent missions from 1909 to 1915 that
served as the foundation for the future Latino Assemblies of God work
in Texas from 1915 to 1922. This first pioneer generation has been almost
completely left out of Latino AG histories. However, they are important
because they laid a sure foundation for subsequent Euro-American missionaries like H. C. Ball and Alice Luce who later helped organize the
movement.

Arnulfo M. López, pictured in Figure 2.1, is an example of one of
those previously unknown Latino AG pioneers. He wrote that he and
his coworkers passed out evangelistic tracts to 2,500 Latinos in San Antonio. He converted a number of people at his nightly services. As a result, López declared in a letter to the *Weekly Evangel*, "Victory is coming
now."[1] His energy and optimism capture the spirit of an entire generation of Latino Pentecostal evangelists who turned South Texas, from
Houston to San Antonio to Brownsville, into a virtual Latino burned-

Figure 2.1. Arnulfo M. López, South Texas, ca. 1920. (Gastón Espinosa Latino Pentecostal History Collection)

over district like that in upstate New York during the Second Great Awakening (1790s–1840s) led by Charles Finney. A new Pentecostal awakening was emerging in the Spanish-speaking Southwest, one that would forever change the Latino spiritual landscape in the United States.

This chapter traces the origins of this awakening through the independent Latino Pentecostal movement in Texas prior to the formation of the General Council of the Assemblies of God in April 1914 and the birth of Henry C. Ball's Mexican Pentecostal ministry in 1915. Ball and Alice E. Luce are often credited as the key founders of the Latino AG in the Southwest. However, although Ball began his Pentecostal ministry in 1915, he was largely unknown among many Mexican Pentecostal

ministers and evangelists until he helped co-organize the first of two Latino AG conventions in Texas in 1918.

Despite their critical role, the independent Mexican origins and contributions to the Latino AG have been left out of most Latino AG historical narratives, many of which were created by Ball himself and then popularized through Victor De Leon's book, *The Silent Pentecostals* (1979).
This was not an intentional oversight by De Leon since he was simply
unaware of the Mexican contributions, because by the 1970s their erasure was so complete that he was simply left with Ball's autobiographi-
cally oriented narrative, wherein Ball and other Euro-American missionaries took center stage. To address this erasure and revise and correct
the historical narrative, this chapter will examine the first conversions of
Mexicans to independent Pentecostal missions from 1909 to 1914, the
decision of many of them to join the AG (independent of Ball) from 1914
to 1918, and then how they helped build up and spread the Latino AG
work across Texas from 1918 to 1922.

This reexamination challenges a number of stereotypes about Latino
AG origins: first, that Ball and Luce were the first people to convert
Mexicans to Pentecostalism in Texas and to the Assemblies of God; second, that Ball baptized the first Mexicans in the Holy Spirit in the AG
movement; third, that Ball and Luce were the first to found, organize, and
run the first Mexican AG missions in Texas and were the first founders of
the Latino AG in the American Southwest; fourth, that Mexicans themselves did not pioneer and play a pivotal role in the founding of the Latino AG; and fifth, that the Mexican leaders did not seek to lead their
own movement until after Ball stepped down from leading the Latino
AG in 1939. In short, this chapter challenges the long-standing view that
Ball, Luce, and other Euro-American missionaries largely founded the
Latino AG. It points out why this is all inaccurate and simply not true for
the origins of the movement.[2]

Seymour's and Parham's Influence on Pentecostal Origins in Texas

The Latino AG movement in Texas traces its spiritual origins directly
back to the followers of Seymour and Parham. Azusa Street participant

F. F. Bosworth ordained a number of Latinos to the ministry in Texas, as did Mack M. Pinson, who was brought into the Pentecostal experience through three Seymour-influenced evangelists, Charles Mason, Gaston Barnabus Cashwell, and William H. Durham. Pinson actively worked with and ordained Mexicans to the Pentecostal movement in Texas. Azusa Street participants George and Carrie Judd Montgomery brought Francisco Olazábal into the Pentecostal movement in 1916, and he went on to pioneer the work in El Paso and south Texas. Olazábal in turn influenced Demetrio and Nellie Bazan and many other Latinos in the AG throughout Texas. The Bazans are important because they not only served as his co-pastors in El Paso, but they also had a profound influence on the Latino AG in Texas and throughout the Southwest. The Montgomerys also influenced Juan Lugo, the person credited with founding the Pentecostal movement in Puerto Rico.[3]

Charles Parham's influence is more difficult to ascertain. Sarah Parham wrote that one "fine looking Spaniard" (often a polite euphemism for a Mexican American or a U.S.-born Latino) attended one of his revival services in San Angelo near Brookshire in late April or May 1909. After Parham spoke in tongues, this "Spaniard" walked up to Parham and said he "heard the Gospel in his own tongue." Parham responded by saying that he had always wanted to speak in Spanish and to know the language. Exactly who this man was and what impact Parham's preaching had on his life or future are unclear. This could have been Enemecio Alaniz, the adopted son of a Presbyterian couple named Mr. and Mrs. McNay. Rev. George Joyner had converted the McNays and Enemecio and Concepción (his sister) Alaniz in 1909 around Deepwater, Texas, outside of Houston. We also know that Alaniz visited and later ministered in the Brookshire area. Robert Mapes Anderson stated that Parham garnered some Mexican followers but does not cite any evidence for this assertion. What is clear is that, unlike Seymour, Parham did not specifically target Latinos for conversion, and he did not have any direct impact on the birth of the Latino Pentecostal movement. Parham did, however, have an indirect influence because some of his followers converted Mexicans in the Houston area.[4]

Mexican Pentecostal Origins in Texas, 1909–1915

The Latino AG movement in Texas was influenced by the pioneer evangelistic work of M. M. Pinson, F. F. Bosworth, George Joyner, John A. Preston, Felix Hale, R. E. Winsett, Joseph Scheumack, G. W. Miller, Rev. Simonton, R. M. Thomas, Enemecio Alaniz, Antonio Ríos Morin, Arnulfo M. López, Rodolfo C. Orozco, and Mr. Isabel Flores, among others.[5] From 1909 to 1915 these Euro-American and Latino evangelists pioneered the first permanent Latino Pentecostal missions in Texas.[6] Their evangelization could not have taken place at a more opportune time. The dislocation and the tremendous suffering caused by the Mexican Revolution (1910–1917), along with a rise in Roman Catholic anticlericalism led by revolutionaries and a desire to fit into U.S. society, created a general openness to Protestantism, including Pentecostalism. In Mexico, Protestantism was almost always associated with political and social liberalism because Protestants promoted the separation of church and state and religious freedom for their proselytism. In fact, Protestantism was banned in Mexico until Benito Juárez's Constitution of 1857 guaranteed freedom of religion. This view was reinforced in the new Mexican Constitution of 1917, though anti-Protestant persecution was still widespread.[7]

Mexican Independent Pentecostal Leaders in Texas: Enemecio and Concepción Alaniz

Rev. George Joyner was one of the first Euro-Americans to convert a Mexican to Pentecostalism in Texas. He began preaching in Deepwater in 1909. At one of his multiethnic tent revivals, a Presbyterian lay leader surnamed McNay received the baptism with the Holy Spirit along with his wife. More significantly for the future Latino Pentecostal movement, Joyner also converted McNay's two adopted Mexican children, Enemecio and Concepción Alaniz. They were possibly the first Mexicans to receive the baptism with the Holy Spirit in the Lone Star State. Enemecio was clearly the first Latino Pentecostal evangelist in Texas and one of the first in the United States. Alaniz conducted evangelistic work from 1909 to 1915. As a result, Alaniz was ordained an AG evangelist by John

Figure 2.2. Manuel Cazares, Houston, Texas, September 12, 1913. (Gastón Espinosa Latino Pentecostal History Collection)

A. Preston on May 10, 1916, although by this time he had already been in the Pentecostal ministry evangelizing Mexicans for seven years.[8]

At revival services in Pasadena, Texas, in 1909, Joyner, the McNays, and Enemecio Alaniz (who usually did all of the preaching and follow-up ministry in Spanish) converted Manuel and Inocencia Cazares along with her three daughters, Luisa, Marcelina, and Isabel. Manuel, pictured in Figure 2.2, went on to pioneer the Pentecostal work in Texas. Two years later Enemecio married Isabel. Inocencia attended the revival thinking it was a circus. After the service, she went forward to the altar to receive prayer for divine healing and was reportedly healed. Indeed, promises of divine healing and the generally exuberant celebratory atmosphere attracted large numbers of Mexicans to the movement during the early twentieth century. In addition to personal evangelism, divine healing was the single most important practice that attracted potential converts. The Alaniz family, along with Manuel and Chonita Cazares, pioneered the Pentecostal work throughout the farm labor camps from Houston to Kingsville to San Antonio, founding the church in Rosenberg. Alaniz, Cazares, Joyner, and McNay also conducted outdoor evangelism and home Bible studies in the Magnolia Park farm labor camp near Houston. As was their practice—and that of many other Mexican–Euro-American evangelistic teams—Alaniz translated or preached a sermon, gave an altar call, and then spent time praying for the sick. Although in some instances when they first started out, Euro-Americans "supervised" the services, Alaniz and other Mexicans did most of the preaching and follow-up ministry because they were fluent in Spanish. They held regular services in the home of an American family, where they converted a number of Mexican families to Pentecostalism, including Tranquilino, Isabel, and Vincente Díaz, who later became leaders in the Texas movement.[9]

John A. Preston

While Joyner focused his evangelistic work in the Houston area largely on Euro-Americans, Alaniz and the two former soldiers, John A. Preston and Antonio Ríos Morin, evangelized along the Rio Grande in South Texas.[10] Preston first became interested in missionary work while serving as a soldier in the Spanish-American War in 1898 and in the Philippines in 1904. In 1907, he joined the Salvation Army and began preaching to Puerto Rican laborers on sugar cane plantations in the Hawaiian Islands. Two years later, he became a Pentecostal and moved to Texas, where he came into contact with some of Parham and Seymour's followers. Shortly thereafter, Preston worked with Morin and Alaniz—partly because he was not fluent in Spanish.[11] The trio conducted evangelistic work in San Antonio and Brownsville and were also among the first to take the Pentecostal message to Mexico, where they preached in Matamoros and Tampico. As a result of Preston's work, future Assemblies of God founders

F. F. Bosworth and A. P. Collins ordained him as an evangelist on August 3, 1911. Bosworth knew Seymour and had attended the Azusa Street Revival, thus establishing a direct genealogical connection between Seymour, Bosworth, Preston, and the Mexican Pentecostal work in Texas.[12]

The trio preached for six months throughout Texas before Preston returned to Little Rock, Arkansas, to attend to his ailing wife. His pioneer work was fraught with many hardships: "I slept on the ground and in barns . . . [and in] vacant houses and went many days without food . . . in one cotton camp on the Brazos [Rio Grande] river I lived with my wife and baby in an old shack that had been surrounded by flood waters washed full of mud. . . . We had to cook with sticks out of doors."[13]

Power Evangelism: Antonio Ríos Morin

The critical role that divine healing played in evangelistic work is borne out by a former Mexican Revolution army officer turned Pentecostal evangelist named Antonio Ríos Morin (born c. 1867). After hearing about Alaniz's healing services, in 1912 he attended a racially integrated meeting in the home of Mr. and Mrs. Perry in Houston. Morin was both skeptical and astonished by Alaniz's teachings and healing practices. His skepticism soon gave way to cautious curiosity about divine healing, miracles, and the baptism in the Holy Spirit after Mrs. Cazares used the Bible to explain and justify these practices in detail to Morin. She then invited him to convert and to receive the Spirit baptism. Morin hesitated, stating that God would never forgive him for the terrible atrocities he had committed in the war. Unfazed, Mrs. Cazares reassured him that God could and would forgive him if he truly repented and consecrated his new life to the ministry. She also stated that God would heal his body. This greatly appealed to him because he was still suffering internal pain from several gunshot wounds from the war. He made the leap of faith and reportedly dropped to his knees, bowed his head, and asked Jesus Christ to forgive him, make him born again, and give him the baptism with the Holy Spirit. He kept his word and set out to convert the Mexican people to Pentecostalism.[14]

The conversion and baptism of Morin mark a critical turning point in the history of Mexican Pentecostalism in Texas. If Alaniz preached to hundreds, Morin preached to thousands. Morin left his makeshift job as a manual laborer and ditch-digger and spent the next four years, from 1912 to 1916, preaching in *colonias* and farm labor camps from Houston to the Mexican border.[15]

In 1912, Alaniz, Morin, and Preston joined forces to conduct an evangelistic campaign in a large hall in San Antonio. As was their practice, Morin and Alaniz did most of the preaching. Their ministry attracted the attention of Mexican Spiritists. Spiritists believe the dead can make contact with the living through séances and mediums who can in turn be possessed by departed spirits. San Antonio was a key center of the Mexican Spiritist movement, which was led by Juan Luís Martínez, a Mexican American.[16] The work of Martínez was just one of many metaphysical and occult traditions in the Spanish-speaking community. South Texas also attracted many Mexican *curandera/o* healers, such as Don Pedrito Jaramillo (1829–1907), who had settled in the Mexican village of Los Olmos. He was famous throughout the Spanish-speaking community for praying for the sick and helped to reinforce the belief in divine healing and the supernatural. The curanderos' focus on healing provided Pentecostals with a key avenue through which to attract and convert the masses.[17]

Given Alaniz, Morin, and Preston's heavy evangelistic work in San Antonio, a Pentecostal-Spiritist showdown was inevitable. Almost nightly, Alaniz and Morin challenged the power of Spiritists, Spiritualists (the less scientific version), *curanderas,* and metaphysical practitioners. Alaniz and Morin claimed that their God was not only real, but also more powerful than the spirits the Spiritists summoned. In one conflict, a Mexican Spiritist leader defied Morin and Alaniz to heal his daughter, who was reportedly vexed by an unclean spirit more powerful than he or his colleagues could cast out. Morin, Alaniz, and the "brothers" moved forward and surrounded the girl, stretched out their hands toward her, and then reportedly unleashed waves of prayers asking God the Father in the name of Jesus by the power of the Holy Spirit to cast out the unclean spirit from the girl. The evil spirit departed at once, her father claimed. As a result, the Spiritist and his entire family of eight people were converted and received the baptism in the Holy Spirit. Similar showdowns between Pentecostals and Spiritists took place not only at the Azusa Street Revival but also in Puerto Rico and New York, as noted later in this book.[18]

The news of the exorcism and conversion of a Spiritist leader spread far and wide and attracted crowds to the evangelists' services. Alaniz and Morin reportedly converted and healed others. One woman testified that God had miraculously healed her of a physical ailment she had been battling for more than twelve years. In a day when doctors were expensive and health insurance unheard of, it is not difficult to see why thousands of Mexican Catholic immigrants might be attracted to Pentecostalism's message of divine healing, spiritual empowerment, and the salvation of the body, mind, and spirit, especially if their own prayers and visits to other healers did not bring about the desired results.[19]

As Alaniz and Preston continued their evangelism in San Antonio, Morin began holding services in the Kingsville area in 1913. His work attracted the patronage of Mrs. King, the owner of the enormous 800,000-acre King Ranch and the company town of Kingsville. She decided to sponsor his evangelistic outreach to Mexicans and provided him with a horse and buggy. Whether she did this to assist his work or to keep her Mexican workers pacified or both is uncertain, although the latter is likely.

From the Kingsville area, Morin, pictured in Figure 2.3, set out on an independent preaching itinerary. He preached in Richmond and then Rosenberg, where he conducted street-corner evangelistic services in the Mexican barrio. In open-air services, he reported singing, preaching, and praying for the sick. Morin and Alaniz joined forces to preach at the famous Clark Ranch in Brookshire. The owner allowed them to conduct their evangelistic services on the ranch, and as a result they converted and baptized fourteen Mexicans and their families.[20]

In July 1914, Alaniz and Morin split up to maximize their impact, with Alaniz traveling to Magnolia Park outside Houston and Morin to Uvalde, where he stayed in the home of a Mexican Baptist, Mrs. Maria Ibarra, and her family. During the day Morin would conduct open-air evangelistic services in front of the Uvalde Town Court House, and at night he held them in the Ibarras' living room, where Alejo, Tomacita, Concepción, and Isabel Gutiérrez were converted and baptized in

Figure 2.3.   Antonio Ríos Morin (man with white beard) pioneered the
Pentecostal work in South Texas from 1912 to 1915. This photograph was taken
around 1914.   (Gastón Espinosa Latino Pentecostal History Collection)

the Holy Spirit. They became a key family in the future spread of the
Pentecostal movement throughout Texas. From there Morin preached in
countless towns and labor camps. He would return to Uvalde every two
or three months to rest at the Gutiérrez home.[21]

After returning to the King Ranch area, Morin boarded with the
Euro–Mexican American family of Josefa McGraw, who assigned him
quarters where he could come and go as needed. He soon learned that
an unclean spirit reportedly vexed her daughter. He prayed and fasted
for three days for the teenager. Eyewitnesses report that as a result of his
prayers the evil spirit left her and her countenance and personality became normal. In the wake of this sensational news, people flocked to the
services at the McGraw home. McGraw stood up in the service to testify
how Morin had prayed for her daughter and how Jesus Christ had completely healed her. She also shared this story with a tall, young, blond-
haired, blue-eyed Iowa farm boy and transplant to South Texas named
Henry C. Ball (a.k.a. H. C. Ball or "Brother Ball").[22]

Mrs. McGraw encouraged the young and inexperienced Ball to team up with the seasoned Morin, who was more than thirty years his senior. As Morin's fame spread throughout Pentecostal circles, Euro-American AG leaders took an interest in his work and tried to persuade him to join the Assemblies of God. Independent Mexican ministers like Morin had a difficult decision to make: remain independent or join a Euro-American denomination and possibly give up their freedom. While some never joined, a growing number decided to align with the AG and other Euro-American denominations. Their positive relationships with white AG leaders, along with the growth of white supremacy, the KKK, and Nativism and xenophobia in the wake of the Mexican Revolution, all made remaining isolated in American society unattractive and potentially dangerous. In light of this, many Mexicans joined the AG because they shared its Pentecostal beliefs and visions and in order to secure ordination credentials with a denomination that was duly incorporated in Texas. This decision afforded them a number of benefits, not the least of which included clergy rail fares; funding from the home missions department; access to tracts, Bibles, and evangelistic and Sunday School literature; spiritual accountability; strategic and limited partnerships with Euro-American missions; sharing church facilities; and the ability to perform weddings and funerals legally recognized by the state of Texas.

Euro-American AG leaders made it clear that the Mexican ministers would not be discriminated against or segregated, and would in fact be treated on a par with any other AG minister. The Mexicans could continue to preach and teach with many of the same rights and much of the same freedom they had enjoyed when they were independent missions. Morin and others believed that securing ordination with a white American Pentecostal body would give them the kind of spiritual, material, and financial support they needed to increase their impact and as a result accepted the AG credentials. Morin was the first of many Mexicans to make this momentous decision and the first of many to realize that the AG movement could not always practice what it preached about full racial equality, despite its good intentions.

On January 14, 1914, AG founders E. N. Bell, Daniel Opperman, and A. P. Collins ordained Morin to the AG ministry.[23] He was the first

Mexican ordained by the Assemblies of God in the United States and the first Latino ordained who specifically targeted Mexicans in Texas. This was a full year before H. C. Ball, the person hailed as the founder of the Mexican and Latino AG movement, was ordained by the AG, on January 10, 1915. Despite Morin's earlier ministry and ordination, Ball mentions Morin only in passing in his own account of the Latino AG's origins.[24]

Sometime after this healing episode at the McGraws, Morin took the Pentecostal message to Piedras Negras, Coahuila, Mexico. We know nothing about his subsequent life and ministry. Notwithstanding his relatively short ministry in Texas, Morin is the first person to pioneer the AG work among Mexicans in Texas and Mexico, and many of his converts and missions helped lay the foundation for the future Mexican AG ministry in the Southwest.

Arnulfo M. López

Morin was not the only Mexican to pioneer the independent Mexican Pentecostal work in Texas before Ball. In 1913, a talented Mexican American Protestant minister named Arnulfo M. López (born ca. 1890) joined him. López first became interested in Pentecostalism after hearing reports about J. D. Scheumack's revival services in Austin, Texas. Scheumack traveled from his Mexican Protestant church in the Rio Grande Valley to Austin, where he persuaded López to join the movement. López decided to do so after witnessing the powerful Pentecostal worship and conversions of Mexicans at the altar. Music was a real lure, especially to Mexicans from traditional Protestant denominations, which used hymnals and practiced formal worship styles. López reports that the services and music were so powerful that he began to weep and went forward for prayer at the racially mixed altar. The next evening after the altar call, he received the baptism in the Holy Spirit. He then rose up and gave his testimony in Spanish since there were several Mexicans in the audience. Afterward, he gave up his twelve-year ministry in the Mexican Evangelical Church (Iglesia Evangélica Mexicana) and his large and financially stable 250-member congregation in order to join the Pentecostal movement, a major sacrifice.[25]

López worked for several months alongside Scheumack and then, at the latter's request, set off in 1914 to work with Rev. Simson in San Antonio, near San Jacinto and Ruiz Streets—the future location of the Latino AG mother church that H. C. Ball would one day pastor. Maggie McCaslin of Belton and Evelyn Campbell of Austin joined López and Simson in their labors, and López supervised their ministry. In 1916 López's ministry received a boost after the Alejo Gutiérrez family joined the church. They helped at the altar services because they were seasoned Christian workers.[26]

López decided to plant an independent Mexican Pentecostal mission. He secured a small tent and started evangelistic services to reach the masses. He attracted a small but growing number of defectors from the Catholic Church. This caught the attention of a Catholic priest at the historic San Fernando Cathedral in San Antonio, the sacred center of the Mexican Catholic community in South Texas. The priest told his parishioners not to attend the Pentecostal services and made it clear that López and his followers were not part of Christ's true church. The priest also seemed to imply that if his parishioners converted, they would go to hell. López and his congregation were harassed by Catholic youth who interrupted the services by standing outside the tent (he kept the canvas walls rolled up to keep the space cool and so that people passing by could hear his message), where they mocked and mimicked his preaching and prayers for the sick. Their boisterous heckling made it difficult to hear and was a major distraction for worshippers and visitors, López stated. After López politely asked them to stop, they grew bolder in their harassment. At one of the largest evening meetings, the youth threw sharp-edged rocks at the worshippers during a time of prayer and worship. One of the stones hit Patricio Flores so hard that it knocked him to the ground and cut a deep gash in his head. As he stumbled to get up, with blood streaming from the side of his face, he reportedly lifted up his hands to heaven and began to praise God. He reportedly stated, "Let not this sin be charged to them."[27]

The attacks grew worse. One night Catholic vigilantes took knives and tore the tent to shreds. Rather than give up, López moved the now homeless congregation to another location—a hay shed made out of corrugated metal. Although the new mission could accommodate up to 200 people, it was stiflingly hot. The heat, however, was preferable to the rock-throwing and heckling they had endured. Despite the harassment, the congregation grew and eventually acquired a large hall. Recognizing the need for coworkers and new evangelists to reach the Mexican masses, López persuaded F. Banda and Rafael M. Flores to become evangelists. He wrote in the *Weekly Evangel*, "Apostolic people are going all over." Despite jeers from his former Protestant colleagues that his work would never reach the size or quality of his last church in the Rio Grande Valley, López defiantly wrote, "I can do better work because I have found the Truth . . . [and] power."[28] He continued his work until Ball arrived in San Antonio, after which he handed over the mission to McCaslin and Campbell. Euro-American missionary Sunshine L. Marshall, Ball's future wife, soon joined these women. Eventually, this mission was given to Ball, for reasons that are unclear.[29]

While López spread the Latino AG movement to other parts of the Rio Grande Valley, the independent Pentecostal evangelist R. E. Winsett began evangelistic services in the strategic border town of El Paso, Texas, during the spring and summer of 1910. Winsett and his coworkers passed out 3,000 evangelistic tracts and attracted "hundreds" of Mexicans to his nightly evangelistic services. However, little remained of the work after he left.[30]

Two years later, a wealthy Pentecostal businessman from California named George Montgomery and a "Mr. Valenzuela" conducted evangelistic services in El Paso under a large tent, where they converted many Mexicans. The Valenzuelas crossed the border into Ciudad Juárez, Mexico, during Pancho Villa's siege of the city and passed out evangelistic tracts to the wounded and dying in hospitals. This Mr. Valenzuela was probably the husband or cousin of Romanita Carbajal de Valenzuela since they pioneered the Pentecostal work across the border from El Paso in Chihuahua in 1914.[31]

Rodolfo C. Orozco

A key shift took place in April 1915 when Alaniz and Joyner converted Rodolfo C. Orozco (1892–1991) near Pasadena, Texas. Orozco received the baptism with the Holy Spirit on May 15, 1915. Afterward, he conducted evangelistic work throughout the region and began pastoring a small independent Mexican Pentecostal church near Houston. Over the next several years, Alaniz persuaded him to join the AG. On November 18, 1918, Orozco was ordained by Hale and Ball and became the latter's associate pastor. He went on to organize the Assemblies of God work in Mexico, one of the largest Protestant denominations in that nation today.[32] He was joined in his work along the border by other key Latino Pentecostal leaders such as Isabel Flores, who began preaching in 1913, and Miguel Guillén, who converted in Los Osos in 1916. Flores, Guillén, Orozco, and two other ministers are pictured in Figure 2.4.

From 1912 to 1915, Mexican Pentecostals converted a number of people, including Isabel Flores, Agapito Martínez, and Manual Cazares, who went into the evangelistic and pastoral ministry. They in turn converted and baptized Mexicans on both sides of the U.S.-Mexico border. They started small missions, Bible studies, and prayer groups in many migrant farm labor communities and ranchos in Magnolia, Rosenberg, Texas City, the Hacienda Houses, Sugarland, Webster, Brookshire, Simonton, Genoa, and Pearland, as well as at the King Ranch and in other places near and around Houston and San Antonio.[33] All of these leaders and missions were independent of Euro-American control, even though they kept in contact with them and even some African American Pentecostal churches, with whom they felt a strong kinship and spiritual unity because of their passion, acceptance, and energetic worship style.

The preaching of these independent Mexican evangelists brought them directly into contact with practitioners of occult traditions. In 1916 Alaniz and Manuel and Chonita Cazares started evangelistic and mission work in Rosenberg, where they met and eventually converted a *brujo,* or male sorcerer, after an encounter in which the sorcerer reportedly witnessed the healing of Pedro Tapia, a paralytic and friend, at one of their revival services. This conversion helped birth the independent Mexican Pentecostal work in Rosenberg.[34]

From there, the Alaniz, Frias, Felix and Manuel Cazares, and Inocencia Cazares families loaded up their burro-pulled wagons and made the slow, dusty trek from Rosenberg to Hondo City, where they worked in the fields by day and conducted evangelistic and revival services at night in their makeshift missions. Three months later, the Frias family went to

Figure 2.4.   Mexican Pentecostal ministers who pioneered the Latino AG work
in Texas. First row (left to right): two unknown ministers. Second row (left to
right): Isabel Flores, Miguel Guillén, Rodolfo C. Orozco. Guillén became
the second president of the Latin American Council of Christian Churches
(CLADIC) from 1937 to 1971, and Orozco pioneered the AG work in Mexico in
1922 and served as the second general superintendent of the AG in Mexico from
1931 to 1940.   (Gastón Espinosa Latino Pentecostal History Collection)

San Antonio and the others to Simonton, just outside of Houston. In
Simonton they became sharecroppers and worked the rich soil, growing
crops and raising their families. They also used the farm town as the
base for their evangelistic work in nearby Rosenberg, Cuero, Sugarland,
and Richmond, where they came into contact with other Mexicans who
had been converted by Morin and Alaniz. The small but rapidly grow-

ing number of independent Latino Pentecostal missions was now developing into an identifiable movement with a network that hosted joint worship, revival, and evangelistic camp services.[35]

In 1918, the Alaniz and Cazares families finally raised enough money to build a small church in Rosenberg on land donated by Mari and Matías García. Manuel Cazares served as pastor, aided by Inocencia. They were soon joined in their evangelistic work by one of the most important pioneers of the early Latino Pentecostal movement, Rev. Isabel Flores. Flores conducted outreach in the Houston area and had very good relationships with almost all of the independent Mexican Pentecostal missions. He was a faithful and hardworking evangelist who made a number of converts and helped plant a number of missions and churches. When he was invited to join the AG, he not only did so but also brought his entire independent mission with him.[36]

Power and Cadence of Latino Pentecostalism
in the Southwest

Pentecostal congregations and social networks became a cultural, economic, and spiritual resource for Mexicans in the United States. Their small, family-style gatherings offered Mexicans a strong sense of community in an often alien, impersonal, and racially hostile world. The racial fault lines of South Texas were deeply carved up by white supremacy and Jim Crow segregation, which restricted where Mexicans could live, work, worship, and eat. In contrast to living in isolation in camps of single male workers, Mexican converts to the independent Pentecostal missions were immediately integrated into an extended family where they often shared meals before and after services. The women took turns in makeshift kitchens—often a basement—making chicken, beef, and corn tamales, tortillas, frijoles, roasted chicken, hot menudo, and Mexican rice, all served with chili peppers and *dulces* for the children.

In a day and age in which Mexicans were considered cheap labor and expected to remain silent and hidden in the kitchens, lumberyards, and restaurants, Pentecostalism afforded bright and energetic men and women the opportunity to speak out, testify, and preach from the pulpit, regardless of their race, class, or education. High standards were required for all ministers and laypersons. They had to live a consistent, holy, and sanctified life. This was especially true of anyone seeking to preach "God's Word" from the pulpit. Faith, passion, holy living, and a thorough knowledge of the Bible were the ordinary credentials for ministry. Much as for members of the black churches in the South, people's whole lives centered around their church, which affirmed not only their language but also many of their customs and traditions. Faith and ordinary life were fully integrated. Their missions and churches were more than just refuges from modernity; they were also resources and places where nobodies became somebodies because they were now the sons and daughters of an almighty and loving Father, who had the power to heal and redeem even the most terrible of sinners.

Missions and churches were also places where the pastor and a small band of believers would try to meet the very real physical and material needs of their followers. If someone lost a job, the congregation would share its meager resources and try to get the person added to a road crew or into maid service. If someone was sick and without medical attention, the pastors and elders would visit the home, lay gentle hands on the sick, and pray for divine healing and comfort. The material and spiritual were inseparable. Indeed, in many ways, Pentecostal missions functioned as Protestant mutual aid societies *(mutualistas),* not unlike those in Catholic churches.

Mexicans found joy, hope, and purpose not only in their new extended families but also in the worship services, where they could fully express their love and joy for God in their own cadence and language as loudly or quietly as they wanted. They no longer had to live lives of invisibility. Their services stood in contrast to the liturgical and often beautiful but still tightly structured Catholic masses and mainline Protestant services, which rarely lasted more than one hour. Theirs were not better, just different. The loud and enthusiastic singing, reported moments of hushed silence in the presence of a holy God, testimonies, speaking in tongues, prophecy, and prayer for divine healing created an atmosphere that seemed drenched in God's spirit, at the same time otherworldly and this-worldly. The services could run two, three, and even four hours on special occasions. Latino AG services often last this long even to this day.

Mexican Pentecostals are a "can-do" people. They believed that the same power of the Holy Spirit that fell on the Apostles on the Day of Pentecost in Acts was now falling in their own day and that signs and wonders would follow holy and faithful preaching. They believed this new outpouring of the Spirit would enable them to overcome all the trials and tribulations they suffered in life. Their sense of spiritual empowerment enabled many of them to reimagine their historical identities. They were no longer simply defined by their race, class, economics, education, or material resources. They believed the Holy Spirit empowered them to overcome their adversities and the daily toil of life. For these reasons, Pentecostalism provided one of the most important ingredients for a fulfilling life: hope.

Pentecostal psychology also offered migrant field workers and domestic laborers a chance to gain a certain measure of power, dignity, and control over their lives. They could step out of the shadows of American society with a sense of dignity and self-respect because they were taught that they were the sons and daughters of an almighty and all-powerful God. Their conversion and newfound family also gave them a degree of historical agency by teaching them that with God's help they could transform and better their lives, their families, and their communities. A Protestant "I can do all things through Christ which strengthens me" optimism replaced the fatalism of Mexican Catholicism. They believed that "greater is He [God] that is in you, than he who is in the world."[37]

However, this optimism was also always tempered by a pessimistic eschatology that declared that the world was controlled by the devil and would soon come to an end. There were certain things one could not change because the problem was part of a larger cosmic struggle. However, even in this conviction Pentecostalism provided hope by teaching that one day God would rapture His children to heaven before Jesus's battle with the Antichrist at the Battle of Armageddon. After He defeated the Antichrist, He would set up his thousand-year millennial kingdom on earth. In this respect, Pentecostalism swung along a sliding scale of hope and pessimism, but, its adherents believed, with hope winning out both in this life and the next.

It would be shortsighted to argue that Pentecostalism simply created a false consciousness that enabled people entirely to escape the realities and problems of everyday life. For a Mexican Pentecostal, the calls to conversion, evangelism, healing, and the baptism with the Holy Spirit were calls for fundamental transformation of body, mind, spirit, and society—in this world. Conversion called for a total reorientation of one's life and attitude toward the world. This has often been overlooked because some tend to look for historical agency and empowerment in those places where the dominant Euro-American society finds them, such as in politics, marches, protests, and hunger strikes. Yet one might argue that an undocumented immigrant preaching that God is no respecter of race, class, or riches in a migrant farm camp on the famous King Ranch or in a contemporary labor camp is also a subversive act in the eyes of those running it. Tent revivals can be reread as Christian transgressive social spaces where people often crossed previously inscribed unbiblical social, spiritual, racial, and class borders and boundaries. The revival platform was the poor man's pulpit. Social status was leveled at the foot of the cross. Thus, Pentecostal conversion provided the ideology and conviction that empowered men and women to take a certain measure of control over their lives and destinies, even if complete control and success seemed for some to be just out of reach. This is one of the reasons why Pentecostalism attracted the poor, marginalized, and disinherited and why it still gives them a ready-made message, pulpit, and method to bring about personal and social change.

Despite the newfound hope and optimism, their historical agency was often hemmed in by Euro-Americans who practiced a pious paternalism that suggested it was their duty and right to maintain a kind of spiritual custody over their Mexican converts, an attitude that turned many Mexicans away from the Pentecostal message. Some Euro-American missionaries could not transcend the racialization of American society. More than just a few described Mexican men, women, and children as "dirty little Aztecs," who were "benighted" and "ignorant" "heathen people" "sunk in the superstitious and idolatrous practices of Rome."[38] John Preston summed up the attitude of the white man's burden and not a few missionaries when he wrote in the *Weekly Evangel,* "Their salvation may depend on us."[39] Clearly, not all missionaries were as paternalistic as Preston, but many shared his views and even Charles Parham's racial views. Many early Euro-American missionaries would agree with

Parham's assessment that despite centuries of Protestant mission work, most Mexicans were "nearly all heathen still."[40]

The Euro-American view that Mexicans were lazy, foreign, and child-like "half-breeds" who were trapped in the "bondage of Romanism" on occasion spilled over into Pentecostalism.[41] Therefore it is not surprising that few Euro-Americans ever personally made significant inroads or mass conversions among Mexicans in Texas in the early twentieth century. When the first Euro-Pentecostal missionaries wrote of their success in evangelizing Mexicans and other Latinos, they almost always left out the fact that it was due not to their preaching alone, but rather to that of their Mexican coworkers, who served as the bridge between the missionary and the Mexican masses. This often created the impression that the white Pentecostal missionaries were doing a great work, while the Mexican native evangelists struggled to find converts. However, the historical record shows that just the reverse was true: in fact, sometimes Euro-Americans took credit for the success of their native Mexican converts.[42]

This was clearly the case with John Preston and Enemecio Alaniz. Hence it is not surprising that in their letters and other early documents the names of the Mexican coworkers are almost never mentioned. The only way we know they participated and actually carried out most of the evangelistic work and ministry is because of written testimonies and notarized letters left behind by Mexican pioneers. Without them, their stories, contributions, and agency would have been completely lost to history. With the exceptions of Preston, M. M. Pinson, and Felix Hale, most Euro-Americans did not minister for more than a year in the Mexican community.[43] Ball was the first Euro-American to make a lasting impact among Mexicans in the Southwest.

The formal origins of the Pentecostal work in Texas began in 1909 through people influenced by Seymour and Parham's ministries. Their converts started a number of independent Mexican missions that worked in loose cooperation and fellowship prior to Ball starting his own small mission in 1915 and more formally organizing the work in 1918 into a loose association. Thus it was these pioneer Mexican and Euro-American

Assemblies of God pastors, missionaries, and evangelists, and not H. C. Ball and Alice Luce, who founded the first Latino AG work in the United States. The latter laid a solid foundation for the future Latino AG work that Ball, Luce, and others formally organized and developed in Texas and throughout the Southwest, though not without tensions.

CHAPTER 3

Their Salvation May Depend on Us

Missionary Origins in Texas

IN 1916 ASSEMBLIES of God missionary John A. Preston wrote that the Pentecostal work in Texas was growing by leaps and bounds. He called on his *Weekly Evangel* readers to partner with him by offering their prayer and financial support because "their salvation may depend on us."[1] Indeed, although Preston, pictured in Figure 3.1 with his wife, was referring primarily to raising funds for evangelistic work among Mexicans, it still reflected a deep belief among many Euro-American AG leaders that the Mexican ministers were largely incapable of saving their own people. This general sentiment led to a quiet but growing level of distrust and eventually conflict between Mexicans and Euro-American missionaries. By 1920, Mexicans were beginning to grumble about not being able to run their own movement—something they had done prior to Ball's corralling the independent Mexican Pentecostal churches in South Texas into the "Latin Convention" in 1918. In many ways, Ball was getting in the way of a natural progression of the Euro-American missionaries handing over complete control of the movement to native workers—something that most of the Mexican pioneers wanted and felt was inevitable.

Although Euro-Americans converted the first Mexicans to Pentecostalism in Texas and often worked alongside them in evangelistic meetings

Figure 3.1.   John A. Preston and spouse, Texas, ca. 1915.   (Gastón Espinosa Latino Pentecostal History Collection)

from 1906 to 1915, almost immediately Mexicans ran their own independent missions because most Euro-American missionaries could not
speak Spanish, a fact often overlooked in the historical literature. This
revises the story on the origins of the Mexican Assemblies of God work
in the Southwest and particularly Texas, by challenging the notions that
the first generation of Mexicans passively followed Euro-American missionary oversight; that the independent Mexican leaders were the cause
of the national conflict and schism that erupted in 1922; and that Mexicans
were incapable of leading their own Mexican district on par with white

districts without Euro-American supervision—a charge that, we shall see, Ball made to AG leaders at their headquarters in Springfield, Missouri.

Although Ball and Luce sounded like they genuinely wanted to hand over the leadership of the Mexican work to native leaders as soon as possible, they invariably thwarted every major attempt by Mexicans to take over the reins of the movement. Ball was perhaps the most conflicted of all. While he clearly stated that it was best for natives to run their own indigenous movement, he personally found it difficult to let go of the Mexican AG's leadership in a timely manner. Although perhaps an unfair assessment of Ball, some Mexicans believed that he had no real and genuine intention of handing over the Latino AG work because he lacked confidence in their leadership abilities. They point to the fact that he did not voluntarily step down in 1939—he did so only after being asked by AG headquarters in Springfield to supervise the entire AG work in Latin America, an offer too good to turn down.

Ironically, Ball and some of his Euro-American coworkers contributed to the leadership gap by systematically removing for various reasons almost all of the most experienced and capable Mexicans leaders. Ball's statements about the lack of quality leaders are thus tinged with irony and were something of a self-fulfilling prophecy because, in the end, he drove out the very Mexicans that had the backbone and capacity to lead the movement. As the Euro-Americans became stronger and stronger, the remaining independent Mexican ministers were increasingly regulated, isolated, and replaced with more compliant converts.

Despite this development, originally it was the independent Mexican ministers who had pioneered the Latino AG work between 1914 and 1918 and had provided the social glue and spiritual authority that held the movement together, all the while persuading other independent congregations to join the AG. In many ways, they really continued to lead the movement until 1920 by which time Ball had solidified his power base with a growing number of new converts. Many of the original pioneer independent Mexican ministers were older and had a lot more evangelistic experience (and success) preaching in Spanish than Ball and the other white missionaries. Early on, Ball struggled to attract and keep Mexicans and to preach in Spanish. Luce and the other missionaries faced a similar problem, though with time both became fluent. Because of their linguistic challenges, Ball, Luce, and the white missionaries naturally gravitated toward the top administrative leadership positions, Bible schools, and the print shop, rather than only pastoring and carrying out evangelistic work in the field—though they did that as well. This practice was not unique to Euro-American Pentecostal missionaries and was true for almost all Catholic and other Protestant traditions as well. This helps explain why it took so long for native leaders to run their own movements in the United States.

This is not to say that Ball and the Euro-American missionaries did not plant their own missions and make their own converts, for they surely did. However, the historical record indicates that the best missionaries simply were not as effective as the best native Spanish-speaking evangelists and pastors in preaching, making converts, or growing their churches. Their missions tended to be smaller than those planted by Mexicans, though on occasion some of their missions were larger because they simply had a permanent church building, more resources, and because they hired native Latino co-pastors. This is evidenced by the fact that from 1915 to 1922, the majority of Mexicans in the Latino AG had been brought into it by the formerly independent Mexican pastors and evangelists and their converts. Furthermore, although it is true that Ball later pastored one of the largest Mexican congregations, what is often omitted from these histories is the fact that he often inherited (or assumed control over) congregations that had been previously founded and developed by native Mexican leaders (e.g., Arnulfo López). This spiritual primogenitor practice was not uncommon in Protestantism in this period and to this day it is often applied to churches with young male or female interim pastors.

Although Ball liked the independent and entrepreneurial spirit of the independent Mexican leaders, he also came to see them as less compliant with his authority. They were much more willing to ask questions than recent converts and knew they could always go back to their independent status if they did not like how Ball and the AG treated them. In short, they demanded that Ball treat them with respect and dignity. They knew their salvation did not depend on Ball or any other white missionary. As long as Ball kept this in mind, there would be peace, equality, and a prosperous movement.

As we shall see later, by the fall of 1922, Ball and the Euro-American missionaries had systematically removed or pushed out many of the most outspoken and strongest independent Mexican leaders. They were moving toward complete and undisputed control of the Latino AG in the Southwest—at least so they thought. Rather than empower Mexicans and other Latinos to begin leading their own movement in the early 1920s, Ball, Luce, and other Euro-American missionaries, along with some of their Mexican supporters, perhaps unintentionally, thwarted this movement toward independence and the creation of a Mexican-led district on a par with their white Euro-American counterparts.

Euro-American Missionary Origins of the Latino AG

Euro-American missionaries can be broken down into periods and types. The first are those who converted the first Mexicans to the movement from 1909 to 1918 and largely treated the Mexicans as equals and ordained them into the larger AG. The second are those invited to join the movement by Ball and Luce after 1918 and who largely saw their work as shepherding Mexicans until they believed they were ready to lead and govern themselves. Both groups contributed to the four major evangelization periods and streams that fed into the origins of the Latino AG, some of which overlapped and blended in with one another: (1) those independent Euro-American and Latino Pentecostals that converted Latinos prior to the formation of the AG in 1914; (2) those independent Euro-American and Latino Pentecostals that converted Latinos after the formation of the AG but who did so independently of Ball and Luce and the Latino AG; (3) those Euro-American, African American, and Latino Pentecostals from other Pentecostal denominations and traditions that converted people who eventually joined the Latino AG; and (4) those Euro-American and Latino AG pastors and evangelists who did so under the leadership and supervision of Ball and Luce after the formation of the district.

Although Euro-American missionaries led or co-led evangelistic work among Mexicans, most could not speak Spanish fluently and had no long-term desire to pastor a Mexican church or *templo* and subsequently handed over their converts to Mexicans, who in turn transformed the group of converts or Bible study group into a mission and eventually a church, though some folded due to lack of resources, charisma, and shifts in employment (most ministered part-time and some had to follow seasonal harvests). Furthermore, many of these first-generation missionary converts went out into the mission field on their own, evangelized Mexicans, and started their own missions, completely independent of Euro-American control.

Although this first generation of Euro-American missionaries harbored some of the same nativist and culturally racialized sentiments about Mexicans as their non-Pentecostal white counterparts, their views were modified and often softened by stories of the interracial nature and harmony in Acts 2 and at the Azusa Street Revival. Since many pioneers were independent and in need of coworkers, they also tended to welcome Mexican pastors from other Protestant traditions who joined the movement and they treated them as equals. Furthermore, right after the formation of the AG, the first-generation Mexican American and other Latinos were often welcomed and treated like any other minister. Many missionaries saw their conversion as a stepping-stone to the evangelization of Mexico and then Latin America. This was another reason why they encouraged converts to start their own missions and take the Christian message back to Mexico.

So, prior to the first Spanish-speaking Latino AG convention in 1918, the work among Mexicans was largely a semi-autonomous and independent movement led by and for Mexicans. While there were some missions jointly pastored by Mexicans and Euro-Americans, the Mexicans did most of the preaching, pastoral counseling, and ran the day-to-day operations, and in little more than a year or two they were normally left in complete control of these missions—if they had not been already. Almost all permanent Mexican Pentecostal missions and churches founded in Texas prior to 1918 were planted or co-planted and led by Mexicans.

The relatively peaceful trajectory and development of the rapidly growing Mexican AG movement took a radical turn that almost destroyed the work after a conflict erupted in 1922 with H. C. Ball over the leadership of the movement. Part of the conflict was due to his management style. Ball's desire to evangelize Mexicans, plant churches, and take a more episcopal (at least in practice) rather than congregational approach to leadership were all shaped by his Methodist upbringing. This top-down approach tended to squelch native leadership and innovation because the Pentecostals seemed to undermine the structure that good Methodists in particular and Euro-Americans in general believed led to healthy churches and a strong organizational movement.

Henry C. Ball

The person responsible for leading the Latino AG movement after 1922 was Henry Cleophas Ball. Ball was born in Brooklyn, Iowa, on February 18, 1896. His father was a Quaker and his mother a devout Methodist. After Ball's father died, H. C. contracted tuberculosis. His mother's doctor advised her to move H. C. to warmer climates. She was now faced with a difficult decision: stay in the world they knew or strike out for a new life with the hope of saving her son. She boldly chose the latter and sold the family farm and moved to Amistad, New Mexico, when H. C. was twelve years old. They lived there for two years before heading south in search of even warmer climes in Morelos, Mexico, where their meager dollars could be stretched to make a difficult life more comfortable. Travel was slow in a covered wagon pulled by a burro, which only made ten to fifteen miles per day. A crisis emerged when the road ended in Rivera, Texas. Rather than go farther and exhausted by their lonely and bumpy travels, the Balls interpreted the end of the road as a sign from God that they should stop and plant roots in South Texas. Mrs. Ball took her meager savings and spent it on a small ten-acre farm in the largely Mexican village of Ricardo, where land was cheap and where they built a one-room shack. Her journey had come to an end, but H. C.'s was just beginning.[2]

Historian David Montejano notes that farmers like the Balls were part of a much larger migration of Iowan and other midwestern farmers that headed to South Texas in search of a new life and cheap farmland. They were hardworking, thrifty, and family-oriented. The Mexican and later American *hacienda rancho* society was paternalistic. Mexican *vaqueros* and their families lived on the vast American ranchos and were treated as part of the extended family. After the influx of midwestern farmers into South Texas, this paternalistic rancho society gave way to different social relations and commercial farming in which the Mexicans were now segregated into little farm labor camps and *colonias* at the edge of the large farm or nearby village. This took place at the same time American society witnessed the rise of Nativism, the Ku Klux Klan, Jim Crow segregation, *Plessy v. Ferguson,* and vigilante justice. This anti-Mexican and anti-immigrant fear was only reinforced by the horrors of the Mexican Revolution broadcast daily in Texas newspapers and by the ill-fated 1915 Plan de San Diego, which called for Mexicans, Mexican Americans, and African Americans to liberate South Texas by exterminating all adult white males in the lower Rio Grande Valley. This, along with the influx of millions of Mexican immigrants, most of whom were uneducated and financially destitute, led to the formation of a new stereotype of Mexicans (and U.S.-born Mexican Americans/Tejanos/Latinos) as poor, uneducated, and dangerous foreigners. All of this led to the fracturing and racialization of Mexican–Euro-American relations in Texas.[3]

Ball later admitted that before his conversion to Protestantism in 1910 and his calling to the ministry in 1914, he had looked down on Mexicans. Although he later became an outspoken advocate for the Mexican people, he still had lingering doubts in the 1920s about their ability to lead their own movement in light of their limited education, cultural values, and Catholic backgrounds. Mexicans picked up on this and it led to mistrust.[4]

Ball's biblical outlook was shaped by frontier Protestantism. He and his mother attended Rev. Hatfield's Kingsville Methodist Church, six miles away from Ricardo. Although they attended services every Sunday, Ball preferred the more fiery and evangelistic Baptists and often slipped out after services to attend Rev. Brice's Kingsville Baptist Church. It was at one of Brice's evangelistic services in the old school house in Ricardo that Ball walked down the aisle to the wooden plank altar and gave his life to Jesus Christ. He was born again. He immediately told his mother, who welcomed the news. Their joy was short-lived when they discovered the Baptists practiced closed communion, which meant he could not take communion with his mother since she was a Methodist, a group that practiced infant baptism. Given his deep attachment and love for his mother, on Christmas Day 1910 Ball left the Baptists for the Methodist Church.[5]

This was a critical decision, for it was after hearing a Methodist missionary from Venezuela share her testimony about evangelizing Latin Americans that Ball felt a divine calling to reach the Spanish-speaking people. This, along with his conversion, also changed his racial attitude about Mexicans. He asked Rev. Hatfield for permission to start a ministry to Mexicans in Ricardo. Hatfield agreed and provided him with evangelistic literature and a few old Sunday school lessons from 1904. He also borrowed an old Spanish New Testament and hymnal from a Mrs. Rowland, a Mexican married to a Euro-American. With all the zeal of a new convert, the tall, blond-haired, blue-eyed Ball walked through Ricardo inviting every Mexican he met to his Sunday school class, which he planned to hold at the same schoolhouse where he had been converted. That Sunday he proudly if nervously rang the school bell twice, calling all Mexicans to his service. Only two showed up: Juanita Bazan and Mr. Villareal. He later liked to joke that he wondered how many people would have attended if he had rung the bell more times.[6]

Since Ball could not read, write, or speak Spanish, he asked Villareal to read the Spanish Sunday school material, the Bible, and copies of Wesley's sermons to his congregation of two—really one—since Bazan was the only one sitting in the room. Despite his meager results, Ball was stubborn and fixated on his call. After six months of studying Spanish, he gave his first sermon, but with no tangible results. However, by the power of sheer determination—and some wise strategic moves like having Villareal give the messages—his ministry grew from two to fifty-two Mexicans, though the numbers ebbed and flowed depending on the seasonal harvests. In truth, much of this growth was due to the preaching and social networking of a Mexican Methodist from Alice Springs named Pablo Verduzco, who also assisted Ball. He admired the young high-school student's desire to lead Mexicans to Christ and as a result persuaded several people to attend his struggling mission. Verduzco's help was a mixed blessing because as soon as he left, Ball's core membership dwindled to eleven. Yet Ball was faithful to his little flock. The Methodist Church rewarded his service by officially recognizing his work as a Mexican mission. Ball continued his ministry all the way through high school until 1914.[7]

Ball worried about the future. He realized that a lot more was at stake than just his little mission, and he started an English-speaking morning service to compensate for his falling numbers and moved the Spanish service to the afternoons. The same year that Alaniz, Morin, López, and other Mexicans were planting new missions and rapidly spreading the Pentecostal message throughout the *colonias* and farm labor camps in South Texas, Ball's mission struggled to survive. Just when it looked as if his Mexican ministry would close, he received a boost by the arrival of the Smalley family, who raised his spirits and told him about an evangelist that had just arrived in town to conduct a revival. Eager to learn how to more effectively evangelize, Ball attended the services to see if there were any biblical insights and techniques he could glean.[8]

The Smalley family introduced Ball to Rev. Felix A. Hale and his two associates Carley Mosaley and Sister Hamilton. Although Hale had already spent a number of years in the evangelistic field before that, John Preston ordained Hale on March 22, 1914. Hale and his associates later joined the Assemblies of God and developed a reputation for preaching across the color line and converting Mexicans. Ball was impressed by their evangelistic work among Mexicans, though not sure what to make of their Pentecostal beliefs. After attending the weekly Methodist service in Kingsville, Ball quietly slipped out the back door and into Hale's tent revival services where he listened to him preaching about the Pentecostal fire and baptism with the Holy Spirit. Desperately seeking to jumpstart his struggling ministry and eager to experience more of God, after the service Ball asked Rev. Hale to pray for him and his Mexican ministry.[9] After attending for three weeks, on November 7, 1914, Ball made the momentous decision to become Pentecostal and receive the baptism with the Holy Spirit.[10] This event forever changed his life and the course of the Latino AG movement.

Ball's understanding of Pentecostalism was incomplete. However, he quickly learned that tongues separated Pentecostals from his Methodist colleagues. The Methodists were also skeptical about claims of divine healings, miracles, and prophecy. After it appeared that Ball would not remain silent about his new convictions, Methodist leaders summoned him to a meeting. After two hours of energetic conversations, Ball refused to recant his newfound views unless they could prove from the

Bible that he was in error—something they could not do to his satisfaction. After it was clear he would not yield, Ball was handed a letter of dismissal. He was out of the Methodist ministry. This turn of events shook his faith and made him uncertain about his calling and future.[11]

Rev. Hale admired Ball's raw determination and deep commitment, precisely the qualities he believed one needed to lead a successful ministry. He immediately invited Ball to join the fledgling Assemblies of God. Ball agreed and found a new home. After tutoring Ball in Pentecostal doctrine over the next year—the only theological training he would ever receive—on January 10, 1915, Hale, A. P. Collins, and E. N. Richey, a former associate of Charles Fox Parham, ordained Ball to the ministry.[12] Although Ball's Methodist mission had been taken away from him, this did not stop him from sharing his Pentecostal beliefs with his former parishioners. As a result, a few of his former Methodist parishioners started attending his Mexican Pentecostal mission.[13]

Ball contemplated taking the Pentecostal message to Mexico, but the chaos of the Mexican Revolution kept him from fulfilling this plan. However, he quickly realized that he could evangelize Mexico right where he lived thanks to the waves of Mexican immigrants arriving daily in South Texas. Without any major financial or material support, he wrote that he stepped out in faith and began conducting evangelistic services in Kingsville. His preaching attracted only a few former parishioners. Discouraged a second time, he contemplated abandoning the Mexican work altogether[14] but changed his mind after Rev. Hale introduced him to Rev. John Preston, who encouraged him to be patient and to faithfully continue the work. Ball heeded his advice. Although Ball had attracted a handful of Mexicans, he was still frustrated that after months of preaching about Pentecost none of them had received the baptism with the Holy Spirit.[15]

A breakthrough came on July 4, 1915, when nine Mexicans received the Holy Spirit in Ricardo. Afterward, Ball celebrated communion for the first time. During the service, two more women received the Holy Spirit. Ball was elated. He joyfully wrote to his supporters: "the power fell from heaven and there was shouting and praising God." Although Victor De Leon cites Ball's January ordination as the birth of the Latino AG work in Texas, Ball later wrote that this event on July 4 "was the [actual] beginning of the spiritual revival that has continued to this day."[16] Until that time Ball was seriously thinking about leaving the ministry because of his lack of success and AG support. All of that was about to change.

The July 4 Holy Spirit baptisms breathed new life into his struggling ministry. He tapped into their newfound enthusiasm to persuade his handful of Mexican parishioners and Euro-Americans to help him build a makeshift mission, or *templo*. They built his first church on his mother's farm in Ricardo out of boards and tent canvas. He held Pentecostal services there for almost a year before it was ripped to shreds by hurricane Martinique on August 18, 1916. Now forced to start over and still struggling to attract Mexicans, he decided to move his mission to Kingsville in 1916, with the hope of jump-starting his ministry. He blended his small mission with a Mexican congregation pioneered by López and Morin from 1913 to 1916. He hoped to reach the hundreds of Mexicans that worked on the King Ranch, six miles south. Kingsville became the first real center of Ball's ministry. The facilities problem was solved when Rev. Hale allowed Ball's congregation to meet in his church. Going one step further, Hale made the critical decision to encourage those seasoned Mexicans converted through Morin and López to blend with and assist Ball's ministry. They served as the bedrock of his new congregation.[17]

Some scholars leave out the critical fact that Ball's Kingsville ministry grew out of the work first pioneered by López and Morin. The very same Josefa McGraw who sponsored Morin's work sold Ball the church lot, which was physically adjacent to the McGraw home. Furthermore, many of the Mexicans that still attended the Bible study Morin started now blended in with Ball's congregation. Thus Ball built on and directly benefited from the foundation laid by the Mexican AG ministry that came before him.[18]

In January 1917, Reverends Hale, Ball, and Ball's Mexican parishioners built a 30- by 40-foot wood chapel that seated 100 people. This was one of the first Latino Pentecostal churches built from scratch in the United States and marked a milestone in the history of the movement. De Leon wrote that this chapel marked the "formal beginning" of the AG work among Latinos in the United States. However, as we have seen, it was the previous Euro-American and Mexican AG evangelists who laid the formal foundations of the Latino AG work in the United States.[19]

The AG work grew so steadily because they stressed not only making converts, but also training new pastors, evangelists, and leaders. Seasoned Mexican leaders like Alaniz, Morin, and López persuaded many of their most talented converts and youth to go into the ministry. An example of this is Isabel Flores, who served as a lay and then later ordained evangelist. Morin and Preston recognized the calling on Flores's life and persuaded him and E. N Richey and A. P. Collins to ordain Flores as an AG evangelist in Pasadena, Texas, on November 2, 1916, all independent of Ball. Another Mexican named Miguel Guillén from Los Indios, who had joined the AG and evangelized along the border, joined him. They were part of a growing generation of Mexican evangelists and pastors who contributed to the growth of the movement.[20] All of this makes it clear that Enemecio Alaniz, Antonio Ríos Morin, A. M. López, Isabel Flores, and other Mexican and Euro-American missionaries, rather than H. C. Ball and Alice E. Luce, were the first persons to pioneer the AG Mexican work in Texas and the United States.

After the church was built in Kingsville, and as a result of the work and support of López and Morin's converts, Ball's ministry finally began to grow. He reported converting followers of Mexican president Francisco I. Madero and revolutionary Pancho Villa.[21] Despite the brief reprieve, the hardships Ball and his congregation faced only deepened with the outbreak of World War I, which had a devastating impact on the Pentecostal work in Texas. Many Mexican Americans were drafted into the U.S. Army. Still others fled to Mexico. Ball reported that by October 1917, not one of the fifteen Spanish-speaking congregations in Texas (the vast majority of which independent Mexican evangelists and ministers had founded) had more than twenty members, except for his own congregation in Kingsville, which numbered twenty-five, more than half of whom came from the earlier work. Although he might have said this to justify the drop in his own mission, almost all Protestant and Catholic churches suffered numerical decline during this period as well.[22]

Unlike the Mexican Apostolic Assembly Pentecostals, who were not allowed to fight in combat positions, the Assemblies of God left the decision of whether or not to fight in the armed forces up to the individual to decide for him- or herself. Many went off to war and some never returned. Still others returned to Mexico due to the growing Nativism and racial profiling that took place in the wake of the Plan de San Diego (1915) and the Zimmerman Telegram (January 16, 1917), in which Germany invited Mexico to invade the United States during World War I. This created further anti-Mexican tensions in Texas.

Ball slowed down the pace of his ministry just a bit after he met Miss Sunshine Marshall in April 1917 at the Texas-New Mexico District Council meeting in Fort Worth. He attended with López, Pinson, and Alice E. Luce. Sunshine was a kind and gracious woman who loved the Mexican people and soon fell in love with Ball. When she first met him, her first impression was that he "was the tallest, thinnest and most blue-eyed fellow I had ever seen." Impressed by her Christian commitment and desire to evangelize the Mexican people, Ball invited her to move to Kingsville to live with Alice Luce and later to attend a Pentecostal camp meeting at Onion Creek. She stayed briefly in Kingsville and then moved

Figure 3.2.   Henry C. and Sunshine Marshall Ball and children, ca. 1939. Henry C. served as the first superintendent of the Latino Assemblies of God. First row (left to right): Henry C., Sunshine, Herschel, Leroy. Second row (left to right): Alvina, Ivah, Myrna.   (Flower Pentecostal Heritage Center)

on to San Antonio, where she studied Spanish from May to August before traveling with Luce to Monterrey, Nuevo León, Mexico. She and Luce carried out evangelistic work for six months. However, the dangers of the Mexican revolution made it unsafe to remain. After the U.S. Consulate warned her about the possibility of being kidnapped, they advised them to return to the United States. Once home, Marshall rekindled her friendship with Ball, which soon blossomed into love. After a short courtship, they were married on June 20, 1918, and raised five children (Figure 3.2).[23]

Ball's Vision: Organizing Independent Mexican Missions into a Convention

Due to the struggles they encountered during World War I, the future of the Mexican AG work did not look promising. A turning point came in the fall of 1917 when Rev. Isabel Flores stopped off in Kingsville and visited Ball. He was on his way to Mexico to minister to the converts of López, Morin, and others. Flores described to a discouraged Ball the growing number of independent Mexican missions sprouting up throughout South Texas. In total, there were at least eighteen missions in the independent Mexican Pentecostal movement in Texas and three in Mexico. While some were loosely affiliated with the AG (though not Ball's ministry), most were not, and those that were loosely affiliated with the AG largely retained their independence.[24]

Ball immediately recognized a golden opportunity. Seeing that Flores already worked well with his parishioners, Ball asked him to take charge of his own mission while Ball traveled to Mexico. As a courtesy, Flores postponed his trip to Mexico to assist Ball. After he returned, Ball proposed to Flores the idea of holding a convention of all of the independent Mexican missions in Texas. Ball made it clear that he was not seeking to take over the movement or independent missions but was simply seeking to help unite everyone under the banner of Christ. They would both jointly lead the event. In order to help defray costs and provide a place to meet, Ball offered to host the event at his church. Because Ball was willing to cover the expenses and share the leadership, Flores agreed. Flores then personally invited all of the independent pastors and workers to the convention slated for January 1918. Although it is often described as the first Mexican AG convention, this is misleading because there was no organized Mexican AG or convention at this time, just a small number of independent Mexican missions, some loosely associated with the AG, but most still independent. To Ball's credit, he acknowledged as much when he later wrote that this convention was "of a district nature" rather than an official AG district convention. Despite this qualification, which is often glossed over in the literature, it is often described as the first AG convention with Ball as its founder.[25] Ball also claims that he was elected leader by the seven Mexican ministers, but other Mexicans claim Ball "informally assumed the role of leader" because he organized and "presided over" the first 1918 Convention and because he served as the liaison between Mexicans and Euro-Americans.[26]

This careful parsing of words, events, and leadership along with independent testimonies by eyewitnesses reveals that the vast majority of those who attended were still running their own independent or quasi-independent ministries. The fact is that some had never heard of Ball or the AG prior to Flores's invitation. Ball was simply one of many Euro-American missionaries co-pastoring a struggling mission. Recognizing the potential that lay before him to unite the independent Mexican Pentecostal movement in South Texas under one banner, Ball asked Flores and Arnulfo López to convince the pastors and missions to attend the convention and later join the AG. He must have felt some authority to do this because at the Texas-New Mexico district convention in Kingsville in 1918 the district asked Ball, rather than any of the Mexican leaders, to organize the Latino AG work "wherever found." This was probably due to the fact that he had blended with and reorganized the Kingsville mission. Ball does claim that the seven Mexican ministers present at that particular meeting elected him leader, though corroborating evidence from Mexican ministers has not been found, and in fact some leaders state that he was not elected leader but assumed the leadership role at his own initiative. Even if Ball's rendering of the events were true, it is unclear if they had the authority via a quorum to do so. Even if they did, one wonders if they didn't do so out of appreciation and gratitude for his co-organizing and personally hosting the convention and serving as a go-between with Euro-American AG leaders in Springfield, Missouri.[27]

Regardless, by all accounts the January meeting in Kingsville was a major success. Although the twenty-two-year-old Ball was publicly praised for his generosity in hosting the event, López was the real key to the event's success because of his seniority and respect among the independents. López and Flores not only persuaded many to attend, but also to join the AG. However, at this stage they were not joining the Latino AG, a Mexican AG district, or a Mexican AG convention run by Ball or any other Euro-American missionary, because none of the above existed at this time. They were simply inviting the AG and independent Mexican pastors and evangelists to attend a convention of like-minded Pentecostals. In contrast to the rapidly growing independent work, by 1918 the AG work among Mexicans was scattered across Texas, New Mexico, Arizona, California, and Mexico and numbered only four churches, eight pastors and Christian missionary workers, and 200 members. Ball sought to expand the work by winning over the remaining independent Mexican ministers and missions and forming a Mexican convention under his administrative leadership and, by inference, control. Because many of the ministers did not speak English very well and some of the first-generation Euro-American missionaries were retiring or moving on to other work, the increasingly bilingual Ball stepped into the gap and became the de facto liaison between the Mexican ministers and the Assemblies of God leaders in Springfield. As a result, he began to exercise greater influence and authority in the emerging Latino AG movement.

Ball soon became the gatekeeper for any Mexican in South Texas who wanted to secure AG credentials. Furthermore, the AG leaders in Springfield increasingly treated him as the point-person and go-to man on all things Mexican in Texas, for while he was not the only AG clergyman evangelizing Mexicans, he was the key person in South Texas. An example of Ball's growing influence is evident in his decision to tell Rev. Cecilio Jacinto, who pastored an independent mission in Kyle, Texas, that he (and thus the AG) would not ordain him until he learned how to read. After Jacinto's wife taught him to read, he returned to the second convention in November 1918 (they had two conventions in 1918) not only able to read, but also now ready to receive credentials, which Ball— true to his word—promptly awarded on behalf of the AG. Ball's power grew after E. N. Richey and the Texas-New Mexico district asked Ball to oversee the entire Mexican AG work. Rather than defer the recommendation to the next convention or to his Mexican associates, Ball accepted the offer without putting it to a formal vote.[28]

Ball was intuitive and smart. He realized that Mexicans would elect their own leader if put to a vote and that he needed to follow up on the success of the first convention by holding a subsequent event to bring more missions into the AG fold. This would expand his power base and neutralize the influence of the formerly independent missions. Rather than wait until the following year, Ball decided to hold the next convention (sometimes called the "second convention") on November 10–18, 1918. This time he strategically called the meeting without Flores or López cosponsoring the event. He then sent out invitations to all of the independent ministers, since he had secured their addresses at what Ball called the first convention and in the intervening period.[29]

Despite Ball's growing prominence, he still needed at least some of the support of the remaining independent Mexican colleagues because few of them had attended the first convention. Although the formerly independent Mexicans no longer dominated the Latino AG, Ball wanted to give the appearance that he was working closely with Mexican veterans. He did so by holding the second convention at Arnulfo López's mission in San Antonio, thus giving the appearance that they were co-leading the event—which was not true. This also served Ball's purposes since López's congregation met in the church actually built and controlled by Euro-American leaders Felix Hale and M. M. Pinson. Given that López was the most distinguished and famous Mexican preacher still remaining in the AG at that time, holding the event at López's mission added clout to the convention and made it less threatening to the independent Mexican pastors and missions Ball was still trying to bring into the fold. A small but growing number of Mexicans and other Latinos attended from California, including a thirty-two-year-old ex-Methodist minister named Francisco Olazábal, pictured in Figure 3.3, who had a brief ministry to the Spanish-speaking at Robert Craig's Glad Tidings Church in San Francisco. Olazábal was asked to preach at the second convention and eyewitnesses reported that it was moved to action by his sermon series. Ten years Ball's senior, with four years of formal theological education and over a decade of experience in the field, Olazábal mesmerized Ball

Figure 3.3. Francisco Olazábal, ca. 1922. (Gastón Espinosa Latino Pentecostal History Collection)

with his sermons. Ball wrote in his convention report published in the *Christian Evangel* that Olazábal's preaching was "from the throne of God," a sentiment he would not hold for very long.[30]

Francisco Olazábal

Olazábal was a powerhouse evangelist. His followers called him "El Azteca" and the Mexican Billy Sunday because of his evangelistic style and campaigns. Although courteous and respectful, Olazábal did not mince words and he recognized the value he brought to the AG. Ball captured a strong dose of Olazábal's confidence after Francisco invited Ball to serve as associate pastor of his AG mission in El Paso. Ball declined the offer and instead sent his assistant pastors in his place, Demetrio and Nellie Bazan. In the racially stratified world of the early twentieth century, Americans gave, Mexicans received—age, education, and experience notwithstanding. Although Ball was sanctified, he would not play second fiddle to a Mexican, no matter what his age or education.

Olazábal's speaking and evangelistic skills had been honed at the Methodist Seminary in San Luís Postosí, Sinaloa, Mexico (1906–1908), Moody Bible Institute (1912), and in the field as an itinerant Methodist evangelist and pastor. He grew up preaching alongside his mother, an itinerant lay Methodist evangelist in the rugged Sierra Madre Mountains in north central Mexico. He conducted evangelistic work on foot, moving from village to village in rural Indian country in Sinaloa, and went on to pastor churches in El Paso (1911), Pasadena (1913–1915), and San Francisco and Sacramento (1915–1916). He was ordained to the Methodist ministry by Bishop A. W. Leonard in 1916. Francisco was as cosmopolitan a Mexican as they come.[31]

In 1902 Olazábal left his mother and went through a rebellious streak. He traveled to San Francisco to visit relatives and hatched plans to travel the world as a sailor. His plans were rudely interrupted after he met George and Carrie Judd Montgomery in Oakland. They persuaded him to rededicate his life to Christ and afterward attend the Wesleyan Seminary. After pastoring in the Methodist circuit ministry in northern California, in 1917 he ran into the Montgomerys again. This time he learned that they had attended William J. Seymour's Azusa Street Revival in Los Angeles and had become Pentecostal. They also believed in faith healing and prayed for his wife, Macrina, who was suffering a physical illness. After she reportedly was healed, the couple decided to receive the baptism with the Holy Spirit. Although the Methodists tried to persuade Olazábal to stay—even promising him a $2,000-a-year salary, and that he might one day become the first Mexican Methodist bishop, he resigned. Robert J. Craig and others persuaded him to join the Assemblies of God. Craig laid hands on Olazábal and ordained him to the AG ministry on February 14, 1918.[32]

In addition to working alongside Craig and pastoring a Spanish AG Mission in San Francisco, Olazábal preached throughout California before pioneering his own Buenas Nuevas Mission in El Paso in 1920, the same city where he had begun his U.S. ministry nine years earlier in 1911. He was invited by Angelo Fraticelli to hold his first major Pentecostal revival in Danville, California, in 1918. There he preached to a large number of Puerto Ricans that had migrated over from the Hawaiian Islands at the turn of the century to work on the sugar cane plantations, including many that had attended Francisco Ortiz's Pentecostal mission on Oahu. After the revival, Olazábal baptized the famous Puerto Rican evangelist Domingo Cruz and many others. Since the Puerto Ricans were migrant workers and without hard currency to provide a love offering, every night after the service every large family that attended offered Francisco and Macrina one pail of cherries, which the Olazábals later sold to cover travel and room and board expenses for their growing family. Afterward, he then traveled to Los Angeles to conduct another powerful revival for Alice Luce in the tiny mission she rented near "La Placita" (Olvera Street) in downtown Los Angeles, the little Spanish colonia.[33]

Ball's Vision and Doubts

The Assemblies of God was attracting a growing number of highly gifted and qualified Mexicans to the ministry. Despite this fact, Ball still believed that the Mexicans needed Euro-American assistance and supervision. Although Ball publicly promoted the idea of an independent Mexican ministry, he foreshadowed future conflict when he wrote: "it will be a long time until they can become entirely self-supporting, but it will come."[34] Indeed, Ball's concerns about the ability of rank-and-file Mexicans to support and lead their own missions was also shared by some but not all of the Euro-American missionaries like Felix Hale, John Preston, Miss Brown, M. M. Pinson, Sunshine Marshall, Emily Kuhn, Minnie Varner, C. Nuzum, Fred and Flora Steele, Laura Kritz, Carl Garrett, Anna Sanders, and others.[35]

As Ball's vision grew, he realized that San Antonio was the premier location for the fledgling movement since it was the largest, most strategically located city in South Texas and home to a large Mexican population. He could use it as a railroad hub to plant missions throughout Texas and eventually Mexico. For reasons that are not entirely clear, in 1918 López stepped down from pastoring his large and flourishing mission in San Antonio and handed it over to Ball. Some writers, following Ball's interpretation, state that M. M. Pinson and R. D. Baker organized the mission. However, as we have seen, it was actually an outgrowth of

Rev. Simson's work, which was first initiated in 1913 and developed through López's careful shepherding from 1914 to 1918. Thus Ball benefited from the labor of López's ministry. Ball's movement from the dusty village of Ricardo to Kingsville and now on to San Antonio created the impression that he was successfully building up the AG work among Mexicans when in fact he was largely inheriting and organizing the work pioneered by formerly independent but now Mexican AG ministers.[36]

As the first generation of Euro-American missionaries left the Mexican ministry for other lines of work, Ball increasingly became the de facto liaison and leader between the Mexican work and AG headquarters. As the movement grew, Ball and the newer missionaries sought to bring structure and cohesion to the movement. One after another, they began to squeeze out outspoken native Mexican leaders, all the while continuing to invite independent Mexican missions and pastors to join their growing fellowship. The real keys to this growth were not only Ball and Luce, but also independent Mexican leaders like López, Morin, Alaniz, Flores, and increasingly, Francisco Olazábal, due to his growing number of evangelistic campaigns. Ball's outreach efforts in conjunction with the independent leaders were not in vain. At the third convention in San Antonio in 1919, Rev. Juan Valadez of Keechi brought his entire independent congregation into the AG. He was one of the last holdouts. By 1920, most of the independent Mexican and Euro-American missions had been brought into the AG fold under Ball's de facto leadership. However, there was still a quiet but growing restlessness at the 1921 convention in Dallas. A number of Mexican pastors told Ball they wanted to organize a Mexican district like their Euro-American counterparts. Ball denied their request because he said there were not enough Mexican ministers present to make such an important decision, and for this reason Ball encouraged them to postpone the petition until the sixth convention in Victoria in 1922.[37]

Ball pacified them for the time being by stating that he would join them in their desire to convert Mexicans in the United States and Mexico. Ball was by all accounts honest and truthful in his claims because he had come to respect many Mexican leaders through his interactions with Alaniz, Morin, López, Flores, and Olazábal. Unlike some Pentecostal groups that placed their emphasis on evangelism alone, Ball also learned (from the independent Mexican movement) to focus on church plant-ing.[38] This approach not only resulted in growth, but also a certain de-gree of freedom and autonomy among the Mexican evangelists and min-isters, whom worked the vast expanse of South Texas. More important, this strategy encouraged the creativity of each Mexican minister, many of who were already seasoned workers. It also contributed to the indi-genization of the movement on a local level. Recognizing the success of independent and indigenous Mexican churches and leadership, Ball and Luce said the goal of each church was to be self-supporting, self-sustaining, and self-propagating—a sentiment that would soon be put to the test.

Extending Ball's Influence through the Power of the Pen

In order to help Latino AG missions and churches become completely self-sustaining, they needed Spanish-language literature. The key to Ball's success and influence lay not only in serving as a liaison and his pastoral leadership, but also in his decision to produce Spanish Pente-costal literature, hymnals, tracts, books, and other resources. All of this enabled him to exercise disproportionate influence in the movement. Drawing on his own Methodist experience, Ball used a small hand-press to print a hymnal in 1916 called *Himnos de Gloria (Hymns of Glory)*. It contained 125 hymns, most of which were Methodist and Protestant. It was remarkably influential not only in the United States but also throughout Latin America. By the late 1920s, Presbyterians in Guatemala and Pentecostals in Peru were using Ball's hymnal. By 1931, thousands of copies were in print. This, along with other publications, led to the birth of Casa Evangélica de Publicaciones.[39]

The hymnal was more than just a songbook. Just as during the Span-ish Catholic Spiritual conquest of Mexico by the missionaries five hun-dred years earlier, when they used music, plays, and dramas to convert and teach the native population, Euro-American missionaries and their converts in the early twentieth century used the songs and music as ve-hicles to attract potential converts and to teach the Bible and doctrine. Ball's hymnal also helped contribute to the movement's heavy emphasis on music. Music and the enthusiastic worship services were two of the

primary reasons why thousands of Mexicans and other Latinos were attracted to the Pentecostal movement. The enthusiastic style gave them
an opportunity to express themselves in ways normally restricted by
the equally rich but liturgical Catholic and Protestant churches. More
important, Pentecostal worship created a fiesta-like atmosphere that offered hope and joy to countless working-class Latinos often expected to
remain silent in public. It gave them a voice and means by which to express their newfound faith through the creation of bands, choirs, poetry
readings, orchestras, and worship teams. This is largely overlooked in
the historical literature.

While *Himnos de Gloria* filled one important gap, Ball published *La
Luz Apostólica (The Apostolic Light)* to fill another: the need for training
in Bible, doctrine, apologetics, evangelism, and related subjects normally taught in seminary. This was especially important since there
were no Latino Pentecostal Bible schools at the time. The first edition of
La Luz Apostólica was printed in Kingsville, Texas, in September 1916.
This four-page, thirty-five-cent publication was the first Spanish-
language Pentecostal periodical in North America and one of the very
first in Latin America, where it was also distributed until the 1930s because the Latino AG work until that time included Mexico and Central
America. López and others published reports, testimonies, and pieces
in this periodical and in the *Weekly Evangel* (later the *Pentecostal Evangel*).[40] Within a year, Ball was printing 500 copies of *La Luz Apostólica* a
month and by 1919 he was sending copies to eleven states and to sixteen
countries throughout Latin America. By 1940, the Latin District Council was mailing 2,000 copies throughout the Americas.[41]

Thanks to his hymnal and periodical, by the early 1920s Ball was becoming a household name in both Springfield and the Spanish-speaking
community and, as a result, later exercised significant influence in the
Americas.[42] Ball also used his periodical to announce the date and location
of revivals, new churches, and annual conventions. In short, he controlled
the media and became the gatekeeper and spokesman to the Euro-American
and Latino Pentecostal communities for all issues related to Latino AG.

Although the first Mexican convention primarily attracted ministers
from the Southwest and Mexico, it also attracted missionaries from
Puerto Rico and Central America, since at that time, the Spanish AG

work in the United States was seen as extending all the way down to El Salvador. As a result, Mr. and Mrs. C. A. Hines came from Guatemala. Their participation along with that of others kept the Spanish-speaking AG movement interconnected throughout North America.

In fact, AG headquarters in Springfield eventually asked Ball to supervise the entire Spanish-speaking work in North America, even though other Euro-American and Latino leaders predated his own rise to power. The AG work formally spread to Mexico in 1917, Cuba in 1923, El Salvador in 1926, and Guatemala in 1926, though individual and independent evangelists arrived earlier. These countries came under Ball's administration until national districts were formed in 1929–1930 because a growing number of countries like Mexico demanded that all foreign religious bodies be nationalized and run by native leaders. The only exception was Cuba, which remained under his jurisdiction until at least the late 1930s.[43] Ball was building a spiritual network that traversed North America. Nothing seemed able to stand in his way.[44]

Ball's growing influence was solidified after he raised funds to build Templo Cristiano in San Antonio in October 1919. Given that Ball used it as the place to publish the hymnal and periodical and to meet with candidates for ordination, it became the mother church and main administrative center of the fledgling North American Latino AG movement. By this time, the Mexican AG work had increased to eighteen ordained workers and over 500 members. This growth was largely due to the influx of the independent Mexican missions, though the handful of Euro-American missionaries also converted Mexicans and led or co-led their own missions.[45]

The church workers' early evangelistic strategies were largely focused on personal evangelism because large crusades were not held in significant numbers until the early 1920s. As early as 1917, Mexican evangelists traveled in wagons from village to village, work camp to work camp to evangelize migrant farm laborers. In 1924, they were given a "Gospel Truck" to conduct this evangelistic work. They often went from house to house, passing out Bibles, evangelistic tracts, and other literature. They prayed for the sick and invited people to attend their revival and worship services.[46]

While it is easy to be critical of Ball's actions, he clearly had a strong commitment to the Mexican people and worked hard to create strong and viable networks that brought a disparate group of loosely affiliated independent churches together into one convention and movement. Unlike other Euro-American missionaries, who quit the Mexican work after a few years or even months, Ball dedicated himself to the work and set out to strengthen it and provide the administrative structure it needed to develop into a regional, state, and eventually national movement—no minor accomplishment in its own right.

The shift from Mexican self-determination to a Euro-American-led movement was subtle. Ball partnered with Flores and López to organize the first two Mexican conventions and used them to gain access to other Mexican missions. As a result, Ball was either elected or—depending on whom you believe—assumed the leadership of convention. After he established relationships with the independent ministers, he no longer needed Flores and López as much and began directing the conventions. He and Luce benefited from the pioneer independent Mexican ministry by assuming the leadership of the missions they had pioneered, by blending his congregation with theirs, or by having their own missions jumpstarted through their revivals. He also had a strong evangelistic streak in him and sought to make as many converts as he could through his preaching and outreach events. Ball's influence grew through his growing leadership, and the publication of *La Luz Apostólica, Himnos de Gloria,* and other Pentecostal literature, which allowed him to define and shape the movement. However, the Latino AG movement was larger than Ball. In California, the AG ordained a former Methodist evangelist named Francisco Olazábal in 1918. He held large revivals and evangelistic campaigns throughout the Southwest, organized a Bible school in El Paso, and soon rivaled Ball's influence. Unfortunately, they had different visions for the Latino AG's future—one run by Mexicans and the other run—at least for the time being by—Euro-Americans. A struggle was bound to follow.

CHAPTER 4

The Gringos Have Control

Francisco Olazábal's Reformation in the Borderlands

A S BALL'S INFLUENCE GREW in San Antonio he heard reports of Olazábal's powerful evangelistic campaigns in the West.[1] Robert J. Craig of Glad Tidings Tabernacle in San Francisco sponsored his application for AG ordination and prophetically wrote that he "preaches with power in English and Spanish" and that "God will greatly use him in organizing and opening up the work among the Spanish-speaking people."[2]

Olazábal felt called to pioneer the AG work in El Paso. As Latino historian Mario T. García points out, the city was strategic for several reasons: millions of Mexicans traveled through El Paso because it was the main railroad hub and gateway into the United States, it was a boom-and-bust town in the 1920s, and tens of thousands of immigrants passed through it in search of a new life. The city was also strategic because Olazábal had pastored a Methodist church there in 1911 and could call on some of his old friends to help him jump-start his ministry.[3]

After he arrived, he immediately organized evangelistic tent services. He preached salvation and healing from the Bible and prayed for the sick. By March 1919 he wrote that a Pentecostal revival broke out. Dozens were converted and a woman was healed of tuberculosis. As his ministry grew, he began to see the importance of connecting divine healing to evangelism. He wrote "God is using divine healing to bring many souls to Christ."[4] This mixing of healing and evangelism soon became an Olazábal trademark. He would preach an evangelistic message from the Bible, pray for the sick, and afterward pray with people to convert and receive the baptism with the Holy Spirit. This laid the foundation for a second revival that erupted that summer and fall.

By July 16, 1920, more than 100 Mexicans had converted in El Paso—more than all of the converts Euro-American missionaries had made combined in the last five years. In January 1921, Olazábal reported that "many were saved . . . others were healed and ten baptized with the Holy Spirit."[5] He and Macrina needed help to minister to the growing number of converts. He wrote: "The power of the Spirit fell as a mighty shower over the seekers. I believe that if we had had workers to help out, we could have seen greater results, but I did not have any help at the altar with seekers."[6] Although he faced stiff opposition from Protestants and Catholics, over the course of two years he reports converting 400–500 people and praying with 100 to receive the baptism with the Holy Spirit. Ball and his colleagues hadn't seen anything like it. Most Euro-Americans struggled to make a handful of converts annually, and few had more than seventy people attending their missions. The El Paso revivals were thus unprecedented. The number of converts grew so large that Olazábal started two missions for them across the border in their hometowns of Ciudad Juárez (Chihuahua) and Hipolito (Coahuila).[7]

This development highlighted another characteristic Olazábal trademark—church planting. One of his most important (if overlooked) evangelistic strategies was to conduct an evangelistic-healing campaign in a city, organize a mother church (usually called Bethel Temple) in the wake of the campaign, and then organize daughter churches (like spokes on a wheel) around the mother church in the surrounding region. This blending of evangelistic healing campaigns and church planting helps explain the phenomenal growth of Latino Pentecostalism in the Americas throughout the twentieth century.

Despite this setback, the work on the U.S.-Mexico border was prospering. Olazábal invited H. C. and Sunshine Ball to serve as co-pastors and help develop the work throughout the region. Ball declined the invitation and instead sent Demetrio and Nellie Bazan. They were an excellent choice. Ball trained them well in the Bible and Pentecostal doctrine and ordained them to the ministry in 1920. They were effective preachers and teachers and helped solidify the work.[8]

Francisco Olazábal's AG Bible School in El Paso and Southwest Ministry

In order to address the growing need for Christian pastors, evangelists, and workers, in 1919 Olazábal proposed to H. C. Ball and J. R. Flower creating a Spanish AG Bible school in El Paso. They liked the idea and Flower told him he could start raising funds from AG churches, which he did from 1921 to 1922. To ensure high ethical standards, he sent all funds directly to Flower's Home Missions Office for safekeeping.[9]

As the number of converts began to swell, Olazábal opened up the first Latino Assemblies of God Bible School in 1922. He had approximately nine students and three teachers (see Figure 4.1). They would have their lessons in the morning and then carry out fieldwork and internships in missions and evangelistic outreach in the afternoon. To their credit, Ball and AG headquarters supported Olazábal's idea—at

Figure 4.1.   First Latino AG Bible School, El Paso, Texas, 1922. First row (left to right): Eva Chacón, Juanita Enriquez, Mrs. Ballinger, Dora Chacón. Second row (left to right): Benjamín Cárdenas, unknown, José Caballero, Roque Ortiz, Conrado Alvarez, Martidiano Durán, Alfonso Zavala, Esteban Cavarillo. (Gastón Espinosa Latino Pentecostal History Collection)

least so he thought. Ball even promised to send chalkboards and other school supplies from his church in San Antonio. Unfortunately, the badly needed supplies never arrived. This undermined Olazábal's ability to provide the resources needed to effectively run the Bible school and teach the students.[10]

Mexican Expansion in the Southwest

Now firmly established in El Paso, Olazábal received a calling to pioneer the work in Los Angeles. The Bazans would take over in El Paso. Alice Luce and Fred Steele led the work in the City of Angels, but there was little growth because of the fierce competition with other Latino Pentecostal and Protestant denominations and their inability to connect with the Mexican people because of linguistic and cultural barriers. Giving a sermon in textbook Spanish was one thing. Preaching with power and persuasion in Spanish was quite another. The city was simply too large and rich a mission field to be left largely vacant. For these reasons, Olazábal laid plans to ignite the AG work in Los Angeles the same way he did in El Paso.[11]

The growth of Olazábal's ministry was part of a larger trend in the growth of Mexican-led ministries across the Southwest, especially in Texas. The region from Houston to the Mexican border was like the Great Awakening burned-over district in upstate New York. Independent Mexican evangelists, now stocked with AG-supplied Spanish tracts and Bibles, spread the Pentecostal message throughout the state. Although true statewide revival had not broken out, in South Texas it sure seemed like it. Hundreds were being converted and new missions—both Assemblies and independent—were springing up. They in turn sent their own pioneers to start new works throughout the state and in Mexico. This decentralized approach and regular supply of fresh evangelists contributed to a thriving entrepreneurial ministry and to a vibrant religious economy that was highly competitive with Catholic and Protestant churches, who complained incessantly about Pentecostal growth.[12]

As Alaniz, López, Flores, and the others continued to bring more and more independent missions and ministers into the AG in South Texas, they began to push for greater Mexican leadership. They called for the creation of a Mexican AG district on a par with their white counterparts. However, they soon became frustrated with Ball and Luce because they seemed to be dragging their feet about handing over the leadership of the work, something they touted as early as 1918 when Ball wrote: "We are teaching them to support themselves and the whole work as soon as possible."[13] In 1921, Luce wrote a series of articles for the *Pentecostal Evangel* about St. Paul's missionary methods. She argued that missionaries should hand over their work to native workers as soon as possible: "When the Lord raises up spiritually qualified leaders in the native churches themselves, what a joy it will be to be subject to them, and to let them take the lead as the Spirit Himself shall guide them."[14] To many Mexican pastors this seemed too good to be true. And so it was.

For despite this public support for native Mexican leadership, Ball, Luce, and Euro-American leaders were gaining a systematic monopoly over the administration and organizational apparatus of the Latino AG Convention, and this invariably marginalized Mexican voices and aspirations. Within just a few years, they controlled virtually all of the main sources of power and influence such as the magazine and publishing house, hymnal, convention organization, ordination certification, and increasingly (especially with their own converts) ministerial and even church assignments. Yet they could not control the bodies, churches, and hearts of the Mexican people. Mexican ministers began to realize that despite all of their promises about wanting Mexicans to "take the lead," Ball and Luce were consolidating their administrative power and undermining their ability to lead the AG. This led to conflict.[15]

Olazábal's Reformation in the Borderlands

At the 1920 Latino AG Convention in Magnolia Park, a group of formerly independent Mexican AG ministers led by López, Flores, and Olazábal called for reform. They began asking Ball and the other missionaries about when they would follow through on their pledge to hand over the leadership to Mexicans so they could create a Mexican-run district. They hoped this would happen at the 1921 convention in Dallas. Olazábal, by now the most powerful and famous evangelist in the movement, tempered their optimism by pointing out Ball's growing influence through his control over the apparatus of the movement. To be fair, Ball claims he was elected superintendent by the seven Mexican ministers at the 1918 convention and by the Texas–New Mexico District that same year. However, others claim that Ball "informally assumed the role of leader" because he organized and "presided over" the first 1918 Convention and because he served as the liaison between Mexicans and Euro-Americans.[16]

By 1921 many Mexicans were unhappy with Ball's leadership. They wanted reform and change. Although Olazábal was unable to attend the Dallas convention, he nonetheless worked with the Mexican ministers who requested they be allowed to organize a Mexican-led district. Ball refused to comply because there were not enough ministers present to vote on the creation of a Mexican district, he said. (Interestingly enough, he did not raise the issue of numbers when he claimed he was voted leader of the convention by the seven ministers that elected him in 1918.) He asked them to be patient and promised that they could vote on the birth of a Mexican district and superintendent at the 1922 convention in Victoria, just outside Houston. The Mexican ministers were placated for now, but concerned that this was just a ploy to further solidify his support.[17]

While some ministers interpreted Ball's decision as an honest procedural matter, others were more skeptical. López and Flores informed Olazábal about the turn of events, because he was the person with the most experience working with Euro-Americans, given his nineteen-year (1898–1917) ministry in the Methodist Church. As a result of these developments, and in order to ensure a smooth transition from American to Mexican leadership, Olazábal began working with them to put forward a series of proposals for the next convention to bring about the creation of a Mexican-led district.[18]

They also knew time was running out. Although many of the churches were pastored by former independent ministers, there were a growing number of missionaries and new converts entering the movement being trained and ordained by Ball, thus increasing his power base and potentially dividing the Mexican clergy's push for reform and independence.

They turned to Olazábal not only because of his successful campaigns in the San Francisco Bay Area, Los Angeles, and El Paso, but also because he was not afraid to stand up to Euro-Americans. In his May 9, 1913, "Mi Pueblo" speech given at the 9th Annual Los Angeles District Epworth League Convention, the young and then Methodist Olazábal warned that the United States should avoid armed intervention in the Mexican Revolution because "the United States would have to exterminate the people of Mexico to the last man."[19] He went on to warn that a war with Mexico would cost the United States thousands if not possibly "millions of lives" and millions of dollars. He predicted that it would lead to "international disgrace" for the United States. What Mexico needed was "another kind of intervention, the intervention of the Gospel and of Christian love," Olazábal stated. The cross, not colonialism and empire, was the answer.[20] Most of the Mexicans at the 1921 convention would have agreed with the last part of this statement.

As a result of his courage, evangelistic campaigns, and leadership, Olazábal received invitations to hold services throughout the nation. On the evangelistic trail, he began dreaming with ministers about the day when they would run their own Mexican Assemblies of God district—like Ball and Luce had promised. That day, he proposed, was now at hand. In 1922, his sentiments echoed those of López, Flores, and others in South Texas, who were also champing at the bit to create a Mexican district. They were all thankful to Ball, Luce, Preston, Fred Steele, and other Euro-American leaders for their honorable service. Now seven years later, however, it was time for them to stand aside and hand over the movement to their Mexican coworkers.[21]

All of this seemed to be good news; after all, the missionaries preached that Mexicans should one day run the convention. Despite the public rhetoric, though, many Euro-Americans privately believed that Mexicans were not ready to govern their own district. A showdown was inevitable. It was only a matter of time before the headstrong thirty-six-year-old Olazábal clashed with the equally stubborn twenty-six-year-old Ball. Ball's initial admiration for Olazábal and earlier praise that his "messages were from the Throne of God" soon reportedly gave way to quiet jealousy and envy.[22] Olazábal stated that Ball was "inspired by selfishness and jealously caused by envy" and this led Ball to "plot" against him with the General Council in Springfield.[23]

Reflecting the pious paternalism of the day, Ball thought he could treat Olazábal the way he treated any other Mexican. He was mistaken. Olazábal found Ball's delays, growing power, and treatment of Mexicans unacceptable, especially in light of his stated desire to hand over the movement "as soon as possible."[24]

As a result, Olazábal, Alaniz, López, Flores, and their followers laid out a new vision for a Mexican district under Mexican control. As his power in the council grew, Olazábal began to gently question the constant delays. He also corrected any attempt by Ball and Luce to exaggerate the success of their ministries, not only because they often built on the pre-existing work other Mexicans pioneered—whose labor often went unnoted—but also because he knew they could use this to justify their continuing leadership and control.[25] He refused to give any credence to Ball's assertion that "while they [Mexicans] are excellent workers they need American oversight."[26]

Olazábal and the Mexican reformers would have none of it. They also did not like the fact that Ball, Luce, and other missionaries did not show the original pioneers the respect they deserved in their annual reports, histories, and letters in the *Pentecostal Evangel*. They were being quietly erased from the historical narrative. While this was partially due to the fact that few Mexicans wrote letters to the *Pentecostal Evangel* (though there are letters by Arnulfo López and others) and no early histories of the Latino AG in Texas were written by Mexicans, it was also because the stories of these original pioneers were simply being left out of Euro-American narratives, which tended to date the start of the Mexican AG with that of their own ministries. After the Euro-Americans took control of the Latino AG publication arm of the movement, their own reports and histories took on canonical-like status and thus contributed to the erasure of the earlier pioneer work. All of this helps to explain why most of it is left out of Latino AG histories, which tended to be written by second- and third-generation leaders socialized and historicized through the institutions and organizations that were founded by H. C. Ball and Alice Luce. In fact, many of them—including Victor De Leon—were simply unaware of these original pioneers because their erasure was so complete.

Another key reason why this earlier history has been left out of the narrative is because Ball and his coworkers, over a five-year period, moved out almost all of the most important Mexican ministers and even some of the noncompliant pioneer Euro-American missionaries like John Preston, and they would have to include this chapter in their story. They would invariably have to answer questions about why they left or were forced out. After a careful review of the AG internal documents and ministerial reports, the real reasons why they left are clear. In 1917, Ball accused Antonio Ríos Morin of coming "close to destroying the [Mexican] work" and thus he and the others "were compelled to recommend his retirement."[27] In 1919, Ball criticized the work of John A. Preston to J. R. Flower at AG headquarters and said he was not very successful in the Mexican ministry, thus undermining his Home Missions funding. This is one of the reasons Preston left the Latino AG work.[28] In 1922, Ball accused Enemecio Alaniz of embracing the Oneness doctrine, even though the Apostolic Assembly had not set up a permanent work in South Texas. Because Alaniz was ordained by AG founder E. N. Bell (on October 19, 1922), and not Ball or the Latin Convention, he fought back and appealed directly to Bell. He asked Bell to support their move to appoint "our own Mexican" leader. He also stated "H. C. Ball . . . never treated me right."[29] When it was clear that Bell was going to back Ball, Enemecio Alaniz, the most important founder and pioneer of the independent Mexican Pentecostal movement and the now blooming Latino AG, resigned, an event that sent shock waves through the movement.[30]

Even more alarming, news was spreading that Ball, Luce, and Steele were "allies against" Olazábal and were planning to "oppose" his "plans of expansion" and the creation of a Mexican-led district. Olazábal learned that Ball had been "plotting against me before the [General] Council" in Springfield. The reason for Ball's action: "selfishness and jealousy caused by envy," Olazábal asserted. Olazábal now saw the handwriting on the wall and decided to act.[31]

By 1922, Olazábal and the majority of Mexican ministers had had enough. At the convention, he could no longer listen to Luce taking credit for the work of Mexican pioneers and recent converts. He rose from his seat and gently corrected Luce in front of the delegates, because, he claimed, she exaggerated the success of one of her campaigns, which he himself had attended and participated in.[32] He also later criticized Ball for his constant delays and for not delivering the promised

Figure 4.2. Latin American AG Convention, Victoria-Houston, Texas, 1922. H. C. Ball is pictured in the top center and Francisco Olazábal is in the top row, fourth person to the left of Ball. Demetrio Bazan is pictured third row, third person from far right. Rodolfo C. Orozco is shown right behind Bazan to his left. The three white women in the second row (left to right) are Lena Howe (missionary to Puerto Rico), Alice Luce, and Florence Murcutt.   (Flower Pentecostal Heritage Center)

supplies for the fledgling Bible school in El Paso. This undermined Olazábal's ability to develop the school, something that not only hurt the work, but also thwarted any attempt on their part to generate and nurture native Mexican leadership. He and others flatly rejected the widespread sentiment that "their salvation may depend on us." Indeed, it amounted to what later Chicano historian Mario Barrera described as internal colonialism.[33]

Olazábal's Call for a Mexican-Led District

The revolutionary call for reform and restructuring the movement came on November 22, 1922, at the AG Convention in Victoria, outside of Houston (Figure 4.2). Nominated by the Mexican pastors to represent them, Olazábal laid out five bold propositions on their behalf that for all practical purposes called for an end to Euro-American missionary rule and internal colonialism. First, they called for the creation of a Mexican district independent of Euro-American control and on a par with other Euro-American districts. Second, they proposed that a Mexican be named leader of this district. Third, they recommended that a Mexican create the curriculum and run the Bible school. Fourth, they requested that a Mexican edit *La Luz Apostólica*, the Spanish-language magazine that was used to disseminate theology, Bible teachings, and spiritual and administrative guidance over the movement. And fifth, they proposed that the headquarters, Bible school, and print shop all be moved to Olazábal's church in El Paso. They ended by stating that they wanted Olazábal, rather than Ball, to be their new superintendent, to lead the Bible institute, and to run the print shop. They took a vote on the proposal. When it was finally tallied, the Mexican delegates approved all five propositions. It was nearly unanimous. Only a few of the American missionaries opposed the proposal. Olazábal wrote in December 1922, "all the brothers in the convention . . . voted in favor of all the propositions that I presented."[34]

The fire had been lit, the reformation begun. "Flushed" red with anger and "humiliated" by the propositions, Ball stood up and stated that, on procedural grounds, AG Headquarters said they could not and would not accept the Mexican vote for a new district, the election of Olazábal, or any of the propositions. De Leon states that they had to wait only one year, while Miguel Guillén says it was four years. Regardless, this move was read as a tactic by Ball and the AG to disavow the Mexican vote, short-circuit Olazábal's election, and undermine the birth of a Mexican-led district. In a veiled allusion to Olazábal and others who received Home Missionary funds from headquarters (e.g., Olazábal received a $3–$5 monthly stipend), Ball also warned that the Mexican missionaries might lose their financial support from headquarters if they didn't comply. All of this seemed to imply that Mexicans were not yet ready or capable of directing their own work and could be dissuaded by financial incentives.[35] This "convinced" some of the Mexican ministers that "the vote of the Mexicans had no value" and that they were subject to the "imposition" and "dictatorship" of Ball and his Euro-American allies.[36]

The fact that they actually voted and passed the motion to create a new Mexican-led district has been left out of almost all Latino AG histories. The event is simply treated as a misunderstanding. However, those that left the movement argued otherwise. Ball himself admitted in a private letter to J. W. Welsh in 1924 that the vote to create a Mexican district took place in 1922, but that he and his followers "did not deem it best to attempt it [organize a Mexican district] then."[37] One can't help but wonder if Ball would have disavowed the vote if he had been elected superintendent and if AG headquarters would have nullified it.

Despite Ball's response at the convention, or perhaps because of it, the propositions became a rallying point for Mexican reformers. Olazábal, López, Flores, and others believed Ball was stalling and using Springfield to justify his actions. Many Mexicans were convinced that their vote and opinions had no real value to Ball and his supporters and that he simply wanted to use this additional time to run noncompliant ministers out of the movement.[38]

Olazábal and the Push for Mexican Independence

López, the most powerful and influential leader in the Houston area, said it was time to leave Ball and the Assemblies of God. He began promoting the idea of joining another Pentecostal Council in Chicago, the name of which is no longer known. López shared this idea with his senior Mexican colleagues after his evangelistic campaigns in San Antonio, Houston, and Rosenberg. He told the Mexican ministers that Ball and the Euro-Americans would not respect their vote and propositions. López said he spoke from personal experience since he was Ball's secretary and often traveled with him and the missionaries to the conventions and thus had a sense for his attitude toward Mexicans.[39]

Concepción Suárez joined the growing independence movement and told Isabel Flores, who was now very close to Ball, what López said and encouraged him to join another Pentecostal denomination in Chicago. After weighing the matter, he said it would be better to return to their independent status rather than join another Euro-American movement. Furthermore, he asked, why exchange one set of Euro-American leaders for another? In the minds of most formerly independent Mexican leaders, the decision to leave was largely a decision to return to the freedom of their independent status in light of their treatment in the AG.[40]

López, Suárez, and now Flores were soon joined by a growing number of Mexican ministers who believed that they should disassociate themselves from the AG because of the "problems," "discrimination," and "mistreatment" they felt they had endured. Flores and López reminded the people that just as God had freed the Hebrew people from the power of Pharaoh, he could now do the same for the Spanish-speaking people. Rather than have Euro-Americans leading them, Flores said they now needed someone to lead them out of their Egyptian captivity. That person was Francisco Olazábal. He stated that to allow the Mexican people to be divided into different Euro-American councils was "treason against the Mexican people" and that they would no doubt suffer the same mistreatment in every other American denomination because of discrimination against Mexicans. For these reasons, the only honorable solution was to create an independent Mexican denomination.[41]

However, not everyone agreed with Flores. Ball had his supporters. The opposition, two members of the Bethel Temple church in Magnolia Park, believed that starting their own movement was not the answer. Rather, they should work through their problems with prayer, fasting, humility, and patience. Possibly drawing on comments made by Ball himself, they also argued that Texas law might not allow Mexicans to legally incorporate their own independent movement. Flores responded by pointing out that he had visited black Pentecostal churches and had not seen a single Euro-American overseer. This along with other comments reassured all but the two who had originally spoken up on Ball's behalf. As a result, the reformers decided to accept the proposal to establish an independent Mexican Pentecostal denomination (*concilio* or "council"). At another conference, López, Flores, Manuel Trujillo, Juan Valadez, and Concepción Suárez decided to notify the churches of the decision. Like Paul Revere sent out to warn the colonists that the British were coming during the American Revolution, Flores was sent out to all of the independent and sympathetic missions to present the call for Mexican independence and to explain their biblical motives and purpose, and the method by which they had reached agreement.[42]

Later, these ministers sent a telegram to Olazábal, who had since traveled back to El Paso, and asked him to travel back to Houston—at once. They provided his train fare and upon his arrival asked him if he would be willing to lead the new council. After spending time in prayer and reflection, Olazábal arose and said he would accept the leadership of the fledgling movement. He said that they needed to pray for God's wisdom and guidance and persevere in their struggle for "our movement for independence." If they did, he said God would bless "our cause" and bring revival and renewal to the Spanish-speaking community. After agreeing to lead the movement, they asked Olazábal to look into whether it was possible for Mexicans to create an independent movement run by and for the Spanish-speaking. After talking to a Pentecostal lawyer named Warren Faye Carothers, a one-time friend of Parham and William J. Seymour and leader of the Apostolic Faith work in Texas, Olazábal relayed to them the good news that Texas law would indeed allow Mexican Americans to organize their own independent Pentecostal council. At this news, the two dissenters defected to Ball and detailed all that had taken place.[43]

Although some people have tried to downplay Olazábal's role in the conflict to create an independent Mexican council, newly discovered internal documents and notarized testimonies by eyewitnesses indicate that Olazábal was one of the key architects behind the struggle for reform, self-determination, and now independence.[44] The clearest evidence that he led the struggle is that Ball, Luce, and the missionaries singled him out by name as the lead instigator of what Ball called the "propaganda" against the Euro-American missionaries.[45]

Ball's Counteroffensive

Ball rightly interpreted the propositions as a direct challenge to his leadership and Euro-American governance. In a preemptive strike to cut off the head of the reform and now independence movement, and with the new testimonies from recent defectors now safely in his hands, Ball wired national missionary secretary J. Roswell Flower at AG headquarters. Ball complained that although "he did not have a thing in the world against Bro. Olazábal," he was duty-bound to report that he was spreading rebellion through false "propaganda" and by saying many "bitter" things against Euro-American missionaries *and* the "American [i.e., AG General] Council."[46] He does not mention any other Mexican leader by name. By juxtaposing Olazábal against the [white] "missionaries" and [white] "American Council," Ball was in fact injecting race and nationality into the conflict, thus tapping into latent nativist fears of Mexican takeovers, which were widespread in the wake of Pancho Villa's raid on Douglas, New Mexico, the ill-fated Plan de San Diego in South Texas, and the Zimmerman Telegram, wherein Germany reportedly sought to create an alliance with Mexico against the United States during World War I.[47]

In December 1922, Flower rallied to Ball's defense. He summoned Olazábal to AG headquarters to "answer charges" that he had made against Ball and Luce. On December 16, Flower chaired a closed-door meeting with Ball, Luce, E. N. Bell, and J. W. Welsh. Ball "heatedly charged him [Olazábal] with instigating" the proposal in Victoria and the move to take over and then leave the AG. Olazábal denied the charges. He stated that he had no intention of inciting rebellion or conflict and that all he and the other Mexicans did was to exercise their right to vote for self-determination and a Mexican-led district. They simply voted on what Ball, Luce, and the other Euro-American missionaries had already promised many years earlier—to hand over the Mexican work to native leaders. After listening carefully to Ball level charge after charge against him, Olazábal finally spoke. He stated that Ball was insincere about providing the promised chalkboards and supplies for the Bible school, and was overreacting to the propositions to reform the Latino AG. Finally, Olazábal asked how could the Mexican work become entirely self-supporting, self-propagating, and self-sustaining—something Ball and Luce called for in their writings and fund-raising letters—if it were still run and controlled by American missionaries? He also pointed out that Ball did not send the promised supplies he needed for the Bible school he had opened in El Paso. Ball said in his defense that he would have sent him the blackboards he promised after the school was built and after he wrote him a letter saying he was ready to receive them. However, they all knew that due to lack of resources most Pentecostal Bible schools were housed in existing churches, and requiring that he build the school first before he sent the chalkboards to help educate the students already enrolled was disingenuous.[48]

Although Flower had wisely remained neutral through most of the discussion, after Olazábal mentioned the Bible school he went on the offensive. Flower demanded to know who gave him permission to start the Bible school in El Paso, a key source of contention. "You did at the last annual convention," Olazábal replied. Furthermore, he told Flower that he sent all of his fund-raising offerings for the Bible school directly to his office, and was thus surprised and disappointed by Flower's statement, which sounded more like an accusation. This was a tipping point in the conversation and turning point in the history of the Latino Assemblies of God. Until that time, Olazábal hoped that Flower and the national AG leadership would remain impartial and not line up along racial lines with Ball and Luce. However, he now realized that race mattered. Feeling cornered by the inquisitorial nature of the meeting, Olazábal later stated: "I left the Methodists [because] I believed I was joining a more Christian people, but now I see that a Russian, a Greek, an Italian or any other nationality can be a missionary [on equally footing with whites] except a Mexican, for no fault . . . [or] transgression [other] than being a Mexican."[49]

In defiance of the racial politics of his day, Olazábal stated that if they planned to treat him "like the Blacks," then you can "consider this my resignation." Startled by his response, Flower, Ball, Luce, and Bell all tried to dissuade him from resigning. Flower attempted to patch up the now disastrous meeting by asking everyone to spend time in prayer, after which they should agree to "forgive and forget." Little was forgiven, less forgotten.[50]

Recognizing the racialized politics he now faced in Springfield, with nine cents in his pocket, Olazábal quietly boarded the train for the long bumpy ride home to El Paso. No sooner had Olazábal walked off the dusty platform than he heard the news: Ball, in a second preemptive strike, had installed one of his own associate pastors in the church that Olazábal had planted in 1919. Ball had barred Olazábal from the church and—by implication—the AG ministry. If he had the authority to take away his church in El Paso, then he could try to stop him from fulfilling his calling in Los Angeles and in just about any other AG outlet. Olazábal would have none of it. He wrote that if Ball and the Euro-Americans "wanted to act with advantage against me" and use that as a "pretext" to thwart "my liberty" and prevent him from opening up a new work in Los Angeles, he would leave the AG. Ball did precisely that by unilaterally stripping him of the church he founded in El Paso. He knew Ball could not have carried out this action without Springfield's tacit approval.[51]

Now publicly humiliated, he could not return to the Latino AG without losing face and submitting to Ball's leadership. As a result, Francisco Olazábal resigned from the AG ministry. His resignation was accepted on January 13, 1923. When later asked by Latino AG pastor Francisco Nevarez why he left, Olazábal simply stated in the Mexican racial parlance of the day: "because the Gringos have control."[52]

Spiritual Revolution and Mexican Independence

Ball knew that Olazábal and his followers would move to consolidate their movement. The result could be disastrous. In a third preemptive strike, Ball attempted to split the rebellion through a divide-and-conquer strategy by going directly to Isabel Flores, the person he had used five years earlier to bring the independent missions into the AG. With Olazábal in El Paso and now out of the AG, he believed he could persuade Flores and the rest to remain and thus break the back of the independence movement. He had to move quickly; once they heard about Olazábal's resignation, they were likely to rally to his cause.

No sooner had Ball arrived and begun speaking to Flores at the doorway of his home when he saw, to his surprise, Olazábal seated comfortably in the living room with a number of ministers around him. Ball had been outfoxed. Flores invited Ball inside to speak with everyone, but Ball declined, refusing to speak in Olazábal's presence. After getting nowhere with Flores, he brushed him aside and walked right into his living room and told everyone they could form their own district if they were patient and abided by Springfield's decision. He said he personally had full confidence in them and that it was Springfield's decision, not his own, that forced him to invalidate their vote and postpone the formation of a Mexican-led district. Seeing this wasn't working, he also implied that Texas segregation laws might not permit Mexicans to organize their own denomination. In time, Ball promised, Springfield would allow them to create their own district. Flores, recognizing that Ball was trying to use him now as he had five years earlier, said that if Ball really loved the Mexican people he could work alongside them as one of their brothers—as an equal, but not as their superintendent. Ball replied: "Your eyes will never see that!" and walked out.[53] Despite the white missionaries' good intentions, the Mexicans knew that it was difficult for them to treat Mexicans—no matter how educated, experienced, or Godly—as complete equals.

Birth of the Latin American Council of Christian Churches, 1923

At the next meeting in Houston, Flores stood before the Mexican AG ministers and proposed that they form their own denomination and elect Olazábal president of the new Interdenominational Mexican Council of Christian Churches (Pentecostal), renamed in the early 1930s the Latin American Council of Christian Churches (CLADIC) since their ministry by that time included Latinos from across Latin America. The proposal was approved. CLADIC was the first completely indigenous and legally incorporated Latino Pentecostal (indeed Protestant) denomination in the United States and one of the first in the Americas. On March

14, 1923, twelve Mexican ministers[54] and their six congregations in Magnolia Park (Houston), Rosenberg, Keechi, San Antonio, Juárez, and El Paso (the second El Paso church Olazábal founded) incorporated the new council. By 1924, CLADIC reported forty churches and almost 2,000 people across the Southwest and Chicago.[55] Olazábal reported, "Our movement is . . . growing more and more each day and if [it] keeps up like that . . . Ball will only have one or two congregations left."[56]

Ball had taken a big gamble by attempting to remain in control of the Latino AG and forcing Olazábal and other seasoned ministers out of the AG.[57] However, his actions almost destroyed the work. Just when it looked like the Latino AG convention might disintegrate in Ball's hands, the movement was resurrected not by Ball, Luce, and the Euro-American missionaries, but rather by the return of Mexican ministers like Rev. Francisco Nevarez, Rev. José Caballero, and Rev. Barrero in March 1923. The real turning point came when Ball's (and Olazábal's) most prized protégés—Demetrio and Nellie Bazan—returned to the AG in November 1924. They did so after Ball showed Demetrio the telegram indicating that it was Springfield's decision, not his own, to invalidate the election and postpone the formation of the Mexican district. They also returned because Nellie never felt entirely comfortable with leaving and had since had a vision that they should return. Ball said the conflict was based on an honest "misunderstanding." He told Demetrio that he had no objections to a Mexican leading the district one day and even implied that Demetrio might make a great superintendent.[58] Today, however, was not that day. Ball remained in control for another fifteen years—until 1939.

The Bazans' return was a critical turning point because they represented a new generation of Mexican American Pentecostal leaders, which Ball desperately needed in order to shore up his otherwise substantial losses. It also signaled a newfound confidence in Ball and the AG and started a small trend of others returning to the AG or other Protestant denominations, among them Arnulfo M. López, Simon R. Franco, Eduardo Rodríguez, and Guerro Durán. This was no doubt disappointing news for Olazábal, since Demetrio and Nellie were his co-pastors and close friends in El Paso.[59]

This exodus of ministers between 1923 and 1924 created a crisis for Olazábal. This, combined with his wife's pregnancy, the children contracting measles, the move to East Los Angeles to pioneer a new work, and other internal concerns, prompted Ball and others to predict that Olazábal's independent Mexican movement would not last. Olazábal asked his followers and family to pray for God's will for "our independent movement and cause" and for "great success" in their forthcoming Los Angeles revival. Despite Ball's prediction of failure, Olazábal not only stayed in the ministry, but also went on to conduct some of the largest Latino revivals in Los Angeles and in American history in the 1920s and 1930s.[60]

Francisco Olazábal's Legacy

Although Olazábal left the Assemblies of God in 1923, his impact on the subsequent history, development, and spirit of the Latino AG movement was substantial. Hundreds, if not thousands, of his converts either returned or eventually joined the AG before and after his death in 1937. He personally baptized and/or touched the lives of many future AG leaders, including Demetrio and Nellie Bazan, Luís Caraballo, Domingo Cruz, Angelo Fraticelli, and Ramón and Nicolasa Camacho—whose mother, Julia Camacho, went on to teach at Mizpa Bible School in Puerto Rico, where she in turn influenced generations of future pastors in Puerto Rico and New York City. Many of the pastors and leaders returned or joined the AG. He inspired Luce and Ball to open two Latin American Bible Institutes in California and Texas in 1926. His converts continued his method of mixing healing and evangelism, and admirers like Domingo Cruz (whom he baptized in the San Francisco Bay Area), Simon Franco (whom he converted in El Paso), and Roberto Fierro all patterned their own revivals after Olazábal's.[61]

He served subsequent generations as a role model of a strong and powerful Latino preacher, teacher, and leader. Olazábal prophetically reminded Ball and Euro-Americans that Mexicans were fully capable of leading their own movement and district. He continued to be a source of inspiration and encouragement for Latino ministers who privately attended his revival services, invited him to speak, and who were invited by Olazábal to speak in his churches and services. Olazábal prompted the Latino AG leaders in the Southwest to be more interdenominational and open to working with other Pentecostal bodies outside of the AG.

He imparted a Mexican can-do spirit and willingness to stand up to mistreatment by Euro-Americans. Finally, he reportedly modeled a passionate commitment to Christ, saving the lost, evangelism, and church planting. Most important, eyewitnesses and his own adult children claim he was a loving father to his ten children.[62]

Just as Olazábal influenced the AG's outlook toward evangelism, so, too, the AG influenced Olazábal and his new council in a number of ways. First, it influenced his strong sense of personal holiness. Although many described him as strict in his views on the Bible and ethics, he also welcomed innovation in evangelistic methods and style. However, he reportedly would not compromise the Bible, Pentecostal doctrine, and personal holiness. Second, his belief in spiritual gifts was formed and developed through AG literature he read and in conversations he had in his first and most impressionable years in the Pentecostal ministry. Third, the overall doctrinal views he imparted to CLADIC were almost identical with the AG, and for this reason some AG ministers even later studied at CLADIC seminary in East Los Angeles. Fourth, he continued to maintain and nurture relationships with AG ministers, Mexicans, and Euro-Americans. He stressed to his followers that it was important to live in harmony with all born-again, Spirit-filled believers, including people in the Assemblies of God. He stated, "I don't believe that God will bless us if the spirit of contention characterizes us in our work. We have to love them in spite of what they do to us," a refrain that both William J. Seymour and later, Martin Luther King Jr., said of whites.[63]

In fact, Olazábal was so close in doctrine and church polity that on at least two occasions he even considered returning to the AG. He wrote Flower on several occasions. However, Flower made it clear that if he wanted to return, he would have to "address" and "apply" for credentials through Ball and the Latin American District "in accordance with our policy." They would not allow Olazábal to hold credentials in a Euro-American district like he had done with Robert Craig in the Northern California AG District, because he was a Mexican. Apparently the new policy was that all new Latino clergy in the Southwest had to be credentialed through Ball's Latin American District. Flower must have known that Olazábal would not submit to such humiliation and racial marginalization. Flower's conditions made Olazábal's reunification all but impossible. Ball states that after learning about Olazábal's desire to possibly reunify, he called him twice, visited two of his conventions, and invited him to go and pray for a sick young man. However, Ball was frustrated that Olazábal would not accept his overtures to work under him in the Latino AG, perhaps because of his past treatment.[64]

Despite Ball's positive statements and overtures, in private letters to pastors and leaders he and Flower were much more critical of Olazábal and his ministry. Flower stated in a letter to one pastor who asked if he should invite Olazábal to preach in his church: "My personal suggestion would be for you not to have him in your assembly. I do not believe he would do you any good. I am personally acquainted with the man. He is a well educated man, far above the average Mexican in education." The reason why he wouldn't invite him was because Flower said he exaggerates the size and success of his campaigns, which have no lasting benefit and are "not very profitable."[65] Likewise, Ball said in a letter to J. R. Evans that Olazábal's style is "autocratic" and that although he has these "big tent meetings," they have "no apparent benefits." Ball also stated that Olazábal "has said many bitter things about me," and that Olazábal said that Ball was "insincere" in his promises and "he withdrew on his own accord."[66]

Olazábal's Future Ministry, 1923–1937

It was indeed unfortunate that the AG would not allow Olazábal to return to the AG as a minister in regular standing and not segregate him to the Latin American District, because he went on to become one of the most important evangelists and faith healers in the early twentieth century. After he set up his mother church in a tent in East Los Angeles in 1923, he began holding evangelistic-healing services. Despite predictions that his ministry would fold without Euro-American AG support, it grew rapidly after the healing of the daughter of Guadalupe Gomez. After the 1924 convention (Figure 4.3) of his newly formed denomination, he began preaching across the United States, Mexico, and Puerto Rico.[67]

Olazábal's dynamic evangelistic-healing ministry was a cross between that of Billy Sunday and Oral Roberts. Called the "Mexican Billy Sun-

Figure 4.3. Francisco Olazábal at the Latin American Council of Christian Churches Convention, Houston, Texas, 1926. (Gastón Espinosa Latino Pentecostal History Collection)

day" by Aimee Semple McPherson, he and McPherson had joint Sunday evening worship services at Angeles Temple, and she on occasion visited his tent revivals in Watts. Olazábal preached to over 250,000 people throughout North America and the Latin Caribbean during his 30-year (1907–1937) ministry. He ignited the Chicago revival of 1929, the Spanish Harlem revival of 1931, and led two large evangelistic campaigns in Puerto Rico in 1934 and 1936. He also regularly preached in David Ruesga's church in Mexico City and elsewhere in Mexico.

The Chicago revival began in 1929 after AG pastor Francisco Paz invited him to lead a revival in the Palace Opera House. He did just that for at least six weeks and filled the house to the brim after healing an Italian gangster wounded in a shoot-out. Word spread like wildfire, and the place was packed with 3,000 souls every night seeking healing and salvation.

Paz next invited him to conduct a revival in the burgeoning Latin American community in Spanish Harlem on 113th street, not far from Robert Orsi's Madonna of 114th Street in Italian Harlem. It was in New York City where Olazábal's ministry took on truly national and even international proportions, after his outreach in a former strip club erupted into a full-blown revival, which quickly spread from the gigantic Calvary Baptist Church to an equally large 1,500-seat former synagogue on 113th Street. It was here that people estimate that he preached and prayed for 100,000 people over the next six years until 1937.

He preached to thousands in Puerto Rico, where leading newspapers covered his campaigns. By the time of his death on June 9, 1937, as a result of injuries suffered in an automobile accident, he claimed 50,000 adherents, started his own periodical *El Mensajero Cristiano* in 1923, planted or helped plant an estimated 130 missions and churches, and contributed to at least fourteen Latino denominations and councils throughout the United States, Mexico, Puerto Rico, and Central and South America. He brought tens of thousands of Latinos into the Pentecostal movement during the 1920s and 1930s. The immense impact of his life and ministry is evident in the accounts of over 40,000 Latinos attending his three-day funeral in New York City and 15,000 attending in East Los Angeles, where he was buried in Evergreen Cemetery—not far from William J. Seymour.

He met and worked with many of the nation's leading Evangelical leaders and evangelists, including R.A. Torrey, Aimee Semple McPherson, A. J. Tomlinson, Smith Wigglesworth, Gerald Winrod, Sweet "Daddy" Grace, and Robert E. Speer. His enormous evangelistic healing campaigns (with as many as 10,000 attending) prompted Spencer Duryee to write in the *Christian Herald* in 1936 that Francisco Olazábal was one of the "most startling stories and personalities in modern religious history."[68] Most important, his prophetic rejection of Jim Crow segregation and racial marginalization was not lost on his followers who called him *El Azteca* or the "mighty Aztec."[69] Although he left the Assemblies, he left an indelible impression on the Latino AG and should rightly be considered one of its most important founders.

This chapter challenged the notions that the first generation of Mexicans passively followed Euro-American missionary oversight and rule, that the independent Mexican leaders were the cause of the conflict and schism that erupted in 1922, and that Mexicans were incapable of leading their own Mexican District on a par with their Euro-American counterparts without Ball's supervision. As noted, independent Mexican and Euro-American Pentecostal evangelists and pastors, along with those who joined the AG prior to Ball's 1918 convention, laid the foundation for the future Latino AG work and were heavily responsible for expanding the Latino AG movement into the 1920s.

What began as a reform movement to elect Latinos to lead a Mexican District turned into a struggle for self-determination since Ball and some missionaries were unwilling to hand over the movement's leadership. Although they stated they wanted to hand it off to Mexican leaders "as soon as possible," over the course of five years Ball seemed to find reasons to remove almost all of the most capable Mexican clergy who could lead the Mexican District. This created resentment, which boiled over into revolt after Ball did not accept the Mexican vote at the 1922 convention and put pressure on Olazábal to submit to his authority or leave the AG ministry. Ball's actions transformed what had once been a simple desire to reform the movement into a struggle for total independence, especially after the Mexican ministers heard how Olazábal—their strongest and most powerful leader—was treated by AG headquarters. As a result of being pushed to the side and trying to reform the movement from within, Olazábal, Flores, and a group of formerly independent ministers broke free of Ball and organized the first completely indigenous and autonomous Latino-led Protestant and Pentecostal denomination in the United States. Ball's actions set into motion a series of events that almost destroyed the Latino AG. It was saved not by Ball and the Euro-American missionaries, but rather by the return of a number of accomplished Mexican and Mexican Americans ministers like Demetrio and Nellie Bazan. They provided the social, cultural, and spiritual glue and vote of confidence that Ball needed to rebuild the work. Although Olazábal contemplated on at least two occasions returning to the AG, leaders at headquarters made it clear that he could only return if he could submit to Ball's leadership and authority in the Latin American District. As a result, what could have been a temporary split, turned into a permanent break. Although the Latino AG suffered an unnecessary loss of leadership, clergy, and churches, Ball and those that remained worked hard and effectively to rebuild and consolidate the movement.

CHAPTER 5

Pentecostal Origins in the Southwest and the Struggle for Self-Determination

ALTHOUGH BALL SURVIVED with his power base intact and would go on to rebuild a remarkably strong movement, he was still disappointed by his own inability to avoid the schism. For despite his personal tensions with many of the Mexican leaders, all accounts indicate that he loved the Mexican people and wanted what was best for them.[1] However, what he and they thought were best were occasionally at odds.

The conflict between Ball and Olazábal's independent movement was largely restricted to Texas. It did not affect the work in California, Arizona, New Mexico, and Colorado. To reduce any simmering tensions and because of the mass defections in Texas, the 1923 convention was held in San Jose, California. Most of the attendees were from California, Arizona, and Puerto Rico, which by this time was developing its own independent movement led by Juan and Isabel Lugo. Although the Latino AG struggled for two years to gain its footing, by 1925 a number of Latinos had returned to the AG and it began to grow, as shown in Figure 5.1.

The Latino AG work in California led by Alice Luce faced its own difficulties. Unlike the robust movement in Texas, which was founded and largely run by Mexicans, the California work was small and largely Euro-American missionary-run. It also had to compete vigorously for

Figure 5.1. Latino AG Convention, Laredo, Texas, 1925. H. C. Ball is pictured second row from the top right of center. Demetrio Bazan is pictured first row, third person from far right with a violin in his hands. Rodolfo C. Orozco (above Ball to the right with a mustache) and a delegation of ministers from Mexico also participated. (Flower Pentecostal Heritage Center)

converts with the Baptists, Methodists, Presbyterians, the Pentecostal Apostolic Assembly, Mormons, Adventists, and Jehovah's Witnesses.[2]

This chapter challenges and revises a number of assumptions about the origins and development of the Latino AG work in California and the Southwest: first, that the Latino AG grew rapidly in California in light of its proximity to the Azusa Street Revival; second, that AG missionaries alone pioneered the Latino work in all of these states; third, that California was easier to evangelize given the strength of the state's larger Euro-American AG movement; and fourth, that Ball finally stepped down from leading the Latino AG in the Southwest because he felt it was time for Mexicans to run the movement without Euro-American interference.

Origins of Independent Latino Pentecostalism in California

The Latino Pentecostal movement in the Southwest traces its roots back to Seymour's Azusa Street Revival. The first Latinos converted to Pentecostalism in April 1906 and continued to attend Azusa Street until 1909 and visit it through the early 1920s. Eyewitnesses claim that "hundreds" of Catholics attended Azusa from 1906 to 1909, "many" of whom were "Spanish" and "Mexican." After a conflict with the mission "leader" in 1909, a growing number of Mexicans began attending one of the other Pentecostal missions in Los Angeles, started their own pioneer ministries, and/or were converted and baptized in the Holy Spirit through one of the Euro-American, African American, or other ethnic Azusa daughter missions.[3]

Between 1909 and 1913, approximately 200 Mexicans attended Elmer Fisher's Upper Room Mission, Finis Yoakum's Pisgah Missions, Thomas E. Liddlecoat's Midnight Mission, and other missions in southern California.[4] Charles Parham noted around 1906 that Liddlecoat's Midnight Mission was crowded with "poor and unemployed . . . white men, Negroes, and Mexicans."[5] Mexicans began attending Fisher's Upper Room in large numbers by 1908.[6] By 1909, at least twenty to thirty Mexicans attended the Pisgah Mission and Faith Healing Homes in Los Angeles and Santa Ana.[7] Many were converted because Pisgah prayed for divine healing and provided free food and clothing.[8] By 1910,

Pisgah evangelists had spread their work to Hispanos in New Mexico, where they converted many to Pentecostalism.[9]

That same year, Elmer Fisher noted the large influx of Mexicans into the Upper Room that were already converted and had received the baptism with the Holy Spirit. This influx prompted Fisher to organize a separate Spanish-language service and mission, and almost fifty people (mostly Mexican) attended the first meeting, where he also officiated at the first Mexican Pentecostal wedding on record. He recalls:

> For many months we have had, in more or less regular attendance in the Upper Room Mission, a number of saved Mexican brothers and sisters, some of who already have received their Pentecost. So it has been in our minds to have a regular Spanish meeting once a week. Saturday was the only night on which we had no other service in the hall, so Saturday night it had to be; and on the night of December 31, 1910, we had the opening meeting. A grand, good meeting it was. Some fifty people were present, mostly Mexicans, and the presence of the Holy Ghost was blessedly manifest throughout. Many burning testimonies were given, and a dear Mexican brother (who under God was in charge of the meeting) gave a good little message from the Word.[10]

The Mexican leader was probably Abundio L. López, who later received ordination credentials from Fisher. He was from Guadalajara, Mexico, and left the Presbyterian ministry and Gospel Detective Mission on 1516 San Fernando Street to serve as a pastor and an evangelist in the Latino Pentecostal movement. He was ordained by Seymour in 1909 and carried out independent evangelistic work throughout southern California. In light of his years of service in Elmer Fisher's Victoria Hall Pentecostal Assembly, Fisher issued ordination credentials to López on July 18, 1914. He pastored the Apostolic Faith Church on 125 South Spring Street. He continued his ministry with Victory Hall until 1943, when he joined Francisco Olazábal's Latin American Council of Christian Churches on May 19, 1944.[11]

Other Mexican Americans who attended the Azusa Revival, such as Adolfo C. Valdez (1896–1988), attended William Durham's Seventh Street Mission. He, his family, and other Mexicans like Rev. Genaro and

Romanita Carbajal de Valenzuela also participated in the Second Azusa Camp Meeting at Arroyo Seco in 1913. While none of these Mexicans worked directly with the AG, they did help lay a foundation for a Latino Pentecostal network that the AG would build on through its converts and evangelistic ministries.[12]

Adolfo C. Valdez and the Assemblies of God

Although none of the Latinos who attended Azusa were ordained by the AG, there were several who sought ordination and several who were indirectly influenced by the revival. The first and most important was Adolfo C. Valdez (a.k.a. A. C. Valdez), depicted in Figure 5.2. In fact, he was a major catalyst in the origins and development of the Latino Pentecostal movement in California. After attending Azusa from 1906 to 1909, he was ordained in 1916 in an Azusa daughter mission in Long Beach. He was popular among Euro-American, Latino, and Native American

Figure 5.2.   Rev. A. C. Valdez, ca. 1925.   (Flower Pentecostal Heritage Center)

churches and swapped pulpits and shared meals on a number of occasions at Francisco Olazábal's home in East Los Angeles.[13]

Valdez sought AG ministerial credentials on at least two occasions. To show good faith, he handed over to the AG the pioneer Pentecostal work he led among Indians in northern California as well as the work he helped create through his evangelistic campaigns in Australia and New Zealand in the 1920s. Despite these overtures and incentives, the AG denied Valdez's requests even though he had strong backing from several Euro-American AG leaders in California. His ministerial files indicate that his applications were variously rejected for three reasons (some of which seemed to echo Olazábal's experience): because he held to a post-tribulation view of the rapture, because he worked with the "Spanish-speaking people," and because the leadership in Springfield felt he was too "restless" and willing to speak his mind. They knew he would not accept ordination through Ball's Latin District or submit to his authority since he was a highly sought-after evangelist among whites as well as Latinos and Native Americans. Nevertheless, Valdez continued to preach in Latino, Euro-American, and Indian AG churches until he retired from the ministry in the 1980s, and for this reason he should be credited as someone who contributed to the Latino Pentecostal movement in California. To their credit, AG leaders later stated that these decisions to deny Valdez credentials were unfortunate because he was doctrinally orthodox and was an accomplished evangelist who had spread Pentecostalism through his large campaigns across the United States, Latin America, Asia, Australia, and New Zealand; in the two latter countries he is credited as one of the founders of Pentecostalism. Valdez's son, Alfred Jr., followed in his father's footsteps and became a prominent crusade and healing evangelist in the 1950s.[14]

George and Carrie Judd Montgomerys' Ministry to Olazábal, Valenzuela, and Lugo

The work of these Mexican evangelists was augmented by Euro-Americans like George and Carrie Judd Montgomery, who also had loose ties with the AG. After the Montgomerys attended the Azusa Street Revival in 1907, they began reaching out to Mexicans, Puerto Ricans, Cape Verde Islanders, and other Latinos through their ministry in Oakland,

California, and to gold miners in San José de los Playitos, Sonora, Mexico. Their travels to Mexico and their ability to speak Spanish put them in a strategic position to reach out to Latinos.

Their most important contribution to Latino Pentecostalism was in ministering to two of the movement's most famous evangelists—Francisco Olazábal and Juan L. Lugo. They prayed with Olazábal in 1902 to rededicate his life to Christ, in 1916 to receive the baptism with the Holy Spirit, and shortly thereafter to join the AG. Juan Lugo stayed in their healing home in Oakland, where they ministered to him and taught him Pentecostal doctrine for a very brief time before he went on to pioneer the Spanish-speaking Pentecostal work in California, New York, and his native Puerto Rico. Like Valdez, the Montgomerys provide a direct link between Seymour's revival and the Latino AG.[15]

The Montgomerys influenced two other important leaders—Genaro and Romanita Carbajal de Valenzuela. The Valenzuelas are important because in 1911 they organized one of the first Latino Pentecostal missions in the United States, which met on 627 Alpine Street. They were also among the first Mexicans to pioneer the Pentecostal work in Mexico,[16] and are considered the founders of the Oneness movement there. Little is known about the Spanish Apostolic Faith Mission except that it met in their home until at least 1914.[17] Around 1911/1912, Genaro's wife or relative, Romanita Carbajal de Valenzuela, was converted to Pentecostalism in Los Angeles, where she sought refuge from the ravages of the Mexican Revolution. More than likely, they began attending when Durham took over as interim pastor and for this reason sided with the Durham faction that embraced the Oneness message at the Arroyo Seco Camp Meeting, which the A. C. Valdez family also attended. However, some Apostolic Assembly historians claim that the Oneness message was revealed to Mexicans before the birth of the Oneness movement at Arroyo Seco in 1913, though without providing any concrete documentary evidence.[18]

Regardless of the origins of the Latino Oneness movement, Romanita is important because she was one of the first people to spread the fires of Pentecost to Mexico in her hometown of Villa Aldama, Chihuahua, in 1914, where she planted a church. This event is often cited as the birth of the Oneness movement in Mexico.[19]

In addition to this work, several early Pentecostal periodicals reference a link between the Valenzuelas and the Montgomerys in 1912 and 1913, stating that the Montgomerys were carrying out evangelistic work in El Paso with "Mr. and Mrs. Valenzuela." The Montgomerys praised them as "evangelists" who loved music and had "blessed results."[20]

Mexican Oneness Pentecostalism

A critical turning point in the larger Latino Pentecostal movement took place in 1913 at the Second Pentecostal Camp Meeting at Arroyo Seco, California. The Oneness message was birthed and the Pentecostal movement split into two theological factions: Trinitarian and Oneness. The Assemblies of God and Church of God in Christ (COGIC) became the main Trinitarian Pentecostal bodies and the United Pentecostal Church (UPC) and Pentecostal Assemblies of the World (PAW) became the leading Oneness denominations.

Though they both stressed that a born-again relationship with Jesus Christ was fundamental, and that the baptism with the Holy Spirit must be evidenced by speaking in unknown tongues, they also believed each other's view on the Trinity to be unbiblical and would not recognize each other's baptisms. Because Oneness leaders believed one has to be baptized in the name of Jesus only, they were also called "Jesus only" Pentecostals. Two Mexicans who attended the Azusa Street Revival, Luís López and Juan Navarro Martínez, joined the Apostolic Assembly.[21] Navarro Martínez traveled to San Diego, where he evangelized migrant farm workers in the Imperial Valley and likely in Mexico as well. In 1912, he converted Francisco F. Llorente (a former Methodist married to a white woman) from Acapulco, Mexico,[22] and together they converted María and Rita Serna in 1913 and Marcial de la Cruz in 1915. Navarro Martínez, Llorente, and de la Cruz preached throughout southern California from 1914 to 1915, after which Navarro Martínez drops out of Apostolic history. In 1916, de la Cruz converted Antonio Casteñeda Nava, an immigrant from Durango, Mexico. That same year the trio founded what is today known as the Apostolic Assembly of the Faith in Christ Jesus, Inc. They worked in association with G. T. Haywood's Indianapolis-based and African American–led Pentecostal Assemblies of the World until 1930, primarily for doctrinal, legal, and ordination purposes, after which time they incorporated in California as a legal religious organization.[23] Despite this PAW connection, the Apostolic Assembly was run by and for the Mexican people.[24] The Apostolic Assembly became the first Latino Oneness Pentecostal tradition in the United States. Its sister organization, the Apostolic Church, became the first Oneness denomination in Mexico. The latter gave birth to other Oneness denominations in Mexico like Iglesia Evangélica del Consejo and a heterodox splinter group called Iglesia La Luz del Mundo, based in Guadalajara, which despite its Apostolic and Oneness roots (which it denies) claims that it is the only true church of Jesus Christ with a living apostle in the world today.[25]

Alice Luce and the Origins of the Latino AG in California

The person often credited by AG historians for pioneering the Latino AG work in California is Alice Evelyn Luce (1873–1955). Born in Cheltenham, England, on January 22, 1873, Luce was the eldest daughter of Anglican vicar J. J. Luce. After receiving a calling to the missionary field, she sailed to India in 1896, where she eventually served as principal of a girls' school. After reading about the Azusa Street Revival in Pentecostal newspapers, she sought the baptism with the Holy Spirit, received the baptism on February 10, 1910, and joined the Pentecostal movement. Two years later she returned home and in 1914 resigned as a missionary from the Church of England and traveled to Canada.[26]

After receiving a calling to evangelize Mexico, she left Canada for the United States en route to Mexico. Luce and Dr. Florence Murcutt (a Jewish doctor and a convert to Pentecostalism) stayed in Kingsville, where they met Ball. Both were ordained in 1915. The now forty-four-year-old Luce traveled with Murcutt, Marshall, and Miss Ester Banda to Monterrey, Nuevo León, Mexico. They arrived on September 21, 1917, and started a Pentecostal mission in their home on 25 Jimenez and M. M. del Llano Streets. They met with little success because of the Mexican Revolution and fierce Catholic opposition, and after growing fears about being kidnapped, returned to Laredo, Texas, on December 18. In January 1918, Marshall returned to San Antonio, and Luce and Murcutt returned to Los Angeles, where the latter organized the first permanent Latino AG mission.[27]

Despite her important work, Luce was not the first AG evangelist to minister to Mexicans in Los Angeles. In April 1916, two Puerto Ricans, Juan Lugo and Francisco (a.k.a. Panchito) Ortiz (both converted by Azusa Street missionaries in Hawaii), traveled from their new home in the San Francisco Bay Area to Los Angeles, where they organized a small makeshift Assembly of God mission, preached to "hundreds" in the Mexican Plaza district in downtown Los Angeles, and converted eight Mexicans. Despite these efforts, and because of their meager results and lack of funding, Lugo and Ortiz abandoned the mission a few months later.[28] In the fall of 1916, Mr. and Mrs. E. Crawford also attempted to organize a Spanish Pentecostal mission, but also gave up several months later.[29]

The Latino Pentecostal movement began in northern California in 1906 with a Cape Verde Islander named Adolph Rosa, who spoke both Portuguese and Spanish. He attended the Azusa Street Revival that year and pioneered the Spanish-speaking work in the San Francisco Bay Area. He converted a number of Latinos to Pentecostalism.[30] Robert J. Craig, pastor of the Glad Tidings Mission (future AG), also converted a number of Mexicans in 1911.[31]

The northern California work received a shot in the arm in 1913 when Juan Lugo and Francisco Ortiz Sr. and Jr. arrived from Hawaii. They attended a small Portuguese/Spanish Pentecostal mission in San Jose pastored by a Reverend Silva. Lugo and Panchito conducted evangelistic work throughout the Bay Area in migrant farm labor camps, and in Oakland. In 1917, Francisco Olazábal joined the movement and preached throughout northern and southern California from 1916 to 1919. He converted a number of Mexicans and Puerto Ricans and laid the foundations of the Latino AG work in California, so that by the time Luce and Murcutt arrived, Latinos had already started several missions and had made a small but growing number of converts.[32]

Inspired by the Latino evangelistic work they saw in Texas and northern California, Luce and Murcutt returned to Los Angeles and began conducting open-air evangelistic meetings in the historic Mexican Plaza district in 1918. They went house to house passing out hundreds of evangelistic tracts and praying for the sick.[33] In order to bring in "a great harvest of souls," they stepped out in faith and rented a large hall that seated over 200 people. But their hopes of mass conversion were dashed on the bitter rocks of indifference and opposition. While crowds of Mexicans would gather around to listen to the novelty of white female evangelists preaching in Spanish, they would not follow them into the mission or convert.[34]

Luce also complained that, like San Antonio, Los Angeles was a stronghold of Spiritism in the Spanish-speaking community. She said there was a large Mexican Spiritist church a few blocks away from her mission and that their "emissaries" attended her meetings and attempted to entice their new converts to join them.[35]

The Oneness Apostolics proved even greater competitors. By 1917, they had established two missions in Los Angeles. Luce lamented that these "false teachers have been among the flock in these parts, and they have been tossed and torn by many winds of doctrine, so that it is hard to find any who are standing together in [doctrinal] unity . . . the 'New Issue' [Oneness or Jesus Only] error is the greatest difficulty here—they are trying to steal away our flock all the time."[36]

Luce had good reason for concern, because unlike the Latino AG, the Apostolics were run entirely by and for Mexicans and were very evangelistic and openly critical of Trinitarian Pentecostalism. Even more disturbing to Luce and her colleagues was their practice of persuading Latino AG pastors and entire churches to join their movement. Reverend Antonio Meza, a pioneer Apostolic minister in southern California, stated that this was a common church growth strategy not because they sought to divide the church, but rather because they genuinely believed that they preached the truth about the Oneness of God.[37]

In spite of the competition, Luce and Murcutt continued their ministry, though with very modest results. Francisco Olazábal led the first major Latino AG revival in Los Angeles in the fall of 1918. At Luce's invitation, he arrived from San Francisco and led a powerful evangelistic-healing crusade that attracted hundreds of Mexicans to Luce's mission, including some Apostolics. He, more than any other Latino AG preacher, checked the Apostolic advance in California. Olazábal's preaching not only attracted Catholics seeking redemption, healing, and the latest entertainment, but also a number of his former Methodist parishioners from Pasadena and Watts. Many Methodists, including two Mexican pastors, decided to join the Latino AG as a result of Olazábal's Los Angeles campaign. Although not a gifted evangelist, Luce was an expert organizer and worked tirelessly to build a firm foundation on Olazábal's and his and Murcutt's own work. Luce was a strong proponent of taking the Christian message to the community, and by December 1918 she and her Mexican converts had preached in virtually every Mexican labor camp within a twenty-mile radius of Los Angeles.[38]

Luce and Murcutt's ministry attracted a disproportionate number of Mexican women, and Luce and her converts were forced to confront domestic abuse and violence. She wrote about one woman who was savagely beaten and abused by her drunken husband for attending Luce's Pentecostal mission and for praying in tongues. When her Catholic husband found his wife praying one day, he took a red-hot iron and burned her face until she screamed and writhed in pain. Luce and her Mexican followers nursed the woman back to health. After about two years of literally torturing his wife, the husband finally converted, and the two became traveling evangelists.[39] Not all Mexican women were so receptive to the Pentecostal message. Indeed, Luce and other AG evangelists noted that many Mexicans thought they were already Christian enough and did not need to repent of their sins and have a personal relationship with Jesus Christ to go to heaven.[40]

The work Luce, Murcutt, and their Mexican followers founded grew slowly between 1918 and 1923. After Olazábal arrived in East Los Angeles in 1923 to found his new mother church and headquarters for his evangelistic ministry, the evangelistic work of Luce and her colleagues became even more difficult. Luce nonetheless laid a solid foundation upon which other Mexican evangelists and pastors built a very strong and vibrant ministry. Her open-air meetings, Bible studies, testimonies, house-to-house visitations, prayers for the sick, and tract distribution made an impact. She and her colleagues ministered in the beet and bean fields and at different fruit ranches throughout California, often following the seasonal harvests along with the migrants. At one Mexican Independence Day parade in Los Angeles, they passed out a thousand tracts in thirty minutes. Despite her efforts to reach this "floating population," her mission only grew from thirty people in 1918 to fifty by 1920. Yet Luce met with her converts and reportedly kept them "continually in prayer." She also taught them the Bible, theology, church history, and apologetics, and many regarded her as a "mother" in the faith.[41]

As a result of this slow but steady growth, in 1923 Luce, Fred and Flora Steele (two AG missionaries), and others built the first Latino AG church in Los Angeles. Flora was a Mexican American and an effective evangelist who ministered with her husband. The work they founded was developed and expanded by Mexican Americans like Francisco and Natividad Nevarez. By the 1930s, their Upper Room (El Aposento Alto) mission became the mother church of the Latino AG work in southern California. Despite these efforts, the Latino AG work continued to grow slowly in Los Angeles because of competition not only with the Apostolics but, after 1924, with Francisco Olazábal's evangelistic-healing ministry and his council's growing number of churches in the 1930s. For these reasons and others, by 1940 the Latino AG counted only four churches in Los Angeles.[42]

Despite the modest growth, Luce made a number of lasting contributions to the Latino AG. She pioneered the work in California, paved the way for women in the ministry, translated and published Spanish-language evangelistic and teaching materials, and founded the second Latino AG Bible school in the United States, the Latin American Bible Institute (LABI), in San Diego; it later moved to Los Angeles and is now located in La Puente. And she also promoted the notion that all Latino churches should be self-supporting, self-governing, and self-propagating. Her decision to promote an indigenous church was influenced by Roland Allen's book, *Missionary Methods: St. Paul's or Ours* (1912), which challenged the Euro-American paternalistic approach to missions. In 1921, Luce promoted these views through a series of articles for the *Pentecostal Evangel* entitled "Paul's Missionary Methods."[43]

Latino Pentecostal Origins in the Southwest-Mexico Borderlands

Although Luce and her followers had to contend with the Oneness and Latin American Council of Christian Churches (CLADIC) movements in California, they largely had a free hand in Arizona, New Mexico, and Colorado, where other groups did not have a strong power base until the late 1920s and 1930s—though virtually all Protestant and Pentecostal denominations had varying levels of outreach.

Arizona

Although Azusa Street evangelists first arrived in Arizona in 1906, the first documented outreach to Mexicans took place in 1911 when Ms. Cornelia Nuzum evangelized Mexicans in Nogales.[44] She wrote: "These border towns are at present golden gates of opportunity. They lie partly in Mexico and partly in the United States. All of them are overflowing with war refugees from all parts of Mexico."[45]

Chonita and Floyd Howard and George M. Thomas joined her. Together they pioneered the Pentecostal outreach to Mexicans in Pirtleville, Bisbee, Douglas (Arizona), and Agua Prieta, Sonora, Mexico. Chonita, the daughter of a Euro-American miner and a Mexican mother, was particularly adept at evangelizing along the Arizona-Sonora border. George and Francisca Blaisdell and a "brother López" also joined Nuzum and the Howards. They pioneered the work along the border prior to 1915. Almost all of them joined the fledgling Assemblies of God. Francisca and Chonita went on to become key leaders in the Latino AG, serving as directors of the women's missionary council and as prominent evangelists and revival speakers.[46] By 1925, Ball claimed that they had seven ministers in the Arizona-Sonora region and that their church in Agua Prieta, Mexico, numbered fifty to one hundred members.[47]

Catholic Harassment and Persecution

Conflict with Catholics was inevitable. As was the case with Arnulfo M. López in San Antonio in 1914, sometimes the Catholic attacks turned violent. Converting to Pentecostalism or any tradition other than Catholicism came at a price. Mexican converts faced religious discrimination, ridicule, scorn, and persecution from family, friends, and Latino employers. Their evangelical fervor, strict morality, and religious practices also made them a target of persecution and religious discrimination. In

1918, Luce wrote that nearly all her Mexican converts were going through some kind of persecution. In Texas, a Euro-American foreman fired a group of Mexican workers after he heard that they had converted to Pentecostalism.[48]

Many Catholic priests fought back by organizing processions on feast days. Ball wrote in 1922, "The day I arrived [in Seguin, Texas] the Mexican Catholic priest had a sacred procession in order to counteract our influence. . . . In the procession he marched with his congregation carrying an image of the Virgin Mary and the child Jesus."[49]

Mexican Catholics worried about Pentecostals in particular because they were very effective at youth proselytism, broke up their community with a "we-preach-the-Truth" attitude, and criticized Mexican Catholicism and traditions like praying to the saints. The main Pentecostal criticism of Catholicism is that it did not call on its followers to have a born-again conversion experience with Jesus Christ. Wrote Ball: "Roman Catholicism . . . produces superstition, ignorance, and even idolatry. . . . The trouble with Mexico is that her Christ is always on the Cross or dead in the grave, and so is their religion, dead. Our Christ was dead, but now He lives at the right hand of God. HE LIVES, praise God, and our religion is life."[50] Similarly, José F. Marez wrote: "I was a strong Catholic for 40 years. I worshipped images and prayed to the saints and lit candles, but I never gave up sin until the day that they [Pentecostals] told me about Christ according to Acts 4:11–12 and 2 Corinthians 5:17. Christ made me a new man."[51] More often than not, conversion meant a decisive break with popular Catholicism rather than a way to maintain continuity with it.

Contrary to recent interpretations of Mexican conversion to Protestantism as a means to significant upward economic mobility, the vast majority of Mexican Pentecostal pastors lived at or below the poverty level. The average church numbered thirty to eighty members and few could afford to support a full-time minister. For this reason, the turnover rate was high. In an attempt to help secure financial assistance, H. C. Ball called on readers of the *Pentecostal Evangel* to financially support Mexican pastors and evangelists.[52] In some cases, the minister's family was so poor that the children had to work in the fields and could not attend school.[53] In 1937, Ball lamented that "our Mexican pastors have been sorely tried during the depression, the majority of their members being on relief; their poverty and suffering have been terrible."[54]

Colorado

Despite persecution and financial struggles, the Latino AG spread throughout the Southwest. Pentecostalism arrived in New Mexico and Colorado by 1906, and by 1909 there was significant outreach across the state. The first major AG work was conducted in 1914. Pentecostal evangelists reported that the native Hispanos in New Mexico were very receptive to their message, no doubt building on and drawing converts from the Protestant work pioneered by the previous Methodists, Presbyterians, and Baptists.[55] The Pentecostal work in Colorado began after Euro-Americans and African Americans started converting Mexican migrant workers. The first known conversion took place in October 1914, in Pueblo, Colorado. The state proved fertile ground and produced a number of independent missions and highly capable ministers who went on to provide important leadership, including Carlos Trujillo, Enrique Lucero, Agustin López, Salomon Mendoza, Edwardo Duran, Sandoval, José F. Marez, and Juan Martínez.[56] Almost all of these leaders and their missions were brought into the Latino AG by Demetrio Bazan by the early 1930s, though not without challenges and conflicts, as we shall see later.[57]

In the 1930s, a group of five Apostolics publicly challenged Assemblies of God leader Demetrio Bazan to a public debate over the doctrine of the Trinity and Oneness of God in an independent church near Denver. The leaders of the independent Mexican congregation agreed to join whichever side won the debate. Bazan won.[58]

The southern California–based Apostolics were not a major concern in Texas until the 1930s, by which time the AG and Olazábal's Concilio had a virtual monopoly over the Pentecostal movement. However, after the Apostolics arrived in Texas they made up for lost time. Ball lamented, "There are . . . many independent Pentecostal Mexican groups now teaching everything from free-love to new-issue" (Oneness theology).[59]

The Pentecostal work in southern Colorado faced many of the same persecutions and hardships experienced by their sister churches in Texas and Arizona. In 1933, the Reverend Agustin López and his small Pentecostal mission faced an onslaught of persecution and hatred in Greeley. Shortly after this former silent film actor for Universal Studios joined the Pentecostal movement in California, he moved to Colorado where he planted a church. After he began converting many of Greeley's Catholic youth, the verbal disapproval turned violent. Right after López and his congregation finished building their church, a mob of angry Catholics stormed in and grabbed López from the pulpit during a worship service and dragged him outside to beat him. When he would not leave town, the men returned one night to his house, and in a scene reminiscent of the Ku Klux Klan in the Deep South, doused gasoline on the front porch and ignited a fire. The terrified family awoke to flames, which they were able to snuff out before the fire consumed the entire home. Despite the harassment, López continued his ministry in Colorado and later joined the Assemblies of God in 1934;[60] by 1939 the Latino AG counted twenty-five churches throughout the state.[61]

New Mexico

The Mexican Pentecostal work in Colorado spread to New Mexico, and by 1919 there were small missions in Raton and Padilla.[62] The movement made strong inroads in the 1930s. The main source of tension in New Mexico was not with Oneness Pentecostals but rather with Roman Catholics, who dominated the social, spiritual, and political landscape of northern New Mexico, especially in rural areas. These conflicts on occasion led to bloodshed and even martyrdom, as happened on May 14, 1936, in the small town of Gallina. Problems had been brewing for some time as the Pentecostal evangelists were converting many of the town's youth. Catholic townsfolk commanded José Girón, Miguel Martínez, and a Mr. Jaramillo to stop their evangelistic services immediately, threatening to kill the preachers if they did not get out of town. After the preachers would not leave, one night townsfolk ambushed and shot Girón in the neck and Martínez in the leg. Lacking funds for proper medical treatment, Martínez died soon after from infections caused by the gunshot wound to his leg and became one of the first Mexican American Pentecostal martyrs in the United States. The very next night, Girón, still recovering from his gunshot wound to the neck, defiantly decided to continue preaching the Pentecostal message.[63]

Hispano Catholics had good reason to fear the inroads Pentecostals were making in rural New Mexico. In 1937, J. B. Johnson wrote in the *Southwest Review* that the Pentecostal "cult" had grown so fast that in some communities of New Mexico, 50 percent of the people belonged to the "aleluyas." He claimed that their success was due to the hypnotic quality of the singing, belief in divine healing, biblical literalism, and the psychological similarities of Pentecostal practices to the rites found among the Indians and Hispanos in New Mexico.[64]

Laying a Firm Foundation:
The Latin American Bible Institutes

The relative isolation of Latino AG missions made them difficult to reach with theological education. Varying levels of illiteracy among immigrants compounded this. Some pastors and evangelists were field laborers with little or no formal education.[65] As a general rule, Ball would not ordain a person who could not read.[66] In response, Ball and Luce began holding free literacy programs two evenings a week in 1917.[67] The Bible was the first book many Mexican converts learned to read.[68] In addition to the night school, Ball and Luce also conducted short seminars at the conventions.[69]

To address the need for ministerial training and theological education—and contrary to what is stated in previous Latino AG histories—Francisco Olazábal founded the first Latino AG Bible school in early 1922 in El Paso. He provided room and board in his own home for five of his nine students, while the rest lived locally. Rev. Narro, Mrs. Julia Ballinger, Juanita Enriquez, and others assisted him. The school met in his church and ran for less than a year because Francisco resigned from the AG in December 1922. In addition to helping them with their studies and mentoring them in the Bible and pastoral ministry, Olazábal provided ministerial internships by having the students help him during his revival and evangelistic services in his churches in El Paso and on the road during his evangelistic travels. He also assigned them to serve alongside the pastors of the other AG missions in the El Paso area.[70]

Four years after Olazábal resigned, Alice Luce opened the Berean Bible Institute in San Diego, California, on October 1, 1926, and Ball opened the Latin American Bible Institute three days later in San Antonio, on October 4. The former was later renamed the Latin American Bible Institute; it was relocated to Los Angeles on November 2, 1941, and ultimately to its present location in La Puente in 1949.[71] In 1926, Adah Wegner opened a third LABI in Venezuela, and in 1927 David Ruesga opened a fourth in Mexico City, which at that time was still under Ball's administrative control, where it remained until 1930.[72] In addition to the Bible schools, by 1930 Luce's correspondence program had attracted seventy students from the United States, Mexico, Puerto Rico, Peru, Argentina, Venezuela, Panama, and Chile. In Figure 5.3, Luce is shown with the graduating class of LABI, La Puente, along with key

Figure 5.3. Latin American Bible Institute, La Puente, June 1, 1942. First row: unknown students. Second row (left to right) are faculty and staff: Rev. Jovita Bonilla, Rev. Alice Luce, unknown, Rev. Josue Sánchez, Rev. Simon Franco, Rev. Demetrio Bazan, Rev. Francisco, and Rev. Natividad Nevarez, and an unknown couple. (Latin American Bible Institute, La Puente, California)

teachers and leaders such as Josue Sánchez, Demetrio Bazan, and Francisco and Natividad Nevarez; the latter two also co-pastored Aposento Alto in Los Angeles.[73]

In order to publish evangelistic and worship literature and later materials for the Bible school in the Southwest and increasingly throughout Mexico and Latin America, in 1924 Ball founded La Casa Evangélica de Publiciónes (later called Editorial Vida) in San Antonio, the first Spanish-language Pentecostal publishing house in North America. It printed hymnals, Sunday school literature, and over 500,000 evangelistic tracts. In 1947, the publishing house was closed in San Antonio and re-opened as a branch of the Gospel Publishing House in Springfield, Missouri, under Ball's administration and leadership.[74] Springfield increasingly looked to Ball as the go-to person for all things related to the U.S. Latino and Latin American AG work.

Race and the Struggle for Survival and Mexican American Self-Determination

J. R. Flower, the AG missionary secretary, had good reason to have confidence in Ball and Luce's work. Despite the schism in 1922, by 1924 a number of key Latino leaders, led by Demetrio and Nellie Bazan, had returned. They provided a solid foundation on which to build a revived movement in the Southwest.

By 1927 the convention had rebounded and was growing rapidly not only in the United States, but also in Mexico, Puerto Rico, Guatemala, and El Salvador. Ball and Luce shaped all these works through their hymnals, periodicals, ordination applications, evangelistic literature, Bible schools, and annual conventions. Yet there were continued and sustained efforts by Latinos in each of these regions to wrest control of their movements from Ball, Luce, and their Euro-American overseers. Notwithstanding this struggle, from 1918 until 1929 the Latino AG was truly a North American movement that stretched from the United States to El Salvador.

The Latino AG was reaching over 90,000 people a year by 1927. Ball reported 2,000 to 3,000 members,[75] largely due to the work of Mexicans evangelizing the thousands of immigrants fleeing the highly secular

Mexican Revolution (1910–1917) and the reactive Catholic Cristero Rebellion (1926–1929). Ball's emphasis on friendship evangelism turned every new convert into a lay evangelist and potential church planter once their Bible study group grew to at least twenty to thirty committed members. For Ball, no person was too poor or uneducated to carry out God's work, provided they were willing to learn how to read, write, and preach the Bible and promote Pentecostal doctrine. The simple message that God was no respecter of class, education, race, or immigrant status was attractive for Mexicans and other Latinos looking for a way to transition into American society as equals and to scale the high walls of segregation, white supremacy, and the racial borders and boundaries that diced up U.S. society. All of this freedom, along with new roles for women in ministry, attracted not only Catholics, but also a good number of Protestants to their ranks, especially Methodists, Presbyterians, and Baptists.[76] This mix enabled Ball to create a new movement that led to remarkable growth, maturity, and long-term stability from the 1920s through the 1970s.

However, the growth of the Latino AG in the 1920s and 1930s was a double-edged sword. It was rapidly outpacing Ball's ability to effectively control and govern the movement. Furthermore, many national leaders, like the feisty David Ruesga (1898–1960), a close associate of Francisco Olazábal, began pushing for independence and a national AG church independent of Ball and the American AG. Ball foresaw this trouble and knew he could no longer control and keep a lid on the growing nationalist sentiment and native calls for indigenous leadership. This pressure, along with his own public statements about self-supporting, self-governing, and self-propagating churches, led Ball and AG Missionary Secretary Noel Perkin to divide the North American movement into separate national churches. This decision was also due at least in part to the fact that the new Mexican government called for all foreign religious bodies to be nationalized and led by native clergy. Although this law was really aimed at the influence of the Roman Catholic Church and its vast wealth and the large number of foreign priests and missionaries, it also affected Protestants. Foreign missionaries who for decades had been allowed to live and work in Mexico were now asked to hand over the work and land holdings to native leaders and in many cases to leave the country.[77]

As a result, from 1929 to 1930 the national AG leaders in Mexico, El Salvador, and Guatemala began severing their administrative ties to Ball's Latino AG mother church in the United States and became completely independent national churches. Ball finally handed over the leadership to native workers in these countries, but not in the United States. By 1930, the transfer of power was largely complete. Ruesga was elected superintendent of the thirty-six AG churches in Mexico, and Francisco Arbizú was elected superintendent of the twelve churches in El Salvador.[78] This newfound freedom unleashed a wave of indigenous creativity that resulted in rapid growth. By 1943, the AG work in Central America had grown to 4,000 adherents, 300 churches and missions, 200 native pastors and evangelists, and 13 missionaries, the latter of whom worked alongside native Central American leaders. In contrast, the U.S. Latino Pentecostal movement remained under Ball's leadership for another decade, though not without grumblings.[79]

The Great Depression and the Struggle to Survive, 1929–1940

Despite the rapid growth during the 1920s, the Latino AG movement in the United States almost completely collapsed in the 1930s due to the Depression. It devastated the economy and created massive job shortages that fanned the flames of Nativism and racial prejudice. Millions were out of work. Americans began demanding that "white men should be given . . . jobs" first. A number of cities and counties passed laws making it virtually impossible to hire Mexican and Latino immigrants for public works projects, and for this reason President Franklin Delano Roosevelt's New Deal public works projects offered little economic relief for Mexican Americans and Mexican immigrants, who were often seen as one and the same.[80]

In reaction to this xenophobia, the U.S. government ordered the mass repatriation of 500,000 Mexicans to Mexico, including many U.S.-born Mexican American citizens.[81] Some were forcibly rounded up, packed into hot rail cars without food or water, and shipped to Mexico, including many Mexican American young people who were born and raised in the United States. As a result, entire Latino AG churches vanished overnight—something other Protestant churches also faced.[82]

By 1941, a staggering 100 Latino AG churches and missions had closed their doors. The largest mission was Ball's own in San Antonio, which counted only twenty-five regular members.[83] The future looked bleak. However, not every Latino Protestant group was suffering equally. Francisco Olazábal's Latin American Council of Christian Churches witnessed massive growth during this period, largely due to the enormous evangelistic-healing crusades he held from East Los Angeles to Chicago to Houston to Spanish Harlem to San Juan, Puerto Rico. Indeed, the 1920s and 1930s witnessed the rapid growth of indigenous Pentecostal bodies throughout the United States.[84]

Despite these obstacles, and in an effort to raise hope in the midst of ashes, Ball claimed that the Depression led to a spiritual awakening and revival along the border in the quality rather than the quantity of the churches and missions that remained. People had to choose between attending church and putting bread on the table. Those that attended church did so under the conviction that if they honored God, God would in turn honor and bless them by providing for them. It was this small but committed remnant that Ball used to rebuild the U.S. Latino AG.[85] Despite these losses, they had a strong convention in 1941 and were slowly beginning to bounce back.

Ball Defending Latinos against Discrimination

Ball realized that the Nativism sweeping the nation was also contributing to a hostile climate for Latinos and evangelism. He recognized that the repatriation movement and much of the anti-immigrant sentiment were both driven by overt and covert prejudice. Although Ball could be stern with recalcitrant and rebellious pastors, he could be even sharper with those who discriminated against U.S. Latinos, especially those in the household of God. He took great personal risks and faced the possibility of social ostracism to speak out against racial discrimination, especially in South Texas, where discrimination against Mexicans was widespread. Ball was described by many who knew him as a "righteous (and stubborn) man in the things of the Lord" and a stalwart defender of his

Mexican flock. He had good reason to be concerned. By the mid-1920s, the Ku Klux Klan had even infiltrated some quarters of the Pentecostal movement. For instance, Raymond Richey, who often preached in AG churches and even occasionally preached in Latino missions, allowed a hooded delegation of the KKK to march down the aisle at one of his Pentecostal crusades in Houston in the mid-1920s. All of these developments created a hostile environment for Ball and Latinos in Texas.[86]

Despite minor support for the KKK in some parts of the Pentecostal subculture, Ball completely disagreed (as did most Pentecostals) with its harsh racial views.[87] It was precisely Ball's commitment to racial equality that led him to publicly protest the shoddy treatment of Isabel Flores, who was arrested in 1917 by a Euro-American sheriff on grounds of loitering. He confronted the sheriff, challenged the charges, and secured Flores's freedom. The problem was so pervasive and persistent that Ball wrote in the *Pentecostal Evangel* in 1931 that the ongoing racial "discrimination" against Mexicans was "unjust." He stated, "Even American born Mexicans have been discriminated against most unjustly." Ball made his views crystal clear when he stated, "They are [just] as much American as we are."[88]

Indeed, despite Ball's advocacy and activism on behalf of Mexican Americans and other Latinos, they continued to face racial marginalization even within Euro-American AG churches. Miguel Guillén (c. 1896–1971), a light-skinned Mexican immigrant who pioneered the AG work in South Texas from 1916 to the 1930s and went on to serve as second president of the Latin American Council of Christian Churches, describes how he personally witnessed whites complain about Mexicans who prayed at the altar during revival and church services. The problem was so widespread in some segments of the AG that sympathetic Euro-American pastors had to sponsor and shepherd a Mexican's application for ordination through the process lest it be denied.[89]

Guillén lamented that there was something of a two-tier racial system in the AG—one for Euro-American missionaries and another for Mexican American missionaries, even if they were of lighter coloration like himself. He argued that AG leaders and parishioners occasionally discriminated against Mexican Americans. He describes, for example, how after Jesús and Abelardo Ramírez had converted at an AG evangelistic meeting in Texas, the white evangelist and pastor directed them to a Mexican church rather than their own, despite the fact that they clearly spoke English and wanted to attend his church—the place where they were converted.[90] The racial problems they faced were also common in Protestant and Catholic churches.[91]

The racialization of ethnic minorities in the AG was not unique to Latinos. African Americans, Native Americans, and Asian Americans also faced similar problems.[92] Mel Robeck argues that even in segregated churches black leaders had to report to white leaders. He claimed that this kind of paternalism reflected the old plantation life in a new form. He pointed out that during this period and through the early 1960s, the AG denomination's list of ministers was carefully highlighted with the notation "colored" following the names of black ministers so that these ministers would not be invited to speak in churches that practiced segregation.[93]

All of these factors created major hurdles for Ball and the Latino AG. The Depression, repatriation, Nativism, and the raw need to survive prompted many Mexicans to return to Mexico or move from city to city and farm camp to farm camp in search of work. Thousands were constantly on the move. As a result, some pastors who were constantly on the move were forced to give up the ministry to care for their impoverished families. In an effort to raise consciousness about the work and raise badly needed funds for their support, in 1932 Ball wrote in the *Pentecostal Evangel* that "our struggling churches even in good times have a hard time, and now it is nothing short of a miracle that they are able to 'carry on.'"[94] Five years later in 1937 little had changed: "Our Mexican pastors have been sorely tried during the depression, the majority of their members being on relief; their poverty and suffering have been terrible."[95]

Relinquishing Control: The Struggle for Self-Determination

The conflict with Olazábal, trenchant poverty, frustration with Ball's inability to stem the decline and even reversal in growth in some regions, and the continuing push for native leadership, forced Ball himself to take seriously the aspiration of the Mexican people to govern themselves. He did so by affording them greater respect and freedom at the local level. Every church was autonomous and did not have to follow any kind of a prescribed national curriculum, although Ball made General Council and Latin District materials available in Spanish via *La Luz Apostólica*. He also sponsored pastoral training seminars at the LABIs, and evening seminars since so many worked in the fields, factories, and as day laborers. However, there was only one superintendent of the "Latin American Convention." Ball allowed each region to create smaller conventions, thus providing relative autonomy at the regional level. While this provided some independence, it also led to a number of problems and a lack of commitment to the Latino AG and General Council, which helps to explain why some churches and missions left the AG for other Pentecostal denominations, most often Olazábal's CLADIC, the Church of God, or the Apostolics.

At the same time Ball afforded greater local freedom, he also moved to secure complete administrative control over the Latino AG movement at the national level. He created the Latino AG District in the Southwest with one general superintendent. During the 1920s and 1930s, the Euro-American missionaries largely ran the movement at the national administrative level, wrote many of the articles for *La Luz Apostólica*, and directed and heavily staffed the LABIs.

Although the pious paternalism of Ball, Luce, and missionaries began to give way to a greater degree of confidence in Mexican leadership by the late 1920s, the Mexicans still harbored doubts about their ability to lead the movement and believed that Euro-American missionaries were necessary to enable them to reach their fullest potential. Thus Luce called on Euro-American churches to "keep a friendly eye on them, encourage them to keep close to Jesus and urge them to press forward in the salvation of souls," all of which seemed to imply that the Mexicans were incapable of doing this themselves.[96] The fact that they continued to promote handing over the movement to Mexicans but then had Ball allow himself to be nominated year after year created a sense of betrayal that stoked the fires of independence and gave birth to an "anti-English spirit." This, combined with the nationalizing of the AG movements in Mexico and Central America, all contributed to a growing anti-Americanism that led to open strife. In her 1931 report on the Latino convention in the

Pentecostal Evangel, Luce admitted that one of the reasons there was friction between missionaries and Latinos was that the former were unwilling to relinquish control of the work. This was reinforced by criticisms from Latino leaders inside and outside (e.g., CLADIC, Apostolics) of the movement that the Latino AG was an "American" (i.e., Euro-American-run) movement. In an effort to address the anti-American spirit, Luce called on Euro-Americans to "urge the native converts to carry on the work themselves and to make them feel that theirs is the responsibility of evangelizing their own country."[97] She believed that if they were willing to do so, then "the gospel as interpreted by them can no longer be called a foreign religion."[98] But despite Luce's push for native leadership, Ball did not relent.[99] He did not believe that Mexicans were fully ready to effectively govern themselves.[100] Along with his sometimes-stern leadership style, this fueled resentment among some prominent Mexican American leaders.

Although Ball claims otherwise, recently discovered internal documents indicate that he had problems not only with Olazábal but with many key Mexican founders such as Enemecio Alaniz, Antonio Ríos Morin, Arnulfo M. López, Isabel Flores, Anastacio Frausto, José Rodríguez, and later leaders like second-generation Mexican American clergy, including Joseph Ramos, who was a major figure in California and someone who had also been nominated for superintendent.[101]

To his credit, Ball realized that his leadership style and conflicts were taking a toll on the Latino AG work. He met with AG Missionary Secretary Noel Perkin in 1927 and offered to resign. Perkin persuaded him not to. In fact, Perkin promised Ball his full and uncompromising support.[102] With Perkin squarely behind him, Ball moved to consolidate his control and root out malcontents. In God's Army, Ball was the general. Insubordination was rarely tolerated. However, Latinos still wanted to exercise self-determination. This led to what Ball and Luce called an "anti-English spirit" on the part of "several natives" at their district council meetings between 1928 and 1932.[103] José G. Castellanos left the AG in 1932 because of Ball and joined Olazábal's CLADIC.[104] The second-generation Mexican American pastor and LABI graduate Joseph Ramos captured the growing frustration of some Mexicans when he wrote in a letter to J. R. Flower, "Brother Ball is under the impression that his word is infallible in your office because the Mexicans [since Olazábal] have never had the courage to stand up for their rights."[105] Ramos's charges were not completely unfounded, as there is not a single instance in which AG headquarters sided with a Latino leader against Ball in key controversies.[106]

Upset that Ramos tried to circumvent his authority by writing directly to Flower, Ball wrote in his letter to Flower that Ramos had a dictatorial spirit, was arrogant, hard, critical, and noncooperative, and taught doctrines similar to those of Jehovah's Witnesses, charges Ramos flatly denied. Ball was not alone in his assessment since some Mexican leaders like Bazan agreed with some, though not all, of his criticisms of Ramos. After an extensive internal discussion, Ball said that he and other AG leaders like Alfonso Lara and Demetrio Bazan had tolerated Ramos long enough. In his letter to AG headquarters, Ball concluded: "He [Ramos] should be out, that is the only hope for the man."[107] Like Olazábal eighteen years earlier, Ramos realized his fate was sealed in Springfield and, despite thirteen years of service in the AG ministry (1927–1940), he resigned.

Although it is easy to criticize Euro-American leaders like Ball, the extant documents also indicate that he served the Latino community, advocated for them in Springfield, fought against their discriminatory treatment, and considered it a "privilege to minister to the Latin-American people."[108] Pioneer evangelists such as Rev. Elvira Perales stated that although Ball could be tough, she still "loved" him very much for all of his service to Latinos and his support for her personal ministry.[109]

Rather than step down, Ball continued to lead the Latino AG through the Great Depression of the 1930s. He found ways to hold on to the movement despite numerous obstacles. However, the quiet pressure to nominate a Mexican leader of the Latino AG movement in the Southwest continued. After years of pressure to step down, in 1939 Ball decided to resign as superintendent to accept a missionary calling to Chile, where he served from 1941 to 1943. The second in command, Demetrio Bazan, was named superintendent of the Latino AG. Ball's decision to serve in Chile may have been a temporary stepping-stone, because two years later AG headquarters asked him to direct the entire AG work in Latin America—an offer too big to refuse. He served as the AG missionary field secretary from 1943 to 1954, although he still kept his headquarters in San Antonio, Texas. While Ball had stepped down as superintendent, after he returned to the United States he decided to become involved again in the Latino AG by running the publications department. He also allowed himself to be elected vice-president of the Latino AG under Bazan in the 1950s, and in 1956 ran against Bazan for superintendent. Although Bazan won the final vote 77 to 55, it created hard feelings. Latinos still lived in the shadow of Ball and their well-intentioned Euro-American friends. Ball continued to exercise influence in the Latino AG until the day he died in 1984. He and Alice E. Luce were celebrated as the primary founders of the Latino AG in the Southwest. However, we have seen that this was only partially true since a number of Mexican leaders, including Alaniz, Morin, López, Olazábal, Flores, Bazan, and many others, were largely responsible for founding, expanding, and creating the spiritual, social, cultural, and linguistic glue that not only held the movement together but enabled it to expand and prosper.[110]

The Pentecostal movement in California and the Southwest trace its origins back to William J. Seymour and the Azusa Street Revival in Los Angeles. A number of Euro-Americans and Latinos embraced his message, and some of them, including A. C. Valdez and George and Carrie Judd Montgomery, went on to influence future key Latino AG leaders like Francisco Olazábal and Juan Lugo. Despite Ball's pious paternalistic attitude toward Latinos, he was also a staunch advocate and would not allow Latinos to be discriminated against in the AG or in society. He created a highly efficient administrative and organizational struggle. While this helped modernize the movement and bring it up to speed with other Euro-American districts, it also seemed to make it difficult to bring in real innovation and make allowances for Mexican cultural patterns and social practices. While Ball never promoted the kind of strict Americanization program some Americans would have wanted, he still used and measured the success or failure of the district by how well it measured up to the mother denomination in Springfield (i.e., the Euro-American AG tradition). While this made communication and the movement of resources and personnel throughout the AG easier, it also put pressure on Latinos to soften their Latino cultural practices. Notwithstanding this, Ball did strongly affirm the use of Spanish and indigenous churches and leadership.

Despite Ball's advocacy for Latinos, his growing power led to conflict, especially with second- and third-generation Mexican Americans in the 1920s and 1930s who felt he was too overbearing. Some left to start their own movements or to join Olazábal's council or another denomination. Although not without flaws, Ball provided badly needed stability for the Latino AG, which helped contribute to its subsequent growth, and he did bring in a certain level of innovation through publications like *La Luz Apostólica* and *Himnos de Gloria,* and even by opening up a Spanish-language publishing house.

Ball continued to exercise influence in the Latino AG until his retirement in 1961 and his death in 1989. With time, he tempered his speech and desires and became a dearly beloved founder and elder statesman of the movement. A tireless worker before and after retirement, he continued to teach at the LABIs and to publish Spanish literature, all of which allowed him to have continuing influence in the United States and Latin America. Although in many ways he and Luce slowed the process of indigenization and growth during their tenure, in other ways they helped lay a very solid organizational, administrative, and publishing foundation for the future movement, which has since helped it blossom into the largest Latino Protestant denomination in the United States. For all of these reasons and others, it is accurate to argue that Ball and Luce were the two most important founders of the AG work among Latinos from 1922 to 1939, even if they were not the first and most important founders and catalysts for its growth from 1914 to 1922. While the Latin American District would experience tremendous growth under Bazan's leadership from 1949 to 1969, it would also face several challenges.

CHAPTER 6

The Challenges of Freedom

Mexican American Leadership in the Southwest

A FTER ALMOST TWO DECADES of struggling for an independent voice and native leadership, Demetrio Bazan was finally elected the second superintendent of the Latino AG on October 20, 1939—eighteen years after Olazábal and the Mexican *independistas* first asked to run their own district. Ball's decision to hand over the work was good news, but the timing was less than ideal. The Great Depression was in full swing and the movement and its ministers were struggling to survive. The organization had lost many churches and missions and its leadership was worn-out and impoverished. While some missions had closed, the Latino AG had also opened up many new missions. The Latino AG grew from 65 congregations, 117 clergy, and 3,000 members in 1930 to 80 churches, 174 ministers, and 4,500 members by 1935.[1]

Bazan was a good pick and ready for the challenge. A smart Mexican American with a sense of humor, he took all of the skills learned under Ball and Olazábal and combined them to build up the movement and lead its rapid expansion during his administration from 1939 to 1959. This growth was due not only to his focus on evangelism, missions, and church planting, but also to his leadership style and emphasis on strengthening and developing existing congregations. He also forged stronger ties to the larger General Council, but on their own terms and largely to secure material resources, equipment, and inexpensive literature for the Latino clergy and their churches. Despite their blind spots, he believed in the general good will and intentions of his Euro-American brethren. They were, after all, he said, one body of believers seeking a similar goal—to convert people to faith in Christ.

Second Superintendent—Demetrio Bazan, 1939–1959

Born on December 22, 1900, in La Pesca, Tamaulipas, Mexico, Demetrio Bazan's father Modesto was a fisherman and his mother Dolores Peña a housewife. A turning point came when Demetrio was nine and his father died and his mother could no longer care for him. He was adopted by a wealthy family, Rafael and Epimenia de los Santos Coy. He soon became their favorite. Rafael had an entrepreneurial streak, which shaped Demetrio's can-do attitude. At various times, his father owned a clothing store, a bar, a silver shop, a grocery store, and he had even worked as a mailman and watchmaker. At one point, he also owned three mule trains, which brought supplies back and forth between towns. He was a trader. Hard work, a dose of Mexican humor, and an entrepreneurial spirit were de los Santos Coy trademarks—and came to describe Bazan aptly as well.

When the fires of the Mexican Revolution swept through northern Mexico, like thousands of others the de los Santos Coy family fled to Matamoros, Tamaulipas, just across the Rio Grande River from Brownsville, Texas. Rafael opened a grocery store. Their hopes for a new life were dashed after revolutionary general Venustizo Carranza's troops arrived and ransacked the town and their shop. They fled across the border into Brownsville, where they stayed with Rafael's cousin Manuel until they settled in Sarita, Texas. They soon worked for the railroad and in the cotton fields in Kingsville, close to where Ball set up his tent ministry. The Bazans first met Ball because Demetrio's mother Dolores washed his clothes. Ball invited her to church. In time, Ball's messages began to sink in, and in the fall of 1917 Demetrio reportedly went forward at one of the altar calls to accept Jesus Christ as his savior and lord. Demetrio was born again. Ball discipled and disciplined him (Demetrio liked to play practical jokes as a youth, such as throwing a cat into Ball's

Sunday morning worship services). When it came to living a disciplined Christian life, Demetrio was in every way Ball's protégé; he taught him how to memorize Scripture and, after he moved out on this own in 1918, Ball allowed Demetrio to rent a room at his home in exchange for chores.

It was not long before Demetrio fell in love with a beautiful Mexican American parishioner named Manuelita ("Nellie") Treviño, originally from Helotes, Texas. Nellie was born on November 19, 1898. Her mother died in December 1914, which left Nellie devastated and depressed. Her depression gave way to a greater sense of hope after AG evangelists M. M. Pinson and R. D. Baker began tent meetings not far from where she was living with her younger siblings. Pinson had been brought into the Pentecostal experience through Gaston B. Cashwell, who had attended Azusa before returning to spread the fires of Seymour's Azusa Street Revival throughout the South. This established another spiritual link between Seymour's Azusa Revival and the Latino AG in Texas. At that first revival meeting, Nellie reportedly asked Jesus Christ to forgive her sins and to be her savior and lord. She wrote about how she found new optimism and purpose in life, and soon was called to preach the Gospel and evangelize the Spanish-speaking people. She became friends with Demetrio, and after a courtship the two were married on February 18, 1920. Ball officiated at the wedding at the newly constructed San Antonio church. Both Demetrio and Nellie felt called to the ministry and were ordained together in March of that same year. This practice of ordaining husband and wife evangelistic, missionary, and/or pastoral teams was and remains a common practice in the Latino AG and is the easiest way for a woman to secure ministerial credentials. The Bazans went on to raise a large family and see a number of their children go into the ministry.

Ball sent the Bazans to assist Olazábal in El Paso three months later, after he himself declined Olazábal's request to join him. The timing was good: Olazábal's evangelistic work was converting hundreds, and he desperately needed workers. The Olazábal and Bazan families became close friends and shared their trials, tribulations, and joys. As a result, when Olazábal left the AG in 1922, the Bazans went with him. Demetrio served in a number of leadership capacities and helped edit and publish their periodical *El Mensajero Cristiano (The Christian Messenger).*

Bazan's defection must have been a stinging rebuke to Ball and no doubt hurt him deeply. In truth, the Bazans were never completely comfortable with having to choose between Olazábal and Ball. Demetrio had a change of heart after Nellie did not feel "the spirit behind the new organization was right." Eager to prove that he was not a tyrant and that Springfield had indeed cabled him to invalidate the vote in 1922, Ball showed Bazan the document proving the cable was not just rumor. Bazan apologized for doubting Ball. This, along with a dream Nellie had in which she felt God calling them back to the AG, prompted them to return to Ball and the Latino AG in November 1924. Ball was elated. Bazan was one of Olazábal's most important protégés, and the return was a major vote of confidence for Ball and one that also inspired others to do the same.[2]

After co-pastoring the church in Kingsville for a short while, Bazan started his own itinerant ministry with Rev. Guadalupe Flores. Like Alaniz, Morin, López, and Olazábal, they conducted evangelistic services in tents throughout the region. After this, Bazan pioneered the AG work in Laredo before moving on to Houston to organize a new church, now that Bethel Temple had joined CLADIC. He erected a 20- by 30-foot tent on the corner of Commerce and Buffalo and began evangelistic services. This is where he met Miguel Guillén, someone first converted in Los Indios in 1916. The Bazans' ministry grew rapidly in just a few years and they sent out a number of evangelists such as Pedro and Elvira Perales, Horacio Menchaca, and Josue Cruz, all of whom went on to illustrious careers in the AG.[3]

As their ministry was booming, in 1929 Ball asked the Bazans to take over his 400-member Templo Cristiano in San Antonio, something that at first sounded great until Demetrio discovered that brother Ball planned to remain in the congregation. He said he had to step down since he was so busy with his publishing, editorial, and supervisory work. The Bazans were not thrilled with the idea of pastoring Ball's congregation and knew they would always be under Ball's watchful gaze. However, they also knew they could not say no to Ball. Recognizing he needed help, Bazan asked Josue Cruz to become his associate pastor. Both then accepted the offers and worked hard to grow the church. [4]

As was his custom, Bazan spent an enormous amount of time in prayer and private devotions. In 1932, he received a strong impression from the Holy Spirit to leave San Antonio and to pioneer the Pentecostal work in Denver, Colorado—a true mission frontier. Bazan relayed his experience to Ball and in effect pulled rank by telling him that God was calling him elsewhere. The church board refused Bazan's resignation. However, after realizing that Bazan might leave the AG if his resignation was not accepted, Ball and the board gave their blessing, and Josue Cruz became senior pastor. They had little choice. Demetrio was Ball's most talented minister and could one day run the movement when Ball retired. Ball led the fund-raising effort to finance the move; though the Bazans were grateful for the help, it also left them in Ball's debt. The San Antonio congregation had grown attached to the Bazans. As they slowly drove out of town, the congregation followed them to the outskirts and waved goodbye as they left to pioneer the work in the Rocky Mountain State in complete freedom and with room to grow.[5]

Bazan's Ministry and Leadership Style

The Bazans arrived on September 12, 1932, without any major funding, cold-weather clothes, or even a place to live. They had stepped out in faith. The first person they met in Denver was a young man named José Arroyo. Arroyo told Bazan that the night before he had had a dream which led him to a certain house. That morning he went over to that house and asked the owner if it was available for rent. The owner said it was and promptly gave him the keys, which he in turned handed over to the Bazans. They raised their family in the home for many years and believed that God provided it to confirm their decision to pioneer the work in Colorado. Although remarkably foolhardy by today's standards, this story of simple faith and "God's providence" in the face of uncertainty was and continues to be repeated in the Latino AG.[6]

The Bazans not only pioneered the AG work in Denver but also won over a number of independent pastors and missions, like J. F. Mares (Grand Junction), Carlos Trujillo, Enrique Lucero, Agustin López and Edwardo Duran (Greeley), and Salomon Mendoza and José Aguilera

(Gill), among others. The Bazans pioneered the work in Trinidad, Pueblo, and La Veta, and other small *colonias* scattered throughout the region. The Bazans' church quickly became the mother church in the region, and many of the pastors patterned their life, work, and even crewcut hairstyle after Demetrio. In 1939, he moved his family and the Latin District Office to the strategic railroad hub of El Paso, where he sought to convert the masses pouring into the United States.

Demetrio Bazan was reportedly a good preacher, an excellent administrator, and a confident but humble and hard-working leader. Although not a graduate of LABI, he was a high-school graduate (something many LABI students had not accomplished), mentored by Ball and Olazábal, and a keen student of the Bible and doctrine, especially of End Times prophecy. His doctrinal studies came in handy in his energetic debates with the Oneness Apostolics in Colorado and in his pastoral training seminars.

In many ways the election of Bazan signaled a decisive turning point in the history of the Latino AG. Although Bazan and Ball were similar in their vision and the organizational structure they used, Josue Sánchez wrote that they "were a study in contrasts. . . . Bro. Ball took an authoritative role in instructing how he wanted things done whereas Bro. Bazan was much more democratic in his way of managing the church."[7]

The Latino AG grew under Bazan because of his democratic style, evangelistic drive, and the influx of thousands of Mexican laborers during the Bracero Program, which was launched in 1942 to meet labor shortages during World War II.[8] The Bracero Program grew from 500 Mexican contract workers in September 1942 to over 220,000 in 1947. This massive influx provided a rich field from which Bazan and his compatriots reaped a harvest.[9] In a matter of just two years, the Latino AG grew from 170 congregations and 3,765 members in 1939 to 172 churches, over 300 ministers, and 5,344 members by 1941. Bazan claimed that the actual number of Latino AG adherents was well over 8,300 people. Figure 6.1 depicts Bazan and a small portion of the 1941 Convention attendees in Houston.[10]

The AG was not the only Protestant work growing during this period as the Methodists also witnessed solid growth. The Methodist church reported in 1939 that they had 46 pastors, evangelists, and Christian

Figure 6.1. Rev. Demetrio Bazan and ministers at the Latino AG Convention in Houston, October 21–23, 1941. To Bazan's immediate right is Paul Finkenbinder, who helped pioneer the Latino AG work in Puerto Rico and New York City before moving to the Southwest to work with Demetrio Bazan and at LABI in Texas. Kenzy Savage is pictured in the last row directly above Bazan. (Gastón Espinosa Latino Pentecostal History Collection)

workers reaching 4,337 members at 66 preaching points.[11] The Presbyterians also saw modest growth, increasing from 61 churches and 3,844 member in 1935 to 62 churches and 4,068 members in 1940.[12] The ability of the Methodists and Presbyterians to keep pace with the AG growth fell off sharply during the 1940s, and the Presbyterians were even forced to close a number of missions. The main reasons were reportedly the shifting nature of the Latino population due to migratory labor patterns, the "secularization" and liberalization of theology, a shift away from evangelism and church planting to social work, a lack of financial support from the denomination and parishioners, and—ironically—racial integration, which resulted in Latinos merging their institutions and missions into Euro-American churches and their leadership structures. Although the goal of racial integration was good, at the end of the day it largely meant that Latinos were forced to assimilate into the dominant Euro-American church; within a few years, the entire Latino leadership structure was assimilated, and many Latino leaders were without a job or a ministry.[13]

Latino AG churches were less susceptible to some of these factors than Latino mainline Protestant churches because they focused heavily on evangelism, never forced racial integration—which enabled them to adapt to the shifting needs of the people—and were never dependent upon Euro-American denominational funding. Every Latino AG church lived or died based on the support and commitment of its members. For this reason, almost everyone was involved in one way or another in setting up the church, leading worship, cleaning the facilities, cooking lunch or dinner after services, and providing follow-up with converts, the sick, and those in need. This not only helped build esprit de corps, but also mobilized the entire congregation to take ownership of their church—no matter how large or small. Despite the Euro-American oversight of the larger AG denomination, Latinos had full and unequivocal freedom and creativity to reach the masses however they saw fit. In this sense, Latino Pentecostal churches were creative free spaces and upstart entrepreneurial ministries that by their very nature adapted to the needs of the market. Those that did not folded.

The Latino AG work prospered in both the United States and Mexico. Bazan kept in regular contact with David Ruesga and Rodolfo C. Orozco, and they often took turns preaching in each other's churches. The Mexican work was pioneered by Ruesga, Loreto, Orozco, Anna Sanders, and many others. After securing its independence in 1930 once the Mexican government nationalized all foreign religious bodies, the AG in Mexico grew rapidly from 125 churches and 3,765 members in 1939[14] to an estimated 50,000 people by 1948.[15]

Despite these developments, Ball still exercised considerable influence in the Latino AG. In a decision that clearly signaled his move away from Ball, Bazan moved the Latino AG headquarters from San Antonio to El Paso (over 550 miles west) in 1939 and then on to New Mexico in 1953. He then reorganized the Latino AG from Ball's eleven conferences to just four. He hired four full-time rather than part-time superintendents. This resulted in better supervision, coordination, and systematic evangelization and spiritual oversight.[16]

When a young Jesse Miranda asked Demetrio Bazan why he moved the headquarters so far west, Bazan told him, "Son, we stay close enough to the General Council in Springfield to learn from them, yet far enough away to do things our own way." Miranda stated that this ability to maintain complete freedom and yet tap the larger denomination for resources and support whenever they were needed was one of the reasons for the Latino AG's success.[17]

Another example of tapping the denomination for its support came in 1945, when Bazan secured inexpensive books and teaching materials for theological education and training for pastors and laity. He passed a resolution to create the first Sunday school director position, installed Epifanio Jaramillo, and in 1948 worked with Jaramillo to create the first Sunday School Convention Teacher's Program. They secured educational material from AG headquarters. In another bold move that signaled his quest for independence from Ball, in 1945 he moved the LABI in Saspamco in South Texas to Ysleta, a suburb of El Paso, the key Mexican gateway into the United States and the location of the first LABI that Francisco Olazábal had opened in 1922. This location also made it easier to reach out to students in Chicago, Denver, and the Midwest. In order to accommodate the growing number of students in California, in 1949 he moved the LABI in East Los Angeles to a larger tract of land in La Puente, California. In an effort to provide theological education for ministers and congregations in rural farm labor camps and *colonias,* Bazan spent a good part of his year traveling from camp to camp conducting "minister's institutes" and setting up special seminars, especially for superintendents, who in turn did the same for the ministers in their respective conferences. All these developments led one eyewitness to state that Bazan brought about "so many changes" that it was simply impossible to enumerate them all.[18] However, the most important decision was to push for greater independence and autonomy.

Bazan's Vision for New York, the Southwest, and Latin America

One key area where Demetrio Bazan differed with Ball was over the treatment of the Puerto Rican movements in New York City and in Puerto Rico. Ball brought the Latino AG work in New York City into the Latino AG in 1946 but also allowed it to develop its own autonomy and create the Spanish Eastern Convention (later District). By 1947 it counted eleven churches and missions.[19] Bazan realized that just as Mexicans had wanted to be free of Euro-American rule in the Southwest, Puerto Ricans wanted to be free from Mexican American oversight in New York City and in Puerto Rico. Remembering his own struggle with Ball in the Southwest, Bazan encouraged the Eastern Spanish Convention, which had been gently pushing for complete separation and autonomy for some time, to create their own independent Spanish AG district. The decision was in part driven by the fact that they were already governing themselves and were growing very rapidly. They simply did not need or desire Bazan's oversight. As a result, the Puerto Rican leaders in the AG formed their own independent Spanish Eastern District on a par with the Latin American District (largely based in the Southwest and Chicago) in January 1957. Bazan could afford to be generous because nationwide the Latin American District was growing by leaps and bounds to 321 churches, 573 ministers, and 19,490 members.[20]

Bazan also differed from Ball in his focus on foreign missions. Sponsoring missions was important because it demonstrated a certain level of maturity, agency, and global vision. For Ball, reaching Latinos in the United States was a foreign missionary enterprise. In fact, he was originally sponsored and funded by the department of foreign missions in Springfield to convert Mexicans as a gateway into Latin America, before eventually being transferred over to home missions. Ball sent relatively few Latinos to the foreign mission field outside of the United States. In light of this fact, the Latino AG missionary movement began not under Ball's leadership but rather under Bazan's. Although the Balls are considered the first AG missionaries sent out by the Latin District (to Chile), the first Latinos who were sent overseas by the Latino AG were Pedro and Piedad Torres, who in 1945 pioneered the AG work in Cuba. They were followed by Antonio Enrique, Ramon Aguilar, and a Rev. Nieves, who assisted the Torreses, all of whom also served in Cuba and the Latin Caribbean. Gaspar Mundo was sent to evangelize the Puerto Rican sugar cane field workers in Hawaii; Agusto and Evelyn Reyes Vereau went to Peru; Ben and Pearl Flores went to Argentina; Larry and Myriam Mora went to Ecuador; and Kerry González and his wife, along with Steve Martínez, were sent to Spain.

Demetrio Bazan's equally smart and energetic wife Nellie reportedly shared his "passion for souls." In addition to raising ten children, she found time to preach door to door, help plant three AG missions, write articles for *La Luz Apostólica,* compose poetry, and write an autobiography entitled *Enviados de Dios.*[21]

The Bazans experienced firsthand how ministerial families were devastated if one of them died or was injured. Many lived in abject poverty alongside their parishioners and most had full-time jobs to supplement the meager Sunday offerings, which sometimes amounted to only a few dollars a week. This life of poverty, suffering, and self-sacrifice began to have a negative impact on the children of the ministers, some of whom wanted nothing to do with the ministry after they left home. For this reason and others, Bazan took an innovative step. He had the Mexican American AG evangelist Roberto Fierro and one of the general presbyters translate the U.S. Social Security laws into Spanish and circulated this pamphlet throughout the district so that pastors and laity could enroll in the Social Security program. He also asked José Girón, his secretary, to enroll ministers in the Metropolitan Life Insurance Plan and Social Security to help them and their families deal with unexpected illnesses and tragedies.[22]

Prior to 1952, most convention superintendents had to both pastor and lead their conventions. This proved exceedingly difficult and taxing on the leader and his family. It also made it almost impossible to effectively run the convention, since there was very little time left after one's pastoral duties to visit all of the churches, send out newsletters and aid, and run the annual conventions and revival and youth camps. For these reasons, Bazan decided to make the position of superintendent a full-time paid job without the burden of pastoral duties. Now the superintendent could dedicate his efforts full time to providing leadership and vision for the convention. However, in order to fund these superintendents, Bazan was also forced that year to consolidate and reduce the number of geographically based conventions from nine to just four.

For most Latinos, Bazan, his Mexican American sensibilities, and his leadership style were a breath of fresh air and a source of national and ethnic pride. He was by all accounts greatly loved and appreciated by

Latinos in the AG. The sources indicate that they particularly singled out his love and care for his family. Bazan worked hard not only to spend time with his family, but also to make that time positive and memorable. Victor De Leon wrote, "This was what made him so great and so respected by the ministry of the [Latino] district which he headed."[23] Indeed, Bazan's nonstop, almost workaholic-prone spirit was tempered by his commitment to his family. He reportedly believed that if you cannot convert, disciple, and love your own children, how can you expect to convert the world? He and Nellie committed themselves to raising the next generation of ministers right in their own household. And so they did. As a result, many of their children, including Alex, have served in the ministry.

Bazan had served the AG well and left a lasting impact on the movement. For despite his brief time with Olazábal from 1922 to 1924, he had served the AG as a pastor, evangelist, and church planter from 1920 to 1939 and as superintendent from 1939 to 1959. In a day and a profession where ministerial turnover was high and the temptations of life lured many to pursue other lines of work, Bazan, like Ball before him, was reportedly a rock of stability in a tumultuous sea. With his confidence, creativity, and spiritual commitment, he provided a role model for rank-and-file ministers. Perhaps this was his greatest gift to the AG— and likewise, Nellie's. Bazan's visionary leadership led to the rapid growth of the Latino AG, and by the 1950s it had surpassed the Latino Methodist and Presbyterian works as the largest Protestant movement among Latinos in the Southwest. In fact, the Presbyterian Church noted with alarm that it had to close a number of churches in the 1940s and 1950s due to "lack of numerical and financial support," though there is little reason to doubt that the growth of the Pentecostal movement also contributed to its decreasing market share. During this same period the Latino AG in the Southwest (not including the Spanish Eastern District) grew from 170 churches and 3,765 members in 1939 to 325 churches, 600 ministers, and 20,000 members (60,000 affiliates) by 1960. As the decade of the 1960s approached, Bazan realized that it was time for fresh leadership. After leading the Latino AG for twenty years, he decided to step down.[24]

Third Superintendent—José Girón, 1959–1971

The two natural leaders to replace Bazan were José Girón and Josue Sánchez, both of whom had proved their mettle and loyalty in the field as evangelists, church planters, and pastors, and as the Latin District secretary, the post usually held prior to being elected superintendent. However, Sánchez did not seek the office. Girón was elected Latin District superintendent on January 1, 1959. Girón, depicted in Figure 6.2, began his administration in 1960.

Unlike Bazan, who was raised in the Pentecostal movement, Girón grew up in the Mexican Presbyterian Church. He was one of many Mexican American Presbyterians during this period who joined the Pentecostal movement. The Presbyterians first pioneered the work in the historic Hispano San Luís Valley in southern Colorado in the late nineteenth

Figure 6.2. Rev. José Girón, ca. 1955, who served as third superintendent of the Latino AG. (Flower Pentecostal Heritage Center)

century. In time, they opened a Mexican Presbyterian Church in Del Norte. By the mid-1940s, they began to witness a decline in membership. In addition to the reasons already noted, this decline was also due to the competitive growth of Pentecostal, Evangelical, and other millennial movements. Between 1930 and 1935, the Del Norte Presbyterian congregation witnessed a little upsurge in numbers, from 51 to 61. However, this did not bring about a major increase in numbers, and the larger Latino Presbyterian movement in the Southwest witnessed a decline from 3,874 to 3,444 members. When Girón first met the Pentecostals in Del Norte in 1932, the Mexican Presbyterian work was undergoing a small revival and he thus would have found Pentecostal revival services attractive.[25]

As part of the revival, the Mexican Presbyterian leaders were constantly on the lookout for young leaders. Girón's interest in the Bible caught the attention of his pastor, Manuel Sánchez. He encouraged Girón to attend seminary and stated that the church had passed a resolution to "subsidize his entire expense." Girón, however, was unsure about the ministry. He also loved business and sports. The poverty he saw around him was a daily reminder of what he wanted to avoid. Although he had an interest in the Bible, he also realized that ministry was tough work and often done without earthly rewards.[26]

A critical turning point came after AG evangelist Paul Jones arrived in town and began street evangelism. He passed out gospel tracts and invited Girón to his revival services. At the end of one of the services on February 3, 1932, Girón, along with a Methodist minister named D. Zook, received the baptism with the Holy Spirit.[27]

Girón was an excellent convert to the Pentecostal movement—smart, educated, athletic, and outward looking. He immediately began to imitate the evangelist by trying to convert his friends and persuade his family to receive the baptism with the Holy Spirit, and as a result "precious souls began to accept the Lord's spiritual blessings." In light of this, Jones wrote a glowing letter to Ball recommending that Girón be ordained to the ministry. Surprisingly, Ball complied and without even meeting him—much less examining his doctrine—sent him an AG ministerial license on June 29, 1932. A Mexican American Pentecostal leader was born.[28]

As a result of his newfound calling, Girón conducted evangelistic and revival crusades throughout southern Colorado and northern New Mexico. He became a church planter, started a Spanish AG church in his hometown of Del Norte (1932–1933), and pastored it for about a year before moving on to the itinerant evangelistic trail. Over the next decade, he planted and pastored eight churches, in Alamosa, Colorado (1934–1935); Questa, New Mexico (1935–1938, 1942–1943); Santa Paula, California; McPhee, Colorado; Taos, New Mexico; Center, Colorado; and Chama, New Mexico.

During this time, he also continued to pursue education. In 1943, he served as a substitute teacher in the Taos elementary schools and from 1944 to 1946 pursued theological education through correspondence and graduated from Light House Bible College in Rockford, Illinois, with a degree in theology. He praised Latino youth who went on to the LABIs and seminary and actively encouraged education.

Yet life in the ministry was hard work. Almost every minister had a regular day job and pastored at night, midweek, and on the weekends. More than one church closed its doors because the flow of workers and internal migrations following seasonal harvests quite literally moved the congregation from one dusty farm town to another. Many ministers were also migrant farm laborers and worked alongside their parishioners, sang Pentecostal *coritos* during their water breaks in the fields, and prayed for and ministered to the sick and injured in the farm labor camps.

Girón's evangelistic and church-planting work made him a natural to serve as Bazan's secretary from 1947 to 1959. While Bazan emphasized taking risks, Girón took a gradual approach to change, in large part because most Latino ministers were not in favor of sweeping changes, given their own precarious existence. This gradual approach also reflected a little of Girón's Presbyterian upbringing, which taught him that everything should be done decently and in order. This measured approach to leading and governing the Latino AG served him and the movement well.

One of the first difficulties he ran into was the fact that the Latino AG was still a set of loosely related conventions without any constitution or bylaws. To address this problem, at the 1960 "Constitutional Convention" in El Paso, Girón completed the process Bazan started by requiring each conference to create and adopt its own constitution and governing by-laws. Although some feared that giving each conference the power to create its own constitution might lead to revolt and possibly schism, this was not the case. Nonetheless, the decision was a major gamble and a real test of Girón's leadership and of the conferences' loyalty and support. However, they knew Latinos preferred fraternal relations over total independence, which could lead to isolation, lack of resources, and other difficulties. Moreover, because the conferences did this together and largely in unison at the convention, and because they drew on their constitutions and bylaws as examples, in an odd way it actually brought them closer to the larger Latino District and General Council. The end result, wrote Girón, was stronger ties to the AG because their "sovereignty was spelled out and so restricted."[29]

The result was a stronger sense of harmony across conventions since they each tended to borrow language from other conventions. Perhaps more important, the restructuring enabled each district to allow the new superintendents to work full-time in providing spiritual oversight and long-term vision for their convention. This also enabled them to provide the funding to send the four new superintendents to the General Council meetings, which they had often been unable to attend due to their pastoral commitments and lack of funds. While at first the superintendents enjoyed attending the General Council meetings, this changed as they realized that their districts were often treated in a very well-intended but still paternalistic manner as an internal colony and home missionary enterprise that was not considered central or important to the larger national General Council of the Assemblies of God. This led not only to disappointment, but also to frustration and eventually to a desire to speak out and exercise their own authority, voice, and agency in the national AG administrative body.

Girón made a number of important contributions to the growth and development of the Latino AG. Like Bazan before him, he promoted personal and citywide evangelism, revivals, and church planting. He was the first superintendent, with the help of Epifanio Jaramillo, to create the "Church Extension Plan" program, specifically aimed at raising funds for the construction of new Latino AG churches, often through

"Penny" and tamale fund-raising drives. He also sought to meet the needs of the ministers, sometimes taking money out of his own pocket to help others. This was the case for one pioneer Fresno pastor, to whom he sent a $100 personal check after the pastor's wife had a baby, a quiet act that, once it became known, won him the praise of countless ministers. The news of his self-sacrificial generosity in this instance and many others enabled him to win the hearts and loyalty of the pastors and people.[30]

Girón's background also led him to place a premium on education. During his administration, he and Epifanio Jaramillo, Juan Romero, José Leyva, and Alex Bazan (son of Demetrio and Nellie) pioneered new educational programs. In 1962, they set up the first National Latino AG Sunday School standards and curriculum, which were actually more popular in Latin America because U.S.-born children preferred to speak in English. This was the first major revision to the format of the Sunday school curriculum since its 1935 initiation. They also translated into Spanish more General Council books, literature, tracts, and Sunday school material in order to promote greater theological harmony with the mother organization. In 1966, in order to build on the work pioneered by Bazan, Girón installed the first District Missionary Secretary (Alex Bazan), a Pastoral Appreciation Program, and oversaw the formal separation of the Spanish Eastern Convention into its own stand-alone Spanish Eastern District in 1956. In all of these labors, he continued to build on the foundation laid by Bazan.

Despite Girón's measured steps, he also realized that it was time for the Latino AG to fulfill the dreams of Olazábal, Bazan, and countless others before him by separating each convention into its own district on a par with Euro-American AG districts. This was a risky proposition, but the African American and Mexican American civil rights movements, along with growing demands for equal rights by former AG evangelists like Reies López Tijerina, were beginning to have their quiet effect on Latino AG leaders and how they viewed their agency and role in the AG. The past history of their struggle for voice and agency, along with the struggles currently taking place in society, created an environment ripe for sweeping changes. This was not easy to accept because many Latino pastors and other leaders liked change in small, measurable doses. However, Girón realized that he and the Latino AG could not continue to grow at its present pace and still remain a marginalized movement in the larger parent organization. The AG and Latinos had to change with the times.

At the 46th District Council Convention in Albuquerque, New Mexico, on August 19–21, 1970, Girón announced that he planned to step down as superintendent. As De Leon notes in *The Silent Pentecostals,* on page 130, he gave three reasons. First, despite all of his labors, the Latino AG "was not satisfying the needs of the people," for there were too many ministers and churches for good supervision, and the one district with four conventions was overextended geographically. Second, he wanted to focus on evangelism and the Charismatic renewal sweeping the nation, rather than administering the district. And finally, he felt a very strong impression from God that he should resign. It was time for new blood and fresh leadership.

Birth of Latino Districts, 1971–Present

The ministers were shocked. They asked him to remain as superintendent. Realizing he was exhausted by his work, the district gave him two months' paid vacation and a $1,000 love offering. He agreed to stay on for another year provided that they agree to his proposals, especially the one that called on them to divide the four conventions into separate districts, each with its own full-time superintendent and administrative support system. This would provide better creativity, oversight, and accountability, all of which he believed would enable the movement to grow and prosper. Despite the fact that Girón's Latin District Council in the Southwest had witnessed remarkable growth, increasing to 403 churches, 827 ministers, and 25,000 members in 1970, the Council agreed to his conditions.[31]

They relayed their decision to the General Presbyter in Springfield, Dr. Thomas Zimmerman. He agreed. So at the 47th District Council meeting on November 10–11, 1971, they formally freed each convention to transform itself into a full district on a par with Euro-American districts. The four districts and superintendents were Josue Sánchez of the Gulf District (142 churches, 254 ministers), Nestor Bazan of the Central Latin District (92 churches, 163 ministers), Zeferino Caballo of the

Midwest Latin District (37 churches, 46 ministers), and José Girón of the Pacific Latin District (142 churches, 364 ministers). Archie Martínez was named superintendent of the LABIs. The Texas school would serve the Gulf, Central, and Midwestern Districts and the California school the Pacific District. From among these men, Girón was elected president of the Latin American District Cooperation and A. F. Vigil, secretary. Girón was asked to help write the new regionally influenced constitutions for the four districts. Including the Spanish Eastern District, there were now five independent and autonomous Latino districts in the Assemblies of God, all on a par with their Euro-American counterparts, at least in theory.

At their historic November 1971 District meeting, the AG official from Springfield faced the new district superintendents and read the Scriptures that described the mandate that Moses gave to Joshua before he entered the Promised Land. In the name of the Lord, he called on the superintendents to evangelize and occupy the land and build new churches for the Kingdom of God and his people. There were now not one but five generals in the fields of the Lord. In his last sermon as Latin District Superintendent, Girón declared that the three roads that would lead to spiritual success and prosperity in the future were the "high spirituality in the life of the ministry and laymen alike," "evangelizing the lost at all cost[s]," and promoting a "better trained ministry" and "losing the fear of an educated clergy."[32]

At the next General Council Convention in August 1973, the AG Euro-American leader welcomed the four new districts and their superintendents into the AG and extended the right hand of fellowship. He proudly stood before the General Convention and declared: "A foreign-language district shall have the same privileges and responsibilities which are accorded district councils within the framework of this constitution and by-laws."[33] History was made. It had been a long time coming.

Girón's proposition was a major turning point in the history of the Latino AG movement. The once marginalized and segregated Latino AG was now fully integrated into nationally recognized districts. As a result of this development, each superintendent and district not only took on more ownership of the work and began to compete with the others in a friendly way for converts and church plants, but also now sent five representatives to the AG General Council meetings and thus started the process of laying out a vision for exercising greater voice and agency within their parent organization. The dream of the first generation of Latino AG pastors led by Olazábal, Flores, Bazan, and Girón had finally come to pass.[34] They would be silent no more.

Growth and Development of the Hispanic Districts

The new leadership structure and tighter governing system seemed to work well and bound the Latino districts together in a spirit of unity with each other and with the larger General Council. This newfound freedom, responsibility, and agency unleashed a new generation of leaders who had to draw on their own creativity to reach the millions of Latinos throughout the United States. This had three key results. First, it forced the new districts to mobilize and bring fresh people into their offices. They needed men and women who were willing to pioneer new works within their districts. They also needed fresh ideas. They had to recruit, disciple, and train their own pastors, evangelists, Christian workers, and Sunday school, youth, and women's leaders. Second, Latinos used every possible cultural, intellectual, and material resource at their disposal to convert the lost and to disciple them, since they could no longer count on any financial support from the former Latino AG District or Springfield. As a result, they not only had traditional revivals, evangelistic crusades, and camp meetings, but also dramas, musicals, plays, and skits—all aimed at reaching the next generation of youth. This variety spawned Latino Pentecostal rock, pop, rap, and hip-hop music and spurred the production of biographies, autobiographies, autobiographical histories, hymns, and poetry. In short, the birth of the Latino districts resulted in a religious and cultural renaissance that is active to this day.

The third major result was the phenomenal growth of the Latino AG movement. This growth has in turn forced the existing "Latin" districts (Spanish Eastern, Pacific, Gulf, Midwest, Central, Puerto Rico) created in 1956 and 1971 to split into fourteen districts today, with one more projected in the near future, largely created in light of geography and size. In 2014, these districts included the Northwest Hispanic District (NHD), Northern Pacific Latin American District (NPLAD),

Southern Pacific District (SPD), Southwest District (SD), Central District (CD), Midwest Latin American District (MLAD), West Texas and Plains District (WTPD), Texas Gulf Spanish District (TGSD), South Central Hispanic District (SCHD), Texas Louisiana Hispanic District (TLHD), Florida Multicultural District (FMD), Southern Latin District (SLD), Spanish Eastern District (SED), and Puerto Rico District (PRD) (see Figure 6.3).[35]

These districts are presently led by the following superintendents: Hilario Garza (NHD), Roger Ovalle (NPLAD—see Figure 6.5), Sergio Navarrete (SPD—see Figure 6.4), Tony Martínez (SD), Dennis Rivera (CD), Clemente Maldonado Jr. (MLAD), Ezequiel Pecina (WTPD), Dino Espinoza (TGSD), José Marines (SCHD), Eleazer Rodríguez Jr. (TLHD), Saturnino González (FMD), David Zayas (SLD), Manny Alvarez (SED), and Juan H. Suárez (PRD).

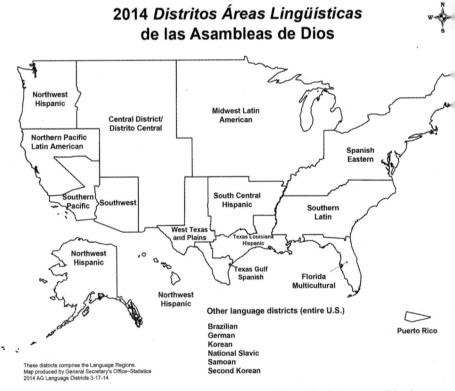

2014 *Distritos Áreas Lingüísticas* de las Asambleas de Dios

Figure 6.3. Map depicts fourteen Latino Assemblies of God Language Districts, 2014. (Assemblies of God, General Secretary's Office–Statistics, 2014)

Figure 6.4.   Southern Pacific District, ca. 2006. Front row (left to right): Rev. Evie Torres, Silvia Martínez, Rev. Silvia Carrizo, Claudia Martínez, Dr. John Perea, Janice Navarrete, Rev. Betty Torres, Jennifer Hernández, Nora Landaverde, Naomi Gamez, and Yanina Espinosa. Back row (left to right): José Beltrán, Rev. Aureliano Flores, Rev. José Luis Camal, Rev. Raul Castro, Danny de León Jr., Rev. Manny Rodríguez, Superintendent Dr. Sergio Navarrete, Rev. José A. Espinosa, Rev. Dimas Flores, Rev. Louis Ortiz, Sammy Ortiz, Jesse Díaz, and Izzy Gamez.   (Southern Pacific District of the Assemblies of God)

The decentralization of the Latino AG movement has led to the unleashing of charisma, innovation, and an entrepreneurial spirituality and a friendly but competitive outlook, since every district rises or falls on the vision, determination, and hard work of its superintendents and his staff and parishioners, who must be persuaded to get behind the leader's vision if the district is to thrive. This highlights a very important principle in religious growth, and that is that the decentralization of charisma often results in the mobilization and development of not just one set of leaders required to run one solitary district, as in Ball's day, but in this case fourteen different districts—each with its own staff and set of leaders, from superintendent on down to the women's council leader,

Figure 6.5. Northern Pacific Latin American District, ca. 2007. Front row (left to right): Rev. Hortencia Noss, Rev. Lee Baca, Rev. Maria Del Pilar Garza. Back row (left to right): Rev. Samuel Rodríguez, Rev. Ramiro Quiroz, Rev. Jesse Galindo, Dr. Richard Tañon, Rev. Wayne Scott, Rev. John A. Gallegos II, Superintendent Rev. Rogelio Ovalle. (Northern Pacific Latin American District of the Assemblies of God)

district youth leader, and so on. This results in higher rates and levels of parishioner mobilization and leadership development and forces people with limited budgets and resources to engage in creative and highly relational outreach, that makes them more sensitive to the needs and trends of rank-and-file parishioners, whom their movements need to survive and thrive. Of course it is equally possible—and no doubt a reality in some cases—that some of these districts could collapse from a lack of leadership and resources. However, this is unlikely because they believe they are divinely called and empowered by God to fulfill their tasks, no matter how challenging and difficult. They can use and invoke this divine calling to leverage the talent of others to build up and develop their respective districts and weather the storms of doubt and conflicts they will no doubt face in the future.

This decentralization principle, along with high degrees of autonomy and entrepreneurial freedom, helps to explain why the Latino AG has grown so rapidly throughout the past fifty years despite not having big-name crusade evangelists, revivalists, megachurch pastors, and divine healers to lure in prospective converts. In fact, this is one of the most startling facts about the Latino AG—the complete lack of huge mega-churches one would think would drive this kind of growth. In many ways, the Latino AG is a Marxist-socialist dream because it succeeded in empowering ordinary people to create an international grassroots movement that has leveled the playing field for the poor, oppressed, and working class. However, another way to look at this movement is the realization of an Acts 2:42–47 house-to-house paradigm of church growth where they:

> devoted themselves to the apostles' teaching and to the fellowship, to the breaking of bread and to prayer . . . and many wonders and miracles signs were done . . . [and] all of the believers . . . had everything in common . . . they gave to anyone as he had need. . . . And they broke bread in their homes and ate together with glad and sincere hearts, praising God and enjoying the favor of all the people. And the Lord added to their number daily those who were being saved. (NIV)

Regardless of the origin, rationale, and impact of these new districts, their creation has mobilized new leadership structures, friendly competition, and ministerial innovation, all of which has led to growth. By 2014, there were 2,665 Latino Assemblies of God churches and missions across the United States and Puerto Rico. Latino AGs make up 9 percent of all Protestants, 23 percent of all Catholics who converted to Protestantism, and 37 percent of all Catholics who converted to Pentecostalism.[36]

In fact, for the past twenty years, it has largely been the Latino AG and other racial-ethnic districts that have enabled the larger General Council to show positive growth rates. The Euro-American AG districts are in slight decline, and if it were not for the growth of Latinos and racial-ethnic minority districts and minorities within their Euro-American district churches, many of them would report declining membership. This reflects a larger socio-demographic shift in the U.S. population. For example, in 2008, there were 418 identifiable Latino congregations in historically Euro-American-serving districts such as Southern California (95), North Carolina (33), and New Jersey (30). The growth of Latinos in the AG movement has resulted in there being at least one Latino AG congregation in forty-four of the nation's fifty states and in forty-five of the AG's fifty-seven districts. Thus Latinos are important not only for the contributions that the Latino Districts bring to the General Council, but also for the contributions they make within non-Latino districts, something often overlooked.

The New Latino Evangelicals: Jesse Miranda

Although each district is separate, Jesse Miranda has often served as a key leader in the development of the districts and as the main spokesperson for all of the districts at national meetings in Springfield. He was the first Latino elected an Executive Presbyter of the AG.

Miranda was promoted by the people to these positions because of his service to the Latino AG. Born on April 9, 1937, in Albuquerque, New Mexico, he worked closely with Bazan and Girón in New Mexico. He attended LABI in Ysleta (near El Paso), Vanguard University (B.A.), Talbot Theological Seminary (M.R.E.), California State University at Fullerton (M.Ed.), and Fuller Seminary (D.Min.), and completed graduate coursework for the Ph.D. in social ethics at the University of Southern California, but due to lack of funding and ministerial and family commitments was unable to finish his doctorate. He served as a pastor (1957–1959), secretary-treasurer (1973–1978), and assistant superintendent of what was then the Pacific Latin American District (PLAD) (1980–1984), and finally as superintendent of PLAD (1984–1992). He has also served as a national presbyter of the AG. Miranda, pictured in Figure 6.6, has taught at Azusa Pacific University, Fuller Seminary, and Vanguard University, and is the author of *Christian Church in Ministry* (1980) and coeditor of *Latino Religions and Civic Activism in the United States* (2005).[37]

In addition to his denominational and regional service, he also served as the leading Latino grassroots Protestant leader in the United States in

Figure 6.6.   Rev. Jesse Miranda, ca. 1990s.   (Flower Pentecostal Heritage Center)

the 1990s. In 1992, he founded the interdenominational Alianza de Ministerio Evangélicos Nacionales (AMEN) and directed this organization until it merged in 2006 with the National Hispanic Christian Leadership Conference (NHCLC), where he currently serves as Chief Executive Director. He has been invited to serve on the Lausanne Committee on World Evangelization, perhaps the largest interdenominational global Evangelical fellowship. In 1999, he and Virgilio Elizondo of the University of Notre Dame and the Mexican American Cultural Center were awarded a $1.3 million grant from The Pew Charitable Trusts to direct the Hispanic Churches in American Public Life (HCAPL) national study. This was the largest study in U.S. history to date on Latino religions, politics, and civic activism. To help solidify the role of Latino Pentecostals and Evangelicals in national politics, in 2002 he cofounded with Luís Cortés of Nueva Esperanza the National Hispanic Presidential Prayer Breakfast in Washington, D.C. Miranda has met with every president from Ronald Reagan to Barack Obama to promote faith-based initiatives for inner-city Latino and racial-ethnic minority churches. As a result of Miranda's lifetime of service, President Obama nominated him to serve on the White House Office of Faith-Based and Community Partnerships, although after three years in review he is still unconfirmed. This offended some Latino national leaders and led to the growing belief that Obama and his administration were using Latinos and Evangelicals for political gain without giving them any real agency and power in the administration. The fact that Obama also did not follow through with his pledge to pass comprehensive immigration reform in his first year in office when the Democratic Party controlled both the Senate and the House and that he changed his views on gay marriage led some Latino leaders to believe that Obama was not following through on his promises.[38]

More important for most Latino pastors and laity, Miranda is an excellent communicator, diplomat, and bridge-builder with Latinos, Euro-Americans, and African Americans outside of the Pentecostal and Latino communities. He is very gracious, soft-spoken, and stable—traits of many of the AG's most effective leaders. For all of these reasons, he has served as the Latino AG's most visible and effective grassroots leader in national denominational and U.S. politics.

For all of these reasons and others, Latinos should play an increasingly pivotal role in the AG. Despite their contributions, however, Latinos are still woefully underrepresented at virtually every level at the national headquarters in Springfield. General Superintendent George O. Wood attempted to take proactive steps to address these gaps, but not everyone was as progressive and forward looking on Latino issues as he was. The denomination's funding, for example, is still completely controlled by Euro-Americans and Latino Bible schools, and ministry projects are at the mercy of these denominational leaders. In short, although the AG has made major strides to accept and welcome Latinos into the mainstream apparatus of the movement, they have yet to give them the denominational representation that their numbers, labors, and churches warrant.

This invisibility and ongoing frustration were evident in 1989 when at the 75th General Convention of the Assemblies of God a historical documentary video was shown at the General Presbytery meeting. For over an hour the four Latino district superintendents watched the story of Euro-American AG leaders without a single reference to Latinos. Afterward, the Latino superintendents walked away and asked, "Where were we in this historical portrait?" Almost twenty-five years later, little had changed. In 2013, the AG commissioned a short history of the denomination. Jesse Miranda and other Latino leaders were shocked to see that not a single reference was made to H. C. Ball or any Latino leaders. The history mentioned only Alice Luce, in part because the AG wanted to spotlight the contributions of women, since it has been heavily criticized in the past for downplaying them. Equally disheartening, while the documentary mentioned the names of female and young district superintendents, not a single one of the then nine Latino district superintendents or any Latinos were mentioned by name, according to Jesse Miranda, who reviewed the first draft of the history. Latinos were invisible. Miranda recommended that the author revise the book in light of literature he sent him on the Latino AG.[39]

This chapter has highlighted the role that Mexican American leaders like Demetrio Bazan and José Girón played in the development of the movement from 1939 to 1971 and the ongoing struggles Latinos face in the national denomination. The Latino AG has exploded in growth from 1971 to the present. This is in part due to the decentralization of the movement, which invariably unleashed an entire new generation of leadership for each and every district, all of which created more buy-in and ownership for each district. Today there are fourteen districts, with one more planned, for a total of fifteen districts. The growth of the Latino districts has been able to keep the larger Assemblies of God in the black, for without them and other ethnic districts the AG would show a net loss in national membership. Despite these facts and the effective leadership by Jesse Miranda and Saturnino González (both Executive Presbyters who sit on the General Council Executive Board), Latinos are still struggling for proportional voice and representation within the General Council.

CHAPTER 7

We Preach the Truth

Azusa Street and Puerto Rican Pentecostal Origins and Expansion

W HILE H. C. BALL WAS BRINGING independent Mexican Pente-costal missions together at the first and second Mexican Pente-costal convention in South Texas in 1918, a Puerto Rican evangelist named Juan Lugo was preaching his own version of the truth on the beautiful island of Puerto Rico. Following the strategy of countless evangelists, Lugo found a street corner in the densely populated city of Ponce on the southern part of the island and then led his small band of followers in singing several hymns and sharing powerful testimonies about how Jesus Christ could save even the most terrible of sinners. Lugo wrote:

> When we finished singing the hymn "We Preach the Truth," we had a crowd [of more than 400] around us. Many of them had heard the Gospel preached in different churches with pompous ceremony and imposing austerity. Now it was presented to them in a different way. . . . Hymns sung with true happiness, testimonies of the marvelous works of God . . . Christian doctrine explained in simple words within reach of all, stories of how God had gloriously redeemed the most horrible sinners and changed them into new creatures. All these things aroused the interest of the audience.[1]

The evangelistic outreach of Juan Lugo and his future wife Isabel (who are pictured in Figure 7.1) attracted nominally Catholic Puerto Ricans by the hundreds and then eventually thousands. His story challenges a number of prevailing assumptions and stereotypes about the origins and development of Puerto Rican Pentecostalism, such as the notion that it was founded and organized by Euro-American missionaries. As with the Mexican AG work in the Southwest, Puerto Rican Pentecostalism was founded by native Puerto Ricans, but unlike in the Southwest, it was never controlled by Euro-American

Figure 7.1. Juan and Isabel Lugo are shown in the front row (second and third from right) at the Seventh Annual Latino AG Convention in San Jose, California, 1923. First row (left to right): Rev. George and Rev. Francisca Blaisdell, Rev. Domingo Cruz, Rev. Juan and Rev. Isabel Lugo, Rev. Jovita Bonilla. Second row (right to left): Rev. Alice Luce, Rev. Francisco Nevarez; the others are unknown. Also present but unidentified: Rev. José Leyva, Rev. Abram Lincoln Vargas, Rev. Juan Aquina, Rev. L. Rodríguez, Rev. Luis Caraballo, and others. H. C. Ball is in the back row on the far left. This image appeared on the front cover of the *Pentecostal Evangel* on February 9, 1924. (Flower Pentecostal Heritage Center)

missionaries. The Puerto Rican Pentecostal movement was almost completely run and developed by natives themselves. In fact, the movement began first among Puerto Rican migrant laborers and sugarcane cutters in the diaspora in Hawaii and northern California and then spread to Puerto Rico.[2] However, this story also challenges another long-standing belief that Juan Lugo was the first to preach Pentecostalism in Puerto Rico, when it was actually a Euro-American missionary evangelist from an Azusa Street daughter mission named Jennie Mishler who first began preaching on the island in 1909. However, despite her labors she left no lasting work; for this reason, it is accurate to assert that Juan Lugo and Puerto Ricans were the driving force behind the organization of the AG on the island and its subsequent evangelization. Finally, despite claims by some scholars that the movement grew slowly in the early years, the primary source evidence indicates that it actually grew by over 1,000 percent between 1920 and 1940.

The Pentecostal movement's phenomenal growth was due to its emphases on prayer, missions, church planting, personal evangelism, evangelistic-healing crusades, leadership development through theological education, raw courage in the face of fierce obstacles, and a firm conviction that "we preach the truth" about God's love, forgiveness, and plan for people's lives. At a larger sociological level, its growth was also due to the weakened state of Roman Catholicism on the island and because its spirituality resonated with the religious and cultural grammar already present in Puerto Rican folk Catholicism, Spiritualism, and Spiritism, with their emphases on the supernatural, divine healing, and spiritual warfare.

Lugo's story, along with that of Puerto Rican Pentecostalism, has not been fully told before in English because the Puerto Rican work was never under the jurisdiction of H. C. Ball and Alice E. Luce and because the sources are admittedly sparse and difficult to secure. Most of the early sources are lost, and almost all of the secondary literature is written by denominationally sponsored Pentecostal writers in Spanish.[3] This story is important because it provides insight into the Latino AG movement in the United States and Puerto Rico.[4]

Precursors to Juan Lugo: Jennie Mishler and Gerald Bailley, 1909–1912

The Pentecostal message first arrived in Puerto Rico after Jennie Mishler from Elmer Fisher's Upper Room Mission in Los Angeles received a calling and commission to spread Pentecostalism to Puerto Rico. Although the documentary evidence is sketchy, in June 1909 Pastor Elmer Fisher and his ministerial team commissioned her to evangelize Puerto Rico. She ministered on the island for at least fifteen months. Mishler wrote to Fisher in 1910, lamenting her lonely struggle to win converts. "I am standing alone, as Elijah on Mt. Carmel . . . I desire . . . that God will send me a helper."[5]

Mishler's ministry ran into trouble after she began attracting Catholics in Santa Isabel. The priest and lay leaders began ridiculing her and persecuting anyone who attended her evangelistic services; the priest organized a brass band, lit gasoline lamps for new alternative evening Masses, purchased new decorations for the church, and increased the number of Masses and novenas the church offered each week, she wrote. In addition to such priestly opposition, male Catholic lay leaders used their connections to create a hostile environment. Feeling blocked at every turn, Mishler lamented in September 1910 that the unrelenting opposition broke up her small band of followers and "caused the interested ones to fall back" to Catholicism. She asked for spiritual reinforcements for the battle she faced on a daily basis, but after her long and lonely battle decided to leave Puerto Rico. Although she did not leave any permanent mission or band of followers behind, this was the first or one of the first times the Pentecostal message was preached in Puerto Rico.[6]

However, Gerald Bailley, a Christian and Missionary Alliance (CMA) missionary to Venezuela in 1896, may have responded Mishler's call, because he arrived in Puerto Rico shortly thereafter. Bailley had received the baptism with the Holy Spirit and was influenced by William J. Seymour's Azusa Street Revival and Elmer Fisher's Upper Room Mission, where he no doubt heard about and perhaps even met Mishler and read her "Cry from Puerto Rico" report in *The Upper Room*. He visited Puerto Rico on one of his return trips to Venezuela and at some point took four Puerto Ricans back with him to Venezuela to prepare them to evangelize Latin America after attending his Bible school near Los Teques, outside of Caracas. In 1912, four of the eight students were Puerto Rican; several of them, like Castulo Rivera, went on to Colon, Panama, to pioneer the work among Amerindians in 1917, after which time Bailley was forced out of the CMA because of its opposition to tongues as the evidence of the baptism with the Holy Spirit. Despite his outreach, he did not organize or plant a permanent Pentecostal mission in Puerto Rico.[7]

Azusa Street, Lugo, and Puerto Rican Pentecostal Origins

One year after Jennie Mishler's lament from Puerto Rico, William J. Seymour commissioned a group of Azusa Street missionaries led by Thomas Anderson and David A. Barth to spread Pentecostalism to China and Japan. During their stopover in Oahu in the spring of 1911, they conducted evangelistic services in the Puerto Rican migrant labor camp and preached Seymour's Azusa Street Revival message about the outpouring and baptism with the Holy Spirit. One of the first persons the Azusa missionaries converted was a thirty-one-year-old illiterate sugarcane cutter named Francisco Decena Ortiz, or Francisco Sr. Recognizing his leadership talent, the missionaries appear to have ordained him to the ministry on November 15, 1911. They taught him Seymour's views on the baptism with the Holy Spirit, the spiritual gifts, divine healing, evangelism, End Times Bible prophecy, and personal holiness. Ortiz converted many to Seymour's Azusa message, including his son Frank Ortiz Jr. ("Panchito"), Juana Lugo (mother of Juan Lugo), Solomon and Dionisia Feliciano, and a number of others. Ortiz opened the first Puerto Rican Pentecostal mission in history right there on the plantation. His conversion and mission planting mark the official birth of the permanent Puerto Rican Pentecostal movement. They also establish a direct spiritual connection between Seymour's Azusa Street Revival and the birth of the Puerto Rican Pentecostal movement.[8]

Although Ortiz played a key role in the first five years of the movement in Hawaii and later in the San Francisco Bay Area from 1911 to 1916, he is not considered the main founder and developer of the movement in Puerto Rico itself, since he lived and ministered primarily in

Hawaii and northern California. This title instead goes to one of Ortiz's first converts, a twenty-two-year-old sugarcane cutter named Juan Lugo.[9]

Conversion of Lugo in the Puerto Rican Diaspora in Hawaii, 1913

Lugo was born to Juana Lugo in Yauco, Puerto Rico, in 1890.[10] Two years after the U.S.-Spanish War of 1898, Juana responded to an American employment advertisement by sugarcane growers for laborers in Hawaii. This decision was driven by Hurricane San Ciriaco, which ripped through the island in August 1899, leaving 3,400 dead and thousands without food, shelter, and work. Because the storm destroyed Puerto Rico's sugarcane economy, it created a spike in demand for sugar grown in the Hawaiian Islands and helped birth the Puerto Rican diaspora as islanders either sailed there via South America or made their way there through New York, New Orleans, Los Angeles, and San Francisco, where some stayed and created Puerto Rican communities. To meet this labor demand in Hawaii, American companies began advertising in Puerto Rico. In 1900 and 1901, the Hawaii Sugar Planters Association shipped in 5,000 Puerto Rican men, women, and children. By 1902, over 1,700 Puerto Ricans were working on thirty-four plantations. Around 1900, Juana, her ten-year-old son Juan, and her sister were part of this migration and left for Oahu. Unable to speak English, she found work as a maid, earning just ten dollars a month. Her precarious financial situation and other frustrations created what Juan later called an "unhappy childhood." Despite her desire for him to finish elementary school, Juan was forced to drop out in the fourth grade to cut cane—backbreaking work. Their financial plight was not ameliorated until Juana remarried while living in Oahu.[11]

In 1912, Francisco Ortiz invited Juana to a Pentecostal evangelistic service. Reportedly surprised and amazed at the energy, love, and down-to-earth otherworldliness of the services, she later converted. Juana immediately set out to win over her cigarette-smoking prodigal son, now living in Kauai. After a long period of letter writing, wherein Juana related the "fantastic joy" she felt, Juan finally returned home to Oahu to placate his mother. She won him over not so much by her words, Lugo later said, but rather by her deeds and ethical behavior. As long as he could remember, his mother had always had a cigarette dangling from her mouth. Now she not only had given up smoking, she also sang Christian praise songs constantly while cooking in the kitchen—something he found positive but annoying. After some prodding, Juan finally agreed to attend church, where almost immediately he was accepted as one of the family. Although not yet converted, he was swept up into the enthusiasm and singing and began attending all of the services. Still, he thought the church was a woman's sphere and something used to domesticate men, and Juan wasn't ready to give up his lifestyle.[12]

A major turning point came in 1913 when Abed Vélez, a "notorious sinner," converted. His conversion caught Lugo by surprise. Their lunch breaks in the stifling hot cane fields, which were once filled with big talk about gambling, vice, and women, now turned to stories of faith, healing, and heaven and hell. What really irritated Lugo was Vélez's insistence that he (Lugo) read aloud the New Testament—because Vélez couldn't read. All of the verses just coincidentally had to do with sin and salvation! Lugo knew he was being preached to. He was a captive audience. He enjoyed his friendship and wasn't willing to give it up over a few Bible passages. However, one passage in particular caught his attention—John 5:24—which Vélez asked him to read very slowly: "Verily, verily, I say unto you, He that heareth my word, and believeth on him that sent me, hath everlasting life, and shall not come into condemnation; but is passed from death unto life."

As Lugo meditated on the passage, he reported that a "feeling of guilt flooded my soul" and with it the conviction that he was spiritually dead to the things of God. He wrote that he realized he was a sinner headed straight to hell. He asked Velez if he could borrow the little New Testament and stole away to read it again and again, to meditate on its message. "He . . . that believeth on him . . . shall not come into condemnation; but is passed from death unto life," Lugo read. For the first time in his life he could finally see his state before an all-holy, all-loving, and almighty God, he later wrote. On June 13, 1913, he answered the divine call and asked Jesus Christ to forgive his sins and become his savior and lord. Lugo was born again. After a lengthy all-night prayer vigil to purify his body, mind, and spirit, Lugo was baptized at Waikiki Beach on June 29.

A few weeks later he was baptized with the Holy Spirit. A new chapter was about to be written not only in Lugo's life, but also in the story of Pentecostalism, Latino religions, and American religious history.[13]

Lugo's conversion was more than just a decision to join a new religion. It was a rite of passage into Pentecostal and Evangelical Christianity. In fact, the central message of the Pentecostal movement was that a person must be "born again" or spiritually reborn to enter the Kingdom of Heaven. This conversionist religion stood in contrast to Lugo's Roman Catholic upbringing, which took a lifelong sacramental approach to salvation.

Lugo interpreted the Spirit baptism as an enduement of power to prepare him for some special work in the future. He wrote, "Even in my ignorance about the work of God—I was still very young in the faith—I could understand that the power God was giving me had to be used for His glory and honor in some unique way that He would show me."[14] Lugo wrote that there was no such thing as chance or fate. God had a plan for his life and used prayer and ordinary events, circumstances, and open and closed doors to communicate his will. During a time in prayer and quiet meditation, Lugo reportedly heard God calling him to California. As a result, on November 9, 1913, Lugo and Francisco and Panchito Ortiz boarded a sailing ship to San Francisco in search of work and the will of God.

Puerto Rican Pentecostalism Spreads to California, 1913–1916

Although Lugo and the Ortizes were unable to find any Spanish-speaking Pentecostal missions in San Francisco, they did find a small Portuguese Pentecostal church pastored by Rodolfo Lima on Columbus Street in San Francisco. They attended for a while because, although Lima primarily targeted Portuguese-speaking immigrants, he also evangelized the Spanish-speaking. Before Lima, Cape Verde Islander Adolph Rosa attended the Azusa Street Revival and then brought the Pentecostal message back to the Portuguese and Spanish-speaking communities around San Francisco.[15]

After joining Lima's church, Lugo and the Ortizes began conducting open-air evangelistic services on the street corners of the most vice-infested sections of San Francisco. Shortly after they began their ministry, a group of drunken sailors offended at Ortiz's preaching rushed over and began beating him. The police rushed over to intervene, which Lugo and the Ortizes interpreted as a sign of divine protection, and they continued their street evangelism.[16]

During Lugo's attempt at preaching the Pentecostal message, he realized that he did not know the Bible or doctrine very well. Because there were no Spanish-speaking Pentecostal Bible schools in the Bay Area, he began to read Pentecostal literature and sought out people to teach him the Bible and doctrine. His first and most important teacher was Mrs. Elsie Johnson, who tutored Lugo in the Bible and theology while he lived with her family in Santa Rosa, California. In 1914, a "sister Brown" also tutored Lugo at a small makeshift Bible school that met in her home, likewise in Santa Rosa. He also learned about the Bible and Pentecostal doctrine and healing through the ministry of George and Carrie Judd Montgomery, and about divine healing through them and the ministry of Maria Woodworth-Etter. He attended one of Woodworth-Etter's evangelistic-healing services in San Francisco and was reportedly healed.[17]

Yet the person who had the greatest influence on Lugo was Assemblies of God leader Stanley F. Frodsham. Lugo devoured his writings and sat under his tutelage when he ministered in the San Francisco Bay Area. Lugo read Frodsham's history of the early Pentecostal movement, *With Signs Following*. It had such a profound impact on his faith and missionary consciousness that he later translated it into Spanish and assigned it at Mizpa Bible school, which he later started in Puerto Rico.[18]

Lugo's contact with Euro-Americans proved decisive in two ways: it helped him to come to terms with his Puerto Rican–U.S. identity, and prompted him to consider taking the Pentecostal message to his native Puerto Rico. A turning point came the same day Lugo was healed by Woodworth-Etter: he reportedly fell into a trance and received a calling to evangelize Puerto Rico. Lugo recalled:

> While I was stretched out on the floor under the power of God, the Lord took me in the Spirit to a high hill at the base of which was spread out a large city . . . the Spirit showed me that the city which I now saw was Ponce. . . . That was the place where I would have to

go now to take the message of health. God told me to go, and the joy in my heart was indescribable.[19]

Although Lugo was happy that God had clearly communicated to him, he was not very happy about returning to Puerto Rico. Now twenty-five years old, he had spent the last fifteen years in Hawaii and California. He was just as much an American in many ways as he was Puerto Rican. Unready to act upon God's will for his life, he pushed the vision to the back of his mind and moved to San Jose, California, where his family had relocated and Ortiz was co-pastoring a multiethnic Pentecostal church with a Euro-American AG pastor.[20]

Although not interested in returning to Puerto Rico, he was still very interested in the ministry. He and the Ortizes decided to become or-dained ministers in the Assemblies of God. After much prayer and pub-lic encouragement by his pastoral mentors, in 1916 Lugo decided to be-come a missionary to the Spanish-speaking. Frodsham ordained the three men on January 16, 1916, in San Jose, California.[21]

Eager to evangelize the throngs of Latinos pouring into California, Lugo and Ortiz Jr. traveled south to Los Angeles, where they began preaching to Mexican immigrants in the Mexican Plaza near Olvera Street. They made a small number of Mexican converts. However, after two months of ministry, family and financial considerations forced Pan-chito to return to San Jose. Lugo stayed behind to continue the ministry—alone. He found the task of leading the small band of Mexican followers very difficult, closed the mission, and returned north.[22]

Although their mission lasted only a few months, it gave them a taste of the rocky road that lay ahead. Converts had to be won over one at a time. They had to be discipled, a difficult task given that so many had to follow the seasonal harvests. In addition to their evangelistic work in Los Angeles, Lugo and Panchito fortuitously came into contact with Bethel Temple, the largest AG church in the city. They attended its youth-group meetings and gave their testimonies. Given the general ex-citement about foreign missions in early Pentecostal culture, Lugo also shared the vision about one day evangelizing in Puerto Rico. In an unex-pected turn of events, the youth leader, Hulda Needham, the senior pas-tor's daughter, claimed that God had revealed to the youth group through an interpretation of tongues that He wanted Lugo to go to Puerto Rico—immediately![23]

The revelation took the now bright-eyed Lugo by surprise. He was used to *talking* about his vision without having to act on it. He decided to cave in to what he and his companions viewed as the will of God. There was one snag; Lugo said, half-sheepishly, that he did not have any money for the trip. To Lugo's surprise, Hulda said the youth group would raise the funds. And they did. He was happy about their confidence and their decision to permanently support his missionary work, but still dreaded the trip. After what seemed like a whirlwind of activity, on August 17, 1916, the youth group accompanied him to the train station, where he boarded a train for AG headquarters in St. Louis, Missouri, then traveled on to New York City and finally Puerto Rico.[24]

The Puerto Rican Religious Marketplace

The threat of Lugo and the Assemblies of God in Puerto Rico was real enough. Although Roman Catholicism had a virtual monopoly until the 1870s, Protestant churches were built for American and European businessmen. The Anglicans, for example, founded the first permanent Protestant Church in Puerto Rico on November 20, 1869, and built the first building in January 1873, just outside the city limits of Ponce. Despite the permission granted to the Anglican Church by the King of Spain, there were strict guidelines regulating Protestant activity.[25]

After the U.S.-Spanish War of 1898, the Roman Catholic monopoly over the island was broken. Puerto Rico became a U.S. territory through the Folkner Act in 1902 and had to abide by the U.S. Constitution, which protected freedom of expression and guaranteed the separation of church and state. This opened the floodgates to Protestant proselytism in Catholic Puerto Rico.[26] The separation of church and state also undermined the centuries-old Catholic monopoly over the island's politics, education, and religious marketplace. Now the Catholic Church had to compete for the hearts and souls of the people on an equal footing, though it still benefited from its 500-year presence on the island in countless other ways. Despite these advantages, the Catholic Church struggled to capitalize on them, because after the war many Spanish clergy fled to Latin America or Spain.[27] The exodus of priests in general was so great that by 1925 there were only twelve native Puerto Rican priests left on the entire island, whereas there were eighteen Puerto Rican Assemblies of God clergy. By 1935 the situation had not improved very much, as there were still only forty-five diocesan priests. The exodus of priests left many parish churches without anyone to administer the sacraments and protect the Catholic laity from proselytism.

The situation within the Catholic Church was further complicated by the fact that the U.S. government and the new Euro-American Catholic hierarchy made Americanization one of their primary goals and so imported Euro-American elementary and secondary school teachers, many of whom were Protestants.[28] The process of Americanization created the perception among Puerto Ricans that progress, upward mobility, and Protestantism were all part of becoming "a good American." This led to a generally uncritical reception of American imports. Jaime Vidal argues that prior to 1930 many Puerto Rican newspapers praised "everything American, from sports and fashions to political institutions, [as] better than its Spanish equivalent."[29] Indeed, "even on the issue of religion, Protestants had as one of their strongest cards the claim that Protestantism was 'the American religion,' associated with the values of progress and democracy embodied in the American ethos, while Catholicism was the religion of the defeated and authoritarian Spanish ethos."[30] As a result, a growing number began attending Protestant churches. The fact that Protestants established a beachfront in Puerto Rico made the transition to Pentecostalism that much easier.

Protestant denominations avoided competition by signing comity agreements, whereby they split up the island into geographical districts and assigned each district to one particular denomination. The Presbyterian, Baptist, Congregational, and Methodist denominations met for a historic prayer meeting in New York City in 1901. There they knelt around a map of Puerto Rico and prayed "that God might help us to enter Puerto Rico in such a way that there might never be any missionary hostility of any kind."[31] Then they divided the island, like spiritual booty, into sections, each board assuming responsibility for one of the sections.[32] Their goal was to "seek the best economy of operation and . . . to impress upon the people of Porto Rico the essential harmony and unity of our common Christianity."[33] Not long after, a growing number of other denominations began demanding a new agreement be drawn up to allow them to join. In 1905, the Federation of Evangelical Churches (later known as the Evangelical Union) was created by ten Protestant denominations, which agreed to systematically evangelize the island. By 1916, Protestant denominations had succeeded in planting churches in just about every coastal town.[34]

The Protestant work met stiff but sporadic opposition from the Catholic Church in the 1920s and 1930s, now somewhat emboldened by U.S. Catholic money, missionaries, and resources. Despite disease, religious skepticism and competition, and a language barrier, Protestant denominations continued to grow until 1915 when Puerto Rico was again divided by Protestant denominations in another comity agreement in which they agreed that the first denomination to establish a mission work in a particular town should have complete control over it until the town grew to over 7,000 residents, after which other denominations could enter.[35]

One of the reasons why the rapid growth of mainline Protestant denominations slowed after 1915 was that they reportedly shifted their emphasis away from evangelism to important social work such as setting up schools, hospitals, missions, and social programs for the poor. The downside to this shift was that the indigenization of the various denominations slowed because few Puerto Ricans had the educational background deemed necessary to teach, work in hospitals, or administer social programs. Furthermore, U.S. missionaries found it much easier to work in and control a mission, school, or hospital in the city than a mission in the *barrio* or the rural countryside, where poverty and disease made life difficult. The process of indigenization was also complicated by the fact that well into the 1930s almost 100 percent of the financial support to build churches and pay Christian workers came from the United States. This created a cycle of economic, spiritual, and intellectual dependency difficult to break in poverty-stricken Puerto Rico. Although there were clearly exceptions, they proved the rule.[36] Perhaps another reason the traditional Protestant growth slowed was because the mainline Protestants now had to compete with new and Puerto Rican-led indigenous movements like Pentecostalism.

By the time Juan Lugo and the Assemblies of God arrived in 1916, eighteen years after the first wave of Protestant missionaries had landed, not one mainline Protestant denomination or congregation was completely self-supporting. A year later things began to change. In 1916–1917, a three-month-long interdenominational evangelistic crusade was launched. In 1919, a number of Protestant denominations joined forces to create the Evangelical Seminary of Puerto Rico, which opened in Río Piedras under the leadership of James McAllister, a noted Euro-American Presbyterian missionary. One of the goals of the seminary was to train native Puerto Rican leaders. As Table 7.1 indicates, by 1916, Protestants claimed 14 church schools, 215 churches, 523 preaching points, and well over 20,000 members and 10,000 affiliates throughout the island.[37] Protestantism was on the island to stay. It was now a permanent fixture in the Puerto Rican religious marketplace.

Protestantism was not the only religion competing for the heart and soul of the people. Spiritism arrived on the island in 1859, and by 1903 its leaders had organized the Federation of Spirits in Mayagüez. The Spiritist movement grew rapidly between 1900 and 1940. By 1939, the Federation of Spiritists claimed more than 150 incorporated societies and thousands of followers, making it and its populist cousin, Spiritualism, two of the largest religious traditions on the island.[38] Spiritualist

Table 7.1.   Largest Protestant denominations in Puerto Rico, 1915

Denomination	Preaching points	Churches	Members	Sunday school
Methodist	132	55	3,218	6,577
Baptist	105	51	2,344	3,289
Presbyterian	115	34	2,675	2,369
United Brethren	40	15	1,252	1,614
Lutheran	21	9	455	1,500
Disciples of Christ	23	7	518	1,392
Congregational	30	11	728	1,197
Missionary Alliance	20	10	312	705
Reformed	10	6	949	327
Protestant Episcopal	12	9	551	696
Christian Church	15	5	248	608
Seventh-Day Adventist	—	3	141	191
Assemblies of God	0	0	0	0
Total	523	215	13,391	20,465

practices centered around an anthropomorphic God, candles, spiritually purified water, spiritual *passas* (laying on of hands), sacred altars,
prayers, images of the saints, spirit mediums, and healing.[39] The 1930
Brookings Institute Report on Puerto Rico observed:

> A large number of our peasants are Spiritualists. They hold meet-
> ings regularly in some barrios, where they gather in a certain house
> and sit around the table 'in meditation.' Then the president opens
> the sessions and spirits are [in]voked. These communicate, and the
> sitters then march in procession to another house. When people are
> ill, one of the so-called 'healing mediums' comes and through cer-
> tain symbolic signs conjures the spirits to depart and leave the suf-
> ferer in peace.[40]

The report further stated that Spiritualism was especially popular
among the poor. Many Spiritualist ritual practices such as the laying on
of hands, prayer for healing, and casting out spirits resembled similar
practices in Pentecostalism. This common religious grammar served as
an immediate cultural and religious bridge in the conversion of their followers to Pentecostalism. Puerto Ricans could have all of the benefits of
both the metaphysical and Protestant traditions. In this respect, Pentecostalism served as a structural *via media* that navigated between the
polarities of the experientialism of metaphysical traditions like Spiritualism and propositional rationalism of traditional Protestantism.

For its part, Spiritualism was far more widespread than the more scientific Spiritism, especially in rural mountainous regions. Spiritualism
consciously blended and combined Roman Catholic symbols, saints,
and traditions with Afro-Caribbean practices. Many Puerto Ricans saw
no major contradiction in attending Mass, a Spiritualist séance, and occasionally a Protestant evangelistic meeting, although such a combination was unusual for committed Protestants because they were taught
that Spiritualism and all metaphysical traditions were of the devil. The
Brookings Institute Report summarized the combinative attitudes of
many Puerto Ricans in the 1930s when it wrote: "Beside the Spiritualists, a large number of people, though members of the Catholic Church
or of a Protestant sect, attend Catholic, Protestant, and Spiritualist meetings indiscriminately. They say that these faiths are all good and that

they see no reason why they should not enjoy all of them."[41] For all this openness, Santería did not play a key role in Puerto Rican religion until after Fidel Castro came to power in Cuba in 1959, at which time large numbers of Cubans immigrated to Puerto Rico.[42]

Pentecostalism was a major competitor not only with Catholicism and traditional Protestantism, but also metaphysical traditions. Nestor Escudero, the official historian of the Spiritist movement in Puerto Rico, claims that the decline of Spiritism was directly linked to the growth of Pentecostalism. In his book on Spiritism, *Saints and Spirits,* David Hess confirmed this and even went so far as to argue, "The ultimate expression of the centrifugal tendency within Spiritism may not be a form of Spiritism at all, but Pentecostalism."[43]

While many Puerto Ricans were initially open to Protestantism and Americanization, by the early 1930s the honeymoon days were over. Many Puerto Ricans began to recognize that although they were in some respects better off under U.S. rule (e.g., in public education), their Spanish language and Puerto Rican traditions were at risk of being erased. Furthermore, many Puerto Ricans recognized that Puerto Rican identity was inextricably linked to the Spanish language and culture.

During the 1930s and 1940s, the charismatic Harvard-trained socialist Pedro Albizu Campos led the Independence Party. Along with Muñoz Marín, he dominated the political scene in the first half of the twentieth century. Campos was an ardent nationalist, took a strong anti-U.S. stand, and called for revolt against U.S. rule and independence for Puerto Rico. In 1937, Campos led an ill-fated nationalistic struggle for Puerto Rican independence. His call for independence led to protest and the "Ponce Massacre," in which government-backed police attacked the protesters after being goaded by their North American overseers. As a result, 17 people died and over 100 were wounded. Despite the revolt, Puerto Rican nationalism was far from dead and would continue to resurface and shape U.S.–Puerto Rican political, social, and religious relations throughout the century. Although Campos's nationalist sentiment did not free the island from U.S. control, it did lead to the election of the first Puerto Rican governor, Jesús T. Piñero, in 1946.[44] More important, it was a major obstacle for many Protestant denominations because they continued to be run by Euro-American missionaries, something that nationalists criticized.[45]

Spreading Pentecostalism to Puerto Rico, 1916–1920

Lugo's historic decision was a decisive turning point in the history of the Puerto Rican Pentecostal movement. Within a period of just twenty-four years (1916–1940), the Pentecostal movement went from being the smallest Protestant tradition on the island to the largest.

Lugo arrived in San Juan, Puerto Rico, on August 30, 1916. Like Jennie Mishler, he came alone and from Los Angeles. However, he had four distinct advantages: he was bilingual, he blended in, his message did not seem to be seen as foreign, as Mishler's had been, and he had prayer and financial support from Bethel Temple Assemblies of God.[46] Bolstered by this support, Lugo believed that God was providentially guiding his every step. In San Juan, he stayed with a "Sister Michaels." He learned about her through a person he met while staying in an AG missionary home run by Robert and Marie Brown of Glad Tidings AG Church in New York City. He made this connection when he visited J. R. Flower at AG headquarters in St. Louis, when he stopped off en route to Puerto Rico. On the advice of Flower, he immediately set out to secure legal permission to conduct evangelistic services from the interim governor of Puerto Rico, Martín Travieso, who granted his request. Lugo interpreted the governor's permission as evidence of God's leading: "I could see clearly how God had been opening the way for me. When I saw how He was going before me every step of the way, I felt new strength, greater enthusiasm, more confidence, and a growing desire to begin to speak of the wonders of the Lord to save souls who were perishing."[47] "I left the governor's room resolved to go to war against the devil, the world and the flesh, and certain beforehand of the victory that was assured me."[48]

Lugo's bold confidence was put to the test the very next night. On August 31, he preached his first sermon not far from Sister Michaels's home, on the corner of Figueroa and Parada Streets in Santurce, a suburb six miles outside San Juan. This first service was, in Lugo's words, "a stinging defeat." He took it hard. Sister Michaels interpreted the defeat as the result of diabolical intervention. After a time of fervent prayer, she predicted "glorious triumph" in the days ahead—if he persevered.[49]

Fortified by Sister Michaels's "prophecy," the very next night Lugo stubbornly went back to the same street corner to reportedly reclaim it for the Kingdom of God. He prayed, sang, and preached to anyone who passed by or glanced over in his direction. His enthusiasm attracted the attention of several curious adults and a few small children, some from the sprawling second-story balconies of the nearby apartment complex. The first ray of light came a few nights later, when he won over a group of eleven "Santomenan believers" from St. Thomas, Virgin Islands. For the next twenty-four nights in a row, Lugo and his newfound coworkers conducted open-air evangelistic campaigns on the street corners of Santurce. For Lugo, every corner was a pulpit and every Puerto Rican a sinner in need of a savior.[50]

The most powerful lure in Lugo's soul-saving arsenal was his message of salvation, divine healing, and a fresh start in life. He testified at every opportunity of the great and marvelous miracles God had wrought in his life and those of other believers.[51] This method was remarkably successful. Lugo's Pentecostal services were a combination of religious fiesta, drama, and modern-day talk show, complete with tears, fears, hopes, and miracles. Unlike most mainline Protestant and Catholic workers, Lugo and his followers took the Pentecostal message directly to the masses in the streets. The small band of Pentecostals had no churches, no tents, and no resources, they wrote, except the Bible, Holy Ghost power, and a passion to save souls from the fires of hell and the coming Armageddon.

The second major breakthrough came in November 1916. Although his street-corner evangelism was moving forward, he really wanted to preach in Ponce and thus fulfill his vision. Ponce was a city of approximately 80,000 and the major port city on the south side of the island. After conducting evangelistic campaigns throughout September and October in Santurce, Lugo left that task in the hands of his coworkers and traveled to Ponce on November 3, 1916. Shortly after he arrived, he was happy to find Solomon and Dionisia Feliciano who became Pentecostal in Hawaii.[52] They had arrived in Ponce on their way to the Dominican Republic, where they believed God had called them to pioneer the Pentecostal work.

After Lugo discovered that the Felicianos did not have enough money to leave right away, he asked them to assist his evangelistic work. They agreed. The trio began the first formal city-wide evangelistic campaign in Puerto Rico that same November 3 evening. On the corner of Aqueduct and Intendente Ramírez Streets, they conducted open-air evangelistic services, and through prayer, music, and impassioned preaching, attracted over eighty people a night.[53]

It was the tremendous conviction that Christ might return any day that propelled Lugo and the Felicianos to conduct nightly services for the next two months straight. Lugo claimed that he doubted there was a single street corner in Ponce that had not served as his pulpit. Indeed, these meetings sparked the first Pentecostal revival on the island. Scores of Puerto Ricans were converted at the nightly meetings. Ponce soon became the sacred center of the Pentecostal movement. At one of their first services, eleven people converted, including a local businessman named José Escamaroni and his wife. Lugo organized the first permanent Puerto Rican Pentecostal church on the island in an unfinished portion of the downstairs of the Escamaronis' home. The first Pentecostal water baptism took place on January 1, 1917, on the beach just outside Ponce. By September 1917, Lugo's mission had grown to over seventy followers. He wrote Hulda Needham at Bethel Temple on a regular basis, and she wrote back and the youth ministry continued to provide key financial support for his ministry.[54]

Conflict between Traditional Protestants and Pentecostals

Not everyone was happy about the open-air preaching of Lugo and the Felicianos, who found themselves at odds not only with Catholics, Spiritualists, and local hecklers who loved to mock and mimic the preachers, but also with smart and cultured Protestants whose criticisms were the sharpest of all. The traditional Protestants accused Lugo of syncretism, that is, of blending Christian beliefs with popular superstitions about divine healing and spirit possession. Lugo's lack of seminary credentials and Euro-American supervision (in contrast to the leaders of almost all of the Protestant churches on the island) made him a serious threat to the religious establishment. He was uncontrolled and unchained. This kind of unregulated, freelance Christianity enabled Lugo to cross denominational borders and boundaries with impunity—and they knew it. He was unaware of the comity agreement set up by the Protestants, who divided the island into sections in which they alone could minister. A comity is an agreement wherein all parties agree not to proselytize members of each other's traditions and that certain traditions have religious jurisdiction over a given area, community, or region. The only exception was cities of over 7,000 residents, in which case all denominations in the comity could evangelize and organize their own missions.

Lugo and his Pentecostal band were not invited to participate in the comity because the Protestants predated Lugo's arrival, nor would Lugo have ever agreed to do so. They reportedly preached wherever they felt led by the Spirit of God. Their message of salvation, divine healing, and the baptism with the Holy Spirit led some to accuse them of Spiritualism and Spiritism, two popular metaphysical movements on the island that emphasized bodily healing and ecstatic speech. Nothing could be further from the truth. Lugo and his followers viewed these movements as satanic counterfeits and, on regular occasions, engaged in criticisms against such beliefs and practices.[55]

The deeper reason behind the accusations was their success in attracting a large number of Protestants to their services. The rising tensions with Protestants led to open conflict in the fall of 1917. Solomon Feliciano's former Methodist pastor, Rev. Wilson, invited Solomon and Juan to hold revival meetings at his church. Wilson heard about Lugo's revival in Ponce and wanted the same in his own congregation. He felt comfortable asking Lugo and Feliciano because Solomon had once been a member of his congregation before he moved to Hawaii. Wilson was unaware of the fact that Solomon had since become a Pentecostal. He was shocked by Lugo's preaching on the baptism with the Holy Spirit. Rev. Wilson asked them to stop the crusade immediately. Just as he was about to claim victory, many of his parishioners left his church and began attending Lugo's revival services.[56]

Frustrated and angered by the loss of some of his parishioners, Wilson, along with several others, called a meeting of all the Protestant ministers in Ponce to discuss Lugo and the growing band of Pentecostal evangelists. Twenty-four Protestant ministers led by American missionaries called a further meeting and invited Lugo and the Felicianos to discuss joint evangelistic services in the city. Once there, the naive Pentecostals quickly discovered that it was an ambush. The Protestant ministers told Lugo and the Felicianos that they were "placing the Gospel on too low a level" and were also causing doctrinal confusion in the Protestant community. They lacked the proper theological educational and financial backing to do a lasting work on the island, the Protestants declared. In order to avoid further chaos in the Protestant community, they said it would be best for everyone involved if Lugo and the Felicianos stopped preaching and left the city at once. As an incentive, they offered Lugo a small mission and regular salary on another part of the island, and they offered to pay the Felicianos' travel fare to the Dominican Republic.

Offended by the condescending and paternalistic attitude, Lugo and the Felicianos politely—but firmly—rejected the proposal. When asked how he planned to minister and survive without a permanent salary, Lugo said that God would provide. He then stated, "Seek ye first the kingdom of God and His righteousness, and all these things shall be added unto you."[57]

Feeling snubbed by working-class sugarcane cutters, and like the Protestant reaction to the Azusa Street Revival in 1906, the frustrated American missionaries and their Puerto Rican coworkers lodged a complaint with the police in an effort to silence Lugo and his followers. They tried to use the law to regulate the spiritual marketplace. They claimed that Lugo and the Felicianos were "spoiling" their evangelistic efforts in the city. The police officials, however, found no evidence for the Protestants' accusations and in fact offered their implicit approval. Lugo and the Felicianos realized that they needed to legally incorporate their work or run the risk of more problems with less sympathetic officials.[58]

Once the Protestant ministers in Ponce realized they could not persuade or legally check the advance of Lugo and the Pentecostal movement, they reportedly turned to slander. Also reminiscent of the accusations first made against Seymour and the Azusa Street Revival, the Protestants accused Lugo and the Felicianos of placing the gospel on too low a level, of lacking theological education, and of practicing hypnotism and Spiritualism, the latter of which was a serious accusation in the

Protestant community since it was tantamount to accusing them of witchcraft.[59]

Lugo and his followers vigorously denied the allegations and reportedly stated that they simply wanted to preach the "full Gospel" in all of its power and glory. However, things were not so simple. Lugo and his colleagues realized they were a threat and had the upper hand, as they were native Puerto Rican preachers who were not bound by the comity agreements. Although they played the role of innocent victims, it is hard to imagine that they were completely unaware of the fact that their growth came at the expense of other Protestant congregations. Tensions between Pentecostals and Protestants continued until the Mexican evangelist Francisco Olazábal was able to win over transdenominational Protestant support in 1934 for his island-wide evangelistic-healing campaign.[60]

Lugo's first major encounter with traditional Protestants left a bitter aftertaste. Why would his brothers in Christ try to run him out of town when they all preached the same message about sin and salvation? Lugo soon realized that talk about the outpouring and baptism of the Holy Spirit and the necessity of speaking in tongues made all the difference. The Protestant leaders, many of whom were Euro-Americans, wanted nothing to do with anyone who preached what they considered an inferior gospel—one that placed too much emphasis on emotionalism and not enough on the mind. The Pentecostal message, they felt, also led to dissension within the Protestant community. Furthermore, there was a real sense that Lugo and his colleagues had a "we preach the truth" mentality, which left little room for compromise or interdenominational cooperation.[61]

This episode created an almost insurmountable division between Pentecostals and Protestants. Deeply wounded by these attacks and others throughout his ministry, Lugo and his colleagues resisted as best they could the temptation to condemn their attackers. However, on several occasions they claimed that while they considered them "brothers in Christ," they were nonetheless "in error" regarding their views on the spiritual gifts and were thus "hiding the fire of the Spirit."[62] Lugo did in fact seek to win over Protestants to the Pentecostal movement, thus in one sense confirming their accusation. While Lugo denies this, an impartial review of his actions indicates otherwise.[63]

Perhaps the greatest reason why traditional Protestants rejected Lugo and the Pentecostal movement was that they were seen as "sheep stealers." The fact is that Lugo and other AG preachers attracted many Methodists, Baptists, Presbyterians, Congregationalists, Disciples of Christ, and other Protestants to their movement, including a number of ministers and lay leaders.[64] One example of this is the story of Pedro Sánchez, who was a deacon at the local Baptist church in Ponce where he had been a faithful member for twenty-one years. After listening to Sánchez describe his service in the church, Feliciano audaciously stated: "So long [a Christian], brother, and the Lord still hasn't freed you from your vices?" After which Solomon quickly snatched the burning cigar hanging from Sánchez's mouth and threw it to the ground. Sánchez was shocked and impressed by Solomon's boldness and conviction. After muttering an incoherent response, Sánchez left. However, he later returned and decided to attend Solomon's evangelistic services to find out more about his church. Shortly thereafter, Sánchez received the baptism with the Holy Spirit, gave up smoking, and joined the Pentecostal movement. Although this encounter was exceptional, it nonetheless provides insight into the Puerto Rican Pentecostal movement's audacity, strong sense of holiness, and spiritual power.[65]

Pentecostal Expansion across Puerto Rico

By 1917 the Pentecostal work in Puerto Rico was growing rapidly and Lugo needed more workers. Reinforcements arrived from California that year in the persons of Panchito Ortiz and Lorenzo Lucena. Together they began evangelizing the island.[66] Panchito printed the first Pentecostal periodical in Puerto Rico, *Nuevas de Salvación (News of Salvation)* in 1918. This one-page newsletter was produced on a hand printer. It contained testimonies of divine healing, conversions, and baptisms with the Holy Spirit, and lessons on the Bible and doctrine.

The Pentecostal movement had grown from a lone missionary in 1916 to 11 congregations, 20 workers, and 600 members by 1920.[67] As the work grew, Lugo began to write letters to the *Pentecostal Evangel*, asking for prayer and financial support and more Christian workers—Puerto Rican or American. The first Euro-American to arrive was Lena S. Howe, a former missionary to Venezuela. She landed in January 1918 and immediately planted a church in Santurce, which by 1929 was one of the largest on the island.[68]

Howe's correspondence offers the reader a rare glimpse into the early Pentecostal spirituality. Describing her Sunday services, she wrote: "We try to have all the reverence possible in the services, each believer kneeling in prayer as he enters his pews, and avoiding conversation before the service. We have prayer as the first step of the service . . . then the usual service of song, prayer again, testimony, and the exposition of the Word. We all are brief so as to have a lovely altar service for the unsaved, the sick and any others who are seeking the Lord. . . . The believers talk with the unsaved, convince them, bring them to the service, to . . . pray with them."[69] Howe was especially successful in attracting women. An energetic evangelist, church planter, and teacher, she served as a role model for women in ministry.[70]

The next Euro-American missionaries to arrive were Frank and Aura Finkenbinder from the state of New York. They arrived in March 1922 and pioneered the work in Arecibo and the mountainous interior, a region where Protestant and Catholic ministers rarely trod.[71] Most of the congregations in the hinterland were small and often met in makeshift chapels, sometimes measuring a mere 8 by 10 feet.[72] In addition to his evangelistic work, Frank also took over the editorial work of *Nuevas Salvación* after Panchito Ortiz died in 1923, an event that had a profound impact on Lugo. Finkenbinder renamed the periodical *El Evangelista Pentecostal* and by 1931 was printing 1,200 copies a month.[73] By 1945, Luís C. Otero was printing 5,000 copies monthly.[74]

In 1924, Clarence T. Radley joined the Finkenbinders and Howe, and others followed. While the role of Euro-American missionaries was important, they played a supporting role by always encouraging the native Puerto Rican leadership. They never dominated the work as Ball and Luce did in the Southwest. Indeed, by 1938 the last Euro-American AG missionaries had left the island. This was different from H. C. Ball's work in the Southwest, for even after Ball and Luce handed over the leadership to Mexicans in 1939 they continued to serve as vice-presidents of the Latin District, LABI teachers, and *La Luz Apostólica* editors, and even as pastors of local churches.[75]

In October 1921, Ball visited Puerto Rico on behalf of the Assemblies of God. He was impressed not only by their tremendous growth, but also by their spirit of unity and the cooperation between Puerto Ricans and American missionaries. He found their enthusiasm and hospitality remarkable in light of their abject poverty: "The majority struggle for life. The people are so poor that I almost wept as I saw their whole-hearted efforts to raise money . . . I wish for once in my life that I was rich, just to help them."[76]

Ball's visit was very important for one reason: he recommended that Lugo and his coworkers incorporate their work as an official branch of the Assemblies of God. In fact, in September 1920 they had already drawn up an organization and named Lugo president and Tomás Alvarez secretary. They also adopted a number of resolutions (for example, see items 1, 2, and 4 in the list that follows) that were fair, strict, and unique compared to AG conventions in the United States, but that resonated with some of the views of William J. Seymour and the Azusa Street Revival, including that (1) no believer could divorce his or her spouse except for infidelity; a minister could not remarry as long as his or her spouse was living; (2) no pastor could leave his or her congregation without the knowledge and consent of the presbyter; (3) no person could be a pastor unless he or she was born again, baptized with the Holy Spirit, and had a thorough knowledge of the Bible and Assemblies of God doctrine; and (4) property purchased on behalf of the movement belonged to the movement.[77]

The second resolution developed into the practice of the superintendent appointing all of the pastors—bishop-style—to all local assemblies on the island. He could also appoint or dismiss them at will, even if their local assembly wanted them to remain. This episcopal style of church government resonated with Seymour's revised Azusa Street Apostolic Faith Movement constitution and differed from the more congregational approach of the Assemblies of God, wherein the local congregation calls the minister and owns the church property. Whether they were actually influenced by Seymour or some other Protestant tradition is unclear. Regardless, it is important to point out these distinctions because they would be the source of problems in the 1950s when the movement would seek integration. However, for the time being they enabled them to consolidate and systematically coordinate their movement.

In response to Ball's proposal, Lugo, Alvarez, Finkenbinder, and the other leaders decided to incorporate. They did not call themselves the Pentecostal Assembly of God because in the wake of World War I and the Red Scare the word "assembly" was viewed with suspicion as suggestive of communist assemblies and the language used by Marxists and socialists. Aguedo Collazo recommended replacing the word "assembly" with "church." As a result, they voted to call their movement the Pentecostal Church of God[78] and legally incorporated it on February 13, 1922. Lugo was elected president and Aguedo Collazo, Tomás Alvarez, Justino Rodríguez, Lorenzo Lucena, Lena Howe, Frank and Aurea Finkenbinder, Isabel O. Lugo, and Eletino Rodríguez signed the articles of incorporation. The first indigenous Latino Protestant, Evangelical, and Pentecostal denomination was born in Puerto Rico. Ironically, if Olazábal and the Mexican *independistas* had been successful in their desire to assume leadership of the Mexican District in 1922, both the Puerto Ricans and the Mexicans would have been able to lead their own movements that same year.[79]

The celebration of the first Puerto Rican Pentecostal organization on the island was short-lived. Frustrated by events surrounding the incorporation and the move toward man-made traditions, Panchito decided to leave and form his own Pentecostal movement. Several churches followed. Before the new movement could gain any steam, Panchito died of tuberculosis. Most of the churches that had joined him either rejoined the AG or later dissolved. His wife and two daughters were left destitute, but not without hope, for Juan Lugo and the other ministers took up an offering for them and looked after the family.[80]

Economic Hardship, Poverty, and Community Evangelism

The conflict between Lugo and Ortiz was too much for the sensitive Lugo to bear. Panchito was his closest friend. His decision to break away from Lugo led to a period of soul searching. As a result of the conflict and his fast-deteriorating health brought on by his almost nonstop preaching and traveling, a month after Panchito's death in the summer of 1923 Lugo returned to San Jose, California. Frank Finkenbinder was elected president of the movement in Lugo's place, while Lugo was named a northern California presbyter of the Assemblies of God, and later took over the pastorate of a Spanish-speaking church in San Francisco. He also drove to El Paso to attend the Latin District Council of the Assemblies of God along with Puerto Ricans Luís Caraballo of Danville and the famous evangelist Domingo Cruz and pastor Cándido Cancel of Haywood. He traveled to San Antonio, where he met with H. C. Ball. Lugo and Isabel were happy. They had finally decided to stay permanently in California when Juan received a call from Hulda Needham. She encouraged him to return to Puerto Rico. After a period of further soul-searching and a visit to Temple Bethel, Lugo decided to go to Puerto Rico. Bethel Temple provided him and his family with the funds for the return trip.[81]

And so Juan, Isabel, and their four children returned to Puerto Rico on April 25, 1925, where Juan assumed the pastorate of the main church he had founded in Ponce nine years earlier. Despite the rapid growth of the Pentecostal movement on the island, no one had built a major church structure. Until that time, virtually all the congregations met in rented facilities or dilapidated small chapels in the countryside. Recognizing the need for permanent church buildings, Lena Howe, Juan Lugo, and Frank Finkenbinder began securing funds to build churches in Santurce and Ponce. In 1928, Howe dedicated the first major Pentecostal church building on the island in Santurce. A year later, in 1929, Juan Lugo did the same in Ponce. Lugo's presence reignited the movement on the island, and it continued to grow.[82]

However, the rapid growth of the Pentecostal movement in Puerto Rico had come at a steep price. Lugo and Finkenbinder had a difficult time finding strong leaders to pastor the new missions. As a result, Lugo, Ortiz, Howe, Finkenbinder, Lucena, Collazo, and many others were forced to take on too many responsibilities. This overload, combined with food shortages, malnutrition, widespread disease, and fatigue exacted a heavy toll on the first generation of pioneers: Panchito Ortiz and Aguido Collazo died from a combination of physical exhaustion and tuberculosis, Lena Howe's daughter Elizabeth died, and Frank and Aura

Finkenbinder's two children were born blind and died from malnutrition. However, their son Paul ("Hermano Pablo") became one of the most famous evangelists in Latin America.[83]

Many early pioneers went hungry, and others fasted in order to help support their churches. Lugo wrote that many people were starving and that "some brethren go without two or three meals in the week so as to bring their Sunday offering, probably two or three pennies."[84] In 1919, Panchito wrote: "It is true we go hungry sometimes, but I take in fasting as a special remedy for stomach cleansing and soul refreshing and I feel good."[85] It was hard for Lugo and Panchito to complain because their parishioners faced even greater financial hardships.

Despite the hardships, many shared what little they had with those who had less. When Panchito was dying of tuberculosis, for example, the Finkenbinders allowed the Ortiz family to stay with them for four months after his family was evicted from their home. After Panchito's death, the Finkenbinders took care of his widow and four children and raised money for them to purchase a small house.[86]

Many of the *hermanas* (sisters) picked up destitute children, bathed and dressed them, and then took them to church every Sunday. Panchito wrote, "Sometimes the children are very dirty and the mothers cannot have them clean early for S.S. [Sunday school], so this sister just goes to work and washes and dresses them and then, like a mother hen, she comes along with ten or fifteen children to Sunday school." This story provides another insight into why the movement grew. For it was the very same conviction that "we preach the truth" that also reportedly prompted them to demonstrate the love of God right then and there in this life with whatever meager resources they had at their disposal, even if it simply meant giving dusty children in tattered clothes a bath, handmade *dulces,* and a warm hug and loving smile.[87]

The parishioners followed the example of their leaders. When a cyclone devastated the island in 1932, the Finkenbinders took the few pieces of clothing they had left and shared them with the Reverend Manuel Rivera and his wife. So while it is true that the early Pentecostal movement did not have an official "social program" or mutual aid societies, it did nonetheless practice relief work and social justice in its day-to-day ministry among the poor.[88]

Pentecostal-Catholic Tensions, Conflict, and Persecution

This de facto social welfare program attracted not only mainline Protestants but also Catholics and Spiritualists. Lugo claimed that the vast majority of their rank-and-file converts came out of Catholicism and Spiritualism, while some leaders came out of Protestant traditions. Because Lugo defined himself over against his Catholic background, he was predictably antagonistic to Catholicism, and particularly critical that it did not teach him about the necessity of being "born again" or about the baptism with the Holy Spirit. Many Puerto Rican Pentecostals in fact believed that Catholicism preached "another Gospel," full of man-made superstitions, traditions, and rituals that had lost their meaning. For this reason, Lugo and others saw it as no better than "heathenism."[89] Convert Sesilia Agostine wrote: "I am a new creature in Him. . . . Where it used to be my pleasure to console myself by going to mass worshipping before idols . . . now I have a taste of real joy."[90]

The antagonism toward Catholicism was not based simply on genuine doctrinal differences, but also on harsh experiences and outright persecution. This was true for Juan's wife, Isabel. After she converted in 1917, her devout and upper-class Catholic family and friends tried to persuade her to leave her newfound faith—until Isabel's mother visited the services and changed her views about it because of its earnest and sincere devotion, according to Lugo. Lugo was impressed by Isabel's commitment and deep spirituality. On her part, Isabel was attracted to Lugo's fervent commitment and desire to spread the Christian faith. As a result, the two were married on July 29, 1917. Isabel was an effective communicator, women's leader, and self-sacrificing coworker in the ministry.[91]

While the competition and conflict between Catholicism and Pentecostalism was usually limited to verbal jousts, sometimes it turned violent. Many of the missionaries wrote home about intense persecution, especially of native workers. In Fajardo, for example, Catholics began showering a small Pentecostal mission with so many rocks that the Reverend Figueroa claimed that it sounded like a torrent of rain. In an experience similar to one described in a previous chapter about the Latino AG in the Southwest, a Catholic vigilante threw a sharp stone through the open door of a mission that cut a great gash in the head of a small child.[92]

Although throwing rocks at the roofs of their makeshift missions was the normal means of assault, sometimes more deadly weapons were used. In one rare instance in 1931 at the height of the Great Depression, a twenty-two-year-old Pentecostal convert named John Corniel began preaching on the plantation where he worked near San Germán. He held a lunchtime Bible study, and after several months of preaching about the need to be born again and Spirit-filled he began to convert some of his coworkers. A Catholic worker reportedly became angry, interrupted him, and claimed that there was no true religion other than Catholicism. He demanded that Corniel stop preaching at once. When Corniel did not comply, as in the story of Cain and Abel, the Catholic worker reportedly ambushed Corniel and, with a large steel machete, hacked him to death in the fields. Corniel is the first known Pentecostal martyr in Puerto Rico.[93] While this kind of violence was rare and was repudiated by Catholic leaders, it does highlight the very real tensions that existed between Catholics and Pentecostals and may help to explain Pentecostals' animosity toward the Catholic Church.

Territorial Spirits: Pentecostal Spiritual Warfare

Attacks against Pentecostalism also came from Spiritists and Spiritualists. However, to be fair, this animosity was also driven by the attempts of Lugo and his colleagues to evangelize them as well as by their sharp criticism of Spiritist and Spiritualist practices and charges that such practices were satanically inspired. Lugo ran into these groups almost immediately after he arrived in 1916. In 1917, he and his colleagues decided to evangelize San Antón, the center of the Spiritualist movement on the island. After some initial conflicts with Spiritualists, Lugo and Ortiz reported a number of conversions. However, most Spiritualists converted as a result of a miraculous healing or acts of kindness and self-sacrifice. So it was in the case of the García family, who had given up any hope of seeing their twelve-year-old son Maximino healed of his "hopeless" lame condition. After taking their son to a Spiritualist and then a medical doctor in San Juan, both of whom were unable to heal him, in desperation they visited an AG church, where they claimed their son was prayed for and instantly healed.[94]

Another example of a "power encounter" and "spiritual warfare" is found in the story of Teresa Ruiz de Vélez of Mayagüez. She offers a rare glimpse into the attraction and transformative power of Pentecostalism. "I could not sleep nights," Vélez wrote,

> because I was so jealous and each day the devil would bring new reasons to me that made me more and more so. So I passed the night smoking and meditating on what I should do to my husband. During the daytime I spent my days lighting candles. One for the spirits, one for my courage, another for St. Joseph, and finally several others so that my children who were angry with me would become content and pacified. I would say my rosaries (machine made prayers) to my idols. Then I would try "Spiritualist Séances" in my home, but with all this I found myself in so many difficulties that I really felt I was losing my mind. I was always sick and found no relief for my sickness. . . . My home was not far from where Pentecostal services were held, and as I would sit and listen to the songs my heart was made tender and was touched by Holy Spirit conviction. I wanted to go to the services, but I did not dare. But the [Pentecostal] minister [Brother Lucena] came to my home and later held a few services there. Jesus spoke to me and said, "Believe on Me and ye shall be saved, you and your house," so I believed and accepted Him and today my whole house, except one has been converted to Jesus.[95]

It was precisely Lucena's zeal and obvious care for Vélez's spiritual and emotional state of mind that were responsible for his crossing the boundaries that separated him from Vélez. Although admittedly hard to quantify, it was also his deep conviction and confidence that Pentecostals preached "the Truth" about God's love, forgiveness, and healing power that was responsible for winning over many converts from Catholicism, Spiritism, and Spiritualism. Tomás Alvarez captured this optimism and confidence when he wrote: "Since the first HEAVENLY PENTECOST fell in Porto Rico [*sic*] we can declare that in several villages and rural districts Pentecost has penetrated with the power and demonstrations of the Holy Spirit . . . we expect very soon to invade the last ends of this Island with HEAVENLY PENTECOST."[96] And so they did.

The most important factor that influenced Pentecostal conversion was divine healing. The literature is full of claims of the blind receiving sight, the lame walking, and the sick being healed.[97] Sesilia Agostine of Mayagüez claimed, for example, that "as a result of sin I came to Jesus a physical wreck, my whole body pained me, and I was especially bothered with kidney trouble and a tumor on my limb, which I felt would never be healed. But this precious Jesus that washed my sins away has also healed me of all sickness and now why should I not rejoice in Him who has done so much to me?"[98]

For many, psychological and physical healing were inextricably linked. Pentecostalism's emphasis on supernatural healing tapped into the existing religious grammar and holistic medicinal sentiments of the day. Divine healing was an accepted part of everyday life in popular Catholicism and Spiritualism. Pentecostalism was the only major Protestant tradition on the island that supported this practice in a major way. This is significant because illness and physical afflictions have a direct bearing on a person's ability to work and provide financially for his or her family. Thus healing led not only to restored health, but also to psychological recovery and economic improvement. It also led to a sense of flourishing.

The above testimonies reveal five key reasons why the Pentecostal movement has planted such deep roots among Latinos. First, Pentecostals believe they preach "the Truth" about heaven and hell, the spiritual gifts, and God's love and forgiveness. Second, they mix evangelism and divine healing and restoration. Third, they target rural districts, the poor, and people across class boundaries. Fourth, they evangelize with spiritual power and authority. And finally, they actively seek to demonstrate God's power in everyday life to make converts. The result was that their movement spread rapidly across the island. While most missions were small, others grew to become large and stable congregations like the one in Fajardo (see Figure 7.2).

Pentecostal Competition, 1930–1940

The San Felipe cyclone, which slammed into Puerto Rico in September 1928, and the Great Depression of 1929 wreaked havoc on the Puerto

Figure 7.2. Assemblies of God Church in Fajardo, Puerto Rico, 1941. (Flower Pentecostal Heritage Center)

Rican economy but helped pave the way for evangelism and conversion of people looking for hope in the midst of despair.[99] Homes were destroyed, lives shattered. Those who stayed on the island faced many hardships. Lugo and AG ministers continued to preach, convert, and baptize converts across the island. The financial disaster in Puerto Rico prompted a growing number of Puerto Ricans to migrate to the United States in search of work, particularly in New York City and Spanish Harlem.

So in 1928 Lugo sent Alvarez to pioneer the Pentecostal work in the Puerto Rican diaspora in the borough of Brooklyn, New York City. The mission struggled until 1931. That year, Juan Lugo migrated to New York City and assumed the leadership of the mission. Despite his departure, the Pentecostal work on the island continued to expand under the leadership of presidents Frank Finkenbinder and Tomás Alvarez, who returned to the island. By 1934, José Martínez, Luís C. Otero, and Frank Finkenbinder had started the first Protestant radio ministry in Puerto Rico. This ministry enabled Pentecostals to reach literally thousands in remote villages and to communicate with people in the comfort of their own homes, all of which neutralized the social stigma attached to attending a Pentecostal church. Otero reportedly preached with power, conviction, and a clear message: Jesus died for their sins and wanted to give them a new life.[100]

As a result, the Latino AG witnessed growth throughout the 1920s and by 1930 held a virtual monopoly over the Pentecostal movement in Puerto Rico. They had organized 29 congregations and missions and an additional 36 preaching points ministering to approximately 2,000 members. However, their monopoly was about to come to an end from an unlikely source—another former AG minister. News broke in early 1934 that the Mexican evangelist Francisco Olazábal was on his way to Puerto Rico to hold a series of massive evangelistic-healing revivals,[101] events that would forever change the history and religious economy of the Pentecostal movement on the island.[102]

Francisco Olazábal and Puerto Rican Revivals, 1931–1936

Olazábal's ministry took him from Texas to East Los Angeles, then to Chicago in 1929, Spanish Harlem in 1931, and Puerto Rico in 1934 and 1936. In 1931, AG minister Eluterio Paz invited Olazábal to conduct a series of evangelistic-healing campaigns in Spanish Harlem. Paz had first met him during his lengthy campaign at the Palace Opera House in Chicago, where thousands of Mexicans and Puerto Ricans were reportedly saved and healed. Olazábal arrived in Spanish Harlem in 1931 with a team of eight workers and over the course of the next year passed out 30,000 circulars announcing his revival campaign. As a result, thousands of Puerto Ricans attended services and were converted. He subsequently founded a church and moved his base of operations from East Los Angeles to Spanish Harlem and transformed a former 1,500-seat Jewish synagogue into the largest Latino Pentecostal church in New York—Bethel Temple. News of Olazábal's evangelistic-healing services spread quickly to Puerto Rico. He then started a number of daughter churches throughout the New York City area.[103]

In 1933, J. L. Rodríguez of the interdenominational Defenders of the Faith in Puerto Rico invited Olazábal to conduct an evangelistic healing campaign in 1934, the first island-wide Pentecostal evangelistic healing crusade. The services were held in a large tent, then in the civic auditorium, and eventually in the sports arena. *El Mundo,* the largest secular newspaper on the island, dubbed Olazábal the "Mexican Billy Sunday" and claimed that 20,000 Puerto Ricans converted. The mass campaigns attracted the attention of poet Luís Villaronga, who immortalized him in his poem "Quién es Olazábal?" This favorable media coverage, the mass turnout, and reports of divine healing caught the attention of Albizu Campos. The two met and spoke about the state of Latinos in U.S. society. Albizu Campos was particularly sensitive to Olazábal's reported ability to heal because of his own public protests against Doctor Cornelius Roades of the Rockefeller Institute, who, he charged, conducted unorthodox medical experiments on Puerto Rican patients at the Presbyterian Hospital in San Juan, which led to many deaths. Thousands of Puerto Ricans were converted and reportedly healed at Olazábal's campaigns. Newspapers covered the revivals and brought a high level of visibility to the larger Pentecostal movement. Olazábal went back to Spanish Harlem to receive a hero's welcome.[104]

By 1936, Francisco Olazábal stood at the height of his popularity. He conducted large evangelistic healing services in Puerto Rico, New York City, Chicago, El Paso, and Edinburg, Texas. Letters arrived from all over the United States, Latin America, and Spain asking him to conduct crusades. He began sketching out plans to conduct services in Latin America and Spain. He also began planning with his son—Frank Jr.— English-language services to minister to the second- and third-generation youth and those Latino Americans outside of the Latino community. By that year, he had already sent or had plans to send missionaries and revivalists to Puerto Rico, Cuba, the Dominican Republic, Mexico, Chile, Argentina, Venezuela, Ecuador, and Spain. These converts became the beachhead for missionary work throughout Latin America. They also stand in sharp contrast to the message of books like David Stoll's otherwise outstanding study, *Is Latin America Turning Protestant?* (1990), with its vintage 1970s cover photo of Jimmy Swaggart, implying that the origins of Latin American Pentecostalism are Euro-American.[105] Olazábal's story points to a parallel, indigenous origin of Latin American Pentecostalism.

The Euro-American Christian community picked up on Olazábal's revivals and plans to convert U.S. Latinos and Latin America to Protestantism. In 1936, the *Christian Herald* magazine and the *Sunday School Times* both published flattering lead articles on his ministry. Writing for the *Christian Herald,* Spencer Duryee described Olazábal as "The Great Aztec" (El Azteca), whose transnational ministry was "one of the most startling stories . . . in modern religious history." He went on to compare Olazábal to the Apostle Paul, John Wesley, David Livingstone, and William Booth.[106]

While the private Olazábal often said that speaking in tongues was the key to his healing ministry, publicly he stated that he was simply "a Christian." This kind of interdenominational spirit attracted the attention of influential Protestant leaders like Presbyterian missionary statesman Robert E. Speer, who agreed to support Olazábal's next Puerto Rican campaign in the spring of 1936. However, Speer decided to withdraw his support after he learned Olazábal spoke in "Tongues."[107]

Although disappointed by the loss of Speer's support, Olazábal refused to repudiate speaking in tongues, the spiritual gifts, or the Pentecostal experience. He struck out for Puerto Rico, arriving in the spring of 1936 ready to repeat his 1934 campaign. Yet the setback with Speer was nothing compared to what he experienced on the island. Roman Catholic leaders looked at Olazábal as farmers look at an oncoming plague of locusts. They reportedly used their influence with the newspapers to criticize Olazábal and to persuade them not to announce his campaign or even his arrival on the island. More disappointing than the predictable Catholic opposition, however, was the resistance he faced from Protestants, even a few in the Assemblies of God, who felt threatened by his growing popularity and would not help him secure meeting spaces. Olazábal wired his wife in New York and asked her to send his large evangelistic tent to protect visitors from the drenching tropical rain and scorching sun. Despite these difficulties, many turned out, including people from the AG churches, though the results were meager compared to 1934.[108]

At every turn, his advance was checked. Yet he pressed forward, conducting as many evangelistic-healing services in the best facilities he could find. However, the lack of support and publicity and proactive opposition made pressing on to other parts of the island almost impossible. Even before his tent arrived, he boarded a ship and steamed home to New York, arriving unannounced and without fanfare. The 1936 Puerto Rico Para Cristo campaign marked a sharp turning point in Olazábal's vision. Prior to that campaign he saw his healing ministry as bridging the racial and denominational divides that fragmented American and Latino Protestantism. He now realized that such bridging would be very difficult, if not impossible.

Despite his disappointment, Olazábal left a lasting mark on Puerto Rican Pentecostalism and the Latino AG in several ways. First, he was responsible for breaking up the AG monopoly on the island. Within ten years of his campaigns, at least eleven new Pentecostal denominations were ministering in the wake of Olazábal's crusades.[109] Second, his large campaigns brought thousands of Puerto Ricans into a Pentecostal movement not affiliated with Juan Lugo or the Assemblies of God.[110] Since Olazábal's CLADIC did not sponsor churches on the island in 1934, most of them joined the AG and many went on to faithfully serve in the ministry. In fact, by 1936 the Latino AG had grown to over 56 congregations and 3,400 members, at least in part as a result of Olazábal's two campaigns, something overlooked in most of the literature. This is not surprising because he maintained warm friendships with Euro-American and Latino AG ministers.[111]

Finally, his campaigns turned Pentecostalism into an island-wide movement and phenomenon and created a kind of Pentecostal/Charismatic social glue that cut across denominational boundaries, because thousands of Protestants (and Catholics) attended his services and took their newfound Pentecostal beliefs back to their traditional denominations. For this reason, to this day many non-Pentecostal denominations affirm the practice of the gifts of the Holy Spirit and are Charismatic in theology, temperament, and outlook. All of this helped bring an entire generation of Puerto Ricans into the movement, and that—along with the work of Juan Lugo and the Pentecostal Church of God—in turn helped lay the foundation for the phenomenal growth from 1930 to 1940, by which time the Pentecostal Church of God claimed 7,100 followers, with no other denomination even approaching 5,000 members. In fact, the movement had grown by over 1,000 percent, going from 600 members in 1920 to 7,100 members (not including adherents) by 1940.[112]

Juan Lugo, Education, and Mizpa Bible Institute

One of the keys to the phenomenal growth and development across the island was a new focus on theological education—systematic instruction in Bible, theology, evangelistic strategies, missions, and church planting. In 1936, Noel Perkin and J. R. Flower asked Juan Lugo to leave La Sinagoga, the church he had founded in 1931 in Manhattan, and return to Puerto Rico to open a Bible school. As a result, Lugo founded Mizpa Bible Institute in Bayamón, Puerto Rico, in September 1937. His wife Isabel and teachers Julia Camacho and John Pérez Hernández joined him. Sixteen students enrolled in the first class.[113] Although the decision to leave La Sinagoga (about which more will be said later) in New York was not easy, it was part of a vision for a Bible school that Lugo first articulated in 1924. Lugo used the Bible school to harness and direct the powerful influx of new converts into a movement. He taught, ordained, and helped commission a new generation of Puerto Rican pastors, evangelists, missionaries, and Christian educators both on the island, in the United States, and overseas, via Puerto Rican missionaries in the Dominican Republic and Cuba. He assigned books written by AG educator Myer Pearlman on Pentecostal doctrines, Stanley Frodsham's *With Signs Following* on church history, and other English and Spanish Pentecostal literature.[114]

Splinter Movements

The need for pastors, evangelists, and educators was enormous. It opened the doors for women in ministry. In fact, women played a more important role in Puerto Rico than in the Southwest. Lugo allowed women to preach, teach, evangelize, and pastor on a more regular basis than some of his colleagues in the United States. Despite this, he did not grant them the exact same freedoms that men had. Women were often ordained at the same time as their husbands and expected to largely support their husbands' ministries. Others were given small and struggling missions and were used, like substitute teachers, to guide a local mission until it was large enough to hand over to a man.

This is one of the reasons why some AG women like Juana García Peraza (1897–1970) left it to found their own denomination. Born in Hatillo, Puerto Rico, in 1897, this former Roman Catholic, department store owner was converted to Pentecostalism after she was healed of a terminal illness in 1940. She began attending an AG congregation in Arecibo, where she reportedly became active in prophecy. Through a series of reported revelations, she deposed the pastor. After the pastor expelled her and eleven followers out of the church, she promptly founded "Mita Congregation" in Arecibo around 1940. In 1949, Fela González claimed a divine revelation during which God stated that the Holy Spirit was to be called "Mita." Peraza's followers believed that the Holy Spirit (Mita) embodied itself in the person of Juanita Peraza and later Teófilo Vargas (Aarón). Many of Peraza's disciples believed that Juanita was the incarnation of the Holy Spirit on earth and referred to her as the "Mita" and the "Goddess." Peraza's triple message of love, liberty, and unity, along with her active cooperatives and social programs that focused on the needs of the poor and women, attracted a growing number of Puerto Ricans. The AG and all other denominations believe the Mita movement is neither Pentecostal nor orthodox in its beliefs.[115]

Emerging Public Voice and Recognition, 1940s–1950s

Despite the rise of new Pentecostal denominations, by 1945 the AG had become the largest on the island. It had grown from 52 congregations and 2,000 members in 1930 to 93 organized congregations, 100 preaching points, and 9,385 members in 1945, with Luís C. Otero editing and publishing *El Evangelista Pentecostal,* which distributed 5,000 copies per month. The growth was in large part due to church planting, evangelism, and self-sacrifice (the salaries were very low).[116] The rapid growth and saturation of Pentecostalism into all facets of Puerto Rican society led to its increasing public recognition in society. Indeed, Pentecostals were finally gaining a public voice and recognition for their positive contributions and service. This was evident as early as 1943 when the mayor of Ponce, the second-largest city on the island, attended the 1943 Pentecostal Church of God Annual Convention and read a public resolution that declared the 1,400 Pentecostal visitors the city's guests of honor.[117] This gesture marked a major milestone in the development of the Pentecostal movement and a radical departure from the attempt by Protestant ministers to run Juan Lugo and his followers out of town twenty-seven years earlier in 1916.

The social stigma attached to Pentecostalism was now waning and Pentecostals were hungry not only for greater public recognition of their positive contributions to society, but also for recognition from the mainstream body of the General Council of the Assemblies of God in the United States. Although Puerto Rican politicians were ready to welcome them into the marrow of Puerto Rican society, the larger Assemblies of God in the U.S. still viewed the island work as a foreign missionary outpost in the larger global AG movement, a sentiment that would lead to conflict and ultimately division.

William J. Seymour's Azusa Street Revival had a direct impact on the origins of Puerto Rican Pentecostalism through its missionaries and daughter missions. The Pentecostal movement first began in the Puerto Rican diasporas in Hawaii and California from 1911 to 1913, then traveled to Puerto Rico in 1916, and finally to New York City in 1928 and to Chicago shortly thereafter.

Lugo's ability to convert the masses in the first five years of the AG's work on the island was largely due to the fact that he was a native Puerto Rican Spanish-speaker and because of his method of taking the Azusa Street Pentecostal message directly to the streets of San Juan, Ponce, and then throughout the island. His practice of transforming new converts into evangelists also created a supply-side surplus of evangelists that were very effective in making new converts.

The Latino AG's phenomenal growth was also due to its emphases on prayer, missions, church planting, personal evangelism, evangelistic-healing crusades, leadership development through theological education, and a firm conviction among Pentecostals that they preached the Truth about God's love, forgiveness, and plan for their lives. Its success also had to do to with the disestablishment of the Roman Catholic

Church's hegemony on the island, and because it resonated with the religious and social grammar already present in Puerto Rican spirituality
with its emphases on the supernatural, divine healing, and spiritual warfare. Although he led the Pentecostalization of the island, Francisco
Olazábal's 1934 and 1936 Puerto Rico Para Cristo campaigns broke open
the AG's monopoly. Despite this fact, many people who were converted
in his campaigns joined the AG. By 1945, if not sooner, the Latino AG
was the largest and most respected Protestant tradition on the island.
With the rapid growth of the movement, second-generation Puerto Ricans were seeking a more organic connection between the Pentecostal
Church of God in Puerto Rico and the Assemblies of God movement in
the United States. However, the push for full integration into the Assemblies of God in the United States as a regular district soon gave way after
their rejection into a call for complete independence.

CHAPTER 8

The "Puerto Rico Problem"

The Struggle for Integration, Independence, and Rebirth

Spirit of Puerto Rican Independence

The growing recognition of the Pentecostal Church of God took place during an upsurge in Puerto Rican cultural and political nationalism. The nationalist push was led by Pedro Albizu Campos and Luís Muñoz Marín, one of whom championed complete political independence and the other full integration but not assimilation into the United States. Although the 1937 Ponce uprising failed in its call for independence, it captured the mood and spirit of the people on the island and throughout the Puerto Rican diaspora who were tired of being treated like an internal colony of the United States.[1]

The next major push for greater freedom and recognition came from the 65,000 Puerto Ricans who returned from U.S. military service in World War II and asked the U.S. government for greater representation in civil society. As a result of these efforts, on April 2, 1943, Senator Millard Tydings introduced a bill to the U.S. Congress calling for Puerto Rican independence. Although the bill was defeated, it represented a growing trend among Puerto Ricans and Americans in how they viewed the island's future. The three main options were independence, statehood, and commonwealth status. In all three cases, Puerto Ricans

sought to exercise greater voice and agency in shaping their future—
something that we shall see had a ripple effect throughout Puerto Rican
denominational churches on the island and in the diaspora.[2]

In response to these calls to end colonialism and push for independence, statehood, or commonwealth status, in 1946 the U.S. government
appointed Jesús T. Piñero the first Puerto Rican governor, and in 1947
the United States granted Puerto Ricans the right to elect their own governor. A year later they elected Puerto Rican poet Luís Muñoz Marín
governor. He worked with Harry Truman to promote the Industrial Incentives Act (also known as Operation Bootstrap), which offered tax
breaks for American corporations that sought to bring work and economic recovery to Puerto Rico. This led to the rapid industrialization of
the island. Over 1,000 U.S. corporations and small businesses moved to
Isla Borinquen, all of which helped to integrate Puerto Rico with the
U.S. mainland. These moves toward integration received a boost when
in 1947 the U.S. Supreme Court ruled in *Mendez v. Westminster School,*
a case that originated in Orange County, California, that educational
segregation on the basis of race was unconstitutional. This had a ripple
effect throughout the U.S. Latino and Puerto Rican diasporic community, with many Latinos becoming increasingly aware of the fact that
their social marginalization was due in part to racial prejudice.[3]

On October 30, 1950, Pedro Albizu Campos and other nationalists
led a revolt against the United States called the Jayuya Uprising, which
resulted in the "Utuado massacre," wherein five nationalists were exe-
cuted in a police station without due process. In response to this and
other grievances, on November 1, 1950, Puerto Rican nationalists
Griselio Torresola and Oscar Collazo attempted to assassinate President Harry Truman. As a result of these conflicts, the U.S. Congress
approved the Constitution of Puerto Rico in 1952 and recognized the island's desire to hold commonwealth status. According to the U.S. Supreme Court, Puerto Rico is "a territory appurtenant and belonging to
the United States, but not a part of the United States."[4] In all major pleb-
iscite referendums on independence and statehood (including that of
2012), the vast majority of Puerto Ricans vote for commonwealth status
or statehood, not independence (the latter is usually favored by less than
5 percent of the population). The *Brown v. Board of Education* Supreme

Court decision outlawing public school segregation on the basis of race, along with the birth of Martin Luther King's civil rights movement, also set the backdrop in the United States for the push for integration and independence in the mid- to late 1950s.

The Pentecostal Church of God's Push for Integration

The Pentecostal Church of God was growing in favor not only with Puerto Rican political, civic, and religious leaders, but also with Euro-American leaders in the United States. A number of its national leaders were attending the AG General Council Conventions in the United States, where they began to conceive a vision for greater integration, voice, and agency in the mother organization. As a result, in the mid-1940s a number of Puerto Ricans led by Superintendent José Martínez, Mizpa Bible School Director Luís C. Otero, and others began dreaming about the Pentecostal Church of God changing its status as a "foreign" national church to an American AG district, with all of the rights and privileges thereof. The reason for this shift was the realization that Puerto Rico would never gain independence from the United States, because in all previous votes over 95 percent of Puerto Ricans had either opted for statehood or commonwealth status rather than independence. They did not support independence because they believed not only that the island would fall into poverty, but also that the Roman Catholic Church would launch a series of persecutions and restrictions against their religious freedom. However, the deeper reason they wanted affiliation was that they—in their own minds—were faithful Puerto Ricans and Americans. Although they had been given the right to citizenship through the Foraker Act in 1917 (in time to draft them into the military for World War I), they still could not vote in presidential elections and were thus treated quite literally like residents of an internal colony. They wanted change. While some pushed for independence, others pushed for full integration without assimilation since they were proud of their Puerto Rican heritage.[5]

Puerto Rican Pentecostals wanted to fully integrate into American society as equals, and they pushed to become an organic U.S. district. They realized they could not do this without the support of the Euro-American missionaries who labored alongside them, and so they turned to missionaries like Frank Finkenbinder. In 1946, Puerto Ricans, through Finkenbinder, asked the General Council to put their proposal for integration as a U.S. district on the agenda for the September 3–10, 1947, General Council Convention in Grand Rapids, Michigan. They proposed that Puerto Rico be recognized as a U.S. district. Their proposal was presented on September 6 at 8:45 a.m. The general response to the proposition was initially positive.[6]

However, their hopes and dreams for acceptance as fully integrated equals on a par with other Euro-American districts on the mainland were dashed on the bitter rocks of race, cultural politics, and history. News broke that Missions Secretary Noel Perkin and Latin American Missions Superintendent H. C. Ball wanted to review the proposal. Prior to that time, the Puerto Rican contingent had sought to avoid Ball and Perkin in order to make their pitch directly to the Euro-American ministers and presbyters, unfiltered by history, biases, and internal U.S. Latino denominational politics. In order to leverage support for their proposal, they won over many Euro-American pastors and leaders, including the influential Executive Presbyter D. P. Holloway from Ohio. They asked him to present their proposal that the Puerto Rican "work" be recognized "on the same level" as a district council in the continental United States. He also indicated that Luís Otero and Frank Finkenbinder were available to present their case further and answer questions. The initial response was again positive. Given the racial tensions in the United States, this was a major endorsement and spoke well of AG leaders who were willing to cross the racial boundaries that divided society and some quarters of the AG.[7]

However, just when it looked as though victory was in sight and the proposal might pass, someone from behind the scenes proposed that it be tabled until Brothers Perkin and Ball could be present to discuss the proposal. Realizing that time was of the essence, Otero and Finkenbinder asked that a decision be quick. Perkin recommended to the Presbytery that the matter be referred to the Foreign Missions Committee and that this committee bring a recommendation to the General Presbytery, but—out of respect for Otero and Finkenbinder and their supporters—as quickly as possible. Hope for full integration teetered in the balance. The delay strategy sounded remarkably similar to what happened to Olazábal and the Mexican *independistas* in 1922.[8]

Perkin and Ball, who also just happened to chair the Foreign Missions Committee, dragged their feet so that no vote or action could be taken at the convention, blaming "the rush of final business." As a result, Perkin and Ball "failed to bring in a report." This inaction killed the proposal that year and gave Perkin, Ball, and their supporters the ability to slow the momentum at the 1947 convention and the time to draw up a rationale for why the Pentecostal Church of God should not be granted full U.S. district status. In 1948, the Foreign Missions Committee finally notified the Pentecostal Church of God that it had decided to *reject* their proposal. Why? "It was decided by motion that it does not seem feasible to consider the Porto [*sic*] Rico work a branch of the Assemblies of God on the same basis as the foreign language groups of the continental United States of America, for the reasons that there is a different standard for the ministry and a different language."[9]

Perkin and Ball transformed the Puerto Rican proposal to be a U.S. district into a proposal for a "foreign language district," something not in the original proposal. These rationales are odd since they had recognized the Puerto Rican AG work, clergy, and Bible school as meeting the same standards as the AG work in the United States—at least enough to warrant their granting them credentials and allowing them to transfer their credentials to the mainland without passing any new polity or theological exams. Furthermore, they already had "foreign language" districts run by Mexican Americans like Demetrio Bazan in the Southwest. Whether or not Perkin and Ball did this because of a lack of confidence in the ability of Puerto Ricans to run their own movement, because they wanted to protect the monopoly the Latin District had in the United States, or for some other reason is uncertain. Regardless, the damage was done. The Puerto Ricans and the Euro-American missionaries read the decision as meaning that they would not be granted an equal status with U.S. Latino and English-language districts. Despite the fact that they all held U.S. citizenship and that Puerto Rico was part of the commonwealth of the United States, they were treated as foreigners and as a national movement, not as Americans. In the language of the Supreme Court's ruling on Puerto Rico's legal relationship to the United

States, the larger message the General Council sent to the Pentecostal Church of God was that they were a territory belonging to the AG, but not an integral part of the AG.[10]

Push for U.S. Integration:
"The Puerto Rico Problem," 1950–1955

Puerto Ricans responded to Springfield's decision in three ways. Some responded by redoubling their efforts to seek integration as a recognized district of the AG. Others decided to withdraw and simply continue their ministry as if nothing had happened. And a third segment decided it was time to break away to form their own denomination.

Despite the rejection, the Pentecostal Church of God was growing by leaps and bounds. By 1950, there were 175 ministers, 133 organized churches, 300 missions, and 13,000 members. They were now sending out missionaries to Cuba and the Dominican Republic.[11] The AG movement was given a boost after T. L. Osborn's island-wide crusades in 1950s, during which he preached to crowds reaching 20,000 in Paquito Montaner baseball stadium. They prayed for the sick and reportedly made 18,000 converts within twelve days, all of whom poured into the AG churches across the island. This was the largest island-wide crusade since Francisco Olazábal's 1934 Puerto Rico para Cristo campaign sixteen years earlier.[12]

In order to investigate the request for full U.S. district status, David J. du Plessis decided to attend the 1951 convention in Puerto Rico. He wrote that the Puerto Ricans were the most "zealous people" he had ever met. The Mexican American Roberto Fierro was the guest evangelist and preached to crowds ranging from 2,000 to 10,000, according to du Plessis. The services ran for four to six hours, and countless people were converted and anointed with oil for divine healing. In an effort to exercise greater public voice and agency, they then organized and led a Pentecostal parade in San Juan on Saturday afternoon, waving colorful banners much as they do today with the International March for Jesus. The San Juan chief of police led the march and estimated that 7,000–10,000 people took part and that another 15,000–20,000 people lined the streets. Many declared it the greatest parade ever organized in San Juan. Although some feared that the Puerto Rican independence movement might exploit the event for political gain, there was no disturbance, du Plessis wrote.[13]

Fierro's campaign was a critical turning point in the struggle for voice and agency in the AG. He had traveled to the island every year since 1940 and had developed strong friendships with the islanders. He was highly sympathetic to the Puerto Rican struggle because of the struggle that Mexican Americans had faced in the Southwest. The Puerto Ricans shared with him their dream of becoming a U.S. district. As a result, they asked him to use his considerable weight and influence as the most famous Latino AG evangelist of the day to push for a Puerto Rican district. After talking with Superintendent Demetrio Bazan and securing his support, Fierro, pictured in Figure 8.1, began promoting the idea to Euro-American district leaders back home in the United States.[14]

Figure 8.1.   Rev. Roberto Fierro at the Assemblies of God General Convention, Grand Rapids, Michigan, September 1947. Fierro was one of the most highly sought after Latino Pentecostal evangelists of the 1940s and 1950s.   (Flower Pentecostal Heritage Center)

In January 1954, Fierro and Bazan met with the Pentecostal Church of God leaders at their annual conference in Guayama, Puerto Rico, and discussed how they might help them integrate and win U.S. district status. They came up with the idea of asking Fierro to make this proposal at the September 1–3, 1954, General Council Convention. True to his word, at the event Fierro made an "impassioned appeal" for Puerto Rico to be recognized as a U.S. district, "instead of as a foreign field." Given that H. C. Ball had stepped down as Field Secretary of the Latin American work in 1953, they now only had to deal with Perkin, who had become more sympathetic in the intervening years. Some said the idea should be delayed further, while others began to worry that all of the nationalist sentiment in Puerto Rico might prompt them to break fellowship and instead become an independent denomination. This would result in a loss of members.[15]

As a result of Fierro's plea, a motion was made to extend an invitation to Superintendent Pedro Juan Alvarado and the Pentecostal Church of God to consider "the privilege of becoming a recognized District Council of the Assemblies of God." They would be "granted equal representation on the General Presbytery with continental District Councils." However, they could only be granted this "privilege" provided that "all conditions are complied with." With these stipulations in mind, the General Council moved to bring the Pentecostal Church of God into an "organic relationship" with the national church. To their relief, the motion was adopted. As a result, they were allowed to have a representative at the General Convention. This was a historic breakthrough. Yet the Puerto Ricans wanted more than just a representative; they wanted full U.S. district status and voting rights. For the first time in history, they wanted a voice in the General Council of the Assemblies of God.[16]

However, Bazan had a change of heart and on September 27 wrote Flower that although the Pentecostal Church of God was ready to send a representative to Springfield, they were not ready for full U.S. district status because, in language reflecting Ball's influence (Ball had since joined back up with the Latino AG in the Southwest), they could not comply with the "standards" required for a U.S. district. Bazan wrote that it would take several years for them to be ready, and he felt that they would be happy for now with simply having a representative at the General Convention. He was right. Pentecostal Church of God Secretary Andrés Ríos wrote to Perkin and said he was "very happy" about the "fine resolution" to give Puerto Rico representation on the General Presbytery. However, he also made it clear that the Pentecostal Church of God still wanted to know how they could make Puerto Rico "qualify" as an American district. At the November 2–4 Executive Presbytery meeting they approved a motion that promised to give Puerto Rico recognition as a district if it met with the standards of the AG work in the United States. This time, no reference was made to the Spanish language as an obstacle to district recognition.[17]

The Puerto Ricans were less than happy about the outcome. They wanted full recognition as a U.S. district with no strings attached and not just a presence on the Executive Presbytery. They were also beginning to have misgivings about the influence that Fierro and Bazan were having behind the scenes. They came to believe that their ultimate loyalty was to the American AG and to the Spanish Eastern Convention (they did not become a district until June 1957) in New York and to the U.S. Latin District in the Southwest, rather than to the Pentecostal Church of God.

The key sticking point was whether the Pentecostal Church of God could maintain jurisdiction over ministers who migrated to the United States or whether jurisdiction automatically transferred to the Spanish Eastern Convention in New York or the Latin District Council in the Southwest, depending upon where they lived. Because 5,000 members and some of their best ministers migrated to the United States, and more seemed ready to do so, they were eager to hold on to their authority over them, especially since some might return to Puerto Rico. However, Bazan and Manuel T. Sánchez of the Spanish Eastern Convention asked that when they arrived in the United States they automatically transfer into the Spanish Eastern or Latin District. To their credit, they also stated that if one of their own ministers moved to Puerto Rico they would have to join the Pentecostal Church of God, although because the migration patterns at that time generally flowed from the island to the mainland, it was less of a concern and liability.

The biggest sticking point of all was what to do with Rev. Abelardo Berrios and the highly influential New York City church La Sinagoga, which was founded by Juan Lugo. It was the most important Latino AG church in the city and the mother church and for a time headquarters of the Spanish Eastern work. The problem was that Berrios was ordained by the Pentecostal Church of God but ministered in the Spanish Eastern Convention area. Should Berrios remain in the Pentecostal Church of God? Should his church now be assigned to the Pentecostal Church of God since he was its minister? Or should Berrios's credentials be transferred to the Spanish Eastern Convention (called the Spanish Eastern District after June 1957)? Despite the agreement that Bazan and Fierro proposed, they decided to make just one exception—Rev. Abelardo Berrios—because La Sinagoga belonged to the Spanish Eastern Convention. Furthermore, Berrios was an outspoken supporter of Puerto Rican cultural nationalism and promoted the Pentecostal work and the more episcopal way of doing things in Puerto Rico, which led to confusion among some Latino AG churches in New York City about which church governance standards they should follow. For this reason, Sánchez wanted Berrios removed as pastor of La Sinagoga. But given the autonomy of the Spanish Eastern Convention churches, he did not have the power to do so himself. However, the Pentecostal Church of God could remove him at will but chose not to do so, not only because he was successful in converting people, but also because he represented their interests among the Puerto Rican diaspora in New York City.

To overcome this impasse, Bazan and Sánchez tried to persuade Berrios to join the Spanish Eastern Convention, return to Puerto Rico, or— they hinted—leave the AG, but leave the church behind. They quickly realized that the quickest solution to the problem was to grant the Pentecostal Church of God status on a par with U.S. districts, because once they did so their ministers would, according to national AG bylaws, automatically have to transfer their credentials to the district in which they served—in this case, because they were a Spanish-language church, the Spanish Eastern Convention or in the Southwest the Latin American District.

The Pentecostal Church of God leaders increasingly realized that the only way they could maintain their influence over their ministers in the United States and elsewhere on the mission field (they were sending missionaries to Latin America and the Caribbean without coordinating this with the AG foreign missions department in Springfield) was to remain a foreign national church or to break off to form their own U.S. denomination. For all of these reasons and others, some Puerto Ricans began thinking that it might be time to leave the AG to protect their freedom and autonomy. However, for these same reasons Bazan again changed his mind and began pushing for Puerto Rico to become a U.S. district.

The Puerto Rican leaders realized that Bazan was trying to use the formation of a district to his advantage and, as a result, protested his involvement. They also protested Roberto Fierro's involvement, even though he was a highly respected and deeply loved evangelist in Puerto Rico. They also disliked the fact that their participation seemed to suggest that they were incapable of representing themselves and that they had not initiated the proposal in the first place, something problematic among Puerto Rican cultural nationalists and those pushing for independence. Finally, they pointed out that they never had any organic relationship to the Latin District Council and thus, for it to represent them was not only paternalistic, but overstepping their fraternal relations.[18]

Bazan fought back by stating in a letter to J. R. Flower that he had listened to complaints and desires for full integration into the national AG denomination for three or four years at their annual conferences and that as a result "promised them I would try to obtain an organic recognition."[19] Bazan also stated that by allowing them to form a district "the Mother Church [in Springfield will gain] . . . the upper hand on them, by helping them with their doctrines and practices in which they differ from us by a good margin."[20]

Knowing how sensitive Puerto Ricans were to honor and racialized politics during this upsurge in cultural nationalism on the island, Bazan presciently warned Flower that the Puerto Ricans were the ones who first sought district status and that if AG headquarters denied their request to become a district, it would never again be given this opportunity. He ended by warning that if they did not grant them district status, they would split the work, go independent, or "fall into a fanatical form of worship," as in Chile under "Dr. Hoover's work." Now pivoting to protect Puerto Rican interests and to secure their district status and playing to AG headquarters' paternalism, Bazan stated that now was the time to "save them from a major future catastrophe."[21]

Notwithstanding these concerns, many Puerto Ricans were delighted at the prognosis that they could become a district with all of the rights and privileges of other "Americans." The General Council and the Pentecostal Church of God planned their historic meeting for Monday, July 25, 1955, in Rio Piedras. At this meeting, J. R. Flower and Melvin L. Hodges, the Field Secretary of the Latin American AG, who replaced H. C. Ball, met with Pedro J. Alvarado, Andrés Ríos, and their Executive Board. After spending Saturday and Sunday attending convention services and preaching in different churches, on Monday, July 25, Flower and Hodges agreed to district status in principle. However, they also stated that if they wanted to make this transition they would have to make key changes. They would have to amend their constitutional standards, recognize the sovereignty of the local assemblies (in Puerto Rico, the superintendent controlled the churches and appointed the ministers of all congregations), and respect the "scriptural organization of the local church," by which they meant organizing elder boards and deacons, and giving every congregation the power to influence the decisions in the local congregations, where the pastor was hitherto really in complete control. Prior to this time, the only officers many congregations had appointed were song leaders and treasurers. The Puerto Rican superintendent would have to adopt a congregational rather than an episcopal form of church governance. He could no longer remove the pastor of a local sovereign congregation at will.[22]

Push for Separation and Independence, 1956–1957

Many of the Puerto Ricans expressed fear that this could lead to chaos, that their hybrid episcopal system had run smoothly for more than three decades, and that therefore there was no need to change their system of governance. However, other younger leaders expressed support for a more congregational form of church governance. Fine speeches were reportedly offered on both sides of the debate. After hours of deliberations it became apparent that the independence contingent would win the day. The key reason, according to Flower, was that they were "not ready" to "conform to the General Council standards" and recognize the congregational form of government and autonomy granted to each local church.

They also realized that they could no longer send out missionaries if they became a U.S. district because all foreign missionaries are processed and sent out in coordination with the Department of Foreign Missions at AG headquarters in Springfield. After wisely moderating the discussion and remaining silent during the deliberations, Pedro Alvarado finally stepped in to throw his weight on the side of the independence movement by recommending that they maintain their present form of church governance. After calling for two votes to confirm this view, he "clinched the argument" for the "status quo" and independence, and the meeting was concluded. The cultural nationalists—who had once pushed for full integration before being rebuffed by the AG leadership in Springfield—had won.[23]

Despite calls by other Puerto Rican leaders for U.S. district status and support from Fierro and Bazan, Flower wrote that they were not ready to assume the responsibilities of a U.S. district.[24] Bazan and Sánchez both feared that the Pentecostal Church of God would continue to exercise authority over its ministers in the United States and could possibly split the Spanish Eastern Convention work if they went independent, with Berrios's La Sinagoga serving as the new mother church of the Pentecostal Church of God work in the United States.[25] Trying to take matters into their own hands, a year later, in July 1956, the Spanish Eastern Convention sent a letter to the Puerto Rican District stating that all ministers from other districts or councils, including Puerto Rico—which was underlined in the letter—should cease in their former affiliation after arriving in New York and should hold only their (Spanish Eastern Convention) credentials or those issued by Springfield.[26]

This brought about a swift response from the Pentecostal Church of God, which roundly condemned the Spanish Eastern Convention for overstepping its boundaries and jurisdiction, because its ministers had always hitherto been able to hold on to their credentials after arriving in the United States. In response, and in a maneuver to pull rank on the Spanish Eastern Convention, the Pentecostal Church of God issued a "Declaration, Status, and Position Report" in which they stated that although they recognized and appreciated the work of the Assemblies of God and their spiritual guidance and support over the years, nonetheless they were—by Springfield's own statements, they pointed out, not without searing irony—"a National and Sovereign Church." As a result, they stated, they exercised the prerogative to send pastors, evangelists, and missionaries anywhere the Holy Spirit permitted. They also wrote that they would not become just "one more district of the General Council," even if this meant being disfellowshipped and starting their own denomination.[27]

Reading the proverbial handwriting on the wall, Noel Perkin wrote to Pedro Alvarado and Andrés Ríos asking them to state clearly what they meant by this functional declaration of independence. Ríos wrote back a two-page letter to Perkin on November 15, 1956, in which he stated that they had no intention of "rupturing" their "friendship" with the AG, but finally agreed with Springfield that they were a "national church," like countless other national AG churches around the world.[28] Ríos wanted to avoid a complete rupture because he realized that the AG and the Spanish Eastern Convention could start their own work in Puerto Rico and divide their movement, which was just as susceptible to schism as any other. For this reason, they took a conciliatory tone, hoping that the AG would not start a new work in Puerto Rico since they were a daughter—and now sister—movement. However, they also made it clear that like all other national churches they would refuse to subordinate their missionary work and church governance to the U.S. church since they were an independent national church.

In what must have been an ironic and bittersweet twist of events, Ríos gave Perkin the same rationale that he had been given in 1948 by Brother Steelberg for why they should not become a U.S. district, but rather remain a national church. Ríos wrote:

> It is perfectly natural that when the sons reach the age of maturity and they separate from the father's home to establish their own homes and to assume their own responsibilities, it does not affect their family relations, the family unity is still maintained, and why not? You know that. That was what brother Steelberg told us in San Juan in 1948. We have just reached the age of maturity to assume full responsibility for our home and foreign work, and why . . . should [it] be interpreted as if we were withdrawing from the Assemblies of God fellowship?[29]

Ríos stated that all they wanted now was to be treated like any other "foreign" national branch of the AG:

> The Assemblies of God of different countries in Europe and also Canada have sent their missionaries where the American Assemblies of God have sent theirs too in different countries, that's true in Latin America. And although each group is raising and supervising it's [*sic*] own work it doesn't affect fellowship, there is no problem in their relations as members of the same family working for a common cause, no matter the difference in the management of their work.[30]

They had no plan or intention of withdrawing from the larger worldwide AG fellowship. They only wanted to follow the advice of Steelberg and others who told them they could not be an American district because they were—in effect—foreigners, not Americans. He wrote: "That's what we have in mind, never have we thought to withdraw from the Assemblies of God fellowship. We only want to develop our own work with the zeal of our own responsibility similar to other Assemblies of God organizations throughout the world."[31]

He ended by ironically calling on AG headquarters to be just as patient and understanding with them as they were asked to be in 1948: "Is it unpleasant or is it hard to be recognized by the Mother Church our right to develop ourselves in and out of our geographical confines?" Reflecting on the consistent rejection by Springfield, he ended by stating: "We are deeply sorry for such a misunderstanding in our relations. Our position is clear before God and before you. No matter whatever you think about our decision we offer you our Christian love and our hand of fellowship . . . with our door and our hearts open."[32]

Realizing that they could not allow Alvarado, Ríos, and the Pentecostal Church of God to still send workers to the United States to compete with the Spanish Eastern Convention and Latin District Council, they made one last attempt to reach out to them. Although a split was unavoidable, both sides hoped that perhaps they could reach a mutually beneficial compromise, a win-win situation. As a result, Melvin Hodges and Howard Bush traveled to Puerto Rico in April 1957. They stated that the Pentecostal Church of God had been the aggressor by declaring itself a national body with plans to establish churches in areas where the national AG church already had Spanish churches, such as the United States, Cuba, and the Dominican Republic.[33]

Pedro Alvarado jumped at this opportunity to "review the . . . history" of the present situation, and calmly pointed out that a decade earlier they—the Puerto Ricans—came to Springfield with a desire to fully integrate into the American General Council but had been "refused" and were "repeatedly told" that they were a "foreign national" church. When Hodges fired back that they, unlike other national churches, were now competing with existing AG churches in the United States, especially New York, and as a result were not working in harmony with Springfield, Alvarado stated that they resented the influence of Bazan on behalf of the Spanish Eastern Convention regarding their decision to allow it to become a district, thus forcing all of their ministers to submit to its leadership. He also stated that they resented being dictated to by the Latin District Council and not being treated with respect as a sister district, although still with no voting rights.[34]

Finally, Alvarado said that Manuel T. Sánchez was not honoring the agreement that the Pentecostal Church of God and the Spanish Eastern Convention entered into and that his actions made this agreement "null and void" after he created the Spanish Eastern District in June 1957, thereby freeing him up to start AG works in Puerto Rico and other places where the Pentecostal Church of God already had churches and missions. Alvarado was particularly unhappy that they were not told for two years about the fact that Sánchez would not honor this agreement and as a result felt like they were not "dealt with fairly." Alvarado ended by stating that the Pentecostal Church of God would send missionaries wherever they liked and wanted equal rights with the Latin District Council to start new churches among the Puerto Rican diaspora in the United States since the AG was not meeting the needs of the people, some of whom were "falling prey" to the Latino Jesus Only people in New York, Chicago, and Milwaukee. They also said that Puerto Ricans have a different style of worship than Mexicans and thus they were better suited to meet their spiritual needs.[35]

In May, Hodges wrote to Flower and Thomas F. Zimmerman about the "Puerto Rico Problem." The struggle, as one letter plainly put it, was now over "their [self]-determination."[36] Despite efforts from smaller factions on both sides to patch up the relationship, the Pentecostal Church of God made the historic decision to formally separate from the AG church on the mainland, with which it had been loosely affiliated. By the time of the General Council Convention in August 1957, Flower and others stated what had become clear to everyone: it was "definitely confirmed" that the Pentecostal Church of God (PCG) of Puerto Rico decided to separate from the Assemblies of God. The split was final. The Pentecostal Church of God of Puerto Rico was no longer part of the AG and now was a completely independent Pentecostal denomination. The Pentecostal Church of God took approximately 300 churches and missions out of the AG and renamed their denomination the Pentecostal Church of God M.I. (Movimiento Internacional). Today, it is the largest Protestant denomination in Puerto Rico, followed by the AG.[37]

Rebirth of the Assemblies of God in Puerto Rico, 1957–1958

Latino and Euro-American AG leaders in the United States now had to decide what to do about the growing Pentecostal Church of God presence in New York City and if the AG should start a new work in Puerto Rico. The AG was left with only three acres of land and a handful of ministers and missions on the island. It decided to start a new AG work. On June 6, 1957, they renamed their Spanish Eastern Convention the Spanish Eastern District, and on June 7, the Spanish Eastern District sent Rev. José Caraballo and Rev. José Cruz to Puerto Rico to assess the situation and draw up plans to begin the new AG work on the island. They met with the few ministers who remained loyal to the AG and with various leaders from independent Pentecostal churches that were now interested in joining the new work. They added two churches under the leadership of Fabriciano Picón and four under Herminio Isern, Manuel Pérez, and Aniano Rivera y Crescencio Santiago. Pablo Clemente, Tony Fonseca, Martin Padilla, and others soon joined them. On October 27, 1958, at Iglesia Cristiana Nazareth, they elected Fabriciano Picón president and Aniano Rivera secretary-treasurer of the Puerto Rican AG work. Within a short time, a number of other people and churches joined them as the Puerto Rico Conference. A short while later they claimed forty-eight churches and missions. Aniano Rivera, Manuel A. Cordero, and Alejandro Pérez were elected to serve as conference presidents until the new AG work in Puerto Rico was granted district status in January 1976. Cordero was important because he had founded the Instituto Bíblico Asambleas de Dios (later Colegio Teológico del Caribe de las Asambleas de Dios) in the Pájaros barrio in Bayamón. This replaced Mizpa Bible Institute. Andrés Rosa was the first president. He was succeeded by the first woman president, Susana Santiago. Doris and Alvaro Rodríguez joined her on the faculty. The Bible School—now a college—offered bachelor's, associate's, and certificate degrees. Today, over 90 students attend at any given time, and more than 500 people have graduated from it since it was founded.[38]

Ruben Nieves served as first district superintendent from 1976–1982. He provided stability and was an effective preacher and leader known for his personal integrity and warm love for his family. He also helped to open up ecumenical dialogue with the governor of the island and other Protestant denominations. He had a broad social vision and desire to change the community, and he even partnered with the government to address drug and alcohol addiction. For all of these reasons, the movement grew rapidly under his leadership, and by 1981 it had increased to 131 churches, 15,485 members, and 271 credentialed ministers.[39]

Nieves laid a solid foundation for the new district. Rafael Miranda (1982–1986), Alejandro Pérez (1986–1991), Saturnino González (1991–2000), and Juan H. Suárez (2001–) followed him as superintendent. The district went through a tumultuous period in the 1980s after Miranda was accused of personal shortcomings, for which he was disciplined. He was restored, but then later dismissed again and expelled from the denomination for falling back into the same pattern of behavior. This executive leadership problem, along with administrative shortcomings, struggles over personality differences, and conflicting visions for the AG's future, divided the leadership. After attempts to address the problem internally, General Superintendent Raymon Carlson and former superintendent Zimmerman intervened to assist the district.[40]

While, in the past, external Euro-American involvement had often led to confusion or problems, in this case Zimmerman was able to offer gentle but helpful guidance about how best to proceed. Pérez was an able leader who not only helped stabilize the district but also was able to redirect its focus to evangelism, education, and renewing the movement throughout the island. He also continued to promote the district's ecumenical outlook and crafted a more biblical yet moderate Pentecostal outlook—and yet one that was also true to the fundamentals of the faith. Given the shift of the second-generation children away from the earlier generation's strict legalism, the AG under Pérez was able to attract a large and growing number of younger Puerto Ricans.[41]

Development, 1990–Present

In 1991, the district leadership was successfully handed to Saturnino González (1991–2000). He was a dynamic superintendent who placed a premium on education and social transformation. After graduating from Bible school, he received his Doctor of Ministry (D.Min.) degree from McCormick Theological Seminary in Chicago. He was a highly effective leader because he was completely bilingual and bicultural. He felt at home in both Puerto Rico and the United States. Although he had a high regard for the Bible, theological education, and interdenominational cooperation, he also stressed that ministers needed to live holy and sanctified lives. As a result of these commitments, he stressed the need to nurture new and old believers alike in the faith. He also placed an emphasis on church growth and helped organize and receive new churches into the AG.

González promoted the triple mission of the church, La Casa Vida (a *hospicio*), and three new Teen Challenge centers to reach youth with drug and alcohol addictions, gang members, and at-risk youth. All of this evangelistic and social outreach resulted in the AG movement expanding the kinds of ministries it offered. In 1996, González organized a pan-Pentecostal celebration of the eighty-year anniversary of Juan Lugo preaching Pentecost in Puerto Rico. He reached out to Pedro Torres of the Pentecostal Church of God, and they had a powerful reunion service. After nine years of serving as superintendent, González decided to accept the senior pastorate at Calvary Church Assemblies of God in Orlando, Florida. He was replaced by Juan H. Suárez, who has carried on the work of González. Suárez and his leadership team, pictured in

Figure 8.2, also led new evangelistic and social initiatives and helped to strengthen the Bible study, mission, and evangelism programs for women, men, and youth.[42]

As a result of their leadership and evangelistic outreach and church planting, the movement grew from just a handful of followers and churches in 1958 to 22,000 members, 192 churches, and 360 ordained (184), licensed (80), and certified/special (96) ministers and leaders in 2010. Today the Puerto Rico District continues its evangelistic work, church planting, Teen Challenge programs, radio ministry, and other social outreach programs. It has softened the hard-edged dogmatism of its early years and has matured into one of the leading Protestant denominations in Puerto Rico today. It has also sought to exercise a voice in public life by balancing the message of the Bible and social responsi-

Figure 8.2. Puerto Rico District Superintendent Rev. Juan Suárez (front row center) and staff, 2006. First row (left to right): Rev. Miguel Arroyo, Superintendent Rev. Juan H. Suárez, Rev. Ivan de la Torre. Back row (left to right): Rev. Ruben D. Figueroa, Rev. Daniel Negron. (Puerto Rico District of the Assemblies of God)

bility via evangelistic-social work. This has challenged the traditional Latino Pentecostal critique of politics as too worldly to get involved with. Instead, leaders like González, Suárez, and others have attempted to find a balance that leads to a healthy spiritual outlook and public life presence. This has in turn led the AG to be an important player in ecumenical dialogue on the island; some leaders and members have even begun entering into Catholic-Protestant dialogue and cooperation on moral and social issues such as the pro-life movement, social justice, and addressing poverty and immigration reform. However, they also hold steadfast to their Pentecostal theological convictions and doctrinal standards without compromise.[43]

Since the 1950s, the Pentecostal movement in Puerto Rico has exploded, in large part due to the competitive Pentecostal Church of God and AG work on the island along with the innumerable splinter denominations and councils. These two denominations alone make up over 30 percent of all Puerto Rican Protestants. Recent studies on Puerto Rican religiosity found that 60 percent of Puerto Rico's 3.7 million people self-identify as Roman Catholic, 39 percent as Protestant and other Christian, and the remainder with no religion or no religious preference. It also found that 45 percent of islanders self-identify as born again, 38 percent as Pentecostal/Charismatic, and 62 percent of all non-Catholics self-identify as Evangelical. Pentecostalism over the past 100 years has been a major vehicle for the evangelization and Evangelicalization of Puerto Rico.[44]

Contrary to popular perception, the Pentecostal Church of God did not break off from the AG in the United States because it was schismatic and influenced by Puerto Rican nationalism. In fact, the church wanted to be fully integrated into the national AG denomination (a move that was similarly being carried out in the 1950s by Latino Presbyterian and Methodist districts), but was rebuffed and told it could not be integrated because it was a "foreign national" church. Some interpreted this as something of a racial slight, which was made all the more pronounced by the upsurge in Puerto Rican cultural nationalism, the 1954 *Brown v. Board of Education* decision, and the newspaper coverage of the African

American civil rights struggle. Although there is no explicit reference to the civil rights struggle in the extant literature, it is hard to imagine that this did not help inform how they interpreted the actions of the American AG. This, combined with the growing nationalist movement in Puerto Rico, persuaded many of those who originally pushed for integration now to call for independence. The schism was more than a Euro-American–Puerto Rican islander conflict. In fact, it was also driven as much by U.S. Puerto Rican versus island Puerto Rican competition as it was by the insensitive treatment by Euro-American AG leaders. Valiant efforts were finally made to respond to the Pentecostal Church of God, but it rejected those efforts because they believed they were now being forced to conform to the U.S. standards that conflicted with how they had been governing their movement for over thirty-five years. A decision to become an "American district" would have created problems on issues such as episcopal-congregational leadership style, church sovereignty, property ownership, and clergy jurisdiction.

As a result of the split, the AG started a new work in Puerto Rico in 1958. It grew from a convention directed and influenced by the Eastern Spanish Convention to its own district in 1976. It has since led the way as one of the most progressive Pentecostal bodies in Puerto Rico in its attempt to mix evangelism and social transformation and interdenominational relations. All of this has resulted in the district exercising a strong public voice in Puerto Rican society. It is ironic that a "liberal" move on the part of the Pentecostal Church of God to go independent resulted in a more culturally insulated and conservative denomination (less willing to engage in ecumenical dialogue and more episcopal and authoritarian leadership style) and that a "conservative" move on the part of the Spanish Eastern District, staying with the AG rather than joining the PCG, led to a more progressive AG movement, both in Puerto Rico and in New York City. Despite the various struggles, the Spanish Eastern District has had a major impact on the growth and development of the Latino AG in the United States, though not—as we shall see in the next chapter—without a struggle.

CHAPTER 9

Spirit and Power

Puerto Rican Pentecostalism in New York City

T HE SPANISH EASTERN CONVENTION played a critical role in the decision of the Pentecostal Church of God to leave the AG. This is ironic because the Spanish Eastern Convention was originally a mission sponsored by the Pentecostal Church of God. However, by the 1950s it had become a hybrid Puerto Rican American work that was increasingly more tied to the General Council in Springfield than to Puerto Rico. This fact, along with the indigenization of the movement with second-generation Puerto Ricans born and raised in New York and the indigenization of their work with the creation of their own churches, Bible school, and headquarters, prompted them to become almost completely independent of the Pentecostal Church of God. By the 1950s they were in every sense of the word an American convention. Because of their loyalty to the General Council in Springfield, along with their rapid growth and strong and independent leadership, on June 6, 1957, the General Council of the Assemblies of God in Springfield awarded the Spanish Eastern Convention full district status with all of the same rights and privileges as the Latin American District in the Southwest and all other American districts—the very thing the Pentecostal Church of God originally requested in the 1940s.

The story of the Spanish Eastern District (SED) differs from that of both the Pentecostal Church of God and the Latin American District Council in the Southwest. In fact, there are a number of myths and stereotypes about its origins and development that are inaccurate, such as the notions that it was founded by Juan Lugo in 1916 and led by Euro-American missionaries. In fact, the Spanish Eastern District was originally pioneered by the Pentecostal Church of God in Puerto Rico, which sent Tomás Alvarez to pioneer the work in 1928. This movement was indigenous from the beginning and differed from Pentecostalism in Puerto Rico, Mexico, and the Southwest in several important ways. It was a largely urban, storefront mission with a completely indigenous tradition whose ministers and parishioners tended to be more educated than those in their above-noted sister movements. Like the movement in Puerto Rico, it was indigenous from the beginning, but like the American movement in the Southwest, it was strongly tied to the General Council in Springfield, despite likewise exercising considerable freedom and autonomy. As a result of this freedom and autonomy and support from both the Pentecostal Church of God and the General Council of the Assemblies of God, along with excellent leadership by Juan Lugo, Frank Finkenbinder, Abelardo Berrios, Manuel T. Sánchez, Ricardo Tañon, and others, the movement grew very rapidly. (See Figure 9.1)

However, it also experienced rapid growth because, unlike Puerto Rico and Mexico in the nineteenth century, where the religious marketplace was dominated and highly regulated by the Catholic Church, in New York City's Spanish-speaking community the Catholic Church was in a weakened state and the religious marketplace was completely unregulated. In fact, many Latino Protestant and Pentecostal churches actually opened up churches around the same time the Catholic Church began designating Spanish parishes to minister to the thousands of Puerto Ricans and other Latin Americans pouring into New York City. In short, the Catholic Church did not have a religious or cultural monopoly over the Latino religious marketplace and found itself in tight competition with mainline Protestants and especially Pentecostals and other Evangelical groups.

Figure 9.1. Rev. Juan and Rev. Isabel Lugo Evangelistic Campaign, La Sinagoga, East Harlem, 1930s. (Gastón Espinosa Latino Pentecostal History Collection)

Origins of *El Barrio* in New York City

Puerto Rican Catholicism and Protestantism largely followed Puerto Rican migration from the island to New York City. However, Puerto Ricans were not the first Latinos to arrive in New York City. Spaniards and Latin American exiles first arrived in New York City during the late nineteenth century. Puerto Rican migration began in earnest after the United States annexed Puerto Rico in the wake of the Spanish-American War of 1898. At first, this migration was primarily of upper-class businessmen and political exiles. By 1910, there were 1,500 Puerto Ricans living in the United States.

The first large-scale migration to New York took place during World War I, when Puerto Ricans arrived to fill the labor shortage during the war and others traveled there en route to the battlefields in France. This migration was facilitated by inexpensive transportation between New York City and the island and by the Jones Act of 1917, which granted Puerto Ricans U.S. citizenship. The second wave of Puerto Rican migration took place in the late 1920s after a devastating hurricane, San Felipe II, ripped through the island in September 1928, destroying its economic infrastructure and leaving 200,000 people homeless. The devastation of the hurricane, the search for employment and housing, and stories about their relatives and friends making almost five times what they earned on the island prompted thousands to migrate to Spanish Harlem between 1926 and 1930. The Puerto Rican migration was supplemented by a large influx of Spaniards, Cubans, and Central and South Americans.[1] By 1931, there were an estimated 175,000 Latinos living in New York City, most of them Puerto Rican.[2] While almost 80 percent of all Puerto Ricans in the United States settled in New York City, the 1920 census reported Puerto Ricans living in fifteen states.[3]

Most Puerto Ricans settled in East (Spanish) Harlem, not far from the Navy Shipyard in Brooklyn, where many worked.[4] During the Great Depression, most Puerto Rican men worked as common laborers, construction workers, laundry workers, factory workers, porters, errand boys, domestics, hotel workers, janitors, painters, cooks, and kitchen workers. The three most common types of employment for women were as domestic maids (42 percent), needleworkers/seamstresses (20 percent), and garment workers (20 percent).[5]

Migration to the United States dropped off sharply after 1930 due to the Great Depression and did not increase again until World War II, when thousands provided muscle in the U.S. war effort.[6] Puerto Ricans were not only drafted but also were offered employment in booming factories in New York and Chicago and across the country. By 1950, over 300,000 Puerto Ricans were living in the United States.[7] The migration to New York City was shaped by overpopulation in Puerto Rico, natural disasters, economic pressures, job opportunities, cheap transportation, and invitations from relatives and friends.[8] Life in in the city was hardly easy because of racial segregation and discrimination, overcrowded housing, the high cost of living, unemployment, lack of upward mobility, deteriorating schools, and a language barrier.[9] While some argue that

Latinos suffered little during the Depression, this is not true for Puerto Ricans, who, because of a rise in Nativism, were the first to be hit by the economic crisis. By 1937, approximately 32,000 Puerto Ricans were on government relief in Spanish Harlem,[10] their hopes and dreams dashed.[11]

Latino Catholicism

In response to the growing Latino presence in New York City, in 1902 the Roman Catholic Archdiocese of New York organized a Spanish-speaking chapel called Our Lady of Guadalupe on West Fourteenth Street in Manhattan. In 1912, a second Spanish chapel called Nuestra Señora de la Esperanza was set up in Washington Heights. Two more chapels were founded in 1926 and 1930. The large-scale migration during World War I and the 1920s prompted the Archdiocese of New York to organize two new Spanish-language parish chapels, Our Lady of the Miraculous Medal (La Milagrosa) in Manhattan and Holy Agony (Santa Agonía) in Spanish Harlem. By 1940, Our Lady of the Miraculous Medal had become the center of the Puerto Rican Catholic community.[12]

Despite the attempt made by the Archdiocese of New York to minister to the growing Latin American population, Ana María Díaz-Stevens argues that these national chapels were unable to meet all of the religious, social, and growing economic needs of the burgeoning community prior to World War II. The few self-help groups and *mutualistas* (mutual aid societies) that did arise, such as El Centro Obrero Español, tended to have secular or anticlerical attitudes. The notable exception was Casa Maria, which was founded by Catholic laypeople in Spanish Harlem around 1934. This center functioned as a settlement house for Spanish, Latin American, and Puerto Rican immigrants and migrants,[13] providing housing, food, clothing, and employment opportunities for the poor.[14] Catholic nuns like Carmela Zapata Bonilla Marrerro also conducted social work in Harlem from 1923 to 1949, which helped alleviate suffering and provided hope.[15]

A major change took place in the Latino Catholic community during 1939, when Archbishop Francis Spellman replaced the national ethnic parish system with a new "integrated parish" model. The new integrated parish church was to serve the immediate community by retaining third-generation Catholics, providing bilingual priests, and desegregating the church. However, the policy invariably undermined the Puerto Rican Catholic community by diluting its resources and its indigenous voice, and by attempting to assimilate the community into the larger Euro-American Catholic Church and U.S. society.[16]

Although the majority of Puerto Ricans who migrated from Puerto Rico to New York City were Catholic, over 50 percent had no formal affiliation with the Church.[17] The disconnect between the Euro-American hierarchy and Puerto Rican popular Catholicism on the island was carried over to New York City. Although Roman Catholicism had had a tremendous impact on the culture and ethos of Puerto Rico, the hierarchy's historic connection to the ruling elites and the new Euro-American governance structure created a socioreligious barrier. As a result, Puerto Rican participation in Catholic services was much lower than for other ethnic Catholics. The low attendance was also the result of having to work on Sundays and due to anticlericalism, especially among men.[18] One Puerto Rican social worker in the 1930s reported that the lack of contact between Puerto Ricans and the Catholic Church was also the result of Pentecostal, Protestant, and nonsectarian organizations.[19] For all of these reasons, by the late 1940s only 29 percent of men and 40 percent of women attended church once a week or more, and only 12 percent of Puerto Rican Catholics said religion was "the most important thing" in their lives.[20] By 1950, only 12 percent attended Mass at least once a week in New York City.[21]

Latino Protestantism

The unregulated nature of the Puerto Rican and Latino religious marketplace in New York City meant that Latino Protestants could compete on a more equal basis. The exact origins of Latino Protestantism in New York City are uncertain. Euro-American and African American Protestant congregations made some efforts to welcome Puerto Rican Protestants into their congregations.[22] The Iglesia Hispana-Americana was perhaps the first Latino Protestant church in New York City, having been founded in 1898.[23] Latino mainline Protestantism did not really begin to expand until after 1912. In 1910, Reverend Samuel F. Cordiano, a

Mexican Baptist, organized one of the first Spanish-speaking Protestant churches in New York City—Calvary Baptist Church. This work grew and moved to the Madison Square Presbyterian Church on 24th Street. In January 1912, the work came under the supervision of the New York City Mission Society, a nondenominational ecumenical Protestant organization. That year, the society took over the First Spanish Evangelical mission and in 1951 renamed it the Church of the Good Neighbor.[24] This church became the symbolic mother congregation of the Spanish-speaking Protestant work in New York City.[25]

The First Spanish Baptist Church of New York City was initiated on May 28, 1920, and by the early 1930s it was one of the largest Spanish-speaking churches in New York City, with over 300 adherents.[26] Despite this growth, Puerto Rican and other Latino Baptists had little say over when and where they would meet because they were at the mercy of the larger Euro-American congregation that hosted them. In 1935, the Euro-American leaders of the Mount Moriah Baptist Church sold their church to a black congregation and forced the Spanish congregation to find a new home. Euro-American–Puerto Rican Baptist relations were further strained when Euro-American Baptists feared that Puerto Rican "blacks" were invading their church, prompting the pastor to ask the Puerto Rican congregation to stop holding services in their church. Though they donated a few chairs to the now-homeless Puerto Rican Baptist congregation, they did little else to help them.[27] The Baptists placed a tremendous emphasis on evangelism and church planting. They organized new Latino congregations in 1928, 1930, 1935, 1941, 1949, and 1954.[28] Almost all these churches started in the homes of Puerto Rican Baptist families, many of which had first converted in their native Puerto Rico.

The Protestant work in New York City grew rapidly. The Fundamentalist-Modernist controversy that raged within the American Baptist Convention had little impact on the Spanish-speaking work in New York City, where the Latino churches tended to be very traditional and pietistic. The notable exception came in 1933, when a number of Puerto Rican American Baptists left the denomination because some felt it was becoming too theologically and morally "liberal."[29]

The New York City Mission Society was the major catalyst in the spread of mainline and Evangelical Protestantism in Spanish Harlem. By the late

1930s the Baptists, Presbyterians, Methodists, Lutherans, and Christian and Missionary Alliance had organized churches and missions throughout the city. The Seventh-Day Adventists and Jehovah's Witnesses also conducted outreach to Latinos.[30] Euro-American and African American churches did little to attract Latinos permanently to their churches.[31]

In addition to these traditional forms of Christianity, Spiritism, Spiritualism, and Marxism were active in Spanish Harlem. Puerto Ricans set up shops, sought out converts, and offered to bring divine healing and/ or hope for marginalized Latinos. They also promised to bring about positive social change. Many Latinos and Puerto Ricans attended their services, converted, and became ardent evangelists for the faith. The growth of Protestantism among the Puerto Rican diaspora help set the stage for the rise of Pentecostalism because it made Protestant churches and beliefs an accepted part of everyday life.[32]

Tomás Alvarez, Juan Lugo, and Latino AG Origins in New York City

The exact origins of the Latino Pentecostal movement in New York City are uncertain, but there is little reason to doubt that Latinos first joined the Pentecostal movement shortly after it arrived in New York City in 1906. That year a group of African American and Euro-American missionaries from the Azusa Street Revival stopped off in New York City en route to Europe, the Middle East, and Africa. Before they left, they organized what was likely the first Pentecostal congregation in New York City. One eyewitness wrote, "Pentecost has surely fallen in New York in a mission there. A number have been baptized with the Holy Spirit and are speaking in tongues."[33] In May 1907, Marie Burgess Brown founded the first major Pentecostal mission in New York City—Glad Tidings Tabernacle. It soon became the center of the Pentecostal movement in New York.[34]

One of the first Latinos to make contact with the Pentecostal movement in New York City was Juan Lugo when, in August 1916, he met Robert and Marie (Burgess) Brown and stayed in their missionary rest home. Lugo realized the need to organize a Pentecostal ministry among the Puerto Rican diaspora. The question was when. Then, in the late

1920s, some of Lugo's former parishioners who had migrated to New York City asked him to organize a church.[35] In response, Lugo and the Pentecostal Church of God sent Tomás Alvarez to pioneer the Spanish-speaking work in New York City.[36]

Alvarez organized the first congregation in the Green Point section of Brooklyn on July 22, 1928. The first person converted was a woman named Belen Nieves, who went on to pioneer the AG work as a missionary in Cuba. Alvarez ministered in Brooklyn until 1931, at which time he returned to Puerto Rico, where he became the third president of the Pentecostal Church of God. Shortly thereafter he resigned from the ministry.[37]

The next major turning point came in March 1931, when Lugo migrated to New York City to take charge of Alvarez's work. In June 1932, he opened the second Pentecostal Church of God congregation in Manhattan. Eleutero Paz, a Mexican evangelist, served as pastor.[38]

Paz suggested that Lugo move his burgeoning congregation to an empty Jewish synagogue on 115th Street. Shortly thereafter, Lugo raised funds to purchase the synagogue and founded La Sinagoga church. It became the sacred center of the Spanish-speaking Assemblies of God and Pentecostal Church of God work in New York City. Lugo used the synagogue to conduct revival meetings and evangelistic-healing campaigns for the sick and lame, with hundreds claiming salvation and healing. By 1933, over 250 people were attending La Sinagoga. Lugo claimed that thousands were converted during his ministry from 1931 to 1936, and he helped plant new churches throughout the city.[39] By 1937, there were seven Latino AG churches in New York.[40]

One problem Lugo faced was preparing pastors and evangelists for the ministry. So in 1935, Edmundo Jordan, a lay leader in La Sinagoga, established a Bible school at the church. In 1939, the school was incorporated as the Hispanic American Bible Institute of the Spanish Eastern Convention of the Assemblies of God. This was the first Spanish-language Pentecostal Bible school in New York City. Students read Myer Pearlman's *Knowing the Doctrines of God,* Stanley Frodsham's *With Signs Following,* and other Pentecostal literature.[41]

In 1936, Noel Perkins and J. R. Flower asked Juan Lugo to open up a Bible school in Puerto Rico to meet the growing need for new clergy.

Lugo agreed and opened Mizpa Bible Institute in September 1937. That same year, Frank Finkenbinder became pastor of La Sinagoga. Finkenbinder's bilingual ministry blossomed to over 440 people by 1939, and he also helped plant new churches.[42]

While the Pentecostal Church of God in New York had its fair share of internal problems between jealous ministers, it had not faced any major schisms. The first major controversy erupted after news broke that Lugo had engaged in misconduct. The Pentecostal Church of God conducted a trial in Puerto Rico and claimed that Lugo was guilty of moral misconduct and playing the lottery. B. R. Colón, Luís C. Otero, and José Martínez recommended that Lugo step down from the ministry. This news spread quickly and shook the Pentecostal movement in Puerto Rico and New York.[43] Lugo denied the charges, said he was falsely accused, and demanded a second trial led by someone more fair-minded. Frank Finkenbinder was brought in to adjudicate the case. Afterward, Finkenbinder wrote to AG headquarters, stating, "There is every evidence that Bro. Lugo has been taken in misconduct morally," though he did not specify on what grounds.[44]

Unwilling to resign in light of the "false accusations," Lugo rallied his followers and led one group out of the Pentecostal Church of God and formed his own independent Pentecostal fellowship in New York City. He accused Finkenbinder of "lacking wisdom" and being unable to rightly judge the accusations. Like Francisco Olazábal in 1922, Lugo appealed directly to J. Roswell Flower, who, after hearing both sides of the argument, asked him to resign voluntarily, which he did in 1940 after twenty-four years of service. Though it took Lugo a lifetime of work to build his ministry, it took only a few accusations or unguarded moments to ruin it—or so it seemed.[45]

Many of Lugo's supporters blamed Finkenbinder for Lugo's dismissal. They interpreted Finkenbinder's actions through an ethnic lens. Indeed, Lugo's dismissal took place during an upsurge in Puerto Rican nationalism; in 1937, Pedro Albizu Campos had led an ill-fated push for Puerto Rican independence that resulted in an overreaction on the part of the police and to the Ponce Massacre. Finkenbinder represented the kind of Euro-American morality, justice, and paternalism that many Nuyoricans no longer wanted.[46]

When Finkenbinder resisted the demand to reorganize the church government structure at La Sinagoga, a majority of the elders demanded his resignation. Finkenbinder lamented that some of his Puerto Rican elders were making "strong propaganda" against him, stating, "They did not want an American Minister any longer . . . that it took too much to keep him." After failing to quell the rebellion, Finkenbinder resigned on August 31, 1940, and Raymond Reyes was elected pastor pro tem.[47] Despite opposition from the board, virtually all the deacons felt that Finkenbinder was wrongly pushed out of the church.[48] After Finkenbinder's resignation, he moved to Denver, where he soon became a leader in the Latin American District. A few years later, in 1950, he moved to Isleta, Texas, where he became director of the Latin American Bible Institute (LABI).[49]

Now that Lugo's testimony was tarnished, he found it difficult to organize a new church. Yet not everyone believed the allegations made against him. Shortly afterward, Lugo was invited by Carlos Sepúlveda and the Assembly of Christian Churches (AIC) to serve as their new superintendent, an office he held for approximately one year. The accusations soon faded or were dismissed by Lugo's supporters. In 1946 he joined the Church of God in Cleveland, Tennessee, and in 1953 he founded a Church of God mission that later became La Tercera Avenida. Although he was heralded as the "Apostle of Puerto Rico," his leadership of the Puerto Rican Pentecostal movement was diminished as a result of the accusations, and his influence faded with time and age—though his stature as one of the movement's key founders remains unchanged.[50]

Origins of the Spanish Eastern District and Second-Generation Leaders

By the time Juan Lugo turned in his ministerial credentials in 1940, the Pentecostal Church of God was the largest Protestant denomination in Puerto Rico and Spanish Harlem. His resignation opened the door to a new generation of young and able leaders like Carlos Sepúlveda, Leoncia Rosado Rousseau, Abelardo Berrios, and Ricardo Tañon.[51] The 1936 election of Manuel T. Sánchez as president of the Spanish Eastern

Figure 9.2.   Rev. Francisco Olazábal Evangelistic-Healing Campaign, Calvary
in the second row, left of center, waving his right hand.   (Gastón Espinosa Latino Penteco.

Conference (later Convention, in 1946, and District, in 1957) began a
trend in Latinos seeking to become more closely affiliated with the
mother church in the United States rather than Puerto Rico. A year later,
in 1937, they began pushing for the creation of a new conference (a larger
organizational unit) organically connected to the AG in the United
States.[52] In 1937, Finkenbinder and a number of Puerto Rican leaders in
New York organized a Spanish-speaking conference within the larger
Eastern District of the Assemblies of God. Manuel T. Sánchez was
elected its first Euro-American president.[53] After six years of back-and-
forth negotiating between Puerto Rican and Euro-American leaders in
Springfield, the Spanish Eastern Convention was organized in 1946[54]
and grew from 11 churches in 1946 to 40 churches and approximately
5,400 members by 1960.[55]

The next major turning point in the Latino AG work in New York
City took place in 1957 after the Pentecostal Church of God officially
severed its affiliation with the AG.[56] The new denomination was called
the Pentecostal Church of God, M.I.[57] That same year, the Spanish
Eastern Convention became the Spanish Eastern District, with Sánchez as its first superintendent. This almost destroyed the AG work in
Puerto Rico and New York. However, a number of Puerto Rican leaders
affiliated with the AG on the island, officially began a new AG work in
1958.[58]

Baptist Church, 120 Lenox Avenue, Brooklyn, September 1931. Rev. Olazábal is
History Collection)

Pentecostal Competitors in New York City:
Francisco Olazábal

The largest Latino Pentecostal denomination in New York City prior to
1939 was not the Assemblies of God but the Latin American Council of
Christian Churches (CLADIC). In 1929, Rev. Paz invited Olazábal to conduct a revival at the Palace Opera House in Chicago; it was attended by
thousands. Two years later, in 1931, Paz then invited him to lead another
revival in New York City. Olazábal accepted Paz's invitation and began
evangelistic work at the gigantic Calvary Baptist Church in Brooklyn and
then in Depression-stricken Spanish Harlem. His preaching to over
100,000 Latinos over the course of the next few years gave birth to the first
major Spanish-speaking Pentecostal revival in New York City, during
which time thousands were converted. His Bethel Temple mother church
met in a former Jewish synagogue on 113th Street in Spanish Harlem, just
one street over from the setting of Robert Orsi's story of the Madonna of
114th Street in Italian Harlem. Olazábal's church quickly swelled to 1,500
members, and he started a number of churches throughout the New York
City metropolitan area. He conducted regular weeklong evangelistic-
healing campaigns until his death in 1937 (see Figure. 9.2).[59]

Olazábal is important to the Spanish Eastern District and the Latino
AG movement because, after he died, many of his ministers, churches,

and converts joined the Puerto Rican, Spanish Eastern, and Latin American Districts, especially after his massive Chicago, Spanish Harlem, and Puerto Rico revivals of 1929, 1931, 1934, and 1936. The Latino AG is in many ways responsible for Olazábal's work and success in New York City, because one of its ministers (Paz) invited him to Spanish Harlem and helped advertise his revival services. Finally, Olazábal's ministry benefited the Spanish Eastern Convention because it forced it to be more proactive in evangelism in order to keep up with the massive gains Olazábal was making throughout the city. Yet despite their common goals and spiritual influences in California, and for reasons that are not entirely clear, Lugo and Olazábal never conducted any joint campaigns or became close friends.

Francisco Olazábal's New York ministry came to a crashing halt when he was killed due to injuries he sustained in a car accident in June 1937. His death stunned his followers and led to fragmentation and schism.[60] In 1939, Carlos Sepúlveda, Gilberto Díaz, Felipe Sabater, and Frank Hernández formed their own New York–based denomination called the Assembly of Christian Churches.[61] By the mid-1940s, Olazábal's Latin American Council of Christian Churches lost virtually all of its churches in New York City and Puerto Rico to the AIC, the AG, the Damascus Christian Church, the Defenders of the Faith, or other councils or denominations.[62]

The primary force behind the formation of the Assembly of Christian Churches was Carlos Sepúlveda (1905–1996), a former Presbyterian and a graduate of the Evangelical Seminary of Puerto Rico. He joined Olazábal during his campaign on the island in 1934 and then became a leader in Olazábal's CLADIC before organizing the first general AIC convention, held May 14–21, 1939, at Bethel Temple in New York City. Sepúlveda saw his ministry in continuity with Olazábal's. During June of that same year, the AIC founded *La Voz Evangélica*, an outgrowth of a smaller periodical published at Bethel Temple called *Ecos de Betel*. The AIC also asked Juan Lugo to serve as superintendent for one year. By 1941, the AIC claimed more than sixty ministers and Christian workers *(obreros)* and 2,000 members in New York, California, Illinois, Michigan, Texas, Mexico, Puerto Rico, Cuba, and the Dominican Republic.[63] The AIC produced a number of very talented female evangelists, such as the mother-daughter team of Julia and Matilde Vargas, who held services in New York, Chicago, El Paso, and Los Angeles.[64] The AIC was strongest in New York City and went from 12 churches in 1940 to 26 congregations and 1,600 members by 1960.[65]

In addition to the growing number of denominations founded in New York City during the 1930s and 1940s, there was also a host of small independent churches and *concilios*. Antonio R. Caquias and his wife founded the Hispanic Church of God (Iglesia de Dios Hispana) in Brooklyn in 1932. They continued their independent ministry until 1940, at which time they had joined the SED. Caquias later became a leader in the movement.[66]

In 1951, after several years of conflict over the fate of La Sinagoga, Abelardo Berrios led the church out of the Spanish Eastern Convention and the AG. Three years later he formed a new denomination called the Latin American Council of the Pentecostal Church of God of New York, Inc. After the Pentecostal Church of God (PCG) split off from the AG in 1957, in the United States it formed an autonomous district of approximately thirty churches. Despite the autonomous nature of the PCG in New York, it still maintained a loose affiliation with the PCG in Puerto Rico during the 1950s and 1960s. A few years later, the PCG organized five churches in the growing Puerto Rican community in New York City. By the 1970s, it had almost 100 churches and 8,000 adult members in the United States, and by 2000 more than 300 churches and preaching points in the States and in twenty-seven countries around the world.[67]

Spanish Eastern District Growth and Development

The fragmentation of the Latino Pentecostal movement, along with a "mighty revival" that Caquias claims broke out in 1945, completely transformed the topography of the Latino religious marketplace in New York City.[68] By the late 1940s, the Church of God (Cleveland, Tennessee), Church of God of Prophecy, the Foursquare, the Pentecostal Church of Jesus Christ, Leoncia Rosado Rousseau's (Mama Leo) Damascus Christian Church, Defenders of the Faith, and the Samaria Evangelical Church all organized churches in New York City.[69] The Latino Pentecostal movement in New York City grew from twenty-five such churches in 1937 to 143 by 1953. That year Pentecostal churches (heavily

AG) made up almost 70 percent (143 out of 204) of all Latino Protestant churches in New York City.[70]

By the 1950s, the largest and fourth-largest Protestant churches in New York City were also Pentecostal, having 612 and 500-plus members, respectively—Abelardo Berrios's La Sinagoga and Ricardo Tañon's John 3:16 Church.[71] Despite their large size, Pentecostal churches in the Spanish Eastern Convention tended to average fewer members (85) than mainline Protestant churches (104) but more than independent churches (68). A full 70 percent of all Latino Protestant churches in New York City had a membership of less than 100 members, and almost 40 percent had less than fifty members. Yet they were the most vibrant, indigenous, self-starting, and self-supporting churches in Spanish Harlem. They received no outside aid, were conservative in theology, had a strong evangelical spirit, were willing to work with other Protestant churches on specific short-term projects, and were very dynamic and evangelistic. While 63 percent of all Latino Protestant churches rented their facilities, only 29 percent owned their own buildings. Almost 50 percent met in storefronts, 25 percent met in regular church edifices, and approximately 25 percent met in private homes, apartments, or other facilities. By the early 1950s, a full 82 percent of all Latino Protestant churches were completely self-supporting, 47 percent of all Latino Protestant churches had full-time pastors, 37 percent worked at other jobs during the week, and 16 percent pastored two or more churches. By 1960 there were approximately 400 churches and 50,000 Latino Protestants in New York City, and a majority of these were Pentecostal.[72]

Texture and Culture of Latino Pentecostalism in New York City

The Latino Pentecostal movement in the Spanish Eastern District differed from its counterparts in Puerto Rico, Mexico, and the Southwest in a number of respects. It was indigenous, urban, largely storefront, and interdenominationally friendly. By contrast, the Latino AG movement in the Southwest was largely rural, Euro-American-controlled, and anti-ecumenical. The greater openness to ecumenism was in large part shaped by their higher educational backgrounds, pluralistic urban environment, and geographic proximity and continued contact with the other Protestant traditions. This also made the SED very competitive with other denominations. One 1959 study argued that the Pentecostal movement posed the greatest challenge to Roman Catholicism, mainline Protestantism, and Spiritualism in Spanish Harlem. It also claimed that little Pentecostal churches and storefronts were almost as numerous as *botanicas* in Spanish Harlem.[73] Their growth and controversial practices left them vulnerable to attack by Protestants and Catholics. Contrary to the stereotype that Latino Pentecostals care more about experience than theology, almost all Latino AG periodicals contained articles on doctrine.[74] Yet despite the relatively high level of education some had achieved, the average Pentecostal parishioner in New York had only a sixth-grade level of education.[75] AG members placed a tremendous emphasis on holy living, which was defined by external observances and practices. They often forbade drinking, divorce, smoking, dancing, and short hair on women, tight clothes, and any other activities that might lead them to compromise their holiness standards.[76]

Pentecostals took their message to the hard areas of New York by conducting house-to-house evangelistic work, and during the spring and summer held as many as five street meetings per day. People would sing praise songs, testify how God had changed their lives, and then pass out evangelistic tracts. Its message and promise of power, divine healing, and personal transformation by way of a God of second chances led to the rapid indigenization of Latino Pentecostalism in New York City.[77] One Pentecostal stated, "The other churches . . . have no power. . . . The Pentecostal church, you know, has the power to heal we have . . . seen people who threw away their crutches and went out of the hospitals healed by the Pentecostal faith. This is the true faith."[78]

The same enthusiasm and "we-preach-the-truth" attitude that attracted some to the Pentecostal movement turned others away. Apostasy was sometimes a problem. The strict morality, the Arminian belief that one could lose one's salvation, and the lengthy nightly worship services simply wore out many people. Burnout and backsliding were common, if unspoken, problems. The well-intentioned but at times overly strict emphasis on morality sometimes led to legalism, backbiting, and division. In fact, most of the divisions in the Puerto Rican Pentecostal movement have been motivated as much by personality conflict as by correct doctrine. Yet, most of those who became disillusioned with the Latino AG did not return to the Catholic Church, but simply attended another Pentecostal or Protestant church.

Ricardo Tañon and Christian Church John 3:16, South Bronx

One example of the new generation of leaders emerging in the Spanish Eastern District was Ricardo Tañon (1904–1997). He migrated from Comerio, Puerto Rico, in 1929, and was converted through the street preaching of Eleuterio Paz in Spanish Harlem in 1934. After graduating from the Spanish American Bible Institute of New York in 1938, Tañon ministered for several years before taking over the pastorate of Antonio Caquias's small mission called Christian Church John 3:16 in the South Bronx in 1943.[79]

Christian Church John 3:16 was originally founded as a youth ministry connected to Francisco Olazábal's work in the 1930s. It became the center of the Spanish Eastern work after Abelardo Berrios led La Sinagoga out of the AG to form his own denomination. During Tañon's thirty-four-year ministry, he helped found seventeen new churches in New York, the Northeast, Puerto Rico, Cuba, the Dominican Republic, and Latin America. He also prepared and sent out fifty-four ministers for the Pentecostal ministry and placed an increasing emphasis on reaching both the spiritual and social needs of Latinos. He sponsored Benevolence Programs and other social service ministries targeting the poor, immigrants, and at-risk youth.[80] Under his leadership, the church grew from eight members in 1943 to over 1,700 by the 1970s, making it the largest Latino Pentecostal Church in the United States. Despite the enormous size of Tañon's church, the average size of Pentecostal churches numbered 85–120 members, with storefront churches averaging 50–75 members.[81]

Tañon is famous in the Latino AG for sending so many young people into the ministry, mission field, and academy. Villafañe noted that in one year alone, Tañon helped support twenty missionaries. He not only had over 1,500 people attending Sunday school, but he also sponsored the largest Latino Christian bookstore in the Northeast, and held evangelistic services with up to 2,000 people in attendance. Despite only going to public school through the fourth grade, he placed a tremendous emphasis on Spirit-infused education and the need for Latino Pentecostal churches and pastors to nurture agents of biblically based social transformation. For this reason, he sent "hundreds" of youth on to Bible schools and in one year alone sponsored a dozen full-time students at the Bible school. Eldin Villafañe, pictured in Figure 9.3 with Tañon, described John 3:16 as a "liberation Citadel" where "thousands upon thousands of lives [were] transformed—finding faith, hope and love." He argues that

Figure 9.3.   Dr. Eldin Villafañe and Rev. Ricardo Tañon, New York City, ca. 1990. Villafañe attended and was mentored by Rev. Tañon in his church, Iglesia Juan 3:16. Villafañe now serves as Professor of Christian Ethics at Gordon Conwell Theological Seminary and served as founding president of the Center for Urban Ministerial Education (CUME) in Boston and as founding president of La Comunidad of Hispanic Scholars of Religion at the American Academy of Religion.   (Eldin Villafañe)

this church is one of the many reasons why the Puerto Rican Pentecostal movement went from 25 churches in 1937 to 560 in 1983. For all of his accomplishments in the field of theological education, Tañon was awarded a doctor of divinity degree, *honoris causa,* from Gordon-Conwell Theological Seminary in 1977.[82]

Latino Assemblies of God-Influenced Scholars: Eldin Villafañe and Samuel Solivan

One of Tañon's most important protégés is Dr. Eldin Villafañe. After earning his Ph.D. from Boston University in social ethics, he founded and directed the Center for Urban and Ministerial Education for the interdenominational Gordon Conwell Theological Seminary. The Center was one of the first cutting-edge urban ministry programs in the United States. Villafañe is important because he wrote one of the first scholarly books on U.S. Latino Pentecostalism: *The Liberating Spirit: Toward an Hispanic American Pentecostal Social Ethic,* which articulated the first Latino Pentecostal social ethic rooted in indigenous expressions of Latino Pentecostalism. Villafañe was a founding member and first president of La Comunidad of Hispanic Scholars of Religion at the American Academy of Religion and the Society for Biblical Literature and platformed Latino Pentecostal issues in the national academy through his visiting professorship at Harvard Divinity School, where he co-taught a class on Pentecostalism and Liberation Theology with Dr. Harvey Cox, author of *The Secular City, The Silencing of Leonardo Boff,* and *Fire from Heaven.* The spirit of Tañon also inspired other Spanish Eastern District–influenced scholars like Samuel Solivan, who, after studying with James Cone at Union Theological Seminary in New York City and teaching at Andover Newton Theological Seminary in Massachusetts, wrote an important book entitled *Spirit, Pathos and Liberation: Toward an Hispanic Pentecostal Theology.* In it, he discusses conditions "under which our suffering and oppression can be transformed by the Holy Spirit into a liberating life full of hope and promise."[83]

In addition to Villafañe and Solivan, still other Latino AG scholars (including Mexican American Tommy Casarez, about whom more will be said later) went on to earn graduate and doctoral degrees from Yale

Divinity School and Princeton Seminary. These are just a handful of third- and fourth-generation Latino AG people who have gone on to serve as key leaders in the Latino scholarly community.

Spanish Eastern District Leadership and Development

The Spanish Eastern District influenced a number of Latino scholars who have left their mark in the academy and the ministry. The anti-intellectualism of earlier generations of Latino Pentecostals has given way to a greater openness due in large part to the rise of second-generation Puerto Rican and Latino AG leaders who supported a move to balance a deep commitment to Jesus Christ, the church, and the Pentecostal faith, with a desire to pursue graduate and doctoral studies at some of the nation's top theological seminaries and universities in order to have a voice and agency in the church, the academy, and society.

Spanish Eastern District superintendents Alejandro Pérez, Vicente Ortiz, Ralph Williams, Augusto Castillo, and Adolfo Carrión not only developed the work of Manuel T. Sánchez and Ricardo Tañon, but also encouraged this balance of faith and education. The Spanish Eastern District grew quickly under their leadership, but especially under that of Carrión and Rafael Reyes II. Carrión was born in Juncos, Puerto Rico, in 1934 and raised Roman Catholic. He migrated to New York City in 1950 and was converted through the preaching of a small group of Evangelicals from the Sea of Galilee Church in 1951. Not long afterward, he went into the Spanish Eastern Convention ministry and became a senior pastor in 1960. He married Elisa Díaz and they had four children. After being elected assistant superintendent, he was elected superintendent of the Spanish Eastern District in 1966 and served in that capacity until 1998 (see Figure 9.4).[84]

Under Carrión's leadership, the Spanish Eastern District became one of the largest in the AG. He placed tremendous emphasis on church planting and spreading the Christian message, especially in new Latino immigrant communities from New England to Miami, Florida. He realized that the most effective means was to create new churches and districts. As a result, he helped create, form, and release the Puerto Rican AG District in 1976. In 1974, he began laying the foundation for the formation

Figure 9.4.   Rev. Adolfo Carrión served as the Spanish Eastern District
Assistant Superintendent and Superintendent from 1964 to 1998.   (Spanish
Eastern District of the Assemblies of God)

of a new district in the South and in 1980 organized the Southeastern
Spanish District based in Florida. He also strengthened the infrastructure of the Spanish Eastern District, organized new churches, and secured new district resources. He further developed the Bible School in
New York, opened a Hispanic Seminary of the East, and created correspondence programs for ministers who could not relocate. He also developed matriculation agreements with Christian colleges (Nyack,
Southeastern, Valley Forge, Central Bible College) so that students
could graduate with a B.A. degree. A strong supporter of missions, he
raised funds to send missionaries throughout the Latin Caribbean and
Central America, and around the world. One of the ways he spread
the Christian message was through a radio station called WWRV
1330—Radio Visión Cristiana.[85]

After Carrión retired in 1998, Rafael Reyes became superintendent.
He has continued the innovative work of Carrion and especially the
need to create a bilingual church (see Figure 9.5).[86] Reyes's vision has
been driven by what he calls the four cardinal doctrines (salvation, divine healing, Spirit baptism, and Christ's second coming) and the four
reasons for the AG's existence (evangelism, worship, discipleship, and

Figure 9.5.   Spanish Eastern District leaders. Left to right: Rev. César Rodríguez, Rev. Adolfo Carrión (superintendent 1998–2013), Rev. Sergio Martínez, Rev. Rafael Reyes, Rev. Nicanor González, Rev. Domingo Valdés, Rev. Manuel A. Álvarez (superintendent 2013–present).   (Spanish Eastern District of the Assemblies of God)

acts of compassion). He argues that addressing these issues will help them meet the Spanish Eastern District's goal of evangelizing the world, developing ministries, planting churches, and bringing about positive social change to prepare people for Christ's second coming.[87] Under Reyes's leadership, the Spanish Eastern District sent out evangelists and ministers to pioneer the work among Latinos up and down the East Coast from Boston to Florida. Nationwide, the Spanish Eastern District has given birth to the new Puerto Rico District in 1958 and the Southeastern Spanish District in 1980. They are in turn laying foundations for future districts on the East Coast and in the South, where the Latino population is growing very rapidly in states like Virginia, North Carolina, and Georgia.

Contemporary Developments of the Spanish Eastern District

The Spanish Eastern District has undergone a number of major developments since the 1990s. It established 118 new churches between 1998 and 2011, transformed its Bible school into the Spanish Eastern School of Theology, strengthened its core curriculum, increased its budget from $3.5 million to $10.7 million, witnessed growth in its men's, women's, youth, and boys' and girls' ministries, sent out missionaries to Latin America and around the world, modernized the district offices, and helped develop the Puerto Rico, Southern Latin, and Florida Multicultural districts. The district has a strong esprit de corps, plants fifteen to twenty new churches a year, and has increased the number of younger ministers. Despite these positive developments, former SED superintendent Rafael Reyes II said that the SED also faces a number of obstacles such as the integration of various national and ethnic groups (i.e., Puerto Ricans, Dominicans, Central Americans, Mexicans, and other Latinos) into one cohesive district; a generation gap, with the median age of its ministers now fifty-five; limited finances; the need to update technology at the district headquarters and in local churches; and a desire on the part of "a few vocal leaders" to create more Spanish districts within the SED territory.[88]

The role of women in the SED has steadily increased. Women now serve as pastors, evangelists, missionaries, youth ministers, and Christian educators. While women have not served as superintendents, they have been elected to the Executive Board. Rev. Virginia Maldonado was elected SED executive secretary—though still a traditional female role— and now serves as the SED director of education. Five women have also been elected to other district offices. As of 2014 there are 300 credentialed Latina ministers in the SED alone, 98 of whom have been ordained into the full pastoral ministry. However, only a modest 15 percent (50) of the 300 are serving as senior pastors. In short, it is hard for a woman to be called directly to a church, though there are a number of exceptions throughout the district. A number of younger women have gotten around this by planting their own churches. The SED reaches out to youth through traditional ministry programs, street evangelism, social events that target at-risk youth, and music festivals (winter, spring, summer) for young people, where they bring out Christian bands to hold live concerts, which attract large numbers of youth. In all of these endeavors, the SED has tried to continue to develop its capacity and increase its presence among the burgeoning Latino community up and down New England and the Mid-Atlantic states. One way it has sought to do so is through its Spanish Eastern School of Theology, which was founded in the Bronx in 1984. It trains pastors, evangelists, missionaries, youth workers, and Christian educators on campus and through correspondence and part-time programs. In a day and age when many denominations are closing or consolidating churches and releasing clergy, the SED is continuing to find ways to empower its people and reach the Latino community with the Christian message.[89] These mobilization, evangelistic, and educational outreach efforts have contributed to continued growth. In 2014, the SED alone reported 440 churches, 1,036 ministers, and more than 60,000 adherents, making it the size of a small denomination.[90]

The Spanish Eastern District has exercised significant influence both within the Latino AG and in the larger Latino Protestant community. It has done so by working with existing ministries like Teen Challenge in Brooklyn and Way Out Ministries in the Bronx; providing leadership for food pantry ministries, prison ministries, and reentry programs and for immigration issues; and by providing leadership of Confraternidad de Líderes conciliares (CONLICO) (an organization of Latino Pentecostal denominational leaders in the New York City metropolitan area which also advocates for social and political issues) and the New York Hispanic Clergy Organization. The SED encourages young people to carry out what Rev. Abigail Alicea has called "evangelism through social services." She pointed out that they not only promote street evangelism, but also seek to connect with the community by identifying its needs and "participat[ing] in its progressive development." They do this, she notes, because they have seen that "providing for the needs of the poor softens up their hearts and opens up their ears and allows them to receive the message of salvation." They are doing this not only at home, but also abroad throughout Latin America through the Ambassadors in Missions ministry. In addition to promoting street ministry and evangelistic social work, they also encourage the youth to add Bible schools, Christian universities, and seminaries. Rev. Alicea represents the sentiment of many in the Latino AG when she stated, "We understand that our future lies in our younger generation and for that reason it is imperative for us to invest in them."[91]

The SED has also generated a number of important scholars and leaders, such as Dr. Eldin Villafañe; Dr. Samuel Solivan; Aimee García Cortese; Dr. Saturnino González, former superintendent of both the Puerto Rico and the Southeastern Spanish Districts; Rev. Maria Correa, who is director of the SED Girls Ministry and an advocate to stop the trafficking and abuse of women; Bishop Dr. Kittim Silva (a former drug addict converted in an SED church) of the Pentecostal Church of Jesus Christ denomination and author of over forty books; and President Samuel Rodríguez of the National Hispanic Christian Leadership Conference. For all of these reasons and many others, the Spanish Eastern District has been the largest and most effective Latino Pentecostal movement in the New York City metropolitan area for the past half a century and has provided important leadership for the larger Latino Protestant Evangelical movement.[92]

The Latino Pentecostal movement in New York City traces its origins back to Puerto Rican Assemblies of God evangelists Tomás Alvarez and Juan Lugo and the Mexican evangelist Francisco Olazábal. It was indigenous from the very beginning and differed from Pentecostalism in Puerto Rico, Mexico, and the Southwest in several important ways. Prior to 1960, it was a largely urban, storefront, semi-ecumenical, and a completely indigenous tradition whose ministers and parishioners were more educated than those in their sister movements in the U.S. Southwest, Mexico, and Puerto Rico. The movement was also initiated and developed by Puerto Ricans sent by the Pentecostal Church of God and later further developed by Puerto Ricans born and/or raised in New York City. Eventually the work became Puerto Rican American and broke away from the Pentecostal Church of God and became the Spanish Eastern Conference, Convention, and finally District. This district also gave birth to the Puerto Rico, Southern Latin, and Florida Multicultural districts.

Despite its small geographical size in the early years, the Spanish Eastern District grew rapidly due to very successful and stable Puerto

Rican leadership and its emphases on evangelism and church planting. Today it also leads the way in the number of women it ordains and places a strong emphasis on education. For this reason it has produced a small but important number of Latino Pentecostal scholars, who have influenced the larger church, the academy, and society.

CHAPTER 10

Your Daughters Shall Prophesy

The Uphill Struggle of Women in Ministry

THROUGHOUT THE HISTORY of the Latino Assemblies of God, women have been ordained to the ministry. They have served as pastors, evangelists, teachers, and missionaries. Despite this fact, they have faced an uphill calling. This struggle is evident in the life and ministry of Aimee García Cortese (Figure 10.1). A young woman with burning passion to preach the Gospel, she ran into a number of roadblocks to full ordination. The biggest obstacle to full ordination, she wrote, was the fact that she was a woman. Although she had the support of every official in her district, she was denied ordination because of "pure prejudice against the ministry of women." As a result, she protested directly to J. Roswell Flower at Assemblies of God headquarters in July 1958:

> I am appealing to the Executive Presbytery of the Assemblies of God, because of the rejection of my application for ordination with the Spanish Eastern District (SED). The rejection was a complete violation of the constitution of the Assemblies of God, Article VI, section 4, part B. I met all the requirements of our Credential Committee and had the full backing and blessing of every Official of my District, but because of pure prejudice against the ministry of women, I was rejected.[1]

Figure 10.1. Rev. Aimee García Cortese, ca. 1970s. She pastored many churches and founded Crossroads Tabernacle in the South Bronx. (Flower Pentecostal Heritage Center)

Despite her plea, we know virtually nothing about the history and con- tributions that women like García Cortese made to Latino Pentecostal- ism.[2] What little has been written on women in ministry has tended to focus on Latina mainline Protestantism, Latina Catholicism, and Euro- American and African American Pentecostal women.[3] Yet this is unfor- tunate because women played an important role in the origins and devel- opment of the Latino Pentecostal movement and thus in the larger stories of Latino Protestantism and North American religions.

The role of women in the Latino AG ministry took a very different trajectory than it did for many Euro-American Pentecostal women. While the AG has licensed and/or ordained Latinas since at least 1916, it never witnessed the kind of "Golden Age" of women in ministry that Charles Barfoot and Gerald Sheppard describe in their article, "Pro- phetic vs. Priestly Religion: The Changing Role of Women Clergy in Classical Pentecostal Churches." Neither was there any great reversal in the accumulation of power or the right to ordination for women in the

Latino AG in the early twentieth century, as there was for Euro-American AG women.[4]

Instead, Latinas have faced a long and steady but uphill struggle for voice and agency in the Latino AG. They have practiced a kind of paradoxical domesticity whereby they are exhorted to be both End-Times prophetesses and evangelists in the public sphere and devoted mothers and good wives in the private sphere. Yet by their own accounts these women are "liberated." In contrast to the Barfoot and Sheppard thesis where the authors argue that there has been a retrenchment against women in ministry in the later twentieth century, the Latino Pentecostal movement adopted an increasingly prophetic and open attitude toward women in ministry during that same time. This is due to increasing levels of acculturation, education, and cultural orientation to U.S. values and gender roles in the AG and American society and to greater openness on the part of Latino AG superintendents and leaders across the districts. Despite this positive development, the actual opportunities for women to exercise their prophetic gifts are relatively limited and are normally regulated by men running the districts and serving on the ordination committees. Women are often assigned to small and marginal missions, church plants, women's ministries and missions, and other forms of youth, musical, and evangelistic-social work, though to be fair so too are younger and older male ministers. As the cultural orientation of Latino Pentecostalism has changed, so too has its attitude toward women. However, unlike during Barfoot and Sheppard's early "Golden Age" for Euro-American AG clergywomen, Latinas have always had the right to preach and have consistently served alongside men—often their husbands—or occasionally on their own. Because their progress has been steady, today there is actually a higher percentage of Latina ministers in the Latino AG than of Euro-American women ministers in the larger General Council. Given the deep-seated patriarchy and machismo in Latino culture, this is indeed a positive development—though there is still room for greater improvement, for reasons outlined in this chapter.

Latinas in Ministry at the Azusa Street Revival

Latinas have been preaching, evangelizing, pastoring, and carrying out evangelistic social work since the birth of the Azusa Street Revival in 1906. Although the first Latinos and Latinas at Azusa Street left few written records of their ministries, the evidence indicates that men *and* women preached. The *Apostolic Faith* newspaper stated: "There are a good many Spanish speaking people in Los Angeles. The Lord has been giving the language, and now a Spanish preacher, who, *with his wife,* are preaching the Gospel in open air meetings" (emphasis added).[5] The couple referred to in the article was Abundio and Rosa López. Originally from Guadalajara, Mexico, Abundio immigrated to the United States around the turn of the twentieth century, joined a Mexican Presbyterian church, and married Rosa in 1902.[6] The Lópezes began attending the Azusa Street Mission on May 29, 1906, shortly after it opened in mid-April. In one of the few testimonies written by Mexicans at Azusa Street, Rosa and Abundio stated:

> We testify to the power of the Holy Spirit in forgiveness, sanctification, and the baptism with the Holy Ghost and fire. We give thanks to God for this wonderful gift, which we have received from Him, according to the promise. Thanks be to God for the Spirit, which brought us to the Azusa Street Mission, the Apostolic Faith, old-time religion. . . . I thank God also for the baptism of the Holy Ghost and fire, which I received on the 5th of June 1906. We cannot express the gratitude and thanksgiving which we feel moment by moment for what He has done for us, so we want to be used for the salvation and healing of both soul and body. I am a witness of His wonderful promise and marvelous miracles by the Holy Ghost.[7]

The Lópezes organized the first major Pentecostal evangelistic ministry to Latinos in the borderlands through their open-air evangelistic meetings in the historic Mexican Plaza District in Los Angeles. While the Apostolic Faith Mission ordained Abundio López in 1909, Rosa's clerical status is less clear.[8] Regardless, both conducted evangelistic work in the Mexican *barrios* and *colonias* of Los Angeles and San Diego and were two of the first Spanish-speaking evangelists at the Azusa Street Revival.

The Azusa Street Revival attracted not only Mexican immigrants like Abundio, but also Mexican Americans like A. C. Valdez and his mother, Susie Villa Valdez.[9] A. C. Valdez was a fifth-generation Mexican American who traced his genealogy back to the founding of Alta California by Father Junipero Serra in the 1780s.[10] A pious Catholic, A. C.'s father, José, was profoundly influenced by Franciscan spirituality, which discussed the role of the Spirit in personal piety. In 1906, Susie attended the Azusa Street Revival, where she was converted and baptized with the Holy Spirit.[11] In a prophetic move not uncommon among early Latinas, Susie took the Pentecostal message not only to her family, but also to prostitutes, single mothers, destitute women, and alcoholics and other marginalized Latinos, blacks, and poor whites living in the "slums" of Los Angeles and in the migrant farm labor camps in Riverside and San Bernardino, California. She also worked at the Azusa daughter Pisgah Mission, which specialized in evangelistic-social work and attending to the social needs of its converts. A. C. Valdez wrote:

> I remember her hard but rewarding spiritual-social work with prostitutes and skid-row alcoholics done in the Lord's name at Pisgah Home . . . my mother visited the slums, playing her guitar and singing sacred songs in the poorly lit streets for anyone who would listen. Without fear . . . she heard the troubles of many lonely and depressed people and usually introduced them to Christ. Around midnight she would walk the long way home, often arriving as late as two A.M.[12]

She continued to preach the Pentecostal message and to work with the poor for the rest of her life.[13] While there is no concrete evidence to prove that Rosa and Susie were ordained to the ministry, evidence indicates that they were actively engaged in evangelistic preaching, social work, and ministry to women and men.

Mexican American Women in Ministry

The practice of ordaining women in the Latino AG is an outgrowth of the larger Euro-American AG's position on women in ministry. The

Euro-American AG technically takes a prophetic view of women in ministry and allows women to be ordained to the ministry, though as Barfoot and Sheppard and Edith Blumhofer noted, after an early Golden Age, there was a retrenchment in the latter half of the twentieth century.[14]

The first Mexican American women to carry out evangelistic work who later joined the Assemblies of God were Francisca D. Blaisdell (ca. 1885–1941) and Chonita Morgan Howard (1898–1983). Blaisdell was converted and then later began preaching in Mexico in 1915, and after eight years in the field she was finally formally ordained an Assemblies of God missionary-evangelist by H. C. Ball and Juan Lugo at the Latin District Convention in San Jose, California, in 1923 (see Figure 7.1). She and her husband, Rev. George Blaisdell, pioneered evangelistic work in Douglas, Arizona, and Nacozari, Sonora, Mexico, and then throughout the Southwest. Around 1922, Francisca helped organize the first women's group in Agua Prieta, Sonora, Mexico, which became the model and forerunner of the Women's Missionary Council (WMC) in the Latin District Council in the United States. Francisca is important not only because she was one of the first Pentecostal AG evangelists in the United States and Mexico, but also because she pastored churches in Douglas, Arizona, Agua Prieta, Sonora, Mexico (1932–1933, 1938–1939), and El Paso, Texas (1933–1935), where she preached to forty to eighty Mexican parishioners every Sunday morning and evening and two or three times a week. She also conducted itinerant evangelistic travels, often on horseback, throughout northern Mexico and the U.S. Southwest.[15]

Like Francisca Blaisdell, Concepción (Chonita) Morgan Howard (Figure 10.2) was a Mexican American whose father was a Euro-American and whose mother was a Mexican. Chonita was converted and baptized in the Holy Spirit in 1913 in the small mining town of San José de las Playitos, Sonora, Mexico. She served as a pioneer Latina Pentecostal evangelist, pastor, and women's leader in Arizona, New Mexico, California, and Mexico from 1915 to 1968. Not long after her conversion and Spirit baptism, she felt called to the ministry and traveled the itinerant evangelistic trail on horseback throughout northern Mexico and Arizona. She eventually traveled to California, where she came under the influence of George and Carrie Judd Montgomery, who had attended the

Figure 10.2. Rev. Chonita Morgan Howard, Agua Prieta, Sonora, Mexico, ca. 1919. She evangelized throughout southern Arizona and northern Mexico in her burro-pulled wagon. (Flower Pentecostal Heritage Center)

Azusa Revival in 1907. The Montgomerys pioneered the Pentecostal work in Mexico in San José los Playitos, where they owned a mine. Chonita began evangelistic work in the United States around 1915. In 1919, she met and married a young Pentecostal preacher named Lloyd Howard, who pastored a small group of Mexicans in the border town of Pirtleville, Arizona. In 1928, the Assemblies of God recognized her evangelistic work and ordained her an evangelist. In addition to her pastoral and evangelistic work, she served as the second president (after Sunshine Marshall Ball) of the Women's Missionary Council (Concilio Misionero Femenil) from 1941 to 1962. From 1966 to 1968, she pastored Betel Asambleas de Dios in Douglas, Arizona. Her fifty-three-year ministry touched the lives of thousands of Latinas and Latinos and helped establish the AG work on both sides of the U.S.-Mexican border.[16]

The first Mexican American woman actually ordained by the AG was Rev. Manuelita (Nellie) Treviño Bazan (1895–1995), wife of the second AG superintendent, Demetrio Bazan. She was not alone. Other key Mexican American and Mexican immigrant women were also ordained, including Francisca Blaisdell, Chonita Morgan Howard, Natividad Nevarez, Elvira González, María Inostroza, Ursula Riggio, Elvira Perales, Ramona Torres, Lillian Torres Valdez, Bertha López García, and Julia Camacho.[17]

Like many other husband and wife teams, the Bazans were ordained together, in 1920 in San Antonio, Texas. They ministered in Texas, New Mexico, and Colorado, where Nellie preached from the pulpit at least thirty times a year and conducted door-to-door evangelistic work. The Bazans, pictured in Figure 10.3, served as associate pastors in Francisco Olazábal's church and revival in El Paso in 1922. Nellie exercised considerable influence in the Latino AG during her seventy-five-year ministry by serving as associate pastor, founding three churches herself in Texas and New Mexico via her door-to-door evangelistic outreach, writing articles for *La Luz Apostólica,* leading women's groups, composing poetry, raising ten children—many of whom went into the ministry— and writing her autobiography, entitled *Enviados de Dios.* Though she exercised a strong prophetic ministry, she was also expected to submit to her husband's spiritual authority at home. Early Latino Pentecostals did not believe that the point of the prophetic gifts was to erase gender distinctions, but rather to empower men and women for Christian service in the End Times drama they now faced. This kind of paradoxical domesticity has remained the norm for many Latino Pentecostal women throughout much of the twentieth century.[18]

Although most credentialed women in the early period were licensed as evangelists, some were ordained as pastors. Natividad Nevarez, for example, was ordained a pastor in 1937 in Los Angeles, where she and her husband Francisco (ordained in 1923) built on the work of Alice E. Luce by co-pastoring the famous Latino AG mother church, El Aposento Alto. She was a key women's leader from the 1930s through the 1960s who taught at the LABI and was one of a handful of Latinas ordained to the pastoral (rather than evangelistic or missionary) ministry prior to 1940. María Inostroza was also ordained in the early 1930s and pastored churches in the 1940s and 1950s.[19] Other Latinas in ministry, such as Elvira González, Ursula Riggio, Elvira Perales, Ramona Torres, Lillian Torres Valdez, Bertha López García, and Julia Camacho, later joined them.[20]

The pioneering work of Mexican American women inspired women in Mexico. Ana Sanders pioneered the AG work in Mexico City in 1921.[21] By 1928, their example inspired women in Mexico, such as Srita Cruz Arenas, Catarina García, Juana Medellín, and Raquel Ruesga, to seek ordination and evangelize their beloved patria.[22]

Figure 10.3.   Rev. Nellie (tambourine in hand) and Rev. Demetrio Bazan. To their left are Macrina, Francisco, and Frank Olazábal Jr. The Bazans served as Francisco Olazábal's associate pastors in El Paso, Texas, ca. 1922.   (Gastón Espinosa Latino Pentecostal History Collection)

Puerto Rican Women in Ministry

At the same time Francisca and Chonita were preaching in Arizona and Mexico, in Hawaii and California Puerto Rican women were also being converted, Spirit baptized, and ordained to the ministry. The first Puerto Rican (and Latina) ordained to the AG ministry was Dionisia Feliciano (see Figure 10.4). Born in Ponce, Puerto Rico, she migrated with her family to Oahu, Hawaii, after 1900 to work on the sugarcane plantations. Some Azusa Street missionaries who were en route to Asia converted her and her husband, Solomon, to Pentecostalism in 1911. They began evangelistic work right after their conversion and were ordained on May 14, 1914. Exactly who ordained them is uncertain, though it may have been the same Azusa Street missionaries they met in 1911 or their colleagues. The Felicianos evangelized Puerto Ricans in Hawaii before moving to the San Francisco Bay Area, where a number of Puerto

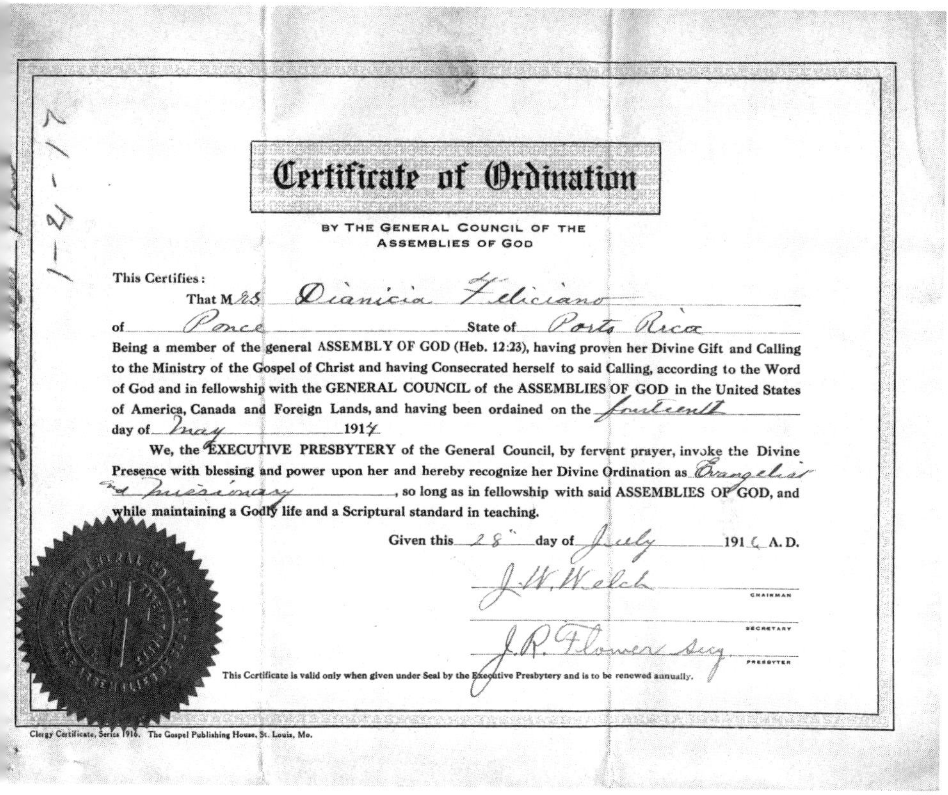
1-21-17

Certificate of Ordination

BY THE GENERAL COUNCIL OF THE ASSEMBLIES OF GOD

This Certifies:

That Mrs Dianicia Feliciano

of Ponce State of Porto Rica

Being a member of the general ASSEMBLY OF GOD (Heb. 12:23), having proven her Divine Gift and Calling to the Ministry of the Gospel of Christ and having Consecrated herself to said Calling, according to the Word of God and in fellowship with the GENERAL COUNCIL of the ASSEMBLIES OF GOD in the United States of America, Canada and Foreign Lands, and having been ordained on the fourteenth day of May 1914

We, the EXECUTIVE PRESBYTERY of the General Council, by fervent prayer, invoke the Divine Presence with blessing and power upon her and hereby recognize her Divine Ordination as Evangelist and missionary, so long as in fellowship with said ASSEMBLIES OF GOD, and while maintaining a Godly life and a Scriptural standard in teaching.

Given this 28 day of July 1916 A. D.

J. W. Welch CHAIRMAN

SECRETARY

J. R. Flower Secy PRESBYTER

This Certificate is valid only when given under Seal by the Executive Presbytery and is to be renewed annually.

Clergy Certificate, Series 1916. The Gospel Publishing House, St. Louis, Mo.

Figure 10.4. Rev. Dionicia Feliciano was originally ordained in May 1914 in Hawaii or the San Francisco Bay area, probably by Francisco Ortiz or some other group. She was later ordained by the AG as an evangelist and missionary to Ponce, Puerto Rico, on July 18, 1916. (Flower Pentecostal Heritage Center)

Ricans had since migrated. Dionisia and Solomon were ordained AG evangelists and missionaries in northern California on July 28, 1916. They helped pioneer the Assemblies of God work in California, Puerto Rico, and the Dominican Republic.

Dionisia pioneered the Pentecostal work in Puerto Rico along with other women such as Isabel Lugo, the wife of Juan Lugo. Isabel, pictured in Figure 7.1, began evangelistic work right after her conversion and was ordained in 1920. She ministered alongside her husband in Puerto Rico, California, and New York City. She also served as a women's leader in the early movement, led some of the Sunday school programs, counseled women, and engaged in evangelistic work. Dionisia and Isabel inspired a number of other Puerto Rican women to go into the ministry, such as Helena Félix, Antonia Laguer, Julia Báez, Rosa Otero, Flora Franceschi, Dolores Estrella, Juana Vélez, Felicidad Andrade, Jacinta Quiróz, Carmen Ortiz, Adela Jesús, America Calvente, Carmen Pacheco, Pura Ortiz, and Nicolas Díaz, among others.[23]

In New York City, AG women were also influenced by the work of female evangelists like María Teresa Sapia and Julia and Matilde Vargas, all of whom were converted through the massive healing crusades of Francisco Olazábal in Spanish Harlem from 1931 to 1937. Matilde gave up a career in early Latino film in order to evangelize her people across the nation. The Vargas mother-daughter team patterned their own ministries after Olazábal and Aimee Semple McPherson, by both praying for the sick and even wearing McPherson's signature cape.[24]

Euro-American Women in Ministry

While Mexican American, Mexican, and Puerto Rican women carried out evangelistic work in the Southwest and Puerto Rico, Alice E. Luce, Sunshine Ball, and other Euro-American missionaries also served as role models for women in ministry and especially in education in the Southwest. Luce was perhaps the most important role model for some because she carried out evangelistic work, planted a church in Los Angeles, founded the LABI in California, and wrote and/or translated much of the Sunday school literature used in the Latino Districts and throughout Latin America, and also because she was by all accounts a very devout woman. Despite her evangelistic work, her primary influence was through preparing the next generation of men and women for the Pentecostal ministry at LABI and through her voluminous publications, all of which may help to explain why the number of women in ministry steadily increased throughout much of the twentieth century rather than going through a period of retrenchment like that experienced by Euro-American women in the larger General Council.[25]

Luce was a former British Episcopalian missionary to India, where she converted to Pentecostalism and later felt called to evangelize Latinos in Mexico and the United States. In 1915, Luce and her friend Sunshine Marshall met H. C. Ball in South Texas and were ordained to the ministry. They, like Ball, were interested in ministering to Mexicans and began Pentecostal work in Monterrey, Mexico, in 1917. After the bloody Mexican Revolution (1911–1917) interrupted their plans, they returned to the United States and helped Ball with his evangelistic work in Texas.[26] Seeking new evangelistic fields, in 1918 Luce traveled to Los Angeles, where she rented a hall in the Mexican Plaza District—where Rosa and Abundio López of Azusa fame had preached twelve years earlier. She began conducting evangelistic services along with a Jewish convert and doctor named Rev. Florence Murcutt.[27] In Los Angeles, they conducted open-air evangelistic services, led Bible studies, organized testimonials, taught Sunday school, led door-to-door outreach, prayed for the sick, and passed out evangelistic tracts.[28] Luce is one of the clearest examples of a prophetic woman's life in early Pentecostalism. Luce, Sunshine Marshall Ball, and other Euro-American women like Aimee Semple McPherson (who served in the AG for a short while) served as role models for Latina clergywomen.[29]

Women in Theological Education and Spanish Bible Institutes

One of the reasons women have played a greater role in the Latino Pentecostal movement is because of their access to theological education through Bible schools and because women helped found and lead the schools.[30] Unlike traditional seminaries, which were geared primarily for men seeking the pastoral ministry, Bible schools sought to train future clergy and lay leaders. They provided a course of study that led to a diploma in biblical studies and ministry and taught Bible, theology, church history, evangelism, missions, apologetics, and related topics. Many lay women were inspired by their training under Alice Luce and other women and men to go into the ministry. For these reasons, women have attended Latino AG Bible schools in relatively high percentages from the very beginning in Texas, California, New York, and Puerto Rico. Indeed, it was Luce who founded the second Latino AG Bible Institute in the United States.[31] The first three graduates from Luce's LABI in San Diego were women: D. Adeline Sugg, Ursula Riggio, and Maria Grajeda.[32] That same year Ball founded the third Spanish-speaking

Bible Institute in South Texas.[33] Edmundo Jordan started the Spanish Eastern District's Instituto Bíblico Hispano del Este in Juan Lugo's La Sinagoga church in Manhattan in 1935 and incorporated it in 1939; it is now located in the Bronx. Mizpa Bible Institute was founded in 1937 by Juan Lugo but left the AG with the Pentecostal Church of God in the 1950s. It was replaced by the Caribbean Theological College.[34]

Women have always made up a significant portion of the graduating classes of the LABIs and the Spanish Eastern District's Instituto Bíblico.[35] For example, from 1939 to 1960, 230 of the 556 people who graduated from the Instituto Bíblico were women. Women also made up a majority of graduates at this Bible institute in 1940, 1943, and 1948. In the Southwest, women made up a majority of the graduating classes at LABI in San Diego in 1935 and at LABI in Ysleta, Texas, in 1955.[36] The training they received has opened doors for women to go into ministry, to teach at these same institutes and others in Latin America and the Caribbean, and to write for Spanish-language periodicals such as *La Luz Apostólica, El Evangelista Pentecostal,* and *The Word.*[37]

The Latino AG Bible schools have provided Latinas with a professional route that is an alternative to child rearing in the secular marketplace. Their education equips and empowers them by giving them the opportunity to nurture and eventually exercise their prophetic gifts alongside men. While the career options after graduation are limited, women nonetheless exercise a certain level of agency that otherwise would have been unavailable to them in the Apostolic Assembly or in other Protestant denominations—let alone the Catholic Church. After graduation, for example, Ursula Riggio pioneered the Latino AG work in Colorado, and in 1957, Cecilia Morfin Velasquez, a graduate of LABI in Texas, pastored a small AG church in northern New Mexico.[38] While some of these women used their Bible school training to pastor their own churches and missions, the majority of them became pastors' wives, co-pastors, Christian educators, and/or women's leaders in the church. Although the exact number of women who studied at (though not necessarily graduated from) the Latino AG Bible schools across the United States and Puerto Rico is impossible to calculate, it would no doubt be in the thousands. While this might not sound very significant, it is important to realize that the Latino AG provided something that was quite rare, because the vast majority of young Latinas were steered into domestic labor tracks at public manual arts schools (which often ended in the eighth grade, after which time students were expected to enter domestic or field work) and because theological education was for most Latinas until quite recently simply out of the question.

Women's Missionary Council (Concilio Misionero Femenil)

The majority of Mexican women who graduated from the Bible schools in Texas, California, New York, and Puerto Rico did not go into the ordained ministry, but instead became actively involved in the national women's organization, the Concilio Misionero Femenil (Women's Missionary Council in the Latin District in the Southwest). The total number of women of all ages in the WMCs reached 44,600 women by 2005. The WMC traces its roots back to Rev. Francisca Blaisdell, who started the first Latino AG Dorcas women's organization in Agua Prieta, Sonora, Mexico, in 1922—which predated by several years the larger Euro-American WMCs founded in the General Council in Springfield.[39] The purpose of the council was to stimulate and propagate missionary work in the U.S.-Mexican borderlands. By 1925, the council had spread to Tacupeto and Colonia Morelos in Sonora, Mexico, and to San Antonio and Mart, Texas.[40] Rev. Blaisdell and women leading the group changed the name from Dorcas to the Concilio Misionero Femenil at the convention in Mexico City in 1927. Sunshine Ball was elected the first president of the WMC, a position she held from 1927 to 1940. Chonita Howard followed as the second president from 1941 to 1962. Their evangelistic social ministry sought to address both spiritual and material needs. H. C. Ball wrote in 1931:

> We have what is known as the Women's Missionary Councils in most of our assemblies, and this organization has been the means of banding the sisters together to work and pray for the salvation of souls as well as for the relief of the poor, and sick visitation. Thousands of tracts and Gospels have been distributed by the sisters, many sick ones healed and revival prayed down upon quite a number of our assemblies. In one of the Los Angeles assemblies the

women meet every morning to pray, and in most of the other places
they hold weekly meetings for Bible study and prayer.[41]

The council saw modest growth under Sunshine Ball, but Chonita
Howard's tenure ushered in a period of unprecedented creativity and
growth, sponsoring Plan Mundial (World Ministries) in 1942 to raise
funds for foreign missions and the Home for the Aged project in the 1950s
and early 1960s. In 1962, Frances Figueroa was elected the third president
of the Women's Missionary Council. She held office from 1962 to 1970
and pushed the Assemblies of God headquarters in Springfield, Missouri,
to begin publishing the denomination's women's literature in Spanish, because approximately 70 percent of all Latinas in the Spanish AG churches
at that time spoke only Spanish. In addition to strengthening the ties between the Euro-Americans' and Latinas women's missionary councils at
AG headquarters in Springfield, Figueroa went on speaking tours throughout the United States and Latin America. Indeed, she was not afraid to use
her prophetic voice to speak on behalf of Latinas at the Euro-American-
dominated AG headquarters in Springfield.[42] After 1970, the Latin District
fragmented into a number of regional districts, each with its own WMC
secretary, who functions as its president. They, along with WMC leaders
from across all General Council districts, meet annually in Springfield,
Missouri, for fellowship and support and to promote unity across the
different geographical, racial, and language districts.

The Concilio Misionero Femenil, now called the Ministerio Femeniles (Women's Ministries Council), is run completely by Latinas. One
of the primary goals of the council is to raise money for foreign missions.
The council has also helped raise funds to build churches and missions.
The primary fund-raising strategy has historically been selling tamales.[43] These and other Mexican delicacies are sold on special holidays
like Christmas and New Year's. Because the food and labor involved are
volunteered, the women's contribution to the AG is a sacred labor of
love, as they see it. The council also allows Latinas who are not formally
involved in the prophetic ministry to contribute directly to prophetic
missionary works and the building of churches throughout the United
States and Latin America. It also provides working-class Latinas with an
opportunity to share the joys and struggles in an environment that af-

firms their language, culture, sacred traditions, and femininity as *mujeres de Dios*—women of God.

Today the Women's Missionary Council provides one of the strongest and best-run ministries across the Latino AG. Over 90,000 Latina women and young girls participate in the Ministerios Femeniles. They are served by 1,718 women's groups across the 2,665 Latino AG churches and missions in the United States and Puerto Rico. They teach, lead, mentor, minister to, counsel, and provide leadership training for more than 66,100 Latina women. More than 2,901 of these women help provide leadership for the 3,565 Latina girls' clubs in churches and missions. They teach, mentor, minister to, and provide leadership training for 24,886 young Latinas across the nation. Although the average club size is only seven girls per group, there can be multiple girls' clubs in the same church for different age groups and needs. These small groups provide a more intimate setting and an engaging learning and mentoring environment for ministry, which many educational studies have argued is more conducive to internalizing one's beliefs, behavioral norms, and social practices. To put these figures in comparative perspective, at 90,000 strong, there are more Latinas (women and girls) involved in the Ministerios Femeniles than in some entire Latino-serving denominations. This is indeed one of the largest and fastest-growing Latina-led religious grassroots religious movements in North America.[44]

Gender Roles at Home and in Society: Prophetic versus Priestly

Although Latina Pentecostal women are actively encouraged by men to enter into the ordained ministry, they are still called upon to submit to the authority of their husbands at home. Rev. Rose Nodal, who began holding Pentecostal revivals among the Puerto Rican diaspora and who served as senior pastor in Santa Maria, California, stated in an interview that she taught that the man was the head of the household,[45] a sentiment echoed by Texas AG women's leader Rev. Gloria Garza, pictured in Figure 10.5.[46] This sentiment remains the common view throughout the Latino AG. This emphasis on headship and domesticity has been taught at an institutional level in churches, Sunday School material, books, and in

Figure 10.5. Rev. Gloria Garza, Kingsville, Texas, October 29, 2008. (Flower Pentecostal Heritage Center)

past and/or present AG periodicals like *La Luz Apostólica, The Word,* and the *Pentecostal Evangel.*[47]

Emphasis on male headship in the home has occasionally caused friction between couples. Rev. Gloria Garza, past president of the Women's Missionary Council in Texas, said that conflict emerged in some homes when the woman was a better preacher than the man in a husband-wife pastoral or evangelistic team. In some extreme cases, husbands would not let their wives preach even though they were both called to preach, Garza said. Garza's advice to women in this situation was to be patient, wait, and pray. However, Garza also underscored that the vast majority of men support and encourage their wives to preach from the pulpit and in evangelistic events. Despite this general support, many women who pastor Latino churches tend to be older and married to pastors. While women are encouraged to preach, they are also expected to be the primary caregivers for their children—though many men are also actively involved. Rev. Garza knows all this from firsthand ministry, since after attending LABI in Texas, she has served in the ordained ministry along with her husband, Manuel, for almost sixty years. For the past forty-eight years they have served as co-pastors of the famous Kingsville Latino AG, which was once pastored by H. C. Ball.[48]

Comportment and the Construction of Latina Pentecostal Identity

Although women have exercised a prophetic voice in the Latino AG, early comportment (dress) codes were conservative, like those of other Latino Pentecostal denominations. Before World War II, Latino AG women were expected to dress very modestly, not cut their hair or wear ostentatious jewelry or makeup, and not wear pants, pantsuits, low-cut dresses, and sometimes even rings. Elvira Perales, who was converted to the AG in South Texas in 1922, recounts how after she was converted, she was admonished to stop wearing her diamond ring. When she wanted to raffle the ring, her Mexican pastor told her that Christians were not encouraged to gamble or raffle things in the church.[49] Rev. Gloria Garza stated that in the 1950s women were encouraged not to wear necklaces or any kind of ostentatious jewelry, which was interpreted as boastful and lacking discretion. This view was not unique to the Latino AG. In fact, it was also common in Pentecostalism and other religious traditions.[50]

Change in Comportment Standards

This attitude began to change in both the broader culture and the AG in the 1950s, according to Rev. Garza. Alex and Anita Bazan stated that from the 1930s to the 1950s, "If you wore makeup or pants you weren't Christian." The Bazans went on to state, "As soon as you got saved you had to get rid of your makeup . . . in those days it was a cultural sin to wear makeup and you never cut your hair," though many styled it or wore it up in a bun or in some other fashion.[51]

As the cultural attitudes have changed, so, too, have the cultural values of men and women in the AG. Expectations of women's comportment in the twenty-first century are now undergoing significant change. While in the past it was not very common for a woman to have short hair, Gloria Garza stated that over 30 percent of all women in the Latino AG today have short hair or a "modern cut." Garza noted that in the 1990s Latino AG pastors criticized her own nape-of-neck-length hair as being like a man's. Rev. Garza defended her short hairstyle by pointing out that many women at the AG headquarters in Springfield also had such short hairstyles, as did many of the wives of the Latino AG superintendents and secretaries.[52]

Reflecting her Euro-American AG cultural orientation, Garza stated that she first began to use light cosmetics in the 1950s after she saw Euro-American AG pastors' wives and women at the AG headquarters in Springfield, Missouri, using cosmetics. While Rev. Garza holds many progressive attitudes toward women's comportment, she also strongly believes that women should not seek to imitate men by always wearing pants and that in deference to Christ should submit to their husbands as the head of the home—all the while respecting their right as women to preach, teach, and pastor, a view that might be considered paradoxical by outsiders.[53]

"Third Class Soldiers": 1950s–1990s

Latinas have been ordained in the AG since at least 1916, yet prior to World War II it was uncommon for a single woman to pastor her own church or be ordained to the pastoral ministry. Typically, women were licensed rather than ordained and served alongside their husbands, as interim pastors, or as pastors of small congregations.[54]

Leoncia Rosado Rousseau (a.k.a "Mama Leo") and Aurora Chávez

The attitudes that Pentecostal women faced were perhaps best summed up by Rev. Leoncia Rosado Rousseau of the Bronx: "We women were treated as third class soldiers by some of our male counterparts." This prompted some women to create their own female-led denominations.

Despite a guarded openness to prophetic women's voices in the Latino Pentecostal movement in general, some Latinas decided to leave their churches to start or cofound their own denominations. No one better illustrates this than Mama Leo. She cofounded the Damascus Christian Church denomination with her husband in New York City in the 1950s. In 1957, she pioneered the Damascus Youth Crusade, one of the first major church-sponsored drug-rehabilitation programs in the United States. Similarly, Juana García Peraza left the Pentecostal Church of God in Puerto Rico in 1942 to start her own unique denomination, Congregation Mita, which sponsored a wide range of social programs and targeted at-risk youth and economically impoverished families.[55]

Other Latinas such as Rev. Aurora Chávez in the Southwest founded their own Spanish-speaking Pentecostal denominations, among them Concilio La Peña de Horeb, which granted greater autonomy to women. Rev. Chávez conducted evangelistic-healing crusades in Los Angeles and throughout the Southwest in the 1950s.

Aimee García Cortese and Julie Ramírez in New York and on the East Coast

The story of Rev. Aimee García Cortese illustrates the innovation and creativity of Latina clergywomen in the latter half of the twentieth century. Born to Puerto Rican parents in New York in 1929, Rev. Cortese was converted in a small Spanish-speaking Pentecostal storefront church in the early 1940s. Reacting against the legalism she saw in this church, she got involved with a Lutheran church and then a Methodist church before returning to the Spanish Eastern District. She was given an exhorter's certificate in 1947 and was licensed to preach in 1951. She later attended the AG-sponsored Instituto Biblico Hispano in New York City and Central Bible College in Springfield, Missouri. A year after her graduation in 1957, she sought ordination. Her request for ordination was denied for no other reason than that she was a woman. Only after key leaders in Springfield intervened was she finally ordained in 1962 by the Euro-American New York AG District. Her cultural orientation toward Springfield and her contact with Euro-American leaders provided her with the leverage and denominational clout to scale some of the barriers she faced.

Because "no one's looking for a female pastor," she said in an interview, García Cortese founded her own church, Crossroads Tabernacle, in 1982 in the Bronx. "If you want to get a church you have to start your own," she stated. Yet, rather than remain bitter, she said she held no grudges against the General Council or the Spanish Eastern District because despite opposition or doubt by some men, others strongly supported her vision and work. Her ministry in the Bronx met with phenomenal success and grew from 37 people in 1982 to 1,500 in 2008, making it one of the largest Latino churches in New York at the time. The gender bias and discrimination she has faced is slowly abating, she stated.[56]

Today there are a growing number of women like Rev. García Cortese and Rev. Julie Ramírez, pastoring very large Spanish District churches. Rev. Ramírez, for example, was ordained along with two highly experienced women ministers by the SED at the convention in 1978. By then, she had already preached in Mexico and Puerto Rico and founded and developed Templo Fe on her own. The congregation blossomed to 1,000 men, women, and children in the 1980s with a million-dollar property in the heart of the Latino community in Hartford, Connecticut. The church was first started as a house church and mission in 1965. By 1973, the congregation purchased from the Catholic archdiocese a large property that used to be Immaculate Conception High School, complete with an attached monastery building, which she turned into a retreat center. Like many women, she gently revised many of the social and comportment views in the Pentecostal movement. Even in her sixties, she still served as senior pastor. Ironically, she arrived in Hartford as a missionary church planter with the intention (and perhaps expectation) of handing over the work to a man—something that still has not happened decades later.[57]

The Struggle Continues

Although the Latino AG has credentialed women for most of the twentieth century, it has largely kept them out of leading administrative positions until relatively recently.[58] Those women who did serve as senior pastors often worked where men were unwilling to go, as interim pastors, or assumed the senior pastorate after their husbands died.[59] Latinas have never served as superintendent of the Latino Districts. However, García Cortese was the first woman ever asked to speak during prime time at the General Council of the Assemblies of God National Convention. Rev. Carmen H. Pérez was the first woman in AG history nominated for the executive presbyter position in the General Council of the Assemblies of God. She did not win the election.[60] Still other women serve on many Latino AG District Executive Boards—usually as secretary. While these moves might be genuine gestures of inclusivity, they might also be a safe way of including women who would never be a real threat to the male leadership of the AG.

Yet, despite the struggles of García Cortese—and perhaps because of them—by the 1990s, the Spanish Eastern District had one of the highest percentages of credentialed and ordained women in the AG. Today it continues to have one of the highest percentages of female ministers in its district in the entire Assemblies of God. Furthermore, it also has a higher percentage of Latina clergywomen than the General Council nationwide. The total number of Latina clergy (ordained, licensed, and certified) in the AG increased from 624 women in 1990 to 741 in 1997 and 815 in 2005. The number of Latinas fully ordained in the AG almost doubled, going from 80 in 1990 to 141 in 1997. While women made up 15.8 percent of all credentialed ministers in the largely Euro-American General Assemblies of God in 1995, they made up 24.8 percent of all credentialed ministers in the then eight Latino districts.[61] The AG now claims more Latina clergy (1,100) than any other denomination in the United States.

By 2014, the SED reported 430 churches and 1,036 ministers, of which over 300 were women and 50 were senior pastors. In 2009, the first female minister—Rev. Virginia Maldonado—was elected to the SED Executive Board and reelected in 2013. She now serves as director of education. The Women's Ministry Department is a highly developed and well-run ministry that provides classes, materials, and resources for women and young girls, but also for the divorced, singles, and widowed women, as well as discipleship, support for mothers of incarcerated children, programs for young mothers with children in public schools, and other ministries. The Women's Ministry Department attracts 3,000 to 4,000 women to its annual conference. In addition, Elisa Carrión (wife of Adolfo Carrion) founded the Confraternidad Esposas de Ministros to minister to the needs of clergy spouses, who often suffer and bear the brunt of the ministry in silence and isolation. Through all of these activities and others, women are exercising a greater voice and level of agency than in the past.[62] Similar positive developments have been taking place across the nation. In the Southern Pacific District, based in Los Angeles, there were 81 clergywomen out of 424 ministers districtwide. They served 296 churches.[63]

Feminism and Mujeres de Dios

When confronted with sexism in the Latino AG, Rev. Garza, like all of the women I interviewed, did not turn to the feminist movement for help or support. She rejected the feminist movement and believes the struggle over the Equal Rights Amendment had very little direct impact on women in the Latino AG. Furthermore, like every other AG woman I interviewed, she stated that Latina Pentecostal women did not support the feminist cause, which they perceived as too radical, tied to the gay movement, pushy, and a luxury that their working-class schedules could simply not afford. Although many Latinas like pastor Garza had little interest in the feminist movement, their strong prophetic personalities surely resonated in their own modest ways with many feminist voices of their day.

As of 2014, women in ministry are dressing in the latest fashions and are using cosmetics and jewelry, though in a way that is not ostentatious given their working-class congregations. Women in general are more confident in themselves and their ministries before the congregation, Garza said.[64]

Despite the obstacles they have faced in the past, women in the Latino AG now have a number of options for the prophetic ministry that are not available to women in other denominations. They can serve as ordained senior pastors, associate pastors, evangelists, missionaries, Bible school teachers, writers, women's missionary council leaders, prophetesses, healers, and church planters. Many female senior pastors are either former pastors' wives or are over fifty years old. Apparently, for many of their male parishioners, the women's age and experience help to off-set the fact that they are female. Many newly converted Latinos, especially those from Mexico and Latin America, are simply not accustomed (in the Roman Catholic tradition) to seeing women preach and teach from the pulpit. Rev. Rose Nodal stated that although it does take some men more time to get used to women serving as pastors than others because of their Latin American cultural values and machismo, most eventually come to recognize her as pastor. All of the women I interviewed agreed that Latinos are not won over to their prophetic ministry by demanding to preach, but rather by preaching the Bible and not showing favoritism based on gender.

As the immigrant generation retired and handed over leadership to the second and third generations, the number of women going into the ministry increased by over 400 percent from the 1970s to the 1980s. The dramatic increase was due to a new generation of leaders, increasing acculturation, a shift in AG denominational policy on women in ministry, and the fragmentation of the Latino AG into a growing number of separate districts, each with its own superintendent and leadership team.

The number of Latina clergywomen receiving credentials increased from the 1990s to 2005. By then, there were over 815 credentialed (ordained, licensed, and certified) Latina AG clergywomen in the United States and Puerto Rico. Yet only 158 of the 815 were actually ordained, while the rest were licensed (310), certified (325), and specialized (22). Furthermore, many licensed and credentialed women are inactive or are serving as youth workers, children's directors, evangelists, missionaries, or associate pastors. Despite the low percentage of ordained Latina clergywomen in the AG, their numbers almost doubled between 1990 and 2005, going from 80 women to 158, and the percentage of clergywomen (approximately 25 percent) in the Latino AG was significantly higher at that time than the percentage for the Assemblies of God (more than 15 percent) nationwide.

U.S. Latina Assemblies of God Clergywomen Profile

Despite the rapid increase in the number of Latina clergywomen in the AG, scholars know little about them. Therefore, the author surveyed and conducted research on 741 Latina Assemblies of God clergywomen in 1997–2000. Although these data are dated, they are still important for the insights they provide into the views and struggles of the sixty Latina clergywomen from across the nation during that time who were studied.

The most important findings are that Latina clergywomen are older, less educated, and less financially secure than most of their Latino Pentecostal male and Euro-American Protestant counterparts.[65] Seventy-two percent of all Latina AG clergywomen are forty years old or older. Fifty percent are between forty and sixty years old, and 22 percent are sixty years old or older. One such older woman is Rev. Anita Soto, who served for many years as a lay leader in her church in southern California. When a sister church in a neighboring city was left without a pastor and the district could not find a man to pastor the small fifty-member church, they asked the then fifty-five-year-old Soto to step in until they could find a pastor. The churches women serve in tend to be small in congregation size. The survey found that most Latinas minister in churches that range in size from 50 to 100 members. However, 35 percent reported ministering in churches with 200 or more members (11 percent with 300-plus members).[66]

The study found that almost 73 percent of clergywomen are daughters of Latin American immigrants and that 97 percent of all Latina Pentecostal clergywomen minister in Spanish or bilingual churches. Three percent minister in English only, although this has no doubt increased with the growing number of third- and fourth-generation English-dominant youth.

Financial problems, along with the inability to master the English language, have served as significant barriers to higher education. Only 29 percent of all Latina Pentecostal clergywomen surveyed had graduated from college and only 12 percent from seminary. However, 24 percent did have Bible school training—usually at one of the LABIs. This is in sharp contrast to the percentage of Euro-American Protestant (94 percent) and Holiness/Pentecostal (44 percent) clergywomen who have graduated from seminary. The lower educational backgrounds of Latina Pentecostal clergywomen can be attributed in part to their immigration status, a language barrier, raising families, their inability to secure higher education, an emphasis on spiritual knowledge over "worldly" knowledge, and/or their often-precarious financial situations.

The small size of their congregations and economically distressed parishioners are the two reasons Latina clergywomen are paid considerably less than their Euro-American counterparts. A full 34 percent of all Latina Pentecostal clergywomen in 1998 earned less than $10,000 a year. More surprising is that 68 percent of Latina Pentecostal clergywomen earned less than $25,000 a year, while only 9 percent earned $35,000 or more, not far from the mean salary of Euro-American AG ($32,750) and Presbyterian ($34,268) women at that time.[67]

Low salaries, small churches, and their auxiliary status are some of the reasons over 40 percent of Latinas have pastored three or more churches in their career. Unlike their Euro-American Protestant counterparts, Latina clergywomen are more likely (60 percent) to work in Christian education or youth ministry for their first job than their Euro-American counterparts (14 percent).[68] Only 25 percent of Latina Pentecostal clergywomen went straight into an associate pastorate position, and only 2 percent went into a senior pastor position. One-half of all Latina clergywomen co-pastor the church with their husbands, 10 percent more (42 percent) than their Euro-American mainline Protestant counterparts. In light of the Latin American cultural orientation, which places a heavy emphasis on marriage and family, it is not surprising to find that Latina clergywomen are almost twice as likely to be married (72 percent) as their Euro-American mainline Protestant counterparts (38 percent). They are also significantly less likely to be divorced (5 percent compared to 24 percent).[69] The low divorce rates are due to denominational policy, the Latin American stigma attached to divorce, and the fact that many who divorce simply leave, or are asked to leave, the ministry. (See Figure 10.6.)

The low divorce rates may help explain why a notable percentage of women are second-generation ministers (19 percent), following in the footsteps of their father and/or mother. One-third (33.9 percent) of Latina clergywomen have either a brother or sister who is also in the ministry. They are also more likely (50 percent) to be married to a minister and to have a larger number of offspring than their Euro-American

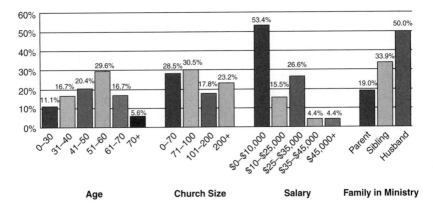

Age   Church Size   Salary   Family in Ministry

Latina Pentecostal Women in Ministry National Survey, 1997–1998 (n=59)

Figure 10.6. Latina clergywomen by age, church size, salary, and family members in ministry.

Protestant counterparts, and to be second-generation (AG) ministers (36 percent).

Whereas 57 percent of all Latina clergywomen came from Roman Catholic backgrounds, almost 92 percent of Latinos who join their churches have Roman Catholic backgrounds. The rest come out of other Pentecostal, Baptist, and Methodist churches, with a few others coming from Spiritualist, Mexican witchcraft *(brujería),* or Adventist backgrounds.

With their predominantly Latin American and Roman Catholic backgrounds, it is not surprising that Latina Pentecostal clergywomen tend to be more theologically and morally conservative than their mainline Protestant counterparts. According to our study, the six leaders who had the greatest influence on Latina Pentecostal clergywomen then were Billy Graham, Aimee García Cortese, Benny Hinn, T. D. Jakes, Luís Palau, and Kathryn Kuhlman. Over 90 percent of all Latina Pentecostal clergywomen supported and agreed with James Dobson's Focus on the Family ministry. They were also strong supporters (68 percent) of the Promise Keepers men's movement.

For this reason, it is not surprising to find that fully 100 percent of the clergywomen surveyed are "pro-life" on abortion and 84 percent believe that the man should be the head of the household. Not one woman stated that the woman should be the head of the household, and only 15 percent took an egalitarian position on gender roles in the home.

Latina Pentecostal clergywomen have mixed feelings about the feminist movement. Many echo Aimee García Cortese's comment that the secular feminist movement was too "tied with homosexuality" to be of interest to most working-class AG Latinas. It is therefore not surprising that only 7 percent of all Latina clergywomen support the secular feminist movement. This finding confirms the recent literature on Euro-American Pentecostal clergywomen as well. Senior pastor Rev. Eva Rodríguez of Cantico Nueva in Sacramento echoed this sentiment when she stated in an interview that working-class Latinas "don't need a secular feminist movement." What they need, she said, "was for men and women to just do the right thing in light of what the Bible teaches about gender roles and how to love and treat women with respect." Men thus needed to get better educated about what the Bible and progressive Christian leaders teach on the role of women in the church and in contemporary society, she said.[70]

Intellectual, Political, and Spiritual Influences and Social Views

Remarkably, a majority of Latina Pentecostal clergywomen in the survey self-identified as "Christian feminists," which to them means the right to preach, be ordained, receive equal pay, be free from sexual harassment, and have equal opportunities in the workplace. Yet it is Pentecostal clergywomen and the progressive values in public schools and the media that shape their opinions, not Latina feminist thinkers like Ada-María Isasi-Díaz and others, who although also listed on the survey were not selected as a source of influence by a single Latina clergywoman.

Figure 10.7 shows that while almost all women supported James Dobson's Focus on the Family ministry (90 percent), they did not support another Evangelical, Pat Robertson. They were also less supportive than men of the Religious Right and the Christian Coalition.

While most women were uncertain (58 percent) about whether or not to support affirmative action, they overwhelmingly rejected (by 91 percent) Proposition 187, a 1994 California ballot initiative to prohibit illegal immigrants from using publicly funded health care, public education, and social services. Latinas/os may prove to be swing voters or influential in

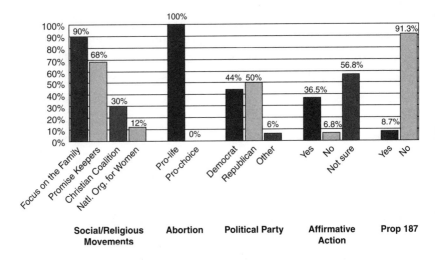

Latina Pentecostal Women in Ministry National Survey, 1997–1998 (n = 59)

Figure 10.7.   Social and political views of Latina clergywomen.

the future, as 82 percent of all Latina clergywomen who were registered Democrats at one point or another crossed over in the past four presidential cycles to vote Republican.

Latina Pentecostal Congregations

Latina clergywomen face an uphill battle in ministering to their immigrant congregations, 70 percent of whom were born outside the United States. Because more than half (55 percent) have not graduated from high school, they find it difficult to secure a well-paying job. This precarious financial situation has forced both men and women into the workplace at a much higher rate than in some parts of Mexico and Latin America. As in the African American Pentecostal churches where women make up a large majority of most congregations, Latinas make up 60–65 percent of the congregations, and though many help run their churches, few are ordained. Although Euro-American and Latina clergywomen share many common struggles, a majority (55 percent) of Latina clergywomen said they did not have regular contact with Euro-American clergywomen. Encouraging greater integration between Latino and Euro-American clergy and congregations could help bridge the isolation some women feel and help promote a more multicultural church that welcomes all people. This could also create a forum and venue wherein women could practice their spiritual gifts across social boundaries. When Latina clergywomen were asked which spiritual gifts women practice more than men, the top responses were helping (84 percent), teaching (83 percent), administration (53 percent), tongues (50 percent), discernment of spirits (38 percent), prophecy (36 percent), and evangelism (36 percent).

Problems and Obstacles for Women in Ministry

Because of traditional Latin American gender roles and machismo, Latina Pentecostal clergywomen are more likely to encounter sexism, gender discrimination, and social problems than some of their Euro-American female counterparts because the latter's churches are much more likely to have an educated clergy and laity and to mask their biases. This overt bias was evident when Rev. Eva Rodríguez, for example, was a candidate for the pastorate in a Latino AG church in the Sacramento area. A few men stood outside the church where the voting took place and encouraged men and their wives to vote for the male candidate instead. At the same time, other men strongly supported Rodríguez's candidacy and her pursuit of her ministerial calling. Recognizing her leadership, preaching skills, and raw talent, Rev. David Espinosa encouraged her to pioneer her own church, which she did when she founded Iglesia Cantico Nuevo in 2006 in Sacramento. In 2014, her ministry has grown to 250 members, with 500 men, women, and children attending church every Sunday.[71]

At the congregational level, however, Latina clergywomen said the number-one challenge facing the Hispanic church (and home) was finances and balancing ministry with family life. Other major problems facing the church include immigration issues, language problems, education, lack of lay leaders, discrimination/racism, lack of commitment, maintaining cultural identity, renting a meeting place, and finding Spanish-language books and literature. Rev. Eva Rodríguez summarized the attitude of many clergywomen when she said she was called on to be both a powerful and prophetic preacher in the church and a good mother and wife at home. This was not a chore or an undue burden, she said, because she found fulfillment in pursuing both her divine calling and being a mother and a wife who was loved and valued by her children, husband, and church community.[72]

The difficulty for many clergywomen lay, she said, in periods when their husbands were gone or on the road. Then women have to pastor, counsel, visit the sick in the hospital, prepare sermons, and come home to clean the house, help the kids with homework, and make dinner, Rodríguez said. Balancing these competing interests was difficult, she admitted. However, what made fulfilling their callings more difficult was when other women—not men—asked why she was not at home in the kitchen and raising the children. They implied that she was sacrificing her children in order to pursue her divine calling. Some even asked if it was really God who called her to the ministry, rather than just her own desires and ambition. Now that her three children have graduated from high school and are all actively involved in the church and ministry, some of these same women have apologized for insinuating that her children would suffer because she stayed true to her divine calling.[73]

Still, the greatest personal obstacles facing Latina Pentecostal clergywomen were low salaries, small church budgets, balancing ministry and family life, bias against women ministers—sometimes even from other women—fatigue, lack of encouragement, and members moving in pursuit of work and housing. Rev. Garza confirmed this when she stated that women still face financial, gender, and generational problems. Despite this, she also noted several positive trends, with women engaging in more effective bilingual ministries (most lead Spanish ministries); graduating from Bible schools, seminaries, and public universities; being elected to executive district positions; and a growing number in senior pastor positions and serving as lead missionaries. She noted that Latina ministers like Maricela Hernández, Doris Loida Espinoza, Maria García, Sarai Luna, and Mary Lou Madrigal, among others, were all carrying out innovative ministries and pastoring or co-pastoring with their husbands. Maricela Hernández founded the Flames of Fire Bible School in Texas, serves in an executive position as the Gulf Latin District secretary-treasurer, and speaks throughout the United States, Mexico, Central America, and Latin America. Doris Espinoza is a pastor, evangelist, teacher, and singer who after graduating from LABI and college now serves as the principal of a Christian school in Crystal City, Texas. Still others like Mary Lou Madrigal are powerful evangelists who speak throughout the Spanish-speaking community in the United States, Mexico, Central America, and Latin America.[74]

Similarly, after Rev. Flora Vegara immigrated to the United States from Guanajuato, Mexico, in 1962 she converted at a Latino AG church in southern California, attended LABI in La Puente for three years, and then went into the ministry in California before going on to help pioneer the AG work in Oregon. Life was difficult after her husband left and she was forced to take care of her children alone. Since 1981, Rev. Vegara has planted six churches in Oregon, ministered to undocumented immigrants, served as a prison chaplain, ministered to prisoners' families by buying them groceries and working with the courts, provided free translation services at social service agencies, and adopted and is raising four young immigrant girls in Portland whose mother was brutally murdered by her boyfriend. They now assist her in the ministry, as does her biological daughter, Rev. Maria Camarillo, who serves as associate pastor at Living Faith Church in La Mirada, California.[75]

Rev. Maria Camarillo, who attended Azusa Pacific University before earning her master's degree in social work from the University of Southern California, has also worked for the Los Angeles County Department of Children and Family for twenty-eight years, leads a number of young women's ministries, and pioneered an interdenominational Third Step recovery program for women. Today twenty-five churches and denominations have partnered with her Third Step recovery ministry. This program is also a kind of evangelistic social ministry, which has been highly effective at attracting and meeting the needs of women. From 2003 to 2014, more than 6,000 women have attended the recovery programs and Bible studies to reportedly find healing, community, and love.[76] Notwithstanding the difficulties that Latina AG women face, all of the women interviewed seemed to find their jobs rewarding and an opportunity to exercise faith, voice, and agency in the Assemblies of God, the Latino community, and American society.

Negotiating Latina AG Space

While this study confirms the findings of a number of previous studies on Euro-American Protestant clergywomen, its findings also challenge existing understandings of clergywomen in American religious history.

Mark Chaves argued that there is a loose connection between the internal and external pressures leading to progress in the struggle for women's ordination. This holds true in the Latino Pentecostal movement. Internally, the growth of Pentecostal Bible schools, denominational women's organizations, and struggles over full ordination have contributed to this trend. Externally, the feminist, countercultural, and Chicano movements applied subtle social and cultural pressure to open the door wider for women in ministry. The "glass ceiling" in the Latino Pentecostal movement did not begin to crack in the AG until the late 1950s. García Cortese's struggle was an important test case that forced leaders to follow through on denominational policy on women in ministry.[77]

Despite the important gains Latinas have made in the struggle for ordination and the right to preach, they still face ongoing gender marginalization at both the local and district levels. As Paula Nesbitt also found among Euro-American clergywomen, Latina clergywomen often bear the brunt of job shortages and are asked to pastor churches that cannot afford a full-time pastor. Many women who pastored churches prior to 1960 did so with their husbands or because of their husbands' absence or death. The same is still true for some women today. Thus, Latinas face an uphill battle to secure positions in stable and sought-after churches. This structural gender bias against women—though not as blatant as in the past—often leaves Latina clergywomen overworked, underpaid, and set up to struggle, though, to be fair, some of these issues are problems for many younger and older male ministers as well.[78]

In spite of the structural gender discrimination some clergywomen face in the Latino AG, they typically reject the secular feminist movement for many of the same reasons Elaine Lawless noted Euro-American Pentecostal women do—but with a twist. Latinas have pressure to reject the feminist movement not only because of their Pentecostal background but also because of their machismo and patriarchal Latin American cultural orientation. Latina Pentecostal clergywomen live a kind of paradoxical domesticity—being virtuous wives and noble mothers as well as End Times prophets and preachers.[79]

Despite the struggle, women continue to pursue ordination for the ministry because it provides one of the few routes to upward social, economic, and ecclesiastical mobility for Latinas that does not require a college degree, seminary training, or the ability to speak fluent English. In this respect, it still is a vehicle for female empowerment, despite the ongoing limitations.

While the number of Latinas in the ministry is increasing, this has not translated into complete gender equality. In fact, in some cases women are deliberately tracked into licensure and certificate programs but not full ordination, though this is not unique to the Latino AG since it is also true in some other denominations as well.

The historical research, interviews, and survey data indicate that Latinas face greater obstacles to going into the ordained ministry than do their Euro-American counterparts—namely, finances, limited theological educational resources and choices, sexism, Latin American patriarchy, and cultural sacramentalism. Nonetheless, Latina clergywomen stated that their number one obstacle in the ministry was financial instability.

Some women in the AG and other Pentecostal denominations have consequently formed their own denominations, such as the Damascus Christian Church and Mita Congregation. Still others have left the Pentecostal movement altogether to join the Methodist, Baptist, Disciples of Christ, or Presbyterian denominations. However, the vast majority of Latina AG clergywomen have chosen to remain within the movement and continue their work in typically small (50- to 150-member) churches and missions.

"We've Got a Voice, but We Know Our Place": Feminism, *Chicanismo*, Evangelicalism, and Latina AG Identity

Latina Pentecostal women construct their identity by drawing on the images of women in the Bible, denominational standards and doctrine, and larger trends in society. The secular feminist movement's upper middle class white orientation, along with its open affirmation of gay relations, is the most difficult hurdle for Latina Pentecostal women to overcome to join the movement. They see same-sex relations as directly contradicting biblical and Latin American cultural values, and because they believe God will not recognize same-sex relations or marriage, they contend.[80] Aware of the perception and critique that Latina Pentecostal women are simply doormats for patriarchal men, one Pentecostal woman summed up the attitude of many Latina AG women when she stated, "I tell my husband that a woman's place is in the house *and* the Senate." She went on to conclude, "We've got a voice, but we also know our place."[81]

The reimagining of what it means to be truly liberated is likewise a theme that ran through all of my interviews. Rev. Gloria Garza, Rev. Rose Nodal, Rev. García Cortese, Rev. Maria Camarillo, Rev. Eva Rodríguez, and many others agreed that the feminist movement had little direct impact on the Latino AG because "there is freedom in the Lord" and because the feminist movement is selfish, self-centered, antimale, antitraditional family and Bible, and "too pushy," they claimed.[82]

Surprisingly, Mexican American clergywomen also had mixed feelings about the Chicano movement in the Southwest during the 1960s and 1970s.[83] Mexican Assemblies of God pastor Rev. Anita Soto stated: "Chicano is a nickname from the world. I don't believe too much in that. We are for the whole world, not just for Chicanos."[84] Yet Latinas like Rev. Garza stated that people in the Latino AG did talk about Chicano activist and former Latin District evangelist Reies López Tijerina, who fought on behalf of the Hispano land-grant struggle in New Mexico. Tijerina was licensed as a Latino AG minister and even attended the LABI in Texas before starting his own independent movement and eventually a utopian commune in the Arizona desert. Latina AG clergywomen also supported, to varying degrees, César Chávez and the United Farm Workers, since many worked in the fields and lived in migrant farm labor camps. Many held Chávez up as a role model for being a man who "was amongst us" and believed in a cause.[85]

Despite this ambivalence toward the racial-ethnic politics of the 1960s and 1970s, many Latina Pentecostal women embraced the broader Euro-American Pentecostal and Evangelical subculture. For example, Latina AG women grew up listening to or currently listened to Pentecostal preachers like Benny Hinn, John Hagee, Oral Roberts, and Kathryn Kuhlman. Next to denominational literature, James Dobson's books on childraising, marriage, and self-esteem, and his *Focus on the Family* radio show were the most popular Christian influences on Latina AG women. None of the women I interviewed seemed terribly interested in mixing politics and religion, although, as we shall see later in this book, this attitude began to change after the election of George W. Bush and Barack Obama.

Latina AG Religious, Social, and Political Views in the 2008 and 2012 Elections

Despite a reticence to become involved in politics, Latina women are more likely to vote than Latino men. Perhaps somewhat counterintuitive given their fairly conservative social and moral views, Latinas are also more likely than men both to be more spiritual and to vote for Democratic candidates. They are also less opposed to controversial moral and social issues like the death penalty, affirmative action, and immigration reform. The 2008 Latino Religions and Politics national survey (n = 1,104) found that AG women are much more likely than AG men to say that religion provides guidance in their daily living (92 percent versus 76 percent), pray every day (82 percent versus 73 percent), attend Bible study or prayer groups (52 percent versus 35 percent), pray for divine healing (73 percent versus 61 percent), evangelize others (42 percent versus 22 percent), and attend church (69 percent versus 68 percent), and only slightly less likely than men to say that they read their Bibles at least once a week or more (62 percent versus 59 percent). On church-state and moral issues, women and men are both overwhelmingly conservative. However, women are more likely than men to favor prayer in school (86 percent versus 77 percent) but less likely than men to favor keeping "under God" and "In God We Trust" in the Pledge of Allegiance and on American currency (83 percent versus 90 percent), though the differential was modest. Although men and women also overwhelmingly oppose abortion (85 percent versus 70 percent), gay marriage (80 percent versus 70 percent), and gay adoption (62 percent versus 54 percent), women were less likely to oppose these issues than men (see Table 10.1).

Perhaps the biggest surprise is that although women are more likely to favor prayer in school and say that religion provides guidance in their daily living, the 2012 Latino Religions and Politics survey (n = 1,075)

Table 10.1.   Latina religious beliefs and practices (percentages)

	Latino AG		All Latino Christians
	Women	Men	
How important is religious guidance in daily living?			
Quite a bit	92	76	76
Some	4	19	18
No guidance at all	4	5	5
Don't know/refused to answer	0	0	1
How often do you attend church?			
Almost every week or more	69	68	60
Once or twice a month	19	20	20
A few times a year or less	8	5	17
Never	4	7	3
How often do you pray?			
Every day	82	73	67
At least once a week	7	14	16
Once or twice a month	7	4	9
Seldom	4	7	6
Never	0	2	2
How often do you read the Bible?			
At least once a week or more than once a week	59	62	41
Once or twice a month	15	10	18
Seldom	15	15	20
Never	11	13	21
How often do you attend Bible study and prayer groups?			
At least once a week	52	35	26
Once or twice a month	9	15	9
Seldom	9	15	18
Never	30	35	47
Don't know/refused to answer	0	0	0
How often do you pray for divine healing?			
Every day	73	61	63
At least once a week	4	5	10
Once or twice a month	11	10	10
Seldom	8	14	10
Never	4	10	6
Don't know/refused to answer	0	0	1
How often do you evangelize and share your faith?			
Every day	43	22	15
At least once a week	21	29	15
Once or twice a month	12	10	13
Seldom	12	15	23
Never/don't know/refused to answer combined	12	24	34

Source: Findings from the LRAP National Survey of 1,104 U.S. Latino Christian voters, October 1–7, 2008.

found that Latina AG women nationwide (52 percent versus 31 percent) were significantly more likely than men (30 percent versus 37 percent) to be registered Democrats (52 percent versus 30 percent). Furthermore, while a slight plurality of Latino AG men planned to vote for Romney (47 percent versus 43 percent), a clear majority of Latino AG women planned to vote for Obama (66 percent versus 24 percent). In short, Latina AG women were 23 percentage points more likely to vote for Obama than men (66 percent versus 43 percent) and 23 points less likely to vote for Romney (24 percent versus 47 percent). Perhaps this is because Latina AG women were less likely than men to say that a political candidate's faith and morals are relevant to their voting decision (55 percent versus 60 percent) in 2012, though again the differential is almost negligible given the margin of error. However, given their high levels of religious practice and conservative views on faith and moral issues, Latina Pentecostal women may also be a soft constituency for Democrats, one that Republicans could possibly target for outreach in future elections. However, Republicans will need to redouble their efforts if they expect to gain ground among Latino Protestants, whose support dropped from between 40 and 44 percent for Bush in 2004 to 27 percent for Romney in 2012. This is especially true since, as we shall see in Chapter 12, Latino Evangelicals are a swing vote constituency, while Latino mainline Protestants and especially Catholics are solid Democratic constituencies. Thus Latino Evangelicals in general and women in particular may lead the way as the target group that Democrats need to shore up and Republicans need to win over to stand a chance at winning in the future. Regardless, it is clear that Latina Pentecostal women are an increasingly important constituency for both the Assemblies of God and Democrats and Republicans in national politics. For these reasons and many others, it would be strategic for these groups to place greater emphasis on targeting and meeting the needs of women throughout the movement leading into the 2016 presidential election (see Table 10.2).

This chapter has demonstrated that there never was a golden age that threw open the doors to Latinas in ministry in the early twentieth century.

Table 10.2. Latina views on politics, church-state, and social issues (percentages)

	Latino AG		All Lati
	Women	Men	Christi
Political party identification in October 2012			
Democrat/lean democrat	52	30	56
Republican/lean Republican	31	37	22
Independent	17	17	22
Vote leaning in October 2012			
Obama	66	43	63
Romney	24	47	26
Other/undecided	10	10	11
Prayer in public schools (2008)			
Favor	86	77	73
Neither favor nor oppose/haven't thought much about it	2	7	6
Oppose	10	10	18
Don't know/refused to answer	2	2	3
Keep "under God" and "In God we trust" in pledge and on currency (2008)			
Favor	83	90	66
Neither favor nor oppose/haven't thought much about it	4	0	9
Oppose	4	10	19
Don't know/refused to answer	9	0	6
View on abortion (2008)			
Favor	23	5	11
Neither favor nor oppose/haven't thought much about it	7	10	10
Oppose	70	85	77
Don't know/refused to answer	0	0	2
View on gay marriage (2008)			
Favor	21	15	21
Neither favor nor oppose/haven't thought much about it	5	5	16
Oppose	70	80	59
Don't know/refused to answer	4	0	4
Registered to vote (2008)			
Yes	46	56	44
No	41	39	53
Don't know/refused to answer	13	5	3
Political party identification (2008)			
Democrat	50	39	55
Republican	32	39	19
Independent	9	22	20
Something else/don't know/refused to answer combined	9	0	6

Sources: Findings from the LRAP Survey of 1,000 U.S. Latino Christian likely voters, October 3–10, 2012, and the LRAP National Survey of 1,104 U.S. Latino Christian voters, October 1–7, 2008.

Instead, Latinas have walked a steady path of progress toward increasing recognition and voice and agency in the Latino AG. While they started off much slower than their Euro-American counterparts, today Latinas make up a larger percentage of the Latino AG than Euro-American clergywomen make up in the AG nationwide. There has not been a reversal for Latinas in ministry in the late twentieth century, but rather steady progress, especially with respect to the number of women credentialed.

This chapter challenges the Barfoot and Sheppard thesis that a prophetic period of early Pentecostalism gave way to a priestly period that later restricted the role of women in the ministry in unprecedented ways. Although the Latino AG has both routinized and institutionalized, this has not kept women from entering the ministry. Today each Latino district is semiautonomous and has its own superintendent. This has created a greater level of freedom and has perhaps inadvertently led to a greater need for participation by women to help pastor and lead the growing number of churches and districts, though not every district is as supportive of women in the ministry as the Spanish Eastern District in New York and the Southern Pacific District in California. Max Weber's theory that religions of the disprivileged classes tend to allot greater equality to women in the early prophetic years but not in the later priestly period does not appear to hold true for the Latino AG in general, though this may be the case for particular districts—just not nationally.[86]

Women sought empowerment through theological education and the Women's Missionary Council, and they have used both to leverage growing influence and voice in the Latino AG. Yet women have been forced to live seemingly paradoxical lives as both prophetesses and loving spouses and mothers. Despite this, they do not see the tension or problems as sharply as some might think. They believe that their Pentecostal faith empowers them, but in different ways from men. Although women have made modest progress over the years and now exercise greater voice and agency than ever before, with over 1,100 credentialed Latina Pentecostal clergywomen, many still face an uphill struggle as third-class soldiers.

CHAPTER 11

Righteousness and Justice

Faith-Based Action for Social Change

CONTRARY TO POPULAR PERCEPTION, Latino Pentecostals have been involved in faith-based social, civic, and political civic action throughout the twentieth century. Although their work is not framed in terms of the Social Gospel or Liberation Theology movements because such movements are not Christ-centered enough for them, Latino Assemblies of God leaders and laity regularly engage in social, civic, and political action and acts of mercy.[1] In fact, because the needs are so great and these acts so common in local churches, most Latino Pentecostals do not see anything special about them but rather assume that is what Christians are supposed to do on a daily basis for their "hermanos/as" and as a way to demonstrate the love of God to unbelievers.

While traditional Evangelical and liberal Protestant churches have split evangelism and social justice into two different types of ministry, Latino Pentecostals blend them together in evangelistic social work and outreach. This approach seeks to use social action, civic engagement, political participation, and acts of mercy as vehicles through which to demonstrate and incarnationalize the love and saving grace of Jesus Christ to a broken and suffering world. To carry this out, they seek to identify with and redeem the suffering and alleviate the material needs people. This biblical framework is rooted in what Samuel Solivan "orthopathos" and Eldin Villafañe calls the "liberating Spirit," ι seeks to identify with people's suffering and provide a path for spiritual liberation through a holistic vision of faith-based social e.[2]

Latino AG leaders such as Jesse Miranda and Samuel Rodríguez call this blending Jesus Christ's "agenda of righteousness and justice," which they liken to combining Billy Graham's vertical reconciling message of salvation and hope in Jesus Christ with Martin Luther King Jr.'s horizontal prophetic focus on civil rights and social justice. In an interview about his book, *The Lamb's Agenda: Why Jesus Is Calling You to a Life of Righteousness and Justice* (2013), Rodríguez stated, "The cross is both vertical and horizontal. It is both redemption and relationship, sanctification and service . . . orthodoxy and orthopraxy, righteousness and justice, John 3:16 and the Matthew 25, the prophetic and the practical, truth and love, worshipping the Lord and welcoming the stranger, preaching the word and feeding the hungry."[3]

This focus on righteousness and justice resonates with similar trends in global Pentecostalism around the world, especially in the global South as documented in Donald Miller and Tetsunao Yamamori's book, *Global Pentecostalism: The New Face of Christian Social Engagement* (2007). Miller and Tetsunao contend that because Pentecostals do not use the traditional liberal Protestant language of social justice, this has led some scholars and writers to conclude that the latter are apolitical and uninterested in addressing the social and material needs of the people. The authors contend that this is a mistake because their survey of 400 denominational, mission, and other experts around the world found that 85 percent of the churches nominated as the fastest-growing self-supporting indigenous churches that had an *active social program* were Pentecostal or Charismatic. They were not trying to reform society, but rather rebuild it from the ground up, Miller and Yamamori noted. However, in this respect Latino Pentecostal leaders such as Miranda and Rodríguez differ because they are seeking to do both—reform society and challenge the political system on immigration reform and pro-life issues and by promoting Judeo-Christian values.[4]

Latino Evangelistic Social Work at the Azusa Street Revival

The first mixing of evangelism and social work goes all the way back to the Azusa Street Revival in 1906, where Susie Villa Valdez, mother of the famous preacher A. C. Valdez, carried out this kind of work in the slums of Los Angeles and in migrant farm labor camps in Riverside and San Bernardino Counties. She and her companions would play worship music on their guitars; pass out tracts; engage in acts of service and mercy; pray for and minister to ex-cons, prostitutes, and alcoholics; and then offer a short evangelistic message about God's ability to heal their broken spirits and bodies through conversion and divine healing. Valdez and her companions would also take some of these people to Christian rehabilitation centers and other skid row missions for food, shelter, and medical attention. Susie Valdez perhaps drew inspiration and insight from Rev. Florence Crawford, a leader at Azusa who later founded her own denomination, the Apostolic Faith (Portland, Oregon). Crawford worked with the police and Los Angeles County jails in a faith-based prisoner rehabilitation and reentry program. Susie Valdez and her son inspired others to carry out evangelistic social work in the Assemblies of God and other missions. Thus, from the beginning, Latino Pentecostals have tended to take a holistic approach to the needs of the community and individuals that sought to address the body, mind, and spirit. Another practical reason why Latino Pentecostals have been so intimately involved with social change is that almost 50 percent of them (and of Catholics) in the United States live at or below the poverty line, which forces them to find real-world solutions to issues that affect more than half of their congregation, but especially immigrants and single mothers.[5]

Faith-Based Social and Civic Action, 1917–1940s

Latino Pentecostal evangelistic-social and civic action is evident in the work of H. C. Ball. He wrote regular articles for the *Pentecostal Evangel* seeking to raise funds for Mexican ministers who lived in abject poverty alongside their parishioners. He also spoke out against injustice when in 1918 he confronted a sheriff on behalf of Rev. Isabel Flores after he was unjustly arrested and thrown in jail for "loitering" and being on the wrong side of the tracks in the segregated city of Edna, Texas. Ball won Flores's release from jail. He complained in the *Pentecostal Evangel* that racial "discrimination" and "other similar insults" against Mexican immigrants and even Mexican Americans were pervasive throughout Texas and "unjust." Echoing sentiments in the current debate over immigration reform in Washington, D.C., Ball wrote, "They are [just] as much American as we are." His activism led the FBI to investigate him and even confiscate copies of *La Luz Apostólica* and other literature to see if he was a spy working for the German or Mexican governments during the Zimmerman Telegram scare during World War I.[6]

This civic activism was joined with evangelistic social ministry. In 1931, at the height of the Great Depression, the Latin District's Women's Missionary Council prayed for the "salvation of souls as well as for the relief of the poor and sick visitation," wherein they demonstrated the love of Jesus through acts of mercy by providing for the material needs of Mexican immigrants in the community.[7] A year later, during the nativist-driven repatriation movement in the United States, Ball publicly protested the way Mexicans were treated. The U.S. government forcibly repatriated an estimated 500,000 people to Mexico, including many U.S.-born Mexican American youth, to reduce job competition during the Depression.[8] In an effort to help alleviate the suffering of Latino pastors who found it very difficult to find work to supplement their meager Sunday offerings, Ball wrote in the *Pentecostal Evangel,* "Our Mexican pastors have been sorely tried during the depression, the majority of their members being on relief; their poverty and suffering have been terrible." He asked readers to send in funds for one Mexican minister in particular he worked with whose family often went hungry. In fact, Ball wrote that in some cases ministers' families were so poor that the children had to work in the agricultural fields instead of attending schools—many of which in Texas were segregated "Mexican schools."[9]

In the wake of poor educational options and out of a desire to provide theological training, from the 1920s through the 1960s H. C. Ball, Alice Luce, Demetrio Bazan, Roberto Fierro, José Girón, and many others sponsored night schools and literacy programs and attempted to raise funds from Euro-American Pentecostals to provide scholarships for those who could not otherwise attend. In an effort to take care of ministers and their families (often left devastated and impoverished if the minister died), in the 1940s Superintendent Demetrio Bazan had Robert Fierro translate information about Social Security and medical benefits into Spanish. Bazan also spearheaded a plan to enroll Latinos into the Metropolitan Life Insurance and Social Security programs.[10]

As we have seen in previous chapters, Latino and Euro-American missionaries tried to alleviate the suffering and hunger many faced in Puerto Rico. During this period, AG women walked through villages and led neighborhood children to church, where they washed their clothes and fed them. Evangelistic social work was a regular practice throughout Puerto Rico and the United States, and no one thought twice about these actions, which were and still are often simply called "outreach."

Faith-Based Social Action, 1950s–1980s

Pentecostal Influences in Gabriel Caride's Cuban Refugee Ministry in Florida

Latino AG civic and social activism was also evident in the Cuban community in the 1960s. In the wake of Fidel Castro's 1959 Cuban Revolution and overthrow of Fulgencio Batista, Latino AG pastors and laity opened up refugee centers in Florida to take care of those fleeing the island. They also sought to minister to some of the 14,000 children boatlifted from Cuba to the United States through President Dwight D. Eisenhower's Operation Pedro Pan. In time, over 800,000 Cubans arrived in Florida, with some 1,500 refugees arriving weekly. The AG opened up the Assemblies of God Refugee Center in Miami in 1961 and by March 3 had ministered to over 300 Cuban refugee families representing an estimated 1,200 men, women, and children. Three former missionaries to Cuba, Howard Coffeys, Virginia Carpenter, and Kathleen Belknap, pioneered this work, but by 1962 only Belknap was left. She and other Pentecostal social workers called on American society, in a refrain often heard in the contemporary immigration reform debate, to "be not forgetful to entertain strangers" (Hebrews 13:2). This very same verse is often cited today by Samuel Rodríguez of the National Hispanic

Leadership Conference and Catholic bishops such as Cardinal Roger Mahoney in their support for comprehensive immigration reform.[11]

Belknap and others were soon led by the pastor of one of the largest Latino AG churches in Havana, Gabriel Caride (Figure 11.1), and his family. In Miami, he opened up and pastored Cuban Chapel Assemblies of God, which targeted refugees with evangelistic social work. The Eisenhower administration freely mixed religion and politics when it required that for immigration purposes all refugees register with a Catholic, international (secular), or Jewish agency, or with the Protestant Church World Service (CWS) relief agency. The CWS was an interdenominational agency that included representatives from the Methodists, Presbyterians, Assemblies of God, and other denominations. Caride was able to use this agency to gain access and minister to refugees. Throughout the 1960s, the AG and CWS provided clothes, blankets, food, Bibles, tracts, and housing for Cubans. The CWS hall, which

Figure 11.1.   Rev. Gabriel Caride led the Assemblies of God Cuban refugee outreach in Florida and the Southeast in the 1960s.   (Flower Pentecostal Heritage Center)

seated about 300 people, was often filled to capacity. Caride was asked to lead the CWS Center and began offering voluntary evangelistic services for the refugees. In time, thousands of Cubans were converted. Caride and others had to fight against racism, Nativism, and xenophobia. As the flow of refugees increased, they began to see signs that read, "Cubans, go home," "Don't buy from Cuban merchants," and "The Cubans have displaced our jobs."[12] Although the first major waves of Cubans arrived in 1961, by 1967 an estimated 12,000 Cuban refugees were still arriving annually in Miami.[13]

Pentecostal Influences in Saturnino González's Ministry in the Mariel Boat Lift

The second major wave of Cuban immigrants began arriving in April 1980 through the Mariel Boat Lift. By July of that year, some 114,000 Cubans had fled to Florida, including a large number of Cuban Pentecostals. The AG provided 19,000 sets of Spanish Bibles and books for the incoming immigrants.[14] Unlike the first Latino AG outreach in 1961, which was part of a larger interdenominational outreach effort, in 1980 the Spanish Eastern District (SED) and the Florida Conference (a smaller regional subunit of the SED) under Gustavo Jimenez and Adolfo Carrión led it from the beginning. They sent out evangelists to work in the refugee camps and to help process refugees' applications for U.S. citizenship and housing. At the Camp McCoy refugee settlement camp in Wisconsin, AG evangelists preached to many of the 14,000 refugees and claimed that some 2,000 raised their hands to become born-again Christians. This was in large part because Rev. Sam Hernández, whom the U.S. government appointed as chaplain for the Hispanic refugees at Camp McCoy, helped to facilitate and organize these services, attendance at which was completely voluntary. Latino AG pastors and evangelists such as Victor M. Chevere, Richard Reyes, and Saturnino González ministered to refugees in resettlement camps in Fort Chaffee, Arkansas, where they passed out 5,600 Bibles, and at Indian Town Camp in Pennsylvania. They reported 125 conversions at Fort Chaffee and sponsored a small mission of about 60 converts.[15] AG Cuban pastors such as José Espinoza, who had spent seven years in Fidel Castro's prisons for preaching and printing Christian literature, joined their efforts. By July 1981, he had converted and baptized almost 70 men at Fort Chaffee, and in total some 210 people were converted and attended Bible study. Latino AG pastors and workers went on to sponsor 350 to 400 Cuban refugees and helped them find places to live and work.[16]

All of these evangelistic efforts helped thousands of refugees transition into American society and find a voice and agency. They were silent no more. Such efforts may help explain why recent studies found that a surprisingly high 26 percent of all people of Cuban ancestry in Florida self-identified as born again, a population that has the highest levels of education of almost any Hispanic group, a variable often associated with secularism and irreligiosity. This evangelical outreach, along with their being sponsored by Republican presidents Dwight D. Eisenhower and Ronald Reagan, may also help explain why Cubans, unlike other Latino groups, have tended to support the Republican Party and President George W. Bush by wide margins, though this support has declined with successive generations.[17]

Pentecostal Influences in Reies López Tijerina's Land Grant Struggle in New Mexico

While Latino AG ministers were reaching out in Texas, Puerto Rico, and Florida, Reies López Tijerina was leading the land grant struggle in New Mexico. In many respects, Tijerina was a whole new breed and generation of militant faith-based activists. While most Latino AG ministers and laity have worked within the law and society, activists like Tijerina were willing to work outside of it.[18] After joining the Latino AG in his teen years, he attended the LABI in Texas from 1944 to 1946 and was ordained an evangelist. After marrying LABI graduate Maria Escobar, he continued preaching in AG churches across the Southwest. His unyielding convictions and what Kenzy Savage called his increasingly "fanatical" and unorthodox beliefs led the AG to take away his credentials and church in Eden, Texas. Sometime in the 1960s, he reportedly returned to Catholicism during his land grant struggle in New Mexico. Whether he did this due to a sincere desire to join the American Catholic Church or to better identify with the Hispano people in New Mexico

is unclear, though the latter or a mixture of reasons is most likely. Whatever the case, it is clear that he kept very strong ties with the Latino AG
not only through his wife, but also through their network of friends,
churches, and followers. Rudy V. Busto points out that the Latino AG
directly influenced Tijerina's flamboyant preaching style and magical-
literalist interpretation of the Bible and worldview, which later influenced his justification for the Hispano land grant struggle.[19]

What people admired most about Tijerina was his uncompromising
commitment to living out his faith and advocating for the poor and willingness to fight for justice on behalf of the Latino people. He often asked
churches to give any love offering for his preaching to the poor. Disappointed by the worldliness of the church and its lack of love for the poor,
he created a Christ-centered community called the Valle de Paz (Valley
of Peace) in the Arizona desert from 1955 to 1957. However, flood, fire,
and harassment by Euro-American locals and law enforcement forced
him to abandon his Latino commune and utopian dreams. He realized
that the social marginalization he and other Latinos faced was due not
only to a sinful world that he had once tried to convert in Texas and then
escape from in the Arizona desert, but also to their marginal social status, lack of resources, and lack of civic and political power, all of which
he believed stemmed from the loss of their ancestral communal lands or
ejidos. Land brought wealth, power, honor, and respect, all of which
were denied many Latinos in the Southwest.[20]

In an effort to rectify the problem, in 1963 Tijerina began his own independent movement, called the Federal Alliance of Free City-States
(Alianza de los Pueblos Libres). He and his followers argued that 33.5
million of the 35 million acres of Hispano communal lands in New Mexico were swindled from their rightful owners by the U.S. government
and unscrupulous land speculators during the past century. For this reason, he argued, these lands should be returned to Hispanos.[21] In a dar-
ing move to give voice and visibility to the Hispano land grant cause on
national television, Tijerina and 350 followers took over a 1,500-acre par-
cel of land in the Kit Carson National Forest. They renamed it the Latino
Free City-State Republic of San Joaquín del Río de Chama.[22]

Tijerina elected an *alcalde* (mayor) and a governing board for San
Joaquín del Río de Chama. He argued that the colonial Spanish Laws of

the Indies granted in "perpetuity" Spain's right to determine the land grants in the Southwest. These laws and land grants, which were still recognized by the Mexican government after it gained its independence from Spain in 1821, and by the U.S. government after the Treaty of Guadalupe Hidalgo in 1848, superseded Euro-American jurisprudence because they were divinely given and because the Southwest was forcibly taken by conquest and what he called a "criminal conspiracy," not legitimate legal means.[23] Most important, the Laws of the Indies were conferred by the pope (God's representative on earth) to King and Queen Ferdinand and Isabella of Spain. Because the laws were enacted on God's behalf, they were still binding in heaven as well as on earth. In short, divine law superseded human law—including that of the United States. Despite his passionate retelling of the story and international law, Tijerina's dream of a new Hispano homeland was cut short when he and five followers were summarily arrested for trespassing.[24]

Tijerina left jail frustrated by what he believed was another example of "gringo" justice. His steel resolve and religious vision for social and political justice would not yield. On June 5, 1967, he and eighteen followers armed with pistols and shotguns shocked the nation when they led an armed raid on the Rio Arriba County courthouse in Tierra Amarilla, New Mexico. Their stated goal was to make a citizens' arrest of New Mexico state district attorney Alfonso Sánchez. His crime was threatening to arrest anyone who attended Tijerina's lawful assembly and send them to jail for six months, all without due legal process, Tijerina implied. The raid went tragically afoul and turned into a shootout. Two police officers were wounded. Tijerina escaped but not before his men took two officers as hostages. The New Mexican National Guard, three tanks, helicopter gunships, and planes were called in to hunt down the wily Tijerina and his rebel band as they roved through the rugged forested mountains of northern New Mexico. Although Tijerina was arrested, charged with attempted murder, and spent thirty-five days in jail, an all-Hispano jury of his peers found him innocent of all charges. Two years later, he was again accused of destroying federal property and resisting arrest by two police officers. He was arrested and put in jail. While awaiting trial, Tijerina wrote his famous Letter from the Santa Fe Jail. In it, he asserted that the U.S. government had conspired to put him in prison for "upholding" Hispano land rights promised under the 1848 Treaty of Guadalupe Hidalgo, under which Mexico ceded the Southwest to the United States in the wake of the U.S-Mexico War of 1846–1848. He argued that after the treaty was signed, the U.S. government began illegally confiscating Hispano ranchos and did not respect Hispanic property rights, civil rights, and culture. He called for a presidential committee to investigate the land grant question in northern New Mexico. Democratic president Lyndon B. Johnson did not support or respond to his call for an investigation. Though his calls for justice fell on deaf ears in Washington,[25] he continued his struggle for Latino civil rights, racial justice, and the rights of the poor.

Recognizing that his struggle was part of a much larger struggle of racial-ethnic minority civil rights in the United States and colonized people of color around the world, in late August 1967 Tijerina met Martin Luther King Jr. and proposed the idea of a Poor People's March. He proposed that blacks, Latinos, Indians, and even poor whites come together to fight for a common cause in their struggle for social and economic justice. King said it was a good idea, and in March formed the Poor People's March coalition and invited Tijerina to be a leader, though Tijerina was not properly acknowledged as the march's initiator. Their plans almost fell apart after King was assassinated. However, Rev. Ralph Abernathy assumed the leadership, and the march took place in May and June 1968 as scheduled, though without the success its organizers had hoped for because of internal strife and a lack of positive media coverage (see Figure 11.2). Despite this fact, the first national brown-black-Indian-white coalition had been created by Tijerina. As a result of his steadfast leadership, he was invited to speak at Abernathy's church and many others. Prior to that time, minorities were often pitted against one another by Euro-American leaders to dilute their collective power, voice, and agency. Now they sought to speak with one common voice to bring about positive social change for the entire nation.[26]

King's assassination had a profound impact on Tijerina. His already fiery rhetoric now began to take on almost apocalyptic tones. In an interview with Berkeley KPFA radio talk show host Elsa Knight Thompson in the aftermath of King's assassination, Tijerina lamented that America had stoned its prophets and mocked God's justice and was in danger of

Figure 11.2.   Rev. Reies López Tijerina, Henry Adams of the American Indian Movement, and Ralph Abernathy of Martin Luther King Jr.'s Southern Christian Leadership Conference (SCLC) at a press conference discussing the Poor People's Campaign and March in 1968. Tijerina was licensed by the Latino AG and preached throughout the Southwest before calling on his Alianza of Latino activists to lead the Hispanic Land Grant Struggle in New Mexico in the 1960s and other faith-based social justice causes. Left to right: Unknown Chicano leader, American Indian Movement leader Henry Adams, Tijerina, Ralph Abernathy. (2000-008-0130, Karl Kernberger Pictorial Collection, Center for Southwest Research, University Libraries, University of New Mexico)

invoking the wrath of God to bring about an end to the American "Empire." Revealing a deep love for King and the African American people, Tijerina sounded the toll of a fiery prophet when he declared:

> God . . . has run out of patience and we have mocked him too many times . . . we've got him fed up, and I think that we are running out of time, and the patience of God is also running out. I don't think we have left him any alternative. . . . We have been mocking and mocking his true justice, his true democracy by destroying mankind. And establishing our own kind of democracy . . . the assassination, cold-blooded murder of the symbol of peace and representation of

the rights of the poor through a meek and wise man, Dr. King. The government, I feel, is responsible . . . by not developing ways for the oppressed. Only ways and means for the bankers, for the powerful, for the whites. And this is why I feel that the federal government of the United States is pushing its own people to destruction, to the end of empire.[27]

After his time in jail, during which his family suffered greatly from abuse, racism, and harassment, Tijerina came out something of a new man. After a period of prayerful reflection, he decided to take a more pacifist and nonviolent resistance approach to social change. He decided to outsmart white America by forming his own political party and running for office. He created the People's Constitutional Party and ran for the governorship of New Mexico. Although he lost the election, he was able to help legitimize his land grant and civil rights causes. His bid for the governor's mansion also marks one of the first times in U.S. history a former Latino Assemblies of God minister ran for state governor.[28]

Tijerina's support among many Hispanos and Mexican Americans began to fade because some secular academics and writers saw him as too radical and eccentric. Still others were wary of his Pentecostal background, despite reembracing his Catholic roots in the 1960s.[29] Busto argues that it was precisely his Pentecostal-influenced high-octane, faith-based approach to social change that relegated him to the margins of Chicano history, while César Chávez's consistently nonviolent Gandhian pacifist approach has been immortalized.[30] Whatever the case, what is clear is that his years in the Latino AG as a parishioner, LABI student, and licensed evangelist influenced not only his fiery rhetoric, but also his fight for the land grant struggle and fight against racism, and his liberating vision and unquenchable thirst for social justice. It is also clear that in all of these things Tijerina mixed the passion of an evangelist with the zeal of a social prophet in his voracious hunger for righteousness and justice.

Pentecostal Influences in César Chávez's Farm Workers' Struggle in California

While Tijerina was leading the land grant struggle in New Mexico, in California Latino Pentecostal evangelists ministered to migrant workers and contributed to César Chávez's United Farm Workers (UFW) union. Latino AG pastor Rev. Pedro Torres and a group of lay ministers from Roseville AG evangelized migrant farm workers from 1961 to 1965. The workers were brought to the United States because of the Bracero Program, until the California legislature put a ban on these migrant workers on January 31, 1964. The Bracero Program was an agreement between the U.S. and Mexican governments in 1942 to provide contract workers to fill the labor shortage during World War II because many able-bodied American men were serving overseas in Europe and Asia. Torres and his coworkers moved systematically from Woodland, Kolo, Esparto, Winters, Clarksburg, Roseville, and on to sixty other farm camps that varied in size from 25 to 800 people. No camp was too small, no soul too unworthy, they stated. They ministered to the workers' material and social needs and then called on people to repent of their sins and ask Jesus Christ to be their personal savior and lord. Praying for the sick, along with enthusiastic worship services, was the greatest lure in their arsenal of faith. In the camps, they also showed movies of Jesus's crucifixion and resurrection. Because the workers had little to do after work hours in isolated farm camps, the ministers had a captive audience. Over the course of four years, the group passed out 3,000 Spanish New Testaments and countless gospel tracts, and held services on Saturday afternoons as well as midweek Bible studies. Although the migrant workers' squalid living conditions and the meager results of the ministry often discouraged these evangelists, the workers who converted energized them. Rev. Torres reported, "It has thrilled our hearts to see the deep interest the men showed as we gave the message. We are all sure God's Word shall not return unto Him void."[31] Indeed, their labors were not in vain, and that is why to this day no matter what city you happen to visit up and down central California, you are likely to find large numbers of Latino AG and other Pentecostal churches and missions evangelizing and ministering to second-, third-, and fourth-generation farm workers.

The growing number of Pentecostal farm workers converted through the ministry of the Latino AG and the Apostolic Assembly of the Faith in Christ Jesus help explain why César Chávez openly welcomed Pentecostals into his Community Service Organization (CSO) and the UFW. The CSO, founded in 1947 by Antonio Ríos, Edward Roybal, and Fred

Ross Sr. to fight against discrimination, bigotry, and suffering in the Latino community, had a largely Catholic flavor. Pentecostals significantly influenced three key faith-based strategies that Chávez employed during his CSO and UFW struggles—the recognition of the organizing power of religion, singing, and small-group organizing in house meetings.

Chávez's biographer, Richard Etulain, wrote that Pentecostals taught Chávez that religion was " 'a powerful moral and spiritual force' that no movement could afford to overlook."[32] From that realization forward, Chávez decided to incorporate religion and spirituality into his struggle in ways that went beyond his already deeply committed Catholic and ecumenical sensibilities. He actively drew inspiration from Catholic encyclicals and social teachings on the rights of labor, the spirituality of St. Francis of Assisi, the faith-based activism of Martin Luther King Jr., as well as Mohandas Gandhi, Saul Alinsky's Industrial Areas Foundation (IAF), and Father Donald McDonald. As a result of Catholic and Pentecostal influences, he called his first strike in a church, told his workers that God would provide for their needs, allowed and even encouraged clergy to open up union rallies and protests with prayers and to walk the picket lines, organized prayer meetings and vigils, partook in spiritual fasts, led pilgrimage marches, and encouraged the use of songs and *coritos* to lift the spirits of the people during the rallies, pilgrimages, marches, and boycotts. For example, the famous Delano strike was called on September 16 (Mexican Independence Day) in Our Lady of Guadalupe Church hall in Delano. The symbolic date and location were not an accident. They were meant to resonate with and encourage the spirit of the people.[33] These were not common union strategies, and in fact some clergy, union, and organizers criticized him for manipulating religion and playing God.[34] Others like Saul Alinsky, founder of the IAF and an agnostic Jew who had hitherto supported César, said that he and the IAF were embarrassed by the religious nature of Chávez's fast. Dolores Huerta sharply criticized Alinsky's anti-Christian and anti-Catholic bigotry and said it was a major problem with their liberal allies.[35]

In 1963, Chávez stated that he was profoundly struck by the joy, deep commitment, and energy he found in Pentecostal worship services he had attended over the previous years. Around 1961, when he was driving from Los Angeles to Delano, he passed a Pentecostal church at night, and it was full of people. He asked himself, "Why do all of these people come there so much?" He pulled off to the side of the road to investigate. After watching the services from a distance and listening to the powerful worship and shouts of "hallelujah" and "Gloria a Dios," he decided it "must be because they like to praise God—to sing." The realization that singing gave farm workers a voice persuaded him to adopt music as an organizing resource and strategy, he later wrote.[36]

The role of music and singing was underscored after Chávez began attending a little Pentecostal house mission in Madera, which was either AG or Apostolic Assembly. The pastor asked Chávez to help him with paperwork, but he also invited him to attend his prayer meetings and worship services. Chávez attended many of them. He wrote that he was moved by the deep authenticity of the worshippers. He said he learned that a small band of true believers fired up for a cause could be more powerful and effective than a large group of uncommitted followers. He also realized that the key to their success was their joy and focus on winning converts to their cause one person at a time—and in small and intimate home fellowships. He said there was more spirit in the little Pentecostal church than in the much larger Catholic masses he attended. Reflecting on the influence of Pentecostalism on his organizing, he wrote:

> So in that little [Pentecostal] church, I observed everything going on about me that would be useful in [union] organizing. Although there were no more than twelve men and women, there was more spirit there than when I went to mass where there were two hundred. Everybody was happy. They were all singing. These people were really committed to their beliefs, and this made them sing and clap and participate like that. I think that's where I got the idea of singing at meetings. That was one of the first things we did when I started at the Union.[37]

This was not simply a one-time visit, because he visited this Pentecostal preacher's home on a regular basis, where they talked about the Gospel and organizing.[38] Chávez realized that they were trying to convert him, but rather than look down on their commitment and convictions, he realized at the end of the day that they each helped and benefited one another. Chávez said, "We were organizing each other. At the end of the [Pentecostal] services, it would turn into a house meeting. Eventually the preacher got everybody in his congregation to join the CSO."[39] Chávez realized that the key to effective organizing and building loyalty to *la causa* was to win over one person at time. In fact, one biographer likened this strategy to a kind of UFW "friendship evangelism" or what we might call evangelistic social and union work.[40]

Chávez's relationship with Pentecostals continued for many years. Despite the separation between Catholics and Pentecostals, as well as his own Catholic heritage, he and his mother regularly attended Pentecostal services at a small mission in the Sal Si Puedes barrio in San Jose. The Pentecostals provided them with food and lodging and invited his mother to attend the services, which she freely did. He worked with Pentecostal ministers and used Catholic *coritos* to rally the people. César and his Pentecostal colleagues soon developed into an organizing team. They persuaded about 300 people to attend regular CSO meetings. Indeed, Pentecostals went on to exercise disproportionate influence in the early farm workers' struggle. César wrote that they served as excellent strike captains, at one point ran the CSO, and provided excellent leadership in the farm workers' struggle. In fact, he noted that the Protestant Pentecostal-led farmworker board "was one of the best CSOs we had." Chávez concluded, "For several years the Protestants, although a minority [in the CSO], were in control of the CSO and provided some excellent leadership."[41]

The growing influence of Pentecostals in the CSO infuriated a local Italian priest, who complained that there were too many Protestants (i.e., Latino Pentecostals) in the organization. Still another Catholic priest jealously accused Chávez of being a communist and implied that he was turning his CSO (later UFW) into a religious (i.e., Protestant Pentecostal) organization. It was not Catholic enough.[42]

Chávez bristled at the charges. He stood his ground and publicly stated in a speech at the very next meeting, "No one on this earth was going to tell us whether there was too much of anything." Worried that focusing too much on Catholicism might alienate Pentecostals, Protestants, Jews, and others who supported them, he said the CSO was "not a religious [i.e., Catholic] movement, and that if anybody wants to make it so, then they had a fight on their hands."[43] As a result, Chávez said that his movement "lost a few Catholics" but "gained many Protestants."[44] The Latino Pentecostal and Protestant California Migrant Ministry contributions to his struggle were significant enough for him to criticize the complacency of the Catholic Church. Chávez wrote, "Why do the Protestants come out here and help the people, demand nothing, and give all their time to serving farm workers, while our own [Catholic] parish priests stay in their churches, where only a few people come, and usually feel uncomfortable?"[45]

Faith infused many aspects of the Mexican American civil rights movement and Chávez's struggle for farmworkers and the UFW. Chávez reached across religious lines with Catholics, Protestants, Jews, and others on behalf of farmworkers. He brought religion into his struggle by calling his famous Delano strike in Our Lady of Guadalupe Church; made the Catholic-theme Cursillo song "De Colores" one of the UFW theme songs; marched behind colorful banners of Our Lady of Guadalupe; went on a 250-mile pilgrimage march from Delano to the state capitol in Sacramento, where he held a Sunday mass to spotlight the struggle of the farmworkers; invited Catholic, Protestant, and Pentecostal clergy to participate in their activism and picketing; opened many of his strikes in prayer; sang lots of religious songs on the picket lines; peppered his famous Plan of Delano (which he authored with Luís Valdez, who took the lead in writing it) with references to faith and spirituality; and ended his twenty-four-day fast for nonviolence in the UFW Delano struggle by taking holy communion with a Catholic priest and U.S. senator Bobby Kennedy, pictured in Figure 11.3.

Pentecostal Ministry to Gang Members and Drug Addicts in New York City and Los Angeles

In addition to the faith-based activism in Florida, New Mexico, and California, in New York City, Puerto Rican AG ministers and lay workers were engaging in social action to address poverty, the growing drug abuse, and hopelessness. Ricardo Tañon and Aimee García Cortese drew on the pioneer drug and rehab work of Leoncia Rosado Rousseau, better known to addicts as "Mama Leo." She pioneered the Damascus

Figure 11.3.   Robert Kennedy having communion with César Chávez at the end of the latter's twenty-four-day fast in Delano, California, 1968. He fasted to purify his own motives for leading the farmworkers' struggle and to role model a peaceful solution to the end of the grape boycott on behalf of his United Farm Workers union.   (Walter P. Reuther Library, Wayne State University)

Youth Crusade in the 1950s to target drug addicts and at-risk youth. This kind of work was also carried out in Rev. Ricardo Tañon's Iglesia Juan 3:16. Tañon, García Cortese, and many others conducted evangelistic social work, both preaching the gospel and providing for the material and emotional needs of many at-risk youth. Eldin Villafañe notes that there was a strong commitment to the poor, immigrants, and social outcasts. Even after Tañon's church became one of the largest Latino congregations in the nation in the 1970s, he refused to move out of the

Bronx, saying, "This is where God wanted them to shine like a beacon to the shipwrecked." Villafañe noted that he went on to influence more than 100 people to go into the ministry and argues that Tañon's church "became a true liberation citadel."[46]

It was through the ministry of a sister Assemblies of God organization called Teen Challenge that evangelist David Wilkerson converted a young Puerto Rican Mau Mau gang member named Nicky Cruz (b. 1938). Cruz went on to work with Latino AG churches to evangelize gang members, drug addicts, and at-risk youth. His life and spiritual journey are documented in Wilkerson's classic *The Cross and the Switchblade* (1963) and Cruz's own autobiography, *Run, Baby, Run* (1968). After attending LABI in La Puente (1958–1961), Cruz went on to conduct citywide evangelistic crusades with Teen Challenge and other organizations throughout the United States, Latin America, and Europe. Cruz served as a role model for a growing generation of Latino social evangelists now targeting the inner city and at-risk youth. For this reason, he served as an important bridge between the first- and second-generation evangelists and a new generation that sought to make the Christian message relevant in contemporary society.[47]

One of Cruz's most important converts was a former Puerto Rican heroin addict, gang member, and ex-con from Riker's Island Prison named Sonny Arguinzoni (b. 1938). After Arguinzoni's conversion, in 1962 Cruz sent him to study at LABI in La Puente for three years, where—like Tijerina before him—he met and married an AG student. Her name was Julie Rivera. Like Cruz, Sonny and Julie worked with the AG-based Teen Challenge before starting their own Victory Outreach ministry in 1967. They targeted at-risk youth in the Boyle Heights section of East Los Angeles. His stated goal was to "bring treasures [people] out of darkness" of drug addition, gang violence, and hopelessness. He has since developed it into a separate denomination that focuses heavily on evangelizing gang members, drug addicts, prostitutes, and other at-risk youth and social outcasts. It has planted over 210 churches and 350 rehabilitation homes throughout the United States and in over 25 countries around the world. Their international ministry conferences attract upwards of 10,000 people. Victory Outreach has preached to over 1.7 million people in the United States and around the world. It has reportedly organized 10,000 gang-prevention rallies and drama events and has distributed over 20 million pieces of evangelistic literature that target a segment of society forgotten about by both the church and mainstream America. It now sponsors its own magazine, *G.A.N.G.* (God's Anointed Now Generation) and its own Victory Outreach School of Ministry. Arguinzoni and Victory Outreach have garnered commendations and endorsements from former Assemblies of God general superintendent Thomas Trask, Evangelical pastor Rick Warren, and Presidents Ronald Reagan, Bill Clinton, George W. Bush, and Barack Obama, among others. Although no longer under the control of the AG, Arguinzoni not only keeps in regular contact with Latino AG leaders but also affirms and reflects many of the AG values, methods, and doctrinal beliefs he first learned at LABI.[48]

Unifying Latino Evangelicals: Jesse Miranda and the Alianza de Ministerios Evangélicos Nacionales

The growth of the Latino Protestant community along with the social action from the 1960s through the 1980s gave birth to a growing spirit of social consciousness and the need for Christian unity across denominations. This new emerging generation of Latino leaders, led by Jesse Miranda and Daniel De León, realized that crime, gang violence, drug and alcohol abuse, out-of-wedlock teen pregnancies, and poverty were also part of deeper structural problems in the fabric of American society. Realizing that the social problems Latinos faced could be remedied—at least in part—by seeking to bring about greater awareness and representation of Latinos in Washington, a growing number of Latinos began to seek ways to exercise a voice in national politics.

One of the first to do so was Jesse Miranda. Miranda was born in Albuquerque, New Mexico, on April 9, 1937, and converted after witnessing the healing of his mother. After joining the AG, he attended the LABI in Ysleta (near El Paso), Southern California College (now Vanguard University), Talbot Theological Seminary, California State University–Fullerton, and Fuller Theological Seminary (D.Min.). He did Ph.D. work in social ethics at the University of Southern California (1978), though he had to withdraw due to lack of scholarships and to support his family and lead his ministry. He has served as pastor (1957–1959), secretary-treasurer (1973–1978), assistant superintendent (1980–1984), and superintendent (1984–1992) of the Southern Pacific District. Since then, he has taught at the LABI in La Puente, Fuller Seminary, Azusa Pacific University, and Vanguard University, where he runs the Jesse Miranda Center for Hispanic Leadership.

Growing up in the 1950s and 1960s, Miranda learned early about the importance of faith-based activism. He remembers as a child that the church bus would load up parishioners and take them to the polling booths on Election Day during his ministry in Chama, New Mexico. In that same spirit, his service as the Executive Presbyter in the General Council of the Assemblies of God gave him a national platform from which to advocate for Latino issues and to promote and address Latino faith issues in the church and in society. In fact, he was the first Latino keynote speaker at the 1985 General Council of the Assemblies of God National Convention in San Antonio, Texas.

In order to raise awareness of the plight of Latino Evangelicals in general and to encourage leadership development, he has written *Liderazgo y Amistad* (*Leadership and Friendship*) and *The Christian Church in Ministry* and numerous articles in *Christianity Today, Apuntes,* and other periodicals. To address the pressing needs of the Latino community and to unite the Spanish-speaking Evangelical community so that they could speak as a common social and civic voice in national politics, Jesse Miranda created the Alianza de Ministerios Evangélicos Nacionales (National Alliance of Evangelical Ministries), also known as AMEN. Because of his leadership in the Latino community, Presidents Ronald Reagan, George H. W. Bush, Bill Clinton, George W. Bush, and Barack Obama have invited him to the White House or to participate on various White House task forces, symposiums, and committees.

From 1992 to 2006, AMEN was the nation's leading Latino Protestant advocacy group in Washington, D.C, and the United States as a whole. In 1992, Miranda and Protestant clergy from half a dozen denominations created AMEN as a national, multidenominational faith-based association of Hispanic Evangelical leaders. Miranda was able to bring together leaders from twenty-seven denominations and seventy-seven parachurch organizations across the United States, Mexico, Puerto Rico, and Canada.

He was elected by his peers to serve as the founding president. The mission of AMEN was fourfold: (1) to represent the collective aspirations of 10 to 11 million Latino Protestants throughout North America and the Latin Caribbean in both church and society; (2) to promote unity among leaders, churches, and parachurch organizations in the Latino community; (3) to develop the effectiveness of its constituents; and (4) to provide a public voice for Hispanic Protestants. In order to build a collective body, AMEN sponsored a number of national conferences, including a joint conference with the National Association of Evangelicals (NAE) in 1999 in Washington, D.C., and a national conference in Los Angeles in 2001 with over 5,000 participants. AMEN was well served by an advisory board that included Daniel De León, Bobby Sena, Pedro Windsor, Ray Rivera, Danny Villanueva, Francisco Colop, Lisa Treviño-Cummins, Jim Ortiz, and Larry Acosta, among others. Miranda had two highly effective vice presidents—both AG—Johnny Mendez and Victor Mendez. AG pastors and leaders, who made up a majority of the executive board and conference attendees, heavily influenced AMEN.[49]

Due to Miranda's service and nationally recognized leadership in the Latino Protestant community and especially AMEN, Luis Lugo and Danny Cortes at The Pew Charitable Trusts invited him to direct the $1.3 million Hispanic Churches in American Public Life (HCAPL) national study from 1999 to 2002. The HCAPL study fielded three surveys on Latino religions, politics, and activism. In the spirit of ecumenical cooperation, Miranda wrote to The Pew Trusts and stated that they should also invite a Latino Catholic to codirect the project since they then made up over 70 percent of the U.S. Latino community. As a result, The Pew Trusts invited Father Virgilio Elizondo of the Mexican American Cultural Center and the University of Notre Dame to codirect the study. Miranda and Elizondo in turn hired and collaborated with Harry Pachon and Rodolfo O. de la Garza of the Tomás Rivera Policy Institute to help carry out the three surveys (national, civic, leader) and field research. This study was the largest study in U.S. history on Latino religions, politics, and activism and generated a number of publications.[50]

For a number of reasons, Jesse Miranda and AMEN represent a critical turning point in the history of Latino AG faith-based political, civic, and social action. First, for the first time in U.S. history, Latino Evangelicals had a public face and organization to represent their collective aspirations. Through Miranda's diplomatic interdenominational leadership, AMEN became the nation's largest Latino Evangelical organization in the United States. For this reason, Miranda and AMEN leaders have been invited to the White House to meet all Presidents from Reagan to Obama. Second, although over twenty-seven Protestant denominations were affiliated with AMEN, it was disproportionately led by Latino Pentecostals in general and Latino AG leaders in particular, although this may be due in part to the fact that the Latino AG is the largest Latino Protestant-serving denomination in the United States. Third, Miranda and AMEN sponsored and organized the first national pan-Latino rallies in the United States since the large-scale interdenominational crusades by Francisco Olazábal and A. C. Valdez in the 1920s–1950s. Yet, while these latter leaders had focused almost exclusively on evangelism and revival, AMEN provided a national collective voice for both the church and social concerns. Fourth, Miranda and AMEN spearheaded the ecumenical HCAPL national study, which helped give birth to a new scholarly subfield in Latino religion, politics, and faith-based activism in the American Academy of Religion. Fifth, Miranda and AMEN partnered with Luis Cortés and Nueva Esperanza to organize the first National Hispanic Presidential Prayer Breakfast in 2002 in Washington, D.C. Since then, every major president, presidential candidate, and national political leader has attended this event, which annually attracts 750 Latino leaders from 49 states. Sixth, Miranda was one of the first Pentecostal and national Latino leaders to work across the religious aisle with Latino Catholics such as Father Virgilio Elizondo, founder of the Catholic Mexican American Cultural Center (MACC), not only to co-lead the HCAPL national study, but also to partner with them to address poverty, education, immigration reform, social marginalization, the family, and other social justice issues.[51]

And finally, Miranda and AMEN provided strong leadership to an emerging generation of Latino AG and Evangelical activists and organizations like Jim Ortiz, John Mendez, Lisa Treviño-Cummins (Urban Strategies), Luis Cortés (Nueva Esperanza), Danny De León (Obras de Amor), Wilfredo de Jesús (NHCLC), Rudy Carrasco, and Samuel Rodríguez (NHCLC).

Daniel De León and Lee De León—Obras de Amor (ODA)

One of the most successful ministries working alongside Jesse Miranda and associated for many years with AMEN is Danny De León's and Lee De León's ministry Obras de Amor (ODA). This is the community development arm of Templo Calvario in Santa Ana, California, which is pastored by Danny De León and is one of the largest Hispanic congregations in the United States. Danny's brother, Lee, largely runs Obras. Together they have established a network of over thirty-five inner-city churches and missions committed to social outreach work. They seek to build what they call a "Kingdom Coalition" of like-minded Latino Pentecostal, Evangelical, and mainline churches to address poverty, education, immigration, youth and family issues, and social justice. The coalition partners with fifty-seven churches and small groups and works with some of the largest Latino and non-Latino faith-based organizations in the United States, such as the Salvation Army and Community Action Partnerships. This is serving as a model faith-based ministry for a growing number of Latino AG churches and missions across the United States.[52]

Training the Next Generation of Latino AG Leaders—LABI

One of the secrets of the Latino AG growth has been its ability to produce indigenous leadership that is stable, visionary, and well educated. The key to this has been the Latino AG Bible schools in Texas, California, New York, and Puerto Rico, along with their almost innumerable satellite and correspondence programs. One example of a new generation of visionary leaders is Dr. Tommy Casarez, pictured in Figure 11.4 leading worship at the Latin American Bible Institute in La Puente, California. Dr. Casarez is president of LABI in La Puente and has made it part of his mission not only to train the next generation of leaders, but also to promote evangelistic social action and new cultural avenues for outreach such as music, art, and drama.

After being converted in Templo de Betania in Dallas, this fifth-generation Mexican American graduated from Vanguard University, Fuller Seminary, and Yale Divinity School before receiving his Ph.D. in theology from Princeton Seminary. In 2010, he was appointed president

Figure 11.4.   Dr. Tommy Casarez, president of the Latin American Bible Institute (LABI) in La Puente, California, leading worship during a chapel service at LABI, 2013.   (Tommy Casarez and Latin American Bible Institute)

of LABI and Latin American Theological Seminary, which offers associate's degrees and serves 136 full-time students on campus, with an additional 800 students enrolled in the part-time diploma program. He promotes what he calls the "H-factor," for training the head, heart, habits, and hands, with the goal of producing agents of spiritual and social transformation. His other goal is to prepare the next generation of both immigrants and young inner-city leaders for a vibrant ministry.[53]

Since 1926, the LABI in La Puente has graduated 2,000 Latino Pentecostal leaders, and since 2011 about 100 future pastors and leaders graduate annually. Historically about half of the LABI students have been men and half women, but today more than 70 percent of the student body are women. Since 2010 approximately 70 percent of graduates have gone into some form of ministry (pastorate, youth ministry, and so on) and 90 percent transfer to a four-year college or university. The LABIs are a key source for the Latino AG pastorates; more than 30 percent of the 400 ministers in the Southern Pacific District are graduates of LABI in La Puente, which today is situated on five acres and offers a diploma in Biblical studies and an associate of arts degree in Bible and ministry.[54]

Samuel Rodríguez and the National Hispanic
Christian Leadership Conference

One of the most important outgrowths of Jesse Miranda's ministry is the work of Samuel Rodríguez, Wilfredo de Jesús, and the National Hispanic Christian Leadership Conference (NHCLC). Born to Puerto Rican parents who migrated to New York City, Rodríguez was called to the ministry in the Spanish Eastern District at the age of fourteen and began preaching to youth rallies at the age of sixteen. At age eighteen he led the Hispanic youth ministry of the Spanish Eastern District, serving more than 300 churches. After pastoring in Staten Island and graduating from Kutztown University and Lehigh University, where he took an M.A. in educational leadership, he (along with his wife, Eva) co-pastored a Spanish-speaking Assemblies of God Church in Sacramento, California. He stepped down to assume the leadership of the NHCLC. Eva continues to serve as senior pastor of the church.[55]

In 1995, he and others began dreaming about the idea of the NHCLC to address Latino faith issues in American public life for all Latino born-again Christians across the United States. The NHCLC mission statement, which he helped draft, states: "The NHCLC is committed to serving the 16 million Hispanic born-again Christians in the United States and Puerto Rico across generational, country of origin, and denominational lines on issues that pertain to the family, immigration, economic mobility, education, political empowerment, social justice, and societal transformation."[56] Rodríguez stated that he and his colleagues, like de Jesús, drew inspiration from Latino leaders like Francisco Olazábal, Ricardo Tañon, Nicky Cruz, Demetrio Bazan, Victor De Leon, and Dr. Jesse Miranda, and from national organizations like the Southern Christian Leadership Conference (SCLC), the NAE, and the National Council for La Raza. He formed the NHCLC to promote spiritual renewal and Latino civil rights. He sees his organization as the counterpart to the NAE and the SCLC and often describes his organization as the Hispanic SCLC or the Hispanic NAE.[57]

The NHCLC represents the Latino Evangelical community via their seven directives: Life, Family, Great Commission, Education, Justice, Stewardship, and Youth. Their purpose and functions are to (1) provide leadership to exert a collective Latino voice before legislative, economic, and ecclesiastical authorities in Washington, D.C., and in state capitals; (2) host annual conferences throughout the nation where Latinos can come together for revival, renewal, and restoration; (3) provide networking opportunities for empowerment and service; (4) create apostolic partnerships with Hispanic churches in America with the purpose of creating faith-based community programs; (5) engage in political and social advocacy and seek to empower Latinos via "spiritual progressive leadership" and through voter registration drives, Latino-African American alliances, and other initiatives that directly affect Latinos; and (6) serve as a prophetic voice on behalf of the voiceless undocumented, and on other key political, social, and cultural issues. They also seek to lead the Hispanic Evangelical churches in America in transforming the culture, preserving the Judeo-Christian value system, and building spiritual, intellectual, and social/political capital within the Hispanic American community, and for this reason Rodríguez differs from those leaders Donald Miller and Tetsunao Yamamori found in their study of global Pentecostal social engagement.[58]

Today, the NHCLC reports representing 75 denominations and faith-based organizations, institutes, and networks, and over 23,000 Latino Evangelical churches and missions. Rather than compete with AMEN, Rodríguez and Dr. Miranda agreed to merge AMEN into the NHCLC in 2006. Miranda was appointed chief executive officer to replace the late Rev. Felix Posos, who was also an AG District superintendent. What is so remarkable about the NHCLC is the level of influence Latino AG leaders exercise in the organization. Latino AG pastors and lay leaders like Miranda, Rodríguez, and de Jesús have served as chief executive director, president, and vice president for social justice since its founding. Furthermore, Latino AG clergy and leaders make up 70 percent of the Executive Board and 35 percent of the National Board. All of this gives the Latino AG disproportionate influence in the NHCLC and in national politics, where it exercises considerable bipartisan support and influence, which will be discussed in Chapter 12.[59]

Struggle for Comprehensive Immigration Reform, 2005–2008

Although in existence for some time, the NHCLC rocketed into the national limelight during the 2006 debate over comprehensive immigration reform and with its protest against HR 4437. It joined a bipartisan coalition led by Senator John McCain and the late Senator Ted Kennedy to challenge the U.S. House of Representatives' immigration reform bill HR 4437, the Border Protection, Anti-Terrorism, and Illegal Immigration Protection Act (see Figure 11.5). They opposed it because it criminalized undocumented immigrants as well as churches and organizations that assisted them and was, in their minds, unbiblical because it did not reflect God's mercy. Rodríguez and NHCLC leaders met with Senators Kennedy and McCain on Capitol Hill (see Figures 11.5 and 12.3). The

Figure 11.5. Rev. Samuel Rodríguez and Ted Kennedy meeting for a press conference on Capitol Hill to promote comprehensive immigration reform, April 2006, Washington, D.C. (Samuel Rodríguez)

contact was so frequent that McCain gave Rodríguez his personal cell phone number. McCain stated in a meeting that 70 percent of criticisms of him among his Republican base in 2006 were due to his leadership of and public support for immigration reform. He called on Latino Pentecostals and Evangelicals to be more outspoken with their Euro-American Evangelical brethren because many of them opposed his efforts.[60]

The NHCLC used the mass media as a vehicle to push for immigration reform. Rodríguez stated in an interview with the *Washington Post* that the immigration reform debate was a "watershed" moment between Euro-American and Latino Evangelicals. He said that if they joined in their efforts, they would forge a positive relationship that would last for "decades." However, he also warned that if white Evangelicals didn't, "there is a possibility of a definitive schism" and that there would be serious "ramifications" in the church and in American politics—an allusion to Latino Evangelicals defecting in even larger numbers to the Democratic Party. His predictions proved prescient since although Latino Evangelicals had given George W. Bush a majority of their vote in 2004, they swung back over and gave Obama a majority of their support in 2008 and 2012, a topic more fully discussed in Chapter 12.[61]

Rodríguez's sharp criticism of his Euro-American Evangelical counterparts was driven by his conviction that immigration reform was both a spiritual and civil rights issue. At the 2007 NHCLC board meeting in Baltimore, Rodríguez and the late Felix Posos declared that the "prophetic role of the Latino church [w]as one of Righteousness and Justice." They went on to state: "We must never be the extension of one political ideology or the other but rather, we must serve as a prophetic role, truth tellers to the government and the church." Despite this goal, Rodríguez and Latino Pentecostals have been criticized by those on the left for opposing abortion and gay marriage and criticized by those on the right for supporting immigration reform and providing Democrats direct access to the Latino Evangelical community via radio and faith forums and personnel support (for example, Wilfredo de Jesús campaigned for Obama in 2008, though not in 2012). Miranda, Rodríguez, de Jesús, and other Latino Pentecostals helped direct two faith-forum conferences that touched on Latino faith, immigration, and the 2008 election. In order to capitalize on their grassroots support, they sought access to over 100,000 Latinos via their database and through other public venues and forums. They also sought to promote immigration reform via the radio and by sending out literature and voting guides to over 18,000 churches and other organizations.[62]

To advocate for immigration reform further, the NHCLC engaged in bipartisan meetings, seminars, and colloquia with key Democratic and Republican political leaders. They sought to steer a "middle path" between HR 4437 and general amnesty.[63] Miranda, Rodríguez, de Jesús, and the NHCLC also sought to win over Euro-American Evangelical support. They wrote an open letter to Evangelicals in April 2006 on immigration reform. In it, he said that Evangelicals had a moral obligation to speak out on behalf of comprehensive immigration reform. They cited findings from The Pew Forum national survey, which found that many white Evangelicals were fearful of Hispanic immigrants. They challenged them to follow the example of World Relief, the development arm of the National Association of Evangelicals, in calling for comprehensive immigration reform. They made it abundantly clear that the NHCLC was not calling for general amnesty but rather a policy that protected the border, stopped undocumented immigration, and applied the rule of law in a matter that is "consistent with a biblical worldview."[64]

Miranda, Rodríguez, and the NHCLC next sent letters to President George W. Bush and Congress in an endeavor to reframe undocumented immigration from a faith perspective. In the first letter, dated March 1, 2006, they encouraged the president and Congress to move beyond the mere enforcement measures in HR 4437 to create a comprehensive immigration reform bill based on biblical mandates, the Christian faith and values, and a commitment to "civil and human rights." They stated that God requires that people show love and compassion to aliens and then cited Deuteronomy 10:18–19, "You are to love those who are aliens, for you yourselves were aliens in Egypt," and Leviticus 19:33–34, that God's people are not to mistreat the aliens but treat them as native-born sons.[65]

On September 1, 2006, they sent a follow-up letter to President Bush and Congress that seemed to go beyond the more diplomatic language used in the earlier letter. They stated that the lack of passage of a comprehensive immigration reform bill resulted in the kind of "racial profiling, discrimination, and hostile ethnic" polarization that they had not faced since the days of the civil rights movement. They pointed out that cities across America were passing ordinances that "in essence legalize racial profiling." They ended by calling on Congress to pass a bill and the president to sign into law legislation that protects the border, ends undocumented immigration, and creates a "market driven guest worker program that facilitates avenues by which the millions of families already in America that lack the legal status can earn such status in a manner that reflects the Judeo Christian value system this nation was founded upon." They secured endorsements from other prominent Latino clergy, professors, seminary presidents, and organizations.[66]

Unlike the efforts of Reies López Tijerina thirty years earlier to spotlight Latino concerns, these efforts did not fall on deaf ears. Democrats such as Nancy Pelosi, Ted Kennedy, Harry Reid, and Ken Salazar, and Republicans such as Bill Frist, John McCain, Lindsey Graham, Sam Brownback, and others met with Rodríguez and NHCLC leaders to listen to their concerns and find alternative strategies to address immigration reform. President George W. Bush responded at the National Hispanic Prayer Breakfast on June 8, 2006, where he stated that the United States had to find a "common-sense" "reasonable middle ground" on immigration reform that treats Latinos with "dignity" and "respect." He stated, "If you've paid your taxes, you've been here for a while, you can prove that you've been working, you've got a clean background; if you want to become a citizen you pay a fine, you learn English, you learn the values and ideals of America that have made us one nation under God," then you should be able to live and work in the United States. For this reason he called on Congress to support a guest worker program. Bush became one of the strongest advocates in presidential history for immigration reform. Internal polling indicated that if Bush were able to get immigration reform passed, Latino Republican support could skyrocket to 50 percent—building on its 40 to 44 percent in 2004. However, conservative Republicans led by Tom Tancredo and Democrats led by Nancy Pelosi and Harry Reid made sure (albeit for different reasons) that Bush did not get comprehensive immigration reform passed from 2006 to 2008, since the latter knew that Democratic strategists warned that if they did not keep the Latino Republican support below 40 percent they could never again win a presidential election because of the growing size and strategic location of Latinos in key swing states. It appears that Barack Obama took this advice to heart.[67]

Although immigration reform was not passed in 2006, it remained a hot topic in the 2008 presidential election. Obama beat McCain on the issue on Election Day among Latino Protestants by a 58 to 31 percent margin. He did this in part because McCain back-peddled on his support for immigration reform and Obama promised to pass comprehensive immigration reform in his first year in office. To strengthen his ties with the Latino Evangelical community after the election, Obama also invited Jesse Miranda and Rev. Samuel Rodríguez to the 2009 presidential inauguration, even allowing Rodríguez to pray at the nationally covered presidential inaugural prayer service. Since that time, the NCHCL has enjoyed regular access to the former Speaker of the House of Representatives, Nancy Pelosi, the Senate majority leader, Harry Reid, and House of Representatives majority leader John Boehner—in addition to a large number of other Democrats and Republicans.[68] Despite these gestures, delays in pushing for immigration reform have understandably led Miranda, Rodríguez, de Jesús, and the NHCLC to criticize Obama and Democrats for not keeping their campaign pledge. However, to shore up his lagging Latino support in 2010 during the midterm elections, Obama spoke out more forcefully on behalf of comprehensive immigration reform.

Immigration, the Law, and Social Action in Arizona, 2010

That same year, the NHCLC formally protested Governor Brewer's decision to sign into law SB 1070 on April 23, 2010, which criminalized undocumented immigrants. This new law, one of the strictest in the United States, included provisions that enabled law enforcement officials and the courts to identify, prosecute, and deport illegal immigrants. The governor and her supporters stated that the law was put into effect because, despite multiple requests for help, President Obama and Secretary of the Department of Homeland Security Janet Napolitano had done nothing significant to help to secure the border with Mexico. Brewer stated that she was forced to protect Americans from violent drug-cartel-related crime, the murder of Arizona ranchers, and the kidnapping and assaulting of young women by undocumented immigrants with criminal backgrounds.[69] The law required state and local police officers to detain and arrest immigrants unable to provide legal documentation, and it also made it a crime to transport and hire undocumented and day laborers. This does not mean they would stop every Latino, she claimed, just those who warranted "reasonable suspicion." She also signed a law that made racial profiling illegal. Arizona's actions are not the only ones: in 2009 alone, over 222 immigration laws were enacted and 131 resolutions were passed in 48 states, most of them restrictive in nature. Many of these statutes and provisions have been overturned.[70]

On April 20, 2010, Miranda, Rodríguez, de Jesús, and the NHCLC sharpened their criticisms of SB 1070 by stating: "Today, Arizona stands as the state with the most xenophobic and nativist supportive laws in the country. We need a multi-ethnic firewall against the extremists in our nation who desire to separate us rather than bring us together."[71] He regularly cited Isaiah 10:1–3, Proverbs 31:8–9, and Leviticus 19 on providing mercy and hospitality to immigrants and chastisement for discriminatory treatment of immigrants. Rodríguez also invoked Republican icons Abraham Lincoln and Ronald Reagan, the latter of whom granted citizenship to over 2.7 million Latinos in his 1986 Immigration Reform and Control Act. Rodríguez stated: "The Arizona Law stands as evidence that in 21st Century America, we may no longer be in the Desert of Segregation or the Egypt of Slavery but we just discovered there are Giants to be slain in the land of Promise. The Arizona Law is without a doubt, anti-Latino, anti-family, anti-immigrant, anti-Christian and unconstitutional. In addition, the law is without a doubt, Anti-Conservative. It runs counter to the Republican vision of Abraham Lincoln and Ronald Reagan."[72]

In a direct effort to persuade the Arizona legislature to change its views and to send a signal that they would be held accountable by Latino Evangelicals for their actions, Rev. Eve Nunez, vice president of the NHCLC and Arizona State Chapter director for the NHCLC, delivered Bibles to all the Arizona legislators who signed Senate Bill 1070, including the two sponsors, Russell Pearce and Steve Montenegro, who is also a former immigrant. Each Bible had the name of the legislator and the following scripture text inscribed in it:

> Woe to the legislators of infamous laws, to those who issue tyranni-
> cal decrees, who refuse justice to the unfortunate and cheat the poor
> among my people of their rights, who make widows their prey, and
> rob the orphan. What will you do on the day of punishment, when,
> from afar off, destruction comes? To whom will you run for help?
> Where will you leave your riches?—Isaiah 10:1–3[73]

Rodríguez and the NHCLC also had a few critical words for President Obama and the Democratic and Republican leadership in Congress:

> We have elected our leaders to lead and it's time that they did so.
> From Republicans, we're hearing they want to wait until next year.
> Democrats like Harry Reid are playing politics with the issue and
> the President appears to be letting Congress off the hook. To the
> Democrats and the President we say, remember your promise. We
> sure do and we will remind you this November and November 2012.
> To the Republicans we say, you are either the party of Lincoln and
> Reagan or David Duke, Tom Tancredo and Pat Buchanan. Remem-
> ber Pete Wilson in California? We sure do. We are tired of excuses,
> Now we want solutions that will end the division and fear in Arizona
> and put our country on the right path again. Where is the leadership
> that we need?[74]

In order to bring about the desired change, Miranda, Rodríguez, and the Assemblies of God-led NHCLC called for a multipronged strategy that drew on approaches employed by César Chávez, Martin Luther King Jr., and other civil rights leaders, strategies such as prayer vigils, periods of fasting, marches, boycotts, letter writing campaigns, and non-violent civil disobedience to "push back xenophobia, nativism and racial profiling."[75] Together they sought a method that, "respects the God-given dignity of every person, protects the unity of the immediate family, respects the rule of law, guarantees secure national borders, ensures fairness to taxpayers, [and] establishes a path toward legal status and/or citizenship." They also supported a "just integration/assimilation strat-egy" that would require criminal background checks of all incoming immigrants, admission of guilt if they illegally crossed the U.S. border and broke U.S. laws, and learning English.[76]

Miranda, Rodríguez, de Jesús, and the NHCLC admitted the challenge was great. However, by emphasizing righteousness and justice, salvation and transformation, they believe that they can find a middle path that can lead to the passage of a balanced comprehensive immigration reform bill that will be acceptable to American Evangelicals and conservatives and liberals and progressives. They wrote: "But here lies the challenge; can we reconcile Leviticus 19 [human treatment of immigrants] and Romans 13 [obeying laws]? Can we repudiate xenophobic and nativist rhetoric, push back on the extremes from both the left and the right and converge around the nexus of the Center Cross where righteousness meets justice, border security meets compassion and common sense meets common ground?"[77]

Drawing on analogies that echo the work of Virgilio Elizondo's *mestizo* Jesus in *Galilean Journey* (1985, 2000), Rodríguez also cited the Exodus story and pointed out that Moses, Jesus, and many other people in the Christian faith were undocumented immigrants at one point in their lives.[78] Rodríguez ended by stating, "As Hispanic Christians, we stand committed to the message of the Cross. However, that cross is both vertical and horizontal. It is salvation and transformation . . . faith and public policy . . . righteousness and justice. . . . [W]e humbly encourage Congress to finally pass and sign into law legislation that will protect our borders, put an end to all illegal immigration . . . in a manner that reflects the Judeo Christian value system."[79]

Miranda, Rodríguez, and the NHCLC have also influenced a number of prominent Evangelicals including Leith Anderson of the NAE, Stephen Land of the Southern Baptist Convention (SBC), Bill Hybels of Willow Creek Community Church, civil rights activist John Perkin, and Bishop George McKinney to go on the record in support of comprehensive immigration reform.[80] After three years of meetings and negotiations, in October 2009, the National Association of Evangelicals Board of Trustees overwhelmingly approved a statement that affirmed the NHCLC's views on comprehensive immigration reform.[81]

Miranda, Rodríguez, and other Latino AG leaders realized that politicians would try to use their faith-based struggle for immigration reform for political purposes. In June 2010, Senator Chuck Schumer (D-N.Y.) unexpectedly added a provision to the comprehensive immigration reform bill that would enable same-sex partners from overseas to become legal citizens. He did this knowing full well that it could seriously and perhaps permanently divide the tenuous coalition that Rodríguez and Obama were trying to bring together. Schumer calculated that blood and ethnicity were deeper than religion. His calculation was challenged and on June 4, 2010, Rodríguez, Leith Anderson (NAE), and Richard Land (SBC) promptly sent Schumer a letter stating that they would withdraw their support for Obama and his comprehensive immigration reform bill on Capitol Hill if he continued to "pander" to "special interest groups"—meaning the gay lobby. They stated, "Same-sex domestic partnerships will doom any effort for bipartisan support of immigration and will cause religious conservatives to withdraw their support." They asked Obama and Schumer if they were willing to forgo helping "tens of millions" of Latinos and other immigrants in order to help "about 36,000" gay and lesbian couples, the number they estimated to benefit from Schumer's provision. They accused Schumer and his supporters of political posturing, not caring deeply about Latinos, and seeking to undermine the bill and hurt millions of Latino immigrants.[82]

In 2010, Obama set out to reassure the Latino community of his commitment to comprehensive immigration reform. Before his speech on immigration at American University in Washington, D.C., on July 1, Obama convened a VIP meeting of five top national Latino leaders for their input on his speech. He invited Rodríguez of the NHCLC, Dolores Huerta—César Chávez's coworker during the UFW struggle, Janet Murguía of the National Council for La Raza, Eliseo Medina of the Service Employees International Union (SEIU), and one more leader. Rodríguez sat right across from President Obama. After asking for their advice about how to frame immigration reform for the next day's speech, Rodríguez proposed that he change his framework from comprehensive immigration reform to "a just integration strategy." Obama, to Rodríguez's surprise, did precisely that, he claims. He reframed the rhetoric in some of his subsequent discussions by calling for a "just integration strategy." After Rodríguez arrived home in Sacramento that night, he received a call from the White House stating that President Obama had decided to use his proposed phrase "just integration solution" in some of his discussions and that he wanted him to fly back to Washington to attend the American University event. To reward and affirm his advice, Obama had Rodríguez seated right in front of him during his immigration reform speech.[83]

Similarly, Rodríguez was invited to meet with Romney and offer his feedback on his National Alliance of Latino Election Officials (NALEO) speech. He told Romney that he needed to replace the rhetoric of "comprehensive immigration reform," since it was so toxic, with new language about a "just integration solution"—just as he had recommended to President Obama. He also stated that Romney needed to resist the nativists and anti-Latino rhetoric in certain wings of the party and to come out boldly and state that although he is against illegal immigration, he is for legal immigration, and that although he is against general amnesty, he is for a pathway to just integration that would deal fairly with those currently in the United States for many years. Romney, Rodríguez stated, incorporated some of this language and tone in his NALEO speech.[84]

In January 2013, Rodríguez continued the struggle by seeking to platform the issue of comprehensive immigration reform by going on a forty-day fast. Similar to César Chávez, his goal was to attract national attention to the plight of an estimated 11 million undocumented immigrants in the United States. When asked why, he stated, "We . . . have this . . . idea that God actually listens to our prayers." He said he was encouraged by the growing support he saw in Washington, D.C., and was "convinced [Republican House of Representatives] Speaker [John] Boehner wants to pass immigration reform." When asked by NBC Latino why he kept the fast going, he said people come to his church and say, "My wife was picked up [deported] this morning." He stated, "I am a pastor, I experience this every single week." The larger goals, Rodríguez and the NHCLC contend, is to promote the twin themes of righteousness and justice and usher in "a new awakening in the Name of Jesus Christ."[85] Jesse Miranda, Wilfredo de Jesús, and Samuel Rodríguez's leadership and evangelistic social ministry have had a ripple effect that has reverberated down through the ranks of Latino AG pastors and laity across the country. This is evidenced by the large number of them on the

NHCLC Executive Board and Board of Advisors and Directors and in other faith-based social, civic, and political organizations, many of which in one way or another are seeking to carry out similar kinds of evangelistic social work in the Latino community.[86]

This chapter has challenged the stereotype that Latino Pentecostals are always socially and politically quietist or apathetic. While there is a strong element that is nervous about mixing religion and civic and political action (often because many of their parishioners are undocumented), this has not stopped a growing number of especially second- and third-generation Latino AG clergy and laity from getting involved in social outreach. In fact, Latino AG clergy and laity have been involved in many of the Latino community's most important struggles in the latter half of the twentieth century. Instead of framing their work in terms of the Social Gospel and Liberation Theology, they look at it as a form of evangelistic social, civic, and political work. What virtually all of the Latino Pentecostals discussed in this chapter share in common is their desire to address the spiritual, social, and material needs of the Latino community and to strengthen the church and exercise a prophetic voice that balances righteousness and justice in American public life. They seek to promote spiritual renewal and social transformation in all sectors of life. The growing spiritual, moral, and civic leadership that Latino AG leaders are providing has helped them attract the attention of Democratic and Republican congressmen and more recently that of Presidents George W. Bush and Barack Obama. As we shall see in Chapter 12, this has given them increasing levels of social and political capital and thus a growing voice and agency in national politics.

Balancing the Horizontal with the Vertical

Latino Growth, Social Views, and Influence in
National Politics

O NE AREA where Latino AG leaders are beginning to exercise greater voice and influence is in American presidential politics. Over the past thirty-five years, they have gone from being largely silent spectators to active participants. They have sought to use their large and growing number of followers and churches and their intersecting Latino, Evangelical, working-class, and immigrant political clout to leverage influence and agency in American public life. They are attractive to presidents because their intersecting value allows presidents to accomplish multiple forms of outreach via one group. President George W. Bush, for example, invited Jesse Miranda and the National Alliance of Evangelical Ministries (AMEN) along with several other leaders and organizations to the White House to both provide feedback on and stand behind him when he announced the faith-based initiatives to the nation at a national press conference in Washington, D.C. (see Figure 12.1). The fact that he sought to invite a Latino Protestant Evangelical group led by Latino AG clergy to help platform his initiative rather than go to traditional mainline Protestants, Catholics, Jews, or even white Evangelicals was a historic first. He did so to strategically spotlight his work with Latinos, racial-ethnic minorities, immigrants, Evangelicals, Pentecostals, and

Figure 12.1. President George W. Bush meets with Rev. Jesse Miranda and Alianza de Ministerios Evangélicos Nacionales (AMEN) and other leaders to discuss his faith-based initiatives program at the White House on May 22, 2001. This was the first of many meetings with President Bush. Left to right: Rudy Carrasco (AG), Rev. Raymond Rivera (CRC), Rev. Jim Ortiz (AG), Rev. Daniel De León (AG), Rev. Luis Cortés (Baptist), Mr. Armando Contreras (Catholic), Rev. Jesse Miranda (AG), Lisa Treviño-Cummins (AG), and Rev. Pedro Windsor (Pentecostal/Evangelical). (White House, Eric Draper)

the working class—a move that took many Democratic strategists by surprise.

For these reasons and many others, George W. Bush and Barack Obama have sought to win over Latino AG leaders to their campaigns, social policies, and administrations. This chapter overturns long-standing stereotypes that Latino Protestants constitute only 12–15 percent of the national Latino population and that Latino Pentecostals are apolitical, mirror Euro-American Pentecostal political party affiliation and voting patterns, and do not engage in progressively oriented religio-political social action on key national issues that affect the entire Latino community. However, it is also true that they are conservative on other key issues like abortion and gay marriage.

The story of Latino Pentecostal political action has been overlooked because it does not neatly fall into the conventional stereotypes of the religious right or left. Politically speaking, Latino Pentecostal rank-and-file voters maintain a Nepantla-oriented, combinative religio-political spirituality that is betwixt and between the polarities of American public life and their Euro-American AG counterparts on a whole range of key political, social, and moral issues.[1] While they support immigration reform, health care, and increasing the minimum wage, and tend to vote Democrat, they also oppose abortion and gay marriage and have swung over and voted Republican. While not technically centrist or even in the center on many social, moral, and political issues, they are left of center compared to other Euro-American Pentecostals and right of center compared to most Latino Catholics. Most importantly, they can and have changed their political support, and while leaning Democratic can and have swung over and voted Republican for Bush in 2000 and 2004. This has made them a potential swing vote constituency in presidential elections since 2000.

Because of their Nepantla-oriented religio-political spirituality, Latino AG leaders have been assailed as agents of both the right and the left. This is because despite their in-between political status and social location on some issues, they tend to be economically and politically progressive, but also morally and socially conservative like black Evangelicals. While some Latino AG pastors (especially immigrant ones) are indeed reluctant to engage in politics because of time constraints, lack of interest and political know-how, and fear that their congregants could be harassed or deported as a result, other second- and third-generation Latino leaders are seeking to exercise greater voice and agency in American public life. Some of their new and emerging leaders are seeking to redefine the goals, framework, and outcomes of their politics through a Pentecostal biblical hermeneutic that is deeply rooted in their combined racialized struggles and Christ-centered vision of social change.[2]

This shift in the religio-political outlook of Latino AG leaders is confirmed in a number of recent surveys and studies cited later in this chapter, which found that AG leaders and laity want their churches and pastors to engage society with a Godly love and socially transformative message of Jesus Christ, who they believe came to proclaim liberty to the captives and to bring sight to the blind and hope and empowerment to the poor and marginalized immigrants.[3] Their in-betweenness is also evident in their desire to, in the words of Samuel Rodríguez, live out a faith that is politically "committed to both elements of the Cross, the Vertical and Horizontal, both Righteousness and Justice . . . Faith and Public Policy, Billy Graham and Martin Luther King, John 3:16 and Luke 4."[4] After briefly examining demographic shifts in the Latino community across the nation and in the Assemblies of God, this chapter will examine the social, moral, church-state, and political views and voting patterns of Latinos in the Assemblies of God and the various ways leaders have sought to find a voice in national politics in the administrations of Ronald Reagan to Barack Obama.

Latino Demographic Shifts in American Society and Politics

The growth of the Latino AG is part of a larger demographic shift in American society. The Census Bureau reports that the U.S. Latino population has skyrocketed from 22.4 million in 1994 to 53 million in 2014 and is expected to climb to 128 million people by 2050, or 29 percent of the U.S. population. Most national surveys report that Catholics make up approximately 66 percent and Protestants and non-Catholic Christians make up 27 percent of the Latino community.[5]

The Latino AG is one of the primary Protestant traditions driving this growth. Today there are more than one million Latinos that self-identify with the AG, 700,000 of which reportedly attend 2,665 AG churches.[6] This makes the Latino AG the largest Latino Protestant movement in the United States. In addition to its size, there are a number of other reasons why the Latino AG is increasingly important in national politics and appropriate to this story: Its leaders have founded and led two of the most important Latino Protestant national organizations in the United States (AMEN, NHCLC); its leaders have met with all American presidents from Reagan to Obama; it is the destination of one out of five (23 percent) Latino Catholics who recently converted to Protestantism annually; it is a swing vote constituency—after supporting Clinton in 1992 and 1996 it voted for Bush in 2000 and 2004 and helped flip the larger Latino Evangelical vote in Bush's favor in 2004; it also helped Bush increase his overall Latino support nationwide to 40–44 percent in 2004; it swung back over and provided strong support for Obama in

2008, and made up 43 percent of Latino Protestants nationwide who were still undecided and 56 percent of Latino Protestant undecided voters in Florida in October 2012.[7] Latino AG voters make up a significant share of Latino Protestant voters, which is about 3 percent of the Election Day vote. This makes them as large as the Asian American vote, larger than the Jewish Election Day vote, and three times the size of the American Muslim vote.[8] The Latino AG along with other Latino Protestants (over 80 percent of which self-identify as born again or attend an Evangelical church) are also heavily concentrated in key electorally rich states like California, New York, Texas, and Florida, and swing states like Colorado, Nevada, and New Mexico.[9] Finally, the Latino AG is important because its leaders have direct access to national political leaders and American presidents.

Sociodemographic Profile of the U.S. Latino AG Population

The relative youthfulness and first-generation immigrant status of the Latino AG is another reason Presidents Bush and Obama have taken an interest in building relationships with its leaders and interdenominational organizations. More than half of Latinos in the AG were born after 1960, and 60 percent are from Latin America. For this reason, the Hispanic Churches in American Public Life (HCAPL) national survey (n = 2,060) found that most Latino AG churches are primarily bilingual (48 percent), although almost a third hold services in English (29 percent) and a quarter in Spanish only (23 percent). Tens of thousands of Latinos were naturalized through Ronald Reagan's Immigration Reform and Control Act of 1986, and for this reason, 64 percent of them are U.S. citizens and can vote. This also helps to explain why that particular generational and immigrant cohort has at times voted more heavily Republican than others. As is true with most religions globally, a majority of Latino AG adherents are female. Because such a large percentage are young, immigrant, and female, and often have had to drop out of school to make ends meet financially, this helps explain why one-third have not finished high school (33 percent) and another third have not finished college or vocational school (28 percent). Only 15 percent have graduated from college, and only 5 percent have earned graduate degrees.

Like their Catholic counterparts, in the recent past one-half lived at or below the poverty level of $35,000 for a family of six. Another 23 percent made $35,000-plus a year, and 12 percent earned $65,000-plus a year.[10]

Latino AG families are attempting to address this educational deficit by sending their children to private church-affiliated schools. Seventy percent have one to four years of religious schooling (often church-associated), and 30 percent have five to eight years. This high level of religious education is due partially to the fact that 62 percent are married and thus can combine their resources to pay their children's tuition, while 21 percent are single and 15 percent are widowed or separated (7 percent) or divorced (8 percent). The recent agreement between the Latin American Bible Institute (LABI) in La Puente and Vanguard University, which allows a student to transfer up to two years of credit from LABI toward a Vanguard B.A., is a positive step in closing this educational gap.[11]

Latino Religious Profile, Conversion, and Switching

Latino AG and Catholic educational and financial profiles resemble one another because so many Latinos have recently converted from Catholicism. While most Latinos who identify with the AG are second or third generation, 38 percent of Latinos in the AG reported that they had "recently converted" from Catholicism, and another 8 percent switched over from Methodist, Baptist, Lutheran, Mormon, Assembly of Christian, and other churches. This does not include those who converted from Catholicism and other traditions in the more distant past.[12] These conversions help explain why the Latino AG is the largest Latino Protestant tradition in the United States, but especially in California, Texas, Florida, New Mexico, Nevada, Colorado, and Arizona, all of which underscores their political value.[13]

Although scholars have speculated that Latinos convert to Protestantism for reasons of economic and cultural upward mobility, social dislocation due to moving from rural villages to urban contexts, and as an attempt to assimilate to their new American context, there are problems with these explanations.[14] First, Latino AG and Catholic parishioners share similar poverty rates, so there is no financial payoff for their family incomes. This holds true even for the clergy, since many pastors have to hold down one or two additional nonreligious jobs to pay their bills.[15] Second, many have migrated from large urban centers, and although the pastor is held in high regard, Latino AG churches tend to have a much more democratic form of governance than exists in many Catholic churches. This democratic style is also shaped by the reality that many clergy need the assistance of the church members to organize, staff, and run their church's ministries, since they cannot afford to hire additional staff or rely on the parish or religious orders to provide assistance.

Finally, rather than serving only as a vehicle for Americanization, which they do encourage at one level (for example, patriotism on the Fourth of July and promotion of naturalization and citizenship), their churches also promote and celebrate their Latino identity (Latinidad), the Spanish language, Latin American customs, values, and traditions, and often the independence day of their members' country of origin. In most Latino AG churches, almost all communication is done in Spanish or Spanglish, a mixture of Spanish and English.[16] For these reasons, many Latino AG churches (and I would add other Latino Protestant churches) also counterintuitively serve as a bulwark, resource, and vehicle for reaffirming and preserving their members' Latin American identity and cultural values. Latino AG churches serve as a spiritual-social space wherein Latin American immigrants can engage in selective acculturation and a Nepantla-oriented combinative Latino Protestant spirituality and subculture in the borderlands. This provides a space and place where they can selectively incorporate both American and Latin American ideals and values, which results in a new hybrid identity.

While some of the above theoretical claims can indeed help explain why some Latinos convert, since socially dislocated people might indeed be more inclined to look for a community that affirms the cultural values they left behind in their home countries, most of the actual reasons Latinos themselves give for their conversions and religious switching are much more personal, immediate, and practical. The 2012 Latino Religions and Politics (LRAP) survey found that the top reasons why Latinos converted from Catholicism to Protestantism were relational: they wanted a more direct personal experience with God; personal evangelism and testimony of a family member or friend; a miracle they reportedly personally saw, heard about, or experienced; a deep personal crisis; inspiration by a pastor or faith community; and because of marriage. For a community without political power and health care, it is not surprising that some—especially undocumented immigrants—might turn to Pentecostalism because of its claim to provide converts with supernatural power and divine healing to overcome their anxieties, afflictions, and social problems (see Table 12.1).[17]

While there is a tendency in the literature to emphasize and exaggerate sensational healing crusades and televangelism, megachurches, the prosperity gospel, and other supernatural occurrences (e.g., the *Time* magazine article cited at the beginning of this book), the Latino AG does not have any famous nationally recognized healers, televangelists, or prosperity preachers. In fact, former Spanish Eastern District superintendent Rafael Reyes said that he could not think of a single church in the SED (440 churches total) with over 1,000 members and that the vast majority of SED churches have less than 500 members.[18] In the Southern Pacific District in southern California, Superintendent Sergio Navarrete stated that there are only 10 churches out of 300 plus that have more than 1,000 members, and only 2 of these 10 embrace any kind of a prosperity gospel.[19] In fact, most megachurches are independent or were denominational churches that decided to break away to form their own independent church and/or movement. Rev. Reyes summed up the attitude of many Latino AG superintendents when he stated that "the Euro-American prosperity Gospel message does not play an important role" in the Latino AG because local churches have had to have a more realistic and "holistic focus" on ministering to the whole person in the Latino community.[20]

Prayer for divine healing is almost always done during or at the end of their Sunday and midweek services. They often invite people to come forward after the services for prayer and to be anointed with oil. Then, with the permission of the person making the request, perhaps two or more women and men (more women than men participate in praying for the sick) will gather around the person and gently lay hands on the person's shoulders to pray for divine healing. It is precisely this kind of individualized attention, consideration, pastoral care, and body life ministry that may help explain why these churches attract new converts into the fold. In an often harsh and impersonal society, the personal touch by seemingly caring people may alone prompt some to think about return-

Table 12.1. Latino religious practices and beliefs (percentages)

	Latino AG		Latino Catholic	Latino Protestant	All Latino Christians
	2012*	2008	2008	2008	2008
How important is religious guidance in daily living?*					
Quite a bit	97 / 78	85	71	85	76
Some	3 / 8	11	22	10	18
No guidance at all/don't know/refused to answer combined	0 / 14	4	7	5	6
How often do you attend church?*					
Almost every week or more	79 / 66	69	55	71	60
Once or twice a month	3 / 7	19	23	14	20
A few times a year or less	15 / 17	6	19	11	17
Never	3 / 10	6	3	4	3
How often do you pray?*					
Every day	91 / 80	79	61	79	67
At least once a week	6 / 3	10	18	11	16
Once or twice a month	0 / 5	6	11	5	9
Seldom, never, don't know/refused to answer combined	3 / 12	5	10	5	8
How often do you read the Bible?					
At least once a week or more than once a week		61	30	63	41
Once or twice a month		12	20	15	18
Seldom		16	23	13	20
Never		11	27	9	21
How often do you attend Bible study and prayer groups?					
At least once a week		43	17	45	26
Once or twice a month		11	8	11	9
Seldom		14	18	18	18
Never and don't know/refused to answer combined		32	57	26	47
How often do you pray for divine healing?					
Every day		64	61	65	63
At least once a week		6	11	9	10
Once or twice a month		11	10	10	10
Seldom, never, don't know/refused to answer combined		19	18	16	17
How often do you evangelize and share your faith?					
Every day		33	11	24	15
At least once a week		24	9	23	14
Once or twice a month		11	10	18	13
Seldom, never, don't know/refused to answer combined		32	70	35	58

(continued)

Table 12.1. *(continued)*

	Latino AG		Latino Catholic	Latino Protestant	All Lat: Christi:
	2012*	2008	2008	2008	2008
Have you led a Bible study or small group?					
Yes		46			27
No		54			73
Have you helped organize religious meetings?					
Yes		57			28
No		43			72

Sources: Findings from the LRAP Survey of 1,000 U.S. Latino Christian likely voters, October 3–10, 2012, and the LRAP National Survey of 1,104 U.S. Latino Christian voters, October 1–7, 2008.

* Single asterisk indicates that the findings are split into two data points: (1) born-again Latino AGs and (2) all Latino AGs (born-again and non-born again).

ing to the church and perhaps even converting. This kind of outreach crosses generational boundaries and may help explain why the Latino AG generational breakdown is more evenly distributed than one might imagine for a movement that targets primarily Spanish-speaking immigrants and youth. This attraction may also be due to the fact that second- through fourth-generation Latinos can attend a small but growing number of churches either in the Latino AG or Euro-American AG, where they can experience Spanish-language Latino churches, English-language Latino-led AG churches, racially mixed AG churches, or Euro-American-led but ethnically mixed AG congregations. These language options provide a greater avenue for generational continuity than immigrant-only indigenous Spanish-speaking Pentecostal denominations, which often do not provide English-language churches or outlets for their youth, something that has caused some of these youth to join the AG or the growing number of bilingual Evangelical/Pentecostal churches.[21]

Interpreting Latino AG Denominational Identity

The Latino AG has done a fair job of teaching their followers that they are part of the larger Protestant, Evangelical, and Pentecostal traditions. Almost seven out of ten (68 percent) Latino AG respondents self-identified as Protestant on the 2012 LRAP survey religion screening question

(1,075), which surveyed all likely Christian and non-Christian voters. However, a sizable number also self-identified as "just Christian" (22 percent) and "other religious tradition" (10 percent). This reflects a trend in the number of Latinos self-identifying as "just Christian," "other religious tradition," and "independent/nondenominational," "something else," "other religion," and even "no religion." Some theorize this proves that Christianity in general and Protestantism in particular are declining because these respondents are choosing to identify with the above-cited generic categories. This kind of unrefined analysis of the survey data has led some social commentators to claim that the percentage of Latino Protestants is 13 percent. However, this study and a number of others have consistently found the actual percentage of Latinos that are Protestant is 25 to 28 percent when survey respondents in these supposedly religiously "unaffiliated" and "other" categories are asked in follow-up questions to specify what church, if any, they are attending or affiliate with and if they are born-again and/or Evangelical Christians.[22]

This finding was confirmed when in a follow-up prompt in the same religious identity question, respondents were asked to *specify* their religious preference, if any. Virtually all of the respondents specified a smaller identifiable Evangelical, Pentecostal, or Protestant church (e.g., Victory Outreach, Foursquare, ELIM, Calvary Chapel, Vineyard, Church of God, Free Methodist, Christian Reform Church, Mennonite), and 48 to 77 percent of these same respondents in the above categories (e.g., "other Christian," "other religion," "nondenominational/independent," and so on) also self-identified as born-again Christian and attended church once a week or more, the highest possible attendance rates. It is highly unlikely that an atheist, an agnostic, or someone who actually had no religion would self-report being born again and attend church once a week or more. Since being born again is highly correlated with being Evangelical Protestant (though some Catholics and others also self-identify as born again) and since it has a negative social stigma in American and especially Latin American societies, these rates are more likely to be under- rather than overreported.[23]

On top of this, the LRAP 2008 and 2012 surveys found that a high percentage of even those respondents who reported having "no religion" actually personally believed in God, were Christian, Catholic, Protestant, spiritual, and/or believed in a higher power. The 2008 LRAP survey for the religion and no religion screening questions (n=2,828, a national bilingual sample of all U.S. Latinos) asked the "no religion" respondents in a separate follow-up question to explain what they personally meant by "no religion." Only 17 percent of them said that they meant, "I literally have no personal religious belief or faith in God or in organized religion." Over 80 percent of "no religion" respondents said they actually believed in God or a higher power or were Christians, and more than a third (34 percent) said they were Christian, Catholic, or Protestant and personally believed in God, and/or did not have any one particular religious tradition they preferred over another at that time. This was confirmed again in the 2012 LRAP survey (n=1,075 Latino Christian likely voters), which found that only 23 percent of the "no religion" respondents said in a follow-up question, "I literally have no personal religious belief or faith in God or in organized religion." Instead, 77 percent of these "no religion" respondents said they believed in God and/or were Christian, Catholic, or Protestant, or spiritual, and/or did not have any one religious preference at that time. This helps to explain why most carefully refined Latino religion surveys put the number of confirmed Latino atheists at around 1 percent, but the number of those having no religion at 5–12 percent depending on the survey. However, as we have seen, many of these "no religion" respondents are not monolithic, and in fact 77–80 percent of them may be religious, spiritual, Christian, and/or believe in some kind of higher power.

What many may actually mean is that they have no religious *preference* or do not see themselves as institutionally religious, something especially true for Latino Evangelicals, Pentecostals, and Charismatic Christians—particularly those that are independent and nondenominational—one of the fastest growing segments in American Evangelicalism today. This should not in any way discount the fact that some Latinos are in fact not religious. However, it is important to make sure that people who are religious are not inaccurately being misclassified as nonreligious when cross analyses indicate that they are religious or spiritual.[24]

All of this points to the larger insight and finding that many respondents that have hitherto been classified as *not* being Protestant, Christian, or even religious may in fact ironically believe in God or a higher power and be Evangelical, Pentecostal, or Charismatic Christian. If these methodological and theoretical insights also hold true for larger U.S. religion surveys (and I believe they will to varying degrees depending on the inclusivity of the sample and survey questions) and the massive numerical growth of racial-ethnic minorities continues, then rather than see a decline in American Christianity and religion in the future, we may actually see what sociologist R. Stephen Warner calls the de-Europeanization of American Christianity and re-Christianization of American society, albeit through both traditional denominations and in new and combinative religious forms, independent churches, and trans-denominational movements. All of this may help to explain why on the one hand the *New York Times* runs stories that proclaim "The Decline of Evangelical America," while on the other hand the National Election Pool (NEP) exit poll indicates that the number of born-again Christian voters in the U.S. electorate increased from 20 percent in 2004 to 26 percent in 2012.[25]

Beliefs and Practices

Because such a high percentage of Latinos in the AG are new converts and because converts are often correlated with higher rates of religious commitment, it is not surprising that they have higher rates of religious belief and practice than Latino Catholics. Although there has been much debate about the reported decline of religion's influence in America, Latinos in general and those in the AG in particular overwhelmingly reported that religion provides a great deal or quite a bit of guidance in their day-to-day living and that they pray daily and attend church almost every week or more. They are also twice as likely as Catholics to read their Bible once a week or more, and two-and-a-half times more likely to attend Bible study or a prayer group at least once a week.

Given their high regard for the Bible as the inerrant and infallible word of God, it is not surprising that they tend to read it literally when it comes to its teaching on divine healing. Almost 64 percent of Latinos in the AG reported praying for divine healing every day, and many cite it as a reason for their conversion. Their conservative biblical worldview also explains why such a high proportion (88 percent) reported that Jesus is the only way to heaven. Latino AG churches teach that the same saving and resurrection power that raised Jesus from the dead is available to all who ask in faith. These convictions may help explain why the vast majority of Latino AG respondents (68 percent) share their faith with non-believers every day (33 percent), weekly or more (24 percent), or monthly (11 percent).

The Latino AG stress on an active faith manifested through personal evangelism, missions, church planting, devotions, and leading Bible studies has invariably led the church to nurture transformational leadership and capacity-building skills that can be transferred into the political, civic, and social arena. This is one of the reasons Latino AG pastors have often been both the ones to organize and then serve as leaders and presidents of the nation's most prominent Latino Evangelical and inter-denominational organizations, such as AMEN, NHCLC, the Association of Hispanic Theological Education (AETH), and La Comunidad of Hispanic Scholars of Religion at the American Academy of Religion. Leadership has been a major focus of Jesse Miranda and the Jesse Miranda Center for Hispanic Leadership at Vanguard University and has served as a theme in his books *The Christian Church in Ministry* and *Liderazgo y Amistad* (Leadership and Friendship).[26]

This focus on leadership development is also evident in Eldin Villafañe's Center for Urban Ministerial Education, which he founded in Boston in 1976. Villafañe also served as a founder and first president of both La Comunidad and AETH. Latino AG support for this capacity- and skill-building orientation is confirmed by the HCAPL survey findings that 46 percent of AG parishioners said they had led a Bible study or small group and 57 percent had helped organize religious meetings, versus just 28 percent of Latinos nationwide. This is one of the hidden benefits of their relatively small AG congregations, which averaged 135 members across the nation versus 97 members for Asian congregations and 155 members for Euro-American congregations. Their small size and lack of full-time paid clergy and staff forces them to mobilize lay leaders to take on leadership roles in the church that generate skills they can use in other settings.[27]

Social, Moral, and Church-State Views

The Latino AG's strong fidelity to the Bible leads them to generally interpret it literally on moral and social issues. This is why they are overwhelmingly pro-life and pro–traditional marriage. As Table 12.2 indicates, they believe that the Bible teaches that human life begins at conception, abortion is the taking of an innocent life, same-sex relations are sinful, and that God ordained marriage as a divine covenant between one man and one woman. They cite passages like Psalm 139:13,

Table 12.2. Latino social and moral views by religious affiliation (percentages)

	Latino AG		Latino Catholic	Latino Protestant	All Latino Christians
	2012*	2008	2008	2008	2008
Women in ministry					
Women should be ordained and allowed to pastor churches		76			52
Women should be allowed to serve in the lay ministry only		11			14
Women should not be ordained or allowed to pastor churches		9			22
Women should be licensed but not ordained		4			12
Death penalty					
Favor		34			39
Neither favor nor oppose/haven't thought much about it		19			16
Oppose		47			45
Abortion					
Favor		14	11	10	11
Neither favor nor oppose/haven't thought much about it		9	12	8	10
Oppose		77	74	81	77
Don't know/refused to answer		0	3	1	2
Gay marriage*					
Favor	15 / 29	18	24	14	21
Neither favor nor oppose/haven't thought much about it	0 / 0	5	19	10	16
Oppose	76 / 59	72	53	72	59
Don't know/refused to answer	9 / 12	5	4	4	4
Gay sexual relations*					
Always wrong	79 / 66	79			65
Almost always wrong	12 / 25	10			6
Wrong only sometimes	0 / 0	3			7
Not wrong at all	9 / 9	8			22

Sources: Findings from the LRAP Survey of 1,000 U.S. Latino Christian likely voters, October 3–10, 2012, and the LRAP National Survey of 1,104 U.S. Latino Christian voters, October 1–7, 2008.

* Single asterisk indicates that the findings are split into two data points: (1) born-again Latino AGs and (2) all Latino AGs (born-again and non-born again).

Luke 1:44, Matthew 19:5, Leviticus 18:22, Romans 1:26–32, and I Corinthians 6:9-10 to support their views. While desiring to share Christ's love and compassion with gays and lesbians, Latino AG leaders like Miranda and others said they could not support same-sex sexual relations and marriage because they contradicted Latin American cultural values, historic Catholicism and Protestantism, and the Bible's teaching on family, human sexuality, and marriage, they contend. They believe that affirming same-sex relations would also mean affirming fornication and/or adultery, since these are the only two contexts in which same-sex sexual relations can take place because God would never bless a same-sex marriage even if the state or liberal churches do. However, Jesse Miranda, Samuel Rodríguez, and other Latino AG leaders also stated that same-sex relations should not be singled out for special derision and that Latino Evangelicals "must repudiate homophobia." Despite their purported efforts to combat homophobia, leaders like Rodríguez have been criticized for not supporting LGBTQ issues and for associating with conservative Evangelical organizations like Liberty Counsel, which provides legal support for traditional marriage and against abortion—both of which are true.[28]

The desire of many Latinos in the AG to see their pastors and laity exercise greater influence in American public life have led most to support Clinton's charitable choice initiative, Bush's faith-based initiatives, and school vouchers (63 percent versus 27 percent for the latter), which would provide taxpayer-funded vouchers so that parents could send their children to private schools, including religious ones. Latino AG respondents also wanted the government to partner with churches to address the nation's social problems such as drug and alcohol abuse, teenage pregnancy, gangs, and violent crime. Their desires were consistent with Presidents Bill Clinton, George W. Bush, and Barack Obama, all of whom promoted limited church-state partnerships to address the nation's social ills. Latino AG parishioners want the private school option because many believe that public schools are deteriorating and promoting views contrary to the Bible. They also believe public schools promote religious and moral relativism, which they believe contradicts the Bible and Jesus's teachings about human origins. For this reason, the vast majority believe that both biblical creation or creation and evolution should be taught in public schools. As Table 12.3 indicates, they also *ble 12.3.* Latino church-state views by religious affiliation (percentages)

	Latino AG		Latino Catholic	Latino Protestant	All Latino Christians
	2012*	2008	2008	2008	2008
ıyer in public schools*					
Favor	94 / 76	81	68	84	73
Neither favor nor oppose/haven't thought much about it	0 / 0	4	7	4	6
Oppose	3 / 14	12	22	10	18
Don't know/refused to answer	3 / 10	3	3	2	3
ep "under God" and "In God we trust" in pledge and on currency					
Favor		85	61	78	66
Neither favor nor oppose/haven't thought much about it		2	11	5	9
Oppose		7	22	11	19
Don't know/refused to answer		6	6	6	6
vernment vouchers for private schools					
Agree		63			60
Neither agree nor disagree		10			6
Disagree		27			34
aching creation and evolution in public schools					
Both should be taught		55			58
Should only teach creation		43			28
Should only teach evolution		2			14

Sources: Findings from the LRAP Survey of 1,000 U.S. Latino Christian likely voters, October 3–10, 2012, and LRAP National Survey of 1,104 U.S. Latino Christian voters, October 1–7, 2008.
* Single asterisk indicates that the findings are split into two data points: (1) born-again Latino AGs and (2) all ἴino AGs (born-again and non-born again).

overwhelmingly want political leaders to promote prayer in public schools (81 percent versus 12 percent) and to keep "under God" on U.S. currency and "In God We Trust" in the Pledge of Allegiance.[29]

While many Latinos in the AG are conservative on a range of issues, they are also liberal-progressive on other issues like the death penalty, immigration reform, affirmative action, government-sponsored health care, government assistance to undocumented immigrants, civil rights, social justice, and the ordination of women to the ministry. In fact, the HCAPL survey found that 76 percent of Latino Pentecostals reported that women should be allowed to serve as pastors of their own churches.

Latino AG leaders have been very critical of the nativist rhetoric in the Republican Party, and for this reason leaders like Jesse Miranda, Wilfredo de Jesús, and Samuel Rodríguez have actively criticized it and Euro-American Evangelicals for tolerating anti-immigrant rhetoric. This is one of the many reasons why a majority of Latinos in the AG are registered Democrats and tend to vote for Democrats on Election Day. It is also why Clinton and Obama have actively courted Latino AG leaders, have sought out their advice, language, and support for key domestic policies speeches and initiatives, and have appointed them to key White House Office task forces.[30]

Views on Political and Social Work

The Latino AG emphasis on leadership and exercising a voice in American public life, along with promoting education, helps explain why the HCAPL survey found that 71 percent of Latino AG respondents said they were personally interested in public affairs, 66 percent said their clergy should try to influence public affairs, 55 percent said they would like their churches to become more involved in public affairs, and 74 percent believed they could have a lot of (36 percent) or some (38 percent) influence in public affairs. This widespread interest and support helps to explain why a growing number are becoming more politically active.

However, because many pastors struggle financially to survive and are forced to hold down multiple jobs, it is not surprising that most are unable to sponsor social and political activities. That is why the HCAPL survey found that despite these above desires, only 27 percent reported that their churches sponsored drug or alcohol rehab programs, 22 percent sponsored daycare facilities, food co-ops, and child care centers, 19 percent sponsored after-school youth programs or ministries for teens, and 19 percent reached out to gangs to reduce community violence. It also reported that Latino AG churches provided resources for the larger community that were slightly greater than or equal to (when controlled for various variables like age, language, and education) those provided by Catholic churches on three out of four social measures, which may help explain why some Latinos convert to the AG. However, Catholics were much stronger in sponsoring after-school programs. Despite these limitations, the HCAPL survey found that 47 percent reported that their

AG religious leaders often talked about pressing social issues of the day, which indicates they are much more aware of political developments than apolitical stereotypes have hitherto indicated.

Latino AG Leaders in Presidential Politics from Carter to Clinton, 1976–2000

Jimmy Carter's clean-cut persona, born-again Christian faith, support for civil rights and Latin American struggles, and perceived honesty in the wake of Richard Nixon's Watergate scandal all contributed to Carter winning 92 percent of Mexican American votes and 82 percent of Latino votes. However, his moralistic calls on Americans to stop complaining about skyrocketing gasoline prices, the Panama Canal transfer, the Iranian hostage crisis, and growing criticisms of Latin American leaders led some Evangelicals to abandon Carter in 1980 in favor of Ronald Reagan, who won 37 percent of the Latino vote.[31]

Ronald Reagan was the first American president to personally invite Latino Evangelicals to the White House. He invited Jesse Miranda and sixty top religious leaders—including ten to fifteen Latino clergy—to secure their feedback on his Immigration Reform and Control Act in 1986, some of which his staff reportedly incorporated. Reagan's "amnesty" bill—as Miranda called it—led to the naturalization of 2.7 million immigrants. As superintendent of the AG's Southern Pacific District, Miranda called the White House and worked with immigration officers to help Latino AG churches set up bilingual screening facilities. Reagan's bill is one of the reasons that the Latino population across the nation skyrocketed and why those naturalized under Reagan have occasionally voted Republican, as they did for George W. Bush in 2000 and 2004. Reagan invited Miranda to the White House on two more occasions to monitor the bill's progress. Like Reagan, George H. W. Bush invited Miranda and a delegation of over sixty clergy to the White House to pray for the nation right before commencing the bombardment and invasion of Iraq. Bush's outreach to Latinos was very limited, despite the fact that his son Jeb married a Mexican immigrant named Columba Garnica Gallo in 1974.[32]

As a result of Bush's limited outreach to Latinos and Bill Clinton's personal charisma and Evangelical roots, Clinton won the Latino vote by a wide margin (70–30 percent) in 1992. Unlike Bush, Clinton understood the changing demographics of the nation, and he and Hillary reached out to Miranda four times from 1992 to 2000, no doubt because in 1992 Miranda created the Alianza de Ministerios Evangélicos Nacionales (AMEN) so that Latino Protestant leaders could exercise a common voice in American public life. President Clinton invited Miranda to breakfast with a group of about twenty religious leaders and assigned Miranda to his personal table, along with Ann Lotz Graham, daughter of Billy Graham, Clinton's Southern Baptist pastor, a black pastor, an Orthodox bishop, and two others. Clinton stated, "I have called you together because you are evangelical leaders and I want you to take James Dobson off my back," Miranda recalled. They were surprised by his request until the news broke shortly thereafter that Clinton had had an illicit relationship with a young White House intern. Clinton next invited Miranda to Washington to discuss and provide feedback on his Latin American foreign policies. Miranda was also invited to attend another White House briefing and a press conference on related topics. Although Clinton was more affable than George H. W. Bush, Miranda did not have any significant political influence on him. However, his mere presence was an indication that Clinton was aware of the growing importance of Latinos and Latino Protestants and Evangelicals. After the 2000 election, Miranda and four other clergy were invited to a private breakfast with then-Senator Hillary Clinton at her home to offer their spiritual support, prayers, and guidance in the wake of Bill's White House intern scandal.[33]

After the 1994 midterm election disaster wherein Democrats lost over 160 House, Senate, and governors' races, Clinton recreated himself by promoting his Puritan-sounding "New Covenant" with America. To increase his Latino support in anticipation of the upcoming 1996 election, Clinton also persuaded Congress to pass the North American Free Trade Agreement (NAFTA) and to fund an $18 billion bailout to help Mexico avoid financial collapse. He also appointed Latinos like Bill Richardson to serve as U.N. ambassador, Federico Peña to serve as secretary of energy, and Henry Cisneros to serve as secretary of housing and urban development. To connect with people of faith, Clinton stressed his education at Georgetown University, his Southern Baptist roots and friendship with Billy Graham, and the new charitable choice initiative, which sought to enable faith-based social service providers to compete for government funds on the same basis as any other organization. Clinton invited Miranda and other leaders to D.C. to discuss charitable choice, and he signed into law the Defense of Marriage Act (DOMA), which defined marriage as the legal union of one man and one woman. Clinton tapped Miranda's Evangelical colleague, José Vicente Rojas, to serve as a Latino Protestant adviser and surrogate at AMEN's events. Dole, by contrast, did little to reach out to and win Latinos. As a result, in 1996 Clinton beat Dole among Latinos by a wide margin both nationwide (76 percent to 21 percent) and among Latinos in the AG (62 percent to 24 percent). This halted and reversed Reagan's Latino inroads and led many Democrats to conclude that Latinos were now a solidly Democratic constituency.[34]

Latino AG Leaders and the Presidency of George W. Bush, 2000–2008

Despite Clinton's victory among Latinos in 1996, they were not permanently wed to the Democratic Party, but rather to Clinton's warm personality and Latino- and faith-friendly policies. Al Gore thought he would simply inherit the same level of Clinton's Latino support. He was mistaken, because a small but notable number of Latino Reagan Democrats were susceptible to Republican outreach, something Texas governor George W. Bush would capitalize on in the 2000 election.

Bush's first Latino outreach began in Texas in the governor's race against the popular and feisty Democrat Ann Richardson. He drew on two factors among many to beat her in 1994—the faith community and Latinos. After a series of financial failures and battles with alcohol, Bush had a born-again conversion experience through the preaching of Pentecostal evangelist Arthur Blessitt. A year later he rededicated his life to Christ through the ministry of Billy Graham.[35]

All of this set the stage for Bush's 2000 presidential campaign. Although the front door to the Latino community was quietly blocked by the Democratic-leaning National Council for La Raza, the League of United Latin American Citizens, and the Mexican American Legal Defense Fund, the back door through the faith community was wide open.

To make inroads, Bush championed their pro-life position on abortion, prayer in school, and school vouchers. He also promised to call for a Constitutional amendment to defend traditional marriage as a covenant between one man and one woman. To personalize his outreach, he proudly emphasized his Mexican American sister-in-law and nephews, gave speeches in Spanish, and stated in his televised debate against Gore that Jesus had the greatest impact on his life.[36]

At the same time that Bush was reaching out to Latinos, Gore had a few missteps. First, he did not aggressively court Latinos because he assumed he would secure Clinton's support. Second, he did nothing to counteract Bush's Latino faith outreach. And third, in 1999 he decided at the last minute not to meet with AMEN's national advisory board and the large number of pastors who attended AMEN's joint meeting with the National Association of Evangelicals (NAE) in Washington, D.C. Instead, Gore sent Robert Seiple, Clinton's U.S. ambassador-at-large for international religious freedom, in his place. Seiple spent thirty minutes berating white and Latino evangelical denominational leaders—many of whom were AG—for their lack of social concern. Latinos in particular were stunned by Seiple's condescending tone, especially since most of them were loyal Democrats who had voted for Clinton-Gore in 1992 and 1996. News spread throughout Latino churches that Gore had canceled his meeting without apology and that he was not friendly to Latinos or people of faith, all of which made Bush a more viable alternative— something he used to his advantage on Election Day. Word of this shoddy treatment was passed on throughout the Latino Protestant community because of the large number of denominational leaders and clergy who participated.[37]

As a result of these developments, the HCAPL survey found that by October Bush's Latino support grew to 38 percent—up 17 points over Dole's support in 1996. Despite this upsurge, the survey found that Gore still led Bush among all Latino Catholics (63–33 percent), Protestants (49–48 percent), mainline Protestants (63–27 percent), Pentecostals (49–46 percent), and born-again Christians (49–48 percent). However, Bush led Gore among all Evangelicals (non-Pentecostals) (56–40 percent), Protestant born-again (53–44 percent) voters, and Latino Assemblies of God voters (56–36 percent), no doubt due—at least in part—to Bush's outreach to Miranda and AMEN and Gore's D.C. misstep with AMEN. Although exit polls indicated that Gore beat Bush among Latinos 62–35 percent on Election Day, Bush still gained a surprising fourteen-point increase, which helped him win Nevada, Colorado, and Florida (the latter by 537 votes) and thus the 2000 election.[38]

To help reward and solidify his Latino support, on December 20, 2000, President-elect Bush invited Jesse Miranda to a small VIP gathering at the First Baptist Church in Austin to promote his new White House Office of Faith-Based and Community Initiatives and to secure their feedback. Miranda asked President Bush if the initiatives' grants would also be open to small independent churches (most of which are Evangelical, Baptist, or Pentecostal/Charismatic), something that Bush indicated would be the case. Bush decided to promote his new White House Office of Faith-Based Initiatives not through the white Evangelical or Catholic community, but rather through the Latino Protestant Evangelical community. On May 22, 2001, President Bush and Director John DiIulio of the White House Office of Faith-Based Initiatives met with President Miranda and AMEN's board of directors and others (including three other leaders with AG backgrounds, Daniel De León, Kittin Silva, and Lisa Treviño-Cummins) to discuss how they might strengthen the initiatives, what programs might be helpful to the faith community, and how they might present them to the nation. They sat around a long table at the White House with President Bush, DiIulio, and their aides discussing the proposal and writing down their suggestions and sharing their own counter-reflections. At the later press conference, Bush asked Miranda and his Latino AMEN leaders and one Latino Catholic leader—and not any other white or black religious leaders—to stand behind him as he lauded not only the new White House office, but also the important role that Latinos played in American public life. This was one of the first times in U.S. history that a sitting president asked a Latino Evangelical and Assemblies of God leader and an organization that he founded to help promote a major domestic policy initiative to the nation.[39]

Jesse Miranda next accepted Bush's invitation to an emergency prayer meeting at the White House on September 20, 2001 in the wake of Osama bin Laden's-inspired 9/11 attacks on the World Trade Centers and the Pentagon. The president asked Miranda and about twenty other

Protestant, Catholic, Jewish, and Muslim clergy to stand beside him in his first speech to the nation after 9/11. At the meeting, Bush asked the clergy to pray for him and the American people, and to call on the nation not to engage in any acts of hatred or violence against Muslims. The clergy, led by Catholic cardinal Bernard Law and assisted by Pentecostal Jesse Miranda, drafted a statement wherein they called on the nation not to engage in any acts of hate and violence against Muslim Americans and instead to pray for peace and tolerance. As the only Latino invited to the event, Miranda stated to President Bush that the Hispanic community stood by him and the nation.[40]

Miranda invited President Bush to speak at the first National Hispanic Presidential Prayer Breakfast in Washington, D.C., on May 16, 2002. The event, which was also cosponsored by Luis Cortés of Nueva Esperanza community development organization, attracted AG and Protestant leaders from over forty denominations and forty-nine states. Bush, Ted Kennedy, Nancy Pelosi, Rahm Emanuel, Tom Ridge, Hillary Clinton, Barack Obama, and others have since spoken at this annual event because it gives them direct access to many of the nation's top Latino religious leaders.[41]

To test Bush's commitment to the Latino community, Miranda worked with Lisa Treviño-Cummins to help Latino AG and other religious leaders apply for government funding for their faith-based social service programs. As a result, the Bush administration delivered on its promise by awarding Miranda's Assemblies of God colleague and AMEN board member, Rev. Jim Ortiz, a $10 million HUD grant for his Coalition for Faith and Community Initiatives in Whittier, California, which he used to fund faith-based job training and skills development projects for at-risk youths in nine states from Connecticut to California. The Bush administration also awarded a total of $11 million in grants to Evangelical Baptist Rev. Luis Cortés of Nueva Esperanza in Philadelphia, to launch a nine-city, three-year project working with at-risk and adjudicated youth. The key to these developments was Miranda's colleague, Lisa Treviño-Cummins. She was a third-generation Latino AG-raised lay leader who had worked for Gov. Bush in Texas and now served as the White House Office of Faith-Based Initiatives Director of Special Grants.[42]

Although because of his stance on political neutrality, Miranda did not give Bush his endorsement in 2004, he nonetheless appreciated the president's outreach to the Latino faith community. To build on his support, Bush also gave speeches in Spanish, invited Mexican president Vicente Fox to his home in Crawford, Texas, highlighted his sister-in-law and nephews' Mexican American identity, and nominated a number of Latinos to high-profile administrative posts, including Mel Martínez (HUD), Miguel Estrada (U.S. Court of Appeals), Alberto González (Attorney General), and a Pentecostal leader named Gaddy Vasquez (Peace Corps), among others.

As a result, in the 2004 election between Bush and John Kerry, Bush won 40–44 percent of the Latino vote (though some contend the figure was only around 40 percent). Although Bush lost the overall Latino vote 53 to 40 percent (or 53 to 44 percent), he actually flipped the Protestant vote from voting Democratic in 2000 to voting Republican in 2004. He won 63 percent of the Latino Protestants to Kerry's 37 percent, although the National Election Pool exit poll reported Kerry over Bush by 57–43 percent. Not surprisingly, Kerry beat Bush among Latino Catholics 69 to 31 percent, in part because Kerry himself is Catholic. Although it is not known how AG Latinos voted, in all likelihood they voted for Bush by over 50 percent, given their level of support in 2000 and Bush's proactive outreach from 2000 to 2004.[43]

In 2006, Rodríguez and the NHCLC publicly supported comprehensive immigration reform, a pro-life position on abortion, and traditional marriage. They wrote letters to President Bush calling on him to support both immigration reform and traditional marriage. In June 2006, President Bush sought out Miranda and now Samuel Rodríguez and the National Hispanic Christian Leadership Conference to support his Marriage Protection Amendment. Although Rodríguez could not attend, Miranda met in the West Wing along with about fifteen other national religious leaders to discuss the president's initiative. As the only Latino at the event, Miranda told President Bush that most Latinos supported traditional marriage and that he and AMEN would support the proposed amendment. After this event, President Bush invited Miranda to another event in June 2008 on the looming tax increases, but he was unable to attend.

In partial response to Miranda, Rodríguez, and other faith leaders, from 2006 to 2008 Bush worked hard to pass comprehensive immigration reform, but was unsuccessful because after the 2006 midterm elections he lost control of the House and the Senate. John McCain and Ted Kennedy joined forces to follow Bush's lead by crafting their own immigration reform bill and worked with Rodríguez to try to get the bill passed, but were unsuccessful. Although the primary reason immigration reform failed was because Republicans like Tom Tancredo vigorously opposed it, to be fair it is also true that Democrats Harry Reid and Nancy Pelosi were determined not to allow the Bush or McCain-Kennedy immigration bill to pass under a Republican administration and repeat what Reagan did in 1986 because they feared Republicans would gain major political inroads in the Latino community. Rodríguez went to Capitol Hill to meet with Speaker Nancy Pelosi and Harry Reid to discuss immigration reform, but with no concrete results—though he was able to meet face to face with Senator John McCain. Despite Reed's and Pelosi's verbal support through their staffers, they were unwilling to allow immigration reform to pass on Bush's watch and thus let Republicans build on their growing inroads in the Latino community. The main reason was because independent polling firms concluded that if Bush persuaded Congress to pass his Republican immigration reform proposal, Latino Republican support might grow from 40 to 50 percent in 2008. Samuel Rodríguez stated that Reid and Pelosi helped indirectly kill the bill by dragging their feet and by adding provisions that they knew would not be passed by Republican politicians facing reelection in 2008.[44]

At his last National Hispanic Prayer Breakfast in 2007, Bush praised the "Hispanic American pastors and priests and community leaders and faith-based activists" from all over the United States for "their compassion" and "abiding faith in the power of prayer." He was proud of the fact that Latinos who were the grandsons of migrant workers could stand in front of the president of the United States and talk about the "promise of America." That, Bush declared, is the "beauty of America." As he waved goodbye, he looked out over the audience and said in his signature style of mixing religion and politics, "Y también, que Dios les bendiga."[45]

In reflecting on Miranda's relationships with American presidents, it is clear that his influence was limited to largely an advisory capacity in several policy initiatives during the post-2000 Bush administration. That aside, the larger point is that Latino AG and other Evangelical leaders went from being asked to occasionally attend photo press releases to actually offering feedback on domestic policy initiatives, which Bush used to help leverage the bipartisan support he needed to get his initiatives through Congress and out to the American people. Although the outreach seems to be genuine on one level, on another level it is clear that he also used this as an opportunity to build up his presence and clout in the Latino faith community and thus the larger Latino electorate. Given the exceedingly narrow margins by which Bush won Florida and New Mexico in 2000, this kind of outreach was a wise and strategic investment of time and resources in light of the lack of traction he could expect to gain among traditional Latino organizations, which are heavily oriented toward the Democratic Party and its platforms. Jesse Miranda, Luis Cortés, and others were aware of this leveraging of their religion, race, immigration, and working-class backgrounds and for this reason were leery and unwilling to formally endorse Bush (or the Democratic candidate) during the primaries. Notwithstanding these factors, after being largely shut out of the White House and national politics they now were beginning to find their footing and voice in small but still important ways, all of which would help lay the foundation for greater involvement after 2006.[46]

Latino AG Leaders and the Presidency of Barack Obama, 2008–2014

In 2005, Miranda began moving toward retirement, and AMEN became less of a factor in national politics. Samuel Rodríguez and a growing number of other younger Latino AG clergy and leaders in their thirties and forties stepped into this gap after they took the lead in working with John McCain and Ted Kennedy to champion comprehensive immigration reform in 2006. Unlike AMEN, the NHCLC focused more not only on bringing about spiritual renewal, strengthening the church, and providing unified leadership in public life, but also social justice and political change in American politics. In 2006, Miranda and Rodríguez agreed to merge AMEN under the umbrella of the NHCLC. Miranda was named the CEO and Rodríguez president. Under Rodríguez's leadership they continued to reach out to a growing number of Latino Protestants across denominations, although the largest number of their core executive and advisory board members remained Latino AG clergy.[47]

When Barack Obama sought to create his 2008 campaign staff to promote his new Democratic religious and racial-ethnic pluralism platform that would welcome both pro-choice and pro-life people of all backgrounds into his new coalition, he made a strategic decision to name born-again Pentecostal ministers Rev. Leah Daughtry to run the Democratic National Convention and Rev. Joshua DuBois to direct his campaign outreach to all faith communities. DuBois was a graduate of Boston University and Princeton University and attended National Community Church in Washington, D.C., which was affiliated with the Pentecostal movement. DuBois was strategic in helping Obama to reach out to the Evangelical, Pentecostal, and Assemblies of God faith communities, since Obama's own ties were largely to liberal Protestant traditions.[48]

Recognizing the size and the critical role of both the Latino AG and the NHCLC, Obama and DuBois regularly contacted Miranda and Rodríguez about their Latino, Evangelical, and faith-friendly policies. At the recommendation of his advisers and Rodríguez, Obama appointed Latino AG pastor and NHCLC vice president of social justice Rev. Wilfredo de Jesús to serve as his 2008 Latino Protestant adviser and outreach coordinator. De Jesús, depicted in Figure 12.2, was pastor of the 4,000-member New Life Covenant Worship Center of the Assemblies of God in South Chicago. He was well positioned to represent Obama to Latino AG and other Evangelical churches throughout the nation. Obama flew him around the nation, financing de Jesús's airfare and room and board, and in some instances even providing him with a personal driver for his surrogate campaign speeches and events.[49] Pastors looked up to de Jesús for growing his church from 100 people to 4,000 in ten years and because his congregation sponsored a homeless shelter for women and children, "Gangs to Grace" programs for at-risk youth, a ministry for homeless men, and a rehabilitation farm in a rural area out-

Figure 12.2. Rev. Wilfredo de Jesús, pastor of New Life Covenant Church, Chicago, ca. 2010. De Jesús served as Senator Barack Obama's 2008 Latino Protestant campaign adviser and spokesperson in the Latino Evangelical community. De Jesús did not support President Obama in 2012 because he reportedly broke his promises to pass immigration reform in his first year in office and to support traditional marriage.   (Wilfredo de Jesús)

side of Chicago for women struggling with drug addiction and those seeking to leave prostitution and start a new life.[50]

De Jesús also brought his pro-life and traditional marriage credentials to the Obama campaign, which enabled him to win over many Latinos who voted for Bush in 2004. He also gave Obama's campaign concrete national visibility and influence in the Latino Evangelical community, almost all of which was pro-life and pro–traditional marriage.[51] He campaigned for Obama for fifteen months on the promise that Obama would pass comprehensive immigration reform in his first year in office, try to reduce abortions, and support traditional marriage.[52] De Jesús publicly praised Obama on the campaign trail for speaking out against the "mistreatment of illegal immigrants" and for understanding "the importance of justice issues such as health care, education, and immigration within the faith community."[53]

Latino AG and NHCLC leaders invited President Obama to meet with Latino pastors and lay leaders at the University of Texas at Brownsville. Before Spanish radio and news reporters, Obama sought to win over Latinos and other people of faith by publicly declaring to the 150-plus leaders and people of faith: "I let Jesus Christ into my life because I learned that my sins could be redeemed and if I placed my trust in Jesus, that he could set me on a path to eternal salvation."[54] Then Obama allowed Latino AG, NHCLC, and other leaders to lay their hands on him and pray for him and his campaign—something covered by Christian media.[55]

In an effort to reward Rodríguez and the NHCLC for their seemingly implicit support, Obama invited Rodríguez to attend a VIP "closed door" meeting on June 10, 2008, with over forty of the nation's top clergy and religious media leaders, including Evangelical leaders such as Franklin Graham, T. D. Jakes, David Neff (*Christianity Today* magazine), Steven Strang (*Charisma* magazine), Max Lucado, Richard Cizik (NAE), and other Catholic, mainline, and black Protestant leaders. Obama stated that part of his job was to make it clear that pro-life and traditional marriage Evangelicals of all races were welcomed into this New Democratic pluralist coalition.[56] Obama then invited Rodríguez to the Compassion Forum at Messiah College, and he went out of his way to walk through the crowd to meet him and shake his hand.[57] This message, along with a string of invitations and promises that he would pass immigration reform in his first year in office and that he would support traditional marriage, prompted many pro-life Latinos who had voted for Bush to take a second look at Obama.

The strategy paid off. Samuel Rodríguez stated in a follow-up interview in July 2008: "It's good to see a nominee engage Evangelical leaders. For too long the Democratic party seemed hostile to Evangelicals."[58] De Jesús stated that Obama was winning over Latinos because in 2008 he "resonated with our people, the Hispanic community and *especially the Evangelical community*" (italics in original).[59] Reflecting the growing muscle of the nation's Latino AG and Evangelical community, de Jesús also told reporters that Latinos like him represented "a new generation of younger Hispanic evangelical Christians . . . [who are] no longer content to remain on the sidelines."[60] Indeed, Latino AG leaders were coming of age and refused to remain silent anymore.

Latino Pentecostal leaders proved critical not only for Obama in 2008, but also for Senator John McCain. Pentecostal leaders like Mark González and Dr. Juan Hernández, depicted in Figure 12.3, voluntarily offered their services to McCain. They tried to promote McCain to the Latino faith community. Hernández had not only helped broker several meetings between Mexican president Vicente Fox and George W. Bush, but he also promoted McCain via Spanish religious and secular television and radio and in church forums. However, Hernández lamented that their Spanish

Figure 12.3.   Meeting of Rev. Samuel Rodríguez and the National Hispanic Christian Leadership Conference with Senator John McCain to discuss comprehensive immigration reform, April 2006. Left to right: Three unknown staffers from Senator McCain's office, Mark González, Rev. Samuel Rodríguez, Senator McCain, Rev. Marcos Witt, Rev. Noel Castellaños, and Dr. Juan Hernández.   (Samuel Rodríguez)

commercials were never aired because everyone was pulling for their own issues, which "constantly squeezed out Hispanics."[61] González, who also served as vice president of communications at that time for the NHCLC, campaigned for McCain throughout the Southwest. Without a significant budget or paid staff, he literally loaded up the trunk of his car with campaign materials and drove from city to city passing out flyers, posters, and other literature to spread McCain's faith-friendly message. On a few occasions McCain would support González's efforts with a brief campaign appearance, but more often than not González had to go it alone or with a handful of other volunteers and with limited funding.[62]

The greatest campaign strategy mistake was McCain's decision to distance himself on comprehensive immigration reform, the signature mark of his loyalty to the Latino community and AG leaders like Miranda and Rodríguez. While President Bush still promoted it, McCain's advisers said he had to back down in order to ensure that his Euro-American base showed up on Election Day. This decision led Rodríguez to write in a *Washington Post* editorial, "Hispanic evangelicals won't be squeezed into a Republican barrio. . . . Is the Republican Party the party of xenophobia, nativism and anti-Latino demagoguery, or is it the party of faith and family values, regardless of skin color or language proficiency?"[63]

To mobilize Latino Evangelical churches, pastors, and laity, the NHCLC launched its own nationwide church-based mobilization drive. They also distributed Latino Christian voter guides and Defense of Marriage flyers. Finally, they used their website, e-mail, and other social media to promote voter turnout on Election Day.[64]

To provide a Latino Evangelical forum for Obama's and McCain's top advisers to promote their candidate's positions on key social, moral, and political issues, Jesse Miranda and Rodríguez sponsored a Latino Evangelical Presidential Forum at Vanguard University, an Assemblies of God–affiliated institution in Costa Mesa, California. Wilfredo de Jesús (who called in) and Juan Hernández (who participated in person) debated about key campaign issues, and who cared the most about Latinos and the faith community. To underscore his interest in the Latino Evangelical vote, Obama had Joshua DuBois participate via conference call, and he sent his Evangelical outreach coordinator, Dr. Shaun Casey, to participate in the event and to network with Latino Evangelical leaders.[65]

When de Jesús pointed out that Obama had just announced plans to invest $20 million toward Latino outreach and asked how much McCain would invest, Hernández was awkwardly silent.[66] When Rodríguez later asked Hernández after the debate how much the McCain camp had given him to win over Latino faith community, he quietly replied: "My business card is made out of printer paper . . . I don't get paid." Hernández was given no major budget, staff, or even business cards. And while Hernández and Mark González normally had to pay their own way to and from events, Obama funded Wilfredo de Jesús to travel around the nation. Whether this violated the separation of church and state is unclear, though clearly in Obama's mind this did not seem to matter since he did so for fifteen months—perhaps arguing that de Jesús did this in his capacity as a private citizen. Either way, it was a smart move, especially given Obama's lack of credentials in the Latino and Evangelical faith communities.[67]

Rodríguez said McCain's failure to win a larger share of the Latino vote was due in part to a lack of personal attention paid to Latinos and Evangelicals during the campaign. He did not allocate enough time, personnel, and money to Latino outreach. He could have increased his Latino support by more face-to-face meetings, conversations, and public policy partnerships with pastors and civic leaders, Rodríguez stated.[68]

This surprised and pleased Obama's advisers. Shaun Casey summed up the attitude of many when he stated in an interview, "The McCain campaign . . . threw the Bush playbook in the trash. They banked on [white] social [rather than religious or moral] conservatives to help them win. . . . The Bush Evangelical outreach was at a high point. It's a mystery to me why McCain did not capitalize on it."[69] For de Jesús, the problem went deeper. McCain needed to say, "This is what I believe in . . ." but instead he showed "no sense of conviction" about Latinos or faith issues, he said.[70]

As a result of de Jesús and other Latino outreach advisers such as Dr. Miguel H. Díaz, who reached out to Latino Catholics, Obama won the U.S. Latino vote 67–31 percent on Election Day 2008. He took 73 percent of Latino Catholics and at least 58 percent of Latino Protestants, most of them Evangelical. Although Latino AG postelection voter results are unavailable at this time, the 2008 LRAP national survey reported that by October 7 Obama had led McCain among Latino AG voters 40–27 percent, with 34 percent still undecided. However, it appears that Obama won two-thirds of these undecided voters, thus reversing their trend in voting Republican. Obama led among Latino AG men and women and across first-generation Latino AG voters, but McCain led among second- and later -generation Latino AG voters. Thus many in the Latino AG constituency that had supported Bush in 2000 and 2004 had now flipped over and supported Obama in 2008.[71]

The Latino AG and the 2012 Election

To reward and solidify his Latino Evangelical support, Obama invited NHCLC president Rodríguez to pray at his 2009 presidential inaugural prayer service. Jesse Miranda was also invited. Miranda, who was unable to attend, was slated to be seated next to Oprah Winfrey—a major honor. This outreach, along with inviting Rick Warren of Saddleback Community Church and other Evangelical leaders to participate, seemed like a good sign that Obama planned to follow through on his campaign pledges to create a religious and racial-ethnic inclusive platform that welcomed pro-choice and pro-life and pro–traditional marriage people into a new Democratic coalition. To seemingly underscore this commitment, he also asked Rodríguez to serve on his White House Fatherhood Task Force and his White House Abortion Reduction Task Force. From 2008 to 2014, President Obama has also sought Rodríguez's personal advice at least ten times in face-to-face meetings regarding public policy issues on immigration reform, homeland security, Latino deportations, civil rights, and faith issues, some of which advice Obama has used in his public policy legislation and speeches on immigration, Rodríguez stated.[72] The president also rewarded Dr. Miguel H. Díaz for his service as a Latino Catholic campaign adviser by appointing him the U.S. ambassador to the Holy See in Rome.

In addition to Rodríguez, Obama appointed another Latino Evangelical leader, Noel Castellanos of the Christian Community Development Association, to the advisory board of the White House Office of Faith-Based and Neighborhood Partnerships. In October 2010, President Obama nominated Jesse Miranda to the same White House board. This recommendation was made in part because Wilfredo de Jesús and Samuel Rodríguez noted they were unhappy that a nationally recognized Latino Evangelical leader was not appointed to the faith-based board, despite their support for Obama during the campaign. However, for reasons that are still unclear, Miranda's appointment was never confirmed, which has led to disappointment with President Obama. This has led some to believe he was intentionally delaying Miranda's appointment because of their reticence to support some his policies and was just engaging in politics as usual.[73]

Realizing that he did not keep his promise to pass comprehensive immigration reform in his first year in office, and worried about his sluggish poll numbers among Latinos heading into the 2010-midterm elections, Obama set out to reassure the Latino community of his commitment by announcing that he would give a speech on immigration reform. Before his speech at American University in Washington, D.C., on July 1, 2010, he convened a VIP meeting of five top national Latino leaders for their input. He invited Rodríguez of the NHCLC, Dolores Huerta (César Chávez's coworker during the UFW struggle), Janet Murguía of the National Council for La Raza, Eliseo Medina of the Service Employees International Union, and one other leader. Rodríguez sat right across from President Obama. After Obama asked for their advice about how to frame immigration reform for the next day's speech, Rodríguez stated that he proposed to President Obama that he change his framework from comprehensive immigration reform to "a just integration solution." Obama, to Rodríguez's surprise, said he liked that idea. Obama and his staff reframed some of their rhetoric in later statements by calling for a just integration strategy, Rodríguez claimed. After Rodríguez arrived home in Sacramento that night, he received a call from the White House stating that President Obama had decided to discuss his "just integration solution" and that he wanted Rodríguez to fly back to Washington to attend the American University event. To reward and affirm his advice and support, Obama had Rodríguez seated right in front of him during his immigration reform speech.[74]

After that event, the Obama White House regularly contacted Rodríguez, twice as many times as Bush had, to discuss religious liberty, marriage, immigration, and health care. Rodríguez has also been contacted numerous times by the Obama White House to attend Capitol Hill briefings and other events. Not all of these meetings were strictly about domestic policy. As depicted in Figure 12.4, Rodríguez was also invited to have breakfast with President Barack Obama along with seven other religious leaders at the White House.

Latino AG leadership proved important not only for Obama, but also for Mitt Romney. Although Romney attempted to reach out to Latinos through his *Juntos con Romney* campaign efforts, these efforts came late in the election season, with little fanfare, and sometimes seemed contrived. He contacted Samuel Rodríguez and asked him to serve as his outreach coordinator and surrogate in the Latino Protestant community. Rodríguez declined Romney's request, since he and the NHCLC were politically nonpartisan. Neither did he recommend anyone to Romney as a replacement. He first met Romney at the Republican National Hispanic Assembly in 2008 when they were both invited to give

Figure 12.4. Rev. Samuel Rodríguez (seated, second from left) having breakfast with President Obama, East Room of the White House, April 19, 2011. To Rodríguez's immediate left is Father Michael Pfleger of Chicago. On his far right is Southern Baptist Dr. Melissa Rogers of Wake Forest University, who is now director of the White House Office of Faith-Based and Neighborhood Partnerships. (White House)

keynote presentations. They sat at the same table and talked, and Romney decided to stay behind to hear Rodríguez's entire speech. His message was very pro-Latino, but that "was the old Mitt Romney," Rodríguez claimed.[75]

Uncertain about Romney's commitment to Latinos, Rodríguez criticized the Romney campaign rhetoric and references to self-deportation, the "47 percent," and "illegals." Still trying to gain ground among Latinos and to help offset his growing liabilities, Romney asked Rodríguez if he would provide feedback and advice on his upcoming National Alliance of Latino Elected Officials (NALEO) speech. Rodríguez did so, since he had also worked in a nonpartisan way with President Obama. He told Romney that he needed to replace the rhetoric of comprehensive immigration reform, because it was so toxic, with new language about a "just integration solution"—just as he had recommended to Obama. He also stated that Romney needed to speak out against the nativist and anti-Latino rhetoric in certain wings of the party and to state boldly that although he was against illegal immigration, he was *for* legal immigration, and that although he was against general amnesty, he was *for* a pathway to just integration and citizenship that deals fairly with those already in the United States for many years. Romney, Rodríguez claims, incorporated some of this language and tone in his NALEO speech and in later speeches on the topic, though with little impact since it came so late in the campaign season.[76]

As a result of Rodríguez's advice, and in a desire to win over Latino Evangelical support as Bush did in 2004, the Romney camp contacted the NHCLC at least once a week from April to November 2012 about their faith-friendly policies. This was no doubt a last-ditch effort to strengthen their sagging poll numbers among Latinos, which were dangerously well below Bush's and McCain's numbers in 2000, 2004, and 2008. Romney also decided to spotlight Latinos in general and Latino Evangelicals in particular at the Republican National Convention. First, he invited Latino AG pastor Samuel Rodríguez to give the closing benediction on the opening night—a prized spot for any national religious leader. Second, he invited Latino Evangelical and Assemblies of God pop music sensation Jaci Velasquez to perform on the first day of the convention. Then he asked a string of the nation's top Latino Republican political leaders to speak on the opening day of the convention, including Florida senator Marco Rubio, Texas senator Ted Cruz, New Mexico governor Susana Martínez, Nevada governor Brian Sandoval, Delaware lieutenant governor Sher Valenzuela, and Puerto Rican governor Luis Furtuño and his wife, Luce. However, not all of these speakers were well received by some of the anti-immigrant hard-liners at the convention. Romney also participated in forums sponsored by Univision in Florida, where he won some support but not enough to ultimately win the state.[77]

Rodríguez stated that if Romney had started much earlier in his Latino outreach, he could have increased his Evangelical vote if he had emphasized his "commitment to faith, family, entrepreneurship and a just immigration reform solution." He needed to "emerge as the defender of religious liberty and 'la familia,' or traditional marriage" as Bush did, which Romney did only half-heartedly, Rodríguez stated.[78]

Rodríguez reported that President Obama also reached out to the NHCLC, though "not as extensively" as he had four years earlier. Perhaps Obama's lack of aggressive outreach was due to his not keeping his promise to pass immigration reform during his first year in office and because he changed his view on gay marriage, both topics that the NHCLC was openly critical of during the campaign. This may have made him more reticent to reach out to Latino Evangelicals. Although perhaps it is also because Obama felt that he had already reached out to Latino Evangelicals by inviting Rodríguez to pray at his inauguration, join task forces on fatherhood and on abortion reduction, and visit the White House on a regular basis and even for breakfast—in addition to appointing other Evangelicals to various positions.[79]

However, prior to Election Day 2012 Rodríguez believed that Obama was "very vulnerable" on the economy, immigration, marriage, and abortion.[80] He stated that Obama moved "far left on gay marriage, abortion, and gays in the military." He reauthorized the pro-abortion Mexico City policy, did not keep his promise to pass immigration reform, and in April 2012 changed his views on gay marriage. As a result, Rodríguez said that Obama did not take a "centrist" approach during his first term and that he was not the "centrist candidate we thought he was and [that he] painted himself . . . to be." Rodríguez concluded that Obama had simply "forgotten about the rest of America that voted for him."[81] But

Rodríguez also energetically pointed to Obama's recent June 15, 2012, support for the DREAM Act, which made it possible for some undocumented young adults brought to the United States as children to defer deportation if they met specific criteria.[82]

Still, for Obama's former Latino Protestant outreach advisor Wilfredo de Jesús, this move came too late. Despite campaigning for Obama in 2008, de Jesús was clearly disappointed with and felt betrayed by Obama in 2012. He said that Obama misled the Latino community and did not keep his promises to pass immigration reform in his first year in office and to support traditional marriage. De Jesús stated, "You can't say I will push through immigration reform in the first year in office and then make health care, gay issues, and other topics a bigger priority than millions of Latinos suffering throughout the nation."[83] De Jesús stated prior to the election, "Latinos don't like being used and tricked. You can't contradict and double-talk. . . . I am responsible to our people. You can't say you'll get immigration reform passed in the first year and then actually deport more Latinos than President Bush. I campaigned for Obama on a platform he promised the Latino community in good faith. What's happening now is not acceptable."[84] He warned, "You threaded the moral needle in 2008, but now the tapestry you wove is coming apart at the seams and unraveling." He ended by saying, "Frankly, I'm disappointed."[85] For this reason, de Jesús said he would not support President Obama in 2012, which was not unlike similar defections from Obama (though for different reasons) by Cornell West, Tavis Smiley, and other African American leaders who felt Obama did not make a good faith effort to champion the rights of the poor and racial-ethnic minorities and fight for economic justice.[86] During his appearance at the Univision forum, Obama had to answer hostile questions about his immigration record. "My biggest failure so far is we haven't gotten comprehensive immigration reform done," Obama reluctantly admitted.[87]

Despite the frustration of many Latino AG leaders with Obama's broken promises, Romney's effort to transform himself in the Latino community was too little, too late. Obama's campaign painted Romney as a rich white Mormon outsider from Massachusetts who wanted "illegals" to self-deport, even though Romney had changed his rhetoric. This rhetoric, combined with late outreach to Latinos and Evangelicals (via Billy

Graham) during the campaign, allowed Obama to effectively paint Romney as an outsider to Latinos and the Evangelical community. Romney also did not promote any major Latino-specific domestic policy initiatives in the community. In short, Obama's success among Latino Evangelicals and perhaps other Latinos had as much to do with Romney's lackluster outreach as it did with Obama's relatively tepid canvassing.

As a result of these factors and many others, Obama won the Latino vote on Election Day 2012 by the wide margin of 71–27 percent. Although not as high as Jimmy Carter's 82 percent in 1980 or Bill Clinton's 76 percent in 1996, it was still a decisive victory. Because Romney did not give Latinos in the AG and other denominations any major public policy reasons to vote for him until very late in the campaign, by October 10 the LRAP survey found that a majority of Latino AG likely voters were registered Democrats (though a majority that were both AG and born-again Christians were Republican) and planned to vote for Obama (54–36 percent), although Obama trailed Romney (42–45 percent) among Latinos in the AG who said they were born again. This general support for Obama reflected his larger lead among likely Latino Catholic voters (67–22 percent), Latino Protestant voters, over 80 percent of whom are Evangelical (53–35 percent), and all Latino Christian voters (63–26).[88] (See Table 12.4.)

Obama won the 2012 election because he disproportionately carried Latinos, blacks, Asians, students, and single females by a wide margin—though with admittedly much less enthusiasm than in 2008. The fact that racial-ethnic minorities grew to 28 percent of the U.S. electorate and turned out in larger numbers than expected proved decisive. By contrast, white Protestants, Catholics, and Evangelicals voted for Romney by stunningly wide margins. The National Election Pool exit poll results indicate that Obama would have lost by a landslide if the election was determined solely by white Protestants (69 percent for Romney versus 30 percent for Obama) and white Catholics (59 percent for Romney versus 40 percent for Obama). The nonwhite vote (80 percent for Obama versus 18 percent for Romney) helped push Obama over the top on Election Day 2012. Likewise, white Evangelicals cast 78 percent of their votes for Romney and 21 percent for Obama, a decline of five percentage points for Obama from 2008.

Table 12.4. Latino political party affiliation and vote by religious affiliation (percentages)

	Latino AG*	Latino Catholic	Latino Protestant	All Latino Christians
Latino vote on November 4 by Obama, Romney, Other—71 / 27 / 2				
Vote lean (October 3–10, 2012)*				
Obama	42 / 54	67	53	63
Romney	45 / 36	22	35	26
Other/undecided	13 / 10	11	12	11
Relevance of a candidate's faith and morals to voting (2012)*				
Very/somewhat relevant	66 / 58	66	64	66
Not very/not at all relevant	30 / 39	30	32	30
Don't know/refused to answer	4 / 3	4	4	4
Political party identification (2012)*				
Democrat/lean Democrat	36 / 41	61	44	56
Republican/lean Republican	45 / 34	18	32	22
Independent	19 / 25	21	24	22
Registered to vote (2008)				
Yes	50	38	54	44
No	40	58	43	53
Don't know/refused to answer	10	4	3	3
Political party identification (2008)				
Democrat	42	59	49	55
Republican	34	16	24	19
Independent	14	20	18	20
Something else/don't know/refused to answer combined	10	5	9	6
Political party identification (2004)				
Democrat	45			
Republican	20			
Independent	35			
Vote lean (2004)**				
Democrat	52 / 57**			
Republican	45 / 40**			
Someone else/do not intend to vote/undecided/don't know	3/3**			
Vote lean (2000)				
George W. Bush	45			
Al Gore	27			
Someone else/do not intend to vote/undecided/don't know	28			

(*continued*)

Table 12.4. (*continued*)

	Latino AG*	Latino Catholic	Latino Protestant	All Latino Christians
Vote (1996)				
Bob Dole	26			
Bill Clinton	61			
Ross Perot	6			
Someone else	7			

Sources: Findings from the National Election Pool (NEP) Election Day exit poll of 26,565 voters, November 6, 2012; LRAP Survey of 1,000 U.S. Latino Christian likely voters, October 3–10, 2012; and LRAP National Survey of 1,104 U.S. Latino Christian voters, October 1–7, 2008. Findings for the 2004 election are drawn for surveys cited in Gastón Espinosa, ed., *Religion, Race, and Barack Obama's New Democratic Pluralism.* Findings from the 1996 and 2000 elections are taken from the 2000 HCAPL National Survey of 2,060 U.S. Latinos (general population).

* Single asterisk indicates that the findings are split into two data points: (1) born-again Latino AGs and (2) all Latino AGs (born-again and non-born again).

** Double asterisks indicate two different national survey results, from the National Election Pool exit poll and the Fourth National Survey of Religion and Politics.

Obama won over Latinos because many believed the economy was stabilizing and slightly improving. Rodríguez stated that many Latinos also voted for Obama because they believed that if a black man could win today, then perhaps a brown Latino could win in the future. Most importantly, Latinos believed that Obama was much more likely than Romney to pass immigration reform. Romney lost, Rodríguez stated, because "he self-deported the Latino vote" and because he did not show any real passion to win over Latinos or Evangelicals or to champion their faith and moral issues, as Bush did in 2000 and especially 2004. In many ways, Romney ran a largely secular campaign that was not faith- or racial-ethnic-minority-friendly until relatively late in the campaign. He placed too great an emphasis on middle-class white voters rather than on Latinos and the demographic shifts taking place across American politics. The best evidence of this was his decision to name Paul Ryan rather than Marco Rubio or Susana Martínez as his vice presidential choice, though perhaps one or both were approached but declined. The fact that Romney was a Mormon also appears to be a factor, since as late as October born-again Christians made up 43 percent of all undecided likely voters nationwide and 56 percent in Florida. Given the final election results, it is clear that a majority of them swung over and voted for Obama. In general, although Latino Evangelicals tend to be very interdenominational in outlook, they also tend to be critical of nontraditional religions.[89]

Does Obama's victory mean that abortion and gay marriage are no longer wedge issues and that liberalism won the day? Not necessarily, just that Romney did not place a great enough emphasis on them early enough in his campaign, and that this neutralized a potential rallying point. For despite claims to the contrary, a very large segment of the Latino and American electorate remain opposed to gay marriage due to their deeply held faith traditions. This is true not just for Latinos and Evangelicals, but also for traditional Catholics, mainline Protestants, Muslims, and conservative Jews, Hindus, Buddhists, and other religious practitioners. The evidence that this may still be a live wedge issue was confirmed in the 2012 LRAP survey (n = 1,000 likely Christian voters), which found that a majority of Latino Protestant likely voters opposed gay marriage (57 percent versus 25 percent) and believed gay relations were a sin and contrary to the Bible's teachings (61 percent versus 25 percent). By an even wider margin, Latino Evangelicals opposed both gay marriage (68–17 percent) and believed gay relations were a sin and contrary to the Bible's teachings (73 versus 16 percent). The National Election Pool exit poll also reported that despite Obama's victories in 2008 and 2012, more Americans reported that on political matters they considered themselves conservative (35 percent) or moderate (40 percent) rather than liberal (25 percent). This seems to confirm Bill Clinton's view that although the U.S. electorate is "operationally progressive" it is also "philosophically moderate conservative."[90]

Although Latinos in the AG were socially active in varying degrees through their outreach ministries for much of the twentieth century, their activism really began to increase in the 1970s and 1980s. This served as a stepping-stone to their political activism in the 1990s and 2000s. Jesse Miranda led the way through the creation of AMEN, and Samuel Rodriguez developed this further after the 2006 push for comprehensive immigration reform. Politically speaking, the Latino AG has often been in the middle between Euro-American Evangelicals and Latino Catholics in their voting patterns, but not in many of their moral, social, and economic views, wherein they can be just as conservative as their Euro-American Evangelical counterparts (if not more so in some cases). Thus their more moderating outlook has to do primarily with their political party affiliation and voting patterns. They began to fall back into their previous Democratic-leaning voting patterns in 2008 and largely continued this in 2012, though with some loss of support for Obama.

They first became personally involved with American presidential politics during Ronald Reagan's presidency. Although they are morally conservative and Democratic leaning, Latino AG leaders have often acted in a bipartisan way by providing advice to both parties and political candidates and have tried to steer a middle path between the religious right's anti-immigrant nativist rhetoric and the Democratic Party's social and moral views on abortion and gay marriage. In many ways, their Nepantla-oriented middle-path political spirituality has sought, in the words of Miranda and Rodríguez, to promote and balance both the horizontal and the vertical, the salvation message of Billy Graham with the faith-based social action of Martin Luther King Jr. In the words of Miranda and Rodríguez, they seek to promote neither the donkey nor the elephant, but rather their message of faith in Jesus Christ. However, their lack of uniform support for the Republican or the Democratic Party has led to criticisms by extremists and activists on both sides that they are not centrists but a Trojan horse for the other side.

While Miranda was sought out by Presidents Reagan, George H. W. Bush, Bill Clinton, and George W. Bush, his influence was largely symbolic and representative until the presidency of George W. Bush. Miranda, Treviño-Cummins, and other Latino AG leaders met with Bush to discuss the White House Office of Faith-Based Initiatives. As a result, Bush followed up on his campaign pledges, and his administration provided at least $20 million in federal funding for Latino AG and Evangelical ministries that sought to serve the poor, immigrants, and inner-city at-risk youth. After Miranda merged AMEN into the NHCLC and went into a phased retirement, Samuel Rodríguez became the key spokesperson for both the Latino AG and the Latino AG–influenced NHCLC. He was able to assist President Obama by allowing his AG vice president for social justice, Wilfredo de Jesús, to campaign for Obama for fifteen months throughout the Latino Evangelical community. While Rodríguez also allowed the NHCLC vice president of communications, Mark González, to campaign for McCain, thus providing bipartisan support and outreach to the Latino community, de Jesús was given the resources necessary to effectively carry out his outreach, while González was not provided with the same level of funding. After the election, President Obama attempted to solidify his gains among Latino Evangelicals by inviting Rodríguez to pray at his inaugural prayer service. Obama also nominated Miranda and appointed Rodríguez to various White House task forces, adopted Rodríguez's recommendations for his immigration reform speech, and regularly invited Rodríguez to the White House and sought out his advice on a wide range of issues. However, Obama did not court the Latino Evangelical vote as aggressively in the 2012 election because of his past outreach and because a growing rupture was occurring as a result of Obama's decision not to pass immigration reform in his first year in office and his decision to change his views on gay marriage. Romney sought out Rodríguez's assistance, but late in the campaign and only after it was clear that he was struggling with both Latinos and the Evangelical community. It was too little, too late, and Latinos decided to go with President Obama in 2012.

In all of these post-1980 developments, it is clear that after almost a century of living in silence in the shadows of the borderlands, a growing number of Latino AG and other Pentecostal clergy and laity are beginning to enter into mainstream national politics and exercise limited but strategic influence on key issues pertaining to the Latino community. For these reasons and many others noted throughout the chapter, the Latino AG will continue to be an important movement to watch for those interested in tracking trends and developments in American religion, politics, and society for many years to come.

Conclusion

THIS BOOK CHALLENGES a number of conventional stereotypes about the Latino Assemblies of God. Chapter 1 challenges the notion that the Latino Pentecostal movement is a recent post-1960 phenomenon. We have seen that the Latino AG movement actually traces its roots back to William J. Seymour's Azusa Street Revival in Los Angeles and Charles Parham's Apostolic Faith work in Houston. Latinos actively contributed to the Azusa Street Revival and helped transform what was a largely biracial English-language domestic prayer meeting on Bonnie Brae Street into a multilingual, international, multiracial-ethnic revival on Azusa Street.

Chapter 2 challenges the notion that H. C. Ball founded the first Latino AG work in the United States by examining the Euro-American and Mexican pioneers who predated him in Texas. The first Euro-American evangelists emerged out of Seymour's and Parham's ministries. They converted a number of Mexicans from 1906 to 1918 who evangelized and planted a good number of independent Pentecostal missions throughout South Texas from Houston to San Antonio to Brownville. After the formation of the Assemblies of God in April 1914, a number of them joined the AG. They, along with their Euro-American missionaries, were really the first to pioneer the Latino AG work in Texas and the United States.

This was before Ball first began preaching Pentecostalism in a small, struggling mission in 1915 and long before Ball rose to prominence in the first convention of Latino AG churches in 1918. The important and hitherto overlooked work of these Euro-American and Latino evangelists and pastors laid the foundation for Ball's work and the Latino AG in Texas. Still other Latino and Euro-American men and women in the AG planted other AG churches in the Southwest, Mexico, and Puerto Rico, all independent of Ball's influence.

Chapter 3 explored how a second set of Euro-American home missionaries led by H. C. Ball pioneered a second wave of evangelistic work among Latinos in Texas. Ball's own ministry struggled to survive, in part due to his broken Spanish and his authoritarian style. His breakthrough came after he and Rev. Isabel Flores invited many of the hitherto independent and AG Mexican ministers to attend a Latino Pentecostal convention, which Ball then stepped in to assume leadership of. He was able to do so because he spoke some Spanish, had an evangelistic ministry to Latinos, was Euro-American, and served as a go-between for the independent Mexican pastors and AG headquarters in Springfield. He provided leadership for the Latino AG for over twenty years and for this reason he should be credited as arguably the single most important founder. However, to be fair, his critical role was due at least in part to the fact that he also drove out many of the most talented Latino leaders and left their contributions out of the early histories of the movement, which he largely wrote as autobiographical accounts which lent themselves to focusing almost exclusively on his own accomplishments and those of other Euro-American missionaries and a few Latinos with whom he worked. When Victor De Leon and others drew on the accounts by Ball and other Euro-American missionaries, this only reinscribed (this time with Latino support) their contributions and glossed over the Mexican origins because De Leon was probably unaware of them and/or they were dismissed as independent Mexican ministers and missions only loosely associated with the AG that eventually joined Francisco Olazábal's CLADIC, and therefore unworthy of inclusion.

Chapter 4 challenges the notion that the Latino AG was and is a largely Euro-American missionary organization wherein Latinos have allowed themselves to be treated like an internal colony without dissent or revolt because of the supposedly passive nature of the Pentecostal religion. The chapter maps out how Francisco Olazábal and a growing number of independent Mexican ministers who had joined the AG pushed for (at least initially with the support of Ball and Luce) the creation of a Mexican District on par with Euro-American districts to be led by and for Latinos. They sought to reform the pious paternalism of Euro-American missionaries and transfer the leadership and administration of the movement from whites to Latinos. After the election of Francisco Olazábal, Ball stepped in and stated that AG headquarters had disavowed the election and that they had to wait until some other unspecified time to hold another election for a new district superintendent. Many saw that as a tactical move on Ball's part and revolted against Ball's heavy-handed leadership and AG headquarters' tacit support. Ball had Olazábal summoned to Springfield to answer charges that he was fomenting "anti-American" sentiment. After seeing the proverbial handwriting on the wall after the Euro-American leaders backed Ball's side of the story, Olazábal told them he would not allow himself to be treated like the blacks (a reference to racism), and not long afterward resigned after they took control of his AG church in El Paso. Olazábal and his compatriots, recognizing that they had no future in the AG, organized the Latin American Council of Christian Churches (CLADIC) in 1923—the first completely indigenous Latino-led Protestant denomination legally incorporated in the United States. Olazábal went on to conduct the largest evangelistic-healing crusades in North American history in the United States, Mexico, and Puerto Rico until his death in 1937.[1]

Chapter 5 discusses how despite Ball's and Luce's public declarations that they wanted to hand over the Latino AG ministry to Mexicans as soon as possible, Ball served as its superintendent until finally stepping down in 1939. He did so at a less than opportune time, since the Great Depression forced many missions to fold, and ministers struggled to survive. Despite this fact, the new Mexican American superintendent, Demetrio Bazan, brought new life and energy to the Latino AG and a more personal and relational leadership style. The Latino AG witnessed significant growth under his leadership, and he sought to modernize the movement in a number of ways, including by providing translations of social security and life insurance information and policies into Spanish and by encouraging Latinos to enroll in them and to participate in other government, state, and citywide social service programs. In 1959, Bazan handed the movement over to a former Presbyterian turned evangelist named José Girón, who sought to decentralize the movement, strengthen the Bible schools and ministry requirements, and focus on church planting and evangelism.

Chapter 6 traces the struggles, indigenization, and the growth of the Latino AG under leaders like Demetrio Bazan, José Girón, Jesse Miranda, and others and why it grew from 170 churches in 1939 to 2,665 churches in 2014. Their growth is due to their relational and transformational leadership styles, indigenization, democratic governance, focus on evangelism, church planting, and social outreach, and their decentralization from one to fourteen districts, which has fostered power sharing and unleashed new generations of charismatic leaders that are innovative, creative, and entrepreneurial in spirit. It also examines how and why its leaders have gained national visibility in U.S. Latino Protestantism and politics.

Chapter 7 challenges the notion that the U.S. Latino and Latin American Pentecostal movements were the product of Euro-American missionaries. After briefly discussing the evangelistic outreach of Jennie Mishler and George Bailey around 1909 to 1911, it shows how it was Juan Lugo and other native Puerto Ricans who founded the first permanent Pentecostal movement on the island in August 1916. Although they were virtually penniless, through sheer vision, determination, and firm conviction that people's eternal destinies were at stake, they fulfilled their divine calling to evangelize every corner of the island, including the hinterland which most Euro-American mainline and Evangelical missionaries avoided due to tropical diseases and the rugged, rain-drenched mountainous terrain. Lugo, the Ortizes, the Felicianos, and others evangelized every town and village and directly challenged (both symbolically and directly) the three most powerful movements on the island: mainline Protestantism, Catholicism, and Spiritualism. They had the distinct benefit of arriving when the Catholic Church was in complete disarray and struggling because of a shortage of Latino priests and at a time when the other Protestant churches had already paved a path of tolerance and acceptance for Protestantism, which was soon associated with progressive ideals and Americanization. While Protestants paved the way for a general toleration of non-Catholic Christian traditions,

Spiritualism paved the way for an openness to the supernatural world, healing, spirit possession, and other practices that resonated with Pentecostal practices and beliefs. Pentecostalism provided a third alternative and via media that resonated with sentiments associated with both Protestant and Spiritualist traditions. For this reason, some scholars speculate that the centrifugal force of Spiritualism may have actually benefited the spread of Pentecostalism, since converts could seemingly have all of the benefits of Spiritualism while still remaining Protestant.

Chapter 8 focuses on the desire of the Pentecostal Church of God (i.e., the Latino AG on the island) to integrate into the larger AG movement in the United States. It shows how, contrary to perception, the Pentecostal Church of God did not—at least at first—break away from the AG due to Puerto Rican cultural nationalism alone, but instead because their overture to integrate into the larger AG was rejected by the national General Council because they were treated as a national, foreign district. After feeling rejected by the mother church, when the AG in Springfield changed its mind because it feared the Pentecostal Church of God in Puerto Rico might go independent, the Puerto Rican leaders decided to do precisely that—become their own independent denomination, not just a district or national branch of the larger AG movement. This move toward independence took place during a great upsurge in Puerto Rican nationalism during the 1950s. Chapter 8 also reveals ethnic fault lines not only between Mexican American and Puerto Rican leaders, but between Puerto Rican leaders on the island and those in the diaspora in New York City. It traces the rebirth of the Latino AG on the island after 1957 and points out how (ironically) a relatively liberal move on the part of those seeking independence led to a more insular church that was less open to democratic governance and styles of government that actually gave more power to local congregations. The chapter challenges the notion that the Latino AG is a monolithic movement and shows how different sectors of the movement engaged in their own struggles for voice, agency, and respect in American religion and society.

Chapter 9 traces the origins of the Latino Pentecostal movement in New York through the work of what is today called the Spanish Eastern District. It reveals that, contrary to popular perception, the Puerto Rican Pentecostal movement first began in the Puerto Rican diaspora in

1911 before traveling to Puerto Rico in 1916 and then to New York City in 1928, where Tomás Alvarez pioneered the work and Juan Lugo built it up after he arrived in 1931. It also reveals that, despite the conflict between Francisco Olazábal and Ball and Luce, many Latino AG pastors still kept in regular contact with Olazábal and invited him to conduct evangelistic-healing crusades in Chicago in 1929 and New York City in 1931. In New York's Spanish Harlem Olazábal founded the most important Latino Pentecostal church in the Puerto Rican diaspora, Bethel Temple. Olazábal led evangelistic crusades throughout 1931 and 1932, and an estimated 100,000 people attended his healing campaigns. Despite their overlap, Lugo and Olazábal never worked together, for reasons that are still unclear. The Latino AG work in New York City was originally a branch and conference of the Pentecostal Church of God in Puerto Rico (the name of the Latino AG on the island) but secured its own independence as a separate district in 1957. Despite the common sympathy for Puerto Rican nationalism and unity, the chapter shows the very real tensions that existed between Puerto Rican leaders in the Spanish Eastern District and in the Pentecostal Church of God on the island.

Chapter 10 spotlights the struggles that Puerto Rican AG women such as Aimee García Cortese faced in seeking ordination and to fulfill their divine calling to the ministry. Contrary to the Barfoot and Sheppard theory of a golden age of openness to women in ministry in the early AG, Latinas have always been able to be ordained, and their numbers have steadily increased throughout the twentieth century. In short, there was no major retrenchment like that among Euro-American AG women. In fact, the Latino districts have a higher percentage of clergywomen today than the average Euro-American AG district, which is surprising given the historic machismo and the uphill calling women faced and continue to confront in the ministry. One of the training grounds for female leadership and empowerment appears to be the young girls' clubs and Women's Missionary Councils, which provide skills and opportunities to exercise leadership. Women have also exercised agency and influence through the Latino AG Bible schools, which at times were led by and enrolled a disproportionate number of women. Women used their education to help offset their gender liability in establishing their authority and leadership in local congregations. However, the most common route to the pastoral ministry for women was and remains to this day co-pastoring a church with their husbands. While in some cases this means largely leading the women's and Sunday school programs for children, it also almost always entails preaching from the pulpit and exercising voice and authority over men. The fact that their husbands are pastors is both a liability and an asset, because men are less likely to challenge a clergy-woman's voice and authority if her husband is the senior pastor, since that would be considered impolite and dishonorable.

Despite their ability to serve as pastors, evangelists, missionaries, and educators, young Latinas did not have any interest in the larger feminist movement, seeing it as undermining traditional family values, which they strongly affirm. However, they were more open to Christian feminism and in many ways exercised feminist agency in the church and society through their divine callings, which they leveraged along with supportive men to fulfill their desires to carry out their ministries. Despite this, they still face the same kind of marginalization and marginal ministerial assignments that other ordained women face in liberal Protestant and Evangelical churches, wherein they are often assigned to small, struggling, or troubled missions and ministries. This has prompted some women who want to strike out to find their own voice and agency to start their own churches, which, along with inheriting the senior pastorate of a church after a husband dies or retires, is the most common route to the senior pastorate. Although progress has been made, as of this writing no woman has ever served as superintendent of a Latino district, though women do regularly serve in the top executive positions in many districts, usually as secretary, treasurer, or director of Christian education. Thus the story of the progress of Latina AG clergywomen is mixed, though the trend is generally on the upbeat in an otherwise still uphill struggle.

Another chief avenue by which women and men carry out creative ministries is through evangelistic social work. Chapter 11 challenges the stereotype that Pentecostals are so heavenly minded that they are no earthly good. Instead, although they do not use the language of liberal Protestantism, the Social Gospel, or Liberation theology, they nonetheless carry out various forms of social outreach. While liberal and Evangelical Protestants have often split evangelism and social work into two different types of ministry, Latinos blend them. Thus what is marketed as an evangelistic outreach may also have a social needs component, and vice versa. Latinos use social action, civic and political engagement, and other acts of mercy as vehicles through which to demonstrate what they describe as the love and justice of Jesus Christ. They seek to blend what Eldin Villafañe calls the "liberating Spirit" with what Solivan calls "orthopathos." In so doing, they carry out what Miranda and Rodríguez term the twin biblical themes of "righteousness and justice." Their social vision is part of a much larger trend that Miller and Tetsunao document in their book on global Pentecostalism and social engagement. This evangelistic social work can be traced all the way back to the work of Susie Villa Valdez, Rosa López, and H. C. Ball, among many others.

Perhaps most surprising is that Latino AG clergy and laity have been involved and/or influential in many of the most important struggles in the Latino community from the Latino AG's ministry to Cuban refugees in Florida, to Tijerina's land grant struggle in New Mexico, to Chávez's United Farm Workers' struggle in California, to Nicky Cruz and Sonny Arguinzoni's ministry to drug addicts and gang members in New York City and Los Angeles, to Miranda's and Rodríguez's struggle for comprehensive immigration reform. One of the vehicles through which this evangelistic social work is taught and encouraged is the Latino AG Bible schools, where students are grounded not only in the Bible and Pentecostal theology, but also in practical evangelistic outreach methods.

This evangelistic social work and the desire to blend righteousness and justice have also inspired a growing number of younger Latino AG leaders and laity to seek greater influence in national politics. Chapter 12 challenges the stereotypes that Latino Pentecostals are apolitical and uniformly conservative in both their morals and their party identification and politics. While segments of the movement are apolitical due to fear of government investigations of their immigrant congregations and lack of time and know-how, a growing number of Latinos recognize the importance of exercising a Christian voice and agency in national politics. Although Latino AG leaders and laity are conservative on moral issues, they are also somewhat liberal in their views on immigration reform and some social and economic justice issues. Furthermore, despite their conservative biblical worldview, they are political moderates who tend to vote Democratic, but who can and do switch over to vote Republican in light of a candidate's relational style and faith-friendly message and policies. Thus their political orientation, and especially their party identification and voting patterns in presidential elections, can be described as more in-between and in the middle (that is, Nepantla) than those of Latino Catholics and white Evangelicals. In this respect, they resonate with African Americans who, despite also being very morally conservative, vote Democrat for a host of historic reasons going back to the civil rights movement's struggle for racial equality and their ongoing struggle for economic, immigrant, and social justice.

Chapter 12 also found that previous studies have underestimated the percentage and number of Latino Protestants, Evangelicals, and Pentecostals because they did not offer a more refined analysis of the relatively large number of survey respondents who reported being "just Christian," "other religious tradition," "other," "independent/nondenominational," and so on. When these groups were cross-analyzed in light of other religious identity and religious practice questions like being born again 48 to 77 percent said they were. Similarly, when those who said they had no religion were asked to explain what they meant by "no religion," we found that over 80 percent of the "no religion" Latino respondents nationwide and 77 percent of "no religion" Latino Christian registered voter respondents respectively stated in a follow-up question that they actually were Christian, Protestant or Catholic, religious, spiritual, meant something else, or believed in God. These findings are very important because they indicate that a large percentage of Latinos are being misclassified as "not religious," when in fact this is not the case according to their own clarifying statements. If these findings also hold true for larger national surveys of the United States, then many of the reports to date will have to be revised and corrected. They may also invariably show not only the de-Europeanization of American Christianity, but also possibly the growth of Christianity in America (albeit nondenominational/independent Evangelical, Pentecostal, or Charismatic) in the future due to high immigration and birth and conversion rates, along with the decline in Euro-American birth rates.

The Future of the Latino Assemblies of God

What does the future hold for the Latino Assemblies of God, and what is-sues do they have to address within their movement? Jesse Miranda ar-gued that in order for the movement to thrive, the Latino AG must address a number of key issues. First, it needs to develop mature leadership that is full of faith, biblical and moral integrity, self-respect, and a sense of pride and history. Second, it needs to address generational differences, transfer of power, and cultural variations in order to effectively reach the entire Latino community. It has to find ways both to reach "non-Christians" and to nurture and develop Christian youth who grow up in the church. Third, the Latino AG districts will have to find ways to develop positive relations with each other and with the Euro-American districts as they compete for scarce resources. Fourth, the Latino AG needs to find a peaceful way to address the fact that more and more Euro-American districts and churches are starting Spanish-language Latino-serving congregations, because this could have profound implications for the future of the fourteen Latino AG districts as they compete for the same people. Fifth, they need to find a way to deal with the language and cultural differences among the twenty-two Latino nationalities that they minister to on a regular basis.[2]

In addition to these internal issues within the Latino AG, Miranda stated that the larger General Council of the Assemblies of God needs to address a number of Euro-American-Latino relational issues. He argues that Latinos are still "outsiders looking in" on matters of education, fi-nancial services, and sharing pulpits, conferences, and facilities. To be "one body in Christ," there has to be a greater and more conscientious effort to fully integrate the Euro-American and Latino assemblies as fully equal partners, Miranda said.[3]

Miranda admits that some progress has been made. First, he was elected to represent all racial-ethnic AG branches at General Council headquarters, which was a new development since prior to that time they had no racial-ethnic representation in Springfield. Second, now there are two Latino Executive Presbyters. Yet Latinos are still under-represented in the national General Council at virtually all levels of administration and leadership. Latinos make up almost 20 percent of all churches and 22 percent of all adherents in the AG, and account for

55 percent of the denomination's growth from 2002 to 2012. In fact, AG leaders admit that the denomination's national growth would be flat without them. There are 2,665 Latino-serving AG churches in the United States and Puerto Rico, and over 700,000 Latinos self-identified with the Assemblies of God in their denominational statistical reports. The top two largest churches in the AG nationwide today are both Latino-led and predominantly Latino-serving congregations. Overall, Latino churches make up three out of the top ten largest AG churches in the United States. Despite these developments, there are relatively few megachurches, and very few preach any kind of prosperity Gospel. Latino presidents, senior administrators, and faculty are also still woefully underrepresented at almost all of the AG General Council Bible schools, colleges, seminaries, and universities. Miranda stated that there is a need to push for proportional representation at all levels of the AG if the movement is to be truly color-blind and fully integrated in the future.[4]

Samuel Rodríguez echoed many of these concerns, but added several others. He noted that the Latino AG is experiencing a greater number of second- and third-generation people leaving for non-AG Evangelical churches "due to language, cultural, and generational specific deficiencies in ministerial outreach." In order to counter this, he believes that the Latino AG must provide a viable integration platform that includes English language acquisition, educational resources, and family and marriage enrichment programs, or "risk losing the next generation of worshippers." Preaching will not suffice, he argues, because these generations seek in their churches a vertical relationship with God and a horizontal community of faith, where they can be encouraged to develop their God-given gifts and talents to transform society for Jesus Christ. He argues that with respect to Euro-American–Latino relations, the AG and its leadership must be more intentionally multiethnic and racially diverse. He stated that some Latino AG leaders are "frustrated" with the lack of proportional leadership, especially in light of their contributions to denominational growth and resources. He said, "The question arises, how long will Hispanic AG leaders accept the current reality . . . when they represent the fastest and soon to be the largest segment of the denomination?" This leads to a third concern that Miranda also raised about the growing overlap between Latino and Euro-American districts competing with one another for outreach to the community. Finally, he said that Latinos must embrace digital platforms, communication, and marketing in order to be both relevant and viable in the modern context. This, along with a push to promote primary and secondary education and biblical and theological literacy, will help prepare Latinos in the Assemblies of God to provide organic and cutting-edge transformational leadership in the twenty-first century, he stated.[5]

Larger Historical Insights and Developments

As we reflect on 100 years of Latino Assemblies of God history, a number of historical insights emerge. First, we see that Latinos have consistently drawn on their Pentecostal faith and community to exercise voice and agency in their lives and ministries. They have fought for self-determination, self-respect, and the ability to shape their destinies. Despite these struggles and in some ways perhaps because of them, their views and stories have been overlooked in prior AG histories. Second, Latinos have not received credit for their pioneering work, leadership, and vision. As an act of deference consistent with Latino culture, they have often allowed Euro-American missionaries to talk and write about their own contributions to the Latino AG at the expense of their own. The result is that Latinos were almost completely left out of the founding narratives, and when they were included, it was almost always in a supporting role to Euro-American missionaries. The driving vision and leadership seemed to be that of Euro-Americans. However, this book challenges that portrayal and shows that Latinos were also responsible for birthing the Latino AG through their pioneer evangelistic, missionary, and educational work. Third, the work of these first Latino and Euro-American missionaries initiated prior to Ball was soon taken over and expanded by Ball and other Euro-Americans in 1918, who consolidated power in 1922 after Francisco Olazábal and the independent faction was de facto expelled from the Latino AG. Despite this fact, low-level pressure persisted until Ball finally stepped down in 1939 and Mexican American Demetrio Bazan was finally elected superintendent. Fourth, the Puerto Rican Pentecostal movement began in the diaspora, then traveled to California and Puerto Rico, and then finally to New York City. Unlike the Mexican American AG movement in the Southwest, the

Puerto Rican work was run by Latinos from the beginning and has remained firmly in their control ever since. Fifth, the Latino-led schisms in 1922 and 1957 were the result of Latinos not being treated with complete respect and cultural sensitivity by their Euro-American coworkers and leaders at AG headquarters in Springfield.

Sixth, women have faced an uphill struggle and have had to struggle with gender discrimination and "glass ceilings." However checkered this history and struggle, they were granted the right to full ordination and to pastor their own churches half a century or more before their Latina sisters in the Methodist, Presbyterian, and American Baptist traditions. Seventh, compared to Latino Presbyterians, Methodists, and other Protestants, Latinos in the Assemblies of God in the Southwest and Puerto Rico went through an earlier indigenization process. This may in part help to explain why they witnessed greater growth after 1950, especially after these other Latino Protestant Spanish-language branches and conventions were merged into their Euro-American mother denominations in the 1950s and as a result lost some of their leadership, autonomy, and agency. Finally, Latino AG pastors, evangelists, and lay leaders consistently struggled for faith-based social change throughout the twentieth century. As a result of their growth and social vision, both Republicans and Democrats have actively sought to use Latino AG leaders to help win over the Latino community in general and the Latino Evangelical/Pentecostal community in particular. Furthermore, American presidents such as Bush and Obama have sought out their political advice and public voice on domestic policy issues like faith-based initiatives, immigration reform, fatherhood, abortion reduction, and on a range of related topics. In all of these efforts, Latino AG leaders have sought to exercise voice and agency in their denomination, in the Latino Protestant community, and now in national politics. After a century of living quietly in the shadows and margins of North American religion and society, Latino AG leaders and laity are increasingly speaking out about their personal faith in Jesus Christ and the needs of the poor and immigrants. They are also increasingly being asked to represent the aspirations of Latinos, immigrants, Evangelicals, and people of faith across the nation and for this reason have shed almost 100 years of silence to be silent no more.

Notes

Index

Notes

AF   The *Apostolic Faith*
EMC   *El Mensajero Cristiano*
LLA   *La Luz Apostólica*
N/t   No title given
TCC   The *Christian Century*
TCE   The *Christian Evangel*
TLRE The *Latter Rain Evangel*
TPE   The *Pentecostal Evangel*
TWE   The *Weekly Evangel*

Introduction

1. Victor De Leon, *The Silent Pentecostals: A Biographical History of the Pentecostal Movement among Hispanics in the Twentieth Century* (Taylors, SC: Faith Printing Company, 1979), v. He wrote the first draft of this book as his M.Div. thesis for the now defunct Melodyland School of Theology in Anaheim, California. Victor De Leon did not use an accent over the "o" in his last name.

2. B. F. Lawrence, *The Apostolic Faith Restored* (St. Louis, MO: Gospel Publishing House, 1916); Stanley F. Frodsham, *With Signs Following: The Story of the Pentecostal Revival in the Twentieth Century* (Springfield, MO: Gospel Publishing House, 1926, 1946); Klaude Kendrick, *The Promise Fulfilled* (Springfield, MO: Gospel Publishing House, 1961); Carl Brumback, *Suddenly . . . from Heaven: A History of the Assemblies of God* (Springfield, MO: Gospel Publishing House, 1961); William Menzies, *Anointed to Serve: The Story of the Assemblies of God* (Springfield, MO: Gospel Publishing House, 1971); Edith Blumhofer, *The Assemblies of God: A Popular History* (Springfield,

MO: Gospel Publishing House, 1985); Edith Blumhofer, *The Assemblies of God: A Chapter in the Story of American Pentecostalism,* 2 vols. (Springfield, MO: Gospel Publishing House, 1989); and Gary B. McGee, *People of the Spirit: The Assemblies of God* (Springfield, MO: Gospel Publishing House, 2012). Recognizing the importance of the Assemblies of God in global Pentecostalism, the John Templeton Foundation funded Margaret M. Poloma and John C. Green's *The Assemblies of God: Godly Love and the Revitalization of American Pentecostalism* (New York: New York University Press, 2010). Although not commissioned by the AG, also see Edith Blumhofer, *Restoring the Faith: The Assemblies of God, Pentecostalism, and American Culture* (Urbana: University of Illinois Press, 1993).

3. The exceptions wherein Latinos are mentioned include the works by Frodsham, McGee, and Poloma and Green, though the latter lacks chapter-length coverage.

4. There are other books, dissertations, and articles on Latino Pentecostalism, including Samuel Solivan, *The Spirit, Pathos and Liberation: Toward an Hispanic Pentecostal Theology* (Sheffield, UK: University of Sheffield Press, 1998); Gastón Espinosa, "El Azteca: Francisco Olazábal and Latino Pentecostal Charisma, Power, and Faith Healing in the Borderlands," *Journal of the American Academy of Religion* 67, no. 3 (September 1999): 597–616; Luís León, "Metaphor and Place: The U.S.-Mexico Border as Center and Periphery in the Interpretation of Religion," *Journal of the American Academy of Religion* 67, no. 3 (September 1999): 541–572; Daniel Ramírez, "Borderlands Praxis: The Immigrant Experience in Latino Pentecostal Churches," *Journal of the American Academy of Religion* 67, no. 3 (September 1999): 573–596; Manuel Vasquez, "Pentecostalism, Collective Identity, and Transnationalism among Salvadorans and Peruvians in the U.S.," *Journal of the American Academy of Religion* 67, no. 3 (September 1999): 617–636; Rubén Peréz Torres, *Poder desde lo alto: Historia, sociología y contribuciones del Pentecostalismo en Puerto Rico, el Caribe y en los Estados Unidos,* 2nd ed. (Barcelona: Editorial CLIE, 2003); Luís León, *La Llorona's Children: Religion, Life, and Death in the U.S.-Mexican Borderlands* (Berkeley: University of California Press, 2004); Sammy Alfaro, *Divino Campañero: Toward a Hispanic Pentecostal Christology* (Eugene, OR: Pickwick Publications, 2010).

5. Juan L. Lugo, *Pentecostés en Puerto Rico o La vida de un misionero* (San Juan, Puerto Rico: Puerto Rico Gospel Press, 1951); Maclovio Gaxiola López, *Historia de la Iglesia Apostólica de la Fe en Cristo Jesús* (México: Libreria Latinoamericana, 1964); Benjamín Cantú and José Ortega, *Historia de la Asamblea Apostólica de la Fe en Cristo Jesús* (Mentone, CA: Sal's Printing Service, 1966); De Leon (1979), *The Silent Pentecostals,* 7–10; Miguel Guillén, *La historia del Concilio Latino Americano de Iglesias Cristianas* (Brownsville, TX: Latin American Council of Christian Churches, [1982] 1991); Davíd Ramos Torres, *Historia de la Iglesia de Dios Pentecostal, M.I.: Una iglesia ungida para hace misión* (Río Piedras, Puerto Rico: Editorial Pentecostal, 1992). For an example of the chapter- and book-length district histories and overviews in Spanish, see Jesse Miranda, "Asambleas de Dios, Distrito Latinoamericano del Pacifico," in *Hacia una historia la Iglesia Evangélica Hispana de California del Sur,* ed. Rodelo Wilson (Montebello, CA: Asociación Hispana para la Educación Teológica [AHET], 1993), 129–138; Spanish Eastern District, *Celebrando mas de seis decades, 1928–1992* (Bronx, NY: Spanish Eastern District, 1992); Samuel Díaz, *La*

Nave Pentecostal: Crónica desde el inicio de las Asambleas de Dios y su travesía por el noreste hispano de los Estados Unidos (Deerfield, FL: Editorial Vida, 1995).

6. Donald T. Moore, *Puerto Rico para Cristo: A History of the Progress of the Evangelical Missions on the Island of Puerto Rico* (Cuernavaca, México: CIDOC SONDEOS, 1969); Clifton L. Holland, *The Religious Dimension in Hispanic Los Angeles: A Protestant Case Study* (South Pasadena, CA: William Carey Library, 1974); Eldin Villafañe, *The Liberating Spirit: Toward an Hispanic American Pentecostal Social Ethic* (New York: University Press of America, 1992); Josue Sánchez, *Angels without Wings: The Hispanic Assemblies of God Story* (New Braunfels, TX: Atwood Printing, ca. 1991), is an autobiography focused on Sánchez's life and ministry; Arlene Sánchez-Walsh, *Latino Pentecostal Identity: Evangelical Faith, Self, and Society* (New York: Columbia University Press, 2003); Sergio Navarrete, "Latino Districts of the Assemblies of God in the United States," in *Los Evangélicos: Portraits of Latino Protestantism in the United States,* ed. Juan F. Martínez and Linda Scott (Eugene, OR: Wipf and Stock, 2009), 38–50.

7. The phrase "Latino Reformation" was coined by Samuel Rodríguez to describe demographic shifts taking place today in the Latino religious community. Elizabeth Dias, "The Latino Reformation: Inside the New Hispanic Churches Transforming Religion in America," *Time,* 15 April 2013, 20–28.

8. Some of the largest U.S. Latino Pentecostal/Charismatic denominations and districts within Euro-American Pentecostal denominations include the Apostolic Assembly of the Faith in Christ Jesus, the Assembly of Christian Churches, the Church of God (Cleveland), the Church of God of Prophecy, the Foursquare Church, the International Pentecostal Holiness Church, the Pentecostal Church of God, M.I., Victory Outreach International, the United Pentecostal Church, the Latin American Council of Christian Churches, the Damascus Christian Church, and the Defenders of the Faith. For a relatively comprehensive list of Latino Protestant Evangelical, mainline, and Pentecostal denominations, see the findings from the database created by Clifton Holland and his Programa Latinoamericano de Estudios Socioreligiosos (PROLADES), "Report on Hispanic Protestant Denominations in the USA, July 2012," http://www.hispanicchurchesusa.net/denominations/hispusa-table-prot -denoms-sort-clascode-15july2012.pdf. For brief overview articles on many of the above Latino Pentecostal/Charismatic denominations, see Stanley M. Burgess and Eduard Van Der Mass, eds., *The New International Dictionary of Pentecostal and Charismatic Movements* (Grand Rapids, MI: Zondervan, 2004).

9. Holland, "Report on Hispanic Protestant Denominations in the USA, July 2012." Holland stated to me in written correspondence that, unlike other estimates based on denominational reports, the Latino Southern Baptist Convention (SBC) church statistic (2,997 Latino churches) is based on information he gathered from SBC leaders. However, he also pointed out that they did not provide any hard denominational-secured statistical data to back up their numerical claims and for this reason were only estimates. Because these SBC data are not confirmed, the Latino AG has the largest number of confirmed Latino Protestant churches in the United States. Gastón Espinosa, correspondence with Clifton Holland, 3 March 2014. Prior to 2004, the SBC sent confirmation to me that there were approximately

1,800 SBC churches in the United States. It is unlikely that in ten years this number would have skyrocketed to 2,997 churches. Gastón Espinosa, "Changements démographiques et religieux chez les hispaniques des Etats-Unis," *Social Compass: Revue Internationale de Sociologie de la Religion* 51, no. 3 (2004): 309–327.

10. The number of Latino AG adherents was provided by Sherri Doty, Statistics Department supervisor, Office of the General Secretary of the Assemblies of God, General Council of the Assemblies of God National Leadership and Resource Center, 8 August 2013. The 2000 Pew Charitable Trusts–funded Hispanic Churches in American Public Life (HCAPL) national survey (n = 2,060) reported that 2.16 percent (1.14 million out of 53 million in 2014) of all Latinos nationwide self-identified with the AG. For more about the HCAPL bilingual survey, see Gastón Espinosa, Virgilio Elizondo, and Jesse Miranda, *Hispanic Churches in American Public Life: Summary of Findings* (Notre Dame, IN: University of Notre Dame Institute for Latino Studies, 2003). The HCAPL Latino AG figure of 2 percent was reaffirmed six years later in the 2006 Pew Forum *Spirit and Power* ten-country survey (which included a U.S. Latino subsample), which also reported the national Latino AG population at 2 percent. For *Spirit and Power* survey results see http://www.pewforum .org/files/2006/10/pentecostals-08.pdf. There are several possible reasons why the number of Latinos reported by the AG does not match the number reported on the 2000 Pew-funded HCAPL and 2006 Pew Forum *Spirit and Power* national surveys. It is possible that the Latino AG response rate was artificially high on both surveys, for unknown reasons. However, another reason for the discrepancy may be that the AG only reports Latinos actively involved in the church, while the HCAPL and *Spirit and Power* surveys report all U.S. Latinos who self-identify with the AG, regardless of whether they regularly attend an AG church. Latinos who self-identify with the AG may not be actively attending an AG church for a whole host of reasons. For example, there may be no AG church near their home; job transfers; personality or stylistic differences with the local AG pastor; found a better local church for themselves or their children despite identifying primarily with the AG; or they simply did not want to attend an AG church at the time of the survey. Since survey responses are strictly optional, respondents' decision to self-identify as AG does indicate that they still see it as an important part of their identity. The HCAPL national bilingual telephone survey was funded by a $1.3 million grant from The Pew Charitable Trusts. The HCAPL study also fielded a religious leaders survey and a civic leaders survey. All three surveys were supervised and/or shaped by Harry Pachon, Rodolfo O. de la Garza, Louis DeSipio, and Jongho Lee of the Tomás Rivera Policy Institute (TRPI) and HCAPL project manager Gastón Espinosa, principal investigators Jesse Miranda and Virgilio Elizondo, and HCAPL advisory board members Wade Clark Roof, Donald Miller, Dean Hoge, Allen Hertzke, David Leege, Edwin I. Hernández, Milagros Peña, Daisy Machado, Elizabeth Conde-Frazier, and others.

11. The Latino AG has consistently been named among the largest Latino Protestant traditions in the United States on the above noted Pew-funded HCAPL and *Spirit and Power* national surveys. Holland, "Report on Hispanic Protestant Denominations in the USA, July 2012." Espinosa, "Changements démographiques et religieux

chez les hispaniques des Etats-Unis," 309–327. The *Religious Landscape Survey* put the proportion of Jews at 1.7 percent and that of Muslims at 0.6 percent of all adult Americans. Latino Protestants and non-Catholic Christians make up 25 to 33 percent of the U.S. Latino community (53 million) depending on the survey, sample size and type, and how respondents are counted, measured, and classified. The Hispanic Values Survey (HVS) reported that Latino Protestants (25 percent) are equally divided between Evangelicals (13 percent) and mainline Protestants (12 percent). However, this may be incomplete because Latinos who attend Evangelical/Pentecostal/Charismatic denominational and nondenominational churches and who are born-again or Pentecostal/Charismatic Christians make up over 80 percent of all Latino Protestants according to the 2000 Hispanic Churches in American Public Life and 2008 and 2012 Latino Religions and Politics (LRAP) national surveys. This 13 percent figure may not include the born-again and Pentecostal/Charismatic Christians in the "just Christian," "independent/nondenominational," and other similar generic categories, the vast majority of whom reported attending smaller Protestant and independent/nondenominational Protestant churches and/or being born-again Christian on other surveys. For example, the HCAPL national survey found that almost all of these "other Christian," "non-denominational/independent," and other respondents in a follow-up prompt specified a smaller Protestant denomination when given the opportunity to do so, and 48–77 percent also reported being born-again Christian, the latter of which is highly correlated with being Evangelical Protestant. The LRAP surveys in 2008 (n=1,104) and 2012 (n=1,075) reported similar results. Furthermore, the most comprehensive study on Latino Protestant churches in America by Clifton Holland and PRO-LADES reported the total percentage of Latino mainline Protestant churches at 12.3 percent (2,863 churches), Pentecostal/Charismatic churches at 41 percent (9,420), and all Evangelical/Pentecostal/Charismatic churches at 88 percent (20,326 churches). At least with respect to the number of Latino Protestant churches, there are seven times more Evangelical/Pentecostal/Charismatic than mainline Protestant churches. For the HCAPL findings, see Gastón Espinosa, "Methodological Reflections on Social Science Research on Latino Religions," in Miguel De la Torre and Gastón Espinosa, eds., *Rethinking Latino(a) Religion Identity* (Cleveland, OH: Pilgrim Press, 1996), 13–45. For the Jewish and Muslim data findings see Luis Lugo et al., *U.S. Religious Landscape Survey* (Washington, DC: Pew Research Religion & Public Life, 2008), 5, 41–43. For a discussion of Latino mainline Protestantism see David Maldonado Jr., ed., *Protestantes/Protestants: Hispanic Christianity within Mainline Traditions* (Nashville, TN: Abingdon Press, 1999), 276–279; Hispanic Values Survey: http://publicreligion.org/site/wp-content/uploads/2013/09/Hispanic-Values-Survey-topline-FINAL.pdf; Holland, "Report on Hispanic Protestant Denominations in the USA, July 2012."

12. These numbers are based on percentages from the HCAPL national survey, published in Espinosa, Elizondo, and Miranda, *Hispanic Churches in American Public Life,* 13–16, 27, and were largely confirmed in the Latino Religions and Politics national survey (n=1,104) in October 2008. Andrew Greeley, "Defection among Hispanics (Update)," *America* 177, no. 8 (1998): 12–15; Gastón Espinosa, *Hemisphere* (Miami: Florida

International University, 2009), 19–21. The 2012 findings are from the LRAP bilingual telephone survey (October 3–10, 2012) of 1,075 Latino likely voters across the United States, of which 1,000 were Latino Christian likely voters. All references to the 2012 LRAP survey refer to the 1,000-person sample unless I am referring to the "Religion" and "No Religion" screening question and sample, which is based on the total sample of 1,075 Latinos. For the percentage of the Latino, Asian American, Jewish, and Muslim electorates in 2012, see the National Election Pool (NEP) exit polls on the CNN website: http://edition.cnn.com/election/2012/results/race/president#exit-polls.

13. U.S. Census Bureau, "Hispanic Heritage Month 2013: Sept. 15–Oct. 15," July 30, 2013, http://www.census.gov/newsroom/releases/archives/facts_for_features_spe cial_editions/cb13-ff19.html.

14. This 93 percent figure differs from The Pew Forum *Religious Landscape Survey,* which put the national Latino Christian community at 84 percent, because it includes all Catholics, Protestants, other Christians, Mormons, Jehovah's Witnesses, and those in broader unrefined categories who also reported in later follow-up questions that they personally identified with a denominational or independent Christian church or with a Christian experience such as being a born-again or Pentecostal/Charismatic Christian. Most surveys do not try to ascertain the religious identities of respondents in these generic categories in follow-up questions. By contrast, the HCAPL and LRAP surveys provide a more detailed picture of the Latino Christian population because they asked all respondents in these broader unrefined categories (e.g., "just Christian," "independent," etc.) to also specify any church or tradition they affiliated with, if they had one. To further ascertain their religious identities, they also ran these respondents against other religious identity questions such as being born-again or Pentecostal/Charismatic Christian. The vast majority of respondents specified a smaller Protestant tradition (e.g., Free Methodist, Christian Reform Church, Mennonite, Calvary Chapel, Vineyard, etc.), as independent/ nondenominational Protestant Evangelical, Pentecostal, or Charismatic, and/or as born-again or Pentecostal/Charismatic Christian. When these individuals were reclassified as Christian, the percentage of Christians rose to 93 percent. Since being born-again and Pentecostal/Charismatic generally have a negative social stigma in Euro-American and Latino/Latin American communities, these figures are not likely to be overreported. If anything, they are more likely to be underreported. For this reason, the respondents in these larger unrefined categories are more likely to be Christians than Muslims, Hindus, Buddhists, atheists, agnostics, or other non-Christian religious practitioners. For these findings and a more detailed analysis of how the religious identities of respondents in these larger categories were ascertained, see Chapter 12 of this book and Espinosa, "Methodological Reflections on Social Science Research on Latino Religions," 13–45; Espinosa, Elizondo, and Miranda, *Hispanic Churches in American Public Life: Summary of Findings,* 14; LRAP national survey (n = 1,104, October 2008); U. S. Census Bureau, "Hispanic Heritage Month 2013: Sept. 15–Oct. 15," July 30, 2013, http://www.census.gov/newsroom /releases/archives/facts_for_features_special_editions/cb13-ff19.html.

15. Espinosa, Elizondo, and Miranda, *Hispanic Churches in American Public Life,* 14–16; Gastón Espinosa, ed., *Religion, Race, and Barack Obama's New Democratic Plu-*

ralism (New York: Routledge, 2013), 215–219; Holland, "Report on Hispanic Protestant Denominations in the USA, July 2012" Pew Hispanic Center 2011 National Survey of Latinos (n = 1, 220).

16. See the discussion in the previous two notes for details and sources and the 2012 LRAP survey of 1,075 Latino Christian and non-Christian likely voters and 1,000 Latino Christian likely voters.

17. Espinosa, Elizondo, and Miranda, *Hispanic Churches in American Public Life,* 14–16; Espinosa, *Religion, Race, and Barack Obama's New Democratic Pluralism,* 215–219.

18. Andrew Greeley, "Defection among Hispanics," 60–61; Andrew Greeley, "Defection among Hispanics (Updated)," *America* 27 (September 1997): 12–13.

19. See Espinosa, "Methodological Reflections on Social Science Research on Latino Religions," 13–45; Espinosa, Elizondo, and Miranda, *Hispanic Churches in American Public Life,* 14–16; Espinosa, *Religion, Race, and Barack Obama's New Democratic Pluralism,* 215–219.

20. 2012 LRAP survey.

21. R. Stephen Warner, "The De-Europeanization of American Christianity," in Stephen Prothero, ed., *A Nation of Religions: The Politics of Pluralism in Multireligious America* (Chapel Hill, NC: University of North Carolina Press, 2006), 233–255.

22. Sherri Doty, Statistics Department supervisor, Office of the General Secretary of the Assemblies of God, General Council of the Assemblies of God National Leadership and Resource Center, 15 August 2013.

23. Caille M. Millner, "Profs. West, Carrasco Seek to Transcend Dialogues on Race," *Harvard Crimson,* 19 March 1998: 1–2.

24. T. Patrick Burke, *The Major Religions* (Cambridge, MA: Blackwell, 1996), 309–312.

25. Catherine Albanese, *America: Religions and Religion* (Stamford, CT: Cengage Learning, 2012); and Mark Noll, *A History of Christianity in the United States and Canada* (Grand Rapids, MI: William B. Eerdmans, 1992).

26. Burke, *The Major Religions,* 309–312; Wayne Grudem, *Systematic Theology* (Grand Rapids, MI: Zondervan, 2000); W. J. Seaton, *The Five Points of Calvinism* (Carlisle, PA: Banner of Truth Trust, 1983), 3–20.

27. Burke, *The Major Religions,* 309–312; Grudem, *Systematic Theology;* Seaton, *The Five Points of Calvinism,* 3–20.

28. John 3:3 states: "You must be born-again to enter the Kingdom of Heaven." John 14:6 states: "I [Jesus] am the way, the truth and the life, no one goes to the Father except through me." Acts 4:12 states: "There is no other name under heaven by which we must be saved." All quotes are from the New International Version (NIV) of the Bible.

29. Marsden, *Fundamentalism and American Culture* (New York: Oxford University Press, 2006); Vinson Synan, "Fundamentalism," *The New International Dictionary of Pentecostal and Charismatic Movements,* 655–658; Maldonado, *Protestantes/Protestants,* 276–279.

30. Vinson Synan, *The Holiness-Pentecostal Movement: Charismatic Movements in the Twentieth-Century* (Grand Rapids, MI: William B. Eerdmans, 1997), 164–165.

31. Ibid., 220–274.

32. For a discussion of the Vineyard Christian Fellowship and Calvary Chapel, see Donald Miller, *Reinventing American Protestantism* (Berkeley: University of California Press, 1999), and for a discussion of Latinos in the Vineyard and Victory Outreach International, see Arlene Sánchez-Walsh, *Latino Pentecostal Identity: Evangelical Faith, Self and Society* (New York: Columbia University Press, 2003). For an overview of Victory Outreach International, see Gastón Espinosa, "Victory Outreach International," *The New International Dictionary of Pentecostal and Charismatic Movements,* 1175. For the influence of the Pentecostal/Charismatic movement among Latino Catholics and mainline Protestants, see Gastón Espinosa, "Catholic Charismatic Movement," in *Hispanic American Religious Cultures,* ed. Miguel de la Torre (Santa Barbara, CA: ABC CLIO, 2009), 1:95–98; Maldonado, *Protestantes/ Protestants,* 273–280.

33. Mircea Eliade, *The Quest: History and Meaning in Religion* (Chicago: University of Chicago Press, 1984), preface, 4, 7–9. For more about what I mean by an ethno-phenomenological approach, see Gastón Espinosa, "Theory and Method in the Study of Mexican American Religions," in *Mexican American Religions: Spirituality, Activism, and Culture,* ed. Gastón Espinosa and Mario T. García (Durham, NC: Duke University Press, 2008), 17–56.

34. The six surveys I directed or managed include the 1998 Latina Women in Ministry Survey of Assemblies of God and Methodist Clergywomen; the 2000 Pew Charitable Trusts HCAPL national (n = 2,060), civic leaders, and religious leaders surveys; the 2008 LRAP (n = 1,104) national survey; and the 2012 LRAP (n = 1,075 Latino Christian and non-Christian likely voters and 1,000 Latino Christian likely voters) survey of Latino Christian likely voters. This study also draws on the 2008 and 2012 National Election Pool exit polls. For a list of the surveys, dates, and sample types and sizes, see Espinosa, "Methodological Reflections on Social Science Research on Latino Religions," 15.

35. Peter Novick, *That Noble Dream* (Cambridge: Cambridge University Press, 1988).

36. The Latino AG has contributed to denominational *and* religious pluralism because it has birthed not only a number of new Pentecostal denominations, but also distinct nonclassical Protestant traditions like Juana García Peraza's Congregation Mita, in Puerto Rico, which broke off from the AG in 1942. Other examples of Latino AG splinter groups could be cited in the United States, Mexico, and Central America, all of which was under the Latino AG District leadership and guidance of H. C. Ball until 1930, after which time almost all of the districts in these various countries were nationalized. This constant fragmentation helps to explain why, of the 1,991 Pentecostal denominations and councils in Latin America, 1,767 are indigenous. Gastón Espinosa, "The Pentecostalization of Latin American and U.S. Latino Christianity," *Pneuma: The Journal of the Society for Pentecostal Studies* 26, no. 2 (2004): 262–292. For a discussion of this fragmentation thesis, see Gastón Espinosa, *William J. Seymour and the Origins of Global Pentecostalism* (Durham, NC: Duke University Press, 2014), 32–33.

37. "The movement toward Protestantism, mostly to fundamentalist, Pentecostal, and Charismatic sects, has been quite recent, and is surprising given the virtual assimilation of Catholicism into Hispanic culture. . . . Protestantism has made few in-

roads among Mexican Americans, except in Texas." Barry Kosmin and Seymour Lachman, *One Nation under God: Religion in Contemporary Society* (New York: Harmony Books, 1993), 138.

38. Ana María Díaz-Stevens and Anthony M. Stevens-Arroyo, *Recognizing the Latino Resurgence in U.S. Religion* (Boulder, CO: Westview Press, 1998), 35, 37, draws on the National Survey of Religious Identity (NSRI) directed by Barry Kosmin and Seymour Lachman and discussed in their previously cited book *One Nation under God;* Espinosa, Elizondo, and Miranda, *Hispanic Churches in American Public Life,* 16.

39. MacGregor Burns argues that there are two kinds of leaders: transactional and transformational. Transactional leaders can be effective because they provide a service or goods in exchange for their followers' support. Transformational leaders help their followers "release" their human potential, gifts and talents now "trapped in ungratified needs and crushed hopes and expectations." Bass and Riggio argue that they are successful because they transform their people into agents of change by helping them to reach their dreams and goals and by paying attention to their individual needs (i.e., "individualized consideration") and talents. They also exhort their followers to try new approaches and reach extraordinary outcomes, all of which builds up their self-esteem. Latino Pentecostal leaders encourage people to engage in transformational leadership through a host of activities, including mentoring and encouraging people to practice their individual spiritual gift(s) and ministries for the benefit of others. Latinos are allowed to experiment with their gifts and leadership skills during services without having to navigate the skepticism they might encounter in Catholic or traditional Protestant churches. For a discussion of transformational leadership, see the introduction to Espinosa, *William J. Seymour and the Origins of Global Pentecostalism,* 33–34; James MacGregor Burns, *Leadership* (New York: Harper and Row, 1978), 3–5, 12–46; and Bernard M. Bass and Ronald E. Riggio, eds., *Transformational Leadership,* 2nd ed. (New York: Psychology Press, 2006), 1–31, 142–166.

40. Gastón Espinosa, interview with Eldin Villafañe, 5 February 2014.

41. The NEP exit poll reported that Bush took 44 percent of the national Latino vote on Election Day 2004, and the *Los Angeles Times* national exit poll reported that he took 45 percent of the Latino vote. Other scholars have challenged these statistics, arguing that they are inconsistent with some of the polling data leading up to Election Day. However, most scholars contend that Bush likely took at least 39–40 percent of the Latino vote. For a discussion of the various arguments, see Espinosa, *Religion, Race, and the American Presidency,* 256–273.

42. For a discussion, see Espinosa, *Religion, Race, and Barack Obama's New Democratic Pluralism,* 213–242.

43. Elizabeth Dias, "The Latino Reformation: Inside the New Hispanic Churches Transforming Religion in America," *Time,* 15 April 2013, 20–28.

44. "Weird Babel of Tongues," *Los Angeles Daily Times,* April 18, 1906, 1.

45. Augustus Cerillo and Grant Wacker, "Bibliography and Historiography," *The New International Dictionary of Pentecostal and Charismatic Movements,* 397–405.

46. This writing about one's own tradition in a somewhat condescending and patronizing tone is evident in Ogbu Kalu, *African Pentecostalism: An Introduction* (New York: Oxford University Press, 2008), 4–10, 47, 64–66, 83.

1. Holy Ghost and Fire

1. Copies of all documents cited in this chapter and others are in the author's general Pentecostal History Collection and Latino Pentecostal History Collection. Abundio and Rosa L. López, "Spanish Receive the Pentecost," *Apostolic Faith* (hereafter *AF*) (October 1906): 4. Because Parham, Seymour, Florence Crawford, W. F. Carothers, and others called their newspapers the *Apostolic Faith,* the city of publication will follow *AF* in parentheses to distinguish the papers from one another, e.g., Los Angeles (Seymour), Baxter Springs (Parham), Houston (Carothers), or Portland, Oregon (Crawford). However, for articles authored by Seymour and Parham, I assume Los Angeles or Baxter Springs, respectively, as the publication location.

2. The exceptions are Benjamin Cantú and José Ortega, *Historia de la Asamblea Apostólica de la Fe en Cristo Jesús* (Mentone, CA: Sal's Printing Service, 1966), 6–7; Cecil M. Robeck Jr., "Evangelization or Proselytism of Hispanics? A Pentecostal Perspective," *Journal of Hispanic/Latino Theology* 4, no. 4 (1997): 42–64; Gastón Espinosa, "Borderland Religion: Los Angeles and the Origins of the Latino Pentecostal Movement in the U.S., Mexico, and Puerto Rico, 1900–1945" (Ph.D. diss., University of California, Santa Barbara, 1999), 117–140; Gastón Espinosa, "'The Holy Ghost Is Here on Earth': The Mexican Contributions to the Azusa Street Revival," Azusa Street Revival Anniversary Edition, *Enrichment: A Journal for Pentecostal Ministry* 11, no. 2 (Spring 2006): 118–125. I have copies of Abundio López's Azusa Mission ordination certificate signed by William J. Seymour, along with two photographs and other primary source materials. I have also been able to secure similar documents and photos of Mexican American Azusa Street Revival eyewitness Adolfo C. Valdez.

3. Walter J. Hollenweger, "Black Pentecostal Concept: A Forgotten Chapter of Black History," *Concept,* Special Issue, no. 30 (Geneva: World Council of Churches, June 1970); Leonard Lovett, "Black Origins of the Pentecostal Movement," in *Aspects of Pentecostal-Charismatic Origins,* ed. Vinson Synan (Plainfield, NJ: Logos International, 1975), 123–141; Douglas J. Nelson, "'For Such a Time as This': The Story of Bishop William J. Seymour and the Azusa Street Revival" (Ph.D. diss., University of Birmingham, England, 1981); Iain MacRobert, *The Black Roots and White Racism of Early Pentecostalism in the USA* (New York: St. Martin's Press, 1988). A notable exception to this line of interpretation is Robert Mapes Anderson, *Vision of the Disinherited: The Making of American Pentecostalism* (Peabody, MA: Hendrickson Publishers, 1992), 69; see also Grant Wacker, *Heaven Below: Early Pentecostals and American Culture* (Cambridge, MA: Harvard University Press, 2003), 226–235. For a discussion of Valdez's preaching across the United States and around the world, see his book, A. C. Valdez with James F. Scheer, *Fire on Azusa Street* (Costa Mesa, CA: Gift Publications, 1988).

4. Sarah Parham, *The Life of Charles F. Parham* (Baxter Spring, KS: Apostolic Faith Bible College, 1977), 212; Miguel Guillén, *La Historia del Concilio Latino Americano de Iglesias Cristianas* (Brownsville, TX: Latin American Council of Christian Churches, 1992), 50–57.

5. Barry Kosmin and Seymour Lachman, *One Nation under God: Religion in Contemporary Society* (New York: Harmony Books, 1993), 138.

6. When citing unsigned editorials I list the title, the newspaper, the date, and the page number. "N/t" indicates an untitled editorial (of which there are many).

7. Robert H. Wiebe, *The Search for Order, 1877–1920* (New York: Hill and Wang, 1967), viii, 56, 76–77, 83.

8. George M. Marsden, *Fundamentalism and American Culture, 1870–1925* (New York: Oxford University Press, 1980), 15–16, 62, 215–221.

9. B. B. Warfield, *Counterfeit Miracles* (Carlisle, PA: Banner of Truth Publications, 1918).

10. Eric Sharpe, *Comparative Religion: A History* (La Salle, IL: Open Court, 1994), 48–49, 54, 56, 94–95, 166.

11. Sandra Sizer Frankiel's *California's Spiritual Frontiers* (Berkeley: University of California Press, 1988).

12. Ann Braude, *Radical Spirits: Spiritualism and Women's Rights in Nineteenth-Century America* (Boston: Beacon Press, 1989).

13. For the origins of Pentecostalism see Walter J. Hollenweger, *The Pentecostals* (Peabody, MA: Hendrickson Publishers, 1988), 22–28; Wacker, *Heaven Below;* Mapes Anderson, *Vision of the Disinherited,* 28–78; Donald W. Dayton, *Theological Roots of Pentecostalism* (Metuchen, NJ: Scarecrow Press, 1987); James R. Goff Jr., *Fields White unto Harvest: Charles F. Parham and the Missionary Origins of Pentecostalism* (Fayetteville, AR: University of Arkansas Press, 1988); Allan Anderson, *Spreading Fires: The Missionary Nature of Early Pentecostalism* (Maryknoll, NY: Orbis Books, 2007).

14. Dayton, *Theological Roots of Pentecostalism;* Wacker, *Heaven Below;* Mapes Anderson, *Vision of the Disinherited;* Nelson, " 'For Such a Time as This.' "

15. The best book-length biographies on Charles Parham and William Seymour are Goff, *Fields White unto Harvest,* and Douglas J. Nelson, " 'For Such a Time as This.' " Also see Gastón Espinosa, *William J. Seymour and the Origins of Global Pentecostalism: A Biography and Documentary History* (Durham, NC: Duke University Press, 2014), and Larry Martin, *The Life and Ministry of William J. Seymour* (Joplin, MO: Christian Life Books, 1999). The best overall history of the Azusa Street Revival is Cecil M. Robeck Jr., *The Azusa Street Mission and Revival* (Nashville, TN: Thomas Nelson, 2006).

16. Hollenweger, *The Pentecostals;* Walter J. Hollenweger, *Pentecostalism* (Peabody, MA: Hendrickson Publishers, 1997); Anderson, *Spreading Fires;* Mapes Anderson, *Vision of the Disinherited.*

17. Charles W. Shumway, "A Study of 'The Gift of Tongues' " (A.B. thesis, University of Southern California, Los Angeles, 1914), 164–168; Charles W. Shumway, "A Critical History of Glossolalia" (Ph.D. diss., Boston University, Boston, 1919), 112–117;

Goff, *Fields White unto Harvest*, 16, 18–37; James Goff, "Parham, Charles Fox," in *Dictionary of Pentecostal and Charismatic Movements*, ed. Stanley M. Burgess and Gary B. McGee (Grand Rapids, MI: Zondervan Publishing House, 1988), 660–661; Mapes Anderson, *Vision of the Disinherited*, 47–52.

18. Goff, *Fields White unto Harvest*, 16, 18–37; Goff, "Parham, Charles Fox," 660–661; Mapes Anderson, *Vision of the Disinherited*, 47–52.

19. Goff, *Fields White unto Harvest*, 16, 18–37; Goff, "Parham, Charles Fox," 660–661; Mapes Anderson, *Vision of the Disinherited*, 47–52.

20. Goff, *Fields White unto Harvest*, 16, 18–37; Goff, "Parham, Charles Fox," 660–661; Mapes Anderson, *Vision of the Disinherited*, 47–52.

21. C. F. Parham, n/t, *AF* (Baxter Springs) (January 1912): 7.

22. Parham wrote: "The difference between these people [created on the sixth day] and the Adamic race of the eighth day was, they were created, had dominion and authority, while Adam was formed from the earth (earthy) and put in the garden to tend it. . . . When Cain killed his brother, he fled to the land of Nod, there took unto himself a wife, one of the sixth day creation. This began the woeful inter-marriage of races for which cause the flood was sent in punishment, and has ever been followed by plagues and incurable diseases upon the third and fourth generation, the off-spring of such marriages. Were time to last and inter-marriage continue between the whites, the blacks, and the reds in America, consumption and other diseases would soon wipe the mixed bloods off the face of the earth." Charles Fox Parham, *Kol Kare Bomidbar: A Voice Crying Out in the Wilderness* (1902; repr., Baxter Springs, KS: Apostolic Faith Bible College, 1910), 82–84, 92–100, 105–107; Goff, *Fields White unto Harvest*, 107–111, 131–132.

23. "Hindoo and Zulu Both Represented in Bethel College: Students Suddenly Begin Talking in Strange Languages," *Topeka State Journal*, 9 January 1901; Sarah Parham, *The Life of Charles F. Parham*, 52; Shumway, "A Study of 'The Gift of Tongues,'" 164–166; Goff, *Fields White unto Harvest*, 38–39, 57–59, 72; Mapes Anderson, *Vision of the Disinherited*, 52–61.

24. For an alternative chronology, see Mapes Anderson, *Vision of the Disinherited*, 56.

25. Shumway, "A Study of 'The Gift of Tongues,'" 167; Mapes Anderson, *Vision of the Disinherited*, 56, 161–165; Edith L. Blumhofer, *The Assemblies of God: A Chapter in the Story of American Pentecostalism*, vol. 1, *To 1941* (Springfield, MO: Gospel Publishing House, 1989), 80–85, 393–394; Goff, *Fields White unto Harvest*, 69–79; Wacker, *Heaven Below*, 35–57.

26. "The Pentecostal Baptism Restored: The Promised Latter Rain Now Being Poured Out on God's Humble People," *AF* (Los Angeles) (October 1906): 1; Goff, *Fields White unto Harvest*, 40–41, 44–49, 66–85. Parham claimed that language interpreters from Chicago corroborated that these tongues were real languages, yet Shumway denied this ("A Study of 'The Gift of Tongues,'" 168).

27. Mapes Anderson, *Vision of the Disinherited*, 57–59; Goff, "Parham, Charles Fox," 660–661.

28. Nelson, "'For Such a Time as This,'" 33–35; Martin, *The Life and Ministry of William J. Seymour*, 65–73.

29. Nelson, "'For Such a Time as This,'" 33–35.

30. The general consensus is that Parham required Seymour to sit either in the hallway or in another classroom adjacent to his classroom. A. C. Valdez states that Seymour asked Parham, "Can I just sit in the doorway and listen to the lessons?" Valdez stated that Parham consented. However, Valdez used that decision as evidence that there was *no* discrimination in his heart. Valdez with Scheer, *Fire on Azusa Street,* 18. Charles Shumway wrote in 1914 regarding Parham's segregated revival services that "colored people were allowed to visit meetings of white people under some circumstances, but they must remain in the *rear* and *keep silent*." Emphasis added. Shumway, "A Study of 'The Gift of Tongues,'" 173. This is consistent with Sarah Parham's statement that at Charles's revival services blacks were segregated and "kept their place." Sarah Parham, *The Life of Charles F. Parham,* 246 (see also 137); Nelson, "'For Such a Time as This,'" 35, 167; H. A. Goss, "Reminiscences of an Eyewitness," *TWE,* 4 March 1916: 4–5; Goff, *Fields White unto Harvest,* 107, 210–212. That Parham was not merely following the racialized social conventions of his day in the Deep South is evident by (1) his views on white supremacy laid out in *Kol Kare Bomidbar,* (2) his racialized attacks on Seymour in his *Apostolic Faith* newspaper, especially in 1912, and (3) that he did not normally allow interracial mixing at the altars in his services in Texas and even outside of the South. While Parham's vision and application of white supremacy was not as harsh as that of other whites in 1906, he became increasingly critical of Seymour, the Azusa Street Revival, and its daughter missions in 1911–1912 and more compliant in his segregationist practices. He also returned again to southern California in February 1913. See C. F. Parham, *Kol Kare Bomidbar,* 81–85, and his *Apostolic Faith* articles: Charles Fox Parham, "Leadership," *AF* (June 1912): 6–9; Charles Fox Parham, "Unity," *AF* (June 1912): 9–11; Charles Fox Parham, "Free Love," *AF* (December 1912): 4–5; and Parham's comments in letters published in Sarah Parham, *The Life of Charles F. Parham,* 163–169, 237–243.

31. Sarah Parham, *The Life of Charles F. Parham,* 212; Miguel Guillén, *La historia del Concilio Latino Americano de Iglesias Cristianas* (Brownsville, TX: Latin American Council of Christian Churches, 1991), 50–77; H. A. Goss, "Reminiscences of an Eyewitness," *TWE,* 4 March 1916: 4–5; Goff, *Fields White unto Harvest,* 107–109; Nelson, "'For Such a Time as This,'" 209, 267.

32. "Tongues as a Sign," *AF* (Los Angeles) (September 1906): 2; William J. Seymour, *The Doctrines and Discipline of the Azusa Street Apostolic Faith Mission of Los Angeles* (Los Angeles: Apostolic Faith Mission, 1915), 10, 95; Stanley H. Frodsham, *With Signs Following: The Story of the Pentecostal Revival in the Twentieth Century* (Springfield, MO: Gospel Publishing House, 1946), 38; Nelson, "'For Such a Time as This,'" 11–13; Shumway, "A Study of 'The Gift of Tongues,'" 173; B. F. Lawrence, *The Apostolic Faith Restored* (St. Louis: Gospel Publishing House, 1916), 64. Mapes Anderson argued that eschatology was at the heart of the movement. Mapes Anderson, *Vision of the Disinherited,* 4, 43, 229–232, 240. Goff argued that tongues were central. James Goff, *Fields White unto Harvest,* 9, 15–16. Martin argued that Seymour's core message was a call to biblical holiness. Martin, *The Life and Ministry of William J. Seymour,* 197, note 84. I contend that his primary ministry emphasis was on converting people and bringing them into a personal born-again relationship

with Jesus Christ and being baptized and filled with the Spirit, or being born again and Spirit-filled. He believed that the Spirit baptism empowered people to transcend the unbiblical national, racial, ethnic, and class boundaries of the day.

33. Nelson, " 'For Such a Time as This,' " 37, 55.

34. Shumway, "A Study of 'The Gift of Tongues,' " 173; "Mother" Emma Cotton, "Inside Story of the Outpouring of the Holy Spirit, Azusa Street, April 1906," *Message of the Apostolic Faith,* April 1939, 1ff.; Nelson, " 'For Such a Time as This,' " 187–189.

35. Shumway, "A Study of 'The Gift of Tongues,' " 174–175.

36. Nelson, " 'For Such a Time as This,' " 57.

37. Shumway, "A Study of 'The Gift of Tongues,' " 175; "The Same Old Way," *AF* (September 1906): 3; "Bible Pentecost: Gracious Pentecostal Showers Continue to Fall," *AF* (November 1906): 1; Frank Bartleman, *Azusa Street* (1925; repr., South Plainfield, NJ: Bridge Publishing, 1980), 43.

38. This Mexican American young adult was already Protestant, but not practicing the faith. Arthur G. Osterberg, "Oral History of the Life of Arthur G. Osterberg and the Azusa Street Revival," transcribed interview by Jerry Jensen and Jonathan Perkin, Flower Pentecostal Heritage Center, 1966, 11.

39. Nelson, " 'For Such a Time as This,' " 58.

40. Espinosa, " 'The Holy Ghost Is Here on Earth,' " 118–125.

41. Hollenweger, "Black Pentecostal Concept;" Lovett, "Black Origins of the Pentecostal Movement," 123–141; Nelson, " 'For Such a Time as This.' "

42. The U.S. Latino Pentecostal movement also traces its origins back to not only William J. Seymour but also Charles Fox Parham's work in Houston, Texas. See Chapter 2 of this book.

43. While the Valdez family was Catholic, Abundio López had a Protestant background before attending the Apostolic Faith Mission. Espinosa, " 'The Holy Ghost Is Here on Earth,' " 118–125.

44. N/t, *AF* (Los Angeles) (September 1906): 1.

45. N/t, *AF* (October 1906): 1; n/t, *AF* (January 1907): 1. The lead articles from the October 1906 and the January 1907 editions of *AF* read "The Pentecostal Baptism Restored" and "Beginning of World Wide Revival."

46. Valdez with Scheer, *Fire on Azusa Street,* 9–11.

47. N/t, *AF* (September 1906): 1; Apostolic Faith Mission, *A Historical Account of the Apostolic Faith* (Portland, OR: Apostolic Faith Publishing House, 1965), 59.

48. *AF,* 1906–1908.

49. Mapes Anderson argues that it is possible but highly unlikely to speak in an unknown human language *(xenolalia).* Mapes Anderson, *Vision of the Disinherited,* 15–20. For a different point of view see Wacker, *Heaven Below,* 40–57.

50. A. W. Orwig, "My First Visit to the Azuzu [*sic*] Street Pentecostal Mission, Los Angeles, California," *TWE,* 18 March 1916: 4; Glenn A. Cook, *The Azusa Street Meetings: Some Highlights of This Outpouring* (Belvedere, CA: Belvedere Christian Mission, ca. 1920), 2.

51. Bartleman, *Azusa Street,* 55.

52. Ibid., 82.

53. Dayton, *Theological Roots of Pentecostalism,* 11.

54. "Arrested for Jesus' Sake," *AF* (Los Angeles) (December 1906): 3; Seymour, *Doctrines and Discipline,* 84.

55. "The Promise Still Good," *AF* (Los Angeles) (September 1906): 3.

56. Bartleman, *Azusa Street,* 13, 15, 19–20, 26. See Seymour's *Apostolic Faith* newspaper for evidence of this theological literacy.

57. "The Pentecostal Baptism Restored: The Promised Latter Rain Now Being Poured Out on God's Humble People," *AF* (October 1906): 1; "Shall We Reject Jesus' Last Words?," *AF* (October 1906): 3; Bartleman, *Azusa Street,* 43, 45–46, 62, 65–66, 77, 89.

58. As cited in A. W. Orwig, "Additional Reports from Los Angeles Covering the Early Pentecostal Work," *TWE,* 8 April 1916: 4; "Tongues as a Sign," *AF* (September 1906): 2; "The Salvation of Jesus," *AF* (January 1906): 4.

59. Shumway, "A Study of 'The Gift of Tongues,'" 172; Dayton, *Theological Roots of Pentecostalism;* Grant Wacker, "Pentecostalism," in *Encyclopedia of the American Religious Experience,* ed. Charles H. Lippy and Peter W. Williams (New York: Scribner, 1988), 935.

60. "The Apostolic Faith," *AF* (Los Angeles) (September 1906): 2.

61. Valdez with Scheer, *Fire on Azusa Street,* 24–25.

62. Bartleman, *Azusa Street,* xviii.

63. Nickel stated that this clubfoot was "completely straightened." Thomas R. Nickel, *The Azusa Street Outpouring as Told by Those Who Were There,* 3rd ed. (Hanford, CA: Great Commission International, 1956), 13.

64. Osterberg, "Oral History of the Life of Arthur G. Osterberg and the Azusa Street Revival," 12.

65. Mrs. Knapp, *AF* (September 1906): 2; no author listed, *AF* (September 1906): 3; Valdez with Scheer, *Fire on Azusa Street,* 27, 34, esp. 39; López, "Spanish Receive the Pentecost," 4.

66. N/t, "A Revival in Los Angeles," *Pisgah* (December 1910): 13; no author listed, "The Camp-Meeting at Pisgah Gardens," *Pisgah* (December 1913): 7.

67. N/t, *AF* (Los Angeles) (September 1906): 2.

68. "Bible Pentecost: Gracious Pentecostal Showers Continue to Fall," *AF* (Los Angeles) (November 1906): 1.

69. Bartleman, *Azusa Street,* xviii; Valdez with Scheer, *Fire on Azusa Street,* 9. Nelson stated that Rev. Lawrence Catley and Mrs. Amanda Smith confirmed this in his discussions with them. Nelson, "'For Such a Time as This,'" 206. See also n/t, *AF* (Los Angeles) (September 1906): 2.

70. "Questions Answered," *AF* (Los Angeles) (October–January 1908): 2.

71. N/t, *AF* (Los Angeles) (January 1907): 3.

72. Seymour, *Doctrines and Discipline,* 40–45.

73. Ibid.

74. Ibid.

75. Ibid.; Nelson, "'For Such a Time as This.'"

76. "God Is His Own Interpreter," *AF* (Los Angeles) (January 1907): 2; n/t *AF* (Los Angeles) (February–March 1907): 1.

77. The Upper Room mentioned in Acts 1:13 is where the outpouring and baptism of the Holy Spirit took place on the Day of Pentecost as described in Acts 1–4. Nelson, "'For Such a Time as This,'" 60.

78. "One Church," *AF* (Los Angeles) (October 1906): 3–4; "Spreads the Fire," *AF* (Los Angeles) (October 1906): 4; "Pentecost with Signs Following," *AF* (Los Angeles) (December 1906): 1; Phineas Bresee, "The Gift of Tongues," *Nazarene Messenger,* December 13, 1906; C. W. Bridwell, "Fanatical Sect in Los Angeles Claims Gift of Tongues," *Rocky Mountain Pillar of Fire,* June 13, 1906.

79. William W. Menzies, *Anointed to Serve,* vol. 1 (Springfield, MO: Gospel Publishing House, 1971), 97, 149, 153.

80. Cook, *The Azusa Street Meetings,* 1–4.

81. Shumway, "A Study of 'The Gift of Tongues,'" 191–192; Nelson, "'For Such a Time as This,'" 62.

82. Nelson, "'For Such a Time as This,'" 59.

83. For a list of all of the countries see Wayne Warner, *The Azusa Street Papers* (Foley, AL: Harvest Publications, 1997), 69–79. Nelson, "'For Such a Time as This,'" 59–64, 213; Valdez with Scheer, *Fire on Azusa Street,* 101–110; Shumway, "A Study of 'The Gift of Tongues,'" 180–182.

84. Nelson, "'For Such a Time as This,'" 61–62.

85. Shumway, "A Study of 'The Gift of Tongues,'" 177; A. A. Boddy, "A Meeting at the Azusa Street Mission, Los Angeles," *Confidence* (November 1912): 244.

86. "The Same Old Way," *AF* (Los Angeles) (September 1906): 3.

87. N/t, *AF* (Los Angeles) (November 1906): 1.

88. Nelson, "'For Such a Time as This,'" 234.

89. Bartleman, *Azusa Street,* xix; Ithiel C. Clemmons, *Bishop C. H. Mason and the Roots of the Church of God in Christ,* Centennial Edition (Bakersfield, CA: Pneuma Life Publishing, 1996), 45.

90. A. S. Boddy, *Confidence* (September 1912): 209–212; Nelson, "'For Such a Time as This,'" 198.

91. W. J. Seymour, "Who May Prophesy?," *AF* (January 1908): 2.

92. Valdez with Scheer, *Fire on Azusa Street,* 25.

93. "Pentecostal Faith Line," *AF* (Los Angeles) (September 1906): 3.

94. Bartleman, *Azusa Street,* 58.

95. N/t, *AF* (Los Angeles) (February–March 1907): 7.

96. Parham described Seymour's Azusa Street Revival as "Darky camp meetings." Charles F. Parham, "Free-Love," *AF* (Baxter Springs) (December 1912): 4–5.

97. Alma White, *Demons and Tongues* (1910; repr., Zarephath, NJ: Alma White, 1949), 67–70, 82, 108; Nelson, "'For Such a Time as This,'" 83.

98. Shumway, "A Study of 'The Gift of Tongues,'" 178.

99. C. F. Parham, "Free-Love," 4–5.

100. C. F. Parham, "Leadership," 7.

101. Nelson, "'For Such a Time as This,'" 95–97.

102. Goff, *Fields White unto Harvest,* 136–142, 223–224.

103. Nelson, "'For Such a Time as This,'" 61.

104. E. N. Bell, "Notice about Parham," *Word and Witness* (Malvern, AR) (October 20, 1912): 3.

105. "Who May Prophesy?," *AF* (Los Angeles) (January 1908): 2; W. J. Seymour, "To the Married," *AF* (January 1908): 3.

106. W. J. Seymour, "Gifts of the Spirit," *AF* (January 1907): 2; Boddy, *Confidence* (November 1912): 244–245.

107. Nelson, "'For Such a Time as This,'" 62–64, 213.

108. Ibid., 64, 216–218.

109. Charles H. Mason stated in 1948: "Seymour told him that Clara Lum had privately made it clear that she fell in love with Seymour and wanted him to propose marriage to her. Seymour had tentatively considered the possibility and discussed the matter in its early stages with Mason who advised him not to even think about the idea." Lum never married anyone. Ithiel C. Clemmons, *Bishop C. H. Mason and the Roots of the Church of God in Christ* (Bakersfield, CA: Pneuma Life Publishing, 1996), 50.

110. Nelson, "'For Such a Time as This,'" 217, 241.

111. Twenty lists were of subscribers in southern California, while the other two were the national and international lists. Seymour had only the southern California mailing lists. Ibid., 217.

112. Emphasis added. Bartleman, *Azusa Street,* 145; Nelson, "'For Such a Time as This,'" 92.

113. Espinosa, "'The Holy Ghost Is Here on Earth,'" 118–125.

114. Ibid.

115. Nelson, "'For Such a Time as This,'" 218.

116. Shumway, "A Study of 'The Gift of Tongues,'" 179; Bartleman, *Azusa Street,* 150–151.

117. Bartleman, *Azusa Street,* 150–151.

118. Nelson, "'For Such a Time as This,'" 249; Shumway, "A Study of 'The Gift of Tongues,'" 179.

119. Bartleman, *Azusa Street,* 143; Nelson, "'For Such a Time as This,'" 253.

120. Shumway, "A Study of 'The Gift of Tongues,'" 191; Nelson, "'For Such a Time as This,'" 253–254.

121. Nelson, "'For Such a Time as This,'" 254; Wacker, *Heaven Below,* 147.

122. Seymour, *Doctrines and Discipline,* preface, 8, 10, 12–13.

123. Ibid., preface, 8, 10, 12–13, 47–51.

124. Shumway, "A Study of 'The Gift of Tongues,'" 179.

125. Ibid.; Nelson, "'For Such a Time as This,'" 260–269.

126. Nelson, "'For Such a Time as This,'" 267–269.

127. Gastón Espinosa, "Francisco Olazábal: Charisma, Power, and Faith Healing in the Borderlands," in *Portraits of a Generation,* ed. James R. Goff Jr. and Grant Wacker (Fayetteville, AR: University of Arkansas Press, 2002), 177–197, 400–404; Nelson, "'For Such a Time as This,'" 267–270.

128. Nelson, "'For Such a Time as This,'" 272–274; Nils Bloch-Hoell, *The Pentecostal Movement* (Oslo, Norway: Universitetsforlaget, 1964), 39.

129. Statistics by Todd Johnson, director of the Center for the Study of World Christianity. Johnson and Peter Crossing direct the World Christianity database, which is the

largest and most comprehensive dataset in the world on global Christianity. Crossing provided this information via an email exchange based on his analysis of the data on January 14, 2012.

130. B. F. Lawrence, *The Apostolic Faith Restored* (St. Louis: Gospel Publishing House, 1916), 73–80; Bartleman, *Azusa Street,* 57.

131. Cecil M. Robeck, "The Past: Historical Roots of Racial Unity and Division in American Pentecostalism," *Cyberjournal for Pentecostal-Charismatic Research,* May 2005, http://www.pctii.org/cyberj/cyberj14/robeck.html; Vinson Synan, *The Holiness-Pentecostal Tradition* (Grand Rapids, MI: Eerdmans, 1997), 180–186.

132. Espinosa, "'The Holy Ghost Is Here on Earth,'" 118–125; Valdez with Scheer, *Fire on Azusa Street.*

133. Espinosa, "'The Holy Ghost Is Here on Earth,'" 118–125; Valdez with Scheer, *Fire on Azusa Street.*

2. Victory Is Coming Now

1. For the full titles of periodicals for which abbreviations are used, see the list of abbreviations at the beginning of the Notes section. A. M. López, "Our Mexican Missionary's Report," *TWE,* 29 September 1917: 12.

2. Victor De Leon stated, "If anyone is to be 'blamed' for this great [Latino AG] move of God besides the Holy Spirit, H. C. Ball would have to be that man." De Leon, *The Silent Pentecostals: A Biographical History of the Pentecostal Movement among Hispanics in the Twentieth Century* (Taylors, SC: Faith Printing Company, 1979), 12. Robert Mapes Anderson reinforces De Leon's view when he writes that Ball was "perhaps the most outstanding leader of the movement among Mexicans in Texas." Mapes Anderson, *Vision of the Disinherited: The Making of American Pentecostalism* (Peabody, MA: Hendrickson Publishers, 1992), 126. Enemecio Alaniz, Arnulfo M. López, Isabel Flores, Francisco Olazábal, Miguel Guillén, and Demetrio Bazan, among others, also played a major role as we shall see in this chapter and those that follow.

3. A. M. López, "Our Mexican Missionary's Report," *TWE,* September 29, 1917: 12; De Leon, *The Silent Pentecostals,* 12. Robert Mapes Anderson reinforces De Leon's view when he writes that Ball was "perhaps the most outstanding leader of the movement among Mexicans in Texas." Mapes Anderson, *Vision of the Disinherited,* 126.

4. Sarah Parham, *The Life of Charles F. Parham* (Birmingham, AL: Commercial Printing Company, 1930; 3rd printing, Baxter Spring, KS: Apostolic Faith Bible College, 1977), 117, 208, 212; Mapes Anderson, *Vision of the Disinherited,* 123.

5. Although Olazábal did not join the movement until after Ball began his work in July 1915, he was ordained as a missionary to the Mexicans in the larger Euro-American AG in California, not by Ball in Texas, and thus was not under Ball's control.

6. Bosworth and especially Pinson ordained a number of Latinos to the AG in Texas, and there is little reason to doubt that they did not in turn share their stories with them about Seymour, the Azusa Street Revival, and his beliefs about the outpouring

and baptism with the Holy Spirit. This may explain why Latinos largely followed Seymour's rather than Parham's explanation that tongues could be both glossolalia (divine language known only to God) or xenolalia (human language one had never previously studied) and why they never embraced any of Parham's other unorthodox theological, social, and racial views, such as annihilation, eighth-day creationism, and British Israelism. For a discussion, see Gastón Espinosa, *William J. Seymour and the Origins of Global Pentecostalism: A Biography and Documentary History* (Durham, NC: Duke University Press, 2014), and W. E. Warner, "Pinson, Mack M.," *The New International Dictionary of Pentecostal and Charismatic Movements,* ed. Stanley M. Burgess and Eduard M. Van der Maas (Grand Rapids, MI: Zondervan, 2002), 989. Also see Manuel Gamio, *Mexican Immigration to the United States* (Chicago: University of Chicago Press, 1930; repr. New York: Dover Publications, 1971), 108–118; Miguel Guillén, *La historia del Concilio Latino Americano de Iglesias Cristianas* (Brownsville, TX: Latin American Council of Christian Churches, 1992), 56, 91.

7. Mario T. García, *Desert Immigrants* (New Haven, CT: Yale University Press, 1981); David G. Gutiérrez, *Walls and Mirrors* (Berkeley: University of California Press, 1995); Deborah Baldwin, *Protestants and the Mexican Revolution: Missionaries, Ministers, and Social Change* (Urbana: University of Illinois, 1990), 3–12, 165–171; George W. Grayson, *The Church in Contemporary Mexico* (Washington, DC: Center for Strategic and International Studies, 1992), 1–21.

8. Concepción Alaniz de Casarez, "Datos dados por la hermana del principio de la obra Pentecostal en Deepwater, Pasadena, Houston, Rosenberg y Sus Alrededores y el Sesarrollo de la Misma," oral history interview transcription, 10 November 1965, Texas; Guillén, *La historia del Concilio Latino Americano de Iglesias Cristianas,* 58–61.

9. Alaniz de Casarez, "Datos dados por la hermana del principio de la obra Pentecostal"; Guillén, *La historia del Concilio Latino Americano de Iglesias Cristianas,* 58–61.

10. Guillén, *La historia del Concilio Latino Americano de Iglesias Cristianas,* 50–53; Rodolfo C. Orozco, "El testimonio: Conmovedor de un consagrado pionero," *LLA* (November 1971): 4.

11. John A. Preston, letter to Frodsham, 19 July 1919.

12. Espinosa, *William J. Seymour and the Origins of Global Pentecostalism.*

13. Preston, letter to Frodsham, 19 July 1919.

14. Guillén, *La historia del Concilio Latino Americano de Iglesias Cristianas,* 58–77.

15. Ibid.

16. June Macklin, "Curanderismo and Espiritismo," in *The Chicano Experience,* ed. Stanley A. West and June Macklin (Boulder, CO: Westview Press, 1979), 217–223.

17. The words *curanderismo* and *curandera* come from the Spanish *curar,* which means to cure or heal. Antonio N. Zavaleta, "The Medieval Antecedents of Border Pseudo-Religious Folk Beliefs," *Borderlands* 5, no. 2 (Spring 1982): 192; Beatrice A. Roeder, *Chicano Folk Medicine from Los Angeles, California* (Berkeley: University

of California Press, 1988), 147; Claudia Madsen, *A Study of Change in Mexican Folk Medicine* (New Orleans, LA: Middle American Research Institute, 1965), 95–98.

18. Guillén, *La historia del Concilio Latino Americano de Iglesias Cristianas,* 60–77.

19. Ibid.

20. Ibid.

21. Ibid.

22. Ibid.

23. Ibid.

24. John A. Preston, "A Plea for Mexicans," *TLRE* (January 1913): 16–17; "God Visiting San Antonio with Mighty Power," *Word and Witness,* 20 February 1913: 1; G. W. Miller, "Falfurrias, Tex.," *Word and Witness,* 20 June 1913: 5; G. W. Miller, "Mission School," *Word and Witness,* 20 October 1913: 3; Guillén, *La historia del Concilio Latino Americano de Iglesias Cristianas,* 60–67.

25. Arnulfo M. López, application blank for Ordination Certificate for the Assemblies of God (1916, 1923); Guillén, *La historia del Concilio Latino Americano de Iglesias Cristianas,* 50–57.

26. Guillén, *La historia del Concilio Latino Americano de Iglesias Cristianas,* 50–57.

27. Ibid.

28. Arnulfo M. López, "A Mexican Pastor's Testimony," *TWE,* 6 January 1917: 16; Arnulfo M. López, "Brother López Makes His Report," *TWE,* 2 June 1917: 13.

29. Guillén, *La historia del Concilio Latino Americano de Iglesias Cristianas,* 50–57.

30. Winsett wrote, "We preach every day to hundreds of Mexicans, who give such earnest attention that it always touches my heart. . . . We had distributed about three thousand tracts, besides many gospels." R. E. Winsett, "El Paso, Texas," *Evening Light and Church of God Evangel,* 15 May 1919: 6.

31. Carrie Judd Montgomery, "El Paso, Texas," *Triumphs of Faith* (December 1912): 275–276.

32. Rodolfo Orozco, "El testimonio: Conmovedor de un consagrado pionero," *LLA* (November 1971): 4.

33. Guillén, *La historia del Concilio Latino Americano de Iglesias Cristianas,* 74–76.

34. Ibid.

35. Ibid.

36. Ibid.

37. Philippians 4:13 and 1 John 4:4 (King James Version). For evidence of this fatalism, see Gamio, *Mexican Immigration to the United States,* 108–127, and the discussion regarding Father Virgilio Elizondo's claim about the fatalistic tendencies in Mexican Catholicism in Andrés G. Guerrero, *A Chicano Theology* (Maryknoll, NY: Orbis Books, 2008), 69, 72–73.

38. Miller, "Falfurrias, Tex.," 5; Preston, "A Plea for Mexicans," 16.

39. John A. Preston, "A Great Opportunity in the Mexican Work," *TWE,* 11 March 1916: 12.

40. Charles Fox Parham, *Kol Kare Bomidbar: A Voice Crying out in the Wilderness* (Baxter Springs, KS: Apostolic Faith Bible College, 1902 [reprint 1910]), 107.

41. Miller called some Mexicans "waifes" and "dirtiest little Aztecs." Miller, "Falfurrias, Tex.," 5. For the claim that Catholics were under spiritual bondage, see H. C.

Ball, "Mexican Work at Ricardo, Tex." *TWE,* 12 February 1916: 12; Alice E. Luce, "Open Doors in Mexico," *TWE,* 17 November 1917; H. C. Ball, "Revival Work among the Mexicans," *TPE,* 26 October 1935: 4.

42. Carrie Judd Montgomery, "El Paso, Texas," *Triumphs of Faith* (December 1912): 275–276; Miller, "Falfurrias, Tex.," 5.

43. Preston ministered until at least 1919. In August of that year, he was accused of being "ineffective" among the Mexicans because he could not speak Spanish very well. Preston vehemently denied these allegations, saying that he ministered to Mexicans throughout the Southwest and northern Mexico. Preston, letter to Frodsham, 19 July 1919.

3. Their Salvation May Depend on Us

1. John A. Preston, "A Great Opportunity in the Mexican Work," *TWE,* 11 March 1916: 12.

2. H. C. Ball, n/t, *LLA* (March 1966); H. C. Ball, "How I Received the Baptism," *TPE,* 18 July 1931: 3; Victor De Leon, *The Silent Pentecostals* (Taylors, SC: Faith Printing Company, 1979), 14–19.

3. David Montejano, *Anglos and Mexicans in the Making of Texas, 1836–1986* (Austin: University of Texas Press, 1994); James A. Sandos, *Rebellion in the Borderlands* (Norman: University of Oklahoma Press, 1992).

4. Ball wrote, "While they [Mexican workers] are excellent workers, they need American oversight." H. C. Ball, "A Call for More Laborers for the Mexican Work," *TWE,* 24 March 1917: 13; H. C. Ball, letter to J. R. Flower, 8 December 1924; J. W. Welch, letter to H. C. Ball, 11 November 1924; H. C. Ball, "Revival Work among the Mexicans," *TPE,* October 26, 1935.

5. H. C. Ball, "A Call for More Laborers for the Mexican Work," 13; H. C. Ball, letter to J. R. Flower, 8 December 1924; J. W. Welch, letter to H. C. Ball, 11 November 1924; H. C. Ball, "Revival Work among the Mexicans."

6. De Leon's history is important because it is based on a number of interviews with now-deceased pioneers. I thus treat it as a primary and a secondary source. De Leon, *The Silent Pentecostals,* 14–17.

7. Ibid.

8. H. C. Ball, n/t, *LLA* (March 1966); Miguel Guillén, *La historia del Concilio Latino Americano de Iglesias Cristianas* (Brownsville, TX: Latin American Council of Christian Churches, 1992), 65.

9. H. C. Ball, n/t, *LLA* (March 1966); Guillén, *La historia del Concilio Latino Americano,* 65.

10. H. C. Ball, "How I Received the Baptism," 3.

11. Ibid.; H. C. Ball, "Revival Work among the Mexicans," 2–3; De Leon, *The Silent Pentecostals,* 16–17, 42.

12. "The origin of the Latin American District [i.e., Latino AG] goes back to the ordination of H. C. Ball, January 10, 1915." De Leon, *The Silent Pentecostals,* 43.

13. H. C. Ball, "How I Received the Baptism," 3; H. C. Ball, "Revival Work among the Mexicans," 2–3; H. C. Ball, "I Remember," *TPE,* 22 March 1964: 7.

14. H. C. Ball, n/t, *TWE*, 24 April 1915: 1.

15. Ibid.; John A. Preston, "Work among the Mexicans in the War Zone," *TWE*, 22 May 1915: 4; John A. Preston, "The Mexican Work," *Word and Witness* (August 1915): 2.

16. Preston, "Work among the Mexicans in the War Zone," 4; Preston, "The Mexican Work," 2; F. A. Hale, "Kingsville," *Word and Witness* (August 1915): 3; De Leon, *The Silent Pentecostals*, 43.

17. H. C. Ball, "Gulf Storm Destroys Pentecostal Property," *TWE*, 9 September 1916: 7.

18. Guillén, *La historia del Concilio Latino Americano de Iglesias Cristianas*, 65–67.

19. De Leon, *The Silent Pentecostals*, 42–44.

20. H. C. Ball, "Gulf Storm," 7; Guillén, *La historia del Concilio Latino Americano de Iglesias Cristianas*, 65–67.

21. H. C. Ball, "Work amongst the Mexicans: One of Villa's Men Captured by the Holy Spirit," *TWE*, 11 November 1916; H. C. Ball, "The Mexican Work," *TWE*, 12 January 1918: 10.

22. H. C. Ball, "The Present Condition of the Lower Mexican Work," *TWE*, 20 October 1917: 9.

23. De Leon, *The Silent Pentecostals*, 46–48.

24. Ibid.

25. H. C. Ball, "Forty-Three Years of Progress in the Latin American District," *TPE*, January 25, 1959: 14.

26. Ibid.; De Leon, *The Silent Pentecostals*, 98–99; Guillén, *La historia del Concilio Latino Americano de Iglesias Cristianas*, 79–80.

27. De Leon, *The Silent Pentecostals*, 44–46, 94; Guillén, *La historia del Concilio Latino Americano de Iglesias Cristianas*, 79–80.

28. De Leon, *The Silent Pentecostals*, 45; Guillén, *La historia del Concilio Latino Americano de Iglesias Cristianas*, 79–81.

29. Participants in the second convention included H. C. and Sunshine Ball, Felix Hale, Francisco Olazábal, Floyd Baker, Concepción Suárez, Mr. and Mrs. Alberto Hines, Demetrio Bazan, Francisco Banda, Isabel Flores, Rodolfo Orozco, Maggie Caslin, Alma English, and Evelyn Campbell. No author listed, "Historia de los primeros 50 años de las Asambleas de Dios Latinas," *LLA* (April 1966): 2.

30. H. C. Ball, "A Report of the Spanish Pentecostal Convention," *TCE*, 28 December 1918: 7; De Leon, *The Silent Pentecostals*, 46; no author listed, "Historia de los primeros 50 años de las Asambleas de Dios Latinas," 2.

31. Gastón Espinosa, "Francisco Olazábal and Latino Pentecostal Revivalism in the Borderlands," in *Embodying the Spirit: New Perspectives on North American Revivalism,* ed. Michael McClymond (Baltimore, MD: Johns Hopkins University Press, 2004), 125–146, 305–309.

32. Ibid., 125–146, 305–309.

33. De Leon, *The Silent Pentecostals*, 27–28, 36.

34. H. C. Ball, "A Report of the Spanish Pentecostal Convention," 7.

35. H. C. Ball, "Mexican Work in San Antonio, Texas," *TCE*, 27 July 1918: 8; no author listed, n/t, *LLA* (March 1966).

36. De Leon, *The Silent Pentecostals*, 46; Guillén, *La historia del Concilio Latino Americano de Iglesias Cristianas*, 52–55.

37. "We believe that the seed to be sown that will fall upon the best ground and bring forth a hundred fold is that sown through the establishment of missions where a pastor, visiting or resident, can pastor the flock and lead them into the truth step by step." H. C. Ball, "Mexican Work in the South," *TCE*, 15 June 1918: 3.

38. Ibid.

39. By 1926, Ball's hymnal was used by Assemblies of God missionaries in Peru and other Latin American countries. H. C. Ball, "Report of the Pentecostal Work in Texas, New Mexico, Colorado, Arizona, and Old Mexico," *TPE*, 1 November 1919: 22; De Leon, *The Silent Pentecostals*, 50; H. C. Ball, "Story of Latin-American Pentecostal Work," *TPE*, 2 September 1931: 1, 14–15.

40. Arnulfo M. López, "A Mexican Pastor's Testimony," *TWE*, 6 January 1917: 16; A. M. López, "Brother López Makes His Report," *TWE*, 2 June 1917: 13.

41. H. C. Ball and A. E. Luce, *Glimpses of Our Latin-American Work in the United States and Mexico* (Springfield, MO: Foreign Missions Department, 1940), 14.

42. H. C. Ball, "Report of the Pentecostal Work in Texas, New Mexico, Colorado, Arizona, and Old Mexico," 22.

43. In 1938, H. C. Ball visited Cuba. Sunshine Ball, "En Route to Peru," *TPE*, 20 August 1938: 7, 11.

44. H. C. Ball, "A Report of the Spanish Pentecostal Convention," 7; José Girón, "Historia de los primeros 50 años de las Asambleas de Dios," *LLA* (November 1966): 9; Sunshine L. Ball, "Yo me acuerdo," *LLA* (December 1968): 9–10.

45. H. C. Ball, "Report of the Pentecostal Work in Texas, New Mexico, Colorado, Arizona, and Old Mexico," 22; no author listed, "Historia de los primeros 50 años de las Asambleas de Dios Latinas," *LLA* (April 1966): 2, 9–10.

46. H. C. Ball, "The Present Condition of the Lower Mexican Work," 9; H. C. Ball, "Mexican Gospel Wagon," *TWE*, 19 January 1918: 11; no author listed, "Historia de los primeros 50 años," *LLA* (May 1966): 3, 11; n/t, *LLA* (June 1966): 3, 10.

4. The Gringos Have Control

1. Gastón Espinosa, "Francisco Olazábal and Latino Pentecostal Revivalism in the Borderlands," in *Embodying the Spirit: New Perspectives on North American Revivalism*, ed. Michael McClymond (Baltimore, MD: John Hopkins University Press, 2004), 125–146, 305–309.

2. Francisco Olazábal, Ordination Certificate, Assemblies of God. He applied for ordination on February 5, 1918, and was ordained by Robert J. Craig in the Northern California District of the Assemblies of God on February 14, 1918.

3. For a discussion of the centrality of El Paso for Mexicans arriving in the United States and of Protestants in the city, see Mario T. García, *Desert Immigrants* (New Haven, CT: Yale University Press, 1981), 3–8, 14–17, 219–222.

4. Francisco Olazábal, n/t, *TPE*, 24 January 1920: 12; Francisco Olazábal, n/t, *TPE*, June 1920.

5. Francisco Olazábal, "A Mexican Witness," *TWE*, 16 October 1920; Francisco Olazábal, "God Is Blessing on the Mexican Border," *TWE*, 1 October 1921: 10; n/t, *TPE*, 4 March 1922.

6. Francisco Olazábal, n/t, *TPE*, 24 January 1920: 2; Olazábal, "A Mexican Witness"; Olazábal, "God Is Blessing on the Mexican Border," 10; no author listed, n/t, *TPE*, 4 March 1922.

7. Francisco Olazábal, n/t, *TPE*, 24 January 1920: 2; Olazábal, "A Mexican Witness"; Olazábal, "God Is Blessing on the Mexican Border," 10; no author listed, n/t, *TPE*, 4 March 1922.

8. N/t, *TPE*, 1 November 1919: 22; Francisco Olazábal, letter to Maria Sandoval, 16 February 1923.

9. H. C. Ball, "Report of the Pentecostal Work in Texas, New Mexico, Colorado, Arizona, and Old Mexico," *TPE*, 1 November 1919: 22; Latin American Council of Christian Churches, *Seminario del CLADIC* (Los Angeles: Latin American Council of Christian Churches, 1979), 7–8; Miguel Guillén, *La historia del Concilio Latino Americano de Iglesias Cristianas* (Brownsville, TX: Latin American Council of Christian Churches, 1992), 104–106; Frank Olazábal Jr., telephone interview by Gastón Espinosa, May 1998.

10. Ball, "Report of the Pentecostal Work in Texas, New Mexico, Colorado, Arizona, and Old Mexico," 22; Latin American Council of Christian Churches, *Seminario del CLADIC*, 7–8; Guillén, *La historia del Concilio Latino Americano de Iglesias Cristianas*, 104–106; Frank Olazábal Jr., telephone interview by Gastón Espinosa, May 1998.

11. Ball, "Report of the Pentecostal Work in Texas, New Mexico, Colorado, Arizona, and Old Mexico"; Francisco Olazábal, letter to Maria Sandoval, 16 February 1923.

12. For Catholic complaints about Protestant growth, see Linna E. Bresette, *Mexicans in the United States* (Washington, DC: National Catholic Welfare Conference, 1929), 33–43; Jay P. Dolan and Gilberto M. Hinojosa, eds., *Mexican Americans and the Catholic Church, 1900–1965* (Notre Dame, IN: University of Notre Dame Press, 1994), 5, 20, 41, 44, 68, 80, 95 131, 155, 159, 259–260, 264, 274, 282–285, 287, 298–300, 302. For Protestant complaints about Pentecostal competition and growth, see Manuel Gamio, *The Mexican Immigrant* (Chicago: University of Chicago Press, 1931), 219–223; Theodore Abel, *Protestant Home Missions to Catholic Immigrants* (New York: Institute of Social and Religious Research, 1933), 52–55.

13. H. C. Ball, "Mexican Work in the South," *TCE*, 15 June 1918: 3.

14. Alice E. Luce, "Paul's Missionary Methods," *TPE*, 8 January 1921: 6–7; Alice E. Luce, "Paul's Missionary Methods," *TPE*, 22 January 1921: 6, 11; Alice E. Luce, "Paul's Missionary Methods," *TPE*, 5 February 1921: 6–7; Alice E. Luce, "Scriptural Methods in Missionary Work," *TPE*, 9 May 1931: 8; Gary B. McGee, "Pioneers of Pentecost: Alice E. Luce and Henry C. Ball," *A/G Heritage* (Summer 1985): 5, 6, 12.

15. Guillén, *La historia del Concilio Latino Americano de Iglesias Cristianas,* 75–114; Espinosa, "Francisco Olazábal and Latino Pentecostal Revivalism in the Borderlands," 125–146; Frank Olazábal Jr., telephone interview by Espinosa, May 1998.

16. Based on eyewitness interviews, Miguel Guillén states that Ball "informally assumed the role of leader of the work among Mexicans for it was he who presided at the convention." Guillén, *La historia del Concilio Latino Americano de Iglesias Cristianas,* 79–80; De Leon, *The Silent Pentecostals,* 98–99; Espinosa, "Francisco Olazábal and Latino Pentecostal Revivalism in the Borderlands," 125–146; Frank Olazábal Jr., telephone interview by Espinosa, May 1998.

17. De Leon, *The Silent Pentecostals,* 98–99; Guillén, *La historia del Concilio Latino Americano de Iglesias Cristianas,* 79–80.

18. De Leon, *The Silent Pentecostals,* 98–99; Guillén, *La historia del Concilio Latino Americano de Iglesias Cristianas,* 79–80.

19. Francisco Olazábal before the Ninth Annual Convention of the Los Angeles District Epworth League, held at Gardena on 9 May 1913.

20. Ibid.

21. Guillén, *La historia del Concilio Latino Americano de Iglesias Cristianas,* 75–114; "Francisco Olazábal and Latino Pentecostal Revivalism in the Borderlands," 125–146; Frank Olazábal Jr., telephone interview by Espinosa, May 1998.

22. Ball, "Report of the Pentecostal Work in Texas, New Mexico, Colorado, Arizona, and Old Mexico," 22; De Leon, *The Silent Pentecostals,* 27; Everett A. Wilson, "Robert J. Craig's Glad Tidings and the Realization of a Vision for 100,000 Souls," *A/G Heritage* (Summer 1988): 8–11.

23. Francisco Olazábal, letter to Maria Sandoval, 8 December 1922.

24. Ball, "Mexican Work in the South," 3. Rev. Elvira Perales noted how Ball could become scornful and angry with his Mexican workers. Elvira Perales, "Una mujer pionera," *LLA* (July 1967): 6, 8; De Leon, *The Silent Pentecostals,* 29–30, 98–99.

25. Guillén, *La historia del Concilio Latino Americano de Iglesias Cristianas,* 75–114; Espinosa, "Francisco Olazábal and Latino Pentecostal Revivalism in the Borderlands," 125–146; Frank Olazábal Jr., telephone interview by Espinosa, May 1998.

26. H. C. Ball, "A Call for More Laborers for the Mexican Work," *TWE,* 24 March 1917: 13.

27. H. C. Ball, letter to J. R. Flower, 10 January 1917.

28. John A. Preston, letter to J. R. Flower, 19 July 1919.

29. Enemecio Alaniz, letter to E. N. Bell, 19 October 1922.

30. Ibid.

31. Francisco Olazábal, letter to Maria Sandoval, 8 December 1922.

32. Frank Olazábal Jr., telephone interview by Espinosa, May 1998.

33. Francisco Olazábal, "The Mexican Work at El Paso," *TPE,* 30 September 1922: 13; Mario Barrera, *Race and Class in the Southwest* (Notre Dame, IN: University of Notre Dame Press, 1979).

34. Francisco Olazábal, letter to Maria Sandoval, 8 December 1922; Guillén, *La historia del Concilio Latino Americano de Iglesias Cristianas,* 75–114; Espinosa,

"Francisco Olazábal and Latino Pentecostal Revivalism in the Borderlands," 125–146; Frank Olazábal Jr., telephone interview by Espinosa, May 1998.

35. Francisco Olazábal, letter to Maria Sandoval, 8 December 1922; De Leon, *The Silent Pentecostals*, 99–101; Guillén, *La historia del Concilio Latino Americano de Iglesias Cristianas*, 82–90.

36. Francisco Olazábal, letter to Maria Sandoval, 8 December 1922; De Leon, *The Silent Pentecostals*, 99–101; Guillén, *La historia del Concilio Latino Americano de Iglesias Cristianas*, 82–90.

37. H. C. Ball, letter to J. W. Welch, 7 October 1924; De Leon, *The Silent Pentecostals*, 99–101.

38. Francisco Olazábal, letter to Maria Sandoval, 8 December 1922; De Leon, *The Silent Pentecostals*, 99–101; Guillén, *La historia del Concilio Latino Americano de Iglesias Cristianas*, 82–90.

39. Guillén, *La historia del Concilio Latino Americano de Iglesias Cristianas*, 80–91.

40. Ibid.

41. Ibid.

42. Ibid.

43. Francisco Olazábal, letter to Maria Sandoval, 8 December 1922; Guillén, *La historia del Concilio Latino Americano de Iglesias Cristianas*, 80–91; Frank Olazábal Jr., telephone interview by Espinosa, May 1998.

44. "All of the brothers in the convention . . . voted in favor of all of the propositions that I presented." Francisco Olazábal, letter to Maria Sandoval, 8 December 1922.

45. Francisco Olazábal, letter to Maria Sandoval, 8 December 1922; H. C. Ball, letter to J. R. Flower, 9 December 1924; H. C. Ball to Robert and Marie Brown, 13 October 1931.

46. Francisco Olazábal, letter to Maria Sandoval, 8 December 1922; H. C. Ball, letter to J. R. Flower, 9 December 1924; H. C. Ball to Robert and Marie Brown, 13 October 1931.

47. Francisco Olazábal, letter to Maria Sandoval, 8 December 1922; H. C. Ball, letter to J. R. Flower, 9 December 1924; H. C. Ball to Robert and Marie Brown, 13 October 1931.

48. The "accusation against me was that I was not 'sincere,' since I had offered to buy some blackboards for a Bible Inst. he was to found in El Paso. Well, I explained to the Council [J. R. Flower] that my offer was then still good; I would have bought the blackboards when the building was up. Moreover, he had never written me that he was ready to receive them." H. C. Ball, letter to Robert and Marie Brown, 13 October 1931.

49. Guillén, *La historia del Concilio Latino Americano de Iglesias Cristianas*, 104–106; Frank Olazábal Jr., telephone interview by Espinosa, May 1998.

50. Guillén, *La historia del Concilio Latino Americano de Iglesias Cristianas*, 104–106; Frank Olazábal Jr., telephone interview by Espinosa, May 1998.

51. Francisco Olazábal, letter to Maria Sandoval, 8 December 1922; Francisco Olazábal, letter to Maria Sandoval, 16 February 1923; Frank Olazábal Jr., telephone interview by Espinosa, May 1998.

52. De Leon, *The Silent Pentecostals,* 99; Frank Olazábal Jr., telephone interview by Espinosa, May 1998.

53. Guillén, *La historia del Concilio Latino Americano de Iglesias Cristianas,* 86–91; Francisco Olazábal, letter to Maria Sandoval, 8 December 1922; Frank Olazábal Jr., telephone interview by Espinosa, May 1998.

54. The twelve core ministers who decided to leave the AG and start CLADIC were Olazábal, López, Flores, C. Suárez, Trujillo, Alaniz, Valadez, Brigido Zavala, Antonio Rodríguez, Salud Robles, Julia Galvan, and Ernesto Saenz. Guillén, *La historia del Concilio Latino Americano de Iglesias Cristianas,* 80–95.

55. Guillén, *La historia del Concilio Latino Americano de Iglesias Cristianas;* Frank Olazábal Jr., telephone interview by Espinosa, May 1998; Francisco Olazábal, "Carta pastoral del presidente del Concilio Mexicano de las Iglesias Cristianas 'Pentecostales,' a las iglesias que lo integran," *EMC* (July 1924): 12–13.

56. Francisco Olazábal, letter to Maria Sandoval, 15 March 1923.

57. "Historia de los primeros 50 años de las Asambleas de Dios Latinas: Epoca de las Conferencias Biblicas," *LLA* (May 1966): 3, 11; De Leon, *The Silent Pentecostals,* 99–100.

58. Ball's letters reinforced the feeling in Springfield that they needed an "American" overseer. H. C. Ball, letter to J. R. Flower, 8 December 1924, San Antonio, Texas; J. W. Welch, letter to H. C. Ball, 11 November 1924, Springfield, Missouri; Nellie Bazan, "Historia de los primeros 50 años de las Asambleas de Dios: Segunda parte de mi testimonio," *LLA* (November 1967): 7–8; Nellie Bazan and Elizabeth B. and Don Martínez Jr., *Enviados de Dios: Demetrio y Nellie Bazan* (Miami: Editorial Vida, 1987), 35–42; De Leon, *The Silent Pentecostals,* 98–100; Francisco Olazábal, letter to Maria Sandoval, 30 March 1923.

59. Francisco Olazábal, letters to Maria Sandoval, 16 February 1923; 30 March 1923; and 26 April 1923. De Leon, *The Silent Pentecostals,* 135–136.

60. Francisco Olazábal, letters to Maria Sandoval, 16 February 1923; 30 March 1923; and 26 April 1923. De Leon, *The Silent Pentecostals,* 98–99, 135.

61. De Leon, *The Silent Pentecostals,* 25–26.

62. Frank Olazábal Jr., telephone interview by Espinosa, May 1998.

63. Francisco Olazábal, letter to Maria Sandoval, 16 February 1923.

64. H. C. Ball, letter to Robert and Marie Brown, 13 October 1931; J. R. Flower to Rev. Kline, 7 February 1933.

65. H. C. Ball, letter to J. R. Evans, 27 October 1931; J. R. Flower, letter to Rev. Kline, 7 February 1933.

66. H. C. Ball, letter to J. R. Evans, 27 October 1931; H. C. Ball, letter to J. R. Evans, 17 December 1931; H. C. Ball, letter to Robert and Marie Brown, 13 October 1931.

67. Guillén, *La historia del Concilio Latino Americano de Iglesias Cristianas,* passim; Espinosa, "Francisco Olazábal and Latino Pentecostal Revivalism in the Borderlands," 125–146.

68. Spencer Duryee, "The Great Aztec," *Christian Herald* (August 1936): 5–8.

69. Espinosa, "Francisco Olazábal and Latino Pentecostal Revivalism in the Borderlands," 125–146.

5. Pentecostal Origins in the Southwest and the Struggle for Self-Determination

1. H. C. Ball, "Pentecost Coming to Latin America," *TPE*, 30 April 1938: 1, 10–11; Elvira Perales, "Historia de los 50 años de las Asambleas de Dios: Una mujer pionera," *LLA* (July 1967): 5, 8.

2. Alice E. Luce, Missionary Update Form, Assemblies of God, ca. 1920; Alice E. Luce, "The Latin-American Pentecostal Work," *TPE*, 25 June 1927: 6–7.

3. Walter J. Hollenweger, *The Pentecostals* (1972; repr., Peabody, MA: Hendrickson Publishing, 1988), 24.

4. This figure is based on references to Mexicans and other Latinos in the early literature, such as the following: no author listed, "Work among Spanish," *Pisgah* (January 1909): 11–12; no author listed, "A Revival in Los Angeles," *Pisgah* (December 1910): 13; no author listed, "Our Spanish Meeting," *The Upper Room* (January 1911): 1; A. C. Valdez with James F. Scheer, *Fire on Azusa Street* (Costa Mesa, CA: Gift Publications, 1980). Arthur Osterberg stated that "hundreds" of Catholics attended the Azusa Street meetings, "many" of whom were Mexican. Arthur G. Osterberg, "Oral History of the Life of Arthur G. Osterberg and the Azusa Street Revival," interview by Jerry Jensen and Jonathan Perkin, transcribed 1966, Flower Pentecostal Heritage Center, 11. The fact that Seymour decided to publish Abundio L. and Rosa López's testimony in English and especially Spanish would also seem to indicate that a large enough number attended and/or were already in the Pentecostal community to warrant such an inclusion. It was also no doubt an evangelistic strategy. This was the only non-English testimony or article ever published in Seymour's *Apostolic Faith* newspaper. No author listed, "Spanish Receive the Pentecost," *AF* (Los Angeles) (October 1906): 4.

5. As cited in Robert Mapes Anderson, *The Vision of the Disinherited* (Peabody, MA: Hendrickson Publishers, 1979), 122–123; Sarah Parham, *The Life of Charles F. Parham* (Baxter Springs, KS: Apostolic Faith Bible College, 1977), 302.

6. No author listed, "Work among Spanish," 11–12.

7. Ibid.

8. Ibid.

9. Hispanos are people of Spanish and Mexican ancestry who live in New Mexico and trace their roots back to the Spanish founding of New Mexico in 1598. They normally do not like to be called "Mexican" or "Mexican American" because they arrived in New Mexico during the Spanish colonization period, before the birth of modern Mexico in 1821. No author listed, "A Revival in Los Angeles," 13.

10. No author listed, "Our Spanish Meeting," 1.

11. This information in based on a review of Abundio López's ordination applications and certificates, which are housed in my Latino Pentecostal History Collection.

12. Shumway notes in his 1914 thesis that people at the Arroyo Seco Camp meeting in 1913 also came from Mexico. He was most likely referring to the Valenzuelas because George and Carrie Judd Montgomery preached alongside Mexican evangelist Genaro Valenzuela and Romanita Carbajal de Valenzuela in El Paso and northern Mexico. Charles W. Shumway, "A Study of the 'Gift of Tongues'" (A.B. thesis, University of

Southern California, Los Angeles, July 1914), 191; Carrie Judd Montgomery, "A Recent Trip to Mexico," *Triumphs of Faith* (December 1913): 269–271; Carrie Judd Montgomery, *Under His Wings* (Los Angeles: Stationers Corporation Printers, 1936), 200–205; Valdez with Scheer, *Fire on Azusa Street*, 27, 41–42; Douglas J. Nelson, "'For Such a Time as This': The Story of William J. Seymour and the Azusa Street Revival" (Ph.D. diss., University of Birmingham, England, 1981), 107.

13. Frank Olazábal Jr., telephone interview by Gastón Espinosa, May 1998.

14. Valdez wrote about his memories in *Fire on Azusa Street*.

15. For more on George and Carrie Montgomery, see Jennifer Stock, "George S. Montgomery: Businessman for the Gospel," *A/G Heritage* (Summer 1989): 12–14, 20; Juan L. Lugo, *Pentecostés en Puerto Rico o La vida de un misionero* (San Juan, PR: Puerto Rico Gospel Press, 1951).

16. Manuel Vizcarra, *Ocupante en enseñar* (Los Angeles: Asambleas Apostólicas, Depto. de Ed., 1977), 3; Clifton L. Holland, *The Religious Dimension in Hispanic Los Angeles* (South Pasadena, CA: William Carey Library, 1974), 356; *Los Angeles City Directory* (1906): 41; *Los Angeles City Directory* (1907): 35; *Los Angeles City Directory* (1911): 31.

17. *Los Angeles County City Directory* (1912): 33, 1552; William McEuen, "A Survey of the Mexicans in Los Angeles" (M.A. thesis, University of Southern California, 1914), 38; Holland, *The Religious Dimension in Hispanic Los Angeles,* 356–357.

18. Nellie Rangel asserts that Valenzuela attended Azusa Street but offers no concrete primary source evidence. While Romanita may not have attended the revival at its peak, there is little reason to doubt that she probably visited the mission around 1911, if not sooner. Nellie Rangel, *Historia de la Confederación Nacional de Sociedades Femeniles "Dorcas"* (Rancho Cucamonga, CA: Apostolic Assembly of the Faith in Christ Jesus, 1986), 23.

19. The work Romanita founded soon spread to the neighboring states of Chihuahua, Durango, Coahuila, and other states in Mexico, so that by 1932 there were over 26 congregations and 800 members. Manuel Jesús Gaxiola y Gaxiola, *La serpiente y la paloma* (South Pasadena, CA: William Carey Library, 1970), 4–5, 81, 140–141.

20. George and Carrie Montgomery, "Notes by the Way: El Paso, Texas," *Triumphs of Faith* (December 1912): 275–276; Carrie Montgomery, "A Recent Trip to Mexico," *Triumphs of Faith* (December 1913): 269–71; Carrie Judd Montgomery, *"Under His Wings"* (Los Angeles: Stationers Corporation Printing, 1936), 203–204.

21. Gaxiola y Gaxiola, *La serpiente y la paloma,* 157; Ernesto S. Cantú and José Ortega A., eds., *Historia de la Asamblea Apostólica de la Fe en Cristo Jesús* (Mentone, CA: Sal's Printing Service, 1966), 5–6.

22. For information on the Apostolic Assembly of the Faith in Christ Jesus, see Cantú and Ortega, *Historia de la Asamblea Apostólica de la Fe en Cristo Jesús,* 6–7; Gaxiola y Gaxiola, *La serpiente y la paloma,* 157–158.

23. Cantú and Ortega, *Historia de la Asamblea Apostólica de la Fe en Cristo Jesús,* 6–7; Gaxiola y Gaxiola, *La serpiente y la paloma,* 157–158.

24. Cantú and Ortega, *Historia de la Asamblea Apostólica de la Fe en Cristo Jesús,* 6–7; Gaxiola Gaxiola, *La serpiente y la paloma,* 157; Holland, *The Religious Dimension in Hispanic Los Angeles,* 356.

25. While H. C. Ball began Pentecostal evangelistic work in 1915, the Apostolic Assembly claims that its roots go back to the work of Juan Navarro Martínez in 1909 and Francisco Llorente in 1912, although some argue that it was not really organized as a definable movement until 1916 by Llorente, Antonio Castañeda-Nava, and Marcial de la Cruz. More importantly, although De Leon claims that the Latino AG work was organized by Euro-Americans like Ball and Alice Luce, it is clear that the work began earlier, in 1909, through the preaching of Euro-Americans and their Mexican converts. De Leon, *The Silent Pentecostals,* 43; Cantú and Ortega, *Historia de la Asamblea Apostólica de la Fe en Cristo Jesús,* 6–21.

26. Alice Eveline Luce, "Declaration of Alien about to Depart for the United States," Form No. 228 (Customs Card), December 13, 1917; Alice E. Luce, U.S. Certificate of Citizenship, January 10, 1930. Also see *LLA* (June 1966): 10.

27. Alice Eveline Luce, "Declaration of Alien about to Depart for the United States," Form No. 228 (Customs Card), December 13, 1917; Alice E. Luce, U.S. Certificate of Citizenship, January 10, 1930. Also see *LLA* (June 1966): 10.

28. John León Lugo, "Among the Mexicans in Los Angeles," *TWE,* June 17, 1916.

29. Mr. and Mrs. E. Crawford, "Mexican Work in Los Angeles," *TWE,* June 17, 1916: 15.

30. Adolph Rosa, "A Portuguese Minister Receives His Pentecost," *AF* (Los Angeles) 1, no. 2 (October 1906): 1; Adolph Rosa, "In San Francisco," *AF* (Los Angeles) 1, no. 6 (February–March 1907): 3.

31. R. J. Craig, "San Francisco, Cal.," *The Pentecostal Herald,* 19 October 1918: 4.

32. Alice E. Luce, "Mexican Work in California," *TWE,* 20 April 1918: 11; Alice E. Luce, "Mexican Work in California," *TWE,* 1 September 1923: 13.

33. Luce wrote: "The Mexican population . . . travels from one place to another for work in the fields of beets, beans, and all the different fruits. So we try to follow them, holding meetings in the various centers which are accessible from here [Los Angeles] . . . we keep in touch with them all, sending them large supplies of Gospels and tracts to distribute, upholding them continually in prayer." Alice E. Luce, "Mexican Work in California," *TCE,* 14 December 1918: 14; Alice E. Luce, "Mexican Work in California," *The Pentecostal Herald* (August 1918): 3.

34. Luce, "Mexican Work in California," *TCE,* 14 December 1918: 14; Luce, "Mexican Work in California," *The Pentecostal Herald* (August 1918): 3.

35. Luce, "Mexican Work in California," *TPE,* 1 September 1923: 13.

36. Luce, Missionary Update Form, Assemblies of God, ca. 1920; Luce, "The Latin-American Pentecostal Work," 6–7.

37. Ball claimed that Apostolics entered and split one Mexican Assemblies of God church in Arizona. H. C. Ball, "Report of the Pentecostal Work in Texas, New Mexico, Colorado, Arizona, and Old Mexico," *TPE,* 1 November 1919: 22; Rev. Antonio Meza, taped interview by Gastón Espinosa, 7 December 1996, Oxnard, California.

38. Luce, "Mexican Work in California," *TCE,* 14 December 1918, 14.

39. Ibid., 3.

40. Ibid.

41. Ibid.; Alice E. Luce, Assemblies of God Annual Missionary Form, 1920; Luce, n/t, *TPE,* 24 January 1920; Luce, "Mexican Work in California," *TCE,* 14 December 1918, 14; De Leon, *The Silent Pentecostals,* 64.

42. Luce, "Mexican Work in California," *The Pentecostal Herald,* August 1918: 3; Luce, Assemblies of God Annual Missionary Form, 1920; Luce, n/t, *TPE,* 24 January 1920; Luce, "Mexican Work in California," *TCE,* 14 December 1918:14; De Leon, *The Silent Pentecostals,* 64.

43. Alice E. Luce, "Paul's Missionary Methods," *TPE,* 8 January 1921: 6–7; Alice E. Luce, "Paul's Missionary Methods," *TPE,* 22 January 1921: 6, 11; Alice E. Luce, "Paul's Missionary Methods," *TPE,* 5 February 1921: 6–7.

44. Carrie Judd Montgomery, "Mrs. Nuzum in a New Field," *Triumphs of Faith* (January 1912): 9; Montgomery, "Pray for Our Workers in Mexico," *Triumphs of Faith* (March 1912): 72.

45. "Each day we visit them in their homes and talk to them of sin, salvation, the cleansing blood, the new birth, the Holy Spirit, eternity and the need for a speedy preparation for it, and the great danger of delay." C. Nuzum, "The Lord Working in Nogales," *Triumphs of Faith* (April 1915): 86–87; C. Nuzum, "Work among the Mexicans," *Triumphs of Faith* (September 1915): 215.

46. H. C. Ball, "Mexican Border Work Prospers," *TPE,* 20 June 1925: 10.

47. Ibid.

48. No author listed, "Historia de los primeros 50 años de las Asambleas de Dios Latinas," *LLA* (April 1966): 2; L. Y. Kenny, "An Appeal," *TWE,* 4 April 1917; Ball, "Mexican Border Work Prospers," 10; H. C. Ball, "The Work Prospering on the Mexican Border," *TPE,* 8 July 1922: 13.

49. No author listed, "Historia de los primeros 50 años de las Asambleas de Dios Latinas," *LLA* (April 1966): 2; Kenny, "An Appeal"; Ball, "Mexican Border Work Prospers," 10; Ball, "The Work Prospering on the Mexican Border," 13.

50. "For centuries the people of Mexico have been in the grasp of Romanism. They worship the Virgin Mary much more than the Lord Jesus Christ, and their religion has never been the one taught in the New Testament or even the old. How much they need the Gospel." A few years later Ball also wrote: "You say, 'They have Romanism.' Yes, but Romanism is certainly not the gospel as we know the gospel. The worship of saints and idols is certainly not in accordance with God's Word. The gospel is the power of God unto salvation . . . I doubt whether in Romanism there are many saved." H. C. Ball, "Our Latin American Work," *TPE,* 20 November 1932; H. C. Ball, "Revival Work among the Mexicans," *TPE,* 26 October 1935: 2–3; H. C. Ball, "Pentecost Coming to Latin Americans," *TPE,* 30 April 1938: 1.

51. Marez went on to pioneer the Latino Pentecostal Movement in Utah, Colorado, and New Mexico. He founded nine churches in these three states. José F. Marez, "Testifica un veterano," *LLA* (December 1966): 7. Around 1930, Isaaco Morfin conducted evangelistic work in Utah and New Mexico. J. B. Johnson, "The Allelujahs: A Religious Cult in Northern New Mexico," *Southwest Review* (January 1937): 131–139.

52. Kenny, "An Appeal"; Ball, "Our Latin American Work," 8; Ball, "Revival Work among the Mexicans," 2–3; Ball, "Pentecost Coming to Latin America," 1.

53. Ball, "Revival Work among the Mexicans," 2–3.

54. Ball, "Our Latin American Work," 8.

55. No author listed, n/t, *AF* (Los Angeles) (May 1907): 2; Ball, "Report of the Pentecostal Mexican Work in Texas, New Mexico, Colorado, Arizona, and Old Mexico," 22.

56. A. L. Casey, "Worker Speaks in Spanish," *TCE*, 10 October 1914: 3.

57. De Leon, *The Silent Pentecostals*, 104–105.

58. Demetrio Bazan's son, Rev. Alex Bazan, claimed that he had a similar experience of Apostolics visiting his church and challenging him to a public debate while he pastored a Latin District Council church in Monterey, California. Gastón Espinosa taped interview with Rev. Alex Bazan and Anita Bazan, 29 November 1996, Escondido, California.

59. H. C. Ball, letter to Noel Perkin, 18 April 1934.

60. Lillian Valdez and Berta García, "Historia," *LLA* (August 1967): 3.

61. Alice E. Luce, "Pentecost on the Mexican Border: A Stirring Story Given by Miss Alice E. Luce at the General Council Meeting," *TPE*, 11 November 1939: 5.

62. No author listed, "Report of the Pentecostal Mexican Work in Texas, New Mexico, Colorado, Arizona, and Old Mexico," 22.

63. José Girón, "Historia de los primeros 50 años de las Asambleas de Dios," *LLA* (November 1966): 9; De Leon, *The Silent Pentecostals*, 121–122.

64. Johnson, "The Allelujahs," 131–139; De Leon, *The Silent Pentecostals*, 154, 173.

65. Ball, "Pentecost Coming to Latin Americans," 1, 10, 11.

66. For example, Ball made Cecilio Jacinto of Kyle, Texas, learn how to read before he would ordain him to the ministry. De Leon, *The Silent Pentecostals*, 45.

67. Ibid., 46.

68. Alice E. Luce, "Report of the Mexican Work," *TPE*, 14 July 1917: 13; no author listed, "God's Work among the Mexicans: An Encouraging Report from the Texas Border," *TWE*, 6 October 1917: 4.

69. No author listed, "Historia de los primeros 50 años de las Asambleas de Dios Latinas: Epoca de las Conferencias Biblicas," *LLA* (May 1966): 3, 11.

70. No author listed, n/t, *TPE*, 1 November 1919: 22; Latin American Council of Christian Churches, *Seminario del CLADIC* (Los Angeles: Latin American Council of Christian Churches, 1979), 7–8; Miguel Guillén, *La historia del Concilio Latino Americano de Iglesias Cristianas* (Brownsville, TX: Latin American Council of Christian Churches, 1992), 104–106; Frank Olazábal Jr., telephone interview by Gastón Espinosa, May 1998.

71. Alice E. Luce, "Latin American Bible Institute in California," *TPE*, June 1942: 7.

72. Alice E. Luce, "Bible School Opens at San Diego," *TPE*, 13 November 1926: 4; H. C. Ball, "Latin American Bible Institute," *TPE*, 4 December 1926: 18; no author listed, "Historia de los primeros 50 años de las Asambleas de Dios Latinas: La Epoca de los Institutos Biblicos," *LLA* (June 1968): 3, 10.

73. Alice E. Luce, "The Strangers within Our Gates," *TLRE* (December 1930): 18.

74. Alice E. Luce, "Latin-American Pentecostal Work," *TPE*, 25 June 1927; De Leon, *The Silent Pentecostals*, 51; Inez Spence, *H. C. Ball: Man of Action* (Springfield, MO: Foreign Missions Department, ca. 1961), 11.

75. H. C. Ball, letter to Noel Perkin, 27 May 1927, San Antonio, Texas; Luce, "Latin-American Pentecostal Work," 6–7.

76. Mario T. García, *Desert Immigrants: The Mexicans of El Paso, 1880–1920* (New Haven, CT: Yale University Press, 1980).

77. Deborah J. Baldwin, *Protestants and the Mexican Revolution: Missionaries, Ministers, and Social Change* (Urbana: University of Illinois Press, 1990), 127ff.

78. For a discussion of the origins of the Assemblies of God in Mexico, El Salvador, and Guatemala, see Luisa Jeter de Walker, *Siembra y cosecha*, vol. 1 (Deerfield, FL: Editorial Vida, 1990).

79. John L. Franklin, "Latin America Calling," *TPE*, 5 June 1943: 1.

80. R. Francisco Brackenridge and Francisco O. García-Treto, *Iglesia Presbyteriana: A History of Presbyterians and Mexican Americans in the Southwest* (San Antonio, TX: Trinity University Press, 1987), 158.

81. David G. Gutiérrez, *Walls and Mirrors: Mexican Americans, Mexican Immigrants, and the Politics of Ethnicity* (Berkeley: University of California Press, 1995), 72; Francisco E. Balderama and Raymond Rodríguez, *Decade of Betrayal: Mexican Repatriation in the 1930s* (Albuquerque: University of New Mexico Press, 1995).

82. Brackenridge and García-Treto, *Iglesia Presbyteriana*, 158; Joel N. Martínez, "The South Central Jurisdiction," in *Each in Our Own Tongue: A History of Hispanic United Methodism*, ed. Justo L. González (Nashville, TN: Abingdon Press, 1991), 50.

83. H. C. Ball, "Story of Latin-American Pentecostal Work," *TPE*, 5 September 1931: 1, 14; H. C. Ball, "Great Blessing at Latin American Council," *TPE*, 13 February 1932: 11.

84. "'*El Azteca*': Francisco Olazábal and Latino Pentecostal Charisma, Power, and Healing in the Borderlands," *Journal of the American Academy of Religion* 67, no. 3 (September 1999): 597–616.

85. Ball, "Great Blessing at Latin American Council," 11.

86. See photograph P8707-Richey in the Flower Pentecostal Heritage Center Archive. The photo shows a delegation of the KKK walking down the aisle at one of Richey's services.

87. Iain MacRobert, *The Black Roots and White Racism of Early Pentecostalism in the USA* (New York: Palgrave Macmillan, 1988); Cecil M. Robeck, "THE PAST: Historical Roots of Racial Unity and Division in American Pentecostalism," *Cyberjournal for Pentecostal-Charismatic Research* (May 2005), http://www.pctii.org/cyberj/cyberj14/robeck.html; Vinson Synan, *The Holiness-Pentecostal Tradition* (Grand Rapids, MI: Eerdmans Publishing Company, 1997), 182–183.

88. Ball, "Story of Latin-American Pentecostal Work," 1, 14.

89. Guillén, *La historia del Concilio Latino Americano de Iglesias Cristianas*, 104–114.

90. Ibid.

91. Moises Sandoval, *On the Move: A History of the Hispanic Church in the United States* (Maryknoll, NY: Orbis Books, 1991), 44–50; Brackenridge and García-Treto, *Iglesia Presbyteriana*, 167–169; Gilberto M. Hinojosa, "Mexican American Faith Communities in Texas and the Southwest," in *Mexican Americans and the Catholic Church, 1900–1965*, ed. Jay P. Dolan and Gilberto Hinojosa (Notre Dame, IN: University of Notre Dame Press, 1994), 76–77, 112.

92. David K. Yoo, *Religion in Korean American History, 1903–1945* (Stanford, CA: Stanford University Press, 2010), 108–110, 135–142.

93. Cecil M. Robeck Jr., *The Colorline Was Washed Away in the Blood* (Costa Mesa, CA: Newport-Mesa Christian Center, 1995), 13.

94. Ball, "Our Latin American Work," 8.

95. Ibid.

96. Ibid.

97. Alice E. Luce, "Scriptural Methods in Missionary Work," *TPE*, 9 May 1931: 8; Gary B. McGee, "Pioneers of Pentecost: Alice E. Luce and Henry C. Ball," *A/G Heritage* (Summer 1985): 5, 6, 12.

98. Luce, "Scriptural Methods in Missionary Work," 8; McGee, "Pioneers of Pentecost," 5, 6, 12.

99. H. C. Ball, letter to J. W. Evans, 31 November 1930; J. W. Evans, letter to H. C. Ball, 5 December 1930.

100. "While they [Mexicans] are excellent workers, they need American oversight." Ball, "A Call for More Laborers for the Mexican Work," 13.

101. H. C. Ball, letter to J. R. Evans, 11 July 1928; Enemecio Alaniz, letter to E. N. Bell, 19 October 1922, Houston, Texas; F. A. Hale and H. C. Ball, letter to J. W. Welch, 10 January 1917, San Antonio, Texas.

102. H. C. Ball, letter to Noel Perkin, 27 May 1927, San Antonio, Texas; Luce, "Latin-American Pentecostal Work," 6–7.

103. Ball, letter to J. W. Evans, 31 November 1930.

104. Ibid.; H. C. Ball, letter to J. W. Evans, 30 November 1932.

105. In his own defense, Ball wrote: "Nobody in all the District was a greater problem to me than Bro. Ramos. I tolerated him year after year in the hopes he might change . . . he was a regular dictator. . . . He should be out, that is the only hope for the man." Joseph C. Ramos, letter to J. R. Flower, October 1940, San Diego, California; H. C. Ball, letter to J. R. Flower, 25 July 1940; Perales, "Historia de los 50 años de las Asambleas de Dios," 6, 8.

106. Joseph C. Ramos, letter to J. R. Flower, October 1940, San Diego, California; H. C. Ball, letter to J. R. Flower, 25 July 1940; Perales, "Historia de los 50 años de las Asambleas de Dios," 6, 8.

107. Joseph C. Ramos, letter to J. R. Flower, October 1940, San Diego, California; H. C. Ball, letter to J. R. Flower, 25 July 1940; Perales, "Historia de los 50 años de las Asambleas de Dios," 6, 8.

108. Ball, "Pentecost Coming to Latin Americans," 1, 10, 11.

109. Perales, "Historia de los 50 años de las Asambleas de Dios," 5, 8; Luce, Missionary Update Form, Assemblies of God, ca. 1920, 6, 8.

110. Kenzy Savage, *The Spirit Bade Me Go* (N.p.: Morris Publishing, ca. 1995), 59.

6. The Challenges of Freedom

1. Victor De Leon, *The Silent Pentecostals: A Biographical History of the Pentecostal Movement among Hispanics in the Twentieth Century* (Taylors, SC: Faith Printing Company, 1979), 52.

2. Ibid., 100–101.

3. Ibid., 100–104.

4. Ibid.

5. Ibid.

6. Ibid.

7. Josue Sánchez, *Angels without Wings: The Hispanic Assembles of God Story* (New Braunfels, TX: Atwood Publishing, 1996), 27.

8. Ibid., 29.

9. David G. Gutiérrez, *Walls and Mirrors: Mexican Americans, Mexican Immigrants, and the Politics of Ethnicity* (Berkeley: University of California Press, 1995), 133–151, esp. 142.

10. Demetrio Bazan, letter to J. R. Flower, 30 June 1941; "New Advances in Latin America," *TPE*, 8 February 1941: 9.

11. Felix Gutiérrez, "The Western Junction," in *Each in Our Own Tongue: A History of Hispanic United Methodism*, ed. Justo L. González (Nashville, TN: Abingdon Press, 1991), 77.

12. R. Douglas Brackenridge and Francisco García-Treto, *Iglesia Presbyteriana: A History of Presbyterians and Mexican Americans in the Southwest*, 2nd ed. (San Antonio, TX: Trinity University Press, [1974] 1989), 161.

13. "In the 1940s and 1950s many of these small churches closed their doors because of lack of numerical and financial support." Ibid., 161.

14. "Pentecost on the Mexican Border: A Stirring Story Given by Miss Alice E. Luce at the General Council Meeting," *TPE*, 11 November 1939: 5.

15. "The fire in Mexico has been burning brightly . . . where some 12,000 are members of the Assemblies of God. The total membership of the Pentecostal people in Mexico may be around 50,000 in the various missions." Ball went on to claim that the number of Pentecostals in Latin America had increased from 128,000 in 1946 to 160,000 by 1948. Ball served as the general secretary of the Assemblies of God missionary work in Latin America from 1943 to 1954. H. C. Ball, "The Latin American Advance," *TPE*, 28 August 1948: 8–9.

16. De Leon, *The Silent Pentecostals*, 108–110.

17. Gastón Espinosa, e-mail interview with Jesse Miranda, 27 August 2013.

18. Ibid.

19. D. H. McDowell, "Latin-American Work in New York City," *TPE*, 10 August 1946: 13.

20. De Leon, *The Silent Pentecostals*, 52, 108–110.

21. Nellie Bazan with Elizabeth B. Martínez and Don Martínez Jr., *Enviados de Dios* (Miami: Editorial Vida, 1987).

22. De Leon, *The Silent Pentecostals*, 110, 123.

23. Ibid., 108–110, 123.

24. Ibid., 52, 108–110, 123.

25. Brackenridge and García-Treto, *Iglesia Presbyteriana*, 157–161.

26. José Girón, "José Girón's Brief Biographical Sketch" (April 1991): 1–4; De Leon, *The Silent Pentecostals*, 120.

27. Girón, "José Girón's Brief Biographical Sketch," 1–4; De Leon, *The Silent Pentecostals*, 120.

28. Girón, "José Girón's Brief Biographical Sketch," 1–4; De Leon, *The Silent Pentecostals*, 120.

29. De Leon, *The Silent Pentecostals*, 127.

30. Ibid.

31. Latin American District of the Assemblies of God Secretary Report, 1970; De Leon, *The Silent Pentecostals,* 52.

32. Ibid., 180–184.

33. Minutes, General Council of the Assemblies of God, 35th General Council, Miami, Florida, 16–21 August, 1973, 133, as cited in De Leon, *The Silent Pentecostals,* 184. In many sources, Puerto Rico was spelled "Porto Rico" until the 1940s.

34. De Leon, *The Silent Pentecostals,* 129–131, 180–182.

35. Photographs of the Southern Pacific District, Northern Pacific Latin American District, Spanish Eastern District, and Puerto Rico superintendents and leaders are shown here because they provided the requested images of their leadership teams. Requests were sent to all nine then district superintendents for a photograph of their leadership team, but only the above four districts provided photos (see Figure 8.2 for the latter).

36. These findings are based on two national surveys I directed: the Latino Religions and Politics National Survey of 1,104 U.S. Latinos in 2008 and the Latino Religions and Politics Survey of 1,075 U.S. Latinos in 2012.

37. See bio in Espinosa, Elizondo, and Miranda, *Hispanic Churches in American Public Life* (Notre Dame, IN: Institute for Latino Studies, University of Notre Dame, 2003), 9; Espinosa, Elizondo, and Miranda, eds., *Latino Religions and Civic Activism in the United States* (New York: Oxford University Press, 2005).

38. This sentiment was expressed by Rev. Wilfredo de Jesús, pastor of the 4,000-member New Life Covenant Church in South Chicago. Although he served as Obama's Latino Protestant adviser and campaigned as an Obama surrogate in the Latino Evangelical community for fifteen months in 2008, by 2010 he stated that President Obama was dishonest in his dealings with the Latino and Evangelical communities on immigration and gay marriage, the latter of which he claims the president could have passed at any time in the first two years of his administration since he controlled both the Senate and the House of Representatives. Gastón Espinosa, *Religion, Race, and Barack Obama's New Democratic Pluralism* (New York: Routledge, 2013), 264–266.

39. Espinosa, e-mail interview with Jesse Miranda, 27 August 2013.

7. We Preach the Truth

1. Juan L. Lugo, *Pentecostés en Puerto Rico o La vida de un misionero* (San Juan, Puerto Rico: Puerto Rico Gospel Press, 1951), 36–37. Unless otherwise noted, all citations to Lugo refer to this autobiography, hereafter cited as *Pentecostés en Puerto Rico.*

2. For books and articles that touch on Puerto Rican Pentecostalism, see Donald T. Moore, *Puerto Rico para Cristo: A History of the Progress of the Evangelical Missions on the Island of Puerto Rico* (Cuernavaca, Mexico: CIDOC SONDEOS, 1969); Jerry Fenton, *Understanding the Religious Background of the Puerto Rican* (Cuernavaca, Mexico: CIDOC SONDEOS, 1969); Anthony LaRuffa, *San Cipriano: Life in a Puerto Rican Community* (New York: Gordon and Breach Science Publishers, 1971); David Ramos Torres, *Historia de la Iglesia de Dios Pentecostal, M.I.* (Río Piedras, Puerto Rico: Editorial Pentecostal, 1992); David Martin, *Tongues of Fire: The Explosion of Protestantism in Latin America* (Oxford: Blackwell Publishers, 1993), 127–128, 191–204; Rubén Pérez Torres, "El marco historico-social entender el Pentecostalismo

en Puerto Rico," *Apuntes* 14, no. 2 (Summer 1994): 52–60; Rubén Pérez Torres, *Poder desde lo alto: Historia, sociología y contribuciones del Pentecostalism en Puerto Rico, el Caribe y en los Estados Unidos*, 2nd rev. ed. (Barcelona: Editorial CLIE, 2003).

3. In LaRuffa, *San Cipriano*, the author lamented that "data" on the origins and early historical development of Puerto Rican Pentecostalism is "sparse." While LaRuffa's comment was made in 1980, my research still confirms his contention about the lack of histories in English. Stephen Glazier, *Perspectives on Pentecostalism* (New York: University Press of America, 1980), 50.

4. Almost all the histories of Puerto Rican Pentecostalism trace the movement's origins back to Juan Lugo's arrival in Puerto Rico in 1916, not 1909. Leading scholars of Puerto Rican religion such as Samuel Silva-Gotay have argued that Pentecostalism grew slowly until the Great Depression. Silva-Gotay is not the only scholar to argue that the growth of Pentecostalism was slow until 1930. Anthony LaRuffa stated, "A few churches were established between 1910 and 1930." This book argues that Pentecostalism expanded quite rapidly between 1916 and 1930 (going from one missionary in 1916 to 56 churches and missions and an estimated 2,500 adherents by 1931). Anthony LaRuffa as cited in Glazier, *Perspectives on Pentecostalism* 50; Samuel Silva-Gotay, "The Ideological Dimensions of Popular Religiosity and Cultural Identity in Puerto Rico," in *An Enduring Flame: Studies on Latino Popular Religiosity* (New York: Bildner Center for Western Hemisphere Studies, 1994), 1, 56. For evidence of the rapid geographical expansion of Pentecostalism in Puerto Rico before the 1930s, see Moore, *Puerto Rico para Cristo*, 3/37–3/50 and the research in this chapter.

5. Jennie Mishler, "A Cry from Puerto Rico," *The Upper Room* (September–October 1910): 6.

6. Ibid.; Allan Anderson, *Spreading Fires: The Missionary Nature of Early Pentecostalism* (Maryknoll, NY: Orbis Books, 2007), 199.

7. Anderson, *Spreading Fires*, 199.

8. Lugo, *Pentecostés en Puerto Rico*, 12–19.

9. Ibid.

10. Through contacts with the Assemblies of God archives in Springfield, Missouri, and Pentecostal denominations and libraries in Puerto Rico, I was able to secure the founder's autobiography and a number of letters written by Euro-American and Puerto Rican Pentecostal missionaries and pastors. Where possible, I have attempted to compare Juan Lugo's autobiography, *Pentecostés en Puerto Rico*, published in 1951, with the early correspondence and other critical outside sources to check the reliability and accuracy of the primary source documents.

11. Lugo, *Pentecostés en Puerto Rico*, 12–19; "Poor Labor Proposition: Porto [*sic*] Ricans Tried and Found Wanting; Hawaiian Planters Have No Use for Them," *Los Angeles Times*, 26 December 1901; "History of Hispanics in Hawaii," *Hawaii Hispanic News*, 6 January 2013, http://www.hawaiihispanicnews.org/HawaiiHispanicHistory.html.

12. Lugo, *Pentecostés en Puerto Rico*, 12–19.

13. Ibid.

14. Ibid., 17–18

15. Ibid., 19–21.

16. Ibid., 12–19.

17. Victor De Leon, *The Silent Pentecostals: A Biographical History of the Pentecostal Movement among Hispanics in the Twentieth Century* (Taylors, SC: Faith Printing Company, 1979), 33.

18. Lugo, *Pentecostés en Puerto Rico,* 20–26.

19. Ibid., 23–24.

20. Ibid., 24–25, 86.

21. Ibid.

22. Ibid.

23. Hulda Needham was the daughter of Harold K. Needham, who served as assistant pastor of Bethel Temple in Los Angeles. J. Roswell Flower, "To Visit the Mission Fields," *TPE,* 3 April 1920: 12; Lugo, *Pentecostés en Puerto Rico,* 27–29.

24. Lugo, *Pentecostés en Puerto Rico,* 27–29.

25. Protestants faced a number of religiously based discriminatory restrictions in Puerto Rico in the nineteenth century. The front door of the church had to be locked at all times; people had to enter through a side entrance; they could not ring a Protestant church bell; no religious sign or symbol was permitted to be displayed on the outside of the church; and advertisements and public notices were prohibited. Furthermore, Puerto Rican Catholics could not be proselytized. Protestants were prohibited from burying their dead in Roman Catholic cemeteries within city limits. Moore, *Puerto Rico para Cristo,* 1/15–1/16. For an examination of the role of the Roman Catholic Church in Puerto Rico, see Jaime Vidal, "Citizens yet Strangers: The Puerto Rican Experience," in Jay P. Dolan and Jaime Vidal, *Puerto Rican and Cuban Catholics in the U.S., 1900–1965* (Notre Dame, IN: University of Notre Dame Press, 1994), 1–135.

26. Jaime Vidal argues that "generations without religious instruction resulted in a dangerously widespread ignorance, which made the people's cultural Catholicism vulnerable to Protestant challenges after 1898." He went on to claim that "the church's lack of touch with the many sections of the masses had reached alarming proportions" during the late nineteenth and early twentieth centuries. Vidal, "Citizens yet Strangers," 21–22.

27. Ibid., 50. Fenton stated, "Without question, the American seizure of the island in 1898 was a disaster for the Catholic church. Many of the already scarce and discredited clergy returned to Spain." Fenton, *Understanding the Religious Background of the Puerto Rican,* 1/G.

28. Vidal, "Citizens yet Strangers," 29, 50.

29. Ibid., 29.

30. There was also significant resistance to Americanization by many Puerto Rican nationalists such as Pedro Albizu Campos. Ibid.

31. No author listed, *Christian Work in Latin America* (New York: Missionary Education Movement, 1917), 2:324, citing C. J. Ryder of the American Missionary Association. As cited in Moore, *Puerto Rico para Cristo,* 2/3.

32. E. D. Thompson, ed., *Charles Lemuel Thompson* (New York: Fleming H. Revell Co., 1924), 139; Moore, *Puerto Rico para Cristo,* 2/3, 2/4, 2/5.

33. No author listed, *Christian Work in Latin America, III,* 27 as cited in Moore, *Puerto Rico para Cristo,* 2/3.

34. Moore, *Puerto Rico para Cristo,* 2/3–2/5.

35. Most of the Roman Catholic opposition to Protestantism came from Catholic priests. Ibid., 2/4, 2/29–2/30, 2/78.

36. Ibid., 2/4, 2/78–2/79.

37. P. W. Drury, "Resúmen estadistico de las misiones Evangélicos en Puerto Rico, Enera 1, 1915," *Puerto Rico Evangélico* 3 (25 June 1915): 7; *Statistical Report of Seventh-Day Adventist Conferences, Missions, and Institutions,* 1916. For the sources and data on which Table 7.1 is based, see Moore, *Puerto Rico para Cristo,* 2/80, 3/7, 3/25.

38. (1) Spiritism, "sometimes called 'Kardecism,' [is] the movement that follows the teachings of Allan Kardec. Some English-language texts use the term 'Spiritist' to mean anyone who accepts the idea of spirit communication, in contrast to 'Spiritualist,' which implies being part of the religious movement"; (2) Spiritualism is "the sibling of Spiritism in English-speaking countries. Spiritualists do not follow Allan Kardec but share many other beliefs and practices with Spiritists. The main doctrinal difference is that reincarnation is an optional belief for Spiritualists." For an examination of Spiritism and Spiritualism in Puerto Rico, see David J. Hess, "Toward a Comparative Study of Spiritism: Historical Development in Brazil and Puerto Rico," in *Spirits and Scientists* (University Park: Penn State University Press, 1991), 230, 210–231.

39. Ibid., 206–207, 227–231.

40. Victor S. Clark, *Porto Rico and Its Problems* (Washington, DC: Brookings Institution, 1930), 569.

41. Ibid.

42. Hess, "Toward a Comparative Study of Spiritism," 210.

43. Ibid., 208, 210; Nestor A. Rodríguez Escudero, *Historia del espiritismo en Puerto Rico* (Aquadilla, Puerto Rico: Privately published, 1989).

44. Vidal, "Citizens yet Strangers," 29–32; Benjamin Keen, *A History of Latin America,* 4th ed. (Boston: Houghton Mifflin, 1992), 528.

45. Moore, *Puerto Rico para Cristo,* 3/15ff., 5/15–5/15.

46. Lugo, *Pentecostés en Puerto Rico,* 27–30.

47. Ibid., 32; Flower, "To Visit the Mission Fields," 12.

48. Lugo, *Pentecostés en Puerto Rico,* 32; Flower, "To Visit the Mission Fields," 12.

49. Lugo, *Pentecostés en Puerto Rico,* 32; Flower, "To Visit the Mission Fields," 34–36.

50. Lugo, *Pentecostés en Puerto Rico,* 32–36.

51. Ibid.

52. Ibid.

53. Solomon and Dionisia Feliciano were both ordained by the Assemblies of God in San Jose, California, in 1916. They met Juan L. Lugo and began their lay ministry in Honolulu, Oahu, in 1912. They attended the same church that the Reverend Ortiz Sr. co-pastored with Peter Davies in San Jose, California. The Felicianos ministered in California for the rest of that year and claimed to have converted thirty-six people (mostly Latino) to Pentecostalism. The San Jose church sponsored the Felicianos as missionaries to the Dominican Republic with a monthly stipend of $20–$30. Peter Davies, "Pentecostal Missionaries Going Forth to San Domingo," *TWE,* 21 October

1916: 9; J. L. Lugo, "A Brief Sketch of the Pentecostal Work in Porto Rico," *TPE,* 20 September 1924: 8–9; Lugo, *Pentecostés en Puerto Rico,* 42.

54. Juan L. Lugo, "Souls Being Saved in Porto Rico," *TWE,* 25 November 1916: 13. Frank Finkenbinder wrote in 1924 that "Porto Rico is receptive to the Gospel, and we must take advantage of the open doors 'ere Jesus comes, or 'twill be too late." Finkenbinder, "Pentecost in Porto Rico," *TPE,* 20 September 1924: 9; Lugo, "A Brief Sketch of the Pentecostal Work in Porto Rico," 8–9; Lugo, *Pentecostés en Puerto Rico,* 43–44, 62.

55. Lugo, *Pentecostés en Puerto Rico,* 45–46.

56. Ibid., 45–47.

57. Ibid., 48–51.

58. J. L. Lugo, "Pentecost Has Fallen in Porto Rico," *TWE,* 10 February 1917: 12; J. L. Lugo, "The Whole Gospel for the Whole Man in the Whole World," *TPE,* 7 July 1917: 12; Lugo, *Pentecostés en Puerto Rico,* 46–53.

59. Lugo, "A Brief Sketch of the Pentecostal Work in Porto Rico," 9; Lugo, *Pentecostés en Puerto Rico,* 58–61.

60. "There were some Methodists who were very bitter against us but God has sweetened them up and five of them are baptized with the Holy Ghost and fire and three of these are preachers." Frank D. Ortiz Jr., "The Pentecostal Work in Porto Rico," *TWE,* 6 April 1918: 11. In 1919 Frank Ortiz stated, "The denominational ministers are confused about our means of support. They know we have no salary or any board [in] back of us, and sometimes they come around trying to persuade us to go with them and have a salary, but, hallelujah! He doth provide and we need not go begging or working for money." Frank Ortiz Jr., letter to *TPE,* 13 December 1919: 13.

61. Lugo, *Pentecostés en Puerto Rico,* 49–51.

62. Ibid., 49–52.

63. Ibid., 49–53.

64. The letters from this period are full of examples of Protestants, Roman Catholics, and Spiritualists deciding to experience the baptism in the Holy Spirit and Pentecostalism. Francisco Ortiz Jr., "The Porto Rican Revival," *TWE,* 22 December 1917: 11; Francisco Ortiz Jr., "The Pentecostal Work in Porto Rico," *TWE,* 6 April 1918: 11; Juan L. Lugo, "Missionary Notes," *TCE,* 20 September 1919: 10; Francisco Ortiz Jr., "A Blessed Report Comes from Porto Rico," *TPE,* 24 January 1920: 13; and Lugo, "A Brief Sketch of the Pentecostal Work in Porto Rico," 8–10.

65. Lugo, *Pentecostés en Puerto Rico,* 47–48.

66. H. C. Ball, "Pentecost Flourishing in Porto Rico: A Thousand Souls in Five Years," *TPE,* 7 January 1922: 6; "EL Evangelista Pentecostal," *El Evangelista Pentecostal* (October 1966): 8; Frank D. Ortiz Jr., Missionary Gleanings, *TPE,* 3 April 1920: 13; Frank Finkenbinder, "The Pentecostal Work in the Island of Puerto Rico" (eight-page typewritten manuscript, ca. 1975), 2.

67. Moore, *Puerto Rico para Cristo,* 3/44.

68. Lena S. Howe, "A Plea from Santurce, Porto Rico," *TPE,* 26 June 1926: 10; Lena S. Howe, "A Voice from Puerto Rico," *TPE,* 26 January 1929: 10–11.

69. Howe, "A Plea from Santurce, Porto Rico," 10; Howe, "A Voice from Puerto Rico," 10–11.

70. Howe, "A Plea from Santurce, Porto Rico," 10; Howe, "A Voice from Puerto Rico," 10–11.

71. See Frank Finkenbinder, "Refreshing Showers in Porto Rico," *TPE*, 16 January 1926.

72. "All our mission halls in the villages are rented halls and perhaps the owner himself is a Catholic, etc. Praise be to God that in the country stations we have some six chapels, and two more under construction. All these have been erected by the natives and without one dollar's help from America. . . . Practically all the lumber in some of these chapels is sawed out by hand by the converts and also erected by them." Finkenbinder, "Pentecost in Porto Rico"; Frank Finkenbinder, "The Lord Blessing in Porto Rico," *TPE*, 11 August 1923.

73. Frank Finkenbinder, "The Tenth Annual Conference of the Assemblies of God in Porto Rico," *TPE*, 21 March 1931.

74. Luís C. Otero, "Puerto Rico Convention," *TPE*, 11 August 1945: 11.

75. Finkenbinder, "The Pentecostal Work in the Island of Puerto Rico," 1–8.

76. H. C. Ball, "Pentecost Flourishing in Porto Rico," 6.

77. Tomás Alvarez, "Minutes of the Council of the Assemblies of God of the District of Porto Rico Convened in Ponce, P.R., September 1 to 6 inclusive 1920," trans. Lena O. Howe, Ponce, Puerto Rico, September 6, 1920.

78. Finkenbinder, "The Pentecostal Work in the Island of Puerto Rico."

79. Lugo, "A Brief Sketch of the Pentecostal Work in Porto Rico," 8–9; Moore, *Puerto Rico para Cristo*, 3/45–3/46.

80. Lugo, *Pentecostés en Puerto Rico*, 79–80.

81. Ibid., 80–86.

82. Frank Finkenbinder, "Dedication of New Church Building, Ponce, Porto Rico," *TPE*, 4 January 1930; Lugo, *Pentecostés en Puerto Rico*, 80–86.

83. No author listed, Missionary Gleanings, *TPE*, 9 March 1935; Finkenbinder, "The Pentecostal Work in the Island of Puerto Rico," 3–7.

84. J. L. Lugo, Missionary Notes, *TWE*, 15 September 1917: 12.

85. Frank Ortiz Jr., letter to *TPE*, 13 December 1919: 13; Frank D. Ortiz Jr., The Missionary Department, *TPE*, 3 April 1920: 13.

86. Finkenbinder, "The Pentecostal Work in the Island of Puerto Rico," 3–7.

87. Frank D. Ortiz Jr., The Missionary Department, *TPE*, 3 April 1920: 13.

88. F. Finkenbinder, "Terrible Effects of Cyclone in Porto Rico," *TPE*, 2 November 1932; no author listed, "A Pitiful Appeal," *TPE*, 21 October 1933.

89. Lugo, "A Brief Sketch of the Pentecostal Work in Porto Rico," 9.

90. Sesilia Agostine, "A Gracious Savior and Healer," *TPE*, 20 September 1924: 10–11.

91. See chapter 7 of Lugo, *Pentecostés en Puerto Rico*.

92. Howe, "A Plea from Santurce, Porto Rico," 10; Frank Finkenbinder, "Trial of Faith—Victory," *TPE*, 25 May 1934.

93. Frank Finkenbinder, "A Martyr in the Pentecostal Work in Porto Rico," *TPE*, 7 November 1931; Finkenbinder, "The Pentecostal Work in the Island of Puerto Rico," 4–5.

94. Lugo, *Pentecostés en Puerto Rico*, 61; no author listed, "Mission Study Course: Latin America, Puerto Rico," *Christ's Ambassadors Monthly* (June 1930): 12–13.

95. Teresa Ruiz de Velez, "A Personal Testimony," *TPE*, 20 September 1924: 10.

96. Tomás Alvarez, "Pentecost Given to U.S. Porto Ricans," *TPE,* 20 September 1924: 10.

97. J. L. Lugo, "The Porto Rican Revival," *TWE,* 13 January 1917: 12; J. L. Lugo, Missionary Gleanings, *TPE,* 11 June 1921: 13; Frank D. Ortiz Jr., The Missionary Department, *TPE,* 9 July 1921: 28; Frank Finkenbinder, "The Blind Receive Their Sight," *TPE,* 24 March 1934.

98. Agostine, "A Gracious Savior and Healer," 11.

99. Frank Finkenbinder, "Porto Rico," *TPE,* 12 May 1931.

100. General Council of the Assemblies of God Minutes (1931), 68; Jesús Pérez Torres, "El ministerio radial de la Iglesia de Dios Pentecostal en Puerto Rico," *El Evangelista Pentecostal* (October 1966): 5, 8.

101. Luís Villaronga, "El evangelista Olazábal en Río Piedras," *El Mundo* (San Juan, Puerto Rico), 5 May 1934; Homer A. Tomlinson, *Miracles of Healing in the Ministry of Francisco Olazábal* (Queens, NY: Homer A Tomlinson, 1939), 10–12, 16–17.

102. Tomlinson, *Miracles of Healing,* 17–19; no author listed, "La campaña en Puerto Rico," *EMC* (April 1936): 3.

103. Villaronga, "El evangelista Olazábal en Rio Piedras"; Miguel Guillén, *La historia del Concilio Latino Americano de Iglesias Cristianas* (Brownsville, TX: Latin American Council of Christian Churches, 1992), 122–131; Spencer Duryee, "The Great Aztec," *Christian Herald* (August 1936): 6.

104. Villaronga, "El evangelista Olazábal en Rio Piedras"; Guillén, *La historia del Concilio Latino Americano de Iglesias Cristianas,* 122–131; Duryee, "The Great Aztec," 6; Frank Olazábal Jr., telephone interview by Gastón Espinosa, May 1998.

105. David Stoll, *Is Latin America Turning Protestant? The Politics of Evangelical Growth* (Los Angeles: University of California Press, 1990).

106. Ernest Gordon, "Revival among Spanish-Speaking," *Sunday School Times,* 24 August 1935: 550–551; Duryee, "The Great Aztec," 5–7; Tomlinson, *Miracles of Healing,* 12, 17, 24.

107. Tomlinson, *Miracles of Healing,* 16–17; Domínguez, *Pioneros de Pentecostés,* 18, 44.

108. Tomlinson, *Miracles of Healing,* 18–19; Domínguez, *Pioneros de Pentecostés,* 45–46; no author listed, "La campaña Olazábal en Puerto Rico," *EMC* (April 1936): 3.

109. The eleven Pentecostal denominations in Puerto Rico by 1941 included (1) Pentecostal Church of God (began in 1916), (2) Foursquare Church (1930), (3) Defenders of the Faith (1932), (4) Universal Church of Christ (1934), (5) Missionary Church of Christ (1938), (6) Pentecostal Church of Jesus Christ (1938), (7) Church of God of Prophecy (1938), (8) Church of God (Mission Board) (1940), (9) Assembly of Christian Churches (1940), (10) Samaria Evangelical Church (1941), and (11) Mita Congregation (1942). No author listed, "Nuestra conferencia en Bayamon," *El Evangelista Pentecostal* 18 (March 1940): 3; Moore, *Puerto Rico para Cristo,* 4/25–4/43; Ramos Torres, *Historia de la Iglesia de Dios Pentecostal,* 126–131.

110. Lugo downplays and hardly alludes to Olazábal's campaigns in New York City and Puerto Rico in his autobiography, *Pentecostés en Puerto Rico.*

111. Luís Villaronga, "El Evangelista Olazábal en Río Piedras," *El Mundo* (San Juan, Puerto Rico), 5 May 1934; Tomlinson, *Miracles of Healing,* 10–12, 16–17.

112. For example, the Pentecostal Church of God grew from 3,400 members in 1936 to 9,300 by 1945. Otero, "Puerto Rico Convention," 11.

113. De Leon, *The Silent Pentecostals,* 39.

114. Lugo, "A Brief Sketch of the Pentecostal Work in Porto Rico," 8–9.

115. Mita Congregation, " 'Congregación Mita': Avance de la obra de Mita, 1940–1990," *El Nueva Dia,* 17 November 1990; Donald T. Moore, "La Iglesia de Mita y sus doctrinas," Siguiendo *La Sana Doctrina* (September–October 1988): 96–104; Ramos Torres, *Historia de la Iglesia de Dios Pentecostal,* 126–131.

116. B. R. Colon, "Pentecost in Puerto Rico," *TPE,* 16 August 1941: 9; Luís C. Otero, "Another Year of Progress in Puerto Rico," *TPE,* 8 May 1943: 11; Otero, "Puerto Rican Convention," 11.

117. Otero, "Another Year of Progress in Puerto Rico," 11.

8. The "Puerto Rico Problem"

1. *Downes v. Bidwell,* 182 U.S. 244, 287 (1901); *Balzac v. Porto Rico,* 258 U.S. 298 (1922).

2. *Downes v. Bidwell; Balzac v. Porto Rico.*

3. Benjamin Keen, *A History of Latin America,* 4th ed. (Boston: Houghton Mifflin, 1992), 527–530.

4. *Downes v. Bidwell; Balzac v. Porto Rico.*

5. *Downes v. Bidwell; Balzac v. Porto Rico.*

6. General Council of the Assemblies of God, General Council Convention Minutes, September 3–10, 1947, Grand Rapids, Michigan; General Council of the Assemblies of God, General Council Convention Minutes, December 16–17, 1948.

7. General Council of the Assemblies of God, General Council Convention Minutes, September 3–10, 1947; General Council of the Assemblies of God, General Council Convention Minutes, December 16–17, 1948.

8. General Council of the Assemblies of God, General Council Convention Minutes, September 3–10, 1947; General Council of the Assemblies of God, General Council Convention Minutes, December 16–17, 1948.

9. General Council of the Assemblies of God, General Council Convention Minutes, September 3–10, 1947; General Council of the Assemblies of God, General Council Convention Minutes, December 16–17, 1948.

10. General Council of the Assemblies of God, General Council Convention Minutes, September 3–10, 1947; General Council of the Assemblies of God, General Council Convention Minutes, December 16–17, 1948.

11. H. C. Ball, "West Indies Conventions," *TPE,* 4 March 1950: 11.

12. Juan L. Lugo, *Pentecostés en Puerto Rico,* 122–126; R. M. Riss, "Osborn, Tommy Lee (1923)," *The New International Dictionary of Pentecostal and Charismatic Movements,* ed. Stanley M. Burgess and Eduard M. Van Der Maas (Grand Rapids, MI: Zondervan, 2002), 950–951.

13. David J. du Plessis, "Caribbean-Area Convention," *TPE,* 21 July 1951: 8.

14. General Council of the Assemblies of God, Minutes from the General Convention Meeting, September 1–3, 1954.

15. Ibid.

16. Ibid.

17. General Council of the Assemblies of God, Minutes of the General Presbytery Meeting, September 1–3, 1954; Andrés Ríos, letter to Noel Perkin, 1 October 1954; Noel Perkin, letter to Andrés Ríos, 15 October 1954.

18. J. R. Flower and Melvin L. Hodges, "Report on the Puerto Rico Situation," 1955, 1–5.

19. Demetrio Bazan, letter to J. R. Flower, 18 July 1955.

20. Ibid.

21. Ibid.

22. Flower and Hodges, "Report on the Puerto Rico Situation," 1–5.

23. Ibid.

24. J. R. Flower, letter to R. J. Bergstrom, superintendent of the New Jersey District Council, 29 July 1955.

25. José Girón, letter to J. R. Flower, 19 August 1955.

26. Letter from Spanish Eastern District Convention, 25 July 1956.

27. Pentecostal Church of God, Inc., "Declaration, Status, and Position of the Pentecostal Church of God, Inc., of Puerto Rico," 3 September 1956.

28. Andrés Ríos, letter to Noel Perkin, 15 November 1956.

29. Ibid.

30. Ibid.

31. Ibid.

32. Ibid.

33. Howard Bush and Melvin D. Hodges, "Report on Conference with Puerto Rican Executive Committee," 16–17 April 1957.

34. Ibid.

35. Ibid.

36. Melvin Hodges, "The Puerto Rican Problem," May 1957; "The Puerto Rican Controversy," 10–11 July 1957.

37. General Council of the Assemblies of God, Minutes from the Annual Convention, August 24, 1927.

38. Rubén Pérez Torres, *Poder desde lo alto: Historia, sociología y contribuciones del Pentecostalism en Puerto Rico, el Caribe y en los Estados Unidos,* 2nd rev. ed. (Barcelona: Editorial CLIE, 2003), 296–301, 312.

39. Ibid., 296–301.

40. Ibid., 302–304.

41. Ibid., 303–304.

42. Ibid., 312–317.

43. Ibid., 303–304, 312.

44. Gaston Espinosa, Virgilio Elizondo, and Jesse Miranda, Hispanic Churches in American Public Life (HCAPL) national survey (n=2,060). The HCAPL survey was fielded October 1–7, 2000. For more about the survey, see Gastón Espinosa, Virgilio Elizondo, and Jesse Miranda, *Hispanic Churches in American Public Life: Summary of Findings* (Notre Dame, IN: University of Notre Dame Institute for Latino Studies, 2003).

9. Spirit and Power

1. The 1930 U.S. Census indicated 175,000 people of Hispanic ancestry in New York City. Lawrence R. Chenault, *The Puerto Rican Migrant in New York City* (Russell & Russell, 1938; repr., New York: Columbia University Press, 1970), 64–65.
2. Donald Keith Fellows, *A Mosaic of America's Ethnic Minorities* (New York: John Wiley & Sons, 1972), 181.
3. Joseph P. Fitzpatrick, *Puerto Rican Americans* (Englewood Cliffs, NJ: Prentice-Hall, 1971), 72.
4. James A. Henretta, W. Elliot Brownlee, David Brody, and Susan Ware, *America's History* (New York: Worth Publishers, 1993), 300. In 1910 more than 50 percent of all Puerto Ricans living in the United States resided in New York City. The proportion increased to 79 percent in 1920 and to 95 percent by 1940. C. Wright Mills, *The Puerto Rican Journey* (New York: Columbia University Press, 1949), 56.
5. Chenault, *The Puerto Rican Migrant in New York City,* 70–75.
6. The largest wave arrived as a result of the War Manpower Commission, which actively recruited workers from Puerto Rico. Mills, *The Puerto Rican Journey,* 44–45.
7. Jaime Vidal, "Citizens yet Strangers: The Puerto Rican Experience," in *Puerto Rican and Cuban Catholics in the U.S., 1900–1965,* ed. Jay P. Dolan and Jaime Vidal (Notre Dame, IN: University of Notre Dame Press, 1994), 56.
8. The most important trade route in Puerto Rico went from San Juan to New York City rather than to Tampa, Galveston, or New Orleans. The low cost of passage between Puerto Rico and New York City, along with a host of other factors, contributed to larger migration there than to Florida or other parts of the United States. Chenault, *The Puerto Rican Migrant in New York City,* 55–56; Fitzpatrick, *Puerto Rican Americans,* 12–15.
9. Henretta et al., *America's History,* 300.
10. Chenault, *The Puerto Rican Migrant in New York City,* 84–86.
11. Ibid., 81.
12. Ana Maria Díaz-Stevens, *Oxcart Catholicism: The Impact of the Puerto Rican Migration upon the Archdiocese of New York* (Notre Dame, IN: University of Notre Dame Press, 1993), 84–85.
13. Ibid., 86.
14. Vidal, "Citizens yet Strangers," 71–72.
15. Virginia Sánchez Korrol, "In Search of Unconventional Women: Histories of Puerto Rican Women in Religious Vocations before Mid-Century," in *Barrios and Borderlands,* ed. Denis Lynn Daly Heyck (New York: Routledge Press, 1994), 142–143; Protestant Council of the City of New York, *Midcentury Pioneers and Protestants: Pathfinding Service for the Churches* (New York: Protestant Council of the City of New York, 1954), 10.
16. Vidal, "Citizens yet Strangers," 72–73; Fitzpatrick, *Puerto Rican Americans,* 124–125.
17. Chenault, *The Puerto Rican Migrant in New York City,* 151.

18. Protestant Council of the City of New York, *Midcentury Pioneers and Protestants,* 10.

19. Chenault, *The Puerto Rican Migrant in New York City,* 152.

20. Mills noted in the late 1940s that 56 percent of men and 45 percent of women never or almost never attended church in New York City. In this respect, most Puerto Ricans were "unchurched." Mills, *The Puerto Rican Journey,* 111. For the 12 percent statistic, see Protestant Council of the City of New York, *Midcentury Pioneers and Protestants,* 3.

21. Jaime Vidal wrote, "In 1953 the figure for Mass attendance for all Catholics in New York was 'slightly more than one third,' while the Puerto Ricans who attended were 'not much more than one in ten.' This would imply that while Puerto Rican attendance was at about 10 to 12 percent, general attendance was about 33 to 35 percent— certainly much better than the Puerto Rican figures, but still 'significantly less than half.'" Vidal, "Citizens yet Strangers," 68.

22. Only five of forty-three Anglo-American Protestant churches had any major outreach to Puerto Ricans. Protestant Council of the City of New York, *Midcentury Pioneers and Protestants,* 12.

23. David Traverzo Galarza, "A New Dimension of Religious Education for the Hispanic Evangelical Church in New York City" (M.A. thesis, New Brunswick Theological Seminary, 1979), 17.

24. In 1961, the Church of the Good Neighbor affiliated with the Presbyterian Church, USA. S. Soto Fontanez, *Misión a la puerta: Mission at the Open Door: Una historia del Trabajo Bautista Hispano Nueva York* (Santo Domingo, Dominican Republic: n.p., 1982), 20, 22.

25. Frederick L. Whitman, "New York's Spanish Protestants," *TCC,* 7 February 1962: 162–164.

26. Fontanez, *Misión a la puerta,* 38, 44.

27. Ibid., 76.

28. Ibid., 46, 74, 98, 124, 126, 170.

29. Parker noted tension in the 1950s and early 1960s between mainline Euro-American Protestants and traditional and Pentecostal Latino Protestants in New York City. Euro-American Protestants accused Latinos of being too theologically and socially conservative. Indeed, Jorge Rivera, pastor of the Spanish-speaking Grace Methodist Church and interim president of the New York Spanish-speaking Protestant Council, stated, "We have no smoking, drinking and dancing places in our churches. Our people come from missionary churches and schools in Puerto Rico. We want our children to be brought up in these ways." Rivera also advocated bilingual education in New York City schools and resisted the attempt to be "Yankeeized." Everett C. Parker, "New York City: Spanish-Speaking Churches," *TCC,* 12 April 1961: 466–467; Fontanez, *Misión a la puerta,* 100.

30. Whitman, "New York's Spanish Protestants," 162; Eldin Villafañe, *The Liberating Spirit: Toward an Hispanic American Pentecostal Social Ethic* (New York: University Press of America, 1992), 64.

31. One 1953 report claimed, "The Protestant churches in the communities where Puerto Ricans are settling are doing little to welcome them, less to discover their

needs and help meet them, and still less to evangelize the unchurched for Christ." Protestant Council of the City of New York, *Midcentury Pioneers and Protestants*, 10, 12, 23.

32. Andrés I. Pérez y Mena, "Puerto Rican Spiritism as a Transfeature of Afro-Latin Religion," in *Enigmatic Powers: Syncretism with African and Indigenous Peoples' Religions among Latinos*, ed. Anthony M. Stevens-Arroyo and Andrés I. Pérez y Mena (New York: Bildner Center for Western Hemisphere Studies, 1995), 137–153.

33. The Azusa Street missionaries who conducted Pentecostal work in New York City were Julia W. Hutchins (African American), G. W. Batman, and S. J. Mead, among others. S. J. Mead, "Pentecost in New York," *AF* 1, no. 4 (December 1906): 3–4.

34. Edith Blumhofer, *"Pentecost in My SOUL"* (Springfield, MO: Gospel Publishing House, 1989), 191–208.

35. Juan L. Lugo, *Pentecostés en Puerto Rico* (San Juan, Puerto Rico: Puerto Rico Gospel Press, 1951), 92; Adolfo Carrión, *Distrito Hispano del este de las Asambleas de Dios* (Deerfield, FL: Editorial Vida, 1991), 9–10.

36. David Ramos Torres, *Historia de la Iglesia de Dios Pentecostal, M.I.* (Río Piedras, Puerto Rico: Editorial Pentecostal, 1992), 79, 344.

37. Alvarez suffered greatly after his wife entered into an adulterous relationship with another man and divorced him, which due to AG guidelines forced him to step aside from the ministry. Since ministry was all he knew, this left him in near-poverty. He struggled to take care of his aged mother and two daughters. He asked for assistance from AG headquarters, but none was given. After falling into temptation, he earnestly asked for forgiveness but was unable to return to the AG ministry. Frank Finkenbinder, letter to J. Roswell Flower, 22 July 1939; J. Roswell Flower, letter to Frank Finkenbinder, 24 July 1939; Ramón Reyes Hernández, Feliciano Pares, and Gabriel Sosa, general letter of endorsement for Frank Finkenbinder to J. Roswell Flower, 30 July 1930; Frank Finkenbinder, letter to J. Roswell Flower, 3 August 1939; J. Roswell Flower, letter to Frank Finkenbinder, 9 August 1939.

38. Lugo, *Pentecostés en Puerto Rico*, 93, 95; Villafañe, *The Liberating Spirit*, 93; Samuel Díaz, *La Nave Pentecostal: Cronica desde el inicio de las Asambleas de Dios y su travesía por el noreste hispano de los Estados Unidos* (Deerfield, FL: Editorial Vida, 1995), 39; Adolfo Carrión, *Celebrando mas de seis decades: Distrito Hispano del Este de las Asambleas de Dios* (Bronx, NY: Spanish Eastern District, 1992), 10; Samuel Díaz, *Comprometidos con Nuestro Pueblo: Historia del Concilio Latino Americano de las Iglesias de Dios Pentecostal de Nueva York, Inc. y su visión misionera a las naciones* (New York: Publicaciones Excelencia, 1999), 52–54.

39. Lugo, *Pentecostés en Puerto Rico*, 96–97; Carrión, *Celebrando mas de seis decades*, 12.

40. Díaz, *La Nave Pentecostal*, 44.

41. Manuel T. Sánchez, "Breves datos del Distrito Hispano del Este de las Asambleas de Dios," *El Embajador* (July–August, 1941), 3–4; Lugo, *Pentecostés en Puerto Rico*, 99; Carrión, *Celebrando mas de seis decades*, 12–13.

42. Frank Finkenbinder, letters to J. Roswell Flower, 22 July 1939 and 24 July 1939; Ramón Reyes Hernández, Feliciano Pares, and Gabriel Sosa, general letter of endorsement for Frank Finkenbinder, copy sent to J. Roswell Flower, 30 July 1939;

Frank Finkenbinder, letter to J. Roswell Flower, 3 August 1939; J. Roswell Flower, letter to Frank Finkenbinder, 9 August 1939.

43. Frank Finkenbinder, letter to J. Roswell Flower, 29 May 1940; J. Roswell Flower, letter to Frank Finkenbinder, 8 June 1940; Lugo, *Pentecostés en Puerto Rico,* 5–11.

44. Frank Finkenbinder, letter to J. Roswell Flower, 29 May 1940; J. Roswell Flower, letter to Frank Finkenbinder, 8 June 1940; Lugo, *Pentecostés en Puerto Rico,* 5–11.

45. Frank Finkenbinder, letter to J. Roswell Flower, 29 May 1940; J. Roswell Flower, letter to Frank Finkenbinder, 8 June 1940; Lugo, *Pentecostés en Puerto Rico,* 5–11.

46. J. Roswell Flower, letter to Gabriel Sosa, 14 July 1939.

47. Frank Finkenbinder, letter to J. Roswell Flower, 6 July 1939, 1–3; J. Roswell Flower, letter to Frank Finkenbinder, 13 July 1939.

48. Esperanza Guadalupe, Juan de Jesús, and Enriqueta Noboa, letter to J. Roswell Flower, 7 July 1939; J. Roswell Flower, letter to Enriqueta Noboa, 13 July 1939.

49. Frank Finkenbinder, letter to J. Roswell Flower, 22 July 1939; J. Roswell Flower, letter to Frank Finkenbinder, 24 July 1939; Ramón Reyes Hernández, Feliciano Pares, and Gabriel Sosa, general letter of endorsement for Frank Finkenbinder, copy sent to J. Roswell Flower, 30 July 1939; Frank Finkenbinder, letter to J. Roswell Flower, 3 August 1939; J. Roswell Flower, letter to Frank Finkenbinder, 9 August 1939.

50. Lugo, *Pentecostés en Puerto Rico,* 119–120.

51. Carrión, *Celebrando mas de seis decades,* 7; Antonio Caquias, letter to J. R. Flower, 14 July 1943; Ramos Torres, *Historia de la Iglesia de Dios Pentecostal, M.I.,* 249–275.

52. Frank Finkenbinder, letters to J. Roswell Flower, 6 July 1939, January 1937, and February 10, 1937; J. Roswell Flower, letter to Frank Finkenbinder, 18 February 1937; Frank Finkenbinder, letter to J. Roswell Flower, 14 April 1937.

53. Díaz, *La Nave Pentecostal,* 44.

54. Lugo, *Pentecostés en Puerto Rico,* 107.

55. Whitman, "New York's Spanish Protestants," 163.

56. Díaz, *La Nave Pentecostal,* 48–51.

57. Ramos Torres, *Historia de la Iglesia de Dios Pentecostal, M.I.,* 225, 249–275.

58. Whitman, "New York's Spanish Protestants," 163.

59. No author listed, n/t, *EMC* (November 1936): 15.

60. Miguel Guillén, *La historia del Concilio de Latino Americano de las Iglesias Cristianas* (Brownsville, TX: Latin American Council of Christian Churches, 1991), 187–213.

61. Ibid., 187–213; Samuel Díaz, *En el umbral de la gloria: Vida obra del Rev. Carlos Sepúlveda, pionero del evangelio entre los hispanos de los Estados Unidos* (Huntington Park, CA: Familia Sepúlveda, 1996), 66–85; Samuel Díaz, *¡Adelante en la carrera! Historia del Concilio Asamblea de Iglesias Cristianas, Inc. y su red misionera a las naciones* (New York: Concilio Asamblea de Iglesias Cristianas, 1997), 58–82; Miguel Guillén, "Historia de los Hechos," *Boletin,* no. 1 (April 1939): 2–32; Miguel Guillén, "En defensa de la verdad," *Boletin,* no. 2 (June 1939): 3–14.

62. Díaz, *En el umbral de la gloria,* 63–73.

63. No author listed, "Crónica sobre la Primera Convención de la Asamblea de Iglesias Cristianas," *La Voz Evangélica* 1, no. 1 (1 June 1939): 11–13.

64. No author listed, "Crónica de la Campaña las Hermanas Julia y Matilde Vargas," *La Voz Evangélica* 2, no. 10 (July 1940): 5, 8, 12; no author listed, "¡Luz, mas luz!," *La Voz Evangélica* 1, no. 4 (October 1939): 10; Díaz, *¡Adelante en la carrera!,* 77–79.

65. Díaz, *¡Adelante en la carrera!,* 82; Whitman, "New York's Spanish Protestants," 163.

66. Antonio R. Caquias, letter to Rev. J. Roswell Flower, 7 July 1945.

67. Díaz, *Comprometidos con nuestro pueblo,* 141; Arthur Piepkorn, "The Pentecostal Church of God of Puerto Rico," *Profiles in Belief 3* (1979): 115–116, 121.

68. Antonio Caquias, letter to J. R. Flower, July 1945; Ricardo Tañon, *Declaraciones del Hermano Ricardo Tañon* (Bronx, NY: Iglesia Juan 3:16, ca. 1983), 2–3; Villafañe, *The Liberating Spirit,* 98–99. For a more detailed description of Tañon's life and ministry, see Ramón Sánchez, *Ricardo Tañon: "El poder y la gloria de Dios"* (San Juan, Puerto Rico: Cooperativa de Artes Graficas "Romualdo Real," 1980).

69. David B. Barrett, ed., *World Christian Encyclopedia* (Oxford: Oxford University Press, 1982), 581.

70. Villafañe, *The Liberating Spirit,* 99–100; Thomas F. O'Dea and Renato Poblete, "Anomie and the 'Quest for Community': The Formation of Sects among the Puerto Ricans of New York," in Thomas F. O'Dea, *Sociology and the Study of Religion: Theory, Research, Interpretation* (New York: Basic Books, 1970), 184.

71. The four largest Latino Protestant churches in New York City in 1953 were the Latin-American Pentecostal Church of God (615 members), founded in 1932; the Church of the Good Neighbor (603 members), founded in 1912; the First Spanish Baptist Church (508 members), founded in 1921; and the Christian Church John 3:16 (500-plus members) founded in 1935. By 1953, the Christian Church John 3:16 was the fastest-growing Latino Protestant church in New York City. Protestant Council of the City of New York, *Midcentury Pioneers and Protestants,* 17, 20.

72. Traverzo Galarza notes that there were 250 Latino Pentecostal churches in New York City by 1960. Traverzo Galarza, "A New Dimension of Religious Education for the Hispanic Evangelical Church in New York City," 9; Protestant Council of the City of New York, *Midcentury Pioneers and Protestants,* 15, 17, 20, 22, 24; Everett C. Parker, "New York City: Spanish-Speaking Churches," *TCC,* 12 April 1961: 466–467.

73. In Wakefield's 1959 study he claimed that Pentecostalism "flourished" in Spanish Harlem, that "Pentecostals pose the greatest challenge to both Catholic . . . [and] traditional Protestant movements," and that "Pentecostals in fact are so strong that they also present a threat . . . to the practice of spiritualism." Dan Wakefield, *Island in the Sun* (Boston: Houghton Mifflin, 1959), 76, 78.

74. W. F. E. Story, "La historia de Jonas Probaba," *EMC* (November 1930): 11–12; S. H. F. "¿Esta sobre nosotros la guerra mas grande del mundo?" *EMC* (June 1930): 2–5; "¿Evolución o envolvimiento?" *EMC* (December 1930–January 1931): 16–17; Antonio Díaz Soto y Gama, "El Cristianismo y la revolución," *EMC* (June 1930): 5–8.

75. Chenault cites one study from the 1930s, which found that 95 percent of all Puerto Ricans in New York had not finished junior high school and that many in the Navy Yard district of Brooklyn were functionally illiterate. By the 1940s, C. Wright Mills found that the median level of educational attainment for Puerto Ricans in New

York City was 6.5 years (6.2 for women and 6.9 for men). He also found that in 1940 only 8 percent of all Puerto Ricans in New York City were illiterate, as compared to 32 percent in Puerto Rico. Chenault, *The Puerto Rican Migrant in New York City,* 145; Mills, *The Puerto Rican Journey,* 30–31.

76. Wakefield, *Island in the Sun,* 80–81; O'Dea and Poblete, "Anomie and the 'Quest for Community,'" 185.

77. One report claimed that Pentecostal churches are "a real indigenous expression of Protestant convictions. They receive no aid from denominational agencies, nor have they flowered from some central group's 'missionary vision.' They have a strong evangelical spirit, a conservative theology, and are willing to work with other Protestants toward a limited number of specific short-term goals. Generally, they are reluctant to identify themselves with institutionalized efforts for Protestant cooperation." Protestant Council of the City of New York, *Midcentury Pioneers and Protestants,* 15, 17.

78. Ibid., 79–80.

79. Sánchez, *Ricardo Tañon,* 79ff.; Villafañe, *The Liberating Spirit,* 97–100.

80. Villafañe, *The Liberating Spirit,* 97–99.

81. Sánchez, *Ricardo Tañon,* 79ff.; Villafañe, *The Liberating Spirit,* 97–100.

82. Villafañe, *The Liberating Spirit,* 97–100; Samuel Solivan, *Spirit, Pathos and Liberation: Toward an Hispanic Pentecostal Theology* (Sheffield, UK: University of Sheffield Press, 1998), 9–13, 97–100.

83. Villafañe, *The Liberating Spirit,* 97–99; Solivan, *Spirit, Pathos and Liberation,* 9–13.

84. Floresmiro Perea Renteria, *Perfil del ministro y líder* (Bogotá, Colombia: Buena Semilla, 1995); Díaz, *La Nave Pentecostal,* 63–67.

85. Spanish Eastern District, *Celebrando mas de seis decades, 1928–1992* (Bronx, NY: Spanish Eastern District, 1992); Díaz, *La Nave Pentecostal,* 68–78.

86. Anthony DePalma, "God's Word, Echoing in English; Hispanic Pentecostal Churches Face Bilingual Problems," *New York Times,* July 2003, http://www.nytimes.com/2003/07/02/nyregion/god-s-word-echoing-english-hispanic-pentecostal-churches-face-bilingual-problem.html?pagewanted=print&src=pm.

87. Rafael Reyes, "El superintendente informa," *Boletín Informativo* (New York: Distrito Hispano del Este Asambleas de Dios, 2011), 1.

88. Gastón Espinosa, e-mail interview with SED Superintendent Rafael Reyes II, 18 January 2014.

89. Ibid.

90. Espinosa, interview with Rev. Abigail Alicea, executive assistant to the superintendent of the Spanish Eastern District (SED) of the Assemblies of God, 21 January 2014.

91. Ibid.

92. Espinosa, e-mail interview with SED Superintendent Rafael Reyes II, 18 January 2014.

10. Your Daughters Shall Prophesy

1. Rev. Aimee García Cortese, letter to J. Roswell Flower, 11 July 1958.

2. For discussions about Latina Pentecostal women in ministry, see Loida Martell Otero, "Women Doing Theology: Una perspectiva Evangélica," *Apuntes* 67 (Fall

1994): 67–85; Maria Elizabeth Pérez y González, *Latinas in Ministry: A Pioneering Study on Women Ministers, Educators, and Students of Theology* (New York: New York City Mission Society, 1994); Virginia Sánchez-Korrol, "In Search of Unconventional Women: Histories of Puerto Rican Women in Religious Vocations before Mid-Century," in *Barrios and Borderlands: Cultures of Latinos and Latinas in the United States* (New York: Routledge, 1994), 141–151; and Elizabeth D. Ríos, "'The Ladies Are Warriors': Latina Pentecostalism and Faith-Based Activism in New York," in *Latino Religions and Civic Activism in the United States,* ed. Gastón Espinosa, Virgilio Elizondo, and Jesse Miranda (New York: Oxford University Press, 2005), 197–217.

3. For a discussion of Latina mainline Protestant women in ministry, see Minerva N. Garza, "The Influence of Methodism on Hispanic Women through Women's Societies," *Methodist History* (January 1996): 78–89; Minerva Garza Carcaño, "Una perspectiva bíblico-teológica sobre la mujer en del Ministerio Ordenado," in *Voces: Voices from the Hispanic Church,* ed. Justo L. González (Nashville, TN: Abingdon Press, 1992), 24–31, 112–121. For the literature on Latina Catholic women, see Ada María Isasi-Díaz and Yolanda Tarango, *Hispanic Women: Prophetic Voice in Church* (Minneapolis, MN: Fortress Press, 1992); Ada María Isasi-Díaz, *En la lucha /In the Struggle: A Hispanic Women's Liberation Theology* (Minneapolis, MN: Augsburg-Fortress Press, 1993); Jeanette Rodríguez, *Our Lady of Guadalupe* (Austin: University of Texas Press, 1994); and Maria Pilar Aquino, Daisy L. Machado, and Jeanette Rodríguez, eds., *A Reader in Latina Feminist Theology: Religion and Justice* (Austin: University of Texas Press, 2002). For a discussion of Euro-American and African American Pentecostal women, see Edith Blumhofer, "The Role of Women in the Assemblies of God," *A/G Heritage* (Winter 1987–1988): 13–17; Elaine J. Lawless, *Handmaidens of the Lord: Pentecostal Women Preachers and Traditional Religion* (Philadelphia: University of Pennsylvania Press, 1988); Edith Blumhofer, *Restoring the Faith: The Assemblies of God, Pentecostalism, and American Culture* (Urbana: University of Illinois Press, 1993), 174–175; R. Marie Griffith, *God's Daughters: Evangelical Women and the Power of Submission* (Berkeley: University of California Press, 2000); Anthea D. Butler, *Women in the Church of God in Christ: Making a Sanctified World* (Chapel Hill: University of North Carolina Press, 2007); Estrelda Alexander and Amos Yong, eds., *Philip's Daughters: Women in Pentecostal-Charismatic Leadership* (New York: Wipf and Stock, 2009); Estrelda Alexander, *Black Fire: One Hundred Years of African American Pentecostalism* (Downers Grove, IL: IVP Academic, 2011), chap. 8.

4. The dichotomy between the prophetic and priestly should not be overdrawn. Clearly, within most Pentecostal traditions there are elements of both. Charles H. Barfoot and Gerald T. Sheppard, "Prophetic vs. Priestly Religion: The Changing Role of Women Clergy in Pentecostal Churches," *Review of Religious Research* 22 (1980): 2–17.

5. No author listed, "Spanish Receive the Pentecost," *AF* (October 1906): 4.

6. The biographical information on Abundio L. and Rose López comes from Abundio's ordination certificate and application from Victoria Hall. Copy in author's possession.

7. López and López, "Spanish Receive the Pentecost," 4.

8. Gastón Espinosa, "'The Holy Ghost Is Here on Earth': The Mexican Contributions to the Azusa Street Revival," Azusa Street Revival Anniversary Edition, *Enrichment: A Journal for Pentecostal Ministry* 11, no. 2 (Spring 2006): 118–124.

9. A. C. Valdez with James F. Scheer, *Fire on Azusa Street* (Costa Mesa, CA: Gift Publications, 1980).

10. Junipero Serra founded most of the Franciscan missions in California, starting in San Diego in 1769.

11. Valdez with Scheer, *Fire on Azusa Street*, 3–4, 23, 25, 45.

12. Ibid., 24–25.

13. Inspired by his mother's vibrant faith, A. C. Valdez was ordained to the Pentecostal ministry in 1916, a profession he remained in for over sixty years. Ibid., 25.

14. However, this has not always been the case. Many men wanted women's roles to be restricted in the Assemblies of God. See, for example, "A Timely Word," *TPE*, 15 September 1923: 9; Minutes of the Fifteenth Annual Session of the Arkansas-Louisiana District Council of the Assemblies of God, 1927, 12; Blumhofer, "The Role of Women in the Assemblies of God," 13–17.

15. Gastón Espinosa, "Blaisdell, Francisca," *The New International Dictionary of Pentecostal and Charismatic Movements,* ed. Stanley M. Burgess and Eduard van de Maas (Grand Rapids, MI: Zondervan Publishing, 2002), 432; Victor De Leon, *The Silent Pentecostals: A Biographical History of the Pentecostal Movement among Hispanics in the Twentieth Century* (Taylors, SC: Faith Printing Company 1989), 146–147; Annual Questionnaire for Ordained Preachers in the Assemblies of God (1930s); Sunshine L. Ball, "Historia: Yo me acuerdo," *LLA* (October 1968): 9.

16. De Leon, *The Silent Pentecostals,* 146–148, Espinosa, "Morgan Howard, Concepción (Chonita)," *The New International Dictionary of Pentecostal and Charismatic Movements,* 907–908; Chonita Howard Morgan Ordination Application Form. Additional information was secured from her ministerial file at the Flower Pentecostal Heritage Center.

17. Lillian Valdez and Berta García, "Historia," *LLA* (August 1967): 3; C. Morgan Howard, "Historia de los primeros 50 años de las Asambleas de Dios," *LLA* (September 1967): 7; Nellie T. Bazan, "Historia: 50 años de Cristiana y de ministerio Cristiano," *LLA* (December 1967): 7–8.

18. Gastón Espinosa, "Bazan, Nellie," *The New International Dictionary of Pentecostal and Charismatic Movements,* 368; Nellie Bazan with Elizabeth B. Martínez and Don Martínez Jr., *Enviados de Dios* (Miami: Editorial Vida, 1987). The material for this section is drawn from this autobiography and an interview I conducted with her son and daughter-in-law; Gastón Espinosa, interview with Rev. Alex Bazan and Anita Bazan, November 1996. Nellie T. Bazan, "Historia: 50 años de Cristiana y de ministerio Cristiano," 7–8; Nellie T. Bazan, "Historia de los primeros 50 años de Dios: Segunda parte de mi testimonio," *LLA* (November 1967): 7–8; Nellie T. Bazan, "Historia de los primeros 50 años de Dios: Conclusion," *LLA* (January 1968): 8–9.

19. This information is from the ministerial files for Natividad Nevarez and Maria Inostroza, both of which are in the author's possession.

20. L. Valdez and B. García, "Historia," 3; Howard, "Historia de los primeros 50 años de las Asambleas de Dios," 7; Nellie T. Bazan, "Historia: 50 años de Cristiana y de ministerio Cristiano," 7–8.

21. Luisa Jeter de Walker, *Siembra y cosecha,* vol. 1, *Las Asambleas de Dios de Mexico y Centroamerica* (Deerfield, FL: Editorial Vida, 1990), 19–20.

22. Minutes of the District Council of the Assemblies of God of Texas and New Mexico (June 1928): 34–36.

23. David Ramos Torres, *Historia de la Iglesia de Dios Pentecostal, M.I.* (Río Piedras, Puerto Rico: Editorial Pentecostal, 1992), 46.

24. Ibid.

25. I have been unable to locate Chonita Morgan Howard's and Francisca Blaisdell's maiden names. L. Valdez and B. García, "Historia," 3; C. Morgan Howard, "Historia de los primeros 50 años de las Asambleas de Dios," 7; Nellie T. Bazan, "Historia: 50 años de Cristiana y de ministerio Cristiano," *LLA* (December 1967): 7–8.

26. De Leon, *The Silent Pentecostals,* 21, 46–47.

27. Alice E. Luce, Missionary Update Form, the Assemblies of God, ca. 1920.

28. De Leon, *The Silent Pentecostals,* 19–23, 47.

29. The following Latinas were among those credentialed by the Assemblies of God in the following years: Isabel Lugo (1920), Mary J. Inostroza (1930), Francisca Blaisdell (1937), Elvira Perales (1956), Josephine López (1956), Rachel Ortíz (1955), Bertha García (1956), and Rebecca Ortíz (1955).

30. Interestingly enough, this is not the case with their sister denomination in Mexico, the Apostolic Church, which does allow women to attend their Bible schools.

31. De Leon, *The Silent Pentecostals,* 68–71.

32. Ibid., 70.

33. Ibid., 77–84.

34. Gastón Espinosa, interview with SED Superintendent Rafael Reyes II, 24 January 2014.

35. Instituto Bíblico Hispano del Este Asambleas de Dios, *El Vencedor 1986: Edicion cincuenteria 1936–1986* (New York, 1986), 155–158. Women also made up the majority of the graduating class of the LABI in Texas in 1952 and 1955, and of LABI in California in 1958 and 1964. "Latin-American Bible Institute," *TPE,* 28 December 1952; Gastón Espinosa, "Bible Institutes, Spanish-Speaking," *The New International Dictionary of Pentecostal and Charismatic Movements,* 380–81.

36. Alice E. Luce, "Latin-American Work in California," *TPE,* 15 June 1935: 8; and Kenzy Savage, "27 Spanish-Speaking Youth Graduate May 10," *TPE,* 1 May 1955.

37. Nellie Bazan and Mary Ruth Prado regularly wrote for both Latin Districts periodicals.

38. No author listed, "Reaching Latin Americans in the U.S.A.," *TPE,* 14 April 1957.

39. The total number of women and young women involved in the Women's Ministries in the entire Assemblies of God (including Latino) is 414,377, of whom 242,394 are adult. Of this last number 44,609 are Latinas. The total number of Latinas (adult and young women) involved in the various denominationally sponsored women's ministries in the 1990s was 67,465. This has since increased to over 90,000 Latina women and young girls, as will be pointed out later in this

chapter. National Women's Ministries Department of the General Council of the Assemblies of God, Women's Ministries and Missionettes 1995 Annual Church Ministries Report.

40. No author listed, "La epoca de los Institutos Biblicos," *LLA* (June 1966): 3.

41. H. C. Ball, "Healed for Service among Mexicans," *TLRE* (January 1931): 11.

42. De Leon, *The Silent Pentecostals,* 144–151.

43. Ibid., 151.

44. Gastón Espinosa, e-mail interview with Sherri Doty, Statistics Department supervisor, Office of the General Secretary and AG National Leadership and Resource Center, 22 January 2014.

45. Rev. Rose Nodal, telephone interview by Gastón Espinosa, June 1996.

46. Gastón Espinosa, interview with Rev. Gloria Garza, 21 January 2014; Gastón Espinosa, interview with Rev. Gloria Garza, January 1996; Gastón Espinosa, interview with Rev. Gloria Garza, June 1996.

47. Josue Sánchez, "La familia: El padre: La cabeza del hogar," *The Word* (January–February 1983): 4–6; Josue Sánchez, "La familia: Le herencia de los hijos," *The Word* (May–June 1983): 10–12, 24.

48. Espinosa, interview with Rev. Gloria Garza, 21 January 2014.

49. Elvira Perales, "Una mujer pionera," *LLA* (June 1967): 6.

50. Espinosa, interview with Rev. Gloria Garza, 21 January 2014; Espinosa, interview with Rev. Gloria Garza, January 1996; Edith Blumhofer, *Pentecost in My Soul* (Springfield, MO: Gospel Publishing House, 1989), 35.

51. Gastón Espinosa, interview with Rev. Alex Bazan and Anita Bazan, spring 1996.

52. Espinosa, interview with Rev. Gloria Garza, 21 January 2014; Espinosa, interview with Rev. Gloria Garza, January 1996.

53. Espinosa, interview with Rev. Gloria Garza, 21 January 2014; Espinosa, interview with Rev. Gloria Garza, January 1996.

54. It is just about impossible to know exactly how many Latinas have been credentialed by the Assemblies of God because they could have been sponsored by the Latin districts, the Euro-American districts, as home missionaries, and as foreign missionaries.

55. For a further discussion of Juana García Peraza and Congregation Mita, see the articles on her and the denomination she founded in Puerto Rico in *The New International Dictionary of Pentecostal and Charismatic Movements,* 659, 901. Also see Ramos Torres, *Historia de la Iglesia de Dios Pentecostal, M.I.,* 126–131.

56. Gastón Espinosa, interview with Rev. Aimee García Cortese, March 1998; Sánchez-Korrol, "In Search of Unconventional Women's Histories of Puerto Rican Women in Religious Vocations before Mid-Century," 149–151.

57. Julie Ramírez, "He Who Does Not Work Shall Not Eat," *TPE,* July 1978: 21; Gastón Espinosa, interview with Efrain Agosto, 19 July 2011.

58. In the 1980s, Latinas began to be elected presbyters to the Latin District Councils. Blumhofer, "The Role of Women in the Assemblies of God," 13–17; Blumhofer, *Restoring the Faith,* 174–175.

59. This is also true of Euro-American Pentecostal women ministers. See Lawless, *Handmaidens of the Lord,* 11.

60. For a copy of her speech at the Assemblies of God National Annual Convention, see Aimee García Cortese, "Together . . . in Christ," *TPE,* 14 October 1979: 4–6; Robert Edwards, "Woman up for AG Post as Doors Begin to Open," *News-Leader* (Springfield, MO), 8 August 1993: 1A, 6A.

61. Sherri L. Doty, Office of Statistician of the General Council of the Assemblies of God, Ministers Marital Status/Gender Summary (1998), 1–2.

62. Gastón Espinosa, e-mail interview with Rev. Abigail Alicea, executive administrative assistant to the superintendent of the Spanish Eastern District of the Assemblies of God, 20 January 2014.

63. Gastón Espinosa, e-mail interview with Yanina Espinoza, executive administrative assistant to the superintendent of the Southern Pacific District of the Assemblies of God, 20 January 2014.

64. Espinosa, interview with Rev. Gloria Garza, 21 January 2014; Espinosa, interview with Rev. Gloria Garza, January 1996; Gastón Espinosa, telephone interview with Rev. Rose Nodal, June 1996; Gastón Espinosa, interview with Patty Galaviz, January 1996. Rev. Nodal lived in Santa Maria, California, where she served as the senior pastor of a large (220–250-member) Spanish-speaking Assemblies of God church.

65. For evidence and discussion, see Barbara Brown Zikmund, Adair T. Lummis, and Patricia Mei Yin Chang, *Clergy Women: An Uphill Calling* (Westminster: John Knox Press, 1998); Paula Nesbitt, *The Feminization of the Clergy in America: Occupational and Organizational Perspective* (New York: Oxford University Press, 1997); Schneider; Frederick W. Schmidt Jr., *A Still Small Voice: Women, Ordination, and the Church* (Syracuse, NY: Syracuse University Press, 1996); and Mark Chaves, *Ordaining Women: Culture and Conflict in Religious Organizations* (Cambridge, MA: Harvard University Press, 1999).

66. Gastón Espinosa, interview with Rev. Anita Soto, spring 1996.

67. Zikmund, Lummis, and Chang, *Clergy Women,* 156.

68. Ibid., 85–86.

69. Ibid., 41.

70. Gastón Espinosa, interview with Rev. Eva Rodríguez of Cantico Nuevo, Sacramento, California, 24 January 2014; Lawless, *Handmaidens of the Lord;* Chaves, *Ordaining Women.*

71. Gastón Espinosa, interview with Rev. Eva Rodríguez, 24 January 2014.

72. Ibid.

73. Ibid.

74. Espinosa, interview with Rev. Gloria Garza, 21 January 2014.

75. Gastón Espinosa, interview with Rev. Maria Camarillo (daughter of Rev. Flora Vegara), 20 January 2014.

76. Ibid.

77. Chaves, *Ordaining Women.*

78. Nesbitt, *The Feminization of the Clergy in America.*

79. Lawless, *Handmaidens of the Lord.*

80. This sentiment was shared by Aimee García Cortese, who stated that the feminist movement did not have an impact on the Latin District Councils because the

"movement was tied with homosexuality." Espinosa, interview with Rev. Aimee García Cortese, March 1998; Espinosa, interview with Rev. Gloria Garza, 21 January 2014.

81. Espinosa, interview with Patty Galaviz, January 1996.

82. Espinosa, interview with Rev. Gloria Garza, 21 January 2014; Espinosa, interview with Rev. Gloria Garza, January 1996; Espinosa, telephone interview with Rev. Rose Nodal, June 1996; Espinosa, interview with Patty Galaviz, January 1996.

83. The Chicano movement (1965–1975) was a political-social student movement that fought for Chicano/Latino civil rights and against the social and racial indignities many Mexican Americans and other Latinos faced in the United States. *Chicanismo* in the Mexican American community is an attitude and a social stance that demands justice and pride in *la raza*. For a discussion of the Chicano movement, see Carlos Muñoz Jr., *Youth, Identity, Power: The Chicano Movement* (New York: Verso Books, 1992).

84. Espinosa, interview with Rev. Anita Soto, spring 1996.

85. Espinosa, interview with Rev. Gloria Garza, 21 January 2014; Espinosa, interview with Rev. Gloria Garza, January 1996.

86. Max Weber, *The Sociology of Religion* (Boston: Beacon Press, 1991).

11. Righteousness and Justice

1. The term *Social Gospel* was coined and popularized by Rochester Divinity School professor Walter Rauschenbusch. He sought to address not only the salvation but also the social needs of the people. Walter Rauschenbusch, *A Theology of the Social Gospel* (1902) as cited in Hugh T. Kerr, ed., *Readings in Christian Thought*, 2nd ed. (Nashville, TN: Abingdon Press, 1990). Peruvian theologian Gustavo Gutiérrez and Brazilian priests Leonardo Boff and Clodovis Boff argued that true and living faith includes the practice of liberation; that Jesus took on oppression to set people free; that the Holy Spirit is present in the struggles of the oppressed; that the church is a sign and instrument of liberation; that the rights of the poor are God's rights; that God has a preferential option for the poor; and that God sides with the oppressed against the pharaohs of this world. Their critiques of exploitation, unregulated capitalism, and structural and social oppression draw on Marxism, but only in an instrumental way. They also draw on Marxist notions of the importance of economic factors in oppression and liberation, attention to class struggle, and the mystifying power of secular and religious ideologies. However, they are also quite critical of Marxism's atheistic framework, assumptions, and lack of Christocentric focus. Liberation theologians (both Catholics and some Protestants) seek to create a theology that arises out of the suffering and social context of the people and that seeks to empower them by raising their consciousness about the root causes of human suffering and oppression and the practical steps they can take to overcome them. Gustavo Gutiérrez, *A Theology of Liberation* (Maryknoll, NY: Orbis Books, 1988 [originally published 1973]), and Leonardo Boff and Clodovis Boff, *Introducing Liberation Theology* (Maryknoll, NY: Orbis Books, 1987). Eldin Villafañe, Sam-

uel Solivan, and other Latino Pentecostal social ethicists and theologians have applied some (though clearly not all) of the biblically consistent insights of liberation theology in their notions of the Pentecostal liberating Spirit and orthopathos. Eldin Villafañe, *The Liberating Spirit: Toward an Hispanic American Pentecostal Social Ethic* (New York: University Press of America, 1992); Samuel Solivan, *Spirit, Pathos and Liberation* (Sheffield, UK: University of Sheffield Press, 1998).

2. For a discussion of Latino Pentecostal social action, see Gastón Espinosa, Virgilio Elizondo, and Jesse Miranda, eds., *Latino Religions and Civic Activism in the United States* (New York: Oxford University Press, 2005), passim, and Gastón Espinosa, "Latinos, Religion, and the American Presidency," in *Religion, Race, and the American Presidency*, ed. Gastón Espinosa (New York: Rowman and Littlefield, 2011), 231–237, 269–273; Villafañe, *The Liberating Spirit;* and Solivan, *Spirit, Pathos and Liberation.* For helpful studies on Latino Pentecostals in the Southwest, see Luís León, *La Llorona's Children: Religion, Life, and Death in the U.S.-Mexican Borderlands* (Berkeley: University of California Press, 2004), and Arlene Sánchez-Walsh, *Latino Pentecostal Identity: Evangelical Faith, Self, and Society* (New York: Columbia University Press, 2003); and for a discussion of Latino Pentecostal Christology, see Sammy Alfaro, *Divino Campañero: Toward a Hispanic Pentecostal Christology* (Eugene, OR: Pickwick Publications, 2010). For the best lay, academic, and Spanish introductions to global Pentecostalism, see Harvey Cox, *Fire from Heaven: The Rise of Pentecostal Spirituality and the Reshaping of Religion in the 21st Century* (New York: Da Capo Press, 2001); Allan Anderson, *To the Ends of the Earth: Pentecostalism and the Transformation of World Christianity* (New York: Oxford University Press, 2013); and Eldin Villafañe, *Introducción al Pentecostalismo: Manda fuego señor* (Nashville, TN: Abingdon Press, 2012).

3. Sherri Huleatt, "Justice and the Lamb's Agenda," *VOICE,* 7 October 2013, http://blog.vyrso.com/2013/10/07/justice-and-the-lambs-agenda/. For a detailed discussion of what Rodríguez means by "righteousness and justice," see Samuel Rodríguez, *The Lamb's Agenda: Why Jesus Is Calling You to a Life of Righteousness and Justice* (Nashville, TN: Thomas Nelson Publishing, 2013).

4. Donald Miller and Tetsunao Yamamori, *Global Pentecostalism: The New Face of Christian Social Engagement* (Berkeley: University of California Press, 2007), 1–12, 34–38, 211–224.

5. A. C. Valdez with James F. Scheer, *Fire on Azusa Street* (Costa Mesa, CA: Gift Publications, 1980), 3–4, 23–25, 45; Espinosa, Elizondo, and Miranda, *Latino Religions and Civic Activism in the United States,* 288.

6. H. C. Ball, "Story of the Latin-American Pentecostal Work," *TPE,* 5 September 1931: 1, 14; H. C. Ball, "Our Latin American Work," *TPE,* 20 November 1932; H. C. Ball, "Historia de los primeros 50 años de las Asambleas de Dios Latinas," *LLA* (April 1966): 2, 12.

7. H. C. Ball, "Healed for Service among Mexicans," *TLRE* (January 1931): 11.

8. David Gutiérrez, *Walls and Mirrors: Mexican Americans, Mexican Immigrants, and the Politics of Ethnicity* (Berkeley: University of California Press, 1995), 72; Ball, "Story of Latin American Pentecostal Work," 1, 14.

9. Ball, "Healed for Service among Mexicans," 11; Ball, "Story of the Latin-American Pentecostal Work," 1, 14; Ball, "Our Latin American Work"; Ball, "Historia de los primeros 50 años de las Asambleas de Dios Latinas," 2, 12.

10. Victor De Leon, *The Silent Pentecostals: A Biographical History of the Pentecostal Movement among Hispanics in the Twentieth Century* (Taylors, SC: Faith Printing Company, 1979), 110–111, 124–129, 151–160.

11. Gustave Kinderman, "Help Needed for Cuban Refugees in Miami," *TPE*, 23 April 1961: 10–11; Gayle F. Lewis, "Helping Cuban Refugees" ('Be not forgetful to entertain strangers,' Hebrews 13:2)," *TPE*, 27/28 August 1961: 14; "Refugee Center Reaches Cubans," *TPE*, 26 November 1961: 10–11; Gastón Espinosa, "'Today We Act, Tomorrow We Vote': Latino Religions, Politics, and Activism in Contemporary U.S. Civil Society," *Annals of the American Academy of Political and Social Science* 612 (July 2007): 152–171.

12. No author listed, "Help for the Evangelical Refugee Center Urgently Needed," *TPE*, 26 December 1964: 21.

13. No author listed, "Cubans Are Still Coming," *TPE*, 16 April 1967: 21.

14. R. C. C., "Cubans and Haitians Flee for Refugee," *TPE*, 18 May 1980: 31; R. C. C., "Many Pentecostals among Cuban Refugees," *TPE*, 20 July 1980.

15. Ruth A. Lyon, "Meeting American's Newest Home Missions Challenge," *TPE*, 10 August 1980.

16. Selby R. Martin, "Fort Chaffee—A Mission Field at Our Doorsteps," *TPE*, 9 August 1981: 12–13.

17. Gastón Espinosa, Virgilio Elizondo, and Jesse Miranda, *Hispanic Churches in American Public Life: Summary of Findings* (Notre Dame, IN: University of Notre Dame Institute for Latino Studies, 2003), 21; Gaston Espinosa, "Latinos, Religion, and the American Presidency," in Espinosa, *Religion, Race, and the American Presidency,* 246–269.

18. See James H. Cone, *Martin and Malcolm and America* (Maryknoll, NY: Orbis Books, 2002). For an analysis of Chávez's faith-based activism, see Luís León, "César Chávez and Mexican American Civil Religion," and Stephen Lloyd-Moffett, "The Mysticism and Social Action of César Chávez," in Espinosa, Elizondo, and Miranda, *Latino Religions and Civic Activism in the United States,* 35–66; and Frederick John Dalton, *The Moral Vision of César Chávez* (Maryknoll, NY: Orbis Books, 2003).

19. Rudy V. Busto, *King Tiger: The Religious Vision of Reies López Tijerina* (Albuquerque: University of New Mexico Press, 2005), 17, 23, 39–50, 88–92.

20. For a discussion of Tijerina's Valle de Paz, see Rudy V. Busto, "Sacred Order, Sacred Space: Reies López Tijerina and the Valle de Paz Community," in *Mexican American Religions: Spirituality, Activism, and Culture,* ed. Gastón Espinosa and Mario T. García (Durham, NC: Duke University Press, 2008), 86–105.

21. Tijerina stated that the U.S. government "conspired" with the Euro-American New Mexican governors to disprove their original land grant claims given during the Mexican period because the titles were intentionally burned and destroyed. He pointed out that five judges, all former Confederate soldiers, who granted Hispanos only 1.5 million of their original 35 million acres of land, adjudicated most of the land grant titles. F. Arturo Rosales, *Testimonio: A Documentary History of the*

Mexican-American Struggle for Civil Rights (Houston, TX: Arte Público Publishers, University of Houston, 2000), 314–316.

22. Tijerina was well aware of the similarities between the struggle of his Alianza and that of the Gorras Blancas (White Caps), as they were called. Ibid., 311–312.

23. Ibid., 314.

24. Rodolfo Acuña, *Occupied America: The Chicano's Struggle toward Liberation* (San Francisco: Canefield Press, 1972), 237–241; Rosales, *Testimonio*, 308–321; Rudiger V. Busto, "'In the Outer Boundaries . . .': Pentecostalism, Politics, and Reies López Tijerina's Civic Activism," in Espinosa, Virgilio, and Miranda, *Latino Religions and Civic Activism in the United States*, 65–75.

25. "Reies López Tijerina Interviewed by Elsa Knight Thompson" (1968), as cited in Rosales, *Testimonio*, 313–316, 322; United States Commission on Civil Rights, *Mexican Americans and the Administration of Justice in the Southwest* (Washington, DC: GPO, 1970), 14–16; Wayne Moquin, *A Documentary History of the Mexican Americans* (New York: Praeger, 1971), 374–377; Busto, "In the Outer Boundaries . . . ," 65–75.

26. Tijerina, as cited in Rosales, *Testimonio*, 308.

27. Tijerina as cited in ibid.

28. Tijerina, as cited in ibid., 308, 321; Acuña, *Occupied America*, 238–239.

29. Acuña, *Occupied America*, 239–240.

30. Busto, "In the Outer Boundaries . . . ," 65–75.

31. Pedro Torres, "Ministering to Mexican Braceros in the United States," *TPE*, 28 February 1965: 19.

32. Richard W. Etulain, *César Chávez: A Brief Biography with Documents* (New York: Bedford / St. Martin's Press, 2002), 23; Jacques E. Levy, *César Chávez: Autobiography of La Causa* (Minneapolis: University of Minnesota Press, 2007), 115–121, 277–278.

33. Moises Sandoval, *Fronteras: A History of the Latin American Church in the USA since 1513* (San Antonio, TX: Mexican American Cultural Center, 1983), 380.

34. F. Arturo Rosales, *Chicano! The History of the Mexican American Civil Rights Movement* (Houston, TX: Arte Público Publishers, 1997), 130–151; Sandoval, *Fronteras*, 381–408; Levy, *César Chávez*, 269–293.

35. In this same passage, Dolores Huerta said Alinsky's lack of support was due to anti-Catholic bigotry. She defended Chávez's fast and then sharply criticized Alinsky and some of her colleagues: "Many liberals and radicals . . . are liberal right up to [the] steps of the Catholic church . . . they can be liberal about everything else but the Catholic church. There the liberalism ends." She said that Chávez, by contrast, "doesn't want to feed the bigotry that the average person has against the church," but rather "tries to overcome that bigotry by his example." Levy, *César Chávez*, 277–278.

36. Wendy Goepel, interview with César Chávez, "Viva la Causa," 1963, n/p, pp. 1–6, as cited in *Farm Labor* 5 (April 1964): 23–38; Levy, *César Chávez*, 115–121

37. As cited in Levy, *César Chávez*, 115–121.

38. Ibid.

39. Ibid.

40. Richard W. Etulain, *César Chávez: A Biography with Documents* (1975; New York: W. W. Norton, 1966), 115–116; Levy, *César Chávez*, 115–121.

41. Levy, *César Chávez*, 115–121.

42. Ibid.; Richard Griswold del Castillo and Richard A. García, *César Chávez: A Triumph of Spirit* (Norman: University of Oklahoma Press, 1995), 28.

43. Levy, *César Chávez*, 115–121.

44. Ibid.

45. César Chávez, "The Mexican-American Church and the Church" (March 8–10, 1968), in *Voices: Readings from El Grito,* ed. Octavio I. Roman V (Berkeley: Quinto Sol, 1973), 215–218, as cited in Antonio M. Stevens Arroyo, ed., *Prophets Denied Honor: An Anthology of the Hispanic Church in the United States* (Maryknoll, NY: Orbis Books, 1980), 118–119.

46. Eldin Villafañe, "Ricardo Tañon: An Apostle in the Bronx," *TPE,* 16 May 1999: 20–22.

47. F. M. Reynolds, "Cruz, Nicky," *The New International Dictionary of Pentecostal and Charismatic Movements,* ed. Stanley M. Burgess and Eduard M. Van Der Mass (Grand Rapids, MI: Zondervan, 2002), 566–567.

48. Gastón Espinosa, "Arguinzoni, Sonny" and "Victory Outreach International," *The New International Dictionary of Pentecostal and Charismatic Movements,* 331–332, 1775.

49. AMEN brochure; Gastón Espinosa, oral history interview with Jesse Miranda, November 14, 2012.

50. The publications that draw on the HCAPL study and research include Espinosa, Elizondo, and Miranda, *Latino Religions and Civic Activism in the United States;* Espinosa, Elizondo, and Miranda, *Hispanic Churches in American Public Life: Summary of Findings;* Espinosa, *Religion, Race, and the American Presidency,* and over a dozen other articles, book chapters, and publications.

51. For more about the HCAPL study and its contributions to the study of religion, politics, and activism in the American Academy of Religion and in American society, see the publications on the sources cited in endnote 50 and in Gastón Espinosa, *Religion, Race, and Barack Obama's New Democratic Pluralism* (New York: Routledge, 2012), among other publications.

52. Gregory C. Stanczak, *Engaged* (New Brunswick, NJ: Rutgers University Press, 2006), 49–57, esp. 55.

53. Gastón Espinosa, interviews with LABI president Dr. Tommy Casarez and administrative assistant Jessica Estrada, Latin American Bible Institute, La Puente, California, 22 January 2014.

54. Ibid.

55. Adrian Campo-Flores, "The Rev. Samuel Rodríguez: Ministering to the Needs of His People," *Newsweek,* 31 December 2007; Gastón Espinosa, interview with Rev. Samuel Rodríguez, 12 April 2009.

56. Their mission statement is taken from the NHCLC website, http://www.nhclc.org /our-mission.

57. These influential leaders are singled out and noted on his NHCLC website as providing inspiration for the NHCLC.

58. National Hispanic Christian Leadership Conference, 2006, http://www.nhclc.org/.

59. The seven AG members of the Executive Board include Rev. Jesse Miranda, Rev. Samuel Rodríguez, Rev. Gilbert Velez, Rev. Dennis Rivera, Rev. Nick Garza, Rev. Efrain Pineda, and Rev. Wilfredo de Jesús.

60. As cited in an interview with Rodríguez. Gastón Espinosa, interview with Samuel Rodríguez, 24 June 2010. Gastón Espinosa, interview with Samuel Rodríguez, 12 August 2010.

61. Alan Cooperman, "Letter on Immigration Deepens Split among Evangelicals," *Washington Post,* 5 April 2006.

62. Campo-Flores, "The Rev. Samuel Rodríguez: Ministering to the Needs of His People"; Ben Smith, "Hispanics Turn Cold Shoulder to McCain," *Politico,* 9 October 2008; Tim Stafford, "The Call of Samuel: Samuel Rodríguez Wants to Build a Bridge between Hispanic and Anglo Evangelicals," *Christianity Today,* September 2006; Gastón Espinosa, e-mail interview with Rev. Samuel Rodríguez, 12 April 2009. Gastón Espinosa, interview with Wilfredo de Jesús, 31 August 2010.

63. For evidence, see Espinosa, " 'Today We Act, Tomorrow We Vote,' " and the NHCLC website press release (http://www.nhclc.org/press-release) and media (http://www.nhclc.org/media-gallery) pages.

64. Samuel Rodríguez, "Open Letter to Evangelicals on Immigration Reform," 1 April 2006.

65. Samuel Rodríguez, David Neff, Ron Sider, Ann Buwalda, Jim Wallis, and Clive Calver, "Open Letter to President Bush and Congress," 1 March 2006.

66. Ibid.; Espinosa, " 'Today We Act, Tomorrow We Vote.' "

67. This statement about the Latino vote growing to 50 percent was made by Rick Hunter of SDR Consulting (http://www.sdr-consulting.com/), who did the polling to test the level of Latino support if Bush was able to get immigration reform passed in 2006. Hunter shared this information with me in a telephone conversation in October 2012. Since 1995, Hunter has supervised the completion of over 200,000 surveys, including for The Pew Charitable Trusts, the Tomas Rivera Policy Institute, Telemundo, and Univision, among others. "President Bush Attends National Hispanic Prayer Breakfast," 8 June 2006, http://www.whitehouse.gov/news/releases/2006/06/20060608-1.html; Espinosa, *Religion, Race, and the American Presidency,* 231; Gastón Espinosa, interview with Rick Hunter, 15 October 2012.

68. See Espinosa, " 'Today We Act, Tomorrow We Vote,' " and the NHCLC website press release (http://www.nhclc.org/press-release) and media (http://www.nhclc.org/media-gallery) pages.

69. David Schwartz, "Arizona Governor Signs Toughest Immigration Law," *Reuters,* 23 April 2010: 1–2; Randall C. Archibold, "Arizona Enacts Stringent Law on Immigration," *New York Times,* 23 April 2010: 1–4.

70. Schwartz, "Governor Signs Toughest Immigration Law," 1–4; Archibold, "Arizona Enacts Stringent Law on Immigration," 1–4.

71. NHCLC press release, "Hispanic Evangelicals Call Arizona Bill SB 1070 'Legislative Nativism,' Declare a 40-Day National Fast for justice in Arizona," April 20, 2010, http://www.nhclc.org/news/Hispanic-evangelicals-call-arizona-bill-sb1070-legislative-nativism-declare-40-day-national-fast.

72. Ibid.

73. Ibid.; Urban Ministry, "Hispanic Evangelicals Call Arizona Bill SB 1070 'Legislated Nativism,'" *Urban Ministry,* April 20, 2010, http://www.urbanministry.org/f/hispanic-evangelicals-call-arizona-bill-sb-1070-legislated-nativism.

74. NHCLC press release, "Hispanic Evangelicals call Arizona Bill SB 1070 'Legislative Nativism'"; Elena Shore, "Arizona Law Spurs Conservatives to Push for Immigration Reform," *New America Media,* April 30, 2010, http://newamericamedia.org/2010/04/arizona-law-spurs-conservatives-to-push-for-immigration-reform.

75. For a discussion on César Chávez's faith-based strategies, see León, "César Chávez and Mexican American Civil Religion," 53–64. For other strategies see chapters 1, 2, 4–6, 9, and 10 of Espinosa, Elizondo, and Miranda, *Latino Religions and Civic Activism in the United States.* NHCLC press release, "Hispanic Evangelicals Call Arizona Bill SB 1070 'Legislative Nativism.'"

76. NHCLC press release, "Hispanic Evangelicals Call Arizona Bill SB 1070 'Legislative Nativism.'"

77. Ibid.

78. Ibid.; Suzy Khimm, "A Right-Wing Schism over Immigration Reform," *Mother Jones,* 2 June 2010.

79. NHCLC press release, "Hispanic Evangelicals Call Arizona Bill SB 1070 'Legislative Nativism.'"

80. Adelle Banks, "Evangelical Voices for Immigration Reform Grow," *Religion News Service,* as cited in *TCC,* 15 June 2010, http://www.christiancentury.org/article.lasso?id=8502.

81. Adelle M. Banks, "Evangelicals Endorse Immigration Reform," *Religion News Services,* posted October 9, 2009, as noted in *Christianity Today,* 14 June 2010, http://www.christianitytoday.com/ct/2009/octoberweb-only/140.51.0.html.

82. Sarah Posner, "So Much for Evangelical Support for Immigration Reform," *Religion Dispatches,* 7 June 2010, http://www.religiondispatches.org/dispatches/sarahposner/2757/so_much_for_evangelical_support_for_immigration_reform/; Baptist Press, "Evangelicals Reject Gay Partners in Immigration Bill," 7 June 2010, http://www.bpnews.net/BPnews.asp?ID=33077; Espinosa, Elizondo, and Miranda, *Hispanic Churches in American Public Life,* 28.

83. Gastón Espinosa, e-mail interview with Samuel Rodríguez, spring 2013.

84. Ibid.

85. Suzanne Gamboa, "Evangelical Pastor Continues 40-Day Immigration Fast as House Set to Leave," NBC Latino, 10 December 2013, http://nbclatino.com/2013/12/10/evangelical-pastor-continues-40-day-immigration-fast-as-house-set-to-leave/; NHCLC, "History," January 20, 2014, http://www.nhclc.org/en/history.

86. For evidence of the large number and percentage of Latino AG clergy and laity on the various NHCLC boards, see their web page link on "Our Leadership," which is a who's who of Latino AG pastors and leaders; http://www.nhclc.org/en/our-leadership.

12. Balancing the Horizontal with the Vertical

1. This was noted in Jim Wallis's foreword to Samuel Rodríguez's book, *Path of Miracles: The Seven Life-Changing Principles that Lead to Purpose and Fulfillment* (New York: Celebra/Penguin Books, 2009). Also see Jim Wallis, *God's Politics: Why the Right Gets It Wrong and the Left Doesn't Get It* (San Francisco: HarperSan Francisco, 2006). For more on Nepantla political spirituality, see Gastón Espinosa, Virgilio Elizondo, and

Jesse Miranda, *Hispanic Churches in American Public Life: Summary of Findings* (Notre Dame, IN: University of Notre Dame Institute for Latino Studies, 2003), 5.

2. Samuel Solivan, *Spirit, Pathos and Liberation: Toward an Hispanic Pentecostal Theology* (Sheffield, UK: Sheffield Academic Press, 1998); Eldin Villafañe, *The Liberating Spirit: Toward an Hispanic American Pentecostal Social Ethic* (New York: University Press of America, 1992).

3. Margaret M. Poloma and John C. Green, *The Assemblies of God: Godly Love and the Revitalization of American Pentecostalism* (New York: New York University Press, 2010), 9–13, 25, 29–32.

4. Rodríguez, *Path of Miracles,* acknowledgments.

5. Gastón Espinosa, ed., *Religion, Race, and Barack Obama's New Democratic Pluralism* (New York: Routledge, 2012), 213–242. See 425n11.

6. For evidence, see the Introduction to this book and Gastón Espinosa, Virgilio Elizondo, and Jesse Miranda, *Hispanic Churches in American Public Life: Summary of Findings* (Notre Dame, IN: University of Notre Dame Institute for Latino Studies, 2003); the 2006 Pew Forum on Religion and Public Life *Spirit and Power* ten-country survey (which included a U.S. Latino subsample): http://www.pewforum .org/files/2006/10/pentecostals-08.pdf; Sherri Doty, Statistics Department supervisor, Office of the General Secretary of the Assemblies of God, General Council of the Assemblies of God National Leadership and Resource Center, 8 August 2013; Clifton Holland and the Programa Latinoamericano de Estudios Socioreligiosos (PROLADES), "Report on Hispanic Protestant Denominations in the USA, July 2012," http://www.hispanicchurchesusa.net/denominations/hispusa-table-prot -denoms-sort-clascode-15july2012.pdf.

7. Ibid.; Gastón Espinosa, *Latino Religions and Politics: Pre- and Post-2012 Election Findings* (Claremont, CA: Claremont McKenna College, 2012), 8. This LRAP 2012 survey found that the AG is the destination for almost one out of four Catholics who switch to Protestantism and that born-again Christians made up 39 percent of Latino Christian voters and 43 percent of Latino undecided likely voters nationwide.

8. Espinosa, *Religion, Race, and Barack Obama's New Democratic Pluralism*, 216; Joe Von Kanel and Hal Quinley, "Exit Polls: Latino Voters Tip Balance," *CNNPolitics. com*, November, 5, 2008, http://politicalticker.blogs.cnn.com/2008/11/05/exit-polls -where-latino-voters-tipped-the-balance/?eref=ib_politicalticker; National Election Pool exit poll, November 5, 2012, http://www.cnn.com/ELECTION/2008/results /polls/#USP00p1. The National Election Pool (NEP) exit poll is a consortium of ABC News, Associated Press, CBS News, CNN, Fox News, and NBC News. The NEP was formed in 2008 to provide information on Election Night about the vote count, election analysis, and election projections. NEP contracted Edison Research to make projections and provide exit poll analysis. In 2012, 26,565 voters were surveyed at polling locations in thirty-one states. In 2012, Edison Research made the controversial decision to not include nineteen states, almost all of which were Republican, to cut down on their costs. However, they have attempted to take these Republican states' voting records into account to create a fair and accurate sampling method and results.

9. Texas, California, New York, and Florida have the largest or among the largest number of Latino Assemblies of God, International Church of the Foursquare, Latin American

Council of Christian Churches, and Southern Baptist churches. Holland and PRO-LADES, "Report on Hispanic Protestant Denominations in the USA," July 2012.

10. These findings draw on the 2000 Hispanic Churches in American Public Life (HCAPL) national survey of 2,060 Latinos, hereafter cited as the 2000 HCAPL survey. For more information on the survey schematics and sampling method of the HCAPL survey and the larger HCAPL study, see Espinosa, Elizondo, and Miranda, *Hispanic Churches in American Public Life*, 13; Gastón Espinosa, "Methodological Reflections on Social Science Research on Latino Religions," in *Rethinking Latino(a) Religion and Identity*, ed. Miguel de la Torre and Gastón Espinosa (Cleveland, TN: Pilgrim Press, 2006), 26–45.

11. Espinosa, Elizondo, and Miranda, *Hispanic Churches in American Public Life*, 13; Espinosa, "Methodological Reflections on Social Science Research on Latino Religions," 26–45.

12. Gastón Espinosa, Latino Religions and Politics (LRAP) survey of 1,075 Latino likely voters, October 3–10, 2012. This 2012 nationally representative bilingual telephone survey builds on the Hispanic Churches in American Public Life national survey in 2000 and the follow-up LRAP national survey of 1,104 Latino voters in 2008. The LRAP 2008 survey drew on a similar framework and questions from the 2000 HCAPL survey and had a large screening segment of 2,828 respondents for almost one-third of the survey questions. The margin of error for the 2012 LRAP survey is +/−3.0 percent at a 95 percent confidence level. More than 93 percent of all Latino likely voters in the 2012 LRAP survey were Christian, and Latino Catholics and Protestants made up 98 percent of Christian likely voters in this sample, with 2 percent self-identifying as Jehovah's Witness and Mormon. The survey was fielded and supervised by Gastón Espinosa and Rick Hunter at SDR Consulting. Hunter has personally supervised the completion of over 400,000 individual surveys during his career. He has consulted for the White House and major corporations on the public's opinion of them and other issues using public opinion research and has overseen surveys for Univision and Telemundo, working in conjunction at different times with ABC, CBS, and CNN. He is one of a handful of professionals to set up, manage, and project elections through exit polls in national and local elections for television stations and networks.

13. Sheri Doty, "Race and Ethnicity of AG U.S. Churches, 2010, National Totals," September 12, 2011, http://agchurches.org/Sitefiles/Default/RSS/AG.org%20TOP/AG%20Statistical%20Reports/2010%20Stats/Acm759%202010%20Sum.pdf.

14. For a summary of the different theories on why Latinos and Latin Americans convert to Pentecostalism, see Brian H. Smith, *Religious Politics in Latin America: Pentecostal vs. Catholic* (Notre Dame, IN: University of Notre Dame Press, 1998), 3–8, 21–49; Andrew Greeley, "Defections among Hispanics (Updated)," *America* 27 (September 1997): 12–13.

15. Gastón Espinosa, Virgilio Elizondo, and Jesse Miranda, eds., *Latino Religions and Civic Activism in the United States* (New York: Oxford University Press, 2005), 288.

16. Smith, *Religious Politics in Latin America,* 3–8, 21–49; Greeley, "Defections among Hispanics (Updated)," 12–13.

17. For more on the LRAP 2012 survey, see 484n12.

18. Gastón Espinosa, interview with SED Superintendent Rafael Reyes, 6 February 2014.
19. Gastón Espinosa, interview with Rev. Dr. Sergio Navarrete, superintendent of the Southern Pacific District of the Assemblies of God, 6 February 2014.
20. Espinosa, interview with SED Superintendent Rafael Reyes, 6 February 2014.
21. See the LRAP 2012 survey. Rev. Juan Hernández, former general superintendent of the Latin American Council of Christian Churches (CLADIC, founded by Francisco Olazábal in Houston in 1923), has stated in numerous conversations that CLADIC has had difficulties retaining some of its second- and third generation English-dominant youth because their preferred language of communication is English (at least in public). He noted that this led some to attend AG or other bilingual Latino Pentecostal or Protestant churches. I have had similar conversations with Latino Apostolic Assembly pastors and ministers who noted the same problems in retaining their youth and who for this reason now in some cases offer bilingual services or one service in Spanish and one in English. Gastón Espinosa, correspondence with Rev. Juan Hernández (CLADIC), 5 January 2013; Gastón Espinosa, interview with Rev. David Jimenez (Apostolic Assembly), 20 October 2013.
22. It is misleading to state that the Latino Evangelical population is only 13 percent of the total Latino population in the United States. When born-again Protestant Christians across denominations are combined with those who attend Evangelical and Pentecostal churches, the number of Evangelicals rises to more than 80 percent of all Latino Protestants. The HCAPL survey found, for example, that 43 percent of Latino mainline Protestants also said they are born-again Christians and that 22 percent of them said they were Pentecostal or Charismatic. When one combines all Latinos who say they are born again and/or attend Evangelical churches, the proportion of Latinos who are Evangelical rises to over 80 percent of all Latino Protestants. Furthermore, when one ferrets out the actual identity of those supposedly "unaffiliated" "other Christian," "independent/non-denominational," and other respondents via follow-up questions or prompts to specify which church or tradition, if any, they currently attend or affiliate with, the HCAPL and LRAP surveys found that most specified (when given the opportunity on the survey) an identifiable Protestant church, almost always Evangelical or Pentecostal/Charismatic or independent/nondenominational Evangelical or Pentecostal/Charismatic. When all of these figures are combined, the number of Protestants ranges from 25 to 33 percent of the United States Latino community, with Evangelicals constituting over 80 percent of them. Espinosa, "Methodological Reflections on Social Science Research on Latino Religions," 26–45. Sarah Posner, "An Immoderate Proposal: Sam Rodriguez, 'Centrist' Evangelical, to Give Benediction at RNC," Religion Dispatches, 26 August 2012, http://www.religiondispatches.org/archive/election2012/6325/an_immoderate_proposal%3A_sam_rodriguez%2C_"centrist"_evangelical%2C_to_give_benediction_at_rnc/. For The Pew Research Hispanic Trends Project data on Latinos, see http://www.pewhispanic.org/2012/04/04/v-politics-values-and-religion/; Laurie Goodstein, "For Some Hispanics, Coming to America Also Means Abandoning Religion," *New York Times*, 15 April 2007; Juan Navarro-Rivera, Barry A. Kosmin, and Ariela Keysar, *U.S. Latino Religious Identification 1990–2008: Growth, Diversity and Transformation* (Hartford,

CT: Trinity College, 2008), 1, 21; Ariela Keysar, Barry Kosmin, and Egon Mayer, *Religious Identification among Hispanics in the United States, 2001* (New York: Graduate Center of the University of New York, 2001), 5, 16–22.

23. These findings draw on the HCAPL national survey.

24. Navarro-Rivera, Kosmin, and Keysar, *U.S. Latin Religious Identification, 1990–2008*, 23; Keysar, Kosmin, and Mayer, *Religious Identification among Hispanics in the United States, 2001*, 6, 22. Neither of these studies specifically reports the percentage of Latino atheists in isolation; instead, they create a composite category called "nones" but then sometimes cite atheists as the first group in that composite, even though they are often the smallest segment of that group when the combined category is disaggregated, all of which creates a perception that this shift toward the nones is a move away from religion. There are other concerns with their classification system, including projecting Latino religiosity based on an English-only sample (in most Latino surveys the Spanish-language response rate is 34–38 percent, thus leaving out a large segment of respondents who are more likely to report being religious and Christian—Catholic or Protestant); misclassifying the Church of the Nazarene as Pentecostal even though it has an explicit denominational statement that rejects Pentecostal tongues; misclassifying the Salvation Army as Pentecostal; and assuming that all Church of God (e.g., Anderson) and Holiness denominations are Pentecostal even though large numbers of them share that label but reject tongues. Equally problematic is misclassifying the Christian Reform Church as a "sect" with Jehovah's Witnesses and Christian Science, and classifying without qualification all "seculars" as "nones." One can be deeply religious *and* secular and even strongly support the separation of church and state (e.g., Baptist and Anabaptist groups). Furthermore, in Latin American history and politics, secularism and the separation of church and state were never strictly tied with having no religion or professing atheism, but rather with religious tolerance and Protestantism, and for these reasons it is not surprising that many religious Latinos from Latin America (and even Evangelicals) might self-identify as secular. All references to the 2012 LRAP survey refer to the 1,000-person sample unless I am referring to the "Religion" and "No Religion" question and sample, which is based on the total sample of 1,075 Latinos.

25. Espinosa, "Methodological Reflections on Social Science Research on Latino Religions," 34–45. While it is also true that some respondents may be genuinely confused or practice a combinative multireligion spirituality, the latter is unlikely with most Latinos in the AG because they are critical of theologically combinative traditions like Santería, *brujería,* Spiritualism, and other occult and metaphysical traditions, arguing that their core beliefs are unbiblical and influenced by malevolent spirits. It is also important to remember that in Latin America most Evangelical Protestants simply call themselves Christians ("soy Cristiano") because almost all Catholics self-identify as Catholic ("soy Católico"). In short, "Christian" is a kind of shorthand for "Protestant Evangelical" in most parts of Latin America and among U.S. Latinos. In addition to the reasons cited previously in the chapter, additional reasons for self-identifying as "just Christian," "independent/nondenominational," "other religion," "no religion," and with other categories are the following: (1) many Latinos are recent converts; (2) many have had no training in church history and

their denominational distinctives; (3) most are unaware of the sociology of religion and the Protestant classification categories it employs, which are usually based on previous mainline Protestant–oriented surveys; (4) many surveys are in English; (5) many surveys do not specify in the religious identity response options Assemblies of God and other indigenous Evangelical and Pentecostal denominations; (6) most Latinos do not believe they practice a "religion" but rather a faith in Jesus Christ; (7) "religion" is often used in Latino circles to denote Catholicism and what they deem largely lifeless human-made rituals and traditions; and (8) because they promote having a personal, living, and born-again relationship with Jesus Christ. There is good reason to believe (based on how they respond to other religious identity questions) that for many Latinos "no religion" may simply or also be shorthand for "no religious preference" at the time of the survey, since clearly more than half of the respondents in some of these categories report being born again and attending church at rates that match some of the most religiously committed survey respondents. R. Stephen Warner, "The De-Europeanization of American Christianity," in *A Nation of Religions: The Politics of Pluralism in Multireligious America*, ed. Stephen Prothero (Chapel Hill: University of North Carolina Press, 2006), 233–255. For a shorter version of this article, see R. Stephen Warner, "Coming to America: Immigrants and the Faith They Bring," *TCC*, 10 February 2004: 19–23.

26. Jesse Miranda, *The Christian Church in Ministry* (New York: International Correspondence Institute, 1980); Jesse Miranda, *Liderazgo y Amistad* (Deerfield, FL: Editorial Vida, 1998); John S. Dickerson, "The Decline of Evangelical America," *New York Times*, December 15, 2012, http://www.nytimes.com/2012/12/16/opinion/sunday/the-decline-of-evangelical-america.html?pagewanted=a.

27. See the HCAPL survey.

28. In an interview with "God in America" for the PBS program *The American Experience*, Samuel Rodríguez stated: "On the issue of marriage . . . would Hispanic evangelicalism be in favor of preserving traditional marriage? One hundred percent absolutely yes, but they would simultaneously say, 'We must repudiate homophobia.' Does that sound oxymoronic or contradictory in terms? We don't find it to be. I've participated personally in conversations, in mobilization strategies in defense of traditional marriage, while I have simultaneously participated in defending the rights of the gay and lesbian community as it pertains to making sure they're not discriminated [against]." American Experience, *God in America: Interview: Samuel Rodríguez*, 13 January 2010, https://www.pbs.org/godinamerica/interviews/samuel-rodriguez.html. Also see Nicola Menzie, "Can Another 'Gay-Friendly' Faith Group Help Steer the Conversation for Christians on Homosexuality?" *Christian Post*, 27 January 2014, http://www.christianpost.com/news/can-another-gay-friendly-faith-group-help-steer-the-conversation-for-christians-on-homosexuality-113274/pageall.html. Despite Rodríguez's public stance against homophobia, Right Wing Watch, a project of Norman Lear's People for the American Way, is unconvinced of his support and has been critical of his association with Evangelical organizations like the Liberty Counsel, which provides legal services to defend traditional marriage and oppose abortion. For more on this topic, see http://www.pfaw.org/category/organizations/national-hispanic-christian-leadership-conference. Gastón Espinosa, interview with

Rev. Jesse Miranda, 11 March 2014; Gastón Espinosa, interview with Rev. Sergio Navarrete, 12 March 2014; Gastón Espinosa, interview with SED Superintendent Rafael Reyes, 12 March 2014; Gastón Espinosa, interview with Rev. Samuel Rodríguez, March 12, 2014.

29. Gastón Espinosa, interview with Rev. Samuel Rodríguez, 24 June 2010; Gastón Espinosa, interview with Rev. Wilfredo de Jesús, 31 August 2010; Espinosa, Elizondo, and Miranda, *Hispanic Churches in American Public Life.*

30. Espinosa, *Religion, Race, and Barack Obama's New Democratic Pluralism,* 213–238.

31. Gastón Espinosa, *Religion, Race, and the American Presidency* (Lanham, MD: Rowman and Littlefield, 2011), 246.

32. Gastón Espinosa, interviews with Rev. Jesse Miranda, 15 and 19 November 2012.

33. Espinosa, *Religion, Race, and the American Presidency,* 231–285; Espinosa, interviews with Rev. Jesse Miranda, 15 and 19 November 2012.

34. Espinosa, *Religion, Race, and the American Presidency,* 231–285.

35. Gastón Espinosa, *Religion and the American Presidency: George Washington to George W. Bush, with Commentary and Primary Sources* (New York: Columbia University Press, 2009), 482–487.

36. Espinosa, *Religion, Race, and the American Presidency,* 231–285.

37. Ibid.

38. Ibid., 219, 231–285.

39. Ibid., 231–285.

40. Ibid.

41. Ibid.

42. Ibid.

43. Ibid.

44. Ibid.; Gastón Espinosa, interviews with Rev. Samuel Rodríguez, 17 and 21 November 2012.

45. Ibid.

46. Ibid.

47. Ibid.

48. Ibid.; Espinosa, *Religion, Race, and Barack Obama's New Democratic Pluralism,* 219–220.

49. Espinosa, telephone interview with Rev. Wilfredo de Jesús, 31 August 2010.

50. Ibid.

51. Espinosa, interview with Rev. Samuel Rodríguez, 24 June 2010.

52. Espinosa, telephone interview with Rev. Wilfredo de Jesús, 31 August 2010.

53. John W. Kennedy, "Preach and Reach: Despite His Liberal Record, Barack Obama Is Making a Lot of Evangelicals Think Twice," *Christianity Today,* 6 October 2008, http://www.christianitytoday.com/ct/2008/october/18.26.html.

54. Jacques Berlinerblau, "Huckobama," *Washington Post,* 3 March 2008; Michelle Vu, "Obama Connects with Hispanic Evangelicals in Texas," *Christian Post,* 3 March 2008.

55. Espinosa, telephone interview with Rev. Wilfredo de Jesús, 31 August 2010.

56. Italics in original quote. Barack Obama, *The Audacity of Hope: Thoughts on Reclaiming the American Dream* (New York: Three Rivers Press, 2006), 198–224; Sarah

Pullman and Ted Olsen, "Q&A: Barack Obama," *Christianity Today*, January 23, 2008, http://www.christianitytoday.com/ct/2008/januaryweb-only/104-32.0.html.

57. Espinosa, interview with Rev. Samuel Rodríguez, 24 June 2010.

58. Samuel Rodríguez, *Hispanic Christian Newswire* (Chicago), http://www.nhclc.org/news/nhclc-and-2008-presidential-candidates.

59. "Two Chicago Latinos That Helped Obama Be President," *Extra* (Chicago) January 21, 2009.

60. Anthony Robinson, "Articles of Faith: Evangelical Group Bucks Tradition, Supports Obama," *Seattle Post-Intelligencer*, July 25, 2008.

61. Gastón Espinosa, interview with Dr. Juan Hernández, 20 August 2010.

62. Espinosa, interview with Rev. Samuel Rodríguez, 24 June 2010. Espinosa, interview with Dr. Juan Hernández, 20 August 2010.

63. Samuel Rodríguez, "Our Flagging Faith in the GOP," *Washington Post*, February 24, 2008: B04.

64. Espinosa, interview with Rev. Samuel Rodríguez, 24 June 2010.

65. Ibid. Dr. Shaun Casey's work for the Obama campaign and thereafter led Secretary of State John Kerry in August 2013 to appoint him to lead the State Department's new Office of Faith-Based Community Initiatives. Lauren Markoe, "Shaun Casey, New Head of State's Office of Faith-Based Community Initiatives, Speaks Out," *Religion News Service*, 8 August 2013, as cited in Huff Post Religion, http://www.huffingtonpost.com/2013/08/08/shaun-casey-state-department_n_3727105.html.

66. Gastón Espinosa, interview with Rev. Samuel Rodríguez, 12 August 2010.

67. Hernández holds a Ph.D. from Texas Christian University, and although he is pro-life, Pentecostal, and a supporter of traditional marriage, Republicans such as Michelle Malkin criticized him for supporting comprehensive immigration reform. Espinosa, interview with Dr. Juan Hernández, 20 August 2010; Jessica Ramírez and Holly Bailey, "Why Won't Juan Come to the Phone? McCain's Hispanic Outreach Chief Is Both Loved and Loathed," *Newsweek*, July 28, 2008; Michelle Malkin, "John McCain's Open-Borders Outreach Director: The New DHS Secretary? Update: A 'Non-paid Volunteer,'" *MichelleMalkin.com*, 25 January 2008; Carolyn Petri, "The Power of the Advisory Council: The Latino Vote Has Already Swung; McCain and Obama's Latino Advisory Boards Could Explain Why," *The American Prospect*, November 4, 2008, web only, http://prospect.org/article/power-advisory-council.

68. Espinosa, interview with Rev. Samuel Rodríguez, 24 June 2010; Espinosa, interview with Rev. Samuel Rodríguez, 12 August 2010.

69. Gastón Espinosa, interview with Dr. Shaun Casey, 18 August 2010.

70. Espinosa, telephone interview with Rev. Wilfredo de Jesús, 31 August 2010.

71. Espinosa, *Religion, Race, and Barack Obama's New Democratic Pluralism*, 232–233.

72. Ibid.

73. Espinosa, interviews with Rev. Samuel Rodríguez, 17 and 21 November 2012.

74. Ibid.

75. Ibid.

76. Ibid.

77. Ibid.

78. Ibid.

79. Ibid.

80. See statistics in Peter Slavin, "Deportation of Illegal Immigrants Increases under Obama Administration," *Washington Post*, July 26, 2010, http://www.washington-post.com/wp-dyn/content/article/2010/07/25/AR2010072501790.html.

81. Espinosa, interviews with Rev. Samuel Rodríguez, 17 and 21 November 2012.

82. Ibid.

83. Espinosa, interview with Rev. Wilfredo de Jesús, 31 August 2010.

84. Ibid.

85. Ibid.

86. Espinosa, *Religion, Race, and Barack Obama's New Democratic Pluralism*, 264–266.

87. Mary Bruce, "Obama Blames GOP for Inability to Pass Immigration Reform," *ABC News*, 20 September 2012, http://abcnews.go.com/blogs/politics/2012/09/obama-blames-gop-for-inability-to-pass-immigration-reform/.

88. Espinosa, *Religion, Race, and Barack Obama's New Democratic Pluralism*, 232–234.

89. 2012 LRAP survey.

90. 2012 National Election Pool exit poll; Bill Clinton, *My Life* (New York: Alfred A. Knopf, 2004), 632.

Conclusion

1. Although the Apostolic Assembly of the Faith in Christ Jesus was initiated by Francisco Llorente in 1912 and organized in Llorente, Marcial de la Cruz, and Antonio Castañeda Nava in 1916, it was administratively under the legal umbrella of the Pentecostal Assemblies of the World until 1930, after which time it became an independent and legally incorporated denomination in the United States. Prior to 1930, all ordination certificates for Latinos in the Apostolic Assembly were issued by the Pentecostal Assemblies of the World.

2. Gastón Espinosa, interview with Rev. Jesse Miranda, 7 July 2011.

3. Ibid.

4. Clifton Holland's study identified 9,420 Latino Pentecostal churches in America. Kate Bowler identified 37 Latino megachurches with more than 2,000 members across the United States. Clifton Holland and the Programa Latinoamericano de Estudios Socioreligiosos (PROLADES), "Report on Hispanic Protestant Denominations in the USA, July 2012," http://www.hispanicchurchesusa.net/denominations/hispusa-table-prot-denoms-sort-clascode-15july2012.pdf; Gastón Espinosa, correspondence with Kate Bowler, 14 February 2014; Sherri Doty, "AG U.S. Vital Statistics, 2010," Statistics Department supervisor, Office of the General Secretary of the Assemblies of God, General Council of the Assemblies of God National Leadership and Resource Center. Gastón Espinosa, email interview with Jesse Miranda, 7 July 2011. See 427n22.

5. Gastón Espinosa, interview with Rev. Samuel Rodríguez, 15 July 2012.

Index

Abortion, opposition to, 308, 317, 343, 389
Adventists, 136, 308
Affirmative action, 309, 317, 377
African Americans, 8, 20, 31, 75, 136, 333; black slave religion, 26; Christian theology and, 39; churches of, 122; civil rights movement of, 180, 253–254; discrimination against, 158; lynching of, 58; Mexican migrant workers converted by, 149; Obama presidency and, 399; Pentecostal women, 283, 310; Protestants in New York City, 260, 262
Alaniz, Concepción, 63, 64–66
Alaniz, Enemecio, 63, 64–66, 68, 77, 92; Ball at odds with, 160; confrontation with Spiritists, 68, 69; documentation of evangelistic work, 81; as founder of Latino AG in Southwest, 162; Mexican expansion in Southwest and, 112; Orozco and, 75; as pioneer of Latino Pentecostal movement, 95
Albanese, Catherine, 427n25
Albizu Campos, Pedro, 207, 226, 233, 264
Alexander, Estrelda, 471n3
Alfaro, Sammy, 422n4
Alianza de Ministerios Evangélicos Nacionales (AMEN), 14, 16, 189, 342–345, 361, 364, 374; Bush (George W.) presidency and, 382–385; creation of, 403; Obama presidency and, 387–388; presidential politics and, 380, 381
Alinsky, Saul, 336, 479n35
Alvarado, Pedro Juan, 240, 244, 246, 247
Alvarez, Tomás, 216, 217, 222, 224, 263, 280, 411, 467n37
American Academy of Religion, 14, 345, 374, 480n51
Americanization, 367, 409
Anderson, Allan, 431n13
Anderson, Leith, 357, 358
Anderson, Robert Mapes, 63, 434n49
Apostolic Assembly of the Faith in Christ Jesus, 141, 335, 423n8
Apostolic Faith, The (newspaper), 28, 285, 430n1, 433n30; circulation of, 46, 50; first issue, 36; healing testimonies in, 40, 41, 42; theological mission of, 39; women as coeditors of, 48
Apostolic Faith Movement (Houston), 15, 29, 33, 216, 406; birth of Latino Pentecostalism in Texas and, 60; Parham's leadership of, 49
Apostolics, 144, 149, 159, 450n37, 452n58

Aquino, Maria Pilar, 471n3
Arizona, 147, 288, 290, 354–360
Armageddon, Battle of, 79, 209
Arroyo Seco Camp Meeting, 140, 448n12
Asians, 28, 365, 400
Assembly of Christian Churches (AIC), 265, 268–269, 366, 423n8
Atheists, 371, 372, 486n24
Australia, 23, 46, 139
Azusa Street Revival (Los Angeles), 15, 67, 102, 141; Bazans and, 166; conflict with Protestant establishment, 44–46, 212; daughter missions, 138; divine healing events at, 40–42; evangelistic social work at, 324; founding of, 33–35; global missions of, 46–47; Latinas in ministry of, 285–286; Latino AG origins in New York City and, 262; *Los Angeles Times* description of, 19, 24–25; message and theology of, 38–42; Montgomerys at, 139; Oneness division and declining influence of, 54–58; origins of Latino Pentecostal movement and, 22, 24, 52, 58, 136, 162, 406; Puerto Rican Pentecostal origins and, 195, 196–197, 231; supernatural events at, 35–36; Texas Latino Pentecostalism and, 88; "Upper Room," 37, 45

Baker, R. D., 103, 166
Ball, Henry C., 15, 60, 70, 190, 194, 406, 438n5; Bazan and, 165–167; Central American Pentecostal movement and, 155; controversy over leadership and, 88–89, 114, 116–117, 127, 136, 158–162; counteroffensive against push for Mexican independence, 123–125; defense of Latinos against discrimination, 156–158; "dictatorship" of, 120; doubts about vision for Mexican AG, 103–105; duties after handover of leadership to Mexicans, 215–216; early life of, 89–90; evangelistic civic action and, 324–325; Foreign Missions Committee and, 236, 237; as founder of Latino AG in Southwest, 61–62, 72, 91–97, 162–163; lasting impact among Mexicans, 81; Latin American Bible Institutes and, 151–153; "Latino Convention" (1918) and, 83, 133; ministry of, 167–168; Olazábal and, 110, 111, 113–114, 130, 158, 408; paternalism of, 85, 159; on poverty of Mexican pastors, 148–149; rebuilding and consolidation of movement, 133, 134; religious development of, 90–91; at "second convention," 442n29; Spanish language and, 85–86, 91, 105–108, 163, 407; vision of Mexican missions in convention, 97–101; women ministers and, 287; on Women's Missionary Councils, 295–296
Ball, Sunshine Marshall, 96–97, 103, 288; as role model for women, 292; at "second convention," 442n29; Women's Missionary Council and, 295, 296
Banda, Francisco, 74, 442n29
Baptism, 6, 26, 27, 276
Baptists, 6, 69, 90, 136, 154; converts to Pentecostalism, 149, 366; former Pentecostals as, 315; indigenization process and, 418; in New York City, 261–262; in Puerto Rico, 203, 205; revivalists, 7; Southern Baptists, 9, 357
Barfoot, Charles, 283, 284, 287, 321, 411
Bartleman, Frank, 36, 38, 39, 48, 59
Batman, G. W., 46, 51
Bazan, Alex, 180, 299, 452n58
Bazan, Anita, 474n51
Bazan, Demetrio, 153, 188, 191, 237, 288–289, 442n29; debate with Apostolics, 149; early life of, 165–166; elected second superintendent of Latino AG, 164–165, 417; evangelistic social work and, 325–326; Latin American Bible Institutes and, 152, 153; at Latino AG convention (1925), 135; Latino AG ministry in Puerto Rican diaspora and, 172–175; leadership style of, 408; ministry in Colorado and leadership style, 168–172; NHCLC and, 348; Olazábal and, 101, 110, 127, 128, 133, 166–167; push for Puerto Rican integration and, 238, 240–241, 243; as superintendent of Latino AG, 161, 162, 163; Texas/Southwest Latino AG and, 63

Bazan, Manuelita (Nellie) Treviño, 63, 101, 110, 127, 153, 175, 288–289; Ball–Olazábal conflict and, 167; as first woman ordained by AG, 288; marriage to Demetrio Bazan, 166

Bell, E. N., 49, 55, 71, 123

Berrios, Abelardo, 241, 242, 256, 265, 269, 270

Bethel Temple (mother church), 121, 167, 411

Bible, 6, 25, 43, 78, 105; distribution of Bibles, 107, 328, 355–356; on human origins, 376; images of women in, 315; Olazábal's legacy and, 129; teaching of, 146, 200

Bible schools, 15, 29, 39, 43, 86, 153, 273, 409; of Olazábal, 111–112, 119, 124; women's involvement in, 293–295, 411–412

Blaisdell, Francisca, 147, 193, 287, 288, 473n25, 473n29

Blaisdell, George, 147, 193, 287

Blumhofer, Edith, 421n2, 471n3

Boddy, Alexander A., 46, 47

Booth, William, 7, 227

Born-again Christians, 5, 8, 10, 39, 67, 198, 382, 485n22

Bosworth, F. F., 45, 63, 64, 67, 438n6

Bowler, Kate, 490n4

Bracero Program, 169, 335

Brewer, Jan, 16, 354

Brown, Marie, 208, 262

Brown v. Board of Education, 234–235, 253

Buddhists, 403, 426n14

Bush, George W., 8, 16, 317, 360, 391, 401, 418, 429n41; Cuban support for, 329; efforts to win over Latino AG leaders, 362; faith-based initiatives, 376, 383, 384, 404; immigration reform and, 352, 481n67; Latino AG leaders and presidency of, 381–387; majority of Pentecostal support to, 351; Miranda invited to White House by, 343, 361, 379; Victory Outreach and, 342

California, 134, 138–139, 365; farm workers' struggle in, 334–339; Latino AG Bible schools in, 346; origins of independent Latino Pentecostalism in, 136–138; Proposition 187 initiative, 309; Puerto Rican Pentecostalism in, 199–202, 231, 290

Calvary Baptist Church, 131, 267

Calvary Chapel (Costa Mesa), 9, 371

Calvin, John, 6, 7

Camacho, Julia, 128, 229, 288, 289

Campbell, Evelyn, 73, 442n29

Cape Verde Islanders, 139, 143, 199

Caquias, Antonio R., 269, 272

Caride, Gabriel, 327–328

Carrión, Adolfo, 275–276, 304, 328

Casa Evangélica de Publicaciones (Gospel Publishing House), 105, 153

Casarez, Tommy, 14, 274, 346–347

Casey, Shaun, 392, 489n65

Cashwell, Gaston Barnabus, 46, 47, 63, 166

Casteñeda Nava, Antonio, 141, 450n25

Castro, Fidel, 207, 326, 328–329

Catholics/Catholic Church, 6, 9, 59, 86, 154, 294, 361, 426n14; at Azusa Street Revival, 35; Charismatic, 9, 10; converts to Pentecostalism, 4, 187, 308, 366, 367; farm workers' struggle in California and, 338–339; fatalism of, 79; Latina, 283; in Mexico, 64, 451n50; in New Mexico, 150–151; in New York City, 256, 257, 259–260, 271; opposition to Pentecostalism, 110, 235; Pentecostals in conflict with, 147–149, 220–221; as percentage of Latino community, 364; political alignments and, 363; presidential politics and, 382, 385, 400, 403; in Puerto Rico, 194, 195, 202–204, 220–221, 231–232, 253, 458nn25–26; self-identification of Catholics, 486n25; Spiritualism and, 206; wealth of Roman Catholic Church, 154

Cazares, Chonita, 66, 75

Cazares, Inocencia, 65, 77

Cazares, Manuel, 65, 66, 75, 77

Center for Urban Ministerial Education (CUME), 14, 273, 274, 374

Central District of the Assemblies of God (Latino district), 182, 183

Charismatics, 3, 4, 6–10, 323, 372, 423n8

Chaves, Mark, 314

Chávez, Aurora, 300, 301

Chávez, César, 16, 316, 334–339, 340, 356, 359, 395

Chicano movement *(Chicanismo)*, 314, 316,
476n83
Chile, 152, 161, 173, 226
China, 46, 196
Christian and Missionary Alliance (CMA),
195, 196
Christian Church in Ministry, The
(Miranda), 188, 343, 374
Christian Church of John 3:16, 270,
272–274, 340, 469n71. *See also* Tañon,
Ricardo
Christianity, 25–26, 371; de-
Europeanization of American Christian-
ity, 5, 373, 414; multicultural, 47, 58;
theological streams in, 39
Christianity Today magazine, 16, 390
Christian Science, 44, 486n24
Churches: attendance, 369; Bethel Temple
(mother church), 110, 121; Euro-
American, 170; evangelism and, 171;
integration of faith and everyday life in,
78; megachurches, 368, 416, 490n4;
Obama presidency and, 388
Church of God (Cleveland, Tennessee),
159, 269, 371, 423n8
Church of God in Christ (COGIC), 38, 141
Church planting, 170, 179, 277, 409
Citizenship, 355, 367
Civil rights, 12, 15, 16, 323, 394, 414; black,
31, 32; immigration reform and, 352,
356; Latino views in HCAPL survey
and, 365, 366, 377, 378, 382
CLADIC. *See* Latin American Council of
Christian Churches (CLADIC)
Clinton, Bill, 16, 364, 376, 402, 403; Latino
vote won by, 379–380; Miranda invited
to White House by, 343, 380–381;
Victory Outreach and, 342
Clinton, Hillary, 380, 384
Collazo, Aguedo, 217, 218
Collins, A. P., 67, 71, 93, 95
Colorado, 149–150, 168, 176, 365
Community Service Organization (CSO),
335–336, 338
Congregationalists, 6, 203, 214
Cook, Glenn, 38, 49, 55
Cortés, Luís, 189, 345, 362, 384, 387
Craig, Robert, 100, 102, 109, 129,
143

Crawford, Florence, 50, 324
Cruz, Josue, 167, 168
Cruz, Nicky, 341, 348
Cuba, 107, 207, 226, 229, 272, 326–328
Curandero/a healers, 68, 439n17

Damascus Christian Church, 269, 301, 315,
423n8
Dayton, Donald, 431n13
Defenders of the Faith, 225, 269, 423n8,
462n109
De Jesús, Wilfredo: emerging generation of
Latino AG leaders and, 345; "Latino
Reformation" and, 2; Obama and, 16–17,
351, 388–391, 393, 399, 404–405, 456n38
De la Cruz, Marcial, 141, 450n25, 490n1
De León, Daniel, 342, 344, 346, 362, 383
De Leon, Victor, 1, 2, 15, 62, 93, 407; on
Bazan, 175; on "formal beginning" of
AG work among U.S. Latinos, 94; on
Mexican-led district, 120; NHCLC and,
348; original pioneers and, 116
Democratic Party, 8, 190, 310, 317, 319,
360, 387; immigration reform and, 351,
352, 354; Latino support for, 381, 401,
404; New Democratic coalition, 390;
racial-ethnic minorities and, 413–414;
Reagan Democrats, 381; swing voters
and, 363
Díaz, Samuel, 422n5
Disciples of Christ, 205, 214, 315
Divorce, 50–51, 307
Dobson, James, 309, 316–317
Dole, Robert, 381, 382, 402
Dominican Republic, 209, 212, 226, 229,
248, 272, 291
Dowie, Alexander, 28, 49
DuBois, Joshua, 388, 392
Duran, Edwardo, 149, 168
Durham, William H., 45, 46, 53–54, 55,
63, 137
Duryee, Spencer, 132, 227

Eisenhower, Dwight D., 326, 329
Elections, presidential, 8, 317–319, 354
Eliade, Mircea, 428n33
Elizondo, Virgilio, 189, 344, 357

El Salvador, 107, 153, 155

End Times prophecy, 50, 169, 196, 284, 289, 315

English language, 2, 47, 99, 109, 237; churches and, 370; citizenship and, 353; dominant among Latino youth, 485n21; immigrants' learning of, 357; mixed with Spanish (Spanglish), 367

Enviados de Dios (Bazan), 174, 289

Eschatology, 18, 32

Euro-American missionaries, 60, 62, 71, 74, 98, 406; Ball's counteroffensive and, 123; Ball's vision and, 103; departure from Mexican ministry, 104; Evangelical leaders, 16; Latinos as internal colony and, 407–408; Mexican control of ministry and, 115, 119; origins of Latino AG and, 87–89; paternalism among, 80–81, 83, 87; in Puerto Rico, 193, 215; push for Mexican independence and, 132; push for Puerto Rican integration and, 235–236; time sent ministering to Mexicans, 81

Euro-Americans, 10, 13, 15, 17, 71, 138; AG districts and, 187; Catholic hierarchy of, 203; "multicultural" history and, 19–20; Pentecostal women, 283; political alignments of Pentecostals, 363; press attention on Olazábal, 227; Protestants in New York City, 260, 261, 262, 466n29; women in ministry, 292–293

Evangelicals, 2, 3, 4, 372, 400; history and definitions of, 6–10; invited to White House, 16, 190, 343; presidential politics and, 403; racialization of, 5; relation to Pentecostals/Charismatics, 8; as swing constituency in elections, 319; traditional, 9

Evangelista Pentecostal, El (periodical), 215, 230, 294, 298, 325

Faith-based social activism: Cuban refugee ministry in Florida, 326–328; in early period (1917–1940s), 324–326; farm workers' struggle in California, 334–339; Latino Evangelical unity and, 342–345; Mariel Boat Lift and, 328–329; ministries to gang members and drug addicts, 339–342

Farrow, Lucy, 31, 32, 45, 46

Feliciano, Dionisia, 196, 209–210, 290–292, 409, 459n53

Feliciano, Solomon, 196, 209–210, 211, 212, 290–291, 409, 459n53

Feminism, 304–305, 309, 314, 412; and secular feminism, 314, 315

Fierro, Roberto, 128, 174, 238–240, 243, 325, 326

Finkenbinder, Aura, 215, 217, 218–219

Finkenbinder, Frank, 215, 217, 256, 460n54, 461n72; bilingual ministry of, 264; children of, 218–219; as president of movement in Puerto Rico, 218, 224; push for Puerto Rican integration and, 236; resignation of, 265

Finney, Charles, 7, 27, 61

First Spanish Baptist Church of New York City, 261, 469n71

Fisher, Elmer, 52, 136–137, 195

Flores, Mr. Isabel, 15, 64, 75, 95, 407; arrested in Texas, 157, 324–325; Ball and, 97, 108, 160; as founder of Latino AG in Southwest, 162; Latino Convention (1918) and, 98; Mexican expansion in Southwest and, 112; as pioneer of Latino Pentecostal movement, 77; push for Mexican independence and, 121, 122; at "second convention," 442n29

Florida, 365, 402, 413

Flower, J. R., 111, 117, 160–161, 208, 248–249; Ball's counteroffensive and, 123, 124–125, 446n48; Lugo and, 263; on Olazábal, 130; push for Puerto Rican integration and, 243, 244; women in ministry and, 282

Focus on the Family ministry, 309, 316

Foursquare, 269, 371, 423n8

Fraticelli, Angelo, 102, 128

Free Methodists, 9, 371

Frodsham, Stanley F., 200, 201, 229, 263

García Cortese, Aimee, 280, 282–283, 301–302, 303, 314; evangelistic social work and, 339, 340, 479n35; on feminist movement, 309, 475n80; influence of, 308

García Peraza, Juana, 230, 301, 428n36
Garza, Gloria, 297–299, 300, 304, 312, 316
Gaxiola y Gaxiola, Manuel, 448n19, 448nn21–24
Gay marriage, 190, 317, 343, 403, 405. *See also* Homosexuality
General Council of the Assemblies of God, 1, 159, 171, 187, 255, 415; Ball's conflict with Olazábal and, 115, 117, 123; Bazan and, 164; conventions, 182, 240, 249; formation of, 61; Latino District superintendents and, 179; Miranda as Executive Presbyter, 343; Puerto Rico District and, 236; recognition for Pentecostals and, 231; women ministers in, 284, 292
Girón, José, 150, 151, 174; evangelistic social work and, 325; Pacific Latin District of the Assemblies of God and, 182; as third superintendent of Latino District, 176
Glad Tidings Church (San Francisco), 100, 109, 143
Glossolalia, 38, 439n6
Goff, James Jr., 431n15
González, Elvira, 288, 289
González, Justo L., 471n3
González, Mark, 391, 393, 405
González, Saturnino (Nino), 184, 191, 250, 251, 253, 280, 328–329
Gore, Al, 16, 381, 382, 401
Graham, Billy, 7, 16, 308, 323, 380, 381, 399–400, 404
Great Awakening, First, 6–7
Great Awakening, Second, 7, 60–61, 112
Great Depression, 155–156, 161, 164, 221, 258–259, 325; effect on Puerto Rican economy, 223–224; ministers' struggle to survive in, 408
Greeley, Andrew, 425n12, 427n18
Green, John C., 422n2
Griffith, R. Marie., 471n3
Guatemala, 107, 153, 155
Guillén, Miguel, 75, 95, 445n16; Bazan and, 167; on discrimination against Mexicans, 157; on Mexican-led district, 120
Gulf District, 182, 183, 312

Hale, Felix, 64, 81, 92, 93, 103, 442n29
Harvard Divinity School, 14, 274
Hatfield, Rev., 90, 91
Hawaii, 196, 232, 290
Haywood, Garfield T., 46, 55
Healing, divine, 26, 27, 109–110, 238; conflicts with Spiritists/Spiritualists and, 221–223; first healing events at Azusa, 40–42, 435n63; percentage of Latino Christians praying for, 369, 373
Health care, 17, 377, 399
Hernández, Juan Dr., 391–393, 485n21, 489n67
Hernández, Juan, 485n21. *See also* Latin American Council of Christian Churches (CLADIC)
Himnos de Gloria (Hymns of Glory), 105, 106, 108, 163
Hindus, 403, 426n14
Hines, Mr and Mrs. Alberto, 107, 442n29
Hinn, Benny, 308, 316
Hispanic Churches in American Public Life (HCAPL) survey, 189, 344, 365, 424n10, 426n14, 484n10; on interest in public affairs, 378; Latino AG views on political and social work, 378–379; on women's role in churches, 377
Hispanos, 149, 151, 329–330, 448n9, 478n21
Hodges, Melvin L., 244, 247, 248
Holiness movement, 7, 26, 27, 28, 35, 39
Holland, Clifton, 423n9, 425n11, 490n4
Hollenweger, Walter J., 430n3, 431n13
Homosexuality, 309, 315–316, 375, 376, 476n80. *See also* Gay marriage
Howard, Concepción (Chonita) Morgan, 147, 287, 295, 296, 473n25
Howe, Lena, 215, 217, 218
Huerta, Dolores, 336, 358, 395, 479n35
Hutchins, Julia, 33, 46

Immigration reform, 16, 317, 323, 327, 387, 456n38; Bush (George W.) and, 352, 481n62; law and social action in Arizona, 354–360; Obama and, 354, 356, 358–359, 395, 399, 405; struggle for comprehensive reform (2005–2008), 350–354

Inostroza, María, 288, 473n29
Isasi-Díaz, Ada Maria, 471n3

Jacinto, Cecilio, 99, 452n66
Jakes, T. D., 308, 390
Jaramillo, Epifanio, 172, 179
Jehovah's Witnesses, 44, 136, 262, 426n14, 483n12, 486n24
Jesus Christ, 6, 26, 31, 90, 404; baptism of disciples of, 37; battle with Antichrist at Armageddon, 79; born-again experience with, 148, 487n25; healing power of, 42; limited atonement and, 7–8; love and justice of, 413; *mestizo* Jesus, 357; salvation of sinners by, 191; saving grace of, 322; Second Coming of, 28, 37, 276, 277; social message of, 363; Trinitarian teaching and, 54
Jews, 3, 338, 361, 365, 403, 425n11
Jim Crow segregation, 31, 47, 77, 90, 132
Jones, Charles Price, 7, 31
Jordan, Edmundo, 263, 294
Joyner, George, 63, 64, 74
Judeo Christian values, 323, 349, 353

Kennedy, Ted, 350, 353, 384, 386, 387
King, Martin Luther, Jr., 16, 129, 323, 332, 333; faith-based social activism of, 336, 404; immigration reform and, 356
King Ranch (Texas), 69, 70, 75, 79, 94
Kol Kare Bomidbar: A Voice Crying Out in the Wilderness (Parham), 28, 433n30
Kuhlman, Kathryn, 308, 316
Ku Klux Klan, 28, 30, 47, 71, 90, 150, 157

Latin. *See* Latino, U.S.
Latin American Bible Institute (LABI), 128, 146, 159, 163, 178, 182, 329; Ball and Luce as teachers at, 152–153, 215–216; Bazan and, 169, 172; education level of graduates, 169; Finkenbinder as director of, 265; former gang members at, 341; Latino education deficit and, 366; Luce as founder of, 292; Miranda and, 342, 343; Olazábal and, 151–152; training next generation of Latino AG members and,

346–347; women graduates, 293–294, 306, 313, 473n29
Latin American Council of Christian Churches (CLADIC), 76, 129, 146, 159, 407, 423n8; Bethel Temple in, 167; birth of, 126–128; criticism of Latino AG as Euro-American-run, 160; English-dominant youth and, 485n21; in New York City, 267–268
Latin District Council of the Assemblies of God (aka Latino District Council of the Assemblies of God), 218, 243, 247
Latino Assemblies of God (AG), 11, 82, 97, 107; Azusa Street Revival and origins of, 24, 57–58; beliefs and practices, 373–374; Bible institutes, 293–295; birth of Latino Districts (from 1971), 181–183; conventions, 119, 169; decentralization of, 185, 305; demographic shifts in religions and, 3–5; denominational identity interpreted, 370–373; denominational pluralism and, 13, 428n36; Department of Foreign Missions, 236–237, 243, 245; feminist movement and, 316; future of, 415–417; growth of, 134, 154, 164, 175, 183–188, 225, 231–232; historical insights and developments, 417–418; history of, 1–2, 15, 116, 182; influence on non-AG denominations, 13, 14; in New York City, 262–265; number of adherents, 3, 424n10; Olazábal's legacy and, 128–130; in presidential politics, 379–381, 394–403; Puerto Rican diaspora and, 172–175; scholars influenced by, 274–275; social/moral/church-state views, 374–378; Spanish Eastern District of the Assemblies of God impact on development of, 254; in Texas, 60, 74; women's positions in, 302–304
"Latino Convention" (1918) (aka Latin Convention–there were two Latino Conventions in 1918), 83, 98, 113, 114
Latino districts, 183–185
Latino Religions and Politics (LRAP) surveys (2008 and 2012), 3, 4, 367, 370–372, 425n11, 426n14, 483n12; on gay marriage, 403; on "no religion" category, 414; on Obama support by Latinos, 393–394; on party affiliation of Latinos, 400

Latinos, U.S., 28, 63, 278; demographic shifts in American society/politics and, 364–365; demographic shifts in religions, 3–5; discrimination against, 156–158; diversity of, 10–11; early participation at Azusa, 36, 58, 59; folk healers consulted by, 41–42; invisibility and underrepresentation of, 190–191; presidential politics and, 393; religious conversion and switching among, 366–370; sociodemographic profile of, 365–366

Lawless, Elaine, 314, 471n3

Leadership, 429n39

Lee, Ed, 33, 34, 50

León, Luís, 422n4

Leonard, Bishop A. W., 102

Liberation Theology, 322, 360, 412, 476n1

Liberty Council, 376, 487n28

Liderazgo y Amistad [*Leadership and Friendship*] (Miranda), 343, 374

Llorente, Francisco F., 141, 450n25, 490n1

López, Abundio, 22, 23, 36, 56, 285, 430n2; crossing of racial lines and, 37; in Mexican Plaza District, 293; ordination of, 51, 52, 53, 137; social conditions of converts and, 40; testimony of, 448n4

López, Agustin, 149, 150, 168

Lopez, Arnulfo M., 60, 64, 72–74, 86, 94, 127; Ball and, 96, 108, 160; Catholic attacks on, 147; as founder of Latino AG in Southwest, 162; Latino Convention (1918) and, 98, 100; Mexican expansion in Southwest and, 112; as pioneer of Latino Pentecostal movement, 95; push for Mexican independence and, 120–122

López, Luís, 36, 141

López, Rosa, 22, 36, 56, 285, 293, 413, 448n4

López García, Bertha, 288, 289

Luce, Alice E., 15, 60, 82, 87, 95, 190, 194, 289; Ball and, 96, 123; California ministry of, 134; duties after handover of leadership to Mexicans, 215–216; evangelistic social work and, 325; as founder of Latino AG in Southwest, 61, 162, 163; "La Placita" mission of, 103; Latin American Bible Institutes and, 151–152; in Los Angeles, 112; Mexican control of ministry and, 115; Olazábal and, 411; origins of Latino AG in California and, 142–146, 450n33; paternalism of, 159; as role model for women, 292; Spanish language and, 85–86

Lucena, Lorenzo, 214, 217, 222

Lucero, Enrique, 149, 168

Lugo, Isabel, 193, 217, 220, 291

Lugo, Juan L., 15, 63, 140, 143, 162, 256, 411; autobiography of, 457n10; in California, 199–201; calling to evangelize Puerto Rico, 200–202; campaign to spread Pentecostalism in Puerto Rico, 208–210; conflict with Ortiz Jr. (Panchito), 217–218; conversion in Hawaii, 197–199; on hymn singing, 192; Mizpa Bible Institute founded by, 229; in New York City, 224, 257, 262–265, 280; La Sinagoga church founded by, 229, 241–242, 263; traditional Protestant critics of, 210–214; women ministers and, 287

Lugo, Juana, 196, 197

Lum, Clara, 50, 51, 55, 437n109

Luther, Martin, 6, 39

Lutherans, 205, 262, 301, 366

Luz Apostólica, La [*The Apostolic Light*], 106, 108, 119, 159, 163, 216; Bazan and, 174; Bazans and, 289; copies confiscated by FBI, 325; women writing for, 294, 298

Madrigal, Mary Lou, 312, 313

Maldonado, Virginia, 278, 303

Marez, José F., 148, 149, 451n51

Mariel Boat Lift, 16, 328–329

Marín, Muñoz, 207, 233, 234

Marriage, defense of traditional, 382, 385, 389, 392

Marsden, George, 427n29, 431n8

Martínez, José, 224, 235, 264

Martínez, Juan F., 423n6

Martínez, Navarro, 141, 450n25

Martínez, Susana, 398, 402

Marxism/socialism, 187, 217, 476n1

Mason, Charles H., 31, 45, 63, 437n109
McCain, John, 350–351, 353, 354, 386, 387, 391–392, 397
McGraw, Josefa, 70–71, 94
McNay, Mr. and Mrs., 63, 64, 65
McPherson, Aimee Semple, 131, 132, 292, 293
Medina, Eliseo, 358, 395
Mendoza, Salomon, 149, 168
Mensajero Cristiano, El [*The Christian Messenger*] (periodical), 132, 166
Methodists, 7, 26–27, 35, 90–91, 136, 154, 253; attracted to AG preachers, 214; Ball's break with, 92–93; Church World Service (CWS) and, 327; converts to Pentecostalism, 145, 149, 366; former Pentecostals as, 315; growth of, 169–170; indigenization process and, 418; in New York City, 262, 301; in Puerto Rico, 203, 205; skepticism about divine healing and prophecy, 92
Mexican AG, 62, 72, 97, 99; Ball and leadership of, 85, 88, 100; call for equality with white counterparts, 113; "second convention" of, 100, 442n29
Mexican Americans, 10, 88, 90, 180; Protestant inroads among, 13, 428n13; supernatural events at Azusa Street and, 35–36; women in ministry, 286–289
Mexican Revolution, 64, 67, 71, 293; chaos of, 93, 140; refugees from, 153–154, 165; U.S. intervention in, 115
Mexicans, 10, 11, 278, 406; expansion of Mexican-led ministries in Southwest, 112–113; first-generation converts, 88; leadership positions in Texas ministries, 83–86; lynching of, 58; movement into American Southwest, 20; self-determination of, 158–162; spiritual revolution and Mexican independence, 125–126; way of life in Texas, 89–90
Mexico, 11, 15, 153, 155, 226, 290; freedom of religion in, 64; Pentecostal membership in, 171, 455n15; Spanish Catholic spiritual conquest of, 105; Spanish land grants and, 331; U.S. bailout funds for, 380
Midwest Latin District, 182, 183, 184

Migrant labor, 1, 48, 79
Miller, Donald, 323, 349, 413
Miranda, Jesse, 14, 16, 171–172, 323, 359, 404; Alianza de Ministerios Evangélicos Nacionales (AMEN) and, 342–345, 380, 388; Bush (George W.) presidency and, 383; election of 2012 and, 394; invited to White House, 343, 361, 379; leadership as focus of, 374; as new Latino evangelical, 188–191; NHCLC and, 348, 349; President Obama (Barack) and, 392, 394, 395; at Obama's presidential inaugural prayer service, 354
Mishler, Jennie, 194, 195, 196, 208, 409
Missionaries, 46–47, 48, 196, 238, 279; in Puerto Rico, 409; women as, 282
Mita Congregation, 230, 301, 315, 462n109
Mizpa Bible Institute (Puerto Rico), 128, 229, 235, 264, 294
Montgomery, George and Carrie Judd, 45, 46, 58, 74, 287–288; ministry and influence of, 139–141, 162, 448n12; Olazábal and, 102; Pentecostal origins in Texas and, 63
Moore (Seymour), Jennie Evans. *See* Seymour, Jennie Evans Moore
Morin, Antonio Ríos, 64, 66, 70, 92, 94; Ball at odds with, 117, 160; confrontation with Spiritists, 68, 69; as founder of Latino AG in Southwest, 162; ordination of, 71–72; as pioneer of Latino Pentecostal movement, 95; power evangelism of, 67–72
Mormons, 44, 136, 366, 399, 402, 426n14, 483n12
Murcutt, Florence, 142–143, 145
Muslims, 3, 403, 425n11, 426n14

National Alliance of Latino Election Officials (NALEO), 359, 397
National Association of Evangelicals (NAE), 344, 348, 352, 357, 382
National Council for La Raza, 348, 358, 381, 395
National Election Pool (NEP), 373, 400, 403, 483n8

National Hispanic Christian Leadership
Conference (NHCLC), 2, 14, 189, 280,
326–327, 364, 374; AMEN merged into,
388, 404; Bush (George W.) presidency
and, 385; immigration politics in
Arizona and, 354–357, 359; immigration
reform and, 16, 350–352, 354; Obama
presidency and, 387–388, 390, 392,
404–405; as outgrowth of Miranda's
ministry, 348–349
National Hispanic Presidential Prayer
Breakfast, 345, 353
Native Americans, 28, 138, 158
Nativism, 47, 90, 155, 158
Navarrete, Sergio, 184, 368, 423n6
Navarro Martínez, Juan, 36, 51, 53
Needham, Hulda, 201–202, 210, 218
Nelson, Douglas J., 431n15
Nevarez, Francisco, 127, 146, 153
Nevarez, Natividad, 146, 153, 288, 289
New Life Covenant Church (South
Chicago), 16–17, 388
New Mexico, 16, 149, 150–151, 329–334,
365, 448n9, 478n21
New Testament, 39, 91, 198, 335, 451n50
New York City, 128, 131, 172–173, 203,
280–281, 417; Bible schools in, 346;
Catholic Church in, 259–260; Latina
clergywomen in, 292, 301–302; Latino
AG origins in, 262–265; Olazábal in,
225, 226; origins of Puerto Rican *El
Barrio* in, 257–259; Puerto Rican
migration to, 224, 257–259, 410–411,
465n4, 465n8; texture and culture of
Latino Pentecostalism in, 270–272
New Zealand, 23, 46, 139
Nodal, Rose, 297, 305, 316
Northern Pacific Latin American District,
183, 456n35
Nueva Esperanza, 189, 345, 384
Nuevas de Salvación [*News of Salvation*]
(periodical), 214, 215

Obama, Barack, 16–17, 190, 317, 354, 360,
364, 418, 456n38; church-state relations
and, 376; efforts to win over Latino AG
leaders, 362; election of 2012 and,

394–403; immigration reform and, 354,
356, 358–359, 395, 398, 405; Latino AG
leaders and presidency of, 387–394;
majority of Pentecostal support to, 351;
Miranda invited to White House by,
343; Rodríguez invited to White House
by, 388–405; National Hispanic Prayer
Breakfast and, 384, 396; Victory
Outreach and, 342
Olazábal, Francisco, 15, 57, 127–128, 145,
154; AG Bible School, 111–112, 119, 151;
Ball's counteroffensive and, 123–125;
Bazans and, 166–167; call for Mexican-
led district, 119–120; Christian Church
of John 3:16 and, 272; church planting
and, 110; CLADIC and, 127, 130, 159,
160, 407, 408, 485n21; on divine healing,
109–110; early life of, 102–103; entry into
Pentecostal movement, 63, 438n5;
evangelistic-healing ministry of,
130–132; expansion of ministry in
Southwest, 112–113; expulsion from
Latino AG, 417; as founder of Latino AG
in Southwest, 162; Latino Convention
(1918) and, 100; legacy of, 128–130; as
Methodist pastor, 109, 114, 144–145; "Mi
Pueblo" speech, 115; Montgomerys and,
140, 162; in New York City, 267–269,
411; NHCLC and, 348; nicknames of,
101, 130–131, 132, 226; Puerto Rican
revivals and, 225–229, 232, 238; push for
Mexican independence and, 120–123;
Reformation in the borderlands and,
113–117, 119; resignation from AG
ministry, 125–126; at "second convention," 442n29; transdenominational
Protestant support won by, 213; Valdez
and, 138, 139; women ministers and, 292
Oneness or One Jesus doctrine, 54, 55, 117,
140, 141–142, 149, 248
Orozco, Rodolfo C., 64, 171, 442n29
Orsi, Robert, 131, 267
Ortiz, Francisco (Panchito), Jr., 143, 196,
201, 214, 217–218, 218, 219
Ortiz, Francisco, Sr., 103, 196–197, 200,
459n53
Ortiz, Jim, 344, 345, 384
Osterberg, Arthur G., 35–36, 41, 45, 448n4

Osterberg, Emma, 40, 48
Otero, Loida Martel, 470n2
Otero, Luís C., 215, 224–225, 230, 235, 236, 237, 264

Pacific District, 182, 183, 188
Parham, Charles Fox, 7, 15, 24, 55, 57, 59; former associates of, 93, 122; on Midnight Mission, 136; Pentecostal origins in Texas and, 62–63, 81; roots of Pentecostalism and, 26–29, 406; Seymour and, 30, 31–33, 48–50, 433n30; teaching on speaking on tongues, 439n6; white supremacist beliefs of, 27–28, 31, 80–81, 432n22, 433n30
Paz, Eleuterio, 225, 263, 268, 272
Paz, Francisco, 267, 268
Pearlman, Myer, 229, 263
Pelosi, Nancy, 353, 354, 384, 386
Pentecost, Day of, 33, 37, 47–48, 79
Pentecostal Church of God, 240, 242, 244, 245, 253, 254; Mita Congregation split from, 301; in New York City, 263; Puerto Rican independence movement and, 247, 409–410; split from Assemblies of God, 249, 269
Pentecostal Church of God, M.I., 235–238, 249, 266, 423n8; split from Assemblies of God, 244–249
Pentecostal Church of Jesus Christ, 269, 280
Pentecostal Evangel, 106, 113, 116, 148, 158, 214–215. See also *Weekly Evangel*
Pentecostals/Pentecostalism: birth of Latino Pentecostalism, 51–53; Catholic harassment and persecution of, 147–149, 235; as competitor in religious marketplace, 207; exoticism in descriptions of, 18–19; history and definitions of, 6–10; "Jesus Only" or "Oneness," 54; Latino Pentecostal origins in Southwest borderlands, 146–147; Latinos in origin of, 23; outbreak of World War I and, 95; power and cadence in Southwest, 77–81; presidential politics and, 382; psychology of, 79–80; public voice and recognition for, 230–231; relation to Evangelicals, 8;

rise of, 7; social and political action by, 322; splinter movements founded by women, 229–230; spread to Puerto Rico, 208–210; theological education and, 39
Perales, Elvira, 161, 167, 288, 289, 299, 473n29
Pérez, Alejandro, 250–251, 275
Perkin, Noel, 154, 160, 229, 236, 240, 246
Piñero, Jesús T., 207, 234
Pinson, Mack M., 63, 64, 81, 96, 103, 166, 438n6
Pisgah Home Mission, 41, 136–137, 286
Plan de San Diego (1915), 96, 123
Poloma, Margaret, 422n3
Premillennial movement, 26, 31, 39
Presbyterians, 136, 154, 175, 176–177, 253; attracted to AG preachers, 214; Church World Service (CWS) and, 327; converts to Pentecostalism, 149; former Pentecostals as, 315; growth of, 170; indigenization process and, 418; PCUSA, 9; in Puerto Rico, 203, 205; revivalists, 7; Scottish, 6
Preston, John A., 64–67, 84; Ball and, 93, 103; Ball's criticism of, 117; documentation of evangelistic work, 81; Mexican control of ministry and, 115; paternalism of, 80; Spanish language and, 441n43; Ball criticisms of, 177
Prophecy, 31, 40, 78, 92, 169
Protestants, 2, 3, 13, 44, 154, 372, 409–410, 426n14; history and definitions of, 6–10; Latino Protestants in New York City, 260–262; liberal, 322, 323; mainline, 4, 9, 271, 283, 307, 361, 382; in Mexico, 64; Pentecostals in conflict with traditional Protestants, 210–214; presidential politics and, 382, 403; in Puerto Rico, 202–208, 458nn25–26; spiritual primogenitor practice, 86
Puerto Rico, 2, 11, 12, 15, 153, 251–254, 417; Assemblies of God reborn in, 249–251; denominations of Pentecostalism in, 228, 462n109; founding of Pentecostal movement in, 63, 208–210; independence movement, 233–235, 244–249, 264; Latino AG Bible schools in, 346; Olazábal's evangelistic campaigns in,

Puerto Rico *(continued)*
131, 132, 225–229; pastors in, 128; Pentecostal Church of God's push for integration, 235–238; Pentecostal expansion across, 214–217; Pentecostals in conflict with traditional Protestants, 210–214, 460n54; public voice and recognition for Pentecostalism in, 230–231; Puerto Rico District of the Assemblies of God, 183, 184, 223–225, 280, 456n35; "Puerto Rico Problem," 238–244; religious marketplace in, 202–208

Quakers, 39, 89

Race, 12, 17–21, 26, 27–28, 47, 55, 153–155
Ramírez, Daniel, 422n4
Ramírez, Jesús and Abelardo, 157–158
Ramos, Joseph, 160–161, 454n105
Reagan, Ronald, 16, 190, 317, 329, 355, 364; immigration reform and, 365; Latino Evangelicals invited to White House by, 343, 379; Victory Outreach and, 342
Reid, Harry, 353, 354, 356, 386
Republican Party, 16, 17, 310, 319, 360, 392; Cuban support for, 329; immigration reform and, 352, 354; Latino support for, 401, 404, 413–414; nativist rhetoric in, 378; swing voters and, 363; top Latino political leaders of, 397–398
Reyes, Rafael, II, 275, 276–277, 278, 368; superintendent of the Spanish Eastern District, 275–280
Richey, E. N., 93, 95, 99
Riggio, Ronald, 429n39
Riggio, Ursula, 288, 289, 293, 294
Ríos, Andrés, 241, 244, 246–247
Rivera y Crescencio, Aniano, 249, 250
Robeck, Cecil M., 430n2, 431n15, 438n131
Roberts, Oral, 130, 316
Rodríguez, Eva, 309, 311–312, 316
Rodríguez, Samuel, 2, 14, 280, 345, 385, 423n7; election of 2012 and, 396–397, 402; emphasis on righteousness and

justice, 16, 323; on future of Latino AG, 416–417; immigration politics in Arizona and, 355, 356; immigration reform and, 326–327, 350–352, 58–359, 403–404; as key spokesperson for Latino AG, 404–405; NHCLC and, 348–349; Obama and, 17, 387, 388, 390, 396, 398–399; on same-sex relations, 376, 487n28
Romney, Mitt, 359, 396–397, 399–400, 403, 405
Rosa, Adolph, 143, 199
Rousseau, Leoncia Rosado ("Mama Leo"), 265, 269, 339–340
Ruesga, David, 152, 154, 155, 171

Salvation Army, 66, 346, 486n24
Sánchez, Josue, 176, 181
Sánchez, Manuel, 177, 241, 242, 265–266, 275
Sánchez-Walsh, Arlene, 423n6, 428n32
Sanctification, 39, 50, 53
Sanders, Anna, 103, 171, 289
Sandoval, Brian, 149, 398
Scheumack, Joseph, 64, 72, 73
Sepúlveda, Carlos, 265, 268
Seventh-Day Adventism, 44, 205, 262
Seymour, Jennie Evans Moore, 34, 44, 50, 56, 57
Seymour, William J., 7, 15, 19, 59, 102, 406; descriptions of, 46; difficulties in personal life of, 50–51; Durham's betrayal of, 53–54; early life, 30–31; final years, 56–57; former associates of, 122; McPherson, Aimee Semple, 56; Mexican American Pentecostal origins and, 35–42, 52–53, 56, 58–63, 88, 100–102, 136–143, 166; ministry standards and leadership of, 42–44; origins of Latino Pentecostal movement and, 22, 24, 26, 162; Parham's relations with, 31–33, 48–50, 433n30; Pentecostal origins in Texas and, 62–63, 81; Puerto Rican Pentecostal origins and, 196, 216; teaching on speaking on tongues, 37; theology of, 38–40; transformational and egalitarian social vision of, 47–48

Sheppard, Gerald, 283, 284, 321, 411
Shumway, Charles, 448n12
Silent Pentecostals, The (De Leon), 1, 62
Silva, Bishop Kittim, 280, 383
Sinagoga, La (New York), 229, 241–242, 257, 263, 264, 265, 269; Berrios and, 270; Instituto Bíblico del Este, 294
Smith, Hannah Whitall, 7, 27
Social Gospel, 322, 360, 412, 476n1
Social justice, 12, 16, 17, 322, 377, 414
Solivan, Samuel, 14, 274, 280, 413
Soto, Anita, 306, 316
Southern Pacific District, 184, 304, 321, 347, 456n35
Spain, 10, 203, 331
Spanish-American War (1898), 66, 197, 202, 257
Spanish Eastern Convention (aka future Spanish Eastern District), 172, 173, 180, 241, 242; Hispanic American Bible Institute, 263; Pentecostal Church of God split from AG and, 255; Puerto Rican independence movement and, 246; renaming of, 249, 266
Spanish Eastern District, 175, 182, 249, 254, 265–266; church memberships in, 368; contemporary developments of, 278–280; growth and development of, 269–270, 280–281; leadership of, 275–277; Mariel Boat Lift ministry and, 328; myths about origins of, 256; Olazábal and, 267; Puerto Rican diaspora and, 410–411; women ministers in, 301, 303, 321
Spanish Harlem, 156, 226, 258, 268; churches in, 270; Latin American community in, 131; Olazábal's healing crusades in, 292; Pentecostalism and its religious competitors in, 271, 469n73; Spanish Harlem revival (1931), 131, 225
Spanish language, 2, 63, 97, 109, 199; Bible Institutes and, 293–294; Bush's speeches in, 382, 385; Charismatic movement and, 10; churches and, 370; Euro-American missionaries and, 84, 85–86, 87, 91, 441n43; mixed with English (Spanglish), 367; in Puerto Rico, 207; religious literature in,

105–108, 294; at Upper Room Mission, 136
Speer, Robert E., 132, 227
Spiritism, 25, 68–69, 144, 459n38; Pentecostals accused of, 211; in Puerto Rico, 194, 205, 207, 221–223
Spiritual gifts (charismata), 39–40, 59
Spiritualism, 25, 44, 68, 205–206, 410, 459n38; Pentecostals accused of, 211, 212–213; in Puerto Rico, 194, 221–223; in Spanish Harlem, 271; women with background in, 308
Steele, Flora, 103, 146
Steele, Fred, 103, 112, 115, 146
Suárez, Concepción, 121, 122, 442n29
Suárez, Juan, 184, 250, 251–252, 253
Sunday schools, 43, 71, 183, 219, 297, 412
Synan, Vinson, 427n29

Tañon, Ricardo, 256, 265, 270; Christian Church of John 3:16 and, 272–274; evangelistic social work and, 339–340; NHCLC and, 348; Spanish Eastern District leaders and, 275
Teen Challenge centers, 251, 252, 279, 341
Templo Cristiano (San Antonio, TX), 107, 167
Texas, 15, 24, 59, 149, 365; discrimination against Latinos in, 156–158; Latino AG Bible schools in, 346; "Latino Convention" in, 83, 88; Mexican Pentecostal origins in, 64; racial fault lines in, 77; racial segregation laws in, 31
Theosophy, 25, 44
Tijerina, Reies López, 180, 316, 329–334, 341, 353, 478n21; and Assemblies of God, 329–330; and Hispano Land Grant Struggle in New Mexico, 330–334
Tomlinson, A. J., 132
Tongues, speaking in, 28, 29, 33, 34, 55, 63; AG teachings on, 37–38; atmosphere of services and, 78; Euro-American Christian disapproval of, 227; Holy Spirit baptism and, 56; opposition to, 196; Pentecostalism separated from Methodism by, 92; purpose of, 40

Torres, David Ramos, 422n5
Torres, Pedro, 173, 335
Torres, Ramona, 288, 289
Torres, Rubén Pérez, 422n2
Treviño, Manuelita ("Nellie"). *See* Bazan, Nellie
Treviño-Cummins, Lisa, 344, 345, 383, 384, 404
Trujillo, Carlos, 149, 168

United Farm Workers (UFW), 16, 316, 334–336, 338, 339, 358, 395, 413
United Pentecostal Church, 55, 141, 423n8
Upper Room Mission (Los Angeles), 52, 136, 137, 146, 195

Valadez, Juan, 104, 122
Valdez, Adolfo C., 23, 36, 137, 430n2, 433n30; Assemblies of God and, 138–139; on divine healings, 41, 42; on end of revival, 52; evangelistic social work and, 324; family of, 286; influence of, 162; ordination of, 472n13; overseas crusades of, 46; social conditions of converts and, 40; on "Upper Room," 37
Valdez, José, 36, 286
Valdez, Susie Villa, 36, 40, 48, 286, 324, 413
Valenzuela, Genaro and Romanita Carbajal de, 36, 52, 56, 74; Montgomerys' influence on, 140–141, 448n12; Second Azusa Camp Metting and, 136–137
Vargas, Julia and Matilde, 268–269, 292
Vasquez, Manuel, 422n4
Victory Outreach International, 9, 341–342, 371, 423n8
Vidal, Jaime, 203, 458n26
Villa, Pancho, 74, 95, 123
Villafañe, Eldin, 14, 273–274, 280, 323; on evangelistic social work, 340, 341; leadership as focus of, 374; on "liberating Spirit," 413

Vineyard Christian Fellowship, 9, 371
Virgin Mary, 6, 148, 451n50
Voting patterns, 12, 310, 318, 320, 393, 429n41, 481n67; election of 2008 and, 16–17, 353–354, 393; election of 1992 and, 380; election of 1996 and, 381; election of 2000 and, 382; election of 2004 and, 385; election of 2012 and, 399–403, 483n8

Wacker, Grant, 430n3
Warner, Daniel S., 7, 31
Warner, R. Stephen, 5, 373, 427n21
Warren, Rick, 342, 394
Weekly Evangel, 60, 80, 83, 106. See also *Pentecostal Evangel*
Welsh, J. W., 120, 123
Wesley, John, 7, 39, 227
White, Alma, 7, 48
White supremacy, 27–28, 31, 77, 432n22, 433n30
William, Ernest S., 45, 46, 57
Windsor, Pedro, 344, 362
With Signs Following (Frodsham), 200, 229, 263
Women, 12, 145, 282–284, 418; in Azusa Street Revival ministry, 285–286; comportment and Latina Pentecostal identity, 299–300; egalitarian social vision and, 47–48; elected to district offices, 278; Euro-American women in ministry, 292–293, 306, 411–412; feminism and, 304–305, 309, 315–317; gender roles at home and in society, 297–299; Latina AG clergywomen profile, 305–309; Latina Pentecostal congregations, 310–311; Latino opinions on women in ministry, 375, 377; Mexican American women in ministry, 286–289; in ministries, 3, 268–269, 281, 473n39; negotiating Latina AG space, 314–315; ongoing struggles of, 302–304; political and social views, 309–310, 317–319; problems and obstacles for, 311–313; Puerto Rican women in ministry, 290–292; splinter movements started by, 229–230; in theological education and

bible institutes, 293–295; "third class soldiers," 300–302, 321
Women's Missionary Council [Concilio Misionero Femenil] (WMC), 287, 288, 295–297, 321, 325, 411
Woodworth-Etter, Maria B., 54, 200
Word, The (periodical), 294, 298
World War I, 95, 96, 123, 217, 235
World War II, 233, 258, 335

Xenolalia, 28, 29, 38, 434n49, 439n6

Yale Divinity School, 274–275, 346
Yamamori, Tetsunao, 323, 349, 413

Zimmerman, Thomas, 181, 248, 250
Zimmerman Telegram (1917), 96, 123
Zion City, Illinois, 28, 49